BEST BOOKS OF 2024

JAMES

by Percival Everett

BookBrowse Rating: 4/5
Critics' Consensus: 5/5
Readers' Rating: 5/5

Published March 2024 in Hardcover, 320 pages

Summary

A brilliant, action-packed reimagining of *Adventures of Huckleberry Finn*, both harrowing and ferociously funny, told from the enslaved Jim's point of view. From the "literary icon" (*Oprah Daily*) and Pulitzer Prize Finalist whose novel

Erasure is the basis for Cord Jefferson's critically acclaimed film *American Fiction*.

When the enslaved Jim overhears that he is about to be sold to a man in New Orleans, separated from his wife and daughter forever, he decides to hide on nearby Jackson Island until he can formulate a plan. Meanwhile, Huck Finn has faked his own death to escape his violent father, recently returned to town. As all readers of American literature know, thus begins the dangerous and transcendent journey by raft down the Mississippi River toward the elusive and too-often-unreliable promise of the Free States and beyond.

While many narrative set pieces of *Adventures of Huckleberry Finn* remain in place (floods and storms, stumbling across both unexpected death and unexpected treasure in the myriad stopping points along the river's banks, encountering the scam artists posing as the Duke and Dauphin...), Jim's agency, intelligence and compassion are shown in a radically new light.

Brimming with the electrifying humor and lacerating observations that have made Everett a "literary icon" (*Oprah Daily*), and one of the most decorated writers of our lifetime, *James* is destined to be a major publishing event and a cornerstone of twenty-first century American literature.

BookBrowse Review

A fresh reimagining of *Adventures of Huckleberry Finn* with Jim at the narrative wheel.

The Oscar-nominated film *American Fiction* (2023) and the Percival Everett novel it was based on, *Erasure* (2001), are about whose voices are heard and in what context. In the movie, Jeffrey Wright and Issa Rae, both playing authors, argue with their white peers against awarding a literary prize to a novel by a Black author that invokes pernicious racial stereotypes. When Wright and Rae try to explain this, one of the white authors responds, "I just think it's essential to listen to Black voices right now," drowning out the only two Black people in the room.

In *James*, Everett brings readers the voice of Jim, the enslaved companion of Huckleberry Finn in Mark Twain's 1885 novel *Adventures of Huckleberry Finn*. Jim's voice, along with the voices of the other enslaved people he knows and meets on his journey, is one of constant code switching. Chapter 2 opens with Jim teaching a group of enslaved children how to speak in a racialized dialect reminiscent of Twain's novel — "Lawdy, missum! Looky dere." — explaining, "White folks expect us to sound a certain way and it can only help if we don't disappoint them...The only ones who suffer when they are made to feel inferior is us." This is a clever detail for creating the world of chattel slavery from the perspectives of the enslaved, and the code switching introduces frequent opportunities for humor (if perhaps a little too frequent). The ignorance-feigning language of minstrelsy also hearkens back to *Erasure*'s book-within-a-book called *My Pafology*, which is written with a white audience in mind, employing the stereotypical language this audience would expect to hear from a streetwise Black criminal.

Everett covers many of the incidents readers will recall from *Huck Finn* — most vividly and disturbingly Huck and Jim's encounter with the confidence men calling themselves the King and the Duke. He also includes, of course, many incidents that are not in the original text, which occur during periods in which Jim and Huck are separated. The plot is stuffed with action and it moves quickly, though Everett finds time to show Jim's philosophical side, as he pores over books stolen from Judge Thatcher's library and engages in imaginary dialogue with Voltaire and Rousseau about the morality of enslavement.

Slavery's violence is unflinchingly captured in all of its horror, but also in its absurdity. At one point, Jim and another person fleeing enslavement are shot at by their pursuers. After the fact, Jim's companion expresses astonishment, declaring, "They were shooting at us...You can't work a dead slave. Why would they shoot?" Jim's response is simple: "They hate us, Norman." Slavery is a matter of capital but it's also fundamentally an expression of hate, rage, and dehumanization.

Of course, Twain was a humorist and *Huck Finn* is, though possibly less so to a modern audience, meant to be comedic in spirit. Perhaps one of the greatest achievements of *James* is that the funniest lines are given to Jim, and humor is a great humanizer. In one scene, Jim tells Huck that he knew his mother, whom Huck doesn't remember. Huck asks Jim if she was pretty, leading to the following exchange:

> "I dunno. I reckon. It's a scary thing for a slave to think such things."
>
> "Why is that?"
>
> "Jest the way the world is."
>
> "You think this here river is pretty?" Huck asked.
>
> "I reckon I do," I said.
>
> "Then why you cain't say if my mama was pretty?"
>
> "River ain't a white woman."

Like the author supposedly standing up for Black voices in *American Fiction*, there are white savior types in *James* held up for satirical ridicule. While separated from Huck, Jim is purchased away from an enslaver by a group of a cappella singers who claim to be anti-slavery. He is ostensibly "free" while among them, but when he discovers they still intend to exploit his labor for profit and care little for his safety around those who would do him harm, he flees. It is clear that without true liberation, sympathetic words from white people are nothing but empty platitudes, or worse, veils that obscure a violence less naked but equally harmful for its insidiousness.

Readers of some of Everett's other work may find themselves yearning for the stranger qualities of books like *Erasure* and *Dr. No*. *James* is a straightforward novel with few frills. However, it features some excellent surprises and the build up to and execution of the final act are expertly done. Everett captures the milieu of slavery at the start of the Civil War with precision and depth and frees his protagonist from the bonds of offensive caricature.

Reviewed by Lisa Butts. This review first ran in the April 17, 2024 issue of BookBrowse Recommends.

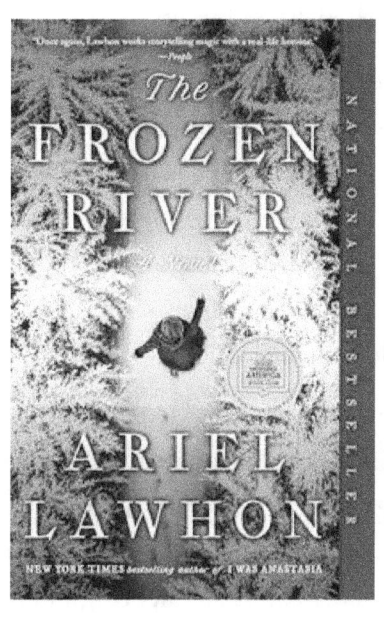

THE FROZEN RIVER

by Ariel Lawhon

BookBrowse Rating: 5/5
Critics' Consensus: 5/5
Readers' Rating: 5/5

Published November 2024 in Paperback, 448 pages

| Summary

Winner: BookBrowse Fiction Award 2024

From the *New York Times* bestselling author of *I Was Anastasia* and *Code Name Hélène* comes a gripping historical mystery inspired by the life and diary of

Martha Ballard, a renowned 18th-century midwife who investigates a shocking murder that unhinges her small community.

Maine, 1789: The Kennebec River freezes, entombing a man in the ice. Martha Ballard is summoned to examine the body and determine cause of death. As the local midwife and healer, Martha is good at keeping secrets. Her diary is a record of every birth and death, every murder and debacle that unfolds in the town of Hallowell. In that diary she also documented the details of an alleged rape that occurred four months earlier. Now, one of the men accused of that heinous attack has been found dead in the ice.

While Martha is certain she knows what happened the night of the assault, she suspects that the two crimes are linked, and that there is more to both cases than meets the eye. Over the course of one long, hard winter, as the trial nears, and whispers and prejudices mount, Martha's diary lands at the center of the scandal and threatens to tear both her family and her community apart.

In her newest offering, Ariel Lawhon brings to life a brave and compassionate unsung heroine who refused to accept anything less than justice on behalf of those no one else would protect. *The Frozen River* is a thrilling, tense, and tender story of a remarkable woman who had the courage to take a stand, and in the process wrote herself into American history.

BookBrowse Review

Thrust into a legal battle concerning sexual assault and murder, midwife Martha Ballard must fight for her friends and family, while continuing her life-saving vocation.

"I cannot say why it is so important that I make this daily record. Perhaps because I have been doing so for years on end? Or maybe – if I am being honest – it is because these markings of ink and paper will one day be the only proof that I have existed in this world. That I lived and breathed."

So run the thoughts of one Martha Moore Ballard after finishing her daily log in the small journal that is her constant companion throughout *The Frozen River*. Beyond the incredibly important role the diary plays in the novel – several keys to the mysteries that unfold throughout the story are held within its pages – Martha's notebook outlived her, and remains a key source for learning about early American history. Although *The Frozen River* is a novel, the protagonist is a fictionalized version of the real-life Martha Ballard whose diary informs the Pulitzer Prize-winning biography <u>*A Midwife's Tale*</u> by Laurel Thatcher Ulrich (1990). Ariel Lawhon weaves together elements of the historical record with strands of her own incredible storytelling to tell a tale worthy of its heroine.

It opens with a shocking discovery: a corpse beneath the ice of the frozen-solid Kennebec River, running beside the small town of Hallowell, Maine, in November 1789. As if that chilling event isn't enough, the identity of the corpse – Captain Joshua Burgess – adds another layer of drama. Just a few months before *The Frozen River* begins, Burgess was accused of rape by the preacher's wife, Rebecca Foster, whose bravery in coming forward about this violent crime has resulted in her ostracization. Many have the motive to kill Burgess: the preacher himself, for example, or Judge Joseph North, an elite member of Hallowell who also stands accused of assaulting Rebecca. As a midwife – and thus an expert both in bringing life into the world and in seeing the tragic ends of mothers and their children – Martha is summoned to the scene. While others claim Burgess's death is nothing but a conveniently timed accident, Martha is convinced otherwise by the signs of rope burn on his neck. When the case attracts attention from higher courts in Boston, her testimonies plunge the residents of Hallowell into a murder trial that occurs alongside the rape trial.

The Frozen River has a multilayered plot that moves at often breakneck pace through the winter of 1789–1790. Within the legal storylines, of course, are the very personal ones at the heart of the matter: Martha's friendship with the traumatized Rebecca; the midwife's growing mistrust of and dislike for Judge North; and even the relationship between Martha and her beloved husband

Ephraim, as the stress of these situations wears on them both. There are plenty of slower-moving moments, too, though, and these are the ones that bring real life and color to Lawhon's 18th-century story. Much in the spirit of Martha's original diary, the fabric of Lawhon's writing captures the small moments, conversations, and tactile details that Martha wanted to remember. Although often gory (merely realistic, some might say!), Martha's stories of attending births and delivering babies are some of the best scenes, allowing Lawhon to demonstrate her talent for capturing dramatic events while also developing full, well-rounded characters, even when they only appear for a few pages.

The characters who return time and time again, however – any one of Martha's six children, for example, or the eccentric old man who runs the general store and shares a book club of sorts with Martha – are the ones who leave the most lasting impact on readers. My personal favorite of these was the enigmatic Doctor, a nomadic, learned Black woman only ever referred to by her title. The relationship between her and Martha – two women whose lives revolve around healing others – is such a unique one among Martha's other relationships in the book that I found myself wishing the Doctor appeared more frequently. Perhaps in the future Lawhon will return to this time period to expand on this character's mysterious backstory.

In any case, *The Frozen River* is Martha Ballard's story, developed down to the finest details (sometimes fictionalized, but mostly believable – Ephraim's friendship with Paul Revere was perhaps the least convincing!) in a way that *A Midwife's Tale*, given its purpose as a work of academic literature and its source's brevity, could not be. For fans of historical fiction, the novel is an excellent path to *A Midwife's Tale* and other stories, historical or fictional, set in the late 18th century. Historians who crave the minute details of everyday life in the past may also be interested in the novel if they're familiar with the source material. Regardless of the nature of your interest, you should read it for the pure enjoyment of letting Lawhon's written universe wash over you.

Reviewed by Maria Katsulos. This review first ran in the February 7, 2024 issue of BookBrowse Recommends.

EVERYTHING WE NEVER HAD

by Randy Ribay

BookBrowse Rating: 4/5
Critics' Consensus: 5/5

Published August 2024 in Hardcover, 288 pages

Summary

Winner: BookBrowse YA Award 2024

From the author of the National Book Award finalist *Patron Saints of Nothing* comes an emotionally charged, moving novel about four generations of Filipino American boys grappling with identity, masculinity, and their fraught father-son relationships.

Watsonville, 1930. Francisco Maghabol barely ekes out a living in the fields of California. As he spends what little money he earns at dance halls and faces increasing violence from white men in town, Francisco wonders if he should've never left the Philippines.

Stockton, 1965. Between school days full of prejudice from white students and teachers and night shifts working at his aunt's restaurant, Emil refuses to follow in the footsteps of his labor organizer father, Francisco. He's going to make it in this country no matter what or who he has to leave behind.

Denver, 1983. Chris is determined to prove that his overbearing father, Emil, can't control him. However, when a missed assignment on "ancestral history" sends Chris off the football team and into the library, he discovers a desire to know more about Filipino history—even if his father dismisses his interest as unamerican and unimportant.

Philadelphia, 2020. Enzo struggles to keep his anxiety in check as a global pandemic breaks out and his abrasive grandfather moves in. While tensions are high between his dad and his lolo, Enzo's daily walks with Lolo Emil have him wondering if maybe he can help bridge their decades-long rift.

Told in multiple perspectives, *Everything We Never Had* unfolds like a beautifully crafted nesting doll, where each Maghabol boy forges his own path amid heavy family and societal expectations, passing down his flaws, values, and virtues to the next generation, until it's up to Enzo to see how he can braid all these strands and men together.

BookBrowse Review

Following a Filipino family across four generations of men, *Everything We Never Had* is a story of immigration, generational trauma, and defining oneself amidst familial and societal expectations.

Francisco Maghabol has recently arrived in California from the Philippines, eager to earn money to send home to his family. But good job opportunities for

Filipinos are scarce, and the threat of violence from the local white men makes life dangerous. Years later, Francisco's son, Emil, is determined to distance himself from his labor organizer father and his Filipino heritage in order to live out the American dream. Emil's plan works so well that Chris, his son, knows nothing about his family history or the suffering that Filipinos have endured. But Chris decides to learn about his heritage and eventually passes on his knowledge to his son, Enzo, who embraces his Filipino background. When the emergence of a global pandemic brings Lolo Emil to live with his family, Enzo can't avoid the rift between his father and grandfather. Following four generations of Filipino men, Randy Ribay's young adult novel *Everything We Never Had* is a story of how our pasts shape our futures and how generational patterns can affect a family for better or worse.

Ribay's novel features four points of view—Francisco, Emil, Chris, and Enzo—in four different settings and times, ranging from 1929 to 2020. Names and relations are mentioned throughout the story as if readers have already been introduced. A family tree included at the beginning of the book is helpful in navigating the jumps between the characters, and switches in points of view are clearly marked. There are numerous untranslated Filipino words and phrases throughout, which is unsurprising as young Filipino American readers are likely the target audience, and the use of several different regional dialects brings authenticity to Ribay's depiction of the lives of early Filipino immigrants. For those unfamiliar with the subject matter, a list of resources at the back of the book provides further reading for a broad understanding of Filipino culture.

This is very much a character-driven novel. Although each timeline has its own small plot, there is no overarching storyline. Rather, the narrative focuses on the typical complexities of father-son relationships compounded by cultural expectations, racial prejudice, and the desire to find one's place in the world. Each generation is significantly impacted by the previous ones, and while some of those impacts are positive—Emil is determined to instill in Chris a strong work ethic, Chris shares his knowledge of his Filipino heritage with Enzo—the book largely explores the negative effects and resulting trauma. This is portrayed in Emil's disgust with Francisco using him to show strikers the importance of family after Emil hasn't seen his father for months, and Chris's return to smoking once Emil moves in with the family—both reactions to the characters having their fathers back in their lives and related issues reemerging. The non-linear nature of the story allows readers to see how one character's choices cause trauma in the other men of the family, even when these choices are made with the best intentions.

Those good intentions and subsequent trauma trickle down over almost a century to Enzo, the fourth generation of Maghabol men. Enzo's story is particularly interesting because it takes place during the lockdown phase of the COVID pandemic; readers will have lived through the events of this time themselves and can see how one family is forced to grapple with personal, relational, and societal problems that are no longer possible to ignore because of social isolation. Enzo's sections are additionally interesting because they bring together three generations of the family—Enzo, Chris, and Emil—rather than just a father and son. Chris and Emil butt heads about almost everything—even a simple family dinner of handmade bulgogi pizza has "Lolo Emil…wondering aloud why Chris can't make a 'normal' pizza"—and the constant tension torments Enzo until he decides to bridge the gap between himself and his grandfather. Enzo's request to join his lolo on his evening walks is the first step in bringing the family together, and the two begin to build a relationship unlike that between any other Maghabol men, proving that generational patterns can be overcome. Although the story ends with a resurgence of tension, there's an air of hopefulness: perhaps family relationships can be mended and generational cycles broken if only people are willing to reach out and listen without judgment or expectation.

Short but impactful, *Everything We Never Had* is an exploration into the lives of the men of one immigrant family, showing how different generations react to the past and how they can begin to understand one another.

Reviewed by Jordan Lynch. This review will run in the December 4, 2024 issue of BookBrowse Recommends.

THE LOVE ELIXIR OF AUGUSTA STERN

by Lynda Cohen Loigman

BookBrowse Rating: 4/5
Critics' Consensus: 4.5/5
Readers' Rating: 4.5/5

Published October 2024 in Hardcover, 320 pages

Summary

It's never too late for new beginnings.

On the cusp of turning eighty, newly retired pharmacist Augusta Stern is adrift. When she relocates to Rallentando Springs—an active senior community in southern Florida—she unexpectedly crosses paths with Irving Rivkin, the delivery boy from her father's old pharmacy—and the man who broke her heart sixty years earlier.

As a teenager growing up in 1920s Brooklyn, Augusta's role model was her father, Solomon Stern, the trusted owner of the local pharmacy and the neighborhood expert on every ailment. But when Augusta's mother dies and Great Aunt Esther moves in, Augusta can't help but be drawn to Esther's curious methods. As a healer herself, Esther offers Solomon's customers her own advice—unconventional remedies ranging from homemade chicken soup to a mysterious array of powders and potions.

As Augusta prepares for pharmacy college, she is torn between loyalty to her father and fascination with her great aunt, all while navigating a budding but complicated relationship with Irving. Desperate for clarity, she impulsively uses Esther's most potent elixir with disastrous consequences. Disillusioned and alone, Augusta vows to reject Esther's enchantments forever.

Sixty years later, confronted with Irving, Augusta is still haunted by the mistakes of her past. What happened all those years ago and how did her plan go so spectacularly wrong? Did Irving ever truly love her or was he simply playing a part? And can Augusta reclaim the magic of her youth before it's too late?

BookBrowse Review

A charming novel of first loves and second chances.

Lynda Cohen Loigman's delightful novel *The Love Elixir of Augusta Stern* opens in 1987. The titular heroine finds her life suddenly turned upside down: her current employer has "encouraged" her to retire (a prospect she's always dreaded), and her niece has arranged for her to move from her Brooklyn apartment into an upscale senior living community in Florida. To make matters worse, on her first morning at the facility she runs into Irving Rivkin, a man from her distant past — and the last person on Earth Augusta wants to see.

The narrative then shifts back to 1922; 15-year-old Augusta is working in her recently widowed father's pharmacy, intent on one day becoming a pharmacist herself. Her great-aunt Esther has moved into their small apartment to help look after Augusta and her older sister. It soon becomes apparent that Esther is a healer in her own right, offering powders and potions to those who can't be helped by modern medicine. Augusta becomes determined to learn all she can from both her father and her aunt, believing each type of treatment has its benefits. Irving is hired as her father's delivery boy, and the two teenagers develop a close friendship.

The timelines unfold in alternating chapters, as the relationship between Augusta and Irving unfolds in both the past and present. Each story has its highlight. The sections set in the 1920s are superb historical fiction, and the author constructs the era beautifully:

> "Her favorite sound was the bell on the door that chimed whenever a customer entered. Not only did she take her very first steps in the aisle between the Listerine and the St. Joseph's Worm Syrup, but when...she slipped and fell headfirst into the display of McKesson & Robbins Cold and Grippe Tablets, family lore had it that the first word she spoke was not Mama, Papa or boo-boo, but aspirin."

This part also contains a bit of magical whimsy as Augusta spies on Aunt Esther, discovering that there's a little more to the latter's healing ability than simply mixing the right herbs.

Loigman displays a remarkable gift for dialogue in the book's 1987 chapters. The banter between Augusta and Irving in particular is both realistic and very funny; these scenes wouldn't be out of place in a 1980s sitcom like *The Golden Girls*:

> "For god's sake, Irving, you scared me half to death!"
>
> "You were worried about me," he said, obviously pleased with the idea.
>
> "*Everyone* was worried," she said. "Eighty-year-old men shouldn't play tennis."
>
> "I'm eighty-two."
>
> "I know that, Irving. I was making a point. But I'm glad that you still remember your age. I guess you didn't have a stroke after all."

Other scenes here, beyond the dialogue, are equally hilarious (there's one in particular involving a Jello mold that had me giggling out loud).

The book does, unfortunately, have some major flaws. Loigman's three main characters are exquisitely drawn, but her skill here doesn't extend to the others and most lack depth. The plot, too, is completely predictable; the author offers so many hints about what exactly happened between Augusta and Irving that by the time we hit that point in the story the revelation has lost all impact. And finally, both storylines rely heavily on coincidence; I can generally forgive one or two chance meetings over the course of a novel — they certainly do happen from time to time — but there are so many here that it strains credulity.

If I were looking at the book's shortcomings alone I'd probably rate it three stars. When all's said and done, though, *The Love Elixir of Augusta Stern* is a lovely little confection of a novel, which boosts it up to a four. There's not a lot to think about, no heavy themes to contemplate, but sometimes that's a good thing. It's cozy; it offers a simple, good-natured, feel-good escape, and for some it will be the perfect respite for a complicated time. I highly recommend it, especially to audiences who enjoy novels about second chances and those looking for a bit of light magic and romance.

Reviewed by Kim Kovacs. This review will run in the December 4, 2024 issue of BookBrowse Recommends.

MY FRIENDS

by Hisham Matar

BookBrowse Rating: 4/5
Critics' Consensus: 5/5
Readers' Rating: 5/5

Published January 2024 in Hardcover, 416 pages

Summary

A luminous novel of friendship, family, and the unthinkable realities of exile, from the Booker Prize–nominated and Pulitzer Prize–winning author of *The Return*

One evening, as a young boy growing up in Benghazi, Khaled hears a bizarre short story read aloud on the radio, about a man being eaten alive by a cat, and has the sense that his life has been changed forever. Obsessed by the power of those words—and by their enigmatic author, Hosam Zowa—Khaled eventually embarks on a journey that will take him far from home, to pursue a life of the mind at the University of Edinburgh.

There, thrust into an open society that is miles away from the world he knew in Libya, Khaled begins to change. He attends a protest against the Qaddafi regime in London, only to watch it explode into tragedy. In a flash, Khaled finds himself injured, clinging to life, unable to leave Britain, much less return to the country of his birth. To even tell his mother and father back home what he has done, on tapped phone lines, would expose them to danger.

When a chance encounter in a hotel brings Khaled face-to-face with Hosam Zowa, the author of the fateful short story, he is subsumed into the deepest friendship of his life. It is a friendship that not only sustains him but eventually forces him, as the Arab Spring erupts, to confront agonizing tensions between revolution and safety, family and exile, and how to define his own sense of self against those closest to him.

A devastating meditation on friendship and family, and the ways in which time tests—and frays—those bonds, *My Friends* is an achingly beautiful work of literature by an author working at the peak of his powers.

BookBrowse Review

A bittersweet study of friendship and loss set against contemporary Libyan history.

The title of Hisham Matar's *My Friends* takes on affectionate but mournful tones as its story unfolds. For the narrator, Khaled, friendships have been both fundamentally necessary and painful. When we first meet him, he has just said goodbye to his friend Hosam Zowa, an author whose work he discovered as a teenager and later met in Paris when the two were exiled from Libya in the era of the repressive Qaddafi regime. In the present, opening timeline, some years after the Libyan Revolution of 2011, Hosam is moving to the US with his wife and child, and Khaled senses their relationship ending. From here, he begins to tell his life story, irrevocably marked by his presence at the 1984 shooting of anti-Qaddafi protesters from the Libyan embassy in London, where as a young man studying literature abroad he was wounded and possibly put on the regime's radar, making it unsafe for him to return to his homeland for the foreseeable future.

Khaled's two closest friends during the decades following the shooting, Hosam and Mustafa (a fellow protester also injured at the embassy), have suffered in ways similar to him but are more eager than he to hit back at the world — both end up participating in the eventual overthrow of Qaddafi. Khaled has no desire to see military action, and the trauma he has experienced seems to separate him from conventional life, leaving him to lose himself in books and to foster meaningful but flexible connections outside the framework of marriage or traditional family. "[V]iolence demands translation," he observes, "I will never have the words to explain what it is like to be shot, to lose the ability to return home or to give up on everything I expected my life to be, or why it felt as though I had died that day." And as relationships between friends, unlike romantic or familial ones, are arguably the most inherently unconventional, the most undefined and open to reinvention but the most difficult in which to find security, it seems only natural that friendships form the stage on which the dramas of his existence play out.

Khaled finds a kindred spirit in a professor at the University of Edinburgh who acts as a mentor figure to him and provides material assistance after the shooting, fabricating an employment reference and offering financial support. His school friend Rana helps him manage the details of safely beginning a new life. Hannah, an off-and-on lover, is the first new person to whom he tells the truth about his injury, and they maintain a bond over time. All these characters have their own lives apart from Khaled, but together they give him a structure that allows him to find himself again, to begin to grow something out of the nothing he was left with.

Still, reminders of a somber reality lie around every corner. He attempts to speak to family members in code during his rare phone calls, envisioning a scrutinizing government official listening in, and considers the difficult choices made by other Libyans abroad — writers, intellectuals, and public figures — such as Mohammed Mustafa Ramadan, a real-life journalist and critic of Qaddafi who worked for the BBC and was murdered in London by men suspected to be associated with the regime. In Matar's novel, Khaled became acquainted with Hosam's work when Ramadan read one of his stories on the air in place of the news.

Khaled meets Hosam years later by near-magical happenstance, and Matar excels at crafting these kinds of fragile, ethereal moments — calling attention to how life thrives on coincidence and intuition, and revealing the wonder of a world connected by literature and other media even (or especially) as art and communication is suppressed. The second half of the book isn't quite as effective as the first in this vein, and the characters' centrality to key historical events begins to feel artificial and unnecessary. But overall, *My Friends* is confident in how it hews close to its protagonist's inner landscape even as it pulls in global concerns, in how it takes unexpected turns past and straight through history.

As Khaled endeavors to tell the story of his friendship with Hosam, a source of heartache and a loose throughline of his narrative, he reveals much about himself alone and the community of people around him, showing the small, delicate ways he has made an adequate place for himself among them. His decisions are not always comprehensible to friends and family, but his presence seems to be as key to others as theirs to him. Hosam will eventually leave London, but only after Khaled helps him build a life there that makes another life possible.

Matar's novel is a quietly humming beast, a low-flying glide over a specific cross-section of contemporary history, but also a bittersweet exploration of how it feels to have vital, formative experiences of friendship, and then to outgrow one's friends or to be outgrown by them in moments that are likewise defining. "My friends never stopped wanting a different life," Khaled reflects at one point, after speaking to his mother on the phone, "But I have managed, Mother, not to want a different life most of the time and that is some achievement."

Reviewed by Elisabeth Cook. This review will run in the December 4, 2024 issue of BookBrowse Recommends.

THERE ARE RIVERS IN THE SKY

by Elif Shafak

BookBrowse Rating: 5/5
Critics' Consensus: 5/5
Readers' Rating: 5/5

Published August 2024 in Hardcover, 464 pages

Summary

In the ancient city of Nineveh, on the bank of the River Tigris, King Ashurbanipal of Mesopotamia, erudite but ruthless, built a great library that would crumble with the end of his reign.

From its ruins, however, emerged a poem, the Epic of Gilgamesh, that would infuse the existence of two rivers and bind together three lives.

In 1840 London, Arthur is born beside the stinking, sewage-filled River Thames. With an abusive, alcoholic father and a mentally ill mother, Arthur's only chance of escaping destitution is his brilliant memory. When his gift earns him a spot as an apprentice at a leading publisher, Arthur's world opens up far beyond the slums, and one book in particular catches his interest: *Nineveh and Its Remains*.

In 2014 Turkey, Narin, a ten-year-old Yazidi girl, is diagnosed with a rare disorder that will soon cause her to go deaf. Before that happens, her grandmother is determined to baptize her in a sacred Iraqi temple. But with the rising presence of ISIS and the destruction of the family's ancestral lands along the Tigris, Narin is running out of time.

In 2018 London, the newly divorced Zaleekah, a hydrologist, moves into a houseboat on the Thames to escape her husband. Orphaned and raised by her wealthy uncle, Zaleekah had made the decision to take her own life in one month, until a curious book about her homeland changes everything.

A dazzling feat of storytelling, *There Are Rivers in the Sky* entwines these outsiders with a single drop of water, a drop which remanifests across the centuries. Both a source of life and harbinger of death, rivers—the Tigris and the Thames—transcend history, transcend fate: "Water remembers. It is humans who forget."

BookBrowse Review

Booker Prize finalist Elif Shafak's mesmerizing novel explores centuries and cultures through the lives of three remarkable characters — and a single drop of water.

Elif Shafak's novel *There Are Rivers in the Sky* follows three disparate individuals separated by time and location. Arthur Smyth (whose full name is "King Arthur of the Sewers and Slums") is born in the stinking muck along the Thames River in 1840. Narin is a nine-year-old Yazidi girl growing up on the banks of the Tigris River in 2014, shepherded by her grandmother. And thirty-year-old Zaleekah Clarke is a hydrologist living on a houseboat in London in 2018, trying to move beyond her failed marriage. As the characters' lives unfold on the pages of this remarkable book, readers gradually learn how they're tied together, with the last pieces falling into place at the very end of the story.

Shafak begins her tale with a sentient drop of water falling on King Ashurbanipal of Ninevah (reigned 669–631 BCE):

> "Dangling from the edge of the storm cloud is a single drop of rain — no bigger than a bean and lighter than a chickpea. For a while it quivers precariously — small, spherical and scared. How frightening it is to observe the earth below opening like a lonely lotus flower. Not that this will be the first time: it has made the journey before — ascending to the sky, descending to *terra firma* and rising heavenwards again — and yet it still finds the fall terrifying."

This tiny observer appears throughout the novel, present at various times in history (the same drop appears at Arthur's birth, and later makes up one of Zaleekah's tears). Indeed, the variability yet permanence of water is a major theme. "While it is true that the body is mortal," the author writes, "the soul is a perennial traveler — not unlike a drop of water." Later, "Many kings have come and many kings have gone…never forget the only true ruler is water," and, "Women are expected to be like rivers — readjusting, shapeshifting." Shafak's writing is lyrical, bordering on poetic, as she weaves this theme into her narrative.

The author's focus varies between her characters, making the experience of reading about each almost like reading three different books. By far the most detailed and appealing story is Arthur's; it fits squarely in the realm of historical fiction as Shafak takes a deep dive into life for the lower classes in Victorian London. Based on George Smith — a self-taught Assyriologist who was the first to translate the *Epic of Gilgamesh* into modern language — this remarkable man rises from tosher (someone who scavenges in the sewers) to expert on cuneiform (see Beyond the Book). The section is crammed with tiny details that bring the period to life. For example, Arthur buys eel pies as a treat for his brothers and reads by the light of the moon because his family has no money for lamps or candles.

Narin's role in the story allows the author to portray the Yazidis, a Kurdish religious minority whose beliefs include elements of Judaism, Christianity, and Islam. Often persecuted throughout history, people from this sect were victims of genocide by the Islamic State from 2014-2017. Yazidi experiences, wisdom, and values are depicted through the character of Narin's grandmother. While this part of the novel is set in more recent times, some of the concepts it contains are ancient.

And finally, Zaleekah epitomizes the struggles of many modern women still trying to establish a place for themselves in the world. She's at a crossroads in her life, wrestling with depression and unable to move forward. Her story might be the least interesting simply because it's so familiar to many of us; she's a typical woman on a voyage of self-discovery. This part of the novel is primarily bildungsroman. Zaleekah's overbearing uncle and a tattoo artist who only works in cuneiform add color.

One of the brilliant aspects of the novel is the author's ability to merge these three completely different storylines into a compelling whole.

I truly enjoyed Shafak's writing, but periodically she itemizes rather than describes:

> "Whatever is unwanted is discarded into the river. Spent grain from breweries, pulp from paper mills, offal from slaughterhouses, shavings from tanneries, effluent from distilleries, off-cuts from dye-houses, night-soil from cesspools and discharge from flush toilets…all empty into the Thames, killing the fish, killing the aquatic plants, killing the water."

These lists are unnecessarily exhaustive; they're included with enough frequency that the technique starts to grate. And while I was enthralled by each character's story, I became impatient waiting for the threads to start coming together. The tie-ins are ultimately brilliant but the author takes her time.

Those complaints aside, *There Are Rivers in the Sky* is a superb work of literary and historical fiction, and I highly recommend it to most audiences. It reminded me very much of Anthony Doerr's excellent novel *Cloud Cuckoo Land*, and readers who enjoyed that title will likely relish this one equally. It would make an excellent book group selection.

Reviewed by Kim Kovacs. This review first ran in the September 4, 2024 issue of BookBrowse Recommends.

THE WOMEN

by Kristin Hannah

BookBrowse Rating: 4/5
Critics' Consensus: 4.5/5
Readers' Rating: 5/5

Published February 2024 in Hardcover, 480 pages

| Summary

From master storyteller Kristin Hannah, #1 *New York Times* bestselling author of *The Nightingale* and *The Four Winds*, comes the story of a turbulent, transformative era in America: the 1960s.

"Women can be heroes, too."

When twenty-year-old nursing student Frances "Frankie" McGrath hears these unexpected words, it is a revelation. Raised on idyllic Coronado Island and sheltered by her conservative parents, she has always prided herself on doing the right thing, being a good girl. But in 1965 the world is changing, and she suddenly imagines a different choice for her life. When her brother ships out to serve in Vietnam, she impulsively joins the Army Nurse Corps and follows his path.

As green and inexperienced as the men sent to Vietnam to fight, Frankie is overwhelmed by the chaos and destruction of war, as well as the unexpected trauma of coming home to a changed and politically divided America.

The Women is the story of one woman gone to war, but it shines a light on the story of all women who put themselves in harm's way to help others. Women whose sacrifice and commitment to their country has all too often been forgotten. A novel of searing insight and lyric beauty, *The Women* is a profoundly emotional, richly drawn story with a memorable heroine whose extraordinary idealism and courage under fire define a generation.

BookBrowse Review

Kristin Hannah's latest historical novel tells the story of one young woman's experiences as a nurse in the Vietnam War and her post-service struggle to return to a normal life.

Kristin Hannah's latest historical epic, *The Women,* is a story of how a war shaped a generation and a tribute to all the women who served in the Vietnam War. Hannah tells the story of Frances "Frankie" McGrath, who, at the age of 20 in 1966, joins the Army Nurse Corps, inspired by a family friend's assertion that women can be heroes, too. After a hopeful, patriotic start, readers are thrown right into the action—bloody uniforms, gaping chest wounds, dying men screaming for their mothers as bombs fall overhead—allowing them to empathize with Frankie's chaotic entry into combat nursing. As soon as Frankie arrives in the war zone, she is repeatedly sent to take care of men suffering from some of the worst injuries imaginable. Although she's wildly unprepared, Frankie does what she can, knowing that even if her nursing skills can't save a man, offering a soothing voice or a hand to hold is sometimes enough. Eventually, Frankie finds her feet, becoming not only an excellent nurse but also a confidante, mentor and friend.

While at war, Frankie is forced to live in the moment, primarily because that may be all she has. None of the service members know if they'll make it out alive, and so they take chances and make decisions that might otherwise seem rash. The dangerous, emotionally intense setting pushes Frankie to form relationships with people with whom she never would have associated in her sheltered, privileged pre-war life in Southern California. The most significant of these relationships are her friendships with fellow nurses Ethel, a white farm girl from Virginia, and Barb, a Black woman from a small town in Georgia. The intense, unyielding bonds among these three women prove to be lifelines for Frankie throughout the rest of the novel.

Upon her return home, Frankie is treated with anger or disdain not only by much of the general public but also by her loved ones. Her service is seen as unladylike rather than heroic, and she's pushed to fit back into a more domestic mold. Although Frankie's rebellions against these expectations are dramatic, they highlight her distance from her former peers. Additionally, the leisurely pace of life contrasts starkly with the constant adrenaline rush of the war, leaving Frankie feeling purposeless. She attempts to find a place in nursing, but her skills are written off by administrators who don't believe combat experience is equal to hospital nursing experience. Further discouraged, Frankie visits a veterans' hospital to get therapy for what readers will recognize as post-traumatic stress disorder, but because she wasn't in active combat, she isn't considered a true veteran and so is ineligible for assistance, instead being told to simply forget about Vietnam the way so many other Americans have seemed to.

Interestingly, although the first part of the novel, set primarily during the war, is traumatic and somber, the second part, which stretches from Frankie's return home in 1971 to the early 1980s, feels much more hopeless. While still suffering from horrific nightmares and internalized shame, Frankie endures several tragedies and betrayals but is repeatedly told to soldier on. Frankie's postwar experiences reflect those of many service members, and, sadly, like many other veterans, Frankie turns to drugs and alcohol to cope. Despite enduring their own struggles, Ethel and Barb are by Frankie's side every step of the way, demonstrating that some experiences can only be fully understood when shared. But Frankie does eventually find support from other, unexpected sources, giving her a long-needed ray of hope.

Frankie takes that hope and passes it on to others, finding relief from her trauma only once she is able to share her story. That is also the reward for readers; having endured Frankie's hardships over many pages, they'll harbor their own hopes that Frankie, after sacrificing so much to help others, will finally find some measure of happiness. The novel ends on an optimistic note, seeing Frankie reunite with other veterans at the dedication of the Vietnam Veterans Memorial and vowing to find a way to remember all the women who served (see Beyond the Book). Based on years of research and guidance from real-life Vietnam War nurses, *The Women* vividly describes the horrors of war and the beauty of friendship and forgiveness while honoring the women whose service in Vietnam has been largely ignored.

Reviewed by Jordan Lynch. This review first ran in the February 7, 2024 issue of BookBrowse Recommends.

CLEAR

by Carys Davies

BookBrowse Rating: 4/5
Critics' Consensus: 5/5
Readers' Rating: 5/5

Published April 2024 in Hardcover, 208 pages

Summary

A stunning, exquisite novel from an award-winning writer about a minister dispatched to a remote island off of Scotland to "clear" the last remaining inhabitant, who has no intention of leaving—an unforgettable tale of resilience, change, and hope.

John, an impoverished Scottish minister, has accepted a job evicting the lone remaining occupant of an island north of Scotland—Ivar, who has been living alone for decades, with only the animals and the sea for company. Though his wife, Mary, has serious misgivings about the errand, he decides to go anyway, setting in motion a chain of events that neither he nor Mary could have predicted.

Shortly after John reaches the island, he falls down a cliff and is found, unconscious and badly injured, by Ivar who takes him home and tends to his wounds. The two men do not speak a common language, but as John builds a dictionary of Ivar's world, they learn to communicate and, as Ivar sees himself for the first time in decades reflected through the eyes of another person, they build a fragile, unusual connection.

Unfolding in the 1840s in the final stages of the infamous Scottish Clearances—which saw whole communities of the rural poor driven off the land in a relentless program of forced evictions—this singular, beautiful, deeply surprising novel explores the differences and connections between us, the way history shapes our deepest convictions, and how the human spirit can survive despite all odds. Moving and unpredictable, sensitive and spellbinding, *Clear* is a profound and pleasurable read.

BookBrowse Review

A minister in 1840s Scotland sails to a remote island to evict its last remaining inhabitant in the exquisite new novel from Carys Davies.

John Ferguson is a principled man. But when, in 1843, those principles drive him to break from the established Church of Scotland, the evangelical minister soon finds himself a poor man, too. Stripped of his income, worried how he'll provide for his wife, he puts scruples aside and agrees to a lucrative but dubious mission: to sail north—armed with a pistol—and "clear" Ivar, the last remaining tenant of a forgotten island halfway between Shetland and Norway.

Ivar has lived alone for decades; the Highland Clearances (see Beyond the Book), a series of mass evictions that began a century earlier, have already forced his family from the land. But if Scottish history would have him for another victim, *Clear* deftly upends the usual narrative. Soon after arrival, John slips on the craggy coastline; Ivar, discovering his unconscious body, takes it upon himself to patch the minister up. In the sudden intimacy of the crofter's bothy (hut)—evoked by Davies with a tenderness as touching as it is unexpected—the difference in the men's power evaporates. They speak no common tongue, but the spark of a connection disarms them both; slowly, as the minister convalesces, each begins to decipher the other, one translated word at a time.

An obsession with language drives this slim yet gripping novel. Ivar speaks Norn, an island relative of Danish and Norwegian on the brink of extinction. To John, it's a language uniquely suited to the unforgiving surroundings; what he would call simply "a rough sea," Ivar terms "skreul," "pulter," or "yog," depending on the peculiarities of the roughness. For the Highlander—who hasn't even set eyes on another human in years—to speak and be understood by John is something close to magic: it "connect[s] their lives in the strongest possible way." Yet as the friendship deepens, so much of *Clear*'s fascination springs from the unspoken. John's mission is never far from his thoughts. The hidden eviction notice, not to mention the pistol to enforce it, lies between the two men like an untranslatable phrase.

Language is an apt theme for an author who wields it so masterfully. *Clear*'s chapters, each a brief, poetic vignette, are lessons in what can be achieved with spare, finely-wrought sentences. Davies is a writer with a painter's sensibility. Like the best landscape paintings, her scenes are precise in their detail and expansive in their scope; and like the best landscape painters, she has a rare sensitivity to the natural world. The prose is exquisitely earthy, her pen clearly at home digging through the peat bogs and limpet-crusted rock pools of the Northern Isles. Rain, when it falls, does so in "big, coarse drops, melting the soil into a soft brown soup"; the cold wind in its wake blows "low over the ground, making the bogs shiver." Beauty is found on every page, and rarely is a word wasted.

Less graceful, however, is the handling of history. Between the Clearances and Church schism, Davies arguably takes on more of the 19th century than her short novel can handle, and it's frustrating to see unwieldy exposition clip the wings of a writer who's already proved herself so majestic in full flight. Some finer points come to feel even more superfluous given the turns *Clear* takes in its final quarter. Disappointingly, those carefully assembled tensions which made the premise so compelling—how Ivar will react to his eviction and how John will see it through with his soul intact—go slack once the novel starts pulling at other concerns. That's not to say Davies's ending isn't timely or affecting, only that it arrives like the answer to a question never asked.

But these are minor quibbles about *Clear*'s major achievements. With precision and lyricism, Davies has crafted a gentle, poignant drama. Great forces of history may convulse the mainland, but the soul of this beautiful novel curls around the hearth of the island bothy. At its core, *Clear* is that: two men, alone together, discovering the quiet miracle of human connection.

Reviewed by Alex Russell. This review first ran in the April 3, 2024 issue of BookBrowse Recommends.

TELL ME EVERYTHING

by Elizabeth Strout

BookBrowse Rating: 5/5
Critics' Consensus: 5/5
Readers' Rating: 5/5

Published September 2024 in Hardcover, 352 pages

Summary

From Pulitzer Prize–winning author Elizabeth Strout comes a hopeful, healing novel about new friendships, old loves, and the very human desire to leave a mark on the world.

With her "extraordinary capacity for radical empathy" (*The Boston Globe*), remarkable insight into the human condition, and silences that contain multitudes, Elizabeth Strout returns to the town of Crosby, Maine, and to her beloved cast of characters—Lucy Barton, Olive Kitteridge, Bob Burgess, and more—as they deal with a shocking crime in their midst, fall in love and yet choose to be apart, and grapple with the question, as Lucy Barton puts it, "What does anyone's life *mean*?"

It's autumn in Maine, and the town lawyer Bob Burgess has become enmeshed in an unfolding murder investigation, defending a lonely, isolated man accused of killing his mother. He has also fallen into a deep and abiding friendship with the acclaimed writer Lucy Barton, who lives down the road in a house by the sea with her ex-husband, William. Together, Lucy and Bob go on walks and talk about their lives, their fears and regrets, and what might have been. Lucy, meanwhile, is finally introduced to the iconic Olive Kitteridge, now living in a retirement community on the edge of town. They spend afternoons together in Olive's apartment, telling each other stories. Stories about people they have known—"unrecorded lives," Olive calls them—reanimating them, and, in the process, imbuing their lives with meaning.

Brimming with empathy and pathos, *Tell Me Everything* is Elizabeth Strout operating at the height of her powers, illuminating the ways in which we our relationships keep us afloat. As Lucy says, "Love comes in so many different forms, but it is always love."

BookBrowse Review

The stories of Olive Kitteridge, Lucy Barton, and Bob Burgess continue, post-pandemic lockdown, in *Tell Me Everything*.

Elizabeth Strout's *Tell Me Everything* picks up where her previous book *Lucy by the Sea* (2022) left off. Author Lucy Barton is now living full-time with her ex-husband, William, in the small town of Crosby, Maine. The 90-year-old Olive Kitteridge lives there as well, and asks their common friend Bob Burgess to send

Lucy to her; she has a story to tell that may interest a writer. As Lucy and Olive become friends, they trade tales of "unrecorded lives" — unremarkable people who nevertheless strike the pair as extraordinary.

At the same time, Bob is trying to be the calm eye of the storm as crises whirl around him. His nature is to help people (Lucy calls him a "sin-eater" — see the Beyond the Book), but he's on the verge of being overwhelmed by the problems of others. One of these others is Matt Beach, a strange, solitary man suspected of murdering his mother, who Bob, in his capacity as a lawyer, agrees to represent. Bob's only solace is his weekly walk with Lucy, but as the two become closer even this begins to add to his growing pile of stressors.

In typical Strout fashion, one can't necessarily say the novel has a firm narrative arc. While these varied plotlines sustain the forward momentum, they almost seem like an afterthought, a loose scaffolding on which to build something simultaneously simpler yet somehow grander. But that's what makes each of Strout's books something to celebrate; they draw us in and enrapture us with uncomplicated prose while capturing all the complexities of an ordinary life. For example, the book begins:

> "This is the story of Bob Burgess, a tall, heavyset man who lives in the town of Crosby, Maine, and he is sixty-five years old at the time we are speaking of him. Bob has a big heart, but he does not know that about himself; like many of us, he does not know himself as well as he assumes to, and he would never believe he had anything worthy in his life to document. But he does; we all do."

The author's literary style borders on unsophisticated, yet the content is profound.

Those who've enjoyed Strout's previous work will likely be delighted to see her main protagonists finally brought together in Crosby. Each one comes with a family and friends, though, and those connections result in a huge cast. All the characters, major and minor, are exquisitely drawn, and I felt Strout clarified who was who quite effectively. The publisher has, however, helpfully provided a chart in their Book Club Kit outlining the characters' relationships.

Tell Me Everything can be read as a standalone novel; it's not necessary to have read other Strout books to fully appreciate it. Readers meet each one of these characters where they are at this specific point in time, and although it's evident that each has a past, the author carefully includes everything we need to know to appreciate them in the current moment. That said, those who haven't will almost certainly want to read the previous novels once they've encountered these marvelous characters, and it may be a richer reading experience tackling the books in order. Those who've read the earlier books will be treated to uncovering new layers of familiar characters. One of my favorite parts of the novel was finding out more about Bob's wife, Margaret, and his brother, Jim (both originally from 2013's The Burgess Boys).

Most of us live pretty unremarkable lives, but Strout is here to point out that each of us is exceptional in our own way. While *Tell Me Everything* contains a number of bleak circumstances (death, illness, suicide, parent-child conflict, marital infidelity, etc.), it nevertheless ends up being an uplifting novel, one that left me feeling just a little bit better about life in general. Strout's fans are sure to love this addition to her oeuvre, and it's likely to win the author many new devotees. Its wide range of themes makes it a great choice for book groups as well.

Reviewed by Kim Kovacs. This review first ran in the October 16, 2024 issue of BookBrowse Recommends.

MODEL HOME

by Rivers Solomon

BookBrowse Rating: 5/5
Critics' Consensus: 4.5/5

Published October 2024 in Hardcover, 304 pages

Summary

Welcome to Rivers Solomon's dark and wondrous *Model Home*, a new kind of haunted-house novel.

The three Maxwell siblings keep their distance from the lily-white gated enclave outside Dallas where they grew up. When their family moved there, they were the only Black family in the neighborhood. The neighbors acted nice enough, but right away bad things, scary things—the strange and the unexplainable—began to happen in their house. Maybe it was some cosmic trial, a demonic rite of passage into the upper-middle class. Whatever it was, the Maxwells, steered by their formidable mother, stayed put, unwilling to abandon their home, terrors and trauma be damned.

As adults, the siblings could finally get away from the horrors of home, leaving their parents all alone in the house. But when news of their parents' death arrives, Ezri is forced to return to

Texas with their sisters, Eve and Emanuelle, to reckon with their family's past and present, and to find out what happened while they were away. It was not a "natural" death for their parents ... but was it supernatural?

Rivers Solomon turns the haunted-house story on its head, unearthing the dark legacies of segregation and racism in the suburban American South. Unbridled, raw, and daring, *Model Home* is the story of secret histories uncovered, and of a queer family battling for their right to live, grieve, and heal amid the terrors of contemporary American life.

BookBrowse Review

A domestic horror thriller with an intricately woven plot and a warm, beating heart.

Rivers Solomon's novel Model Home opens with a chilling and mesmerizing line: "Maybe my mother is God, and that's why nothing I do pleases her." The book is narrated by Ezri Maxwell, who grew up Black and nonbinary in a white gated community, and who wonders, upon reentering the area as an adult, what the point is of having a guard regulating entry: "To keep the bad people out? Every guard will fail at that because the bad people are already inside. This is their fort."

In this scene, Ezri, who left for an Oxford education when they were sixteen, has returned from the UK to the Dallas suburbs and to their sisters Eve and

Emmanuelle, with their teenage daughter Elijah in tow. After entering their childhood home, they find their parents dead in the backyard — police are soon declaring it a murder-suicide. Ezri and their sisters experienced many eerie occurrences in the house in their youth for which there seems to be no readily available explanation: Emmanuelle was burned by sulfuric acid that somehow got into her bathwater, animals mysteriously died, a boy who agreed to stay in the house alone once on a dare disappeared and was never seen again. The reader has limited perspective into what Eve and Emmanuelle (and even Ezri, whose first-person narration features incomplete and confusing memories) really think about these happenings, but now, reunited years later and in mourning, the siblings are forced to reckon with what power the house has and what role it may have played in their parents' deaths.

Ezri still feels resentful towards their parents, and particularly their mother, who they perceived as stubborn, proud, and elistist for having insisted on remaining in a neighborhood harmful to them in more ways than one. The first line of the novel ignites an ongoing, pulsing poetic meditation that repeats the incantation-like phrase "Mother is God." Reflections on Ezri's actual mother are countered and muddled by their memories of (and seeming interactions with) someone referred to as Nightmare Mother and the "woman without a face." As Ezri and their siblings seek to resolve the mystery of their parents' death and the reader explores the unfolding chaos of Ezri's thoughts, Ezri's childhood experiences begin to cohere with current reality. Meanwhile, a subplot forms around Elijah's secret relationship with a woman named Lily, whom the reader can identify as a predator but of whose presence and influence Ezri is wholly unaware, preoccupied as they are by thoughts of the house and their parents' funeral.

Model Home is openly a horror story built on social and political realities, in which the lurking evil is understood to be racism and the horrors it enables. This is not the revelation or even the lesson of the novel, but a given, and the riches of the plot that ensues — terrifying but also entertaining, sweet, and sometimes hilarious in a way that can scarcely be described (in one flashback, when Ezri's mother thinks they aren't being enthusiastic enough about a night out, they proclaim, "I want to go more than I've ever wanted to go anywhere in my entire life! I have dreamed about going to a restaurant on a Wednesday night since I was a wee child. A wee sick Victorian child!") — are for those who accept this premise without needing to be convinced. It is a book generously and unapologetically for the victims, without interest in laboring over the complexity of racists and abusers, but rather in tending the nuanced perspectives of those forced to deal with the blunt damage done to them, those already keenly aware of the layers of humanity employed by others as a device to gain and take advantage of their trust.

In fact, the novel interrogates the concept of "humanity" as a perceived moral good, asking whether it might be more accurate to see it as a notion associated with sensitivity, intelligence, multifacetedness, and greater understanding that is used to obscure violence and maintain racial hierarchy. In another flashback, the siblings' mother, an academic who gave up her career for her children, refers to "the white colonialist assumption that humankind is separate from and above the rest of animal kind, justifying human dominion over it. How powerful it would be for us to be called animals and say, Yes, yes, of course. And what does that make you? Not animal? Not flesh? Not alive

Solomon's novel retains a mood of classic horror, of shadows lurking in dark corners, but in structure, it ends up feeling more like a thriller with horror elements than the reverse. It has a genuine mystery. Readers need not fear an ambiguous ending. Some may find the neat lining up of plot incidents a bit hard to swallow, but the story, while it eventually reveals the strings being pulled behind the curtain, is content to create its own reality, which feels deliberately constructed at every turn. It is, finally, a tale of the recovery and reinvention of a family broken from its traditional base, of sibling bonds and love that has persisted even without being named or understood.

Reviewed by Elisabeth Cook. This review first ran in the October 2, 2024 issue of BookBrowse Recommends.

SMALL RAIN

by Garth Greenwell

BookBrowse Rating: 5/5
Critics' Consensus: 5/5

Published September 2024 in Hardcover, 320 pages

Summary

A medical crisis brings one man close to death—and to love, art, and beauty—in a profound and luminous novel by award-winning author Garth Greenwell.

A poet's life is turned inside out by a sudden, wrenching pain. The pain brings him to his knees, and eventually to the ICU. Confined to bed, plunged into the dysfunctional American healthcare system, he struggles to understand what is happening to his body, as someone who has lived for many years in his mind.

This is a searching, sweeping novel set at the furthest edges of human experience, where the forces that give life value—art, memory, poetry, music, care—are thrown into sharp relief. Time expands and contracts. Sudden intimacies bloom. *Small Rain* surges beyond the hospital to encompass a radiant vision of human life: our shared vulnerability, the limits and possibilities of sympathy, the ideal of art and the fragile dream of America. Above all, this is a love story of the most unexpected kind.

BookBrowse Review

When a poet ends up in the ICU after a medical emergency, his world both contracts into the daily rituals of hospital life and expands into wider meditations on life, death, love, and art.

At the beginning of Garth Greenwell's novel *Small Rain*, the protagonist, an unnamed poet in his early forties, is stricken with acute abdominal pain. The COVID pandemic is raging and he's reluctant to visit the hospital, but after suffering at home for a few days, he finally capitulates to his alarmed partner and ends up in the ER, where doctors discover that he has a life-threatening aortic tear.

The rest of the novel is mostly set in the ICU, where the narrator is tethered to his hospital bed with IV lines and sensors, but where his mind roams freely and widely. Greenwell is a master at creating intimacy; the poet seems to speak directly to the reader, and his narrative voice is compelling: sometimes self-critical and dismissive of his perceptions, but also empathic and reflective.

> "I sat in a chair while she took my blood pressure and temperature....I disliked her, I realized, I felt an antipathy she hadn't earned. Probably she was exhausted; I can't imagine it, day after day seeing people in pain, at their worst moments, over years; how could you protect yourself from that, I wondered, there was some human regard I wanted from her that I had no right to demand."

The protagonist in *Small Rain* bears a close resemblance to Greenwell himself: a writer raised in Kentucky and living in Iowa City with his partner. Greenwell's previous novels, *What Belongs to You* and *Cleanness*, shared a similar first-person voice, but the landscapes of the novels are very different. Both earlier novels are set in Sofia, Bulgaria and explore queer sexuality and desire. In *Small Rain*, the subject of illness and its attendant concerns appear alongside the protagonist's quiet, domestic life in Iowa.

The poet also meditates on art and beauty; in one particularly significant section, he reflects on his attempt to introduce his literature students to a favorite poem by American poet George Oppen (see Beyond the Book), about a sparrow: "I wanted to tell them, this record of a mind's noticing, a moment of particularizing attention. From a flock of sparrows this sparrow, in a forest." The sparrow of Oppen's poem is both individual and representative of other sparrows—perhaps all sparrows—throughout time. This is a key to the novel's larger ideas about art: the poet thinks about the core challenges of creating art, wanting to be "faithful to the concrete, particular thing," but "wanting too to pull away from the concrete, to make it representative."

It's also a key to the novel's own form, which continually adjusts its narrative lens from the close-up and personal to the wide-angled and universal. As the poet is experiencing his own unique medical crisis, the outside world faces an unprecedented pandemic; both the individual and the larger world suffer from anxiety about the uncertain future. The novel's title, too, reminds us how connected this one man and his experience is to all of humankind. "Small rain" is taken from the medieval poem "Westyrn Winds":

> Western wind, when wilt thou blow
> That the small rain down can rain
> Christ, that my love were in my arms
> And I in my bed again!

The lament of this poem reminds us that people throughout history, like Greenwell's narrator, have turned to poetry to help articulate the depth of their desire and pain, and that the yearning for home and family is universal.

As the poet in the novel processes his time in the hospital—the vague and inconclusive tests; the cheerful but evasive jargon of doctors and nurses; the days that blur into one another; the sharp and constant fear—his appetites for the world are sharpened. He eats a potato chip, and it is like eating one for the first time. He drinks a coffee, and coffee has never tasted better. As he realizes how close he has come to death, his life becomes very sweet. In his newly weakened state, he holds the world close. This is Greenwell's gift: to ask the reader how one can live a life with true appreciation, paying close attention to the full gamut of sorrow and joy in the world.

Reviewed by Danielle McClellan. This review first ran in the September 4, 2024 issue of BookBrowse Recommends.

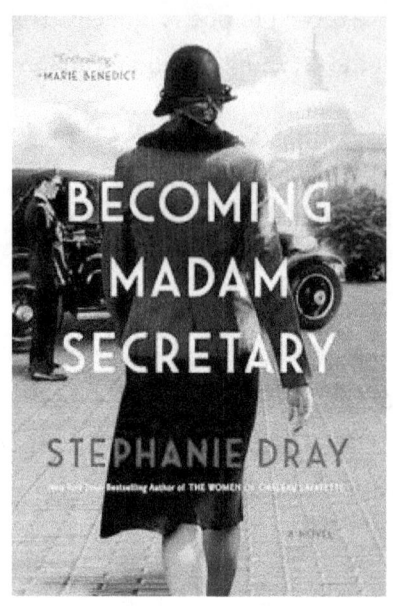

BECOMING MADAM SECRETARY

by Stephanie Dray

BookBrowse Rating: 5/5
Critics' Consensus: 5/5
Readers' Rating: 5/5

Published March 2024 in Hardcover, 528 pages

Summary

New York Times bestselling author Stephanie Dray returns with a captivating and dramatic new novel about an American heroine Frances Perkins.

Raised on tales of her revolutionary ancestors, Frances Perkins arrives in New York City at the turn of the century, armed with her trusty parasol and an unyielding determination to make a difference.

When she's not working with children in the crowded tenements in Hell's Kitchen, Frances throws herself into the social scene in Greenwich Village, befriending an eclectic group of politicians, artists, and activists, including the millionaire socialite Mary Harriman Rumsey, the flirtatious budding author Sinclair Lewis, and the brilliant but troubled reformer Paul Wilson, with whom she falls deeply in love.

But when Frances meets a young lawyer named Franklin Delano Roosevelt at a tea dance, sparks fly in all the wrong directions. She thinks he's a rich, arrogant dilettante who gets by on a handsome face and a famous name. He thinks she's a priggish bluestocking and insufferable do-gooder. Neither knows it yet, but over the next twenty years, they will form a historic partnership that will carry them both to the White House.

Frances is destined to rise in a political world dominated by men, facing down the Great Depression as FDR's most trusted lieutenant—even as she struggles to balance the demands of a public career with marriage and motherhood. And when vicious political attacks mount and personal tragedies threaten to derail her ambitions, she must decide what she's willing to do—and what she's willing to sacrifice—to save a nation.

BookBrowse Review

A stirring work of historical fiction tracing the life of Frances Perkins, the first woman to serve in the US Cabinet.

Our First Impressions reviewers enjoyed reading about Frances Perkins, Franklin Delano Roosevelt's Secretary of Labor, in Stephanie Dray's novel *Becoming Madam Secretary*; out of 33 reviewers, 32 gave the book four or five stars.

What it's about:

The prologue begins with a scene in FDR's office in 1933 where he is asking Frances Perkins to be his Secretary of Labor. For reasons we learn later, she has already decided she will not accept the appointment. She lays out what she would do if she had the position, assuming that her agenda is so radical that he won't agree to it. To her amazement, he does. How could she say no? Chapter One takes us back in time to the summer of 1909, when Frances is getting a master's degree in economics. Upon graduation, she begins a career of fighting for workers' rights. She observes the tragic Triangle Shirtwaist Factory fire, which makes her an unstoppable force for safety in the workplace. Her successes attract the attention of New York Governor Al Smith and Theodore Roosevelt, as well as FDR.

The author delves into Perkins' personal life, a happy marriage that gradually disintegrates due to her husband's mental illness, which seems to be genetically transmitted to their daughter as well. It was for this reason that she was reluctant to take the position offered by FDR. But she did, and brought about legislation that even today affects every citizen of the US. Without Frances Perkins, there is some doubt that we would have ever had Social Security, minimum wage, unemployment insurance, child labor laws, and so many other safety net programs (Jim T).

Readers loved learning more about Frances Perkins' work and were impressed with all she was able to accomplish at a very misogynist time in history.

But the real story here is how she had to endure hatred, lies, death threats, scorn in the press, and sabotage by other members of the Cabinet; yet she maintained her dignity, pressing forward to get the programs she knew were needed by the American people. This is a book about history, but more importantly an inspiring story about courage and persistence in the face of seemingly impassable barriers (Jim T). Her struggles to overcome the horrors of unfair, cruel, and unsafe work environments, poverty and her own personal struggles at home are a testament to her strength and character so very well portrayed in the book (Miss Liz).

In addition to her professional accomplishments, readers found Dray's depictions of Perkins' personal life compelling.

Her support of her husband and daughter during their struggles with mental illness and her deep friendships attest to her strength of character. The author, Stephanie Dray, did an excellent job bringing Frances Perkins to light in this book (Ellen H). Dray also portrays Perkins' struggles, so pertinent to many working women, to juggle her commitment to being a loving, available mother to her daughter throughout their lives with her commitment to her equally demanding and fulfilling work life (Dianne S).

***Becoming Madam Secretary* has what many see as the markers of a successful work of historical fiction.**

The job of writing historical fiction about a larger-than-life character like Ms. Perkins and all the important people she had to push, cajole, and convince, requires not only extensive research but also the creativity to try to discern and write what plausibly could have been her thoughts and her conversations. Stephanie Dray does a masterful job of all of the above. As she says in her Author's Note, "Novelists can go where historians rightly fear to tread." (Jim T). What a great book! I'm embarrassed to say I knew nothing of Frances Perkins nor her incredible achievements. A fiction book that sends the reader searching for more information must be a great book and this is one of them. I continue to be astonished that a book about the woman deeply involved in FDR's New Deal and the architect of Social Security could be such a page-turner! (Jeanne W).

While some found the writing style to be less than desirable…

The book is often repetitive and provides overly exhaustive detail, especially regarding her relationships with Paul and Ramsey. I often found I skipped whole pages to avoid some details (Dianne S). At times her characters felt rather flat, and the tone seemed superficial. The novel was a bit long, but there was so much territory to cover. This was an easy read, interesting and informative (Ruthie A).

...others found it exceptional.

Her writing pace matches the intense drama and passion of Perkins and likeminded women who sought out justice and fair labor practices. Because of her ability to tell a good story while revealing significant facts about women in history, the reader comes away from each chapter breathless for the next one (Ricki A).

And many felt it would be a good choice for a book group discussion.

The influence of Frances Perkins continues to this day. Book groups will find much to discuss about Ms. Perkins' personal life, professional life, and the balance between them (Shawna L). Dray, true to her previous books, has woven an interesting dialogue covering some very important parts of the history of our nation. A book worth reading for your personal illumination as well as a book destined for book clubs and the many different directions the conversations can flow (Carole A). I have suggested to the members of my book club we read *Becoming Madam Secretary* and look forward to a great discussion with other thoughtful women on a subject that has benefited us in our own life endeavors (Ricki A).

Reviewed by First Impressions Reviewers. This review first ran in the April 3, 2024 issue of BookBrowse Recommends.

THE GOD OF THE WOODS

by Liz Moore

BookBrowse Rating: 5/5
Critics' Consensus: 5/5
Readers' Rating: 5/5

Published July 2024 in Hardcover, 496 pages

Summary

When a teenager vanishes from her Adirondack summer camp, two worlds collide.

Early morning, August 1975: a camp counselor discovers an empty bunk. Its occupant, Barbara Van Laar, has gone missing. Barbara isn't just any thirteen-year-old: she's the daughter of the family that owns the summer camp and employs most of the region's residents. And this isn't the first time a Van Laar child has disappeared. Barbara's older brother similarly vanished fourteen years ago, never to be found.

As a panicked search begins, a thrilling drama unfolds. Chasing down the layered secrets of the Van Laar family and the blue-collar community working in its shadow, Moore's multi-threaded story invites readers into a rich and gripping dynasty of secrets and second chances. It is Liz Moore's most ambitious and wide-reaching novel yet.

BookBrowse Review

Liz Moore returns with a compelling double mystery set in the heart of the Adirondack Mountains.

Bestselling author Liz Moore's latest novel, *The God of the Woods*, begins with a disappearance. On a summer morning in 1975 at Camp Emerson in the Adirondacks, camp counselor Louise realizes that one of her charges, 13-year-old Barbara, is not in her bunk. It soon becomes apparent that no one knows what's become of her. Complicating matters is that Barbara is the daughter of the wealthy Van Laar family (who own the camp and a mansion abutting it), and Barbara's brother, Bear, went missing 14 years earlier from the same area and was never found. Oh, and a serial killer who was active at the time of Bear's disappearance has recently escaped from prison and is believed to be in the area.

Moore's narrative structure is intricate; non-sequential chapters bounce among several points between 1950, when the children's mother Alice first meets their father Peter, and 1975, as the investigation into Barbara's whereabouts progresses. Chapters are also written from the viewpoint of different characters, so diverse voices and perspectives are explored. And finally, the plot concerns not only two separate mysteries but abounds with subplots, examining themes such as family dysfunction, class structure, and the roles of women during these decades. Although this sounds horribly complex, the author is so skilled that one never feels lost and not one line feels unnecessary or out of place.

Her writing, too, is brilliantly descriptive. At one point, Alice muses on how her marriage has changed over time ("It was funny, she thought, how many relationships one could have with the same man, over the course of a lifetime together"). Elsewhere, we see the Van Laar estate through the eyes of newly minted investigator Judy, as she observes:

> "The lanky young people sprawled out on all the furniture in the great room are the people she is least eager to speak to. They look somehow like they should be feeding one another grapes; like young gods—in their own minds, at least."

Keen observations like these are sprinkled lavishly throughout the narrative.

The novel's main characters are female, and we get a detailed look at several of them; Alice, Louise, Judy, and Barbara's bunkmate Tracy are each awarded several chapters devoted to their lives, not only narrating the current investigation, but filling in their backstories as well. Others, such as TJ, the camp's director, are equally well described through the eyes of others. These characters are so vivid that readers are compelled to empathize with the challenges they face; grieving mother Alice, in particular, is heartbreakingly real. Rounding out the vast cast are assorted police officers, family members, boyfriends, staff, and fellow campers. Again, Moore's skill shines as she balances this enormous group of individuals, painting each with such a fine brush that even minor characters are distinct.

The only exceptions to Moore's skillful characterizations are a couple of her wealthy male antagonists. In contrast to the complex, sympathetic character of Alice, Moore's depictions of the men of Alice's class are less nuanced, generally portraying them as either narcissistic or vapid. A couple of plot points also felt like stretches. The book is so well-written overall that these minor transgressions jump out, though in the end they aren't significant enough to mar what is otherwise an exquisite reading experience.

The God of the Woods is an engrossing mystery that expands the genre into character study and a discussion of social norms. The book is highly recommended for those looking for a top-notch summer mystery, as well as anyone interested in an outstanding work of literary fiction.

Reviewed by Kim Kovacs. This review first ran in the July 31, 2024 issue of BookBrowse Recommends.

THE MIGHTY RED

by Louise Erdrich

BookBrowse Rating: 5/5
Critics' Consensus: 5/5
Readers' Rating: 4/5

Published October 2024 in Hardcover, 384 pages

Summary

In this stunning novel, Pulitzer Prize and National Book Award–winning author Louise Erdrich tells a story of love, natural forces, spiritual yearnings, and the tragic impact of uncontrollable circumstances on ordinary people's lives.

History is a flood. The mighty red ...

In Argus, North Dakota, a collection of people revolve around a fraught wedding.

Gary Geist, a terrified young man set to inherit two farms, is desperate to marry Kismet Poe, an impulsive, lapsed Goth who can't read her future but seems to resolve his.

Hugo, a gentle red-haired, home-schooled giant, is also in love with Kismet. He's determined to steal her and is eager to be a home wrecker.

Kismet's mother, Crystal, hauls sugar beets for Gary's family, and on her nightly runs, tunes into the darkness of late-night radio, sees visions of guardian angels, and worries for the future, her daughter's and her own.

Human time, deep time, Red River time, the half-life of herbicides and pesticides, and the elegance of time represented in fracking core samples from unimaginable depths, is set against the speed of climate change, the depletion of natural resources, and the sudden economic meltdown of 2008-2009. How much does a dress cost? A used car? A package of cinnamon rolls? Can you see the shape of your soul in the everchanging clouds? Your personal salvation in the giant expanse of sky? These are the questions the people of the Red River Valley of the North wrestle with every day.

The Mighty Red is a novel of tender humor, disturbance, and hallucinatory mourning. It is about on-the-job pains and immeasurable satisfactions, a turbulent landscape, and eating the native weeds growing in your backyard. It is about ordinary people who dream, grow up, fall in love, struggle, endure tragedy, carry bitter secrets; men and women both complicated and contradictory, flawed and decent, lonely and hopeful. It is about a starkly beautiful prairie community whose members must cope with devastating consequences as powerful forces upend them. As with every book this great modern master writes, *The Mighty Red* is about our tattered bond with the earth, and about love in all of its absurdity and splendor.

A new novel by Louise Erdrich is a major literary event; gorgeous and heartrending, *The Mighty Red* is a triumph.

BookBrowse Review

Louise Erdrich's latest novel is a patient, intense story of how people and communities grapple with unaddressed trauma.

Permit me to break the fourth wall. Like any good reviewer, I aim to analyze a book dispassionately, on its own terms. But personally, the true sign of a powerful work of fiction is if I dream about it—if I find myself in a character's shoes, feeling all the dread or confusion or exhilaration that they felt.

And that is exactly what happened with *The Mighty Red*, Louise Erdrich's latest novel. The action built slowly—Erdrich's specialty—until one night I awoke sweating and grasping for consciousness to escape the book's suffocatingly small town and its desperate personalities. This is a fundamentally human story, suffused with elements of the supernatural, resulting in something both relatable and fantastical—and moving enough to influence your subconsciousness.

The Mighty Red takes place from 2008 through the early 2010s, with the Great Recession as a backdrop and the rural Red River Valley in North Dakota as its setting. Casual high school lovers Kismet Poe and Gary Geist stumble into an ill-advised marriage immediately after graduation. Kismet is actually in love with someone else and isn't ready to commit to either man, but a family crisis and Gary's overwhelming desperation push her into the marriage.

She quickly realizes that she's become the supposed savior and linchpin of a family torn apart by a horrible tragedy that was in many ways Gary's fault. Not only does Kismet have no desire to play this role, but it's obvious that no one person can wipe away the trauma the way she wipes away months' worth of filth in her in-laws' neglected house. Practically held hostage by the family, Kismet begins to realize what she wants and what she truly values. The slow burn of her captivity with the Geists—and her making the best of it through cleaning, gardening, and learning the truth about the terrible accident that changed them—builds expertly and keeps the reader entranced.

Meanwhile, other narrative threads and perspectives are interwoven with Kismet's story. Kismet's wayward father is on a crime spree, robbing the town church's fundraising haul and a string of banks; left to clean up the mess, Kismet's mother tries to fend off foreclosure, bankruptcy, and the townspeople's suspicions that she's in on all of it. Kismet's true love, Hugo, heads to the oil fields and returns as a man with a career and a nest egg. The landscape surrounding everyone becomes increasingly barren, as pesticides on the Geists' farm kill all insects, birds, and wildlife, resulting in an arms race between herbicide-resistant weeds and ever-more-powerful chemicals (see Beyond the Book), and families throughout the town struggle to survive and adapt to this new reality.

Erdrich expertly switches between characters' perspectives and pulls the reader into their inner lives; the effect is never disorienting, but rather provides a 360-degree view of this insular community and its lightly magical realist world.

As the tension builds, the reader waits on edge of her seat for the characters to finally face their traumas, whether by confronting what happened the night of the tragedy or by reflecting on even earlier misfortunes and mistakes that led them to their current lives. As we watch their stories unfold, the Red River silently looms in the background as a source of pain, a recipient of pesticides, a regional water supply, and a purifying force all at once.

The Mighty Red bears many resemblances to Erdrich's earlier novels; scenes of overnight shifts in grueling workplace conditions are reminiscent of *The Night Watchman*, and the depressed, depopulated parts of North Dakota are familiar territory for her. But this story progresses with a momentum all its own. It is an intimate study of characters, with a dash of the thriller genre in the crime spree storyline—it frightens and excites, but never overly so. Above all, the novel explores what happens to individuals, families, and communities when trauma is buried, and what happens when it inevitably resurfaces.

Reviewed by Rose Rankin. This review first ran in the October 2, 2024 issue of BookBrowse Recommends.

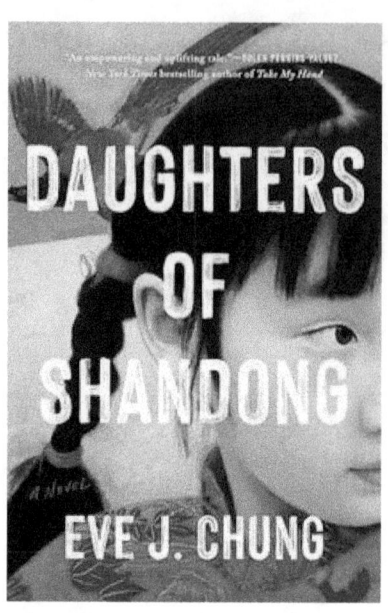

DAUGHTERS OF SHANDONG

by Eve J. Chung

BookBrowse Rating: 5/5
Critics' Consensus: 5/5
Readers' Rating: 5/5

Published May 2024 in Hardcover, 400 pages

Summary

Winner: BookBrowse Debut Book Award 2024

A propulsive, extraordinary novel about a mother and her daughters' harrowing escape to Taiwan as the Communist revolution sweeps through China, by debut author Eve J. Chung, based on her family story.

Daughters are the Ang family's curse.

In 1948, civil war ravages the Chinese countryside, but in rural Shandong, the wealthy, landowning Angs are more concerned with their lack of an heir. Hai is the eldest of four girls and spends her days looking after her sisters. Headstrong Di, who is just a year younger, learns to hide in plain sight, and their mother—abused by the family for failing to birth a boy—finds her own small acts of rebellion in the kitchen. As the Communist army closes in on their town, the rest of the prosperous household flees, leaving behind the girls and their mother because they view them as useless mouths to feed.

Without an Ang male to punish, the land-seizing cadres choose Hai, as the eldest child, to stand trial for her family's crimes. She barely survives their brutality. Realizing the worst is yet to come, the women plan their escape. Starving and penniless but resourceful, they forge travel permits and embark on a thousand-mile journey to confront the family that abandoned them.

From the countryside to the bustling city of Qingdao, and onward to British Hong Kong and eventually Taiwan, they witness the changing tide of a nation and the plight of multitudes caught in the wake of revolution. But with the loss of their home and the life they've known also comes new freedom—to take hold of their fate, to shake free of the bonds of their gender, and to claim their own story.

Told in assured, evocative prose, with impeccably drawn characters, *Daughters of Shandong* is a hopeful, powerful story about the resilience of women in war; the enduring love between mothers, daughters, and sisters; and the sacrifices made to lift up future generations.

BookBrowse Review

The captivating tale of a mother and daughters' treacherous escape to Taiwan during the Communist revolution in China.

Daughters of Shandong is the debut novel of Eve J. Chung, a human rights lawyer living in New York. Overall, First Impressions readers loved the book, awarding it an outstanding average rating of 4.8 out of 5 stars.

What *Daughters of Shandong* is about:

This book is a work of fiction, but it's based on the real life of the author's grandmother. A mother and three daughters are left behind when the more powerful members of their Nationalist family flee to escape Communists during the revolution. The story is told from the perspective of the oldest daughter, Li Hai, and the author does an astonishing job of capturing the thoughts of an adolescent girl dealing with both inconceivable trauma and everyday concerns (Kathleen L). This is also a character study of the women, both young and old, their strengths, the cultural rules accepted by the mother, and the awareness of the daughters that these rules are not fair (Susan W).

Readers were immediately swept up in the story's fast pace and absorbing details.

This novel was one which I could not stop thinking about. When I wasn't reading it, I couldn't wait to return to the story. There were some difficult scenes throughout but reading about Hai and the treacherous journey from Shandong to Taiwan was ultimately gratifying and I rooted for these women through every step. I cannot recommend this novel enough! (Darlene B). A fast-paced historical fiction novel that keeps the reader turning pages until the end (Cindy B).

Many felt that the book was thoroughly enjoyable despite its difficult subject matter.

If a book taking place during a war can be called enjoyable, this is it. I say enjoyable based on the mother/daughter relationships, the three-dimensional characters and the rising above the circumstances, which almost makes the reader forget the horrors in favor of the power of the storyline (Marie M). Chung's writing is descriptive without being overly expansive. *Daughters of*

Shandong was a real pleasure to read and I hope Chung continues to write (Laurie B).

Reviewers also thought that the novel's exploration of the treatment of girls and women was substantial and important.

As a Chinese daughter myself, I resonated deeply with Hai and many of the struggles she went through in trying to reconcile her identity with her culture…More than any other novel I've read in recent years (specifically ones written in contemporary times), this one does a great job exploring the internal battle that many of the women who grow up in restrictive cultures face (Lee L). From the story's emphasis on gender inequality, I learned about the damage that it has done to individuals and its harsh effects on society. I was moved by the relationships and the portrayal of the mother and her daughters in their relentless struggle to survive as their lives were continually torn apart (Patricia W).

In general, readers found *Daughters of Shandong* to be a fascinating and stunning work of historical fiction.

Daughters of Shandong is now on the top of my list of historical fiction novels. The author transports the reader into the eye of Chinese history and shows the incredible strength and fortitude of women who refused to be oppressed so that their daughters could rise above the hardships of cultural and political challenges and injustice (Melissa C). So many great details about the times and places, I could not put this book down! I look forward to reading other books by Eve J. Chung and want to share this story with my teenage granddaughter (Ruth H). Amidst the backdrop of resistance and resilience, Chung weaves a tale of hope and love that empowers this family to conquer insurmountable odds. Her storytelling skillfully explores the bonds of family and the strength that emerges from adversity, delivering a narrative that is both heart-rending and hopeful (Lani S).

Reviewed by First Impressions Reviewers. This review first ran in the May 15, 2024 issue of BookBrowse Recommends.

PROPHET SONG

by Paul Lynch

BookBrowse Rating: 5/5
Critics' Consensus: 5/5
Readers' Rating: 4/5

Published November 2024 in Paperback, 320 pages

Summary

Exhilarating, terrifying and surprisingly intimate, *Prophet Song* offers a shocking vision of a country at war and a deeply human portrait of a mother's fight to hold her family together.

On a dark, wet evening in Dublin, scientist and mother-of-four Eilish Stack answers her front door to find two officers from Ireland's newly formed secret police on her step. They have arrived to interrogate her husband, a trade unionist.

Ireland is falling apart, caught in the grip of a government turning towards tyranny. As the life she knows and the ones she loves disappear before her eyes, Eilish must contend with the dystopian logic of her new, unraveling country. How far will she go to save her family? And what—or who—is she willing to leave behind?

BookBrowse Review

The life of a suburban Dublin family is upended when the ruling Irish nationalist party introduces policies that lead to a totalitarian state, societal collapse and civil war.

Paul Lynch's 2023 Booker Prize–winning *Prophet Song* is a speedboat of a novel that hurtles the reader through ever-heightening waves toward a dark shore, a stark vision of total societal breakdown.

The narrative follows Eilish Stack, a microbiologist living in suburban Dublin with her husband, Larry, the deputy general secretary of the Irish teachers' union, and their four children, the oldest a teenager and the youngest an unexpected, late-in-life baby. Her father, showing early signs of dementia, lives nearby. Eilish's mind perpetually buzzes with the kinds of thoughts about work and kids and home that sustain a privileged, ordinary life held together by the almost invisible braces of a functioning civil society.

Lynch sets this world to spinning when the police arrive at the family home, looking for Larry. The authoritarian ruling party has introduced emergency measures in response to an unstated crisis. The government suddenly appears darkly inscrutable as it sidesteps the usual legal protocols and arrests dissenters, trade unionists—really, it quickly becomes clear, any person who is declared to be a domestic threat. This includes Larry, who after a late-night interrogation is later summarily arrested at a union march without even a nod to his civil rights, which so recently had felt like bedrock to the Irish state. The family's all-too-fragile edifice collapses as the city transforms around them.

Lynch understands that totalitarianism doesn't simply storm into power; all too often it creeps in, exploiting minor, seemingly harmless administrative policies and incrementally asphyxiating democratic mores, leaving only the specter of terror as the ruling party, their ambitions unmasked, declares that those who are not with us are against us. As the novel proceeds, readers follow Eilish through a cold Kafkaesque nightmare in which family members can get no information about missing relatives, and residents of the city can only seek the false safety of silence, as dissent is dangerous. Those who enter the prisons and military hospitals do not return, and those who disappear leave no trace.

Curiously, as Eilish's world collapses, her rational mind begins to work against her. She cannot grasp the gravity of the situation, it seems. How can she make sense of what she experiences, when it falls so far beyond the pale of what she had dreamed possible in a democratic country such as Ireland? Her only sanctuary, then, is denial. She lies to her children about the situation to protect them and explains away the evidence of danger shadowing over her. Stubbornly, she resists help from her sister, across the ocean in Toronto, who reminds her that "History is a silent record of people who did not know when to leave."

Some readers might find Lynch's break from standard formatting and punctuation unsettling—there are no quotation marks or paragraph breaks, so that each section of a chapter consists of long, solid blocks of text. The overall impact of these stylistic choices, however, echoes the intense, immersive description of the novel's world, the creeping dread of no exit and the clutching fear that gains momentum with the book's pace as the nightmare gallops towards its perhaps inevitable end.

Offering some solace to the reader, Lynch's prose can be both unusual and beautiful: "once the lie is known it will remain outgrown from the mouth like some dead-tonguing poisonous flower."

Prophet Song plays into a deep fear—that civilization will fall into conflict and ruin, that fascism will invade from democracy's back door, opening the way for history's never-ending line of bullies and thieves. But, in the end, Lynch reminds us that a democracy's demise may also occur through the stealthy creep of far subtler agents, whether the slow strangulation of individually innocuous statutes or our stubborn insistence that an old reality remains.

Reviewed by Danielle McClellan. This review was originally published in *The BookBrowse Review* in February 2024, and has been updated for the November 2024 edition.

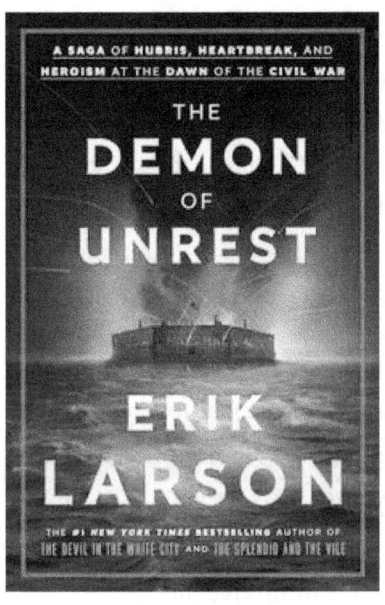

THE DEMON OF UNREST

by Erik Larson

BookBrowse Rating: 5/5
Critics' Consensus: 5/5
Readers' Rating: 5/5

Published April 2024 in Hardcover, 592 pages

Summary

Winner: BookBrowse Nonfiction Award 2024

The #1 *New York Times* bestselling author of *The Splendid and the Vile* brings to life the pivotal five months between the election of Abraham Lincoln and the start of the Civil War—a simmering crisis that finally tore a deeply divided nation in two.

On November 6, 1860, Abraham Lincoln became the fluky victor in a tight race for president. The country was bitterly at odds; Southern extremists were moving ever closer to destroying the Union, with one state after another seceding and Lincoln powerless to stop them. Slavery fueled the conflict, but somehow the passions of North and South came to focus on a lonely federal fortress in Charleston Harbor: Fort Sumter.

Master storyteller Erik Larson offers a gripping account of the chaotic months between Lincoln's election and the Confederacy's shelling of Sumter—a period marked by tragic errors and miscommunications, enflamed egos and craven ambitions, personal tragedies and betrayals. Lincoln himself wrote that the trials of these five months were "so great that, could I have anticipated them, I would not have believed it possible to survive them."

At the heart of this suspense-filled narrative are Major Robert Anderson, Sumter's commander and a former slave owner sympathetic to the South but loyal to the Union; Edmund Ruffin, a vain and bloodthirsty radical who stirs secessionist ardor at every opportunity; and Mary Boykin Chesnut, wife of a prominent planter, conflicted over both marriage and slavery and seeing parallels between them. In the middle of it all is the overwhelmed Lincoln, battling with his duplicitous secretary of state, William Seward, as he tries desperately to avert a war that he fears is inevitable—one that will eventually kill 750,000 Americans.

Drawing on diaries, secret communiques, slave ledgers, and plantation records, Larson gives us a political horror story that captures the forces that led America to the brink—a dark reminder that we often don't see a cataclysm coming until it's too late.

BookBrowse Review

A master of popular history explores the fraught six months between Lincoln's election in November 1860 and the April 1861 Confederate bombardment of Fort Sumter, revealing the depths of sectional differences and their eerie parallels to today.

In the aftermath of the 1860 presidential election, the divided United States began to collapse as South Carolina seceded from the Union, followed by another six Southern states. Among the countless contentious points between the Union and the fledgling Confederacy was the existence of a 75-man Federal garrison in Charleston Harbor that would become the flashpoint for civil war. In *The Demon of Unrest*, Erik Larson weaves a gripping tale of America's slow-motion lurch toward war, placing the reader inside events as they unfold.

In seeking to answer what "malignant magic" could lead Americans to consider the unthinkable—a bloody civil war—Larson prefaces his narrative with the parallels between the "national dread" felt during the run-up to the certification of the Electoral College and the presidential inauguration in 1861 with that during the Capitol assault of January 6, 2021 (as electoral votes were counted). Dread is the watchword, and readers will experience it anew in Larson's taut telling.

In seven dramatic parts, *The Demon of Unrest* unfurls those eventful months in 1861, centering the stories of memorable individuals such as Major Robert Anderson, Union commander of Fort Sumter; Edmund Ruffin, fire-eating evangelist for Southern secession who fired the first shot at Fort Sumter; Mary Chesnut, the acclaimed Southern diarist and wife of a prominent planter and politician; and, of course, an embattled Lincoln ringed round by presumptuous allies and politicians who believed they knew better how to handle the crisis.

Traveling from Washington, D.C., where lame duck president James Buchanan's inaction bordered on treason, to the heady excitement of the newly formed Confederate government in its first capital of Montgomery, Alabama, Larson sharply dissects the Union's fresh cadaver in the months prior to the Sumter attack and posits that a wounded sense of honor warped Southern political sensibilities and befuddled Northern peacemakers eager to bring the secessionists back into the fold. Lincoln's stubborn belief, based "on basically no evidence," that a vast swathe of pro-Union sentiment still existed in the South after the defection of seven states reveals a startling naivete, Larson observes, and may account for the exceeding caution with which the new administration considered whether to resupply and reinforce Fort Sumter.

Larson's most incisive analysis scrutinizes the Southern planter aristocracy that called themselves "the chivalry." Here, Larson reveals a society bred and fed upon the tales of Sir Walter Scott, enamored of military titles and uniforms. Their simulacrum of nobility, Larson writes, was "affirmed on a daily basis by the fact of their possession of, and dominion over, a subservient population of enslaved Blacks." Valuing honor above all human traits, the chivalry "would happily kill to sustain it." It was a *code duello* mentality, and it symbolized a South stuck in time. Larson's most powerful analogy is that of South Carolina as Miss Havisham from Charles Dickens's *Great Expectations*: left at the altar of the Railroad Age, she stops her clocks and leaves the world behind, retreating into her "own world of indolence and myth."

Excavating a wealth of official documents and secret communiques, Larson crafts a thrilling tale with tick-tocking suspense around the book's prime target: Fort Sumter. Indeed, the true hero in Larson's telling is Anderson, a U.S. officer sympathetic to the South who nevertheless did everything in his purview (and beyond) to maintain his position and protect his soldiers from imminent attack. It was Anderson's secret decision—made without consulting the then-Secretary of War John B. Floyd, soon to defect to the Confederacy—to move his command, under the cover of Christmas night, from Fort Moultrie on the coast to the more defensible Fort Sumter in the middle of the harbor (see <u>Beyond the Book</u>). His cunning and situational awareness is even more impressive in the wake of long silences and confusing directions from Washington; Larson clearly admires him, as will the reader. Anderson's steadfast defense of Sumter, which became "a cauldron of heat, smoke, and lacerating shrapnel" for two April days under intense Confederate artillery fire, would cement his celebrity in the North after the stockade surrendered on April 13 and sailed for home on April 14.

Interspersed with the politics and intrigues are a raft of other appealing and appalling characters who orbited the Sumter drama, with James Henry Hammond a prime example of the latter. An ex-governor of South Carolina and senator who gave the historic 1858 Senate address that "Cotton *is* King," Hammond was a member of the chivalry, a pro-slavery advocate who "worked his slaves hard" and barely recovered politically from a sexual scandal including four of his nieces. More palatable is the bemused and observant Sir William Howard Russell, *The Times* of London's special correspondent, who wrote about his meetings with prominent people North and South. Larson outlines Russell's keen conviction that "Northerners had little understanding of their brethren below the Mason-Dixon Line" and that Southerners viewed their Northern counterparts as cowards. Russell's writings captured both sides' central misunderstanding of "the other," which led to missteps and miscommunications between Lincoln's administration and the Confederacy during these key months.

Adding an indelible sparkle to the narrative are Larson's plumb pickings from Mary Chesnut's diary. A reliable source of comedic relief, Chesnut chronicles the mood and spirit of the Confederacy as she goes "social spelunking" in Montgomery and Charleston. Included is Chesnut's lighthearted "flirtation" with South Carolina's handsome ex-governor and bon vivant John L. Manning, a source of friction with Mary's husband, James: "After dinner, Mr. Chesnut made himself eminently absurd by accusing me of flirting with John Manning, &c. I could only laugh—too funny!" Known mostly from her folksy inclusion in Ken Burns's iconic documentary *The Civil War*, she is discussed in all her contradictions by Larson. "Mary had a clear-eyed view of slavery," Larson writes, accepting it as a foundation of Southern society even as she was honest about and spoke against the sexual abuse of enslaved girls and women at the hands of white slaveowners. She is an enigma of sorts, but a categorical delight to discover through the pages of her diary.

Covering the dicey days leading up to war, *The Demon of Unrest* is cinematic in scope, intimate in detail and charmingly written. Even more importantly, the parallels of 1861 with the electoral riots of 2021 make this book an urgent call to learn from history's mistakes. This is narrative history at its best: instructive, timely and utterly enthralling.

Reviewed by Peggy Kurkowski. This review first ran in the May 1, 2024 issue of BookBrowse Recommends.

THE LION WOMEN OF TEHRAN

by Marjan Kamali

BookBrowse Rating: 4/5
Critics' Consensus: 4.5/5
Readers' Rating: 4/5

Published July 2025 in Paperback, 336 pages

Summary

From the nationally bestselling author of the "powerful, heartbreaking" (*Shelf Awareness*) *The Stationery Shop*, a heartfelt, epic new novel of friendship, betrayal, and redemption set against three transformative decades in Tehran, Iran.

In 1950s Tehran, seven-year-old Ellie lives in grand comfort until the untimely death of her father, forcing Ellie and her mother to move to a tiny home downtown. Lonely and bearing the brunt of her mother's endless grievances, Ellie dreams of a friend to alleviate her isolation.

Luckily, on the first day of school, she meets Homa, a kind, passionate girl with a brave and irrepressible spirit. Together, the two girls play games, learn to cook in the stone kitchen of Homa's warm home, wander through the colorful stalls of the Grand Bazaar, and share their ambitions for becoming "lion women."

But their happiness is disrupted when Ellie and her mother are afforded the opportunity to return to their previous bourgeois life. Now a popular student at the best girls' high school in Iran, Ellie's memories of Homa begin to fade. Years later, however, her sudden reappearance in Ellie's privileged world alters the course of both of their lives.

Together, the two young women come of age and pursue their own goals for meaningful futures. But as the political turmoil in Iran builds to a breaking point, one earth-shattering betrayal will have enormous consequences.

BookBrowse Review

Set against the backdrop of Iran's turbulent twentieth century and spanning decades, *The Lion Women of Tehran* chronicles a story of betrayal and redemption between two best friends, Ellie and Homa.

Seven-year-old Ellie, living in Tehran in the 1950s, has just lost her father. She and her single mother are forced to leave their lavish life behind and move to a tiny home downtown. Grieving her father and struggling to cope with the outbursts of her proud and volatile mother, Ellie fantasizes about the best friend she will meet when she starts school: a polite, sweet girl with whom she can share her secrets. The wild, brash Homa is hardly who she has in mind, but after a rocky start, the girls become inseparable despite the protests of Ellie's mother, who fears that Homa, with her working-class background and communist father, will be a bad influence on Ellie.

When Ellie's mother remarries and relocates the family back uptown, regaining their former social status, Ellie and Homa lose touch. Later, Homa transfers to Ellie's high school, and Ellie, now rich and popular, is mortified when Homa makes no effort to fit in with their classmates as she has. Nevertheless, Homa soon charms her way back into Ellie's life. As the two girls grow up together, Ellie finds that she admires her friend's fearlessness and political activism, but while Homa gets involved with a communist organization at university, all Ellie can do is think about her engagement and dream about being a wife and a mother. Ellie's naivety ends up having dire consequences when an error in judgment puts Homa's life in danger, altering the course of both girls' lives.

Set during a particularly turbulent period of Iranian history, *The Lion Women of Tehran* highlights the growing conflict between those like Ellie's mother who support the royal family, and those like Homa's father who advocate for Mohammad Reza Shah's deposition. But when the Shah is overthrown by the 1979 Iranian Revolution, the religious extremists who take power plunge the entire country into a period of darkness that is only exacerbated by the Iran-Iraq War of 1980-1988.

Author Marjan Kamali distills Iran's complex contemporary history into a compelling narrative that centers on the intertwined lives of the two main characters. In emphasizing the contrast in the girls' upbringings, Kamali presents the reader with a multifaceted picture of Iran, and as personal and political conflicts build, she underscores how the differences between Ellie and Homa are not nearly as significant as their similarities as women living and surviving in a systemically misogynistic society.

There are a few moments where the novel could have used sharper editing—dialogue about narcissism and emotional abuse feels anachronistically articulate for the 1980s; a final confrontation between Ellie and Homa is brought on by an event whose melodrama feels silly. The last few chapters almost abandon the narrative in favor of acting as a manifesto for women's rights in Iran—and while the author's passion for this important subject shines through, it feels a little shoehorned in rather than serving as a logical culmination of Ellie and Homa's story.

But on the whole, this is a gripping, eye-opening narrative about a fascinating period of Iranian history, that tells the story of two complicated, bright young women who are committed to fighting for each other through numerous personal challenges and moments of political upheaval.

Reviewed by Rachel Hullett. This review will run in the December 4, 2024 issue of BookBrowse Recommends.

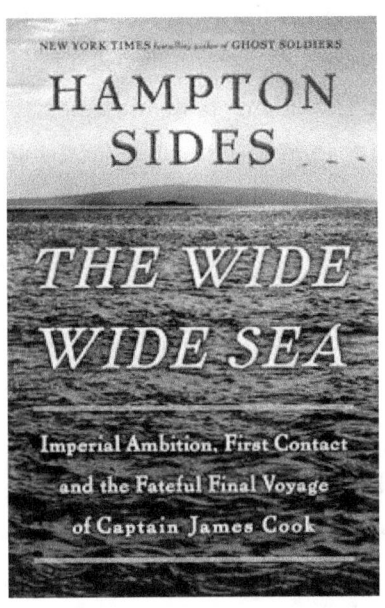

THE WIDE WIDE SEA

by Hampton Sides

BookBrowse Rating: 5/5
Critics' Consensus: 5/5

Published April 2024 in Hardcover, 432 pages

Summary

From *New York Times* bestselling author Hampton Sides, an epic account of the most momentous voyage of the Age of Exploration, which culminated in Captain James Cook's death in Hawaii, and left a complex and controversial legacy still debated to this day

On July 12th, 1776, Captain James Cook, already lionized as the greatest explorer in British history, set off on his third voyage in his ship the *HMS Resolution*. Two-and-a-half years later, on a beach on the island of Hawaii, Cook was killed in a conflict with native Hawaiians. How did Cook, who was unique among captains for his respect for Indigenous peoples and cultures, come to that fatal moment?

Hampton Sides' bravura account of Cook's last journey both wrestles with Cook's legacy and provides a thrilling narrative of the titanic efforts and continual danger that characterized exploration in the 1700s. Cook was renowned for his peerless seamanship, his humane leadership, and his dedication to science--the famed naturalist Joseph Banks accompanied him on his first voyage, and Cook has been called one of the most important figures of the Age of Enlightenment. He was also deeply interested in the native people he encountered. In fact, his stated mission was to return a Tahitian man, Mai, who had become the toast of London, to his home islands. On previous expeditions, Cook mapped huge swaths of the Pacific, including the east coast of Australia, and initiated first European contact with numerous peoples. He treated his crew well, and endeavored to learn about the societies he encountered with curiosity and without judgment.

Yet something was different on this last voyage. Cook became mercurial, resorting to the lash to enforce discipline, and led his two vessels into danger time and again. Uncharacteristically, he ordered violent retaliation for perceived theft on the part of native peoples. This may have had something to do with his secret orders, which were to chart and claim lands before Britain's imperial rivals could, and to discover the fabled Northwest Passage. Whatever Cook's intentions, his scientific efforts were the sharp edge of the colonial sword, and the ultimate effects of first contact were catastrophic for Indigenous people around the world. The tensions between Cook's overt and covert missions came to a head on the shores of Hawaii. His first landing there was harmonious, but when Cook returned after mapping the coast of the Pacific Northwest and Alaska, his exploitative treatment of the Hawaiians led to the fatal encounter.

At once a ferociously-paced story of adventure on the high seas and a searching examination of the complexities and consequences of the Age of Exploration, *The Wide Wide Sea* is a major work from one of our finest narrative nonfiction writers.

BookBrowse Review

Bestselling history writer Hampton Sides takes a fresh look at Captain James Cook's final voyage.

By 1775, 48-year-old Captain James Cook had completed two highly successful voyages of discovery and had earned a comfortable retirement. The Admiralty gave him a plum position: an honorary post at Greenwich Hospital near London, where his only responsibility was to "keep a paternal eye on the thousand or so Navy pensioners" who lived there. He quickly became bored, however, and longed to be back on the open ocean. His restlessness was exacerbated when he learned that the Admiralty was planning an expedition to look for the fabled Northwest Passage from the Pacific side—something that had never been attempted—and had assigned his former ship, the HMS *Resolution*, to the task. The powers that be, too, felt that Cook was the only man who could pull off such a journey, and so manipulated him into asking for the commission (which doesn't appear to have been much of a challenge). In July 1776 Cook left England on his final—and fatal—voyage. It's this tale of exploration and tragedy that Hampton Sides relays in his nonfiction account, *The Wide Wide Sea*.

The author tidily sums up his task: "This is not a biography but a narrative history with a large, diverse cast of characters…It's the story not only of James Cook but of the men who accompanied him on his swan-song voyage to the Pacific. They took part in a monumental enterprise that left lasting impacts, good and bad, on the world." It would seem like an enormous task to describe all that occurred on the expedition—over three years, Cook sailed from England to New

Zealand, Tahiti, Hawai'i and the Bering Strait. But in *The Wide Wide Sea*, Sides does what he does best: condenses a complex subject into an eminently readable, compelling story—a true account that reads like a novel. Although he doesn't break new ground—Cook and his voyages have been the subjects of many books—he does approach his topic with fresh eyes, acknowledging Cook's tale is a "morally complicated" one and allowing current debates about the explorer's cultural impact to inform the narrative.

It's unfortunate that there are so few records of Cook's actions from the perspective of the residents of the lands he "discovered," but many of Cook's men left behind journals. Sides laboriously combed through an extensive trove of documents squirreled away across the globe, combining the many sources to paint a nuanced picture of the captain and events that transpired on the journey. He's an expert in providing enough detail to get readers hooked on a story without allowing it to bog down the book's flow, and his skill is on full display here.

Also quite interesting is the author's attempt to understand Cook's increasingly erratic behavior as the journey wore on. I've read a number of books about Cook's expeditions, but I don't recall conjecture as to why he became so irrational toward the end of his life. Sides clearly draws the line between fact and speculation on this matter and others throughout, something I appreciate in works of narrative nonfiction.

The author claims not to "lionize, demonize nor defend" Cook, but I still found the portrayal fairly sympathetic. The captain and crew certainly had a negative impact on the people and cultures they met, but nevertheless Sides claims that Cook was one of the more socially enlightened navigators of the age. The author sees him as an anthropological observer, interested in understanding the cultures of those he met rather than dismissing them as inferior. He also excuses some of the side effects of European contact (e.g., venereal diseases, rats) as happening regardless of this specific voyage; the ills likely would have been introduced by the first European vessel to land, and that ship just happened to be Cook's.

Although I understand the points he makes, I found I wasn't completely convinced by them, at least not enough to overcome my discomfort with the interactions between the explorers and the Indigenous populations they encountered. That said, the account is a factual one, and Sides makes no attempt to ignore the expedition's misdeeds, even though he might try to rationalize them.

The Wide Wide Sea's subject matter is challenging from a 21st-century perspective; statues of Cook have been torn down worldwide, viewed as symbols of European exploitation. But we should keep in mind that the book is, at its core, history, and as such the events portrayed here need to be understood and remembered. And readers can't go wrong with a book by Hampton Sides, a master at penning marvelously readable history. I highly recommend it for a wide audience, including those who don't usually read nonfiction.

Reviewed by Kim Kovacs. This review first ran in the April 17, 2024 issue of BookBrowse Recommends.

THE MISSING THREAD

by Daisy Dunn

BookBrowse Rating: 5/5
Critics' Consensus: 5/5

Published July 2024 in Hardcover, 480 pages

Summary

A dazzlingly ambitious history of the ancient world that places women at the center—from Cleopatra to Boudica, Sappho to Fulvia, and countless other artists, writers, leaders, and creators of history

Around four thousand years ago, the mysterious Minoans sculpted statues of topless women with snakes slithering on their arms. Over one thousand years later, Sappho wrote great poems of longing and desire. For classicist Daisy Dunn, these women—whether they were simply sitting at their looms at home or participating in the highest echelons of power—were up to something much more interesting than other histories would lead us to believe. Together, these women helped to make antiquity as we know it.

In this monumental work, Dunn reconceives our understanding of the ancient world by emphasizing women's roles within it. *The Missing Thread* never relegates women to the sidelines and is populated with well-known names such as Cleopatra and Agrippina, as well as the likes of Achaemenid consort Atossa and Olympias, a force in Macedon. Spanning three thousand years, the story moves from Minoan Crete to Mycenaean Greece, from Lesbos to Asia Minor, from the Persian Empire to the royal court of Macedonia, and concludes with Rome and its growing empire. The women of antiquity are undeniably woven throughout the fabric of history, and in *The Missing Thread* they finally take center stage.

BookBrowse Review

A delightful and paradigm-shifting history of the ancient world weaves in "the missing thread" of women's pivotal and powerful roles that male-centric historiography often leaves out.

The fabric of ancient history is stitched heavily with stories of dramatic politics, conquest, and war, all with men firmly at the center of action. But women played just as vital and central a role in antiquity's most consequential events, as classicist Daisy Dunn (*The Shadow of Vesuvius*) elegantly details in *The Missing Thread*.

Dunn observes that countless histories of the ancient world are "ineluctably male" and shares her vision of the classical world as one that is not so much about women as "a history of antiquity written *through* women." Mining a wealth of archaeological and literary sources, Dunn also includes previously undiscovered material to present 3,000 years of ancient history with women doing more than just weaving or baking: many possessed property, ran businesses, oversaw estates, wrote poetry, and even went to war.

Beginning in Minoan Crete and concluding with the collapse of the Roman Julian-Claudian dynasty, Dunn's story is a global one that moves through Greece, Italy, Asia Minor, Macedon, and North Africa, while also staying true to its classicist focus (the worlds of Greece and Rome [see Beyond the Book]). Throughout, Dunn refuses to ignore the intrinsic contribution of women even though the majority of surviving male sources "simply wrote them out."

In ancient Minoa, Dunn claims, women were often more prominent than men, as the society's rich artwork and architecture can attest. The Minoan religion included a cult of "Snake Goddesses" who mastered snakes the same way Minoan Crete men mastered bulls. The quantity of Minoan artworks with women as the central focus has led some historians to suggest Minoan society was matriarchal or matrilineal, and Dunn agrees to the extent that there is no evidence to indicate women were secondary to men in Minoan Crete.

Although Dunn acknowledges men's primacy in the arenas of power, she underscores the myriad ways women influenced the course of history through their actions. During the epic Greco-Persian Wars, Dunn argues, "exceptional women and girls demonstrated both fortitude and ingenuity." She tells the fascinating story of Gorgo, a Spartan princess and future wife of King Leonidas, whose "quick thinking as an early code-breaker" deciphered a cleverly concealed warning on wax tablets about the invasion of Xerxes' Persian forces in 490 BCE that alerted Sparta and other communities to imminent danger. Women also engaged in violence…and ferociously, too.

A case in point was Queen Tomyris of the nomadic Massagetae tribe on the eastern borders of the Caspian Sea. When Tomyris turned down his marriage proposal in 530/29 BCE, Cyrus of Persia invaded her lands and targeted her people. When Tomyris's son, Spargapises, was captured by Cyrus and died by suicide rather than be held hostage, Tomyris sought vengeance. After massacring Cyrus's forces in battle, Tomyris was reported to have filled an animal skin with human blood and deposited Cyrus's head inside, to fulfill her earlier threat that he would have his "glut of blood" for stealing away Spargapises. No mere hidden sidenote of history, Dunn says Roman writers of the period considered it "one of the most memorable deeds ever performed by a woman in ancient history."

From Artemisia, the sole female commander on either side of the Greco-Persian Wars, to the equally fierce women behind Roman senators and emperors, Dunn's range is sweeping yet sharply focused on her subjects' often-overlooked contributions. In a chapter entitled "This One's for Fulvia," Dunn resuscitates the character of Fulvia, Mark Antony's second wife, who not only warned Cicero about a plot to assassinate him (the infamous Catiline Conspiracy) but also organized a war to protect Antony's reputation. The Perusine War of 41-40 BCE was "truly Fulvia's war," Dunn argues, and recent excavations reveal how close Fulvia was to the action. Lead bullets hurled over the city walls by Octavian's besieging forces were inscribed with vulgar messages to Fulvia. Dunn shares Fulvia's troops' response with her own witty riposte: "'I'm aiming for Octavian's bumhole,' read a counter missile, which was of such a size as to make the threat feasible, though extremely unlikely to be fulfilled."

Fulvia was just one among Dunn's broad cast of exceptional women whose "loyalty and fortitude" was disregarded by their male counterparts, "as women's so often were." Dunn ably brings to the fore women's roles in antiquity—whether writing poetry like Sappho, fighting like Tomyris, or acting as "mistresses of guile" in the palace halls—without pandering to ideology or distorting the reality of patriarchy in ancient cultures.

Dunn answers the many male-centric histories of antiquity with this shimmering volume that celebrates women as true "creators of history" instead of passive bystanders. *The Missing Thread,* with its rich erudition and sprightly narrative, is an engrossing addition to antiquity studies that readers will want on their shelves for years to come.

Reviewed by Peggy Kurkowski. This review first ran in the July 31, 2024 issue of BookBrowse Recommends.

BEST BOOKS OF 2023

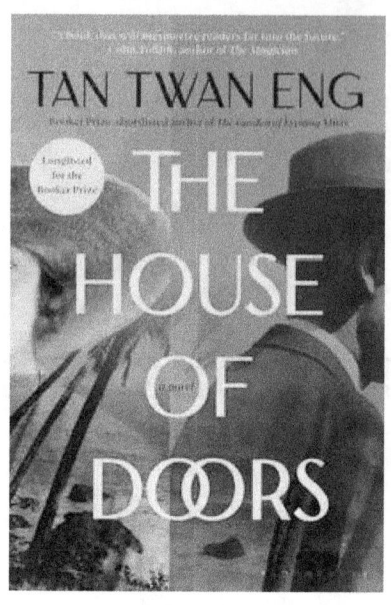

THE HOUSE OF DOORS

by Tan Twan Eng

BookBrowse Rating: 5/5
Critics' Consensus: 5/5
Readers' Rating: 5/5

Published October 2024 in Paperback, 320 pages

Summary

From the bestselling author of *The Garden of Evening Mists*, a spellbinding novel about love and betrayal, colonialism and revolution, storytelling and redemption.

The year is 1921. Lesley Hamlyn and her husband, Robert, a lawyer and war veteran, are living at Cassowary House on the Straits Settlement of Penang. When "Willie" Somerset Maugham, a famed writer and old friend of Robert's, arrives for an extended visit with his secretary Gerald, the pair threatens a rift that could alter more lives than one.

Maugham, one of the great novelists of his day, is beleaguered: Having long hidden his homosexuality, his unhappy and expensive marriage of convenience becomes unbearable after he loses his savings—and the freedom to travel with Gerald. His career deflating, his health failing, Maugham arrives at Cassowary House in desperate need of a subject for his next book. Lesley, too, is enduring a marriage more duplicitous than it first appears. Maugham suspects an affair, and, learning of Lesley's past connection to the Chinese revolutionary, Dr. Sun Yat Sen, decides to probe deeper. But as their friendship grows and Lesley confides in him about life in the Straits, Maugham discovers a far more surprising tale than he imagined, one that involves not only war and scandal but the trial of an Englishwoman charged with murder. It is, to Maugham, a story worthy of fiction.

A mesmerizingly beautiful novel based on real events, The House of Doors traces the fault lines of race, gender, sexuality, and power under empire, and dives deep into the complicated nature of love and friendship in its shadow.

BookBrowse Review

This novel reimagines the events surrounding the 1921 visit by writer W. Somerset Maugham to friends in Penang, Malaysia, which would inspire his book of short stories *The Casuarina Tree*.

Every July, I take on the overly ambitious goal of reading all of the novels chosen as longlist finalists for the celebrated Booker Prize award, and every year I fail miserably. This year, of the seven novels that I read (out of thirteen), six involved traumatized children as central characters. Reading these books in quick succession made for some harrowing hours. The welcome exception to this thematic run was *The House of Doors* by Malaysian writer Tan Twan Eng. Set on the island of Penang, Malaysia, in the early years of the twentieth century, the novel directs the reader with grace and humor to the contradictions lurking beneath the ice of Victorian convention in British high-colonial society. This may sound familiar to readers of the English writer W. Somerset Maugham (1874–1965), who, fittingly, shows up as one of this novel's main characters, but Twan Eng introduces a contemporary, nuanced take on the psychological complexity of the period.

The central narrative follows Maugham (here called Willie) on his visit to Penang in 1921 with his secretary and romantic partner Gerald Haxton. The two stay with old friends Lesley and Robert Hamlyn. Over the course of several evenings, Lesley shares with Willie intimate stories about her life in Penang a decade earlier. Her account involves a friend's murder trial, extramarital affairs, and her political work for the Chinese revolutionary Sun Yat-sen (see [Beyond the Book](#)), who had based his campaign in the British colony to raise funds for the revolution that by year's end would make him the first president of the new Republic of China. Lesley well understands that by sharing with Willie these significant and revealing details of her life she is tacitly accepting that they might one day become public. As Robert reminds her, "He's my friend, but he's also a writer, and there's nothing he loves more than snuffling out people's scandals and secrets." And, indeed, in this story, Willie eventually does incorporate some elements of Lesley's stories—such as the murder trial she recounts—into his fiction.

The upper altitude of early-twentieth century British colonial society on Penang provides the milieu for Twan Eng's novel. Social conventions are sacrosanct, and even transgressors do anything in their power to uphold the social contract. Willie maintains the façade of a straight man in a happy marriage so that he can travel freely with his male companion. Lesley and Robert struggle to sustain their own fiction of an idyllic married life, while each seeks solace in publicly unacceptable partnerships; their fear of exposure safeguards their union's bond.

Lesley's friend Ethel chooses to risk being branded a murderess rather than admit to an adulterous affair. Thus, many of the British characters lead double lives, adhering to strict societal mores while simultaneously contravening them. But this same leeway is not afforded to others, and at the margins of Penang's white mischief, the serious work of Sun Yat-sen's revolution moves forward.

In writing *The House of Doors*, Twan Eng effectively reverse engineers the work of the real-life Maugham, using his book of short stories *The Casuarina Tree* to envision a context within which the author might have been sparked to create his fiction. In so doing, Twan Eng crafts a novel that has much to say about the very art of narrative crafting, and structurally functions as something of an infinity mirror held up to a repeating interplay between fiction and nonfiction.

The intertwined voices and time periods make the plot gallop along, and I enjoyed the way the narrative dips in and out of true biographical detail and imagined fictional detail. In plot and execution, the novel reminds us that fiction writers are magpies who collect the materials that support their vision, discarding elements that they assign less importance, even when these elements are the very things that others commit their lives to.

Reviewed by Danielle McClellan. This review was originally published in *The BookBrowse Review* in November 2023, and has been updated for the December 2023 edition.

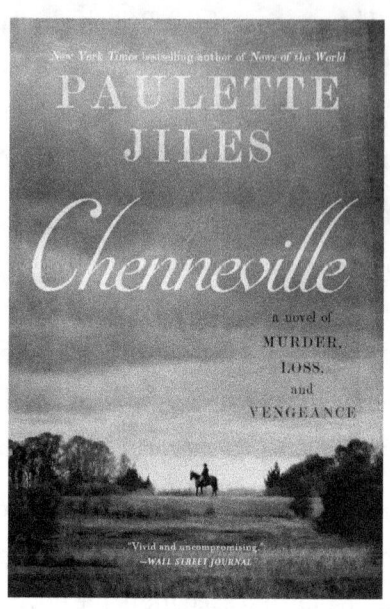

CHENNEVILLE

by Paulette Jiles

BookBrowse Rating: 5/5
Critics' Consensus: 5/5
Readers' Rating: 5/5

Published September 2024 in Paperback, 320 pages

Summary

Consumed with grief, driven by vengeance, a man undertakes an unrelenting odyssey across the lawless post–Civil War frontier seeking redemption in this fearless novel from the award-winning and *New York Times* bestselling author of *News of the World*.

Union soldier John Chenneville suffered a traumatic head wound in battle. His recovery took the better part of a year as he struggled to regain his senses and mobility. By the time he returned home, the Civil War was over, but tragedy awaited. John's beloved sister and her family had been brutally murdered.

Their killer goes by many names. He fought for the North in the late unpleasantness, and wore a badge in the name of the law. But the man John knows as A. J. Dodd is little more than a rabid animal, slaughtering without reason or remorse, needing to be put down.

Traveling through the unforgiving landscape of a shattered nation in the midst of Reconstruction, John braves winter storms and confronts desperate people in pursuit of his quarry. Untethered, single-minded in purpose, he will not be deterred. Not by the U.S. Marshal who threatens to arrest him for murder should he succeed. And not by Victoria Reavis, the telegraphist aiding him in his death-driven quest, yet hoping he'll choose to embrace a life with her instead.

And as he trails Dodd deep into Texas, John accepts that this final reckoning between them may cost him more than all he's already lost…

BookBrowse Review

In the post-Civil War South, a wounded man finds his life shaped by memory in a saga of vengeance, resolve, and consequence.

Reading Paulette Jiles' revenge western *Chenneville*, it's easy to remember she's a poet. She plays with language, painting her characters and scenery in vivid color. The story follows a former Union soldier named John Chenneville as he searches for revenge and his memories, narrated in Jiles' lush prose.

He wakes in a Virginia army hospital in 1865, suffering from a head wound and amnesia. After months recovering, John is finally released home to Missouri. But it's hard to remember who he was before. Fragments of feeling return first, "unbidden and intensely real."

> "Ghosts of a memory, impressions. His brain had gone back to the basics, remembering and re-remembering. This is truly what we are to each other: a shape, a feeling, phantoms of love or threat of laughter, those who are lucid and speak in a strange old archaic French and smell of well-worn wool, of tobacco, of apples and wine."

When he hears of his sister's murder by a man named Dodd, John becomes someone new, grieving and seeking retribution. His quest leads to Texas, and he expects it will not end well no matter the outcome. But his forgotten character soon reemerges. Hardened and steadfast, introspective and considerate. John's warmth shines when he hears women laughing, or when he cares for starving puppies and their mother.

Chenneville reminded me why reading is true magic. Jiles is a very observational writer; the flicker of an eyelid and gentle grip of the wrist are two of the many minute details she uses to display emotion and build a balanced scene. She has that rare gift of putting the reader directly in the character's shoes, and this is a character study of the highest order. When John remembers something new, you feel the elation alongside him. He feels ready to walk out of the page, or at least into a movie. This is a novel that would work beautifully as a screen adaptation.

Another of Jiles' talents is crafting characters in only a few pages of storytime. In this journey of vengeance, John crosses paths with transitory characters who often linger in rippling effects. Like a web, everything is connected. Though most of the narrative lives in John's mind, the few third-person point-of-view transitions are seamless.

The writing is restrained and never self-indulgent — exploring characters John directly encounters and remembers, such as Aubrey Robertson, the chess-loving English telegrapher who shelters him during a blizzard. Through Aubrey, John first hears of the deft skill of another telegrapher: Victoria Reavis, known as Belle. Belle captures his attention with her distinctive Morse code and sign-off. It feels deeply intentional that John learns of Belle and Dodd secondhand through others. This allows him to imagine them freely, creating expectations that guide him forward.

Chenneville's tone feels appropriate for its setting, the recent Civil War haunting all. The people and land are unforgiving; no one has time for frivolity or wishful thinking. Though chased by a stubborn marshall, John is hell-bent on avenging his sister, and he cannot be steered from this arduous task. He rides until he falls ill with fever and can only slowly recall pieces of his life.

But as his wounded mind heals and he finds his life tangled with Belle's, he begins to see a better purpose: "She seemed to him a lamp in a dark place and a saving grace from the cesspit of human waste from which he had just come. He felt an uncoiling inside himself, an unbending perhaps."

It's John's true nature that saves him more than anything. Though he fails often, he handles trials with resolute grace. He cares about all living things and never stoops to Dodd's level in an effort to win. This kindness of character is John's greatest advantage. In every situation, he chooses the decent thing, and in the end this makes all the difference.

Chenneville seems to be about how our minds shape our reality — whether they're our ideas of a person or our true memories. Who are we without them? Is a sense of duty more important than innate humanity — the ability to feel, to love, to get angry? Without it, we're hollow shells. As one man says of Dodd's kind: "They are not human...We always want to give them human motivations but they don't have any." *Chenneville* hearkens back to westerns long past, <u>Riders of the Purple Sage</u> in particular. But with Jiles' thoughtful care, it truly is one of a kind. Give this masterful novel a shot. It is highly recommended.

Reviewed by Christine Runyon. This review was originally published in *The BookBrowse Review* in October 2023, and has been updated for the December 2023 edition.

REMEMBER US

by Jacqueline Woodson

BookBrowse Rating: 4/5
Critics' Consensus: 5/5
Readers' Rating: 4.5/5

First published October 2023 in Hardcover, 192 pages

Summary

Winner: BookBrowse YA Book Award 2023

National Book Award winner Jacqueline Woodson brings readers a powerful story that delves deeply into life's burning questions about time and memory and what we take with us into the future.

It seems like Sage's whole world is on fire the summer before she starts seventh grade. As house after house burns down, her Bushwick neighborhood gets referred to as "The Matchbox" in the local newspaper. And while Sage prefers to spend her time shooting hoops with the guys, she's also still trying to figure out her place inside the circle of girls she's known since childhood. A group that each day, feels further and further away from her.

But it's also the summer of Freddy, a new kid who truly gets Sage. Together, they reckon with the pain of missing the things that get left behind as time moves on, savor what's good in the present, and buoy each other up in the face of destruction. And when the future comes, it is Sage's memories of the past that show her the way forward. *Remember Us* speaks to the power of both letting go ... and holding on.

BookBrowse Review

A bittersweet meditation on the nature of friendship, memory, and finding one's place in the world.

BookBrowse YA Book Award 2023

Remember Us is set largely across a single hazy summer of the 1970s in Bushwick, New York. With the neighborhood nicknamed "The Matchbox" by the press due to an ongoing spate of deadly housefires, 12-year-old Sage has grown up against a backdrop of sirens, ash, and dread over whose home will be next to burn. Basketball is her escape from the anxiety, and despite being the only girl on the local courts, she dreams of pursuing a future in professional sports. That is, until an encounter with a bully and the echo of his words — "What kind of girl are you, anyway?" — leaves her shaken.

Scared away from the courts for the first time in her life, Sage feels her entire identity is unmoored. Should she continue to strive for success as a girl in the male-dominated world of basketball, or should she conform and attempt to fit in with the popular girls at school, from whom she feels adrift? As Sage wrestles with who she is and what she wants for her future, her mother saves to try to move them to a safer neighborhood, despite the potential wrench of leaving loved ones behind.

Though never heavy-handed, there is definite commentary on class divide and the correlation between wealth and safety. As the cheaper, older, wood-built properties of Sage's working-class community continue to go up in flames, the neighboring middle-class streets lined with modern brick houses remain untouched. Bushwick is easy for outsiders to write off as condemned, but author Jacqueline Woodson shows that many moments of beauty and joy can make up childhoods even in troubled areas. Sage spends hours playing with friends, singing and dancing with loved ones, and sharing food with neighbors. These seemingly small moments stay with her as much as the fear of the fires, showing that moving on is rarely a straightforward decision.

Woodson strikes an excellent balance of accessibility and poignancy with her writing, lending the novel genuine appeal to a broad readership. While *Remember Us* is aimed at younger audiences and her adolescent protagonist feels authentic, its themes of place, memory, identity, and belonging will ring true for readers of any age. It never seems as though Woodson is patronizing younger readers by simplifying the complex themes and emotions at play, and she never resorts to clichés or saccharine prose. Take this moment of clarity for Sage, which considers the mindsets of adolescents and adults alike:

> "I had finally come to understand the hollowness in my chest. All year, I had already been missing all of this, even though it was right in front of me. Right in front of me but, building by building, burning away. When I finally asked my mother about it, she said *That's what growing up feels like.*"

Though relatively slight and easy to devour in a single sitting, Woodson's novel rarely feels rushed. It captures the mood of a very specific time and place by maintaining a focus on character over action. Understated and ruminative, *Remember Us* is the kind of book that leaves its mark on you subtly, over time. The relatively scant narrative follows a linear and predictable path, arguably lacking a stand-out gut-punch moment, but a heady feeling of melancholy hangs over the story, reflecting the sad reality of saying goodbye to the people and places that shaped us as children so that we may become the adults we want to be.

Reviewed by Callum McLaughlin. This review was originally published in *The BookBrowse Review* in November 2023, and has been updated for the December 2023 edition.

LET US DESCEND

by Jesmyn Ward

BookBrowse Rating: 4/5
Critics' Consensus: 5/5
Readers' Rating: 3.5/5

Published September 2024 in Paperback, 320 pages

Summary

From Jesmyn Ward—the two-time National Book Award winner, youngest winner of the Library of Congress Prize for Fiction, and MacArthur Fellow—comes a haunting masterpiece, sure to be an instant classic, about an enslaved girl in the years before the Civil War.

"'Let us descend,' the poet now began, 'and enter this blind world.'" —*Inferno*, Dante Alighieri

Let Us Descend is a reimagining of American slavery, as beautifully rendered as it is heart-wrenching. Searching, harrowing, replete with transcendent love, the novel is a journey from the rice fields of the Carolinas to the slave markets of New Orleans and into the fearsome heart of a Louisiana sugar plantation.

Annis, sold south by the white enslaver who fathered her, is the reader's guide through this hellscape. As she struggles through the miles-long march, Annis turns inward, seeking comfort from memories of her mother and stories of her African warrior grandmother. Throughout, she opens herself to a world beyond this world, one teeming with spirits: of earth and water, of myth and history; spirits who nurture and give, and those who manipulate and take. While Ward leads readers through the descent, this, her fourth novel, is ultimately a story of rebirth and reclamation.

From one of the most singularly brilliant and beloved writers of her generation, this miracle of a novel inscribes Black American grief and joy into the very land—the rich but unforgiving forests, swamps, and rivers of the American South. *Let Us Descend* is Jesmyn Ward's most magnificent novel yet, a masterwork for the ages.

BookBrowse Review

In pre-Civil War America, the enslaver of teenage Annis and her mother separates and sells them in New Orleans. On a new plantation, Annis tries to survive brutalities while being haunted by a spirit.

Separated from her mother and everyone she loves by her enslaver, Annis tries to figure out what remains. A spirit, Mama Aza, has been following Annis's lineage for generations, waiting to be seen. When Annis's enslaver sells her to a plantation in New Orleans, five states away from her birthplace in Virginia, Mama Aza asserts her presence. Annis navigates surviving the brutalities of slavery while learning how to live a life of freedom on her own terms — and how that may involve divine intervention. Jesmyn Ward's *Let Us Descend* is as horrific as it is beautiful, the definition of grief itself. The way Ward manipulates language is as demanding of attention as Mama Aza; this novel is a force to be reckoned with.

Something that appealed to me on a narrative, structural level is the story's main points of tension. By default, slavery offers its horrors as a tension. Annis's overwhelming grief as she loses people close to her is also a relatively expected narrative layer. Mama Aza's mystical, sometimes sinister presence is a fascinating, unexpected tension that complements Annis's experiences very well. But these tensions are not the only moving pieces of the plot as it unfolds: Ward's novel is also a coming-of-age story. Alongside the bleak reality of her life, readers grow up with Annis, hearing her interests and her desire for freedom, seeing how what freedom means to her evolves.

We cannot talk about *Let Us Descend*, or even Jesmyn Ward for that matter, without talking about how her novels drip with descriptive language. I especially love the descriptions Ward gives her characters: "Safi's neck flashes with the sun that cuts through the leaves: fresh-cut wood set aflame." Among countless impressive images and phrasings, one linguistic decision especially stuck with me. Ward makes a very intentional choice of referring to those who have bought Annis as "slavers" or "sires" — never as "masters." The absence of "master" throughout is *very* loud. Language as a tool — both as a weapon to hurt and an instrument of healing — is an important theme, so it is inevitable to consider the omission of the word in the context of Ward's narrative. I observed some of the connotations "master" has for me.

Think, for example, especially in a spiritual sense, of how a being can be described as a "master of fate." A master is something or someone who commands. The word has this dominating aura and, in *Let Us Descend*, the power to deplete Annis of any control or means to truly direct herself. Definitions of "master" that support these connotations include "gain control of" and "overcome" (from Oxford Languages), as well as "victor" and "superior" (synonyms from Merriam-Webster). Yes, Annis being a slave with no legal rights informs the de facto dynamics at play between her and her enslaver, but her enslaver is not a "master" of her entire being. Her narrative is her own, and it is not only commanded by the people or things that subjugate her.

As intriguing as Ward's novel was to me, there are aspects I questioned and that may not be for everyone. One of the hardest challenges of writing a story from the point of view of a slave is creating a sense of hope. By default, slaves lived a life trying to find hope in a world fundamentally devoid of it. Though a little goes a long way to keep Annis afloat, the ending threw me for an unsatisfactory loop, as Ward stretches the novel's sense of hope into something that feels artificial and convenient; I couldn't find the final direction believable. Another part that I had a hard time with was the spiritual aspect. A huge subplot involves the spirit: Is she benevolent? Is she not? What role does she — or should she — play in Annis's life? Many descriptions are ambiguous, and sometimes this got in the way of me visualizing what the spirit looked like or did. I absolutely adore Ward as a writer, and I do enjoy magical realism, however, there were critical moments where I needed to know what was actually going on. I needed more reality, fewer metaphors, to get some narrative clarity. I'm no stranger to novels that require you to work as you read. I just questioned some of the work I was doing to understand Ward's writing for the sake of the story.

Overall, the labor required for reading this book is demanding, but by virtue of what it is, that's unavoidable. We're talking slavery, lyricism, mysticism. These are very tall orders that, depending on your disposition and tastes, you might think drive too hard a bargain.

Nonetheless, it is a beautiful, contemplative read. Every ounce of this book was clearly made with both pain and love; sometimes Ward packs a wrenching mixture of both into a singular page. In these ways, *Let Us Descend* is worthy of everyone's time and attention.

Reviewed by Lisa Ahima. This review was originally published in *The BookBrowse Review* in October 2023, and has been updated for the September 2024 edition.

NORTH WOODS

by Daniel Mason

BookBrowse Rating: 4/5
Critics' Consensus: 5/5
Readers' Rating: 4.5/5

First published September 2023 in Hardcover, 384 pages

Summary

A sweeping novel about a single house in the woods of New England, told through the lives of those who inhabit it across the centuries—a daring, moving tale of memory and fate from the Pulitzer Prize finalist and author of *The Piano Tuner* and *The Winter Soldier*.

When two young lovers abscond from a Puritan colony, little do they know that their humble cabin in the woods will become the home of an extraordinary succession of human and nonhuman characters alike. An English soldier, destined for glory, abandons the battlefields of the New World to devote himself to growing apples. A pair of spinster twins navigate war and famine, envy and desire. A crime reporter unearths an ancient mass grave—only to discover that the earth refuse to give up their secrets. A lovelorn painter, a sinister con man, a stalking panther, a lusty beetle: As the inhabitants confront the wonder and mystery around them, they begin to realize that the dark, raucous, beautiful past is very much alive.

This magisterial and highly inventive novel from Pulitzer Prize finalist Daniel Mason brims with love and madness, humor and hope. Following the cycles of history, nature, and even language, North Woods shows the myriad, magical ways in which we're connected to our environment, to history, and to one another. It is not just an unforgettable novel about secrets and destinies, but a way of looking at the world that asks the timeless question: How do we live on, even after we're gone?

BookBrowse Review

Daniel Mason's playful, imaginative fifth work of fiction crosses centuries and genres to tell the history of one patch of forested Western Massachusetts land and its inhabitants.

"History haunts him who does not honor it." This incidental line from Daniel Mason's *North Woods* encapsulates the spirit of the whole. In surveying the lives and land use changes that have defined one Western Massachusetts site over four centuries, Mason recalls major groups and events in American history — the Puritans, colonial-era conflicts, slavery and abolition — as well as perennial experiences like love, escape, pride, jealousy, devotion, deception, and mental illness. As the years pass, ghosts linger, their presence manifested in unexpected ways in a creative work that also incorporates epistolary elements and biblical allusions.

The book is rather like a linked short story collection. Each chapter is set at a different time and interspersed with documents such as almanac pages, historical reports, journals, letters, photographs, and songs. The style shifts to suit the period and mimic a certain literary genre. A Puritan man and woman run away from their restrictive community to start a new life. An anonymous writer recounts a period of being held in captivity by Native people. Charles Osgood, an Englishman injured in the French and Indian War, plants an apple orchard and leaves it to his twin spinster daughters, Alice and Mary.

The Osgoods' large yellow house becomes the setting for many of the stories that follow. The catamount, a wild cat sometimes literal and sometimes legendary, is another linking element (see Beyond the Book). In one miniature tale, a slave catcher masquerading as an insurance salesman searches for a person fleeing enslavement. In another sequence, a nineteenth-century painter embarks on an illicit relationship with his friend; his nurse tries to protect his legacy by keeping the secret, but it emerges through a haunting that necessitates a séance.

Along with the Osgoods, members of the S. family become pivotal to the narrative. Readers first meet Robert S. through case notes written by his psychologist that say the young man's strange behavior can be explained by his paranoid schizophrenia. His mother, Lillian, takes him for consultations and considers a lobotomy. Later, through volunteering with a prisoner pen pal program, she nearly falls victim to a con man. In 1977, Robert's sister Helen finds a manuscript and trove of Super 8 recordings relating to his beloved woods and the "soul heirs" he believed they harbored.

Helen and Robert are among the characters who muse about what went on in the yellow house over the centuries. William Henry Teale, the Victorian painter, writes about what is known, and what he imagines, about its previous owners ("the place is *rank* with Time—why shouldn't I wish to scrape away the strata?"). Closer to the present day, an elderly amateur historian named Morris Lakeman stumbles upon the dilapidated residence and uses a metal detector and a published true crime report to locate evidence of human remains. What he actually finds is a surprise connection to a former owner. Nora, a woodland flora researcher whose car runs off the road nearby, hitches a ride with a peculiar local businessman who lives in the house without permission.

The natural history of New England's forests is central as the novel mourns how chestnut blight and Dutch elm disease have decimated the woods. The book also ponders how people's decisions affect the landscape. Mason presents dueling visions: a utopian future where trees are restored to life, versus a dystopian one where heat and fire threaten survival. "Succession," to refer to ecological variations or human generations, is a crucial term here.

I found it rewarding to spot biblical echoes: The fleeing Puritans enact an expulsion from Eden; the Osgood sisters have a Cain and Abel dynamic; and Teale's intimate relationship with his friend is in the tradition of King David's with Jonathan. The focus on history and myth feels somewhat at odds with the matter-of-fact reappearances of the (un)dead. Mason doesn't explain what's going on but appears to be enjoying the intellectual gymnastics, in a way that reminded me of Julian Barnes's *A History of the World in 10½ Chapters*.

While I admired the novel's sweep and ambitious blend of forms, I felt limited emotional commitment. The historical pastiches of the early chapters, though convincing, are rather dull, making for a slow start. There is then insufficient time with certain players; longer sequences are better in that it is possible to become more involved with the characters. I was therefore most engaged with the story of the S. family, followed by Teale and the Osgood sisters. Although there is a sense of humor, my overarching impression, as with [The Overstory](#) by Richard Powers, is of cerebral experimentation. Other readers are sure to feel differently. I'll keep my ears open for National Book Award or Pulitzer Prize buzz for Mason.

Reviewed by Rebecca Foster. This review was originally published in *The BookBrowse Review* in November 2023, and has been updated for the December 2023 edition.

THE HEAVEN & EARTH GROCERY STORE

by James McBride

BookBrowse Rating: 4/5
Critics' Consensus: 5/5
Readers' Rating: 5/5

First published August 2023 in Hardcover, 400 pages

Summary

From James McBride, author of the bestselling Oprah's Book Club pick *Deacon King Kong* and the National Book Award–winning *The Good Lord Bird*, a novel about small-town secrets and the people who keep them.

In 1972, when workers in Pottstown, Pennsylvania, were digging the foundations for a new development, the last thing they expected to find was a skeleton at the bottom of a well. Who the skeleton was and how it got there were two of the long-held secrets kept by the residents of Chicken Hill, the dilapidated neighborhood where immigrant Jews and African Americans lived side by side and shared ambitions and sorrows. Chicken Hill was where Moshe and Chona Ludlow lived when Moshe integrated his theater and where Chona ran the Heaven & Earth Grocery Store. When the state came looking for a deaf boy to institutionalize him, it was Chona and Nate Timblin, the Black janitor at Moshe's theater and the unofficial leader of the Black community on Chicken Hill, who worked together to keep the boy safe.

As these characters' stories overlap and deepen, it becomes clear how much the people who live on the margins of white, Christian America struggle and what they must do to survive. When the truth is finally revealed about what happened on Chicken Hill and the part the town's white establishment played in it, McBride shows us that even in dark times, it is love and community—heaven and earth—that sustain us.

Bringing his masterly storytelling skills and his deep faith in humanity to *The Heaven & Earth Grocery Store*, James McBride has written a novel as compassionate as *Deacon King Kong* and as inventive as *The Good Lord Bird*.

BookBrowse Review

***The Heaven & Earth Grocery Store* extols the power of community and brings an expansive spotlight to the affections between Black and Jewish families in the 1930s.**

The Heaven & Earth Grocery Store by James McBride takes place in Pottstown, Pennsylvania, primarily within the confines of a real-life settlement called Chicken Hill, during the racially contentious 1930s. Chicken Hill's population was largely Jewish and Black, and included Irish, Italian, and Greek immigrants. It was a place where all types of people, united by impoverished circumstances, "pretty much got along," as McBride explains in an interview with NPR, which inspired him to recreate the congenial relationships between his characters. It is this sentiment — of people from different backgrounds relying on the kindness of their neighbors — that holds the novel together.

Opening in 1972 as investigators discover a skeleton at the bottom of an old Chicken Hill well, McBride hits the ground running, setting the stage for an engaging whodunit thriller. But the novel soon turns back the clock to the 1930s and traces the mystery from the source. It evolves into a winding and all-encompassing look at Chicken Hill, its history, and the cast of characters that give it life. Among them is a Jewish couple, strong-willed Chona, the proprietor of the Heaven & Earth Grocery Store who suffers from epileptic seizures and a limp, and her theater-owning husband Moshe. Moshe desperately wants to move off the Hill, to follow other Jewish families to an area of more financial promise, but Chona refuses to leave the grocery store — or the population of children and families she helps through handouts — so on the Hill they stay.

Nate Timblin, a seemingly serene man who is revered by the other Black residents, works under Moshe at the theater, and his wife Addie works with Chona in the Heaven & Earth Grocery Store. Nate and Addie have recently taken guardianship over young Dodo, who was the victim of an explosive kitchen accident that killed his mother and left him almost completely deaf. Soon, Nate gets word that the State is sending men after Dodo, keen on admitting him into Pennhurst, a local mental institution. When Dodo's safety is put in jeopardy, Nate's fatherly affections for the boy give way to an intense inner power struggle — he wants to save Dodo, yet fears undertaking such an emotional and difficult journey might "unleash the evil poison in him" that he fights to keep hidden and under control. One of the most engaging elements of McBride's plot is Nate's secretive past and his gallant efforts to control his demons.

Knowing what the conditions in establishments such as Pennhurst are like (see Beyond the Book), he and Addie immediately take action, going to the community for help. Chona rises above the rest, taking Dodo's safety into her own hands. However, her mysterious illness continues to worsen, limiting her ability to protect him. Worse yet, she is plagued by the ominous and blundering presence of Doc Roberts, the only doctor on Chicken Hill — and a member of the KKK — who harbors a dark obsession with her. Nearly everyone in the neighborhood rallies to protect Dodo — an enduring and poignant example of the power of community that smolders at the center of the novel.

One of the most compelling elements of McBride's writing is its interconnectedness. The finale is a thrilling, Rube-Goldberg-esque sequence of events that culminates in a near perfect ending. The denouement slotted together so well, it redeemed the novel of some of its slower expository segments. Reading some of the chapter-long, detail-heavy sections, I found myself wondering why McBride was tearing me away from the plotline for these tangents. However, I see now that he was playing the long game, setting up future events and hiding little circumstantial Easter eggs. I have a feeling this novel would be an even bigger and more satisfying delight upon the second or even third read. Ultimately, McBride sacrifices some plot momentum in exchange for a shimmering mosaic of characters and histories that we can only see in full once the final page has been read.

At the heart is community, and the tenderness to be found within enduring bonds to one's neighbors. Whether your heartstrings are pulled by the rekindling of a childhood friendship, or Dodo clutching desperately to his only friend as darkness surrounds them, rest assured, they will be pulled. Yet this novel is not without its nuances. You will feel fear, rage, nostalgia, joy, frustration. *The Heaven & Earth Grocery Store* shows readers that it is possible to connect with people who are radically different from you without relinquishing the things unique to your own experience. Love bursts from the pages of McBride's novel, shining its golden light on the miracles we can accomplish as a community.

Reviewed by Abby Edgecumbe. This review was originally published in *The BookBrowse Review* in September 2023, and has been updated for the December 2023 edition.

TOM LAKE

by Ann Patchett

BookBrowse Rating: 5/5
Critics' Consensus: 4.5/5
Readers' Rating: 4.5/5

Published April 2025 in Paperback, 320 pages

Summary

In this beautiful and moving novel about family, love, and growing up, Ann Patchett once again proves herself one of America's finest writers.

In the spring of 2020, Lara's three daughters return to the family's orchard in Northern Michigan. While picking cherries, they beg their mother to tell them the story of Peter Duke, a famous actor with whom she shared both a stage and a romance years before at a theater company called Tom Lake. As Lara recalls the past, her daughters examine their own lives and relationship with their mother, and are forced to reconsider the world and everything they thought they knew.

Tom Lake is a meditation on youthful love, married love, and the lives parents have led before their children were born. Both hopeful and elegiac, it explores what it means to be happy even when the world is falling apart. As in all of her novels, Ann Patchett combines compelling narrative artistry with piercing insights into family dynamics. The result is a rich and luminous story, told with profound intelligence and emotional subtlety, that demonstrates once again why she is one of the most revered and acclaimed literary talents working today.

BookBrowse Review

***Tom Lake* centers on a woman telling her grown daughters about her past, including a brief romance with a now-famous movie star.**

"The thing about picking cherries is that you can look only at the tree you're on, and if you have any sense, you'll just look at the branch you have your hands in," says Lara, the narrator of Ann Patchett's *Tom Lake*. Lara and her husband own a cherry orchard in Michigan, and the book takes place during the harvest of the summer month, for which her three grown daughters are onsite to help. It's the middle of the pandemic, so there isn't much else to do, and they beg Lara to tell them the story of how she came to date heartthrob actor Peter Duke when she was younger.

When Lara says you can only look at the tree you're on, she's also stating one of the novel's themes. Just as some of their cherries are sweet and some are tart, so are her memories (like everyone's), and it's wisest to focus on what's in front of you. Though the characters describe problems that may befall their crop at other times, the harvest is abundant and ripe. The scenes of Lara telling her story probably cover only a few days, but they have an eternal present tense about them, as long days of a summer spent in pandemic isolation do. When Lara revisits the past, those stories are told with the same immediacy, giving the reader a sense that the past and present are happening simultaneously.

I couldn't believe how easy it was to get into the book and absorbed in Lara's story. As a writer myself, I took a lot of notes about Patchett's style here. Rather than crafting shimmering passages that call attention to her skill, Patchett's gift is to make herself disappear so we can better connect with the characters. Lara is likable and unpretentious. From the start we learn of her unlikely path to fame: while in high school, she observed auditions for the role of Emily in her New Hampshire town's production of Thornton Wilder's *Our Town* (see Beyond the Book). She didn't think anyone did justice to the character and decided to audition herself. A Hollywood producer happened to see one performance and offered her a movie audition. Lara wasn't fame-hungry or ambitious; she just had a naturalness about her that worked (echoed by her unpierced ears and unprocessed hair). Lara's daughter Nell wants to be an actress too and can't believe her mother gave it up. Lara pithily observes, "[A]nd that is the difference between us: I was very good at being myself, while Nell is very good at being anyone at all." (Meryl Streep, also known for being capable of playing anyone at all, narrates the audiobook for *Tom Lake*).

The titular lake is the place in Michigan where Lara spends a summer doing *Our Town* and meets the pre-fame Peter Duke. The lake has a powerful presence in the story. As the characters spend endless hours in rehearsals, they start wearing swimsuits under their clothes so they can jump in for a swim as quickly as possible. The lake comes to represent the innocence and freedom of that summer, even in moments that lack these qualities. Lara learns that Peter is not as perfect as she thought, yet she's able to look back and appreciate that summer as a pivotal time in her life. In *Our Town*, the past and present converge into a reminder to appreciate everything, and the detailed nature of Lara's story reflects this sentiment. Yet, she omits details of a sexual nature for the sake of her daughters. Given that she regularly shares things with the reader she doesn't say aloud, I'd hoped for at least a few lines about sex.

The events of Lara's life flow perfectly together, which makes it exciting when we learn how she goes from swimming with a movie star to owning a cherry orchard with a husband and kids. Also, that's really how life is: we never know if a single moment will turn out to be important or not, or when we'll see someone for the last time, or how what we will come to learn about them in future will change how we see the past.

About *Our Town,* Wilder said, "It is an attempt to find a value above all price for the smallest events of our daily life." In *Tom Lake,* a pandemic summer on a cherry orchard is the place to observe these small events—and to retell them so that the telling becomes an event as well.

Reviewed by Erin Lyndal Martin. This review was originally published in *The BookBrowse Review* in October 2023, and has been updated for the December 2023 edition.

DISOBEDIENT

by Elizabeth Fremantle

BookBrowse Rating: 5/5
Critics' Consensus: 5/5
Readers' Rating: 5/5

First published August 2023 in Hardcover, 368 pages

Summary

A riveting novel based on the life of Artemisia Gentileschi—the greatest female painter of the Renaissance—as she forges her own destiny in a world dominated by the will of men.

This is the ring that you gave me, and these are your promises.

A young woman is put on trial. She has accused her painting teacher of the darkest betrayal - he accuses her of being an immoral liar. What really happened, and why will this trial scandalise seventeenth-century Rome?

Rome 1611. A jewel-bright place of change, with sumptuous new palaces and lavish wealth on constant display. A city where women are seen but not heard.

Artemisia Gentileschi dreams of becoming a great artist. Motherless, she grows up among a family of painters - men and boys. She knows she is more talented than her brothers, but she cannot choose her own future. She belongs to her father and will belong to a husband.

As Artemisia patiently goes from lesson to lesson, perfecting her craft, a mysterious tutor enters her life. Tassi is a dashing figure, handsome and worldly, and for a moment he represents everything that a life of freedom might offer. But then the unthinkable happens. A violent act that threatens Artemisia's honour, and her virtue.

In the eyes of her family, Artemisia should accept her fate. In the eyes of the law, she is the villain.

But Artemisia is a survivor. And this is her story to tell.

BookBrowse Review

A rousing fictionalized account of the early life of Artemisia Gentileschi, a pioneering feminist and master painter of the Renaissance.

Born in Rome in 1593, Artemisia Gentileschi led a successful career as an artist throughout the early 17th century. In recent years, she has come to be regarded by many as one of the most influential and talented artists of the era. However, her career was almost over before it even began, when, aged just 17, she was raped by fellow artist Agostino Tassi. At this time, Christian society was wholly unforgiving when it came to women accused of being engaged in any form of sexual activity outside of wedlock, as it was tied to the social stigma surrounding prostitution. Gossip spread quickly throughout her community, with

Gentileschi soon dubbed an immoral "whore" by former friends and neighbors. Her family's reputation in ruins, she was faced with three options: marry her rapist, take Holy orders, or take Tassi to court for his crime and attempt to clear her name. Gentileschi chose the latter, even while knowing the law favored the accused, with women forced to prove they were victims of sexual violence not only under oath, but under torture.

It is a difficult task to imbue real events with the dramatic flair of fiction without sensationalizing them, but author Elizabeth Fremantle strikes a sensitive balance. She also does well to showcase Gentileschi's inherent rebellious nature and more modern outlook from the beginning, establishing her as a young woman unafraid to challenge the norm. By age 17, for example, when the majority of the novel is set, she already regularly stands up to her father's drunken temper, in a time when children – especially girls – are expected to toe the line. The author also has Gentileschi show complete acceptance of her best friend Piero's homosexuality. These quiet yet powerful rebellions pave the way for her later determination to bring the truth to light following the assault, a mission that forms the crux of the novel.

There are further layers to her decision to go to trial, however. Early chapters lay out just how difficult it was for women to advance their standing — be it financially or socially. Greatly limited in terms of education and employment opportunities, they were regarded in many ways merely as commodities to be passed from fathers to husbands. Following her rape, Gentileschi is all too aware of the impact it will have on those she loves: "her virtue is the whole family's business." As such, her fight to clear her name is not just for her own benefit, but for her father's and brothers' too. The selfless nature of her actions makes her resolve even more poignant.

The prose pays tribute to the subject's art in its own subtle yet effective way, painting vivid scenes with words much like Gentileschi would with her brush. Specifically, there is often a focus on describing the colors of a scene, a nice nod to the artist's celebrated use of intense color in her work to add depth. More generally, passages of rich, descriptive text call to mind the sumptuous, detailed quality of Gentileschi's paintings:

> "The cobbles in the piazza, slick and dark, are spotted with fallen almond blossom that has gathered in wet drifts. The rain thins to a fine mizzle and the sun forces a few rays through a break in the clouds, gilding the far rooftops, making the scene like a painted backdrop. A distant shadow moves fast towards them, transforming, as it nears, into a flock of starlings. They land on the wet ground in a chaos of oily black, moving, flitting, gossiping, taking off once more into the air, each bird seeming part of some secret unifying harmony."

Despite capturing a sense of time and place so well, and sticking closely to factual accounts of the events, Fremantle keeps her focus firmly on the personal, human aspect of Gentileschi's story, lending it a timeless, universally relatable quality. Consequently, *Disobedient* is just as likely to stir passionate art historians as it is those who have never heard the name Artemisia Gentileschi before.

Reviewed by Callum McLaughlin. This review was originally published in *The BookBrowse Review* in September 2023, and has been updated for the December 2023 edition.

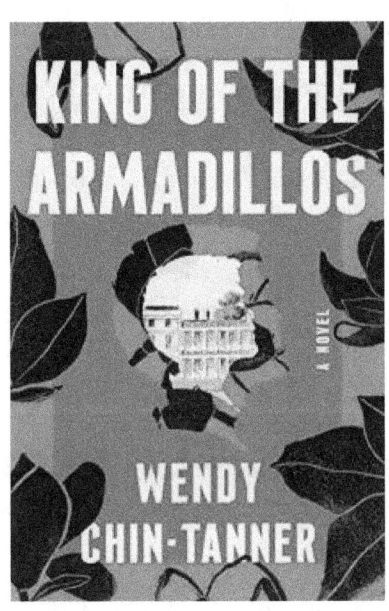

KING OF THE ARMADILLOS

by Wendy Chin-Tanner

BookBrowse Rating: 5/5
Critics' Consensus: 4.5/5
Readers' Rating: 4.5/5

Published September 2024 in Paperback, 336 pages

Summary

A transcendent debut novel about family, love, and belonging, set against the backdrops of 1950s New York City and a historical leprosarium in Louisiana, following one young man's quest to not only survive, but live a full and vibrant life.

Perfect for fans of Jacqueline Woodson's *Red at The Bone*, Netflix's *Atypical*, and *The Guernsey Literary and Potato Peel Pie Society*.

Victor Chin's life is turned upside down at the tender age of 15. Diagnosed with Hansen's disease, otherwise known as leprosy, he's forced to leave the familiar confines of his father's laundry business in the Bronx – the only home he's known since emigrating from China with his older brother – to quarantine alongside patients from all over the country at a federal institution in Carville.

At first, Victor is scared not only of the disease, but of the confinement, and wants nothing more than to flee. Between treatments he dreams of escape and imagines his life as a fugitive. But soon he finds a new sense of freedom far from home – one without the pull of obligations to his family, or the laundry business, or his mother back in China. Here, in the company of an unforgettable cast of characters, Victor finds refuge in music and experiences first love, jealousy, betrayal, and even tragedy. But with the promise of a life-changing cure on the horizon, Victor's time at Carville is running out, and he has some difficult choices to make.

A groundbreaking work of historical fiction, *King of the Armadillos* announces Wendy Chin-Tanner as an extraordinary new voice. Inspired by her father's experience as a young patient at Carville, this tender coming-of-age novel is a captivating look at a forgotten radical community and a lyrical exploration of the power of art.

BookBrowse Review

A historical coming-of-age story that deals with stigma, family, community, love and teenage angst in the 1950s.

Wendy Chin-Tanner has authored two poetry collections: *Turn* and *Anyone Will Tell You*. Our First Impressions readers awarded *King of the Armadillos*, her first novel, an average rating of 4.5 out of 5 stars.

What the book is about:

In 1954, Chinese American teenager Victor Chin is diagnosed with leprosy (Hansen's disease). Victor lives with his father and brother in New York City, where his father owns a laundry. His mother remains in China caring for elderly relatives. It is decided that Victor will go to a federal institute in Carville, Louisiana (see Beyond the Book) for treatment of his disease due to the stigma, fears and costs of leprosy. During his stay in Carville, Victor finds friends and a first love, and discovers his talent as a pianist. The reader learns about the Carville institute and treatment of Hansen's disease as well as immigration, family dynamics and teenage angst (Cindy B).

Readers found Chin's storytelling engrossing, and were quickly drawn into the plot.

Wendy Chin-Tanner's style is reminiscent of Anne Tyler and Ann Patchett in that she is an excellent storyteller and her command of language envelops you, so much so that I found myself frequently fully engrossed in her world and paid no attention to what was happening around me (Mary S). I had a hard time putting this book down. I needed to find out what happened to Victor, his family and his friends. Chin-Tanner made them real people and I was invested in them from the first pages of this coming-of-age novel (Becky H).

Several specified that *King of the Armadillos* is more than your typical coming-of-age story.

Although really a coming-of-age story, this book has an added dimension because it has the side story of Hansen's disease included. This brings an interesting and enlightening element (Donna W). I really enjoyed this not-so-typical coming-of-age novel that entails the life of a Chinese teenage immigrant who has to come to terms with not only Hansen's disease but the chaos of feelings that a typical teenager goes through. Throw in the upheaval of moving from the only home and family he knows and any reader will become engulfed in Victor's life through the amazing writing of Wendy Chin-Tanner (Marinel D).

Reviewers seemed to especially appreciate the lesser-known historical details included in the novel…

Although fiction, this coming-of-age novel sheds light on the reality of dealing with a rare, debilitating and feared disease. It is dedicated to the author's father, who was a patient at Carville, where there is today a museum of artifacts on the grounds of the now-closed leprosarium near New Orleans (Laura C). I grew up not far from Carville and often heard stories and rumors about the "leper colony." Reading *King of the Armadillos* was shocking for me as I had no idea what life was truly like inside the Hansen's facility and figured it was just a locked-down hospital. The description of the treatments and the effects of the disease were eye-opening to say the least! (Margot P).

…and thought it would be a great selection for a book discussion.

There are so many layers in this book and much to discuss. Discussion topics could include the historical aspect of a dreaded, shameful disease, discrimination, cultural characteristics, family — both biological and found — the angst of adolescence, and emerging stronger than you were. This would make a great book club read! (Carol R). This book would make a great book club selection because of the large number of themes and topics to explore in discussion. There is a great opportunity for the facilitator to present additional information about Hansen's disease — historical information as well as current-day treatment. Themes include family relationships, secrets/sacrifice, medical ethics, societal discrimination and group dynamics, among numerous others! (Judy G).

Reviewed by First Impressions Reviewers. This review was originally published in *The BookBrowse Review* in July 2023, and has been updated for the September 2024 edition.

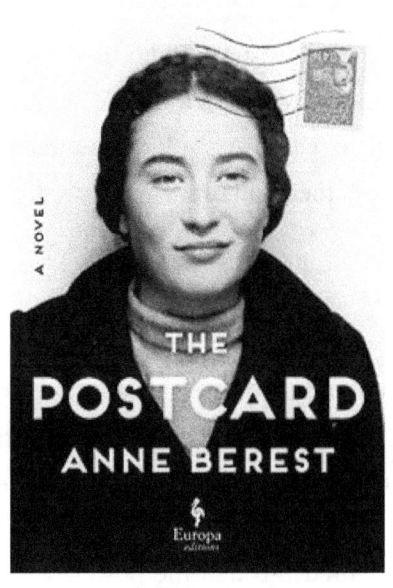

THE POSTCARD

by Anne Berest

BookBrowse Rating: 5/5
Critics' Consensus: 5/5
Readers' Rating: 5/5

Published May 2024 in Paperback, 480 pages

Summary

Anne Berest's *The Postcard* is among the most acclaimed and beloved French novels of recent years. Luminous and gripping to the very last page, it is an enthralling investigation into family secrets, a poignant tale of mothers and daughters, and a vivid portrait of twentieth-century Parisian intellectual and artistic life.

January, 2003. Together with the usual holiday cards, an anonymous postcard is delivered to the Berest family home. On the front, a photo of the Opéra Garnier in Paris. On the back, the names of Anne Berest's maternal great-grandparents, Ephraïm and Emma, and their children, Noémie and Jacques—all killed at Auschwitz.

Fifteen years after the postcard is delivered, Anne, the heroine of this novel, is moved to discover who sent it and why. Aided by her chain-smoking mother, family members, friends, associates, a private detective, a graphologist, and many others, she embarks on a journey to discover the fate of the Rabinovitch family: their flight from Russia following the revolution, their journey to Latvia, Palestine, and Paris. What emerges is a moving saga of a family devastated by the Holocaust and partly restored through the power of storytelling that shatters long-held certainties about Anne's family, her country, and herself.

BookBrowse Review

The Postcard **traces a Jewish family's life in Nazi-occupied France and meditates on the ways in which their fate impacted the lives of their descendants.**

Anne Berest's *The Postcard* — with an elegant translation from the French by Tina Cover — is marketed as a novel about a Jewish family during the German occupation of France but in fact skirts quite close to the line dividing fiction from memoir. Berest applies the narrative liberties afforded by fiction to augment an otherwise accurate account based on well-researched history, family documents and archival sources.

In January 2003, twenty-four-year-old Anne and her sisters are summoned to their parents' Paris home. Lélia, Anne's mother, shows them a postcard that arrived earlier in the week. Written on the unsigned card, in an unfamiliar script, is a short list of names: "Ephraïm, Emma, Noémie, Jacques." These are the names of Lélia's maternal, Rabinovitch grandparents, her aunt, and her uncle. All four died at Auschwitz in 1942. Anne's family is baffled and distressed by the strange postcard. Who could have sent it? And why?

In the chapters that follow, which transform the names listed on the postcard into fully imagined, vital characters, the novel does not adhere to strictly chronological rules. The central story of the Rabinovitch family in occupied France is approached from several directions: the years leading up to the Holocaust as the family flees Russia and makes its way to France via Latvia and British Palestine, and, equally, from the near-present reflecting back. The narrative voice is layered, often one family member recounting pieces of the story to another, reminding the reader that history is a living thing, reanimated through its telling.

Within this layering of time and place, the novel is at once a closely depicted, meticulous account of the lives of the Rabinovitch family and the ways in which their terrible fate has resonated in the lives of their descendants; a fascinating, true-life mystery involving detectives and handwriting analyst, as Anne and her mother investigate the identity of the postcard writer; and a powerful account of the occupation of France and the unfurling, systemic reinforcement of antisemitism through the Vichy government's administrative practices.

In tracing the strategic way that Jews were isolated from full membership in French society, paving the way for public acceptance of their arrests, Berest explains that "they existed in the gray area of indifference." She then follows this with an unsettling question to the reader: "Which victims living in tents, or under overpasses, or in camps way outside the cities are your 'invisible ones'?" The intentional processes by which antisemitism became increasingly normalized within European society are recognizable tactics for the alienation of marginalized groups in today's political arena.

The author also reflects on identity as she explores how inheritances of loss and trauma can realign generational values. For Berest's grandmother, Myriam, the only survivor in her family, "God had died in the death camps." Believing that "her children and grandchildren should be born into a new world, with no links to the old one," Myriam never again entered a synagogue. Berest acknowledges that this movement towards a fully secular life has also been a part of her inheritance. She recognizes that her history is a deep, living thing as she grapples to fully engage with the complex reverberations of her family's virtual erasure: "And that struggle is what constitutes me."

Reviewed by Danielle McClellan. This review was originally published in *The BookBrowse Review* in June 2023, and has been updated for the May 2024 edition.

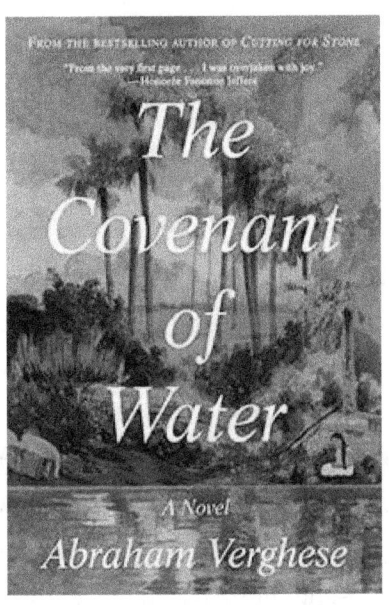

THE COVENANT OF WATER

by Abraham Verghese

BookBrowse Rating: 5/5
Critics' Consensus: 5/5
Readers' Rating: 4.5/5

First published May 2023 in Hardcover, 736 pages

Summary

Winner: BookBrowse Fiction Award 2023

From the New York Times–bestselling author of *Cutting for Stone* comes a stunning and magisterial epic of love, faith, and medicine, set in Kerala, South

India, and following three generations of a family seeking the answers to a strange secret.

The Covenant of Water is the long-awaited new novel by Abraham Verghese, the author of the major word-of-mouth bestseller *Cutting for Stone*, which has sold over 1.5 million copies in the United States alone and remained on the New York Times bestseller list for over two years.

Spanning the years 1900 to 1977, *The Covenant of Water* is set in Kerala, on South India's Malabar Coast, and follows three generations of a family that suffers a peculiar affliction: in every generation, at least one person dies by drowning—and in Kerala, water is everywhere. At the turn of the century, a twelve-year-old girl from Kerala's long-existing Christian community, grieving the death of her father, is sent by boat to her wedding, where she will meet her forty-year-old husband for the first time. From this unforgettable new beginning, the young girl—and future matriarch, known as Big Ammachi—will witness unthinkable changes over the span of her extraordinary life, full of joy and triumph as well as hardship and loss, her faith and love the only constants.

A shimmering evocation of a bygone India and of the passage of time itself, *The Covenant of Water* is a hymn to progress in medicine and to human understanding, and a humbling testament to the difficulties undergone by past generations for the sake of those alive today. It is one of the most masterful literary novels published in recent years.

BookBrowse Review

A sumptuous literary masterpiece recreates a bygone era in South India through a family whose strongest bonds are linked to a mysterious affliction that haunts multiple generations.

BookBrowse Fiction Award 2023

Along the Malabar Coast of South India in 1900, a 12-year-old girl grieving her father's death sets off to a rambling estate called Parambil to marry a man almost

30 years her senior. Three generations later, her granddaughter and namesake begs her for a story about their ancestors and a genealogy "chock-full of secrets." So begins an unforgettable journey of faith, medicine and love in Abraham Verghese's magisterial novel *The Covenant of Water*.

Mariamma, the young bride, arrives at the 500-acre Parambil farm missing her mother and uncertain of her future. Finding strength in her faith as a Saint Thomas Christian (see Beyond the Book), she throws herself into her duties as a wife and homemaker. As the years go by and she bears a child, her stepson JoJo calls her Big Ammachi ("Big Little Mother"), and the name sticks. She becomes the matriarch and mainstay of a family with a peculiar affliction, one she refers to as the "Condition": every generation, one person dies from drowning. Early in her marriage, after an unimaginable tragedy occurs, her husband unrolls a fragile parchment revealing a family tree (what she will call "the Water Tree") going back seven generations:

> "The tree on her lap lacks symmetry and is devastatingly accurate. She understands at once that it is a catalog of the malady that has shattered the Parambil family, but unlike Matthew's gospel, this is a secret document, hidden in the rafters, to be viewed only by family members, and only when they absolutely must see it."

Now knowing, Big Ammachi protects her children from situations that might portend tragedy. What she cannot protect them from, however, is a caste system that "is so ancient that it feels like a law of nature, like rivers going to the sea." When her son, Philipose, witnesses the humiliation of a friend in school, she must explain this system, "conscious of how absurd it must sound." Verghese explores themes of caste further through Digby Kilgour, a young man from Glasgow whose storyline eventually intersects with that of the Parambil family. Digby struggles to become a surgeon in British medical establishments biased against Catholic physicians (not to mention Irish, of which he is half). Circumscribed by this hierarchy that forms a caste system of its own and nursing the emotional scars of his mother's death, he peels "off his past like a soiled glove" and takes ship to Madras in 1933 to join the Indian Medical Service, where he develops his skills in a native surgical ward.

Here is where Verghese's wealth of experience as a practicing physician and professor at Stanford University's School of Medicine is on full display through the book's description of the esoteric ins and outs of surgery and pathologies found in tropic climes. One memorable and humorous episode is Digby's first surgery at his new clinic, when he realizes a "routine" hydrocele removal is anything but:

> "Digby stares at the most astonishing sight framed by the surgical towels: a scrotum ballooned beyond the size of a watermelon, now reaching the kneecaps. The penis is buried in the swelling like a belly button in an obese abdomen."

Digby's panic is allayed by the appearance of the head matron, the no-nonsense Honorine, who reassures him the operation is no different than what he has already done back in Scotland, only the pathology is magnified. In Verghese's elegant prose, the moment moves from the absurd to the transcendent: "That word captures Digby's first impression of India. It is a term he'll use often when a familiar disease takes on grotesque proportions in the tropics: 'magnified.'"

Magnified is also an apt way to characterize a book weighing in at 736 pages. Verghese sustains this massive story with numerous enigmatic and vividly drawn characters like Big Ammachi, Digby, a Swedish physician named Rune who runs a colony for lepers, Philipose and his love Elsie, who is born to be an artist of staggering genius if only the world will let her. However, running like a riptide beneath the waters of the Malabar Coast, the Condition strikes the family in new, unbidden and heartbreaking ways. It will reach a crescendo with Mariamma, Big Ammachi's granddaughter, who becomes a neurosurgeon to unlock the secrets of this affliction, only to face the secrets "that can bind them together or bring them to their knees when revealed." She will come to understand how the Condition takes away but also gives gifts one may not have wanted.

Set against the backdrop of India's journey from the yoke of British colonialism to partition, independence and violent Naxalite revolutionary movements, Abraham Verghese's first novel since *Cutting for Stone* (2009) is a lush, literary masterpiece—written with a surgeon's skill and an artist's eye—that delivers a rich, emotional return on the reader's investment.

Reviewed by Peggy Kurkowski. This review was originally published in *The BookBrowse Review* in May 2023, and has been updated for the December 2023 edition.

THE WAGER

by David Grann

BookBrowse Rating: 5/5
Critics' Consensus: 5/5
Readers' Rating: 4.5/5

First published April 2023 in Hardcover, 352 pages

Summary

Winner: BookBrowse Nonfiction Award 2023

From the #1 *New York Times* bestselling author of *Killers of the Flower Moon*, a page-turning story of shipwreck, survival, and savagery, culminating in a court martial that reveals a shocking truth. The powerful narrative reveals the deeper meaning of the events on *The Wager*, showing that it was not only the captain and crew who ended up on trial, but the very idea of empire.

On January 28, 1742, a ramshackle vessel of patched-together wood and cloth washed up on the coast of Brazil. Inside were thirty emaciated men, barely alive, and they had an extraordinary tale to tell. They were survivors of His Majesty's Ship the Wager, a British vessel that had left England in 1740 on a secret mission during an imperial war with Spain. While the Wager had been chasing a Spanish treasure-filled galleon known as "the prize of all the oceans," it had wrecked on a desolate island off the coast of Patagonia. The men, after being marooned for months and facing starvation, built the flimsy craft and sailed for more than a hundred days, traversing nearly 3,000 miles of storm-wracked seas. They were greeted as heroes.

But then ... six months later, another, even more decrepit craft landed on the coast of Chile. This boat contained just three castaways, and they told a very different story. The thirty sailors who landed in Brazil were not heroes – they were mutineers. The first group responded with countercharges of their own, of a tyrannical and murderous senior officer and his henchmen. It became clear that while stranded on the island the crew had fallen into anarchy, with warring factions fighting for dominion over the barren wilderness. As accusations of treachery and murder flew, the Admiralty convened a court martial to determine who was telling the truth. The stakes were life-and-death—for whomever the court found guilty could hang.

The Wager is a grand tale of human behavior at the extremes told by one of our greatest nonfiction writers. Grann's recreation of the hidden world on a British warship rivals the work of Patrick O'Brian, his portrayal of the castaways' desperate straits stands up to the classics of survival writing such as *The Endurance*, and his account of the court martial has the savvy of a Scott Turow thriller. As always with Grann's work, the incredible twists of the narrative hold the reader spellbound.

BookBrowse Review

An intricate and thrilling account of an 18th-century shipwreck and its aftermath.

BookBrowse Nonfiction Award 2023

David Grann is a journalist, a staff writer for The New Yorker and the author of several nonfiction books, including the bestsellers Killers of the Flower Moon and The Lost City of Z. The Wager was popular with our First Impressions reviewers, with 17 out of 20 rating it 4 or 5 stars.

What the book is about:

Set in the 1740s, this is the story of the treacherous journey of six English warships, the Wager among them, with the secret mission of capturing Spanish silver and gold near the tip of South America. While rounding Cape Horn, and battling an outbreak of scurvy, the weather conditions turned atrocious, and the Wager became separated from the rest of the squadron. Shipwrecked on a desolate island, the surviving crew struggled against the elements, splitting into two groups: one that mutinied against their captain, David Cheap, and a smaller group that remained loyal to him. Based on personal and detailed diaries of the captains and seamen, this book has elements of true crime and history (Anke V). The book is broken into four sections: pre-mission preparation, the disastrous voyage, the desperate struggle for survival after the shipwreck and the improbable return of the few survivors to England. The conflicting accounts of the voyage and shipwreck by these survivors add to the drama (Mary G).

Readers found themselves drawn into the book by the power of its descriptions and "characters"...

Coincidentally, I had just returned from a trip through the Strait of Magellan and the Drake Passage to Cape Horn so I have personally experienced the wind, sleet, fog, clouds, rocky cliffs and raging seas that he so vividly describes. Reading this book swept me right back to this wild place (Linda M). An interesting cast of characters from all ages and strata of society: David Cheap, captain of the flagship Centurion; gunner and log keeper John Bulkeley; 16-year-old John Byron of poet Lord Byron's family; carpenter Cummins, who cobbled together a fragile boat (Gail B).

…and were intrigued by the deep intellectual and moral questions the story raised, as well as the historical details.

What makes this story so fascinating is it covers so many facets; it is not just a shipwreck story. The focus changes to a mutiny (or is it even a mutiny if the ship is no longer at sea?), to a survival story, to a moral conflict story (who should be sacrificed and based on what?), to a legal story…and finally a good refresher of this fascinating time in history (Suzanne B). An unbelievable but true story of hardship, fortitude, betrayal, human folly and survival. It's also a look at the pervasiveness of England's 18th-century societal class structure, its government and its imperialistic ambitions (Brenda D).

A few readers warned that the book may not be best for those looking for something light…

There are so many characters, so many positions/ranks among the crew, diseases, scurvy, burials overboard, storms and eventually mayhem, murder, mutiny and cannibalism (Sherry K). This is a book for someone who enjoys digging into the backstories in history. This would be a fitting discussion for a book club that discusses personalities, events and motivation for actions. I would not recommend to a book club that prefers lighter subjects (Jan B).

…but many found it to be thrilling, entertaining and an overall great read.

I found this book to be well-researched, well-written and extremely easy to read. It was actually quite a thrilling read to be honest. It felt more like I was reading an adventure book than a nonfiction book (Tara T). Although the subject matter was not of great interest to me when I started reading the book, my opinion quickly changed when more of the narrative was developed. The author takes a maritime scandal and engulfs the reader in a suspenseful historical thriller! (Dan

W). It's a riveting, page-turning adventure, complete with shipwreck, mutiny and murder (Lois K).

Reviewed by First Impressions Reviewers. This review was originally published in *The BookBrowse Review* in June 2023, and has been updated for the December 2023 edition

ONLY THE BEAUTIFUL

by Susan Meissner

BookBrowse Rating: 5/5
Critics' Consensus: 5/5
Readers' Rating: 5/5

Published March 2024 in Paperback, 400 pages

Summary

A heartrending story about a young mother's fight to keep her daughter, and the winds of fortune that tear them apart by the *USA Today* bestselling author of *The Nature of Fragile Things* and *The Last Year of the War*.

California, 1938—When she loses her parents in an accident, sixteen-year-old Rosanne is taken in by the owners of the vineyard where she has lived her whole life as the vinedresser's daughter. She moves into Celine and Truman Calvert's spacious house with a secret, however—Rosie sees colors when she hears sound. She promised her mother she'd never reveal her little-understood ability to anyone, but the weight of her isolation and grief prove too much for her. Driven by her loneliness she not only breaks the vow to her mother, but in a desperate moment lets down her guard and ends up pregnant. Banished by the Calverts, Rosanne believes she is bound for a home for unwed mothers. But she soon finds out she is not going to a home of any kind, but to a place that seeks to forcibly take her baby – and the chance for any future babies – from her.

Austria, 1947—After witnessing firsthand Adolf Hitler's brutal pursuit of hereditary purity—especially with regard to "different children"—Helen Calvert, Truman's sister, is ready to return to America for good. But when she arrives at her brother's peaceful vineyard after decades working abroad, she is shocked to learn what really happened nine years earlier to the vinedresser's daughter, a girl whom Helen had long ago befriended. In her determination to find Rosanne, Helen discovers a shocking American eugenics program—and learns that that while the war had been won in Europe, there are still terrifying battles to be fought at home.

BookBrowse Review

The story of two women caught up in the eugenics movements of America and Nazi Germany and their fight to bring a young girl back to her rightful home.

Roseanne "Rosie" Maras' life has imploded. Her family is dead, her new guardians, the Calverts, treat her like a maid, and she's just discovered she's pregnant. Even worse, her darkest secret—she sees colors when she hears sounds—has been revealed, making her circumstances even more dire. Robbed of her freedom, Rosie finds herself fighting for her future and the future of her unborn child. Years later, her old friend Helen Calvert returns home to America after spending World War II in Europe. Expecting to find Rosie still living with her brother and sister-in-law, Helen is shocked to hear what became of her. Determined to find Rosie, Helen finds herself encountering the same discrimination against differently abled individuals as she did living under the Nazi regime. Spanning from the 1930s to the 1950s, Susan Meissner's *Only the Beautiful* explores the eugenics movement in America and Nazi Germany through the eyes of two women determined to reunite a young girl with her family.

Only the Beautiful is told from the points of view of both Rosie and Helen, with each woman's story encompassing two timelines. In each section, the two timelines serve as a before-and-after, with chapters alternating between years until the timelines eventually catch up to one another. Rosie's section begins with her being taken away in disgrace, her pregnancy and her secret—a condition known as synesthesia (see Beyond the Book)—both revealed; the next chapter returns to the year before, shortly after the deaths of Rosie's parents and younger brother. This back-and-forth chapter set up allows readers to slowly understand the events that have led to Rosie's current circumstances while also keeping them glued to the page. While the "past" chapters are slower-paced and informational, the "present day" chapters are nerve-wracking and eye-opening. Readers will continue not only to get the answers to the two biggest questions of Rosie's story—who is the father of her child and does Rosie's synesthesia make her unfit to be a mother? —but also to satisfy their morbid curiosity of what terrible thing will happen next for Rosie.

Helen's story is likewise shocking. Having served as a nanny in Europe for decades, Helen eventually goes to work for an Austrian family whose youngest child has both physical and developmental disabilities. After the occupation of the country by the Nazis, Helen discovers the true horrors of Hitler's regime and is faced with a heartbreaking decision. Although readers will be familiar with the Holocaust, fewer are likely aware of the true extent of the Nazi belief in "racial hygiene" and the T4 Euthanasia Program. Under this program, any individual who the Nazi regime deemed a burden to society or with a life "not worth living" was killed. This list of people included not only those with fatal diseases but also the elderly and people with physical or mental disabilities.

Even less commonly discussed is America's eugenics movement, which began in the early 1900s and continued in some places up through the 1960s. This movement led to the lawful sterilization of tens of thousands of individuals without their consent in order to prevent them from passing on their "feeblemindedness". When Helen returns home to America, she finds that these opinions and procedures closely align with Hitler's vision for hereditary purity, and she begins to speak out against such atrocities. Meissner's extensive research into this time period and movement is clear in her detailed descriptions of mental institutions and the resistance Helen meets as she advocates for the differently abled; although the accuracy of her writing is often gut-wrenching, the stories of these men and women and the terrible treatments they were forced to endure deserve to be shared, and Meissner has found a way to, like Helen, serve as a voice for these individuals to a new generation of readers.

Brutal and heartbreaking, yet ultimately joyful, Susan Meissner's book not only shines a light on a dark period in American history but shows the importance of speaking out for what's right. *Only the Beautiful* is a story of determination, family, and hope that will appeal to readers of historical fiction with strong female leads or anyone looking for a World War II story that's rarely been told.

Reviewed by Jordan Lynch. This review was originally published in *The BookBrowse Review* in May 2023, and has been updated for the March 2024 edition.

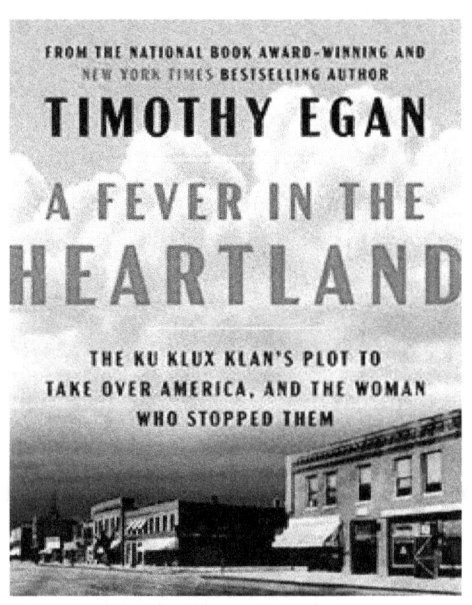

A FEVER IN THE HEARTLAND

by Timothy Egan

BookBrowse Rating: 5/5
Critics' Consensus: 5/5
Readers' Rating: 5/5

Published June 2024 in Paperback, 448 pages

Summary

A historical thriller by the Pulitzer and National Book Award-winning author that tells the riveting story of the Klan's rise to power in the 1920s, the cunning con man who drove that rise, and the woman who stopped them.

The Roaring Twenties—the Jazz Age—has been characterized as a time of Gatsby frivolity. But it was also the height of the uniquely American hate group, the Ku Klux Klan. Their domain was not the old Confederacy, but the Heartland and the West. They hated Blacks, Jews, Catholics and immigrants in equal measure, and took radical steps to keep these people from the American promise. And the man who set in motion their takeover of great swaths of America was a charismatic charlatan named D.C. Stephenson.

Stephenson was a magnetic presence whose life story changed with every telling. Within two years of his arrival in Indiana, he'd become the Grand Dragon of the state and the architect of the strategy that brought the group out of the shadows – their message endorsed from the pulpits of local churches, spread at family picnics and town celebrations. Judges, prosecutors, ministers, governors and senators across the country all proudly proclaimed their membership. But at the peak of his influence, it was a seemingly powerless woman – Madge Oberholtzer – who would reveal his secret cruelties, and whose deathbed testimony finally brought the Klan to their knees.

A Fever In the Heartland marries a propulsive drama to a powerful and page-turning reckoning with one of the darkest threads in American history.

BookBrowse Review

In the 1920s, the Indiana Ku Klux Klan had popularity, power and prestige. Then it fell from grace.

Award-winning author Timothy Egan turns his attention to the Ku Klux Klan in the 1920s in his whale of a book *A Fever in the Heartland*. The story begins in segregated Evansville, Indiana, where a con man named D.C. Stephenson set up shop. His grift: to idealize racial disgust for profit, embracing white supremacy.

At the time, the Ku Klux Klan had shifted from its original conception in the post-Civil War South. Egan explains it this way: "This was a new and expanded roster of enemies for the new and expanding Klan...Hate was tailored to the region—Asians on the Pacific coast, Mexicans in the Southwest, Mormons in the Rocky Mountains, Blacks in the South, Jews on the East Coast, and immigrants and Catholics everywhere."

Stephenson was an odd choice to shepherd a white supremacy movement, since he failed at almost everything he tried. But there he was. Bribing a bunch of Protestant ministers to promote the Klan during Sunday worship services. Sermons preaching white supremacy as a Christian ethic, specifically, preaching that white men were the true Americans, spread throughout Indiana.

Intimidation was the Klan's calling card. Because there was strength in numbers, they visited towns for rallies and parades in large groups. It was a display of force that didn't always land well. For example, when a cohort of Klansmen held a rally in South Bend, home of the Catholic University of Notre Dame, students were enraged and confronted the marchers without care or concern for their own safety. The Klansmen's white hats were ripped off their heads as the protestors mocked their intelligence. "Dunce cap, dunce cap," they chanted, affixing the hats to their own heads.

It was a small victory for resistance. But it didn't change much. Jews were still forced out of their businesses. Black families were run out of their homes. The pointless violence was often based on lies, as when three black teenagers in Marion, Indiana were accused of raping a white woman. Two of the three were lynched in the town square in a picnic-like atmosphere. The woman later confessed she made the story up. Egan's epilogue of the incident: "No one was ever charged with a lawless execution witnessed by thousands of Hoosiers in the public square."

Seeping through Egan's story are similar injustices, examples of how Jews, Catholics and blacks were threatened, bullied and/or killed. It's difficult reading but not alarming. The mild surprise is that a white woman from an Indiana town was brutalized and tormented, not for reasons directly related to white supremacy, but because she was in the clutches of a predator. This supports the idea that angry white men unleash their rage randomly.

Her name was Madge Oberholtzer. She attended the inaugural ball of the newly elected Indiana Governor Edward L. Jackson and sat directly across from Klan leader Stephenson, who was constantly on the lookout for new prey. Oberholtzer was a former sorority girl, a teacher who lived with her parents four blocks from Stephenson. At the ball, he asked her to dance and then gave her his phone number.

Oberholtzer was enamored by Stephenson's charisma. She was naïve about sexually sadistic men, and unaware that he took pleasure in inflicting pain upon women. If any one thing had happened differently — had Oberholtzer not gone to Stephenson's house one night when he called asking her to come, had she stayed home with her parents — perhaps the Klan's presence in Indiana would have remained intact and she would not have died. But she went to Stephenson's house only to endure a 38-hour ordeal of rape and torture. Before her death from taking bichloride of mercury, a poison, she told her story to Asa Smith, an attorney who painstakingly transcribed her version of events, which was read at trial by state prosecutor Will Remy.

Egan's research of this nearly 100-year-old story is detailed and he makes the case that the details were imperative to the results. Oberholtzer's death triggered the death of the Klan. The Klan strategy of bribing and influencing rural men triggered boundless fantasies. One of the more ridiculous ones was that the Klan had the political capital, chops and numbers to win the White House and rule the United States.

There's an argument that such horrifying stories, like those in this book, must be buried forever, cannot see the light of day. But we must revisit the past. Not because we will repeat it. But because we won't. And therefore, we can't make sense of the terrible things our neighbors have done to our neighbors. It's not a leap to say that the worst of people have always damaged the best of people. But what Egan illustrates through this foray into a history rarely told is how American culture continually survives the trauma of its countrymen.

Reviewed by Valerie Morales. This review was originally published in *The BookBrowse Review* in June 2023, and has been updated for the July 2024 edition.

POVERTY, BY AMERICA

by Matthew Desmond

BookBrowse Rating: 5/5
Critics' Consensus: 5/5
Readers' Rating: 5/5

Published March 2024 in Paperback, 320 pages

Summary

The Pulitzer Prize–winning, bestselling author of *Evicted* reimagines the debate on poverty, making a new and bracing argument about why it persists in America: because the rest of us benefit from it.

The United States, the richest country on earth, has more poverty than any other advanced democracy. Why? Why does this land of plenty allow one in every eight of its children to go without basic necessities, permit scores of its citizens to live and die on the streets, and authorize its corporations to pay poverty wages?

In this landmark book, acclaimed sociologist Matthew Desmond draws on history, research, and original reporting to show how affluent Americans knowingly and unknowingly keep poor people poor. Those of us who are financially secure exploit the poor, driving down their wages while forcing them to overpay for housing and access to cash and credit. We prioritize the subsidization of our wealth over the alleviation of poverty, designing a welfare state that gives the most to those who need the least. And we stockpile opportunity in exclusive communities, creating zones of concentrated riches alongside those of concentrated despair. Some lives are made small so that others may grow.

Elegantly written and fiercely argued, this compassionate book gives us new ways of thinking about a morally urgent problem. It also helps us imagine solutions. Desmond builds a startlingly original and ambitious case for ending poverty. He calls on us all to become poverty abolitionists, engaged in a politics of collective belonging to usher in a new age of shared prosperity and, at last, true freedom.

BookBrowse Review

Princeton professor Matthew Desmond tackles the question of why American poverty exists and, in the process, unpacks the complex systems that impact the poor and the decisions they make.

It wasn't a cruel accident that Crystal Mayberry entered the foster care system at the age of five and stayed there her entire childhood. Through no fault of her own, she was born into a family intimately acquainted with generational poverty, drug abuse, and violence. Following dozens of placements and a revolving door of group homes, even Crystal's aunt threw in the towel after trying to parent her, and Crystal abandoned her education at the age of sixteen. Financially supported by SSI (Social Security Income), she took the monthly $754 for granted until it was suddenly removed. While she had been eligible as a minor with a sexual abuse and mental illness history, she was ineligible as an adult. Now Crystal Mayberry was a woman in deep poverty.

Crystal's heartbreaking struggle is one of many absorbing passages in *Poverty, by America*, authored by Princeton sociologist Matthew Desmond. The data Desmond offers is sobering, upsetting, and stark. One in eight children live in poverty. Thirty-eight million Americans cannot afford basic necessities. One million public school students are homeless, living in motels, cars, shelters, and abandoned buildings. Two million people don't have running water or a flushing toilet.

A writer and educator who won the 2017 Pulitzer Prize for General Nonfiction for his first book *Evicted: Poverty and Profit in the American City*, Desmond has an innate sensitivity towards those stigmatized by poverty. He notes that rents and incomes are no longer proportional. Rents have soared while incomes have stagnated. It's not a supply and demand problem, either. In 2021, rental units in Birmingham, Alabama, and Syracuse, New York, had a vacancy rate of 19% and 12%, respectively. Yet the rents in those cities increased by 14% and 8%.

Often invisible to others, poor families spend more than 50% of their incomes on rent, yet capitalist theory and public opinion view any kind of government aid, even for housing, as a threat. Early in the COVID pandemic, when businesses shut down and the government handed out stimulus checks and rental assistance, poverty numbers plummeted among every demographic, and the child poverty rate declined the most. Nevertheless, pandemic benefits were criticized for inciting laziness.

"Poverty isn't simply the condition of not having enough money," Desmond explains, "It is the condition of not having enough choice." It can be difficult, impossible even, for those with only a high school diploma to get ahead. This demographic made 2.7% less in 2017 than they made in 1979, with numbers adjusted for inflation. In Desmond's view, the lack of a unionized workforce is responsible, because unions protect wages. Without this protection, profits ascend and labor costs fall. Real wages (also known as inflation-adjusted wages) have grown by only 0.3% a year since 1979, when the growth was 2% a year. "The real wages for many Americans today," Desmond writes, "are roughly what they were forty years ago."

Desmond is an advocate for an increased minimum wage, arguing that if the minimum had been higher in New York City from 2008 through 2012, more than five thousand premature deaths could have been prevented, as poverty contributes to anxiety and financial stress. "A higher minimum wage is an antidepressant." When the minimum wage increases, child abuse reports decrease, as do teen births.

Poverty, by America leans upon history, since poverty is like an old oak tree with a million gnarly roots. I was surprised to learn that tipping waitstaff began after slavery, when former slaves who worked at restaurants were not paid and had to depend on the charity of diners. Desmond wants to do away with the sub-minimum wage for waiters. In another section of the book, he compares the aftermath of the 2008 recession with the financial effects of the COVID pandemic. After the 2008 recession, families in the bottom half of income levels had to wait a decade for their incomes to return to pre-recession levels. But after what Desmond calls "the COVID-induced recession," the same families had to wait just a year because of government intervention by way of stimulus payments and rental assistance. He introduces the term "poverty abolitionist" to describe those who are committed to eliminating poverty by creating and supporting policy, organizing, and strategizing for those who are financially vulnerable.

In *Evicted*, Desmond follows eight struggling families in Milwaukee, documenting their troubles. He elevates their humanity above their financial insecurity. This second book is more of a sociological document, and while it may lack the kind of personal narratives readers devour, Desmond's scholarship and his unpacking of the multi-layered systems that keep poverty intractable, like housing, employment, banking, and government, is brilliant.

Having read both books in different years, I have reached the same conclusion from each. Matthew Desmond is optimistic but also out of patience. He wants us to care. He wants us to ask ourselves what kind of country we want to pass on to our children. He is begging those of us who haven't fallen through the cracks to shake off our self-absorption and myriad distractions and think of those who are suffering. While he loathes the "why" of poverty, as we all should but sadly don't, he is demanding for us to shake off our emotional malaise and do something. Do better.

He believes passionately in the capacity of the unseen and the poor, but also, and this is the important part, he believes that we have the potential to change how we approach the system of poverty and the people caught in its heavy-handed grip. Because poverty, he repeatedly reminds us, isn't an accident.

Reviewed by Valerie Morales. This review first ran in the December 6, 2023 issue of BookBrowse Recommends.

IN MEMORIAM

by Alice Winn

BookBrowse Rating: 5/5
Critics' Consensus: 5/5
Readers' Rating: 3.5/5

Published March 2024 in Paperback, 400 pages

Summary

Winner: BookBrowse Debut Book Award 2023

A haunting, virtuosic debut novel about two young men who fall in love during World War I.

It's 1914, and World War I is ceaselessly churning through thousands of young men on both sides of the fight. The violence of the front feels far away to Henry Gaunt, Sidney Ellwood and the rest of their classmates, safely ensconced in their idyllic boarding school in the English countryside. News of the heroic deaths of their friends only makes the war more exciting.

Gaunt, half German, is busy fighting his own private battle—an all-consuming infatuation with his best friend, the glamorous, charming Ellwood—without a clue that Ellwood is pining for him in return. When Gaunt's family asks him to enlist to forestall the anti-German sentiment they face, Gaunt does so immediately, relieved to escape his overwhelming feelings for Ellwood. To Gaunt's horror, Ellwood rushes to join him at the front, and the rest of their classmates soon follow. Now death surrounds them in all its grim reality, often inches away, and no one knows who will be next.

An epic tale of both the devastating tragedies of war and the forbidden romance that blooms in its grip, *In Memoriam* is a breathtaking debut.

BookBrowse Review

A heartrending romance between two young soldiers set against the horrific backdrop of WWI.

BookBrowse Debut Book Award 2023

Alice Winn's remarkable debut, *In Memoriam*, opens in 1914 at Preshute College, a fictional British boarding school for wealthy young men. World War I has just begun, and each student longs to enlist; in their youthful ignorance they romanticize battle and dream of committing acts of daring-do in the name of God and country. Two such innocents are close friends Henry Gaunt and Sidney Ellwood. The 18-year-olds are attracted to each other but can't express their feelings, each believing the other doesn't reciprocate the sentiment. Gaunt, whose family has strong German ties, enlists at his mother's urging to prove his family's loyalty to England, and Ellwood follows him soon thereafter, even as casualties mount among their classmates already fighting on the other side of the Channel. The boys are soon disillusioned as they're exposed to the horrors of trench warfare and their own deaths seem imminent.

The author's descriptions of the WWI battlefront leave an indelible image. As Gaunt arrives in the trenches for the first time, he finds, "The smell was overwhelming, but worse than that were the bits of corpses sticking out of the walls. The men had evidently tried to bury them, but in the rain the earth did not hold together. Feet and hands and faces poked at him as he walked by." Ellwood observes that the sandbags "were a sickening mixture of sand and gut-smeared earth. They reeked of decomposing flesh, and sometimes would burst open, showering passers-by with gore and maggots." The story is filled with men ordered to their deaths out of petty revenge or simple ignorance, with officers often displaying a callous disregard for the young lives wasted for no good reason. The author realistically conveys the various ways conflicts like this can leave someone permanently scarred, both physically and emotionally. As an anti-war book it can't be beat, comparing favorably to classics like *All Quiet on the Western Front*.

As well-written as the novel's battle scenes are, its highlight is the love story between Ellwood and Gaunt, and the dynamic between the two sets up the primary tension in the narrative. Winn completely captures Ellwood and Gaunt's terrible longing for each other and the ache of their unexpressed love. The novel is heartbreaking at times, peppered with misunderstandings and missed opportunities: "Ellwood did not come to him, and Gaunt didn't know how to ask him to." As death rains down around the pair, readers yearn for them to tell each other how they feel before it's too late, and we're constantly reminded how painfully young these men are.

A few aspects of the book don't quite meet the high bar set by most of the narrative. Winn goes out of her way to illustrate how WWI was experienced from many viewpoints, such as how some women supported the war effort, the pride and pain parents felt in seeing their sons enlist, how different classes experienced war, and the ordeal that those wounded in battle underwent. While most of these perspectives are exceptionally well-written and seem dead-on accurate, a long section about a POW camp for officers comes across as a bit cartoonish -- a little reminiscent of a sitcom – and seems out of step with the intensity of other chapters. In addition, those around Ellwood and Gaunt seem to know they're gay but are completely accepting – even encouraging – of their love for other men. This seems anachronistic, particularly when other scenes depict men committing suicide rather than enduring the "disgrace" of being outed (until the late 1960s, sexual relations between men were illegal in Great Britain and could lead to imprisonment). Finally, the author employs heavy foreshadowing in the first half of the novel that seems manipulative and largely unnecessary. But although I was aware of these flaws, they did not impact my very high opinion of the novel, and I expect most readers will be more than happy to overlook them.

In Memoriam is one of the most poignant novels I've come across in quite some time, and it made a lasting impression on me. Winn's elegant writing and emotionally intense tableaux make this one a winner. I highly recommend it to anyone looking for top-notch historical fiction or a truly affecting love story.

Reviewed by Kim Kovacs. This review was originally published in *The BookBrowse Review* in May 2023, and has been updated for the April 2024 edition.

GO AS A RIVER

by Shelley Read

BookBrowse Rating: 5/5
Critics' Consensus: 5/5
Readers' Rating: 5/5

First published February 2023 in Hardcover, 320 pages

| Summary

Set amid Colorado's wild beauty, a heartbreaking coming-of-age story of a resilient young woman whose life is changed forever by one chance encounter. A tragic and uplifting novel of love and loss, family and survival—and hope.

Seventeen-year-old Victoria Nash runs the household on her family's peach farm in the small ranch town of Iola, Colorado—the sole surviving female in a family of troubled men. Wilson Moon is a young drifter with a mysterious past, displaced from his tribal land and determined to live as he chooses.

Victoria encounters Wil by chance on a street corner, a meeting that profoundly alters both of their young lives, unknowingly igniting as much passion as danger. When tragedy strikes, Victoria leaves the only life she has ever known. She flees into the surrounding mountains where she struggles to survive in the wilderness with no clear notion of what her future will bring. As the seasons change, she also charts the changes in herself, finding in the beautiful but harsh landscape the meaning and strength to move forward and rebuild all that she has lost, even as the Gunnison River threatens to submerge her homeland—its ranches, farms, and the beloved peach orchard that has been in her family for generations.

Inspired by true events surrounding the destruction of the town of Iola in the 1960s, *Go as a River* is a story of deeply held love in the face of hardship and loss, but also of finding courage, resilience, friendship, and, finally, home—where least expected. This stunning debut explores what it means to lead your life as if it were a river—gathering and flowing, finding a way forward even when a river is dammed.

BookBrowse Review

An exceptional coming-of-age novel from debut author Shelley Read, set in a Colorado peach orchard.

Shelley Read's debut novel, *Go as a River*, follows the life of Victoria Nash from her teenage years through early adulthood. When readers first meet Victoria – "Torie," to most – she's the matriarch of her family at the tender age of 17. We learn almost immediately that her mother, aunt and cousin died in a car crash five years prior to the book's start, and she was left to keep house for her father, brother and disabled uncle while also working in their peach orchard. Ripe for love and adventure, she meets Wil Moon – an encounter that will change both their lives forever.

The story unfolds in Victoria's voice as she navigates a world of love and loss over the ensuing 26 years, from the aftermath of World War II in 1948 through 1971, touching on the Vietnam War. Although the conflicts bracket her story and each has a huge impact on her life, the book is about much more than the effects of war. The author also touches on important themes such as racism, mental health and spirituality. These issues are mostly in the background, though, as the author stays laser-focused on Victoria's determination to thrive despite the obstacles she faces.

Read's prose is gorgeous from start to finish; Victoria's observations are especially superb:

> "The old house smelled like only old houses do, like stories, like decades of buttery skillet breakfasts and black coffee and dripping faucets, like family and life and aging wood."

Writing this descriptive can in some cases slow down a book's action, but the author includes just enough of it to draw us into her heroine's world without allowing the elegant language to overwhelm the narrative. It's a difficult balancing act that Read achieves masterfully.

The best part of the novel, though, is Victoria herself. Read creates such a lifelike, three-dimensional character that I woke up one morning wondering how my friend was doing, only realizing after a second that the person I was worried about wasn't flesh and blood. While her life is filled with tragedy, Victoria herself is not a tragic figure. She reminded me a bit of Scarlett O'Hara from *Gone with the Wind*, a naïve young woman confronted with hardship. At first she's overwhelmed but then she rallies, revealing a hidden strength – and it's that strength that readers both admire and love her for.

My only quibble is with the book's ending, which was more abrupt than I would have liked. In some regards it was perfect; adding a few words or paragraphs as an epilogue may have satisfied my need for closure but it would have lessened the impact. I'm certain that one of the reasons the novel's characters remained in my thoughts long after I finished it is because their stories are left unfinished; I'm not sure that would have been the case had all the narrative threads been neatly tied up. Still, I found myself wanting more, and I was shocked upon turning the last page to find the book had ended.

In short, *Go as a River* is a truly stellar work, so nearly perfect that it's hard to believe it's Shelley Read's first book. It earns my highest rating and is one of my favorites of the year. I recommend it to most audiences, particularly those who enjoy brilliantly written coming-of-age works. Book groups, too, will want to put this one on their reading lists, as many great discussion topics can be found within its pages.

Reviewed by Kim Kovacs. This review first ran in the December 6, 2023 issue of BookBrowse Recommends.

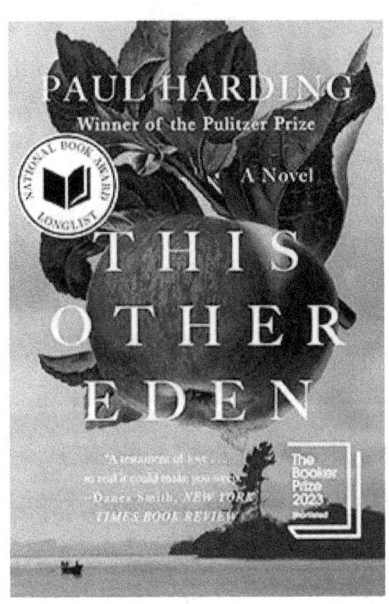

THIS OTHER EDEN

by Paul Harding

BookBrowse Rating: 5/5
Critics' Consensus: 5/5
Readers' Rating: 4.5/5

Published December 2023 in Paperback, 224 pages

Summary

From the Pulitzer Prize–winning author of *Tinkers*, a novel inspired by the true story of Malaga Island, an isolated island off the coast of Maine that became one of the first racially integrated towns in the Northeast.

In 1792, formerly enslaved Benjamin Honey and his Irish wife, Patience, discover an island where they can make a life together. Over a century later, the Honeys' descendants and a diverse group of neighbors are desperately poor, isolated, and often hungry, but nevertheless protected from the hostility awaiting them on the mainland.

During the tumultuous summer of 1912, Matthew Diamond, a retired, idealistic but prejudiced schoolteacher-turned-missionary, disrupts the community's fragile balance through his efforts to educate its children. His presence attracts the attention of authorities on the mainland who, under the influence of the eugenics-thinking popular among progressives of the day, decide to forcibly evacuate the island, institutionalize its residents, and develop the island as a vacation destination. Beginning with a hurricane flood reminiscent of the story of Noah's Ark, the novel ends with yet another Ark.

In prose of breathtaking beauty and power, Paul Harding brings to life an unforgettable cast of characters: Iris and Violet McDermott, sisters raising three orphaned Penobscot children; Theophilus and Candace Larks and their brood of vagabond children; the prophetic Zachary Hand to God Proverbs, a Civil War veteran who lives in a hollow tree; and more. A spellbinding story of resistance and survival, *This Other Eden* is an enduring testament to the struggle to preserve human dignity in the face of intolerance and injustice.

BookBrowse Review

Based on real events, Paul Harding's *This Other Eden* narrates the destruction of a mixed-race community in early 20th-century Maine.

Our First Impressions readers were fascinated by Pulitzer-Prize winning author Paul Harding's historical novel *This Other Eden*, with 23 out of 28 reviewers rating it four or five stars.

What it's about:

Some of the most wrenching novels are based on fact, and so it is here: this novel is inspired by the forced resettlement of the mixed-race population of a small island community in Maine at the start of the 20th century.

For craven eugenicists and greedy politicians and developers, Apple Island is a cauldron of sin. The island consists of those considered perverse: incestuous siblings and their mentally impaired children, a righteous Civil War veteran named Zachary Hand to God Proverbs who lives in a hollowed tree, the formerly enslaved Benjamin Honey and his Irish-born wife with their children of various skin colors, and so on. Of course, things are bound to head south when a well-meaning Christian schoolteacher-turned-missionary decides to better the lot of the island's children — particularly if that missionary feels a visceral repulsion toward Black people.

This Other Eden echoes themes and events that humanity grapples with to this day. Must those who are different and misunderstood be considered "less than" and be deprived of dignity and community? Will intolerance always reign? (Jill S).

Some readers noted that *This Other Eden* was their first exposure to the real-life story of Malaga Island.

What happens to the people of Apple Island is based on events that took place on Malaga Island in Maine in 1912 (see Beyond the Book). I knew nothing of this shameful and ignored history. This book was a catalyst for me to research the setting (Catherine H). This is an outstanding work of historical fiction, so beautifully written, but also, sometimes painful to read. I had never heard of Malaga Island off the coast of Maine, and how it fit in with America's ongoing history of racism, intolerance and injustice before reading Paul Harding's latest novel (Kathrin C).

Readers were profoundly moved by Harding's depiction of the people of Apple Island.

This book blew me away. It is such an intimate tale about people who want to be left to themselves — a small group of social outcasts in every sense of the word, except among themselves. With each other, they are a community. Gorgeously written and terribly sad — I know that doesn't make you want to read the book, but do! This is worth it (Nicole S). The resilience, faith and perseverance of the families living on Apple Island are at once heartbreaking and inspiring. Harding's lyrical prose brings the characters and the island they inhabit to vivid life, transporting the reader right into the hearts and minds of the families (Nancy M).

While challenging in some ways, readers felt the book was profoundly worthwhile.

Gracefully written in magisterial and poetic language, Apple Island itself becomes a fully developed character. Despite its slimness (a bit over 200 pages), the book demands concentration and focus but the rewards are abundant (Jill S). It is not an easy story to read, and many parts are shocking, but the narrative voice treats the main characters with respect and gentleness. I was swept into its time and location, and found myself caring deeply about the residents of Apple Island. There's so much depth in theme, richness in detail and beautiful prose to savor that I have no qualms in calling it a masterpiece (Joan R). Author Paul Harding is a master of his craft. The writing is simply sublime, even though it is not my typical favorite style. Long paragraphs, little dialogue, much description, and yet, I could not put this short book down. I became invested in the lives of every person living on Apple Island (Laurie M).

It was also deemed a good potential book club selection.

This remarkable, understated, luminous novel is well worth reading. Given the issues Harding explores, it would make an outstanding book club selection (Eileen C). It touches on many contemporary topics like prejudice, cruelty, interdependence and family. It illuminates and educates, both lovingly and with the cold "science" of eugenics. It has much meat for discussion and examination for book clubs, for families, for those who are wondering how we got where we are and where we might go from here (Susan S). The book highlights tragedy bred by prejudice, and brilliance found in unexpected places. Book clubs will find weighty topics for discussion (Marian Y).

Reviewed by First Impressions Reviewers. This review was originally published in *The BookBrowse Review* in April 2023, and has been updated for the December 2023 edition.

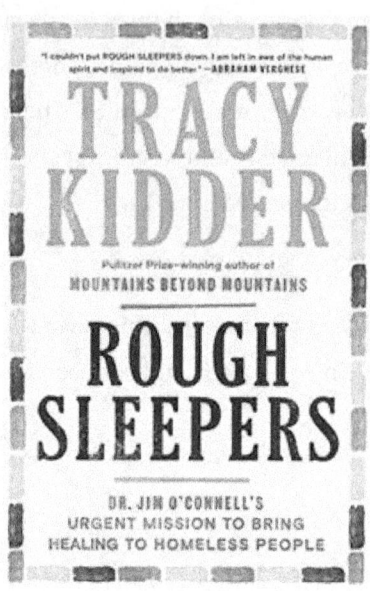

ROUGH SLEEPERS

by Tracy Kidder

BookBrowse Rating: 5/5
Critics' Consensus: 4.5/5
Readers' Rating: 5/5

Published January 2024 in Paperback, 320 pages

Summary

The powerful story of an inspiring doctor who made a difference, by helping to create a program to care for Boston's homeless community—by the Pulitzer Prize–winning, *New York Times* bestselling author of *Mountains Beyond Mountains*.

Tracy Kidder has been described by *The Baltimore Sun* as a "master of the nonfiction narrative." In *Rough Sleepers*, Kidder shows how one person can make a difference, as he tells the story of Dr. Jim O'Connell, a gifted man who invented ways to create a community of care for a city's unhoused population, including those who sleep on the streets—the "rough sleepers."

When Jim O'Connell graduated from Harvard Medical School and was nearing the end of his residency at Massachusetts General Hospital, the chief of medicine made a proposal: Would he defer a prestigious fellowship and spend a year helping to create an organization to bring health care to homeless citizens? Jim took the job because he felt he couldn't refuse. But that year turned into his life's calling. Tracy Kidder spent five years following Dr. O'Connell and his colleagues as they served their thousands of homeless patients. In this illuminating book we travel with O'Connell as he navigates the city, offering medical care, socks, soup, empathy, humor, and friendship to some of the city's most endangered citizens. He emphasizes a style of medicine in which patients come first, joined with their providers in what he calls "a system of friends."

Much as he did with Paul Farmer in *Mountains Beyond Mountains*, Kidder explores how a small but dedicated group of people have changed countless lives by facing one of American society's difficult problems instead of looking away.

BookBrowse Review

Tracy Kidder presents the captivating story of a Boston doctor's work with the city's unhoused community.

Pulitzer Prize-winning author Tracy Kidder's *Rough Sleepers* follows the career of Dr. Jim O'Connell, a Harvard-educated physician who has spent over 30 years providing care to Boston's unsheltered community.

In 1985, as O'Connell was finishing his residency at Mass General, he was asked ("conscripted," in his words) to spend one year building a program called "Health Care for the Homeless." Sponsored by a grant from the Robert Wood Johnson

Foundation, it was a trial to determine if the "poorest of the poor" could be integrated into the city's mainstream medical care system. He quickly realized that the program's patrons "seemed to believe that by 1990, when the grants ended, the big problems of health care for the homeless would be solved," but it was obvious to him that the root causes of his patients' misery weren't being addressed. "How do you treat HIV in a person who has no place to live?" he asks, "How do you treat diabetes in patients who can't even find their next meals?" After just one year working with this population O'Connell decided to spend his career addressing these issues to the best of his ability.

Kidder's portrait of O'Connell is vivid, painting his subject as a caring individual who is both frustrated and fascinated by his profession. He chronicles the doctor's journey from his first enthusiastic but naïve efforts to his becoming savvy about getting care to his patients, even if he has to use unconventional methods to do so (he decides, for example, to leave some patients' medications with a bartender who agreed to make them take their pills before giving them a drink). It's a finely-tuned portrayal that avoids the temptation of casting the physician as overly saintly or heroic; his flaws are evident, as are his strengths, and as a result, readers feel they know O'Connell well by the book's end.

The author also helps his audience understand how complicated the issue of homelessness truly is. He writes about a presentation he attended where a slide "displayed in sequence the forty-two different steps that six agencies and a landlord had to complete to get one homeless veteran housed." In another example, he quotes O'Connell as saying, "I like to think of this problem of homelessness as a prism held up to society, and what we see refracted are the weaknesses in our health care system, our public health system, our housing system, but especially in our welfare system, our educational system, and our legal system – and our corrections system." The author makes it clear that there's no easy solution. He does include statistics and demographic data, but the information is widely distributed throughout the narrative, keeping it from getting bogged down in facts and figures.

As the book progresses, Kidder gradually shifts focus from O'Connell to the individuals he has come to know through his profession, such as Santo, a man who'd been homeless for 40 years, and BJ, who lost both legs due to infections from frostbite. The author takes a deep dive into the life of Tony, another long-time resident of the streets who had been unable to find housing after serving 17 years in prison, and it's through Tony's experiences that we begin to understand the unrelenting trauma of homelessness. The book as a whole is fascinating, but it's these individuals' stories that make the narrative truly affecting and unforgettable.

Kidder spent many hours joining O'Connell in his clinic as well as on the "house calls" he made to his most vulnerable patients – van trips at night to the alleys and doorways where he knew they'd be sleeping. Toward the end of *Rough Sleepers*, he makes it clear these experiences left him a changed person. "[A] certain coffee shop," he writes, "was no longer just a place to get a good muffin, but also the shop across the street from where Harmony and Jake liked to camp, with their caravan of shopping carts and roller bags…Certain sights had acquired meaning—walking up Bromfield Street around dawn, I saw a man in a janitor's uniform sloshing a bucket of water across the pavement of a doorway, and I wondered if I knew the person who had spent last night on that patch of concrete." And I think that might encapsulate the main takeaway from this book; after reading it, I felt I had a better understanding of the issue and had developed more empathy for those experiencing homelessness – the "rough sleepers" in my own neighborhood. I think it should be required reading, and it's one of those books I find myself wanting to discuss with others, so it would make an excellent book group selection. I highly recommend it to all audiences, particularly those wishing to know more about this complex topic.

Reviewed by Kim Kovacs. This review was originally published in *The BookBrowse Review* in February 2023, and has been updated for the February 2024 edition.

IN THE TIME OF OUR HISTORY

by Susanne Pari

BookBrowse Rating: 5/5
Critics' Consensus: 4.5/5
Readers' Rating: 5/5

First published January 2023 in Paperback, 384 pages

Summary

Inspired by her own family's experiences following the 1979 Islamic Revolution, Susanne Pari explores the entangled lives within an Iranian American family grappling with generational culture clashes, the roles imposed on women, and a tragic accident that forces them to reconcile their guilt or forfeit their already tenuous bonds.

Set between San Francisco and New Jersey in the late-1990's, *In the Time of Our History* is a story about the universal longing to create a home in this world – and what happens when we let go of how we've always been told it should look.

Twelve months after her younger sister Anahita's death, Mitra Jahani reluctantly returns to her parents' home in suburban New Jersey to observe the Iranian custom of "The One Year." Ana is always in Mitra's heart, though they chose very different paths. While Ana, sweet and dutiful, bowed to their domineering father's demands and married, Mitra rebelled, and was banished.

Caught in the middle is their mother, Shireen, torn between her fierce love for her surviving daughter and her loyalty to her husband. Yet his callousness even amid shattering loss has compelled her to rethink her own decades of submission. And when Mitra is suddenly forced to confront hard truths about her sister's life, and the secrets each of them hid to protect others, mother and daughter reach a new understanding—and forge an unexpected path forward.

Alive with the tensions, sacrifices, and joys that thrum within the heart of every family, *In the Time of Our History* is also laced with the richness of ancient and modern Persian culture and politics, in a tale that is both timeless and profoundly relevant.

BookBrowse Review

An intriguing, uniquely written tale of the bonds and tensions within an Iranian American family.

Susanne Pari's *In the Time of Our History* was highly praised by our First Impressions reviewers, who gave it an average rating of 4.7 out of 5 stars.

What the book is about:

In the Time of Our History by Susanne Pari is the story of the Jahani family adapting to life in the United States after the 1979 Iranian Revolution. Shireen is the dutiful, obedient wife dominated by her overbearing husband. Mitra is a rebellious first-generation American daughter fleeing the expectations of her father and is struggling to find her identity after her sister's tragic death. The book explores generational and cultural differences in immigrant communities. The characters are flawed and well-developed. The story is raw and hopeful, and the characters feel authentic as they experience challenging circumstances. They deal with grief, infidelity, trauma and sponsorship. They also struggle with class, political and cultural barriers (Mitzi K).

Readers were taken in by the novel's captivating drama...

This book was a page-turner for me. As new information and characters are revealed, the reader is drawn into the lives and drama of a group of immigrants from Iran and their families (Stephanie K). The many plot twists work well and kept me wholeheartedly engaged (Rebecca G). I read the last third of the book in one sitting; I could not put it down (Janet H).

...and praised the realistic, well-drawn characters.

I felt I was witnessing an unraveling of an artful web of multiple viewpoints and history. The story effortlessly describes each character's contribution or thread in that web. I felt emotionally invested in each angle of the various dynamics and family relationships, such as the push and pull of the bond between sisters, the strong love between mother and daughter, and the love-hate struggle of a patriarchal father-daughter duo (Diane J). The depth of the characters made me want them to walk off the page so we could sit down, share tea and have deep conversations (Mary L). This is one of those stories that makes you sad when you reach the last page because you just aren't ready to let the characters go yet (Rebecca H).

Some felt the book was a little slow to start and a bit overloaded with description...

Pari's novel has a slow start and is a little difficult to become invested in. The early portion of the novel has a lot of descriptive passages that don't particularly add anything to the plot or characters (Kathy). My only criticism of Susanne Pari's book is that sometimes the writing imposes itself on the reading. Similes, while descriptive, sometimes do not fit the context (Connie K).

...but others particularly enjoyed Pari's unique writing and stylistic choices.

I like the writing style of this author: oftentimes the characters are recounting past events in the present, which adds a flavorful layer to the story (Sonia F). The author gives us a one-to-two-page "introduction" to each chapter by telling a brief story that does not name names, then proceeds into the heart of the story. I liked that new-to-me style (Janet H). A novel may just tell an interesting story or it may also have beautiful literary value. *In the Time of Our History*, a fascinating tale, is told in elegant language, satisfying the reader who appreciates an excellent story and beautiful writing (Jean B).

Reviewers noted that the novel includes great fodder for reflections and discussions on family dynamics...

This would be an excellent novel for book clubs to discuss, and simply for individual readers to ponder, how we stay in or leave the families we originate in (Stephanie K). Susanne Pari covers topics that are familiar to many families: children rebelling against parental expectations, "good" girls or boys who morph into different personas to keep the peace and please their families while still being true to who they are and what they want, and people whose perceptions of themselves are incredibly flawed (Sally H). This book will be hard to put down and will draw you into a more reflective consideration of cultural differences and family dynamics no matter your origins (Mary G).

...and felt grateful for having had the opportunity to read it.

In a very few words: I loved this book. I couldn't put it down and was sorry it ended. I wanted to spend more time with the Iranian American Jahani family (Judith C). I feel very lucky to have had the opportunity to read this lovely book...I look forward to spreading the word about this novel with my friends who share my love of beautifully written contemporary fiction (Cynthia V).

Reviewed by First Impressions Reviewers. This review was originally published in *The BookBrowse Review* in January 2023, and has been updated for the December 2023 edition.

BEST BOOKS OF 2022

DINOSAURS

by Lydia Millet

BookBrowse Rating: 5/5
Critics' Consensus: 4.5/5
Readers' Rating: 4.5/5

Published August 2023 in Paperback, 256 pages

Summary

Over twelve novels and two collections Lydia Millet has emerged as a major American novelist. Hailed as "a writer without limits" (Karen Russell) and "a stone-cold genius" (Jenny Offill), Millet makes fiction that vividly evokes the ties between people and other animals and the crisis of extinction.

Dinosaurs is the story of a man named Gil who walks from New York to Arizona to recover from a failed love. After he arrives, new neighbors move into the glass-walled house next door and his life begins to mesh with theirs. In this warmly textured, drily funny, and philosophical account of Gil's unexpected devotion to the family, Millet explores the uncanny territory where the self ends and community begins—what one person can do in a world beset by emergencies. In the shadow of existential threat, where does hope live?

BookBrowse Review

A man moves to Phoenix to heal from heartache and rediscovers himself through his connections with other people.

Our First Impressions readers were charmed by Lydia Millet's novel *Dinosaurs*, with 20 out of 25 reviewers awarding the book four or five stars.

What the book is about:

In this gentle novel, Lydia Millet uses deceptively simple prose to explore the psychological intricacies of a wealthy, 45-year-old white man, uncomfortable with his privilege, who is trying to do good in the world (Eileen C). The main character, Gil, is looking for a new start and for purpose in his life, having no need to "make a living." Along the way he exemplifies his humanity in his daily life with his neighbors and others. He cares for the desert birds, the surviving dinosaurs, and we're asked to wonder if they can survive the changing world. Gil doesn't see violence as the answer to conflict, but rather, it's relationships that give us life and freedom (Lynn D).

Reviewers appreciated the novel's well-crafted, compelling characters, particularly the protagonist.

I was touched that the main characters, though flawed, are all trying to be decent, good people. I especially came to appreciate Gil, who recognizes, after many unlucky years, that he is incredibly grateful for the friends who become his surrogate family (Rosemary C). Gil's observational skills allow him to understand and be empathetic to humans and animals alike. Ultimately, he touches and changes (for the better) virtually every character in the book. The world needs more Gils! (Mary Ann S).

They also applauded Millet's stylistic choices.

Millet is a beautiful writer, with a calm and expansive style. She ties up some loose ends of the story, but not all, so that the reader will find it pleasing to contemplate what may happen to these characters down the road (Susan K). Gil is a rather quiet man, but very kind and big-hearted. The story is about relationships he forms with his new neighbors, and others. I ended up falling a little bit in love with Gil by the end of the book (Jennie R). This is a simple story — dryly funny, insightful and emotionally moving. I enjoy Millet's writing and would also recommend *A Children's Bible* and Mermaids in Paradise (Catharine L). The story, while rather simple, is rich with material to discuss and ponder. The allegory of the castle next to the glass house, the birds of the desert evolved from dinosaurs, friendships and life and death are all woven into this lovely story (Sharon J).

A few readers felt the book was somewhat lacking in its structure and characters...

I like a beginning, a plot, an ending, and some relatable characters. *Dinosaurs* is a beautifully written novel, but it is lacking these elements (Leslie R). If I have a criticism, it is that I was left feeling that the world I was experiencing as I read was not fully imagined but, rather, sketched in like a photographer's backdrop (Lorelei S). I read the book but could not find anything climatic to get involved (Ruth H).

...but others were entirely captivated by the writing.

This is an outstanding book and a short read that goes down so smoothly that you will easily finish it in one day (Susan K). I read this book in one sitting — that's how much it captivated me. Lydia Millet has created characters and a setting that are incredibly compelling (Rosemary C). I love this book so much I'd marry it if I weren't already married. As things stand, my rushed affair with Millet's novel left me feeling bereft when it was over. At about 230 pages, the book is slim and easy to gobble up in two sittings (Helia R).

Readers also deemed *Dinosaurs* a great choice for book clubs.

I highly recommend this book for book club discussions. This was the best book I've read this year. Moderately paced writing that describes daily life for the key characters yet consistently and deftly introduces new and timely discussion topics throughout (Judy G). This seemingly quiet novel is actually a powerful and moving exploration of ordinary human cruelty, all the different forms love can take, and the importance of human relationships. It would make an excellent book club selection (Eileen C).

Reviewed by First Impressions Reviewers. This review was originally published in *The BookBrowse Review* in October 2022, and has been updated for the September 2023 edition.

OUR MISSING HEARTS

by Celeste Ng

BookBrowse Rating: 5/5
Critics' Consensus: 5/5
Readers' Rating: 4.5/5

Published August 2023 in Paperback, 352 pages

Summary

From the #1 bestselling author of *Little Fires Everywhere*, comes one of the most highly anticipated books of the year – the inspiring new novel about a mother's unbreakable love in a world consumed by fear.

Twelve-year-old Bird Gardner lives a quiet existence with his loving but broken father, a former linguist who now shelves books in a university library. Bird knows to not ask too many questions, stand out too much, or stray too far. For a decade, their lives have been governed by laws written to preserve "American culture" in the wake of years of economic instability and violence. To keep the peace and restore prosperity, the authorities are now allowed to relocate children of dissidents, especially those of Asian origin, and libraries have been forced to remove books seen as unpatriotic—including the work of Bird's mother, Margaret, a Chinese American poet who left the family when he was nine years old.

Bird has grown up disavowing his mother and her poems; he doesn't know her work or what happened to her, and he knows he shouldn't wonder. But when he receives a mysterious letter containing only a cryptic drawing, he is pulled into a quest to find her. His journey will take him back to the many folktales she poured into his head as a child, through the ranks of an underground network of librarians, into the lives of the children who have been taken, and finally to New York City, where a new act of defiance may be the beginning of much-needed change.

Our Missing Hearts is an old story made new, of the ways supposedly civilized communities can ignore the most searing injustice. It's a story about the power—and limitations—of art to create change, the lessons and legacies we pass on to our children, and how any of us can survive a broken world with our hearts intact.

BookBrowse Review

A chilling novel set in an alternate present in which state-sanctioned violence against Asians and Asian Americans tears families and communities apart.

Celeste Ng's dystopian novel *Our Missing Hearts* wowed readers in our First Impressions program. All 22 who reviewed the book gave it four or five stars.

What it's about:

The author holds up a mirror to our present world with all its division, anger and paranoia. Bird and his father are forced to live apart from Bird's mother, who is Chinese American, to keep them all safe from the new law of the land – the Preserving American Culture and Traditions (PACT) Act. Anyone of Chinese birth or ancestry is considered a danger to PACT. Chinese children are removed from their homes, books are banned and freedom of speech is only acceptable if you agree with PACT. As disturbing as the premise is, it is still a story of a family, of love, of faith in humanity and the fallibility of people trying to do the best that they can (Peggy S). It tells the story of a 12-year-old boy, Bird, who lives with his father in Cambridge, MA. Bird's mother has left the family because her Asian ethnicity could put them at risk. It's been three years since she left but Bird still misses her, and, without his father's knowledge, decides to find her based on a letter he receives with a New York return address (Joyce M).

Though the book has a dystopian premise, it was appreciated by many who do not normally read this genre:

Our Missing Hearts is a story that should be classified as dystopian but is so close to reality that to call it dystopian would diminish its impact. Ng has done something wonderful and heartbreaking with her third novel. She takes a mirror to our society, one that presents reality with just enough distortion to both reflect it and warp it into something unsettling but no less true (Lori S). I do not enjoy reading dystopian novels. They make me angry and anxious. But Celeste Ng wrote this and I would read a phone book if she wrote it. Although the setting and plot are both very dark, the characters are so well drawn and loving I found this novel to be uplifting, hopeful and inspiring (Shirley L). I'm not usually a fan of dystopian fiction. But this novel held my attention and I suspect will be a big bestseller. I hope the message is heard loud and clear (Karen S).

Some readers admired how *Our Missing Hearts* attests to the power of books and libraries:

The author addresses how poetry is a life force; folktales preserve the past's wisdom; society unlearns lessons and then must go to extremes to stop repeating the past's dysfunctions; art is protest; and written and spoken words matter because of their potential power for both good and evil. I was touched by the example of the efficacy of libraries in the communities' resilience and librarians as a vital source of protection for the survival of both literature and children (Rule B). Among other things it is a love letter to libraries and those who protect free speech (Pam S). The characters are well-developed and Ng's use of public art displays, rallies, poetry and folktales to spread messages about the past and the future add depth to the story (Amy A).

As well as how it reflects our current political climate:

This book is set in a dystopian world that is scarily comparable to where we may be heading. Many of the themes are ones that have already occurred, are presently happening, and could happen if we continue down the path some people in power want us to follow (Donna C). This is one of the best books I have read in a long time. It is a terrifying and all too believable fable that imagines a not-too-distant future America (Pam S). This book hit close to home for me as someone who has lived on the edge between being a Chinese person and being an American — finding it hard to fit in at school or in the community because of looking and acting different. Ever since the rise in Asian hate crimes across the country, my parents have constantly told me to keep a low profile and keep my head down. This book gave me chills (Alice L).

Many also noted that it's a great read for book clubs:

Our Missing Hearts would be an excellent choice for a book club. The masterfully written subplots broaden our understanding of real-life situations encountered by many Americans in our current (and past) cultural climate. I can't wait to discuss this book with my own book group! (Laurie L). This book is dark, emotional, and also hopeful. I definitely recommend it and think it will be great for readers that have loved Celeste Ng's other books and a great one for book club discussions (Alice L).

Reviewed by First Impressions Reviewers. This review was originally published in *The BookBrowse Review* in October 2022, and has been updated for the September 2023 edition.

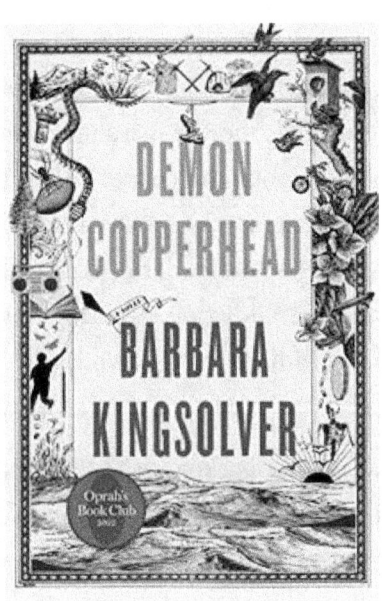

DEMON COPPERHEAD

by Barbara Kingsolver

BookBrowse Rating: 5/5
Critics' Consensus: 5/5
Readers' Rating: 4/5

Published August 2024 in Paperback, 560 pages

Summary

From the *New York Times* bestselling author of *Unsheltered* and *Flight Behavior*, a brilliant novel which enthralls, compels, and captures the heart as it evokes a young hero's unforgettable journey to maturity.

"Anyone will tell you the born of this world are marked from the get-out, win or lose."

Demon Copperhead is set in the mountains of southern Appalachia. It's the story of a boy born to a teenaged single mother in a single-wide trailer, with no assets beyond his dead father's good looks and copper-colored hair, a caustic wit, and a fierce talent for survival. In a plot that never pauses for breath, relayed in his own unsparing voice, he braves the modern perils of foster care, child labor, derelict schools, athletic success, addiction, disastrous loves, and crushing losses. Through all of it, he reckons with his own invisibility in a popular culture where even the superheroes have abandoned rural people in favor of cities.

Many generations ago, Charles Dickens wrote *David Copperfield* from his experience as a survivor of institutional poverty and its damages to children in his society. Those problems have yet to be solved in ours. Dickens is not a prerequisite for readers of this novel, but he provided its inspiration. In transposing a Victorian epic novel to the contemporary American South, Barbara Kingsolver enlists Dickens' anger and compassion, and above all, his faith in the transformative powers of a good story. *Demon Copperhead* speaks for a new generation of lost boys, and all those born into beautiful, cursed places they can't imagine leaving behind.

BookBrowse Review

A retelling of Charles Dickens' *David Copperfield* set in modern-day Appalachia.

Barbara Kingsolver's novel *Demon Copperhead* is a captivating coming-of-age tale set in rural Virginia. Her protagonist, Damon Fields (aka Demon Copperhead for his fiery temperament and red hair), narrates his life's story, beginning with his inauspicious birth in a mobile home. On the path to adulthood he encounters adversity as well as the occasional lucky break and more than a few surprises.

I confess I usually find the *bildungsroman* genre challenging, primarily because these novels' story arcs tend, by their very nature, to follow a predictable pattern. Consequently only a truly exceptional entry in the genre will make its way onto my reading list; *Demon Copperfield* is such a book.

First and foremost, the novel's narrator is one of the most fully developed, multi-faceted characters I've encountered in a very long time — no easy task when a story is told entirely in the first person. Demon's singular voice claims to be a worthless, throwaway individual ("the Eagle Scout of trailer trash"), while at the same time exhibiting admirable self-reliance and a steely determination to rise above his circumstances even when so much lies beyond his control. He's a clear-headed survivor who will undoubtedly succeed in the end.

Kingsolver's writing, too, is stellar. Her prose brilliantly captures the rhythm and humor of rural Appalachian speech. In telling the story of his birth, for example, Demon colorfully relays the role played by his neighbors:

> Mr. Peggot was outside idling his truck, headed for evening service, probably thinking about how much of his life he'd spent waiting on women. His wife would have told him the Jesusing could hold on a minute, first she needed to go see if the little pregnant gal had got herself liquored up again. Mrs. Peggot being a lady that doesn't beat around the bushes and if need be, will tell Christ Jesus to sit tight and keep his pretty hair on.

Finally, the story itself is riveting. When confronted by other hefty novels (this one tops out at nearly 600 pages), I often find myself thinking they could have used a good editor. Not so here; the plot moves along quickly, and I never once felt it was a slog. I enjoyed each and every word and found myself consistently eager to get back to the story.

As you might have guessed, *Demon Copperhead* is a contemporary retelling of Charles Dickens' *David Copperfield*, spanning the late 1990s to the present day; and perhaps hidden inside the book's title Kingsolver has included a subtle nod to Dickens himself, because in the 19th century dickens was a euphemism for the devil, as in "what the dickens", which is why Dickens initially wrote under the pseudonym of "Boz."

Attempting to rewrite such a well-known, beloved work is either very brave or foolhardy, but Kingsolver achieves the impossible, creating a narrative that stands up to its source material and, by some measures, may even surpass it. The plots certainly share a lot of similarities (e.g., both boys' mothers get involved with abusive men) but Kingsolver tailors the details to make them more appropriate to the time or place (David works in a wine-bottling business, for example, while Demon harvests tobacco). Each also has, at its core, the central theme of weak, helpless individuals being mercilessly taken advantage of by those in power. Kingsolver's themes go beyond Dickens', however, addressing opioid and other drug addiction while condemning both "Big Pharma" and the US healthcare system. Although Kingsolver incorporates many clever nods to the original (Uriah Heap becomes Ryan "U-Haul" Pyle, Agnus is named Angus, etc.) readers need not be familiar with *David Copperfield* to fully appreciate *Demon Copperhead*. Those who do know the Dickens novel, though, will likely get a kick out of how Kingsolver adapts the plot to a new time, place and set of social circumstances.

I have no doubt that *Demon Copperhead* will spend weeks at the top of bestseller lists, and deservedly so; the novel is nothing short of excellent and may well be Kingsolver's best work to date. It's a must-read for the author's legions of fans, and certainly those who enjoy well-constructed, entertaining literary fiction will want to pick up a copy.

Reviewed by Kim Kovacs. This review was originally published in *The BookBrowse Review* in November 2022, and has been updated for the September 2024 edition.

SHRINES OF GAIETY

by Kate Atkinson

BookBrowse Rating: 5/5
Critics' Consensus: 5/5
Readers' Rating: 4/5

Published May 2023 in Paperback, 416 pages

Summary

The #1 national bestselling, award-winning author of Life after Life transports us to a restless London in the wake of the Great War--a city fizzing with money, glamour, and corruption--in this spellbinding tale of seduction and betrayal

1926, and in a country still recovering from the Great War, London has become the focus for a delirious new nightlife. In the clubs of Soho, peers of the realm rub shoulders with starlets, foreign dignitaries with gangsters, and girls sell dances for a shilling a time.

The notorious queen of this glittering world is Nellie Coker, ruthless but also ambitious to advance her six children, including the enigmatic eldest, Niven, whose character has been forged in the crucible of the Somme. But success breeds enemies, and Nellie's empire faces threats from without and within. For beneath the dazzle of Soho's gaiety, there is a dark underbelly, a world in which it is all too easy to become lost.

With her unique Dickensian flair, Kate Atkinson gives us a window in a vanished world. Slyly funny, brilliantly observant, and ingeniously plotted, *Shrines of Gaiety* showcases the myriad talents that have made Atkinson one of the most lauded writers of our time.

BookBrowse Review

Award-winning author Kate Atkinson transports readers back to the heady years between World Wars in this delightful Jazz Age caper.

A few years ago, magazines ran pieces about how the 2020s were likely to be the 1920s all over again, full of excess and abandon on the heels of a global recession and much political divisiveness. Little did we know that we'd be spending the first years of these "Roaring Twenties" hiding out in our homes. Whether or not it was Atkinson's intention to give readers who feel disappointed by our current era a little literary escapism into the previous '20s, that's what's on offer in her novel *Shrines of Gaiety*, a delightfully manic journey into London's Jazz Age underworld, which she so brilliantly brings to life.

Atkinson's novel opens outside Holloway prison, where a crowd has gathered to witness the release of one of London's most unlikely criminals: middle-class, Irish-born, diminutive Nellie Coker, who's been locked up for licensing violations at one of the many nightclubs she operates throughout the city. The clubs have been in the more than capable hands of Nellie's oldest daughter since then, but for London's so-called Bright Young Things, Ma Coker's release is sure to usher in even more frivolity and licentiousness at her opulent clubs, which have names like the Sphinx and the Amethyst (named for the ill-gotten jewel that provided the seed money for her first club).

Looking on the scene with less gaiety is Detective Chief Inspector Frobisher, recently relocated from Scotland Yard to Covent Garden's Bow Street station to investigate a string of missing girls, who may or may not have connections to the dozens of dancers Ma Coker employs in her nightclubs. He's joined by a surprising but very eager sidekick, Gwendolen Kelling, a former librarian who has traveled from York to London to look into the disappearance of Freda Murgatroyd, a friend's sister—and perhaps to find a bit of adventure for herself.

Suffice it to say that Gwen is successful in this last pursuit, as she is quickly drawn into the glamour and intrigue of the Coker family. Freda, whose story we also learn, is perhaps less fortunate in her ambition to act and dance on the London stage. And as for the tragicomic character of Frobisher, as he gets closer to Gwen, he might find that Ma Coker's nightclub empire is the least of his concerns.

Much as she did skillfully and delightfully in her Jackson Brodie mysteries, Atkinson segues from character to character and from scene to scene, cleverly utilizing overlapping chronologies and well-placed coincidences in techniques reminiscent of the best Victorian novels. But she also folds in issues of sexuality, women's rights, reproductive health, drug use, sexual harassment and other topics that ring true to the time but wouldn't have been written about so openly as the author is free to do here. Real-life historical figures make cameos, but not in a distracting or manipulative way; instead, Atkinson's focus is on the characters she's created and the many layers of loyalty and betrayal built up between them, making it clear that she—like the master storyteller she is—is entirely in control of the boisterous history she shares with her lucky readers.

In a way, it feels like Kate Atkinson's entire literary career has been leading up to *Shrines of Gaiety*. Here she melds the perceptive character studies and layered storytelling of the Jackson Brodie series with the sharp observation of previous historical novels like *Life After Life* and *Transcription*. This is a novel that is overstuffed in the best possible way, a suspenseful, propulsive narrative that will have readers sneaking time out of their schedules to spend as long as possible in the raucous version of history Atkinson has created on the page.

Reviewed by Norah Piehl. This review was originally published in *The BookBrowse Review* in October 2022, and has been updated for the May 2023 edition.

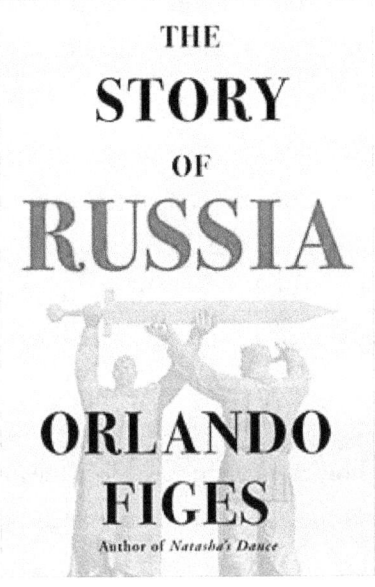

THE STORY OF RUSSIA

by Orlando Figes

BookBrowse Rating: 4/5
Critics' Consensus: 4.5/5
Readers' Rating: 4.5/5

Published September 2023 in Paperback, 368 pages

Summary

From "the great storyteller of Russian history" (*Financial Times*), a brilliant account of the national mythologies and imperial ideologies that have shaped Russia's past and politics - essential reading for understanding the country today.

The Story of Russia is a fresh approach to the thousand years of Russia's history, concerned as much with the ideas that have shaped how Russians think about their past as it is with the events and personalities comprising it. No other country has reimagined its own story so often, in a perpetual effort to stay in step with the shifts of ruling ideologies.

From the founding of Kievan Rus in the first millennium to Putin's war against Ukraine, Orlando Figes explores the ideas that have guided Russia's actions throughout its long and troubled existence. Whether he's describing the crowning of Ivan the Terrible in a candlelit cathedral or the dramatic upheaval of the peasant revolution, he reveals the impulses, often unappreciated or misunderstood by foreigners, that have driven Russian history: the medieval myth of Mother Russia's holy mission to the world; the imperial tendency toward autocratic rule; the popular belief in a paternal tsar dispensing truth and justice; the cult of sacrifice rooted in the idea of the "Russian soul"; and always, the nationalist myth of Russia's unjust treatment by the West.

How the Russians came to tell their story and to revise it so often as they went along is not only a vital aspect of their history; it is also our best means of understanding how the country thinks and acts today. Based on a lifetime of scholarship and enthrallingly written, *The Story of Russia* is quintessential Figes: sweeping, revelatory, and masterful.

BookBrowse Review

A revelatory journey through Russia's unique history.

In *The Story of Russia*, British historian and writer Orlando Figes shares panoramic and authoritative insight into the heritage of this vast and complex country. Figes posits the theory that an understanding of Russia's past is crucial if one is to unpack the logic of contemporary politics and access the mindset of ruling elites: "Contemporary Russian politics are too often analyzed without knowledge of the country's past."

Traveling back to the foundation of the state of Rus in the ninth century, Figes leads his readers on a revelatory journey that terminates with Russia's expansion of its invasion into Ukraine in February of 2022. This sweeping chronology is comprised of numerous micro-stories, stretching from the days of the commonwealth-style Kievan Rus to Putin's exploitation of history to achieve his own vision of Russia. Figes shows how recorded events are open to reimagined versions of history, that they can be molded to legitimize the ruling ideology of the day and shape collective memory, thus blurring the boundaries between mythology and historical fact.

This disingenuous tendency to hijack history to suit purpose is clearly illustrated in the opening pages of *The Story of Russia*. Figes prefaces his narrative by recalling the unveiling of a memorial to Vladimir the Great — known for expanding the Kingdom of Kievan Rus — in Moscow on November 4, 2016. The date coincided with National Unity Day, a holiday celebrating patriotism, which served to promote the leader's quest for a wider Russia. For Putin, the statue — only the latest in a salvo of iconic monuments springing up around the country — is emblematic of Russia's revised past, and is a counterpoint to an existing monument of Volodymyr the Great (as he is known in Ukraine) overlooking the River Dnipro in Kiev. The Moscow version of Vladimir, Figes informs us, is taller and more imposing than its Kiev counterpart, promoting Russia's self-image as a country that is robust and founded on the strength of paternalistic leadership. Reading between the lines, the monument could be a metaphor for Putin himself, although Figes does not go so far as to say this directly. Ukrainians claim this legendary figure, who ruled Kiev from 980 to 1015. The Moscow statue, Figes explains, is the latest attempt by Russia to take advantage of its history of fluid borders and signal to its people that all former Russian states belong under the national yoke.

The warring narratives of Vladimir versus Volodymyr convey the covetous flavor of current politics. From this standpoint, details of Russia's history unfold and illuminate recent events. Figes expounds these events in remarkable detail, demonstrating an astonishing breadth of knowledge and scholarship. He crams his narrative with a glut of specifics and lesser-known facts. For this reason, even aficionados of Russian history are likely to learn something new from this book.

For the lay reader, *The Story of Russia* provides an informative historical overview, written in straightforward, measured prose. The scale of Figes' account means that it can be used as a springboard for more in-depth study of a discrete topic — for example, further reading about Ivan IV (better known in the West as Ivan the Terrible) may be triggered by a desire to learn more about Putin's motivations. Despite the book's merits, the sheer volume of detail that is jam-packed into it can seem a little intense and difficult to absorb, especially as some may find Figes' style on the dry side. A more novelistic exposition would have perhaps helped flesh out the "characters" and lent more engagement to the storytelling.

Reflecting on the book as a whole, three motifs of Russia's unique identity emerge. Firstly, fluid borders have always rendered the country vulnerable to attack (the Mongol invasion is an early example of this), mitigating both the aggression and defensiveness of its rulers; secondly, religion and rulership are historically mortgaged together, making any attack on the nation's leader seemingly heretical; and thirdly, the prevalence of autocratic rule, whereby the ruler is imbued with both spiritual and paternalistic power. What Figes provides is the minutiae surrounding these themes, knitted into a coherent "story," making this book an invaluable read for anyone interested in the foundations of modern Russia.

Reviewed by Amanda Ellison. This review was originally published in *The BookBrowse Review* in September 2022, and has been updated for the September 2023 edition.

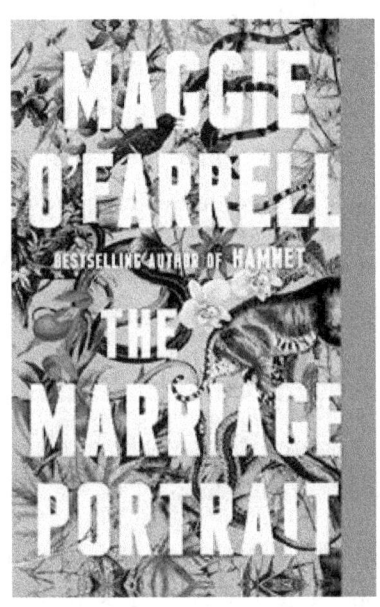

THE MARRIAGE PORTRAIT

by Maggie O'Farrell

BookBrowse Rating: 5/5
Critics' Consensus: 4.5/5
Readers' Rating: 5/5

Published July 2023 in Paperback, 352 pages

Summary

The author of *Hamnet* - *New York Times* bestseller and National Book Award winner - brings the world of Renaissance Italy to jewel-bright life in this unforgettable portrait of the captivating young duchess Lucrezia de' Medici as she makes her way in a troubled court.

Florence, the 1550s. Lucrezia, third daughter of the grand duke, is comfortable with her obscure place in the palazzo: free to wonder at its treasures, observe its clandestine workings, and devote herself to her own artistic pursuits. But when her older sister dies on the eve of her wedding to the ruler of Ferrara, Modena and Reggio, Lucrezia is thrust unwittingly into the limelight: the duke is quick to request her hand in marriage, and her father just as quick to accept on her behalf.

Having barely left girlhood behind, Lucrezia must now enter an unfamiliar court whose customs are opaque and where her arrival is not universally welcomed. Perhaps most mystifying of all is her new husband himself, Alfonso. Is he the playful sophisticate he appeared to be before their wedding, the aesthete happiest in the company of artists and musicians, or the ruthless politician before whom even his formidable sisters seem to tremble?

As Lucrezia sits in constricting finery for a painting intended to preserve her image for centuries to come, one thing becomes worryingly clear. In the court's eyes, she has one duty: to provide the heir who will shore up the future of the Ferranese dynasty. Until then, for all of her rank and nobility, the new duchess's future hangs entirely in the balance.

Full of the beauty and emotion with which she illuminated the Shakespearean canvas of *Hamnet*, Maggie O'Farrell turns her talents to Renaissance Italy in an extraordinary portrait of a resilient young woman's battle for her very survival.

BookBrowse Review

A historical thriller that merges art, history and power politics into a compelling alternate biography.

The idea of marrying for love is a startlingly recent development. It seems natural, in our society that has built stories, movies and an entire wedding industry around the idea that marriage is an expression of true love. But in earlier centuries, marriage was a political and economic arrangement with love considered, at best, a happy accident, and as Maggie O'Farrell shows in her historical novel *The Marriage Portrait*, those arrangements could have fatal consequences for wives.

O'Farrell brings to life early modern Italy while also masterfully inhabiting the mind of a bright yet awkward girl. The lead character and object of the portrait in the title is Lucrezia de' Medici, an actual daughter of Cosimo I de' Medici, Grand Duke of Tuscany, who is believed to have been born in 1545. O'Farrell presents an alternate telling of the life of this obscure yet tragic character from Renaissance history.

The book begins with Lucrezia's realization that her husband means to murder her while they're at a remote castle. The story then loops back through her childhood and adolescence, with chapters periodically jumping to her in the castle trying to avoid her husband's violent intentions. This structure lets the reader watch Lucrezia grow from a smart, artistically gifted girl into a perceptive young woman.

Lucrezia's happy childhood is upended when her eldest sister, who was betrothed to Alfonso II d'Este, Duke of Ferrara, suddenly dies, and the duke requests Lucrezia's hand instead. O'Farrell's attention to detail and historical accuracy are outstanding, from the names of Cosimo's advisors to Alfonso's family history, and she crafts his contradictory character skillfully.

Lucrezia is terrified of marriage and leaving home, particularly since she is barely a teenager when she marries Alfonso, who is in his mid-20s. At first, however, her husband seems caring and kind. Alfonso indulges Lucrezia's love of animals and painting, and he betrays no disappointment in marrying the quiet and bookish girl rather than her older, more glamorous sister.

Yet warning signs appear almost immediately — that beneath his calm exterior, Alfonso is a cruel and vindictive man; that his political position is tenuous and he'll kill to maintain it; that the people surrounding Lucrezia are using her for their own ends.

Alfonso and Lucrezia soon travel to the city-state of Ferrara in northern Italy, the seat of his power. Yet Alfonso's mother, a Protestant refusing to practice Catholicism, has caused chaos by fleeing to France along with one of her daughters. With no heir to guarantee succession and his mother and sister politically protected in France, Alfonso runs the risk of being replaced by his sister's child, which would allow his mother, sister and their faction of the family to gain power.

Alfonso's other sisters who stay in Ferrara quickly pull Lucrezia into their power politics, but she learns that their acts of friendship are insincere. She also realizes that only by providing Alfonso with an heir can she ensure her own safety. Her role as a wife is to guarantee that the dynasty continues, and Alfonso is not a man to let feelings interfere with that fact.

But the heir doesn't come — and everyone at court knows Alfonso has never even fathered a bastard out of wedlock. As a result, rumors swirl that he can't safeguard the succession. All the while, Alfonso's chosen artists are working on a portrait of Lucrezia, a beautiful work that mirrors her own love of painting yet begins to take on a life of its own. O'Farrell correctly depicts how master artists worked in groups during the Renaissance, with apprentices and assistants handling different aspects of sketching and painting a commission like this one. Lucrezia's sessions with the artists become one of her few outlets in an increasingly claustrophobic life at court.

Alfonso's attempts to impregnate his wife grow more fervent, with medieval doctors prescribing cures and barring Lucrezia from her only joys, painting and exploring the castle. His anger with his sisters becomes more violent, as does his frustration with the still-childless Lucrezia, and she finally understands that not giving birth to an heir will be her downfall.

As the story builds, O'Farrell circles back to where the novel began, with Lucrezia at the castle, cognizant that Alfonso wants to murder her. The pace of the two timelines crescendos perfectly, coming together in the terrifying yet exhilarating resolution that brings together Alfonso, Lucrezia and the artists and courtiers around them.

This structure gives the book the feel of a murder mystery — Will he or won't he do it? What is he capable of? — and the simmering undercurrents of danger draw the reader in, enveloping us in Lucrezia's fear and confusion, but also her intelligence and bravery. At the same time, O'Farrell's historical accuracy avoids dryness, and while she takes some artistic liberties with the actual biography of Lucrezia de Medici, her depiction of life in 16th-century Florence and Ferrara are lively and colorful, made real for a 21st-century audience.

By shortening the distance between Lucrezia's lifetime and our own, O'Farrell also makes the risks of succession and reproduction patently clear for modern readers. She provides a glimpse of the terror, pride, hope, danger and sometimes affection that marriage entailed for early modern women, all within an exciting and fast-paced tale.

Reviewed by Rose Rankin. This review was originally published in *The BookBrowse Review* in October 2022, and has been updated for the August 2023 edition.

AFRICA IS NOT A COUNTRY

by Dipo Faloyin

BookBrowse Rating: 5/5
Critics' Consensus: 5/5
Readers' Rating: 5/5

Published November 2023 in Paperback, 400 pages

Summary

An exuberant, opinionated, stereotype-busting portrait of contemporary Africa in all its splendid diversity, by one of its leading new writers.

So often, Africa has been depicted simplistically as a uniform land of famines and safaris, poverty and strife, stripped of all nuance. In this bold and insightful book, Dipo Faloyin offers a much-needed corrective, weaving a vibrant tapestry of stories that bring to life Africa's rich diversity, communities, and histories.

Starting with an immersive description of the lively and complex urban life of Lagos, Faloyin unearths surprising truths about many African countries' colonial heritage and tells the story of the continent's struggles with democracy through seven dictatorships. With biting wit, he takes on the phenomenon of the white savior complex and brings to light the damage caused by charity campaigns of the past decades, revisiting such cultural touchstones as the KONY 2012 film. Entering into the rivalries that energize the continent, Faloyin engages in the heated debate over which West African country makes the best jollof rice and describes the strange, incongruent beauty of the African Cup of Nations. With an eye toward the future promise of the continent, he explores the youth-led cultural and political movements that are defining and reimagining Africa on their own terms.

The stories Faloyin shares are by turns joyful and enraging; proud and optimistic for the future even while they unequivocally confront the obstacles systematically set in place by former colonial powers. Brimming with humor and wit, filled with political insights, and, above all, infused with a deep love for the region, *Africa Is Not a Country* celebrates the energy and particularity of the continent's different cultures and communities, treating Africa with the respect it deserves.

BookBrowse Review

A witty, biting collection of essays that skewers negative perceptions and stereotypes about Africa while shining light on the diverse lived experiences of Africans.

It does not seem possible that people in the 21st century could believe the continent of Africa is a single country. But Dipo Faloyin, journalist and senior editor at *VICE*, begs to differ in *Africa Is Not a Country: Notes on a Bright Continent*. This expert collection of reflections pushes back — often humorously

— on the various, maddening ways the wider world treats Africa and speaks of it as a single country, "devoid of nuance and cursed to be forever plagued by deprivation."

Africa is a continent with 54 nations, more than 2,000 languages, and home to 1.4 billion people. According to Faloyin, however, for too long the continent has been thought of as a "buzzword for poverty and strife…where nothing but misery grows" or as "one big safari park." These lazy assumptions and perceptions make easy targets for the author, who begins his portrait of modern Africa with a healthy infusion of historical context.

"A map is a divided thing," he says, made more so by the meeting of 14 European and Eurasian nations under a large map of Africa in 1884, scrambling after pieces of the resource-rich continent. Dubbed the Berlin Conference, this gathering of "White Men in Khaki" laid out the "principle of effective occupation" that began the mad European rush to confiscate large swathes of the African interior, without the consent of the Indigenous ethnic groups already there. Colonization attempts in Africa were made long before this meeting, but Faloyin describes this event as pivotal to explaining a prevailing attitude toward the continent: "That Africa's fate should not be left to Africans has been the West's go-to strategy in the region for almost every one of the 137 years since" that meeting.

Just as disastrous as the oppressive colonization and landgrabs perpetrated against generations of Africans were the arbitrary and "straight line" borders the Europeans created, "geometrical shapes that bear no relation to the topography, culture or languages of the land they apportion." Why is this important? Faloyin provides keen insight supported by hard data:

> "Only 30 per cent of all borders in the world are in Africa, yet nearly 60 per cent of all territorial disputes that have made it to the International Court of Justice come from the continent."

The drawing of these uninformed borders across Africa resulted in the splitting up of hundreds of ethnic groups among multiple countries. In addition to the psychological violence of having one's land forcibly drawn and quartered were the physical and material tensions created within these made-up states, Faloyin contends. This "created nations born of a melding of adversaries," and "far from creating bonds of unity, the colonial borders forced groups to compete for treasured prizes, not only for personal enrichment but to survive."

With the march of democracy across Africa during the widespread independence movements of the 1950s and '60s, Faloyin tackles one of the more stubborn tropes, that of the "violent African dictator…searching for villages to pillage, children to abduct and blood diamonds to harvest." Admitting that "the continent has tangled with its fair share of authoritarians," he surgically debunks the offensive and pernicious notion that Africans cannot govern themselves and that the continent is "somehow predisposed to evil despotism." The reality, he says, is far more intricately layered than people realize, requiring a fundamental understanding that Africa "is a rich mosaic of experience, of diverse communities and histories, and not a singular monolith of predetermined destinies."

In addition to the weightier sections pertaining to colonialism, dictatorships and looted artifacts, Faloyin unleashes his acerbic wit on the various representations of Africa in media and popular culture, taking sharp jabs at the "white savior" complexes and imagery he finds everywhere in movies, documentaries, and now, social media (see Beyond the Book). In particular, he makes the reader laugh (and at times, squirm) at the ridiculously self-congratulatory feel-good projects of the 1980s, or as he terms this era, "the golden age of charity campaigns." Songs like "We Are the World" and "Do They Know It's Christmas?" sung by a star-studded assortment of artists, raised money to help fund famine relief efforts, but the lyrics of these insipid songs were often inaccurate and insulting. With "Do They Know It's Christmas?" Faloyin critiques the lyrics:

> "For the record: it does snow in parts of Africa; water runs in streams and rivers and emerges from kitchen taps as needed; crops grow, flourish and are exported to help feed

the rest of the world; and people exchange gifts at Christmas that range far beyond staying alive."

Joys and revelations abound in *Africa Is Not a Country*, but perhaps the most satisfying aspect is Faloyin's ability to weave together Africa's painful past with its infinite promise for a brighter future — on its own terms. Highlighting the more positive developments, such as the "significant rise in the number of elected female legislators and women selected for high-ranking government positions" throughout Africa, Faloyin circles back around to the power of individual human beings to be effective in their communities, through grassroots political activism but also through art, literature and music. He calls for the world to engage more genuinely with the continent:

> "Engage with all of it: each language and climate; each political and social framework; each nation trying to form its identity specifically. Engage with the majestic game animals, and communities bursting with kin like mine whose idea of the wild is a small town still to be touched by a reliable Wi-Fi network."

Reviewed by Peggy Kurkowski. This review was originally published in *The BookBrowse Review* in October 2022, and has been updated for the November 2023 edition.

PROPERTIES OF THIRST

by Marianne Wiggins

BookBrowse Rating: 5/5
Critics' Consensus: 5/5
Readers' Rating: 5/5

Published May 2023 in Paperback, 544 pages

Summary

Fifteen years after the publication of *Evidence of Things Unseen*, National Book Award and Pulitzer Prize finalist Marianne Wiggins returns with a novel destined to be an American classic: a sweeping masterwork set during World War II about the meaning of family and the limitations of the American Dream.

Rockwell "Rocky" Rhodes has spent years fiercely protecting his California ranch from the LA Water Corporation. It is here where he and his beloved wife Lou raised their twins, Sunny and Stryker, and it is here where Rocky has mourned Lou in the years since her death.

As Sunny and Stryker reach the cusp of adulthood, the country teeters on the brink of war. Stryker decides to join the fight, deploying to Pearl Harbor not long before the bombs strike. Soon, Rocky and his family find themselves facing yet another incomprehensible tragedy.

Rocky is determined to protect his remaining family and the land where they've loved and lost so much. But when the government decides to build a Japanese-American internment camp next to the ranch, Rocky realizes that the land faces even bigger threats than the LA watermen he's battled for years. Complicating matters is the fact that the idealistic Department of the Interior man assigned to build the camp, who only begins to understand the horror of his task after it may be too late, becomes infatuated with Sunny and entangled with the Rhodes family.

Properties of Thirst is a novel that is both universal and intimate. It is the story of a changing American landscape and an examination of one of the darkest periods in this country's past, told through the stories of the individual loves and losses that weave together to form the fabric of our shared history. Ultimately, it is an unflinching distillation of our nation's essence—and a celebration of the bonds of love and family that persist against all odds.

BookBrowse Review

Pulitzer Prize finalist Marianne Wiggins returns with an epic tale of love and loss in World War II-era California.

Properties of Thirst, Marianne Wiggins' long-awaited ninth novel, is a sprawling story set in California's Owens Valley. Widower Rockwell "Rocky" Rhodes lives on a ranch with his twin sister, Cas, and his daughter Sunny. He is consumed by his decades-long battle with the Los Angeles Water Department, which he believes laid waste to the area's farmland with the construction of an aqueduct (see [Beyond the Book](#)). Irascible and bitter, Rocky's world is thrown into turmoil by the bombing of Pearl Harbor, where his estranged son Stryker may have been stationed aboard a U.S. Navy vessel. Adding to the confusion is the arrival of Schiff, an idealistic lawyer from the Department of the Interior tasked with building an internment camp across the road from Rocky's property on a defunct apple orchard named Manzanar.

The book's intricate plot shifts focus frequently, and it's consequently a challenge to succinctly say what, exactly, it's about. Large swaths of it address the devastation wrought by the misuse of California's water, while other chapters emphasize the challenge of creating facilities in a barren desert to accommodate 10,000 internees. A lengthy section describes a trip Sunny takes with her aunt that serves to explain how she developed a love of food and cooking, while another focuses on Stryker's fate. The author also writes at length about the plight of the Japanese Americans at Manzanar, really bringing home to readers the devastation the United States inflicted on a segment of its population. What ties these disparate plotlines together is the concept of thirst — thirst for justice, thirst for a sense of purpose, thirst for meaning, and, perhaps most crucially, thirst for love.

Wiggins' writing is lyrical and vivid throughout, almost reading like poetry at times:

> "The past is carried to us on simple things — a written page, a spoon, a glove, a bowl of water: carried by the souls who touched them, those plain relics emanate a language freed of time, a language without cadence — mute and eerie as the sound a granite planet makes giving birth to mountains, coursing its way through space."

Perhaps one of the most surprising things about the book's narrative style, though, is how varied its tone is, sometimes contemplative and elegiac, occasionally gut-wrenching, and often very funny. There's one scene in particular — involving an elephant, of all things — that remarkably manages to be all three simultaneously.

The author is equally adept in her characterizations; Rocky, Sunny, Cas and Schiff leap off the page, becoming like friends — people readers come to know and love. Schiff, in particular, goes from being a fish out of water (a native Chicagoan whose only previous exercise was going up the steps of his apartment building, and for whom "eating outside" meant grabbing a hot dog at the corner vendor's cart) to a character of great depth and caring. His metamorphosis is really the heart of the novel. He at first undertakes the camp's construction feeling uneasy about his task but treating it as a job to be done. As the internees arrive at Manzanar and he gets to know them, he begins to realize how unjust their situation is and how much the government — his employer — has taken from them. As the guilt he feels over their plight increases, he goes about trying to improve their lives.

In 2016, when she was 80% finished with this novel, Wiggins suffered a stroke that left her unable to read or write. Her daughter, Lara Porzak, worked tirelessly with her to help complete the work. Her hand is undetectable — the prose is wonderful, start to finish — but the ending leaves a number of plotlines hanging. I'm not sure if that's a result of the interruption in the writing process or if it was a deliberate choice designed to make readers experience a thirst themselves, (i.e., a thirst for resolution). Regardless, I found myself stunned when I turned the last page, expecting more story only to encounter Porzak's afterword.

While the book's narrative is lush and evocative, the print layout is rather idiosyncratic. Sometimes conversations are formatted with quotes, other times not, making it challenging to determine if a statement is said out loud or just thought. The prose contains many long sentences ala William Faulkner or Virginia Woolf, with asides interjected in parentheses, making them difficult to follow. And the point of view may shift halfway through a paragraph, leading to confusion about who's thinking which thoughts. Although I felt these stylistic choices slowed the narrative and were disorienting at first, once I settled into the novel they seemed oddly appropriate.

Properties of Thirst is a worthy addition to Wiggins' canon, perhaps her best work to date. It's a big, beautiful epic that deserves wide readership, and I highly recommend it to audiences looking for first-rate literary fiction.

Reviewed by Kim Kovacs. This review was originally published in *The BookBrowse Review* in October 2022, and has been updated for the June 2023 edition.

DAUGHTERS OF THE FLOWER FRAGRANT GARDEN

by Zhuqing Li

BookBrowse Rating: 5/5
Critics' Consensus: 4.5/5
Readers' Rating: 5/5

Published June 2023 in Paperback, 368 pages

Summary

Sisters separated by war forge new identities as they are forced to choose between family, nation, and their own independence.

Jun and Hong were scions of a once great southern Chinese family. Each other's best friend, they grew up in the 1930s during the final days of Old China before the tumult of the twentieth century brought political revolution, violence, and a fractured national identity. By a quirk of timing, at the end of the Chinese Civil War, Jun ended up on an island under Nationalist control, and then settled in Taiwan, married a Nationalist general, and lived among fellow exiles at odds with everything the new Communist regime stood for on the mainland. Hong found herself an ocean away on the mainland, forced to publicly disavow both her own family background and her sister's decision to abandon the party. A doctor by training, to overcome the suspicion created by her family circumstances, Hong endured two waves of "re-education" and internal exile, forced to work in some of the most desperately poor, remote areas of the country.

Ambitious, determined, and resourceful, both women faced morally fraught decisions as they forged careers and families in the midst of political and social upheaval. Jun established one of U.S.-allied Taiwan's most important trading companies. Hong became one of the most celebrated doctors in China, appearing on national media and honored for her dedication to medicine. Niece to both sisters, linguist and East Asian scholar Zhuqing Li tells her aunts' story for the first time, honoring her family's history with sympathy and grace. *Daughters of the Flower Fragrant Garden* is a window into the lives of women in twentieth-century China, a time of traumatic change and unparalleled resilience. In this riveting and deeply personal account, Li confronts the bitter political rivals of mainland China and Taiwan with elegance and unique insight, while celebrating her aunts' remarkable legacies.

BookBrowse Review

A poignant and informative nonfiction account of two sisters torn apart by the Chinese Civil War.

Our First Impressions readers found Zhuqing Li's nonfiction account of her aunts' lives during and after the Chinese Civil War moving and enlightening.

Daughters of the Flower Fragrant Garden received an exceptional average rating of 4.7 out of 5 stars.

What it's about:

The author's aunts, Jun and Hong Chen, were two years apart in age, living as privileged and educated women in Nationalist China due to their father's position in the government. The family lived in a spectacular house with gardens, maids and all the trappings of wealth and power in China in the 1930s. All that changed when the Communists defeated the Nationalists in the Civil War. Through sheer accident, the sisters were separated and would not see each other again until they were well into their 80s. Jun ended up in Taiwan married to a general in the Nationalist army and became an entrepreneur. Hong lived her entire life in Communist China as a doctor. As each sister pursued the life she was thrown into, one can see the pain of separation they suffered. Each eventually succeeded in her chosen path but that pain was always there (Patricia C).

Many readers noted that they learned a lot about the history of China and Taiwan from the book:

I truly enjoyed the book. In addition to being a great story, I gained a much better understanding of the contrast between life in mainland China and on the island of Taiwan after the Communists came to power (Dianne Y). Coming from a background of zero knowledge of the history of China's civil war and subsequent horrors, I found *Daughters of the Flower Fragrant Garden* both heart-wrenching and fascinating. To have a biographical story telling of two sisters who, by chance, found themselves on opposite sides (physically and literally) of a war that ripped families apart gives this major historical event a human touch that quite literally left me stunned and lost in thought after many late night readings (Melissa S). Out of all the books I've read set in China, this one gave me the most abundant sense of what life was really like during China's civil war and behind the bamboo curtain. Highly recommended! (Sharon P).

And several noted that the historical background information is very relevant today:

I highly recommend this compelling historical account of those living in China during a time of political upheaval. One cannot fail to see the parallels in the story between China and Taiwan then and tensions now in the forefront of current events (Carol S). This is an important personal recounting of Chinese history that brought about the splitting of China and Taiwan and will certainly provide understanding as we face the uncertainties of that situation in our present time (Lynne B).

Readers also appreciated Li's depiction of the bond between Hong and Jun, and found both women to be inspiring:

As I was reading the well-written story of the two sisters, I could not decide which one was the bravest. The important part, however, was obvious — the love each had for the other even though their lives and political views were so different (Patricia C). Li has crafted a marvelous account of how these two very different women, her aunts, acclimated to their respective political climates, raised children and still managed to forge a path ahead. Li's perceptive rendering of their different approaches to life provides added depth. I was immersed in this book from the moment I began reading! (Jean F). This riveting and deeply personal account is a celebration of these remarkable ladies' legacies (Carol N). Blending the personal with the political, Li is a sensitive chronicler as she invites the reader into her family's intriguing story. It is a story of two ambitious, intelligent and talented women who make the best of their lives (Peggy K). This was, without a doubt, not an easy read by any means — hearing Jun's and Hong's stories, with the unflinching descriptions of harrowing experiences they had to endure and the political undercurrents that dominated their entire lives, it was hard not to be moved by the resilience and endurance of these two remarkable women (Louisa Liu).

The book was also deemed a great choice for book clubs:

Zhuqing Li places her family history in the context of the Chinese Civil War and the many cultural and economic changes that took place in China in the 20th century. I think this would be a great book club choice. The themes of war, endurance and strong family ties could spark an interesting discussion (Ellen H). This is a well-written book full of historical facts that keeps the reader's interest — one I will recommend to my book club (Sylvia F). I found it fascinating to read about the lives of people who lived during this time. The writing is excellent; even though this is a true history, it almost reads like a novel. I will definitely recommend this book to my book club and other friends (Doris K).

Reviewed by First Impressions Reviewers. This review was originally published in *The BookBrowse Review* in August 2022, and has been updated for the July 2023 edition.

HORSE

by Geraldine Brooks

BookBrowse Rating: 5/5
Critics' Consensus: 5/5
Readers' Rating: 5/5

Published January 2024 in Paperback, 464 pages

Summary

Winner of the 2022 BookBrowse Fiction Award

A discarded painting in a junk pile, a skeleton in an attic, and the greatest racehorse in American history: from these strands, a Pulitzer Prize winner braids a sweeping story of spirit, obsession, and injustice across American history.

Kentucky, 1850. An enslaved groom named Jarret and a bay foal forge a bond of understanding that will carry the horse to record-setting victories across the South. When the nation erupts in civil war, an itinerant young artist who has made his name on paintings of the racehorse takes up arms for the Union. On a perilous night, he reunites with the stallion and his groom, very far from the glamor of any racetrack.

New York City, 1954. Martha Jackson, a gallery owner celebrated for taking risks on edgy contemporary painters, becomes obsessed with a nineteenth-century equestrian oil painting of mysterious provenance.

Washington, DC, 2019. Jess, a Smithsonian scientist from Australia, and Theo, a Nigerian-American art historian, find themselves unexpectedly connected through their shared interest in the horse—one studying the stallion's bones for clues to his power and endurance, the other uncovering the lost history of the unsung Black horsemen who were critical to his racing success.

Based on the remarkable true story of the record-breaking thoroughbred Lexington, *Horse* is a novel of art and science, love and obsession, and our unfinished reckoning with racism.

BookBrowse Review

Historical artifacts related to the legendary thoroughbred racehorse Lexington serve as the backdrop to this dual timeline novel reckoning with racial inequality in America.

Winner: 2022 Best Fiction Award.

Geraldine Brooks creates a powerful backstory for 19th-century thoroughbred racehorse Lexington, weaving a rich tapestry of historical and current-day narratives that aptly reflect how the legacy of slavery still ripples through America.

Horse truly does offer something for every reader. Brooks seamlessly weaves fact and fiction, past and present, to tell the story of the remarkable Lexington and examine race in America. The real-life Lexington was not only known for his breathtaking speed and agility on the track, but also for his equally talented progeny. Brooks engineers a plausible biography for the horse, filling in the blanks with intriguing research as she traces the history of thoroughbred racing, including the impact of Black jockeys and the Civil War on the industry. This is complemented by compelling contemporary narratives that explore the complex dynamics of race and relationships today.

The novel begins in 2019 with the dueling narratives of Theo, a Nigerian graduate student of the arts working on his thesis, and Jess, a white scientist working for the Smithsonian. Theo salvages a painting of a horse from his neighbor's garbage; Jess unearths horse bones discarded in a neglected attic space. These discoveries bring the characters together and a romantic relationship ensues, complicated by their divergent racial heritage. Jess is Australian and relatively new to the US, and is naive to the myriad concessions and considerations Theo must make due to the color of his skin. Alternately, while a victim of racism both subtle and overt, Theo purposefully tries to look beyond race. At one point, he discloses that he was judged by his former girlfriend as "insufficiently steeped in an experience of American Blackness" to date a Black woman. Despite Jess's protestations that race is not an issue, she first meets Theo when she mistakenly believes he is stealing her bicycle. Jess and Theo's narratives are entrancing enough to stand on their own as an engrossing read. Brooks is deft at characterization; more than once I found myself wanting to meet Jess or Theo at a local coffee shop so I could hear more of their stories.

On the heels of Jess's and Theo's narratives comes Jarrett's, or as Brooks notably titles these sections, "Warfield's Jarrett," reflective of Dr. Warfield's ownership and underscoring Jarrett's status as a slave. Jarrett's story, beginning in 1850, narrates Lexington's time as a foal and Jarrett's deep and abiding connection with the horse. Jarrett is the son of trainer Harry Lewis, and is sold along with Lexington to various affluent, white horse owners. His tale traverses the early halcyon days of thoroughbred racing (as Jarrett becomes Lexington's primary caretaker and ultimately his trainer), through a daring escape from Confederate clutches during the Civil War, and Lexington's later days as a successful stud.

The historic underpinnings of the work are as spellbinding as the characters. Whether Brooks is chronicling the history of thoroughbred racing, exploring the impact of the Civil War on African American jockeys, or detailing the nuances of American equestrian art, it is all equally engrossing. Likewise, each character's backstory is transfixing. The novel ends with a resounding and shocking crescendo that demands an examination of race in America today.

Horse will buoy your soul, break your heart, educate your mind and leave you waiting for Brooks's next work. It is just that spectacular.

Reviewed by Jane McCormack. This review was originally published in *The BookBrowse Review* in June 2022, and has been updated for the January 2024 edition.

THE COLONY

by Audrey Magee

BookBrowse Rating: 5/5
Critics' Consensus: 5/5
Readers' Rating: 3/5

Published June 2023 in Paperback, 384 pages

Summary

In 1979, as violence erupts all over Ireland, two outsiders travel to a small island off the west coast in search of their own answers, despite what it may cost the islanders.

It is the summer of 1979. An English painter travels to a small island off the west coast of Ireland. Mr. Lloyd takes the last leg by curragh, though boats with engines are available and he doesn't much like the sea. But he wants the authentic experience, to be changed by this place, to let its quiet and light fill him, give him room to create.

He doesn't know that a Frenchman follows close behind. Masson has visited the island for many years, studying their language. He is fiercely protective of their isolation; it is essential to exploring his theories of language preservation and identity.

But the people who live on this rock—three miles long and half a mile wide—have their own views on what is being recorded, what is being taken, and what ought to be given in return. Over the summer, each of them— from great-grandmother Bean Uí Fhloinn, to widowed Mairéad, to fifteen-year-old James, who is determined to avoid the life of a fisherman—will wrestle with their own values and desires. Meanwhile, all over Ireland, violence is erupting. And there is blame enough to go around.

An expertly woven portrait of character and place, a stirring investigation into yearning to find one's own way, and an unflinchingly political critique of the long, seething cost of imperialism, Audrey Magee's *The Colony* is a novel that transports, that celebrates beauty and connection, and that reckons with the inevitable ruptures of independence.

BookBrowse Review

Having based her debut novel in mainland Europe during World War II, Audrey Magee sets her follow-up, *The Colony*, closer to her own roots: an Irish island in the late 1970s, at the height of the Anglo-Irish Troubles.

The Colony opens with Mr Lloyd, a London artist, being transported to a Gaeltacht (Irish-speaking) island in a hand-rowed currach, eschewing the more convenient passenger ferry. This attempt at immersing himself in the local customs results in the regurgitation of his breakfast. A rather innocuous episode, it could nevertheless be read as symbolic of much larger issues that erupt when one culture gate-crashes another: exploitation, dilution of indigenous identity, conflict — all of which are examined by Magee in this discomfiting narrative.

Lloyd is traveling to the nameless island in search of solitude and inspiration; the painter's imagination is freighted with clichés of "raw, rugged, violent beauty," conveying all the innocence — ignorance? — of the outsider. The island's undesignated status in the novel may itself be significant: It implies stolen identity as a result of foreign dilution, or perhaps signifies that it is representative of all colonized habitats. Stylistically, Lloyd's pretensions are wrought through Magee's prose, which shifts into lyrical columns to illustrate her protagonist's interior monologue, punctuated with italicized captions — *Self-portrait: alone*, for example — that he imagines for each vignette.

The Englishman's hosts on the sparsely-populated island, the Gillans, are a multi-generational Irish-speaking family. They immediately have their visitor's measure, with the youngest family member, James, denouncing Lloyd's patronizing bearing as "obnoxious." Lloyd's disagreeable disposition is brought further to the fore when he discovers that the cottage next door has been rented for the summer by a French linguist, Jean-Pierre Masson (JP), who is working on a thesis founded on the moribund Irish language. Neither incomer has been forewarned of the other's presence, and they immediately clash, much like "[t]wo bulls in a field." Both become territorial: Lloyd because he had imagined himself to have some sort of exclusive entitlement to the island (at one point the family has to remind him that he "rented the cottage ... Not the island"); JP because he perceives the proximity of an English-speaking inhabitant as something that will skew his research and speed up the decline of an already diminishing language. The interlopers' conflict is weighted with the baggage of history, which the Gillans astutely recognize: "They've been squabbling over our turf for centuries."

As the story unfolds, it is revealed that JP's Algerian mother was abused by her French partner — this may account for the linguist's abhorrence of foreign influence. He even goes so far as to insist on addressing James as Séamus (the boy's Irish name), against the young man's express wishes. With all the blinkered arrogance of the colonist, JP pillages his subjects — irrespective of the standpoint of the colonized — while, paradoxically, earnest in his pursuit of preserving their linguistic heritage.

Teenager James becomes a pivotal individual in the novel, epitomizing the impact of external influence. Unlike his great-grandmother, pipe-smoking monoglot Bean Uí Fhloinn, who "has no English," James's language is thoroughly Anglicized. For JP, Lloyd's residence on the island means that the "linguistic evolution" — which he acknowledges is taking place — will alternate to a "sudden and violent" monolingualism in the form of English. Meanwhile, James becomes an apprentice to Lloyd, exhibiting a raw talent the mentor himself does not possess. For James, whose father and grandfather both drowned while out fishing, it is deemed "[b]etter to be an artist drawing death, instead of being death." James's desire to break with tradition does, therefore, lend some credence to JP's assertion that outside influences exacerbate the death of tradition. Interestingly, Magee chooses not to use speech punctuation; consequently, all communication — verbal or internal — becomes an organic element of the tapestry of the island: Traditional language and behaviors intermingle with incoming influences — including the two foreign visitors. What becomes clear is that both men have mythologized the community, consumed by their own agendas — perhaps the hallmark of the colonist.

But the two summer inhabitants are not the only source of territorial conflict in *The Colony*. Stark, bulletin-style accounts of real-life atrocities on the mainland coldly explode from the page in chapters that are brief, factual, clinical. They are a forceful reminder that this is 1979, when terrorist acts carried out by both Loyalist paramilitaries and the Provisional IRA are at their peak. Attacks are savage and frequent; each chapter's end is marked by a jolting reminder of their existence. Historical fiction and historical fact are juxtaposed, indicative of the nature of history itself. And at the root of this brutal bloodshed is colonization, enmeshed in the long and complicated history of England's violation of Ireland.

Traditionally, the island is a literary trope used to represent a refuge, and a simpler, purer way of life. Magee unmasks this misconception. The pace of life may be slower and more detached, as echoed in her unhurried, dispassionate prose, but is never impervious to infiltration; the aggressors are never too far off. After the cultural looters have gleaned their treasures, the islanders, and others like them, are left to navigate the aftermath.

Reviewed by Amanda Ellison. This review was originally published in *The BookBrowse Review* in May 2022, and has been updated for the July 2023 edition.

REMARKABLY BRIGHT CREATURES

by Shelby Van Pelt

BookBrowse Rating: 5/5
Critics' Consensus: 5/5
Readers' Rating: 4/5

Published March 2025 in Paperback, 368 pages

> ## Summary
> Winner of the 2022 BookBrowse Debut Award
>
> For fans of *A Man Called Ove*, a charming, witty and compulsively readable exploration of friendship, reckoning, and hope that traces a widow's unlikely connection with a giant Pacific octopus.

After Tova Sullivan's husband died, she began working the night shift at the Sowell Bay Aquarium, mopping floors and tidying up. Keeping busy has always helped her cope, which she's been doing since her eighteen-year-old son, Erik, mysteriously vanished on a boat in Puget Sound over thirty years ago.

Tova becomes acquainted with curmudgeonly Marcellus, a giant Pacific octopus living at the aquarium. Marcellus knows more than anyone can imagine but wouldn't dream of lifting one of his eight arms for his human captors—until he forms a remarkable friendship with Tova.

Ever the detective, Marcellus deduces what happened the night Tova's son disappeared. And now Marcellus must use every trick his old invertebrate body can muster to unearth the truth for her before it's too late.

Shelby Van Pelt's debut novel is a gentle reminder that sometimes taking a hard look at the past can help uncover a future that once felt impossible.

BookBrowse Review

A warmhearted look at grief and aging set in the Pacific Northwest.

Winner: 2022 Best Debut Award.

Shelby Van Pelt's debut novel, *Remarkably Bright Creatures*, is set in the fictional town of Sowell Bay in upper Washington State, one of those coastal villages where the best restaurant in town is a deli attached to the area's only grocery store and everyone is "up in everyone else's business," as one character puts it. It is, however, large enough to support a small aquarium that houses, among other animals, a giant Pacific octopus named Marcellus — a "remarkably bright creature" according to the plaque near his tank. He is, indeed, so intelligent that he can understand human speech and escape at will to snack on the sea cucumbers one tank over.

Septuagenarian Tova Sullivan has lived in Sowell Bay since childhood, in the home her father built by hand after immigrating from Sweden. She began cleaning the aquarium at night following her husband's passing, five years before the story opens, to keep busy. Although she has many friends, she's lonely, mired in grief not only over her spouse but also the unexplained disappearance and presumed death of her 18-year-old son decades ago. One night she discovers Marcellus stuck in a tangle of electrical cables and rescues him, and an unlikely friendship ensues.

Meanwhile, there's Cameron Cassmore, an extremely bright young man who, at the age of 30, still can't get a handle on adulting. After losing yet another job, he uses the last of his money to fly to Seattle in the hopes of finding the father he never knew. His search leads him to Sowell Bay, and as the three main characters' lives intersect, Tova and Cameron learn how to move beyond their pain to find happiness.

Van Pelt pens a truly beautiful tale, rife with humor and insight, and there's a lot to love about it. Marcellus's musings are especially entertaining. At one point he hears a man tell his son that "ignorance is bliss," and thinks:

> "Ah, to be a human, for whom bliss can be achieved by mere ignorance! Here, in the kingdom of animals, ignorance is dangerous. The poor herring dropped into the tank lacks any awareness of the shark lurking below. Ask the herring whether what he doesn't know can hurt him."

The book is peppered with a vast array of quirky characters, all of whom are well-rounded and unique. And they're not just padding inserted to add interest to the story or up the page count; they all play roles that are important to the novel's action and are so well-drawn that each makes a lasting impression. The main characters in particular are outstandingly written — three-dimensional individuals readers can relate to and sympathize with.

What I find exceptional about *Remarkably Bright Creatures* is the author's ability to capture those pivotal times in a life when one knows things are changing and must figure out how to adapt. Tova, for example, has endured the death of her husband and the decline of her peers over the past few years, and has to come to terms with the fact that she herself is aging and can no longer live in her vast, multi-storied house: "[S]he sometimes catches a glimpse of her profile reflected in a shop window, the way her shoulders have begun to stoop. She wonders how this body can possibly be hers." As she grapples with what to do with all the items she's accumulated in her 70 years, she ends up discarding those that she finds meaningful. With no family to leave them to, she knows they will only burden someone else if she doesn't dispose of them herself. Cameron, too, has his periods of self-reflection and revelation, and these scenes add an unexpected richness to the novel.

The book combines realism with the supernatural; certainly an octopus capable of intervening in human affairs is an unlikely beast. But while Marcellus's actions are critical to the plot's ultimate resolution, it's the novel's underlying themes of grief, loneliness and change that propel it along. As a result, those who might generally avoid the magic realism genre will probably not find the story particularly objectionable. Despite its unusual elements, the plot is rather predictable, but it's so delightful that most won't mind this either.

Remarkably Bright Creatures is one of those rare, warmhearted novels that feels like the perfect antidote to the worries of the world — a marvelous escape. It has definitely earned its place on the "best of" lists this year, and I heartily recommend it to most audiences; its feel-good ending is sure to leave readers smiling.

Reviewed by Kim Kovacs. This review first ran in the December 7, 2022 issue of BookBrowse Recommends.

TAKE MY HAND

by Dolen Perkins-Valdez

BookBrowse Rating: 5/5
Critics' Consensus: 4.5/5
Readers' Rating: 5/5

Published April 2023 in Paperback, 368 pages

Summary

Inspired by true events that rocked the nation, a profoundly moving novel about a Black nurse in post-segregation Alabama who blows the whistle on a terrible wrong done to her patients, from the *New York Times* bestselling author of *Wench*.

Montgomery, Alabama, 1973. Fresh out of nursing school, Civil Townsend has big plans to make a difference, especially in her African American community. At the Montgomery Family Planning Clinic, she intends to help women make their own choices for their lives and bodies.

But when her first week on the job takes her down a dusty country road to a worn-down one-room cabin, she's shocked to learn that her new patients, Erica and India, are children—just eleven and thirteen years old. Neither of the Williams sisters has even kissed a boy, but they are poor and Black, and for those handling the family's welfare benefits, that's reason enough to have the girls on birth control. As Civil grapples with her role, she takes India, Erica, and their family into her heart. Until one day she arrives at the door to learn the unthinkable has happened, and nothing will ever be the same for any of them.

Decades later, with her daughter grown and a long career in her wake, Dr. Civil Townsend is ready to retire, to find her peace, and to leave the past behind. But there are people and stories that refuse to be forgotten. That must not be forgotten.

Because history repeats what we don't remember.

BookBrowse Review

A moving novel based on a 1973 lawsuit filed on behalf of two young Black girls who were sterilized as part of a federally funded family planning program.

First Impressions readers were moved by Dolen Perkins-Valdez's *Take My Hand*, a novel that illuminates the dark chapter of eugenics in American history. The book received an average rating of 4.8 out of 5 stars.

What it's about:

Take my Hand by Dolen Perkins-Valdez is a tour de force of a novel. Inspired by true events, the story follows Civil Townsend, a woman fresh out of nursing school and working at a reproductive health clinic in Montgomery, Alabama.

Civil quickly discovers that impoverished Black women are being sterilized without their consent. When to two young sisters are sterilized, Civil jumps into action and a lawsuit follows. As she becomes more entwined with the sisters and their family, we also learn more about Civil's family. Each character in this novel is so well developed that you feel as if you know them. Watching Civil try to effect change in the sisters' lives is uplifting and painful. A second timeline features the protagonist as a woman on the verge of retirement from a successful career as a doctor (Mary S).

Some readers were surprised to discover that the real-life events of this story happened in the recent past:

Take My Hand is a deeply touching book. I would have liked to think this forced sterilization of poor Black women happened much longer ago than it actually did (Shirley H). I enjoyed this book because the subject was a revelation for me. It read like a crime novel exposing the extent and enormity of the practice of racial sterilization. This book is intended to bring these past atrocities to light and broadcast awareness to those who can voice dissent (Bonne O). *Take My Hand* is a profound, enlightening and heartbreaking book. I will never be the same after reading it. I was a young adult back then and for the life of me I can't remember this happening or the trial that took place. We can't forget these things. This broke the summer after we learned of the Tuskegee experiments. How could this happen in our great nation? This is a book I will never forget (Phyllis P).

And many drew parallels to present-day events related to reproductive freedoms and racism:

This book, while historical fiction, tackles topics still very relevant to our time. It is a "must-read" for book clubs willing to have meaningful, and possibly tough, discussions — not only about the book, but about the topics of civil rights, structural racism and women's reproductive rights (Gay J). The tragedy of our nation's shameful medical abuse of people of color, especially women, is laid bare here. It begs the reader to understand the mistrust in our society's public health initiatives some people of color have after being betrayed so many times in the past and remaining underserved in many ways today (Jo S).

Readers appreciated the excellent characterization in the novel:

This expertly written historical novel will appeal to readers interested in civil rights and strong intelligent female characters (Jennifer W). The writing is so strong, the characters are well-developed and you get caught up in their emotions; the story is compelling and repelling; messy in a way that life is (Dominique G). The unfolding story is powerful, the characters are brave and unforgettable, and what happened is a story that must be told. Thank you, Dolen Perkins-Valdez, for opening my and other readers' eyes to this unconscionable tragedy (Diane S).

And recommend *Take My Hand* as an ideal choice for book clubs:

This is an emotional compelling and heartwrenching story. I found that the author's superbly drawn characters evoked my emotions, and the seamless integration of the meticulously researched historical details provided the outrage that is needed to make sure this does not happen again. This is a great book club discussion book for those who like to discuss weighty and timely issues. A much-needed book to understand the legacy of injustice! (Beverly J). Book clubs will love this book as it really invites deep thought and discussions about medical ethics and institutional racism. Anyone who enjoys truthful historical fiction will like this hard-hitting and well-written book for the warm characters and the unapologetic descriptions of past US medical abuses (Jo S).

Reviewed by First Impressions Reviewers. This review was originally published in *The BookBrowse Review* in April 2022, and has been updated for the April 2023 edition.

LESSONS IN CHEMISTRY

by Bonnie Garmus

BookBrowse Rating: 5/5
Critics' Consensus: 4.5/5
Readers' Rating: 4.5/5

First published April 2022 in Hardcover, 400 pages

Summary

A must-read debut! Meet Elizabeth Zott: a "formidable, unapologetic and inspiring" (Parade) scientist in 1960s California whose career takes a detour when she becomes the unlikely star of a beloved TV cooking show in this novel that is "irresistible, satisfying and full of fuel. It reminds you that change takes time and always requires heat" (The New York Times Book Review).

New York Times Bestseller • *Good Morning America Book Club* • One of NPR's Best Books of 2022 • One of the Most Anticipated Books of the Year—*New York Times, Bustle, Real Simple, Parade, CNN, Today, E! News, Library Journal*

Chemist Elizabeth Zott is not your average woman. In fact, Elizabeth Zott would be the first to point out that there is no such thing as an average woman. But it's the early 1960s and her all-male team at Hastings Research Institute takes a very unscientific view of equality. Except for one: Calvin Evans; the lonely, brilliant, Nobel–prize nominated grudge-holder who falls in love with—of all things—her mind. True chemistry results.

But like science, life is unpredictable. Which is why a few years later Elizabeth Zott finds herself not only a single mother, but the reluctant star of America's most beloved cooking show Supper at Six. Elizabeth's unusual approach to cooking ("combine one tablespoon acetic acid with a pinch of sodium chloride") proves revolutionary. But as her following grows, not everyone is happy. Because as it turns out, Elizabeth Zott isn't just teaching women to cook. She's daring them to change the status quo.

Laugh-out-loud funny, shrewdly observant, and studded with a dazzling cast of supporting characters, *Lessons in Chemistry* is as original and vibrant as its protagonist.

BookBrowse Review

A charming, funny debut novel about a chemist turned cooking show host.

Bonnie Garmus's debut, *Lessons in Chemistry,* introduces readers to an exceptional woman struggling to succeed in a male-dominated field. When we first meet 30-year-old Elizabeth Zott, the year is 1961, and we quickly learn she's the single mother of a precocious child and the unlikely star of a wildly popular weekday cooking show, *Supper at Six.* We also discover that behind her TV persona, she's a talented research chemist who has taken what she feels is a demeaning position solely as a means of supporting her daughter. The narrative then rewinds to 1952 to explain how Elizabeth got to this point in her life.

Garmus sets her novel in the days before the Equal Rights Amendment and the #MeToo movement, when most men — and many women as well — believed that any woman who dared to enter a traditional men's profession was either "a lightweight or a gold digger," in the author's words. Worse, attractive single women in the workplace were often seen by powerful men as mere prey. Elizabeth experiences the worst of the worst: she's sexually assaulted; she's given a lab coat with her initials — "EZ" — rather than her last name; her work is openly ridiculed by her peers who then plagiarize it; and when her employer uses those breakthroughs to lure investors, they're told the discoveries were made by a "Mr. Zott." And that's just a small sample of the inequities this resilient woman must overcome.

Given the difficult subject matter at its core, one might think the novel is a dark, weighty exploration of the sexual discrimination rampant during the 1950s and early 1960s. Amazingly, it's really not; although the book's substance depends largely on this theme, its overall tone is positive and affirming.

Garmus's narrative reads a bit like a fable, often employing a simple, straightforward writing style and using repetition:

> [Harriet Sloane] was unattractive and she knew it. She also knew that [Elizabeth's partner] was unattractive, and the sloppy dog Elizabeth brought home one day was unattractive, and there was a good chance Elizabeth's future baby would be unattractive too. But none of them were — or would ever be — ugly. Only Mr. Sloane was ugly, and that was because he was unattractive on the inside.

There's something comforting about a cadence like this — a subtle reassurance that all will be right in the end.

The writing is also frequently quite funny. At one point, for example, Elizabeth's producers insist she feature one of their sponsor's canned soups on her program.

It looks like she's agreed when she holds up the soup can and, on live TV, tells her audience it's a real time-saver:

> "That's because it's full of chemicals," she said, tossing it with a clunk into a nearby garbage can. "Feed enough of it to your loved ones and they'll eventually die off, saving you tons of time since you won't have to feed them anymore."

What truly makes the book work, though, is the main character. In addition to being smart, Elizabeth is endlessly logical, practical and clear-headed; she simply refuses to be undervalued. "The reduction of women to something less than men…is not biological: it's cultural," she tells her audience as she proceeds to ignore the boundaries some would impose on her because of her sex. We fall in love with her not so much for the fact that she pushes back against these limits but because she points out their irrationality and proceeds accordingly.

The book does have a few flaws, partially stemming from its overall storybook feel. The author's simplified writing style is especially apparent in the novel's first chapters, which almost read as if they were pitched to a young adult audience. The technique is less noticeable as the narrative proceeds, but some readers may be turned off before the story really gets rolling. In addition, the characters who surround Elizabeth lack nuance; with few exceptions, the "good" characters are all very intelligent and supportive while the bad characters are stupid and evil. Finally, much of the plot — including its fairytale ending — relies heavily on coincidence.

Some might consider *Lessons in Chemistry* "chick lit," but I think that label does the book a disservice. Although its audience will likely be predominantly female, its themes are weighty and relevant, and any romance in it is much like Elizabeth herself: logical, analytical and not at all "frothy." The novel's exploration of gender roles will make it a good choice for book group discussions, and its unforgettable heroine and feel-good ending will almost certainly garner the author a host of avid fans.

Reviewed by Kim Kovacs. This review first ran in the December 7, 2022 issue of BookBrowse Recommends.

PEACH BLOSSOM SPRING

by Melissa Fu

BookBrowse Rating: 5/5
Critics' Consensus: 4.5/5
Readers' Rating: 5/5

Published February 2023 in Paperback, 400 pages

| Summary

A "beautifully rendered" novel about war, migration, and the power of telling our stories, *Peach Blossom Spring* follows three generations of a Chinese family on their search for a place to call home (Georgia Hunter, New York Times bestselling author of *We Were the Lucky Ones*).

"Within every misfortune there is a blessing and within every blessing, the seeds of misfortune, and so it goes, until the end of time."

It is 1938 in China and, as a young wife, Meilin's future is bright. But with the Japanese army approaching, Meilin and her four year old son, Renshu, are forced to flee their home. Relying on little but their wits and a beautifully illustrated hand scroll, filled with ancient fables that offer solace and wisdom, they must travel through a ravaged country, seeking refuge.

Years later, Renshu has settled in America as Henry Dao. Though his daughter is desperate to understand her heritage, he refuses to talk about his childhood. How can he keep his family safe in this new land when the weight of his history threatens to drag them down? Yet how can Lily learn who she is if she can never know her family's story?

Spanning continents and generations, *Peach Blossom Spring* is a bold and moving look at the history of modern China, told through the story of one family. It's about the power of our past, the hope for a better future, and the haunting question: What would it mean to finally be home?

BookBrowse Review

A multigenerational saga about a Chinese family unsettled by war, and the rootless searching that often comes with a life defined by diaspora.

Our First Impressions reviewers loved Melissa Fu's debut novel *Peach Blossom Spring*, about a family fleeing the Second Sino-Japanese War and the immigrant experience in America. Out of 36 reviews received, 34 rated the book 4 or 5 stars, with an average rating of 4.7.

What it's about:

Against a backdrop of war, political upheaval and human displacement, readers are introduced to Meilin and her young son Renshu. The story begins in 1938 when the family is forced to flee their home in Hunan Province and begin a long and perilous journey that ultimately ends in Taiwan. Faced with the violence of war, extreme poverty, betrayal and a country in chaos, one marvels at the courage and resiliency of Meilin and the talent and dedication of Renshu (Janet OP). *Peach Blossom Spring* tells us the story of a mother's struggles, hardships, sacrifices and hopes for her only son as they run for their lives from Changsha to, eventually, Taiwan. It also tells the story of Dao Renshu's immigration from Taiwan to the United States, his complicated transformation from Dao Renshu to Henry Dao and the issues that challenge him. And it tells the story of his struggles to understand who he is just as his daughter Lily later struggles to understand who she is and who she wants to be (Paula K).

Readers appreciated Fu's insight into family dynamics and inter-generational trauma:

Fu not only looks at the historical events, she also examines the consequences and generational impact of the trauma associated with the war, aftermath and political fallout. Sensitive subject matter is carefully handled. The passion the author has for this story is evident in her research and attention to detail (Mitzi K). It reminded me a bit of *The Four Winds* by Kristin Hannah in regard to the bonds of family and the choices you make and lengths you go to to keep them safe, along with questioning whether those choices turn out to be the right ones when you see the effects they have down the line (Gina V).

The novel covers elements of Chinese history that were unknown to many readers, and the author's particular view of that history was deemed enlightening:

All my life, I've only known mainland China as communist, but I never knew how that came about. Reading *Peach Blossom Spring* opened my eyes to the brutal history of China's war with Japan in 1938, the subsequent communist takeover, and the displacement of so many Chinese citizens to Taiwan and elsewhere (Diane S). This heartbreaking and inspirational novel enlightened me to a period of history I didn't know much about (Gina V). One understands in this novel that history is a very personal thing, that it evolves day by day, experience by experience, person by person. History is sights, sounds, food, and above all, stories. I know too little about the history of China, but reading Ms. Fu's novel inspires me to learn and understand more (Lynne L).

Overall, the reviewers thought *Peach Blossom Spring* an exceptional read and a great pick for book clubs:

I absolutely loved this book. Melissa Fu evoked a time and place I am wholly unfamiliar with by using language as delicate and precise as the artistry of the Chinese handscroll that figures so prominently in Meilin's story (Elizabeth VF). I thoroughly enjoyed reading *Peach Blossom Spring* and will recommend it to my many book-loving friends and members of my book club (Doris K). Characters were well-developed and realistic. I would recommend this book to anyone, but especially to book clubs (Sally H). This is a beautiful book, well worth reading. A great book for book clubs — lots of discussion material and lots of material for personal reflection (Marcia C).

Reviewed by First Impressions Reviewers. This review was originally published in *The BookBrowse Review* in April 2022, and has been updated for the March 2023 edition.

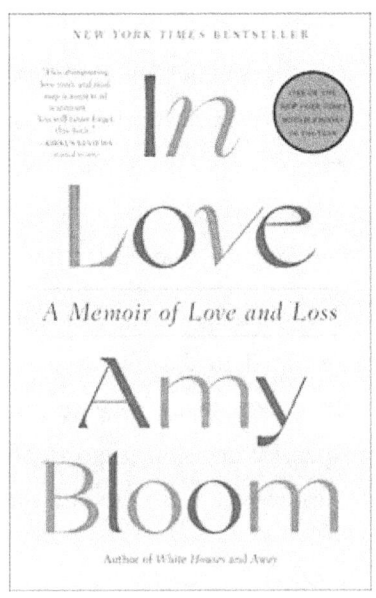

IN LOVE

by Amy Bloom

BookBrowse Rating: 4/5
Critics' Consensus: 5/5
Readers' Rating: 4.5/5

Published February 2023 in Paperback, 240 pages

Summary

Winner of the 2022 BookBrowse Nonfiction Award

This powerful memoir by *New York Times* bestselling author Amy Bloom is an illuminating story of two people whose love and shared life experiences led them to find a courageous way to part - and of a woman's struggle to go forward in the face of loss.

Amy Bloom began to notice changes in her husband, Brian: He retired early from a new job he loved; he withdrew from close friendships; he talked mostly about the past. Suddenly, it seemed there was a glass wall between them, and their long walks and talks stopped. Their world was altered forever when an MRI confirmed what they could no longer ignore: Brian had Alzheimer's disease.

Forced to confront the truth of the diagnosis and its impact on the future he had envisioned, Brian was determined to die on his feet, not live on his knees. Supporting each other in their last journey together, Brian and Amy made the unimaginably difficult and painful decision to go to Dignitas, an organization based in Switzerland that empowers a person to end their own life with dignity and peace.

In this heartbreaking and surprising memoir, Bloom sheds light on a part of life we so often shy away from discussing—its ending. Written in Bloom's captivating, insightful voice and with her trademark wit and candor, *In Love* is an unforgettable portrait of a beautiful marriage, and a boundary-defying love.

BookBrowse Review

A heartfelt memoir about choosing death with dignity.

Winner: 2022 Best Nonfiction Award.

In 2019, author Amy Bloom and her husband of 12 years, Brian Ameche, received life-altering news: a neurologist diagnosed Ameche with Alzheimer's disease. Although he'd been experiencing symptoms for years, Ameche's cognitive decline was still at the mild stage, enabling him to fully understand his predicament. He knew the disease was degenerative and debilitating, and he made it clear that he had no desire to spend his last years gradually losing his memories and sense of self. Bloom agreed to help him find a way to end his life early, and her memoir, *In Love*, describes their experiences during the months between the diagnosis and her husband's death.

Bloom quickly discovers their options are limited. They discuss methods of suicide they could accomplish themselves, but Ameche doesn't think those will work for him. They investigate physician-assisted suicide, a procedure permitted in 10 US states and Washington D.C., but find Amache doesn't meet the criteria. Finally, they discover Dignitas, a Swiss non-profit that offers "accompanied suicide" using sodium pentobarbital (see [Beyond the Book](#)).

Bloom's account vividly describes what it was like to embark on this journey: "Every day is an up-and-down," she writes, "Roller-coaster ride makes it sound thrilling; it is not thrilling. The ups and the downs both hurt, it's a mistake to scream, and nothing moves quickly." Ameche seems certain of his decision, never wavering, while all Bloom can do is support him in every way possible. It's evident that she loves him and is loath to lose him, but at the same time she realizes his death is inevitable.

One of the most engaging aspects of the memoir is Bloom's willingness to lay her feelings bare. She freely admits that there were times when she was angry or frustrated with her husband, even while realizing their time together was coming to a close. She talks about the need to "practice being a widow," doing things like taking down the holiday lights, which soon she'd have no choice but to do on her own. And she describes the many times all she could do was hold her husband in bed and cry. She achieves a candidness that few authors convey.

The account also relays in fascinating detail all the decisions and considerations one must make after choosing death. The pair has to determine, for example, what or how to tell their four young granddaughters. (They opt to tell them nothing; Ameche writes each a goodbye letter, and Bloom figures they can read her memoir when they are older.) Ameche particularly dreads informing others because he is concerned that they won't understand, and will try to talk him out of his decision; several people close to the couple weren't informed until the pair were at the airport headed for Zurich.

It seems a bit callous to critique such a personal narrative, but I felt that for the most part, the work lacked emotional depth. I found it an informative and, above all, an honest account, but to me, the author seemed to keep the subject at arm's length. It almost appears to have been written by an outside observer, one reporting on the facts but failing to fully capture the pain beneath them. Empathetic readers will likely be able to put themselves in Bloom's shoes and imagine what she must have been going through, but the story generally wasn't as visceral as I would have expected. Given the subject matter, that lack of emotional connection may be preferred by some, allowing the reader to understand the process without becoming overwhelmed with grief.

In Love is a fine addition to the genre of books that deal with the decline of a loved one. Those who enjoy memoirs will likely want to put this one on their list, and it's recommended for anyone interested in exploring death with dignity. Book groups in particular will find it offers many topics for discussion, such as assisted suicide and how one copes with knowing their time with a partner is reaching its end.

Reviewed by Kim Kovacs. This review was originally published in *The BookBrowse Review* in March 2022, and has been updated for the March 2023 edition.

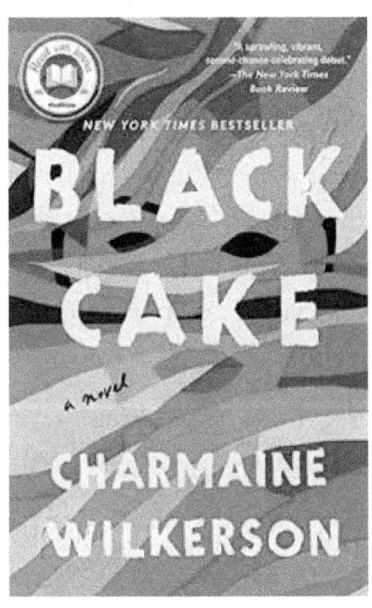

BLACK CAKE

by Charmaine Wilkerson

BookBrowse Rating: 4/5
Critics' Consensus: 5/5
Readers' Rating: 4.5/5

Published November 2022 in Paperback, 416 pages

Summary

In this moving debut novel, two estranged siblings must set aside their differences to deal with their mother's death and her hidden past - a journey of discovery that takes them from the Caribbean to London to California and ends with her famous black cake.

We can't choose what we inherit. But can we choose who we become?

In present-day California, Eleanor Bennett's death leaves behind a puzzling inheritance for her two children, Byron and Benny: a traditional Caribbean black cake, made from a family recipe with a long history, and a voice recording. In her message, Eleanor shares a tumultuous story about a headstrong young swimmer who escapes her island home under suspicion of murder. The heartbreaking tale Eleanor unfolds, the secrets she still holds back, and the mystery of a long-lost child, challenge everything the siblings thought they knew about their lineage, and themselves.

Can Byron and Benny reclaim their once-close relationship, piece together Eleanor's true history, and fulfill her final request to "share the black cake when the time is right"? Will their mother's revelations bring them back together or leave them feeling more lost than ever?

Charmaine Wilkerson's debut novel is a story of how the inheritance of betrayals, secrets, memories, and even names, can shape relationships and history. Deeply evocative and beautifully written, *Black Cake* is an extraordinary journey through the life of a family changed forever by the choices of its matriarch.

BookBrowse Review

***Black Cake* is a captivating debut that centers around the revelation of one woman's secrets.**

Charmaine Wilkerson's first novel, *Black Cake*, tells the story of Eleanor Bennett and her adult children Byron and Benedetta (aka Benny). As the story opens, the siblings are meeting with their mother's estate lawyer, who tells them she's left a long recording, stipulating that upon her death, they must listen to it together, in his presence. He ominously tells them, "You need to be prepared." The pair are reluctant at first; the family had a falling out eight years ago and the two haven't spoken since, but the attorney insists. As the tape plays, Byron and Benny hear their mother talk about her past, revealing secret after secret that sets them reeling.

There are two major threads interwoven to make up the book's intriguing plot. The first is Eleanor's tale, about which not much can be said here without introducing spoilers; suffice it to say it's a story of a person doing what they must to survive. The other is about the relationship between Byron and Benny, the latter of whom feels rejected by her family after revealing her own secret, prompting her to sever all communication with her mother, father and brother. Both plotlines are absorbing and well-written. Eleanor's is fast-paced and unpredictable, propelling the story along at a good clip, but I was particularly drawn to the narrative involving her children. I found their interactions especially realistic; neither understands the other's point of view, and they each blame the other for the rift that's occurred. They long for reconciliation, but each is angry, feeling they're owed an apology that never comes. Both stories ask whether it's possible to truly know another person, and contemplate the risk we take when we show others our true selves. These themes struck a deep chord with me.

The characters, too, are exceptionally well-drawn. Wilkerson states in her Author's Note:

> Most of the characters in *Black Cake* are people who do not quite fit into the boxes that others have set up for them. They struggle against stereotypes and the gulf between their interests and ambitions and the lives that other people expect them to lead, based on gender, culture, or class.

This is one of those uncommon cases when an author's statement of what she was trying to achieve is a perfect description of the result. It's her success here that makes the book a real gem.

Although I absolutely loved the novel in general, it certainly has its flaws. Many of the major plot points depend on coincidence; one or two such occurrences might be overlooked, but there are several that strain credulity. Additionally, the timeline jumps around a lot, particularly toward the end of the book, making it feel somewhat disjointed. This is exacerbated by very short chapters as well as the wrapping up of every single last loose end. While I enjoyed knowing what happened to all the characters, I think it would have been a tighter book had some of these sections been edited out. Finally, *Black Cake* includes a few chapters about issues that are important to acknowledge, notably racial prejudice and climate change, but that do not contribute to the plot.

While *Black Cake*'s technical difficulties might be a turnoff for some, its highlights more than make up for its imperfections. I found it an interesting and entertaining read, and a truly exceptional one given it's Wilkerson's first effort. I thoroughly enjoyed the story and recommend the novel for most audiences. Book groups will find it offers a number of great topics for discussion surrounding family dynamics and how one reconciles with one's past.

Reviewed by Kim Kovacs. This review was originally published in *The BookBrowse Review* in April 2022, and has been updated for the December 2022 edition.

HONOR

by Thrity Umrigar

BookBrowse Rating: 5/5
Critics' Consensus: 4.5/5
Readers' Rating: 5/5

Published October 2022 in Paperback, 352 pages

| Summary

A Reese's Book Club Pick! In this riveting and immersive novel, bestselling author Thrity Umrigar tells the story of two couples and the sometimes dangerous and heartbreaking challenges of love across a cultural divide.

Indian American journalist Smita has returned to India to cover a story, but reluctantly: long ago she and her family left the country with no intention of ever coming back. As she follows the case of Meena—a Hindu woman attacked by members of her own village and her own family for marrying a Muslim man—Smita comes face to face with a society where tradition carries more weight than one's own heart, and a story that threatens to unearth the painful secrets of Smita's own past. While Meena's fate hangs in the balance, Smita tries in every way she can to right the scales. She also finds herself increasingly drawn to Mohan, an Indian man she meets while on assignment. But the dual love stories of Honor are as different as the cultures of Meena and Smita themselves: Smita realizes she has the freedom to enter into a casual affair, knowing she can decide later how much it means to her.

In this tender and evocative novel about love, hope, familial devotion, betrayal, and sacrifice, Thrity Umrigar shows us two courageous women trying to navigate how to be true to their homelands and themselves at the same time.

BookBrowse Review

An Indian American journalist returns to the nation of her birth to report on the story of a Hindu woman whose brothers murdered her Muslim husband.

First Impressions readers enjoyed being transported to India via Thrity Umrigar's novel *Honor*, with 36 out of 38 rating the book four or five stars.

What it's about:

Smita—a Mumbai native who is now an American journalist, reluctantly returns to India on an assignment she accepted as a favor to a friend. Her assignment is to profile Meena, a Hindu villager whose Muslim husband was burned to death in an "honor killing" by Meena's brothers. Meena, left disfigured in the attack, has brought charges; a verdict pends. Umrigar's strength is her great storytelling. As always, not a word is wasted as she moves us through urban Mumbai and into Meena's rural village, and into complex encounters and confrontations that

Smita views with double vision as an Indian American. Her investigation stirs up painful memories of her youth in Mumbai, during the years when rising Hindu nationalism reawakened the violence of partition, now a fact of life in India. At the center of the story is Smita's developing bond with Meena and with Mohan, the friend of her friend, who is acting as her guide, driver and protector in a village where women are not supposed to work, let alone as journalists (Janice P).

Readers appreciated the insight into different facets of life in India:

You will be transported to India where you will learn about the American journalist who tells the story of Meena and Abdul. These pages are written with reality, tenderness and insight into how we are more alike than different (Helen P). Umrigar brings the city of Mumbai to life with her descriptions of the crowds, the heat, the beauty and the cultural disparities. You feel as if you are on the journey with them whether they are in a large city or a remote village (Joan V).

Though the subject matter can be difficult, the book has an approachable style:

While it is painful to read some scenes, Umrigar allows the reader to look into the windows of goodness in the hearts of people who attempt to make change in this world of sadness (Maribeth R). I feel the author's talent lies in delving into and describing the atrocity of acts of misogyny and other inequalities while not pushing the reader away in the process. This is a book and author not to be forgotten, both for subject matter and for her skill in drawing the reader into a place that's not easy to be in (Becky D). It is hard subject matter to read, but Umrigar does it in such a way that you feel the injustice, the hate, the pain, but can continue reading. She is a master at balancing the horror of what mankind is capable of, while also showing the love, loyalty, and compassion that lives within so many (Kate S).

Those familiar with Thrity Umrigar's work appreciated this book's place in her oeuvre:

I have read many of Thrity Umrigar's earlier works and found them all to be thoughtful and rich, and *Honor* is no exception (Nancy L). This was an easy book to rate: five stars, no hesitation (Joan V). I am a loyal fan of Umrigar's work, and she did not disappoint. *Honor* was well-written, with a compelling storyline. Heartbreaking, and anger-inducing. All in all, an excellent and important book, highly recommended (Cheryl S). I've been a fan of Thrity Umrigar's fiction since the 2006 publication of *The Space Between Us*. A Mumbai native who emigrated to the United States at 21, her novels all explore the various "spaces" between us — caste or class, religion, race, above all gender — within the social context of modern India, but with timely parallels to the United States (Janice P).

Many noted that *Honor* offers rich topics of discussion for book clubs:

Thrity Umrigar is a masterful writer whose characters are well-developed. I highly recommend *Honor* to all readers. Book clubs will have lots to talk about (Esther L). The book offers much to discuss for book clubs: oppression, opportunity, hope, religious differences, familial devotion, misogyny, friendship, betrayal, love and honor. I loved this book and I will recommend it to my book club (Helen P). *Honor* is a captivating read, an intriguing window into a culture as well as a really good story. Book clubs will find endless areas of discussion (Donna M).

Reviewed by First Impressions Reviewers. This review was originally published in *The BookBrowse Review* in January 2022, and has been updated for the December 2022 edition.

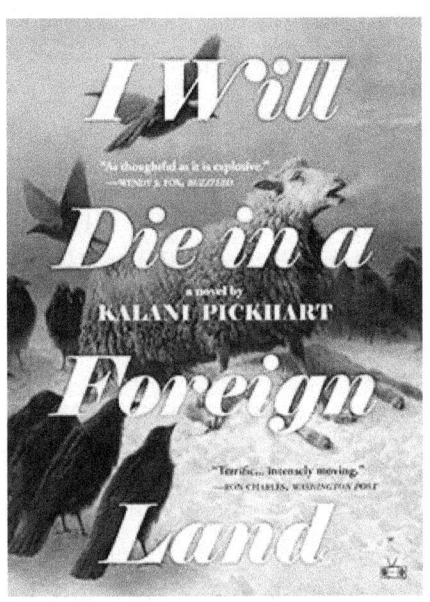

I WILL DIE IN A FOREIGN LAND

by Kalani Pickhart

BookBrowse Rating: 4/5
Critics' Consensus: 5/5
Readers' Rating: 5/5

Published May 2022 in Paperback, 320 pages

> ## Summary
>
> Set in Ukraine in 2013, *I Will Die in a Foreign Land* is an especially moving story of quiet beauty and love in a time of terror; an ambitious, intimate, and haunting portrait of human perseverance and empathy.

In 1913, a Russian ballet incited a riot in Paris at the new Théâtre de Champs-Elysées. "Only a Russian could do that," says Aleksandr Ivanovich. "Only a Russian could make the whole world go mad."

A century later, in November 2013, thousands of Ukrainian citizens gathered at Independence Square in Kyiv to protest then-President Yanukovych's failure to sign a referendum with the European Union, opting instead to forge a closer alliance with President Vladimir Putin and Russia. The peaceful protests turned violent when military police shot live ammunition into the crowd, killing over a hundred civilians.

I Will Die in a Foreign Land follows four individuals over the course of a volatile Ukrainian winter, as their lives are forever changed by the Euromaidan protests. Katya is an Ukrainian-American doctor stationed at a makeshift medical clinic in St. Michael's Monastery; Misha is an engineer originally from Pripyat, who has lived in Kyiv since his wife's death from radiation sickness; Slava is a fiery young activist whose past hardships steel her determination in the face of persecution; and Aleksandr Ivanovich, a former KGB agent, who climbs atop a burned-out police bus at Independence Square and plays the piano.

As Katya, Misha, Slava, and Aleksandr's lives become intertwined, they each seek their own solace during an especially tumultuous and violent period. The story is also told by a chorus of voices that incorporates folklore and narrates a turbulent Slavic history.

While unfolding an especially moving story of quiet beauty and love in a time of terror, *I Will Die in a Foreign Land* is an ambitious, intimate, and haunting portrait of human perseverance and empathy.

BookBrowse Review

A powerful look at the persistence of love despite the heavy human cost of political and social unrest in Ukraine.

Though *I Will Die in a Foreign Land* follows multiple perspectives across a span of several years, the majority of the novel is centered around the Euromaidan protests of 2013-2014 in Ukraine. Tension was sparked by the government's decision to abandon a proposed agreement with the European Union, choosing instead to form closer ties with Russia and the Putin administration. Kyiv's Maidan Nezalezhnosti (Independence Square) became the epicenter of the demonstrations, with thousands of Ukrainians gathering to call for the resignation of President Viktor Yanukovych. Legislation was quickly introduced to try and strip the public of their right to protest, with pro-Russian activists and riot police descending on the square. Violence soon erupted, resulting in well over 100 deaths.

Kalani Pickhart chronicles all of this political intrigue, but chooses to place the focus firmly on her characters, ensuring the book never reads like a history lesson. Though they are embroiled in the turmoil caused by the riots, we also see the enduring nature of the characters' more personal hardships. Each of them is struggling with grief in some way: Misha is an engineer mourning the loss of his wife; Katya is a doctor treating the wounded while contemplating her own son's death; Aleksandr, a former KGB agent, is searching for his long-lost daughter; and Slava is a young activist estranged from her parents after a difficult childhood, now forced to hide her blossoming relationship with another woman due to rampant homophobia. While violence rages around them, each is simply fighting for the chance to be with those they love.

By exploring their complex backstories in this way, we gain valuable insight into the myriad obstacles the people of Ukraine have had to overcome throughout the country's turbulent history — from the Chernobyl disaster to Russian oppression, and from poverty to Nazi invasion. Having already suffered so much loss, their dogged determination to preserve their land and culture makes all the more sense. Beyond this, focusing primarily on the intimate costs rather than the wider furor emphasizes the humanity of those caught up in the crisis, refusing to let them become mere statistics by showcasing how flawed and multi-faceted people can be.

For some, the narrative structure may prove alienating at first. Told in a non-linear fashion and incorporating multimedia formats such as newspaper articles, flight manifestos and audio transcripts, it can be tricky to keep track of the timeline and the various connections between each thread. That said, these somewhat removed, fact-based sections create a tonal contrast that accentuates the passion and emotion of the individual characters' stories, while providing further context for the carnage unfolding around them.

In many ways, the book feels like an ode to the everyman of Ukraine. With a deft hand, it celebrates those who strive to heal when the world around them feels broken, and the bravery required to love against the odds. Never shying away from the brutal reality of living through troubled times, its message of resilience has proven more prescient than anyone could have predicted, given the book's publication mere months before Russia invaded Ukraine in February 2022, forcing Ukrainians to defend their autonomy once again. *I Will Die in a Foreign Land* is at once a detailed snapshot of a very specific time and place, and an enduring, universal rallying call for hope in the face of tyranny.

Reviewed by Callum McLaughlin. This review was originally published in *The BookBrowse Review* in March 2022, and has been updated for the June 2022 edition.

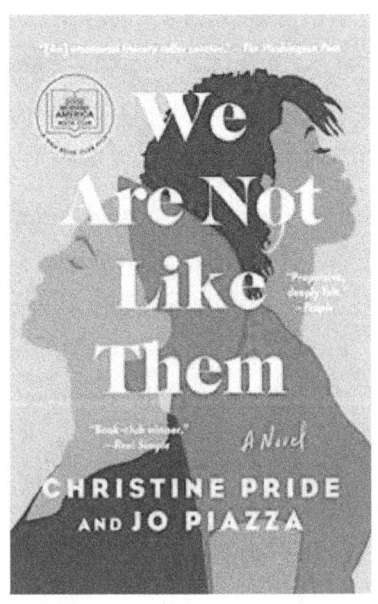

WE ARE NOT LIKE THEM

by Christine Pride, Jo Piazza

BookBrowse Rating: 5/5
Critics' Consensus: 4.5/5
Readers' Rating: 5/5

Published August 2022 in Paperback, 336 pages

Summary

Told from alternating perspectives, an evocative and riveting novel about the lifelong bond between two women, one Black and one white, whose friendship is indelibly altered by a tragic event—a powerful and poignant exploration of race in America today and its devastating impact on ordinary lives.

Jen and Riley have been best friends since kindergarten. As adults, they remain as close as sisters, though their lives have taken different directions. Jen married young, and after years of trying, is finally pregnant. Riley pursued her childhood dream of becoming a television journalist and is poised to become one of the first Black female anchors of the top news channel in their hometown of Philadelphia.

But the deep bond they share is severely tested when Jen's husband, a city police officer, is involved in the shooting of an unarmed Black teenager. Six months pregnant, Jen is in freefall as her future, her husband's freedom, and her friendship with Riley are thrown into uncertainty. Covering this career-making story, Riley wrestles with the implications of this tragic incident for her Black community, her ambitions, and her relationship with her lifelong friend.

Like Tayari Jones's *An American Marriage* and Jodi Picoult's *Small Great Things*, *We Are Not Like Them* explores complex questions of race and how they pervade and shape our most intimate spaces in a deeply divided world. But at its heart, it's a story of enduring friendship—a love that defies the odds even as it faces its most difficult challenges.

BookBrowse Review

A powerful story of friendship set against a backdrop of racial tension.

Newcomer Christine Pride joins veteran author Jo Piazza for *We Are Not Like Them*, a novel exploring friendship and race set in Philadelphia. Protagonists Riley and Jen have been friends for 30 years, since meeting in preschool and forming a near-instant bond. The two women couldn't be more different; Riley is an unmarried Black news reporter who has her eyes on the anchor chair of her local station, while Jen is a white receptionist at a dental clinic, married to a Philadelphia police officer. The pair have always considered themselves best friends, but their relationship is put to the test when Jen's husband shoots an innocent, unarmed Black teenager and Riley is chosen to cover the incident and its aftermath (an assignment she feels will bring her one step closer to her dream job).

Chapters alternate between these two first-person narrators, with each woman giving voice to her thoughts and feelings as she reacts to events transpiring around her. Although the book has an interesting plot that deals with the shooting itself, its main focus is on Riley and Jen's inner turmoil as each struggles to understand her friend's point of view. Through their eyes, readers are asked to contemplate questions about friendship and family, love and loss, racial equity and culpability for racial tension.

The authors are precise in their depictions of each character's concerns, and each woman's voice feels authentic. Jen, for example, grapples with her husband's career choice, thinking, "I will never get used to the constant, relentless fear. Every day Kevin puts on his uniform and walks out the door is a day I wonder if he's going to make it home." When Jen says a conversation isn't about race, Riley thinks, "Are you kidding me? It's always about race, Jen. That's what I wanted to scream back at her. She may have the luxury of pretending that it isn't, but I don't. Her naivete was stunning." Each woman is under extreme stress, and the tension is palpable through every page of the novel. Their anxieties and their reactions to the media storm around them are portrayed brilliantly; the two are so realistic that I found myself in complete sympathy with each, as if Jen and Riley were my own close friends.

Pride, who is Black, and Piazza, who is white, present a relatively balanced view of how people of different races might approach a tragedy such as this one. I appreciated their nuanced portrayal of Jen, who comes across as a sweet, well-meaning person who is clueless about her friend's experiences of racism. Riley is less complex but no less compelling; the shooting and her coverage of it force racial identity to the forefront of her contemplations. She sees Jen primarily as a white person, someone who doesn't comprehend how much she's benefitted from her skin color. It's Riley's narration that lingers in the mind, particularly her descriptions of daily microaggressions she experiences (like a waiter who ignores her, incorrectly assuming Jen is the person who'll leave the tip – something Jen misses entirely). While both points of view resonated deeply with me, it was Riley's that forced me, as a white woman, to reevaluate my thoughts and actions towards people of color.

Somewhat less successful is the portrayal of the book's secondary characters, in particular Jen's family, who come across as formulaic racists with little sense of accountability or sympathy regarding the death of a young Black man. Riley's family and co-workers, too, aren't completely fleshed out. Her grandmother is better developed yet still something of a stock character — the wise woman on her deathbed. And, there's a romance between Riley and a white man toward the end of the book that brings her clarity about her friendship with Jen, but this relationship seems forced and lacks the depth of the rest of the book.

With increased awareness of the Black Lives Matter movement, many books have been released in the past couple of years about racial injustice. *We Are Not Like Them* is a fantastic novel for those who want to further explore the subject, as it encourages readers to think critically and consider racial issues from multiple perspectives. I highly recommend it for most audiences, teens through adults. It's also a novel I found myself eager to discuss with others; I think it would make a perfect book group selection.

Reviewed by Kim Kovacs. This review was originally published in *The BookBrowse Review* in January 2022, and has been updated for the December 2022 edition.

BEST BOOKS OF 2021

FIREKEEPER'S DAUGHTER

by Angeline Boulley

BookBrowse Rating: 5/5
Critics' Consensus: 5/5
Readers' Rating: 4.5/5

Published April 2023 in Paperback, 496 pages

Summary

Winner of the 2021 BookBrowse Award for Best Young Adult Novel

In *Firekeeper's Daughter*, debut author Angeline Boulley crafts a groundbreaking YA thriller about a Native teen who must root out the corruption in her community, for readers of Angie Thomas and Tommy Orange.

Eighteen-year-old Daunis Fontaine has never quite fit in, both in her hometown and on the nearby Ojibwe reservation. She dreams of a fresh start at college, but when family tragedy strikes, Daunis puts her future on hold to look after her fragile mother. The only bright spot is meeting Jamie, the charming new recruit on her brother Levi's hockey team.

Yet even as Daunis falls for Jamie, she senses the dashing hockey star is hiding something. Everything comes to light when Daunis witnesses a shocking murder, thrusting her into an FBI investigation of a lethal new drug.

Reluctantly, Daunis agrees to go undercover, drawing on her knowledge of chemistry and Ojibwe traditional medicine to track down the source. But the search for truth is more complicated than Daunis imagined, exposing secrets and old scars. At the same time, she grows concerned with an investigation that seems more focused on punishing the offenders than protecting the victims.

Now, as the deceptions—and deaths—keep growing, Daunis must learn what it means to be a strong Anishinaabe kwe (Ojibwe woman) and how far she'll go for her community, even if it tears apart the only world she's ever known.

BookBrowse Review

An Ojibwe teen must uncover the truth behind the new strain of drug that is ravaging her community.

Voted 2021 Best Young Adult Award Winner by BookBrowse Subscribers.

Angeline Boulley's young adult novel *Firekeeper's Daughter* follows 18-year-old Daunis — biracial member of the Ojibwe tribe, former ice hockey star and traditional herbal medicine savant — as she witnesses the horrifying murder of her best friend at the hands of her meth-addicted ex-boyfriend. Due to her unique knowledge and connections, she is soon recruited by the FBI to assist in an ongoing investigation into a new strain of crystal meth that is devastating her community. Tasked with looking into local medicines and how they could be influencing the new strain, she fears that the information she uncovers could lead to the demonization of her culture and even risk the future of Ojibwe herbal medicine. Daunis must figure out how far she is willing to go.

From the beginning, Ojibwe culture plays a significant role in the novel. Not only does it create a vibrant and lush background for the events taking place around Daunis — as we see her taking part in the rituals and celebrations of Ojibwe life — but her heritage and her role in the tribe play a major part in the investigation itself. Ojibwe spiritual beliefs offer her extra insight into clues that may help her, and her knowledge of herbal medicine as well as her understanding of the land — and the politics surrounding it — prove valuable.

Alongside these positive and beneficial aspects of Ojibwe culture, Boulley tackles the less pleasant realities of indigenous life head-on. Throughout the book, we witness Daunis experiencing anti-indigenous microaggressions from those around her. She and a friend even create a "microaggression bingo" game that shows just how common such incidents are. Boulley also includes discussion of the systemic racism indigenous people face from the government and other legal entities, including the police. Furthermore, the devastating impact of meth addiction in indigenous communities, particularly in the early 2000s when the book is set, is central to the plot.

Daunis is a proud Anishinaabe kwe (Ojibwe woman) who is nevertheless somewhat on the outside looking in, as her Ojibwe and white backgrounds cause people of either identity to dismiss her based on her differences. Despite this, she is heavily involved in her tribe's culture and takes great joy in her heritage. She frequently spends time with and seeks the help of her Elders. However, it is refreshing to see that Daunis is not a perfect person. For example, she struggles with internalized misogyny and scrambles to "not be like those other girls," and instead be just "one of the guys." As a result, she sometimes misses significant clues that may point her in the right direction, and we see the devastating effect that her oversights have both on the investigation and her personal life.

Jamie, a new recruit of the local hockey team that Daunis' brother plays on, is another compelling character — appearing out of nowhere and stepping into a prestigious spot on the team, immediately being adored by girls yet staying true to a mysterious girl back home. Daunis finds herself intrigued by him, yet it is evident to her that he is hiding much about himself. As the reader, we find out more about Jamie at the same time Daunis does. Getting to piece together who he is, bit by bit, is just as exciting as learning about the investigation that the pair are embroiled in.

Despite being almost 500 pages, the novel never drags, but keeps a slow and sustained pace. This adds an extra layer to what would otherwise just be your average thriller, as it allows the reader to truly digest every new piece of information that comes to light and become fully immersed in the world of the book. However, the faster-paced, more adrenaline-filled chapters will have you on the edge of your seat.

All in all, *Firekeeper's Daughter* is an exciting debut novel headed by a complex female lead that is sure to intrigue you. The meandering but steady pace contrasted with occasional dynamic, action-filled sequences offers a sensational reading experience that will have Angeline Boulley at the top of your authors-to-watch list.

Reviewed by Althea Draper. This review was originally published in *The BookBrowse Review* in May 2021, and has been updated for the May 2023 edition.

THE LINCOLN HIGHWAY

by Amor Towles

BookBrowse Rating: 4/5
Critics' Consensus: 5/5
Readers' Rating: 4.5/5

Published March 2023 in Paperback, 592 pages

Summary

Winner of the 2021 BookBrowse Fiction Award.

The bestselling author of *A Gentleman in Moscow* and *Rules of Civility* and master of absorbing, sophisticated fiction returns with a stylish and propulsive novel set in 1950s America.

In June, 1954, eighteen-year-old Emmett Watson is driven home to Nebraska by the warden of the juvenile work farm where he has just served fifteen months for involuntary manslaughter. His mother long gone, his father recently deceased, and the family farm foreclosed upon by the bank, Emmett's intention is to pick up his eight-year-old brother, Billy, and head to California where they can start their lives anew. But when the warden drives away, Emmett discovers that two friends from the work farm have hidden themselves in the trunk of the warden's car. Together, they have hatched an altogether different plan for Emmett's future, one that will take them all on a fateful journey in the opposite direction—to the City of New York.

Spanning just ten days and told from multiple points of view, Towles's third novel will satisfy fans of his multi-layered literary styling while providing them an array of new and richly imagined settings, characters, and themes.

BookBrowse Review

In Towles' third novel — a big, old-fashioned dose of Americana — brothers and pals set out from Nebraska on road and rail adventures to find a fortune in 1950s New York.

Voted 2021 Best Fiction Award Winner by BookBrowse Subscribers.

Things look bleak for Emmett Watson in June of 1954. The 18-year-old has just been released from a boys' detention center in Kansas, where he served a little over a year for his role in an accidental death. When the warden drops him back at the family farm in Nebraska, Emmett learns that the loan on the property was recalled after his father died. He and his eight-year-old brother, Billy, will soon be homeless, with the bank giving them three weeks to clear out.

Luckily, Emmett still has his pride and joy, his 1948 Studebaker (see Beyond the Book), as well as a cash inheritance from his father. Grateful for the excuse to get away from Nebraska, he intends to light out for Texas to flip houses. Billy has another idea: taking the continent-spanning Lincoln Highway to find their mother in San Francisco — the last place she mailed a postcard from after she disappeared eight years ago. However, the brothers soon discover that Duchess and Woolly, teens from the detention center, escaped and stowed away in the warden's car to the Watson farm. They propose heading east to Woolly's wealthy family's upstate New York getaway to collect his hidden $150,000 trust fund and split it four ways.

Like all the best-laid plans, this one goes awry through a variety of mishaps and tricks; Duchess and Woolly take off in the Studebaker, and Emmett and Billy have to hop the Sunset East train to head them off in New York City. The novel is set over just 10 days, with its chapters counting down from 10 to 1. Billy's favorite book, *Professor Abacus Abernathe's Compendium of Heroes, Adventurers, and Other Intrepid Travelers*, includes tales of figures in history and legend, and he imagines their own adventures rivaling those of the Three Musketeers or Homer's heroes. Indeed, we meet a character called Ulysses — who fought in World War II and has been separated from his wife and child ever since — and other plot points seem to be inspired by *The Odyssey*.

The Lincoln Highway features some fantastic characters. Precocious Billy steals every scene he appears in. Duchess is a delightfully flamboyant bounder, peppering his speech with malapropisms and Shakespeare quotes — he takes after his father, a roguish traveling actor who abandoned him at an orphanage. Woolly is a dozy, melancholy young man, described as being "not all there" or "away with the fairies."

However, Emmett is a dull protagonist; with little inner life, he's always outshone by the supporting cast. The Watsons' Nebraska neighbor, Sally, has always been sweet on Emmett. It's disappointing that she, as one of just two main female characters — and one of the two first-person narrators (Duchess is the other) whose testimonies are interspersed with the third-person omniscient narration of the rest of the novel — plays such a minor role.

A danger with an episodic narrative like this one is that random events and encounters pile up but don't do much to further the plot. At nearly 200 pages in,

I realized little of consequence had happened yet, and there were later points, too, where the book seemed endless (I felt the same about [A Gentleman in Moscow](#)). Despite the condensed timeframe here, it's a meandering story that can try one's patience.

Other readers, no doubt, will appreciate the old-fashioned American road trip vibe. There is something appealing about the conjunction of bravery and mischief, and it's reassuring how the novel comes full circle and promises further adventures ahead. A long road, then, with some ups and downs along the way, but Towles' fans will certainly want to sign up for the ride.

Reviewed by Rebecca Foster. This review was originally published in *The BookBrowse Review* in November 2021, and has been updated for the April 2023 edition.

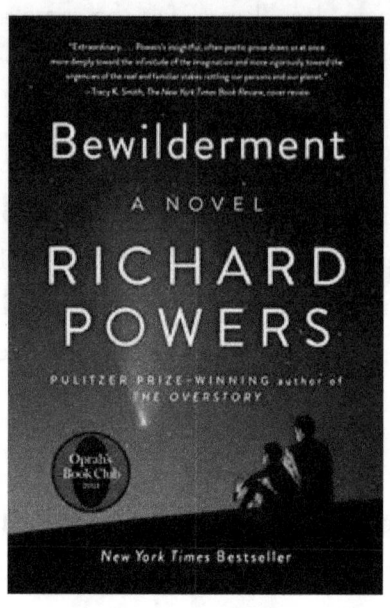

BEWILDERMENT

by Richard Powers

BookBrowse Rating: 5/5
Critics' Consensus: 4.5/5
Readers' Rating: 5/5

Published November 2022 in Paperback, 288 pages

Summary

A heartrending new novel from the Pulitzer Prize–winning and #1 New York Times bestselling author of The Overstory.

The astrobiologist Theo Byrne searches for life throughout the cosmos while single-handedly raising his unusual nine-year-old, Robin, following the death of his wife. Robin is a warm, kind boy who spends hours painting elaborate pictures of endangered animals. He's also about to be expelled from third grade for smashing his friend in the face. As his son grows more troubled, Theo hopes to keep him off psychoactive drugs. He learns of an experimental neurofeedback treatment to bolster Robin's emotional control, one that involves training the boy on the recorded patterns of his mother's brain...

With its soaring descriptions of the natural world, its tantalizing vision of life beyond, and its account of a father and son's ferocious love, Bewilderment marks Richard Powers's most intimate and moving novel. At its heart lies the question: How can we tell our children the truth about this beautiful, imperiled planet?

BookBrowse Review

In Powers' poignant 13th novel, a widowed astrobiologist struggles with raising his troubled son in a time of political and environmental crisis.

In 2019, Richard Powers won the Pulitzer Prize for *The Overstory*, a sprawling novel whose characters are obsessed with protecting magnificent trees. Although his follow-up, *Bewilderment*, has just as much of an environmentalist conscience, its scope is more intimate. It focuses on the experiences of one family and is narrated as a first-person retrospective by Theo Byrne, an astronomy professor at a midwestern university who models earthlike planets in the search for extraterrestrial life. His wife, Alyssa, died in a car accident two years ago. Their volatile nine-year-old son, Robin, named after his mother's favorite bird, is on the autism spectrum and has been violent towards his father and schoolmates.

Father and son journey together in memory and imagination as well as in real life. They connect during time spent in nature: hiking in the woods of the Great Smoky Mountains, swimming in streams and watching birds. For bedtime stories, Theo alternates between anecdotes about Robin's mother, who was an animal rights lawyer, and tales of exoplanets, some of them borrowed from the plots of his extensive science fiction collection. Robin is fascinated by plants and animals, and his father encourages his curiosity.

Theirs is a cozy, comforting relationship, a cocoon of safety after the loss of Robin's mother. But as the novel goes on, the outside world starts to intrude. In this alternative near-future scenario, perhaps one in which the 45th president was re-elected, the funding for Theo's project is at risk and political dissidents are being locked up. Meanwhile, news about the accelerating environmental crisis has Robin increasingly on edge. Angry after hearing a rumor about his mother, he throws a metal thermos at a friend and breaks the boy's cheekbone.

Theo, under renewed pressure from the school to put Robin on mood-altering medication, tries a different tactic. Alyssa's friend Martin Currier researches decoded neurofeedback, a way of locating emotional states in the brain and, through artificial intelligence, giving subjects empathy targets to work toward. She and Theo had volunteered to model emotions for the study and their results are still on file. Currier proposes enrolling Robin in a series of neurofeedback sessions in an fMRI scanner. These are a little like mindfulness training, but because they involve interacting with his mother's recording from years ago, they are also almost like spending time with her again. Robin shows tremendous progress; with his mood now on an even keel, he can have calm dealings with his father and classmates. The case is such a success that Currier reports it to the national news, and Robin becomes the subject of a viral documentary.

Powers is in full control of his myriad themes and packs a lot into 200-some pages. The plot leaps between spheres: between the public eye, where Robin is a scientific marvel and an environmental activist (see Beyond the Book), and the privacy of family life; between an ailing Earth and the other planets Theo can study or imagine; and between the humdrum of daily existence and the magic of another state where Robin can reconnect with his late mother. Within the limited timespan of a school year, much changes for Robin, but regression threatens. The novel opens at the Great Smokies, and returns there for a dramatic finale. I admired this full-circle structure, and the way in which other incidents meaningfully repeat.

In an author's note, Powers discusses his inspirations for the novel. One was his nephew, who loved nature and might have benefited from decoded neurofeedback. Another was the growing feeling of solastalgia, especially among young people. The third was Daniel Keyes's *Flowers for Algernon* (1959), a sci-fi classic Powers first read at age 11. Theo and Robin listen to it during their Great Smokies road trip. (The plot of *Bewilderment* apparently draws on that of *Flowers for Algernon*. If you've read it, you may have an inkling of what's coming; if you haven't, it's probably best not to read up on it unless you're not concerned about spoilers.)

When I came to the breathtaking final paragraph of *Bewilderment*, I felt despondent and overwhelmed. I wasn't sure I could forgive Powers for the ending. But as time has passed, the book's feral beauty has stuck with me, and Robin in particular won't leave my mind. His neurodivergence, viewed as a problem by authority figures in the novel, seems to allow him greater communion with other species, and perhaps even with the dead. The pure sense of wonder that Robin embodies is worth imitating. For while "bewilderment" connotes the confusion of modern life, it also suggests the value of embracing wild creatures and places. As Powers writes in the prefatory note, "A childlike love for our wild, entangled home is the only thing large enough to cure what is wrong with us."

Reviewed by Rebecca Foster. This review was originally published in *The BookBrowse Review* in September 2021, and has been updated for the November 2022 edition.

PROJECT HAIL MARY

by Andy Weir

BookBrowse Rating: 5/5
Critics' Consensus: 4.5/5
Readers' Rating: 5/5

Published October 2022 in Paperback, 496 pages

Summary

A lone astronaut must save the earth from disaster in this incredible new science-based thriller from the #1 *New York Times* bestselling author of *The Martian*.

Ryland Grace is the sole survivor on a desperate, last-chance mission—and if he fails, humanity and the earth itself will perish.

Except that right now, he doesn't know that. He can't even remember his own name, let alone the nature of his assignment or how to complete it.

All he knows is that he's been asleep for a very, very long time. And he's just been awakened to find himself millions of miles from home, with nothing but two corpses for company.

His crewmates dead, his memories fuzzily returning, Ryland realizes that an impossible task now confronts him. Hurtling through space on this tiny ship, it's up to him to puzzle out an impossible scientific mystery—and conquer an extinction-level threat to our species.

And with the clock ticking down and the nearest human being light-years away, he's got to do it all alone.

Or does he?

An irresistible interstellar adventure as only Andy Weir could deliver, *Project Hail Mary* is a tale of discovery, speculation, and survival to rival *The Martian*—while taking us to places it never dreamed of going.

BookBrowse Review

Andy Weir returns with another engrossing space opera.

Imagine, if you will, waking up to a mechanized voice incessantly asking, "What is two plus two?" As it intrudes on your consciousness you realize you're naked, lying on some sort of wall-mounted bed, you have tubes coming out of every orifice, and you share the sterile space with two people who are obviously long dead. To top it off, you can't remember who you are, what this facility is, or why you're there. So begins Andy Weir's science fiction adventure, *Project Hail Mary*.

Our narrator for this entertaining romp is Ryland Grace, and once he can articulate the answer to the simple math problem, he's able to determine he's on a spacecraft. As he familiarizes himself with his surroundings, he has flashbacks that remind him who he was before he left Earth — and what exactly a junior high science teacher is doing alone on a rocket ship light-years from his home planet. His bursts of insight continue throughout the novel, helping him problem solve and eventually revealing shocking information about his presence aboard the craft.

Weir employs a tried-and-true formula to weave his tale that is much like the structure he used in his debut novel, _The Martian_ (and appearing as well in countless space operas like the *Flash Gordon* or *Doctor Who* series). A life-threatening crisis presents itself, the hero comes up with some sort of ingenious solution, and then they do their best to survive in spite of the odds; rinse and repeat. There are a number of factors that keep this novel from feeling trite, however. First and foremost is the central character, Ryland Grace, whose narration is captivating, funny and informative. He comes across as the cool teacher you wish you'd had growing up, able to explain complicated concepts while retaining a sense of humor:

> Light is a funny thing. Its wavelength defines what it can and can't interact with… That's why there's mesh over the window of a microwave. The holes in the mesh are too small for microwaves to pass through. But visible light, with a much shorter wavelength, can go through freely. So you get to watch your food cook without melting your face off.

As always with Weir's writing, I'm impressed with his reliance on credible technologies and his ability to explain these complex notions to even scientifically illiterate readers such as myself. With the exception of one major plot point that occurs about a quarter of the way through the novel, I never found myself thinking, "Well, that seems unlikely." Sometimes these scientific expositions go on a little too long for my taste, but generally I appreciated feeling like the problems Grace encountered and the solutions he came up with were plausible.

One criticism often lobbed at Weir's previous novels is that his main characters are quite foul-mouthed. He seems to have taken this critique to heart in *Project Hail Mary*, as Grace truly curses just once (and it fits, given the circumstances). It's not that he doesn't use expletives at all, but as someone who spends most of his time with kids he defaults to G-rated invectives like "pain in the patoot" and "the poop hit the fan." Although at times the language feels a little forced, it's probably a wise move, as it may allow parents and teachers to feel more comfortable recommending the book to younger audiences. And as written, it's certainly appropriate for teen readers.

I've had serious love for Weir's writing since *The Martian*, and *Project Hail Mary* has only added to my high opinion of his work. Those who count themselves among his fans will undoubtedly be delighted with the book, and I unhesitatingly recommend it to anyone who enjoys well-written, creative science fiction. It's sure to be another huge hit for this author, and I can't wait to read whatever he comes up with next.

Reviewed by Kim Kovacs. This review was originally published in *The BookBrowse Review* in June 2021, and has been updated for the October 2022 edition.

THE PHONE BOOTH AT THE EDGE OF THE WORLD

by Laura Imai Messina

BookBrowse Rating: 5/5
Critics' Consensus: 4.5/5
Readers' Rating: 5/5

Published October 2022 in Paperback, 416 pages

Summary

The international bestselling novel sold in 21 countries, about grief, mourning, and the joy of survival, inspired by a real phone booth in Japan with its disconnected "wind" phone, a place of pilgrimage and solace since the 2011 tsunami.

When Yui loses both her mother and her daughter in the tsunami, she begins to mark the passage of time from that date onward: Everything is relative to March 11, 2011, the day the tsunami tore Japan apart, and when grief took hold of her life. Yui struggles to continue on, alone with her pain.

Then, one day she hears about a man who has an old disused telephone booth in his garden. There, those who have lost loved ones find the strength to speak to them and begin to come to terms with their grief. As news of the phone booth spreads, people travel to it from miles around.

Soon Yui makes her own pilgrimage to the phone booth, too. But once there she cannot bring herself to speak into the receiver. Instead she finds Takeshi, a bereaved husband whose own daughter has stopped talking in the wake of her mother's death.

Simultaneously heartbreaking and heartwarming, *The Phone Booth at the Edge of the World* is the signpost pointing to the healing that can come after.

BookBrowse Review

A phone booth in a garden in Japan offers the grieving the chance to speak to their deceased loved ones; the lives of two strangers on a journey of healing intersect.

Our First Impressions reviewers found *The Phone Booth at the Edge of the World* by Laura Imai Messina to be poignant and inspiring; it scored an average rating of 4.6/5 stars. Messina is a Japanese transplant originally from Italy and this novel is her English-language debut, translated from the Italian by Lucy Rand.

What it's about:

This book tells a gentle and powerful story that is still with me days after finishing it. Set in Japan after the 2011 tsunami, it centers around a real phone booth with an unconnected phone in a Japanese garden. According to an introductory note, every year thousands come to use the phone and speak with those they have lost. The main characters, Yui and Takeshi, each grieving the loss of loved ones, meet at the phone booth and come to know others who are grief-stricken (Joan R).

Our First Impressions readers appreciated the book's nuanced understanding of grief — how it is both universal and deeply individual...

As each human processes the loss of a beloved person, grief changes its face. One can feel sadness, anger, pain, denial and even fear, culminating, hopefully, in acceptance. In *The Phone Booth at the Edge of the World*, main character Yui struggles with loss and seemingly unending grief. She is not alone, however, as others she meet have their own personal, yet similar, journeys to walk (Frances I). From tragedy to hope, the novel carries you on a journey of the human soul. It shows how grief is a personal thing for each one of us (Windell H).

...And for many, this theme resonated with their own experiences.

This book was exactly what I needed at this time, and I think it will touch so many, as we all deal with loss in many ways throughout our lives (Elyse R). Anyone who has ever experienced loss (and that's most of us), will be moved by Laura Imai Messina's beautiful *The Phone Booth at the Edge of the World* (Gloria F). This is a perfect book to read during our current tragic times (Joan R). In this time of so much tension, Yui's story is needed. We need to go to the phone booth and hear the wind (Mary Anne R).

Many readers commented on the author's exceptional writing and character development.

This book is beautifully written! It's easy for the reader to become immersed in the deep feelings and concerns of the many who made the journey to the phone booth (Susanna K). From the beginning I was touched by Laura Imai Messina's poetic manner of writing. She developed her characters in a delightful and loving way. I cared about each one and wanted the best for them. Yui's story is developed in many dimensions: physically, emotionally and spiritually (Mary

Anne R). I loved all the characters and the development of each one in their grief and the impact the phone booth had on their healing. A wonderful book! (Jana G).

Overall, readers agreed that *The Phone Booth at the Edge of the World* is a moving novel with a much appreciated message of hope.

I was moved to tears on more than one occasion. I needed the reminder that after the storm, after the wind, after the loss, there is still room for love, room for hope. It's one of those beautiful reads that ended too soon! (Ed R). The characters were believable and memorable and I loved how their stories intertwined to form a beautiful tapestry of healing and hope (Theresa M). The book asks fundamental questions: how is it possible to live with joy when everything comes to an end? How can we learn to live with the loss of those we loved who have died? The answers suggested by the story are profound, deeply moving and, perhaps most importantly, hopeful (Joan R).

Reviewed by First Impressions Reviewers. This review was originally published in *The BookBrowse Review* in March 2021, and has been updated for the October 2022 edition.

CLOUD CUCKOO LAND

by Anthony Doerr

BookBrowse Rating: 5/5
Critics' Consensus: 5/5
Readers' Rating: 5/5

Published September 2022 in Paperback, 640 pages

Summary

From the Pulitzer Prize-winning author of *All the Light We Cannot See*, perhaps the most bestselling and beloved literary fiction of our time, comes a triumph of imagination and compassion, a soaring novel about children on the cusp of adulthood in a broken world, who find resilience, hope, and story.

The heroes of *Cloud Cuckoo Land* are trying to figure out the world around them: Anna and Omeir, on opposite sides of the formidable city walls during the 1453 siege of Constantinople; teenage idealist Seymour in an attack on a public library in present day Idaho; and Konstance, on an interstellar ship bound for an exoplanet, decades from now. Like Marie-Laure and Werner in *All the Light We Cannot See*, Anna, Omeir, Seymour, and Konstance are dreamers and outsiders who find resourcefulness and hope in the midst of peril.

An ancient text—the story of Aethon, who longs to be turned into a bird so that he can fly to a utopian paradise in the sky—provides solace and mystery to these unforgettable characters. Doerr has created a tapestry of times and places that reflects our vast interconnectedness—with other species, with each other, with those who lived before us and those who will be here after we're gone.

Dedicated to "the librarians then, now, and in the years to come," *Cloud Cuckoo Land* is a hauntingly beautiful and redemptive novel about stewardship—of the book, of the Earth, of the human heart.

BookBrowse Review

A tour de force from the Pulitzer-prize winning author of *All the Light We Cannot See*.

Anthony Doerr's Cloud Cuckoo Land may be even more remarkable than his Pulitzer-prize winning work All the Light We Cannot See. This marvelously imaginative tale crosses time and genre, ultimately weaving a story that captivates readers in a way few can; simply put, it's dazzling.

The third-person narrative rotates between several storylines. Konstance is a teenager, a colonist living on a spaceship headed to a far-away planet in the 22nd century. Born in transit, she has never set foot on Earth, and the ship's journey is long enough that her generation will be long dead before the vessel reaches its destination. Zeno, an octogenarian, is at a library in current-day Boise, Idaho, rehearsing children for a play he wrote, while a young man, Seymour, is committing an act of ecoterrorism elsewhere in the building. Other plot lines explore Zeno's and Seymour's youths, leading readers to understand how they each arrived at this point. And finally, Anna and Omeir are children during the Fall of Constantinople (1453 CE, see Beyond the Book), one Christian and one Muslim, on opposite sides of the city's famous Theodosian Walls.

Doerr ties these disparate tales together through a story called Cloud Cuckoo Land, a book he imagines to have been written by the ancient Greek author Antonius Diogenes. In it, Aethon, a shepherd, desires to fly to a utopian civilization in the sky and seeks a magical means to transform into a bird to achieve this end. The fact that the book's extended title is Aethon: Lived 80 Years a Man, 1 Year a Donkey, 1 Year a Sea Bass, 1 Year a Crow is some indication of how he fares. Each of Doerr's characters encounters this work in their youth and attaches great sentimental significance to it, and their love for the story is what allows it to be preserved for future generations.

There are so many extraordinary things about this complex novel that it's hard to know where to begin. It defies classification, alternating between contemporary fiction, historical fiction, science fiction and fantasy, and Doerr handles each of the genres superbly. The stories themselves are fascinating, too. When I encounter books with multiple plot lines, I often find myself preferring one over the others, but not so here. Each of the narratives drew me in completely, and while sorry to transition away from a story I was enjoying, I nevertheless greeted the next with eager anticipation. Every last character is unique and vibrant, and I grew to love and understand each of them, even a young man about to cause death and destruction. And, of course, there's Doerr's prose, which is heartbreakingly beautiful at times; there's plenty of gorgeous description, but it's never so dense that it slows down the book's pace. It's truly amazing that he is able to weave so many people, events and themes into such an immensely satisfying tale, and I'm in awe of his achievement.

Cloud Cuckoo Land is much more ambitious than All the Light We Cannot See. It's longer, more complex, and has a lot of moving parts that don't seem to relate to each other until the book nears its conclusion. I personally found Cloud Cuckoo Land considerably more entertaining and believe it's a stronger work than Doerr's previous novel. If I have any complaint at all, it's that the book's ending isn't as complete as I'd have liked. All the plot threads wrap up nicely except for Konstance's, and although her story's conclusion is appropriate it still left me with questions. Every other aspect is so outstanding, though, that this minor nitpick should deter no one from reading this wonderful work.

I've been fortunate to have read some truly exceptional books this year, but absolutely nothing compares to Cloud Cuckoo Land. It's one of those books that's sure to generate a lot of buzz and garner much acclaim — it may well be the "must-read" book of the year — and I highly recommend it for all audiences.

Reviewed by Kim Kovacs. This review was originally published in *The BookBrowse Review* in October 2021, and has been updated for the October 2022 edition.

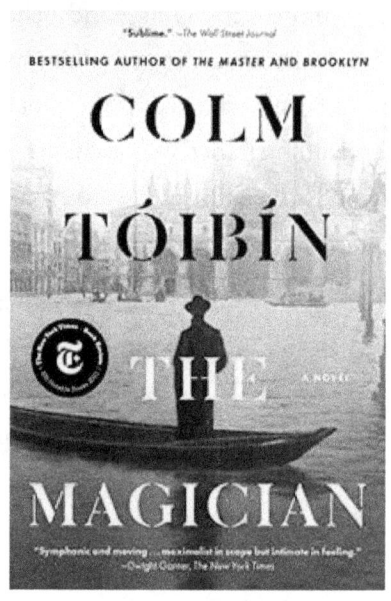

THE MAGICIAN

by Colm Toibin

BookBrowse Rating: 5/5
Critics' Consensus: 5/5
Readers' Rating: 3/5

Published September 2022 in Paperback, 512 pages

Summary

From one of today's most brilliant and beloved novelists, a dazzling, epic family saga centered on the life of Nobel laureate Thomas Mann, spanning a half-century including World War I, the rise of Hitler, World War II, and the Cold War.

Colm Tóibín's magnificent new novel opens in a provincial German city at the turn of the twentieth century, where the boy, Thomas Mann, grows up with a conservative father, bound by propriety, and a Brazilian mother, alluring and unpredictable. Young Mann hides his artistic aspirations from his father and his homosexual desires from everyone. He is infatuated with one of the richest, most cultured Jewish families in Munich, and marries the daughter Katia. They have six children. On a holiday in Italy, he longs for a boy he sees on a beach and writes the story *Death in Venice*. He is the most successful novelist of his time, winner of the Nobel Prize in literature, a public man whose private life remains secret. He is expected to lead the condemnation of Hitler, whom he underestimates. His oldest daughter and son, leaders of Bohemianism and of the anti-Nazi movement, share lovers. He flees Germany for Switzerland, France and, ultimately, America, living first in Princeton and then in Los Angeles.

In a stunning marriage of research and imagination, Tóibín explores the heart and mind of a writer whose gift is unparalleled and whose life is driven by a need to belong and the anguish of illicit desire. *The Magician* is an intimate, astonishingly complex portrait of Mann, his magnificent and complex wife Katia, and the times in which they lived—the first world war, the rise of Hitler, World War II, the Cold War, and exile. This is a man and a family fiercely engaged by the world, profoundly flawed, and unforgettable. As *People* magazine said about *The Master*, "It's a delicate, mysterious process, this act of creation, fraught with psychological tension, and Tóibín captures it beautifully."

BookBrowse Review

A vivid, imaginative rendering of the inner life of one of the 20th-century's greatest writers — Thomas Mann.

Thomas Mann — the subject of this biographical novel by Colm Tóibín — is regarded as a major 20th-century German writer, perhaps one of the best known of the so-called "Exilliteratur" writers — Germans in exile who opposed the Hitler regime. Author of works such as *Buddenbrooks* (1901), *Death in Venice*

(1912) and *The Magic Mountain* (1924), Mann was awarded the Nobel Prize for Literature in 1929.

Against a historical backdrop which includes World War I, the rise of Hitler and Nazism, World War II, the Cold War and McCarthyism in the United States, Tóibín's novel examines the life of Thomas Mann from age 16 in 1891 to just before his death at age 80 in 1955. Although Mann lived through what can only be described as an eventful period in world history, the novel focuses on his personal and family life, his emotions and thoughts, and his art.

At 16, Mann was already writing poetry and developing a deep appreciation of music. Music and literature continued to be the essential threads in the fabric of his life; but, like a darker thread which is only suggested in the novel, there is his repressed homosexuality, which in later years found an outlet in his writing.

In 1897, Mann began to write *Buddenbrooks* – his first and perhaps his most loved novel. In describing the genesis of this work, Tóibín brilliantly sets out Mann's creative process, explaining how, as with all his novels, Mann drew deeply on the experiences of his own family. Consequently, Mann was criticized for writing a roman á clef – a novel which overlays historical fact with a façade of fiction. This is of course not unlike *The Magician*, where biographically and historically accurate events in Mann's life are given an added depth and breadth by the author's imagining of Mann's emotions and thoughts as the events unfold.

In 1933, while vacationing in France, Mann was told by his adult children in Munich that it would not be safe for him to return to Germany. Consequently, the family moved to Zürich. In 1939, as the Nazi stranglehold on Europe tightened, the Manns emigrated to the United States, living first in New Jersey where Mann taught at Princeton University, and then in Los Angeles. Tóibín demonstrates how Mann and Katia became prominent figures in the German expatriate community, with Mann recording speeches that were broadcast in Germany by the BBC. The essential theme of the speeches was the significant cultural difference between the German people and National Socialism.

The title of the book originates from an episode in which Mann's son Klaus was frightened by what he believed to be a monster in his room. Mann told Klaus he was a magician and would use his magic to send the monster away. The stratagem was successful and, from then on, his children called him the magician. But in Tóibín's novel, the word takes on a greater significance — Mann is a person who can wield magic with words, whether in his books, his letters or his speeches.

Tóibín has created magic in this book. In beautiful prose, he has brought Thomas Mann to life and given the reader an intimate look at a great author who lived with contradictions — his acclaim as one of the great 20th-century writers set against his hesitant and secretive inner life; his successful marriage to Katia and their six children set against his repressed homosexuality; and his love for Germany and its culture set against the Nazi ideology he detested.

In most of his novels, Tóibín explores the themes of living abroad, the creative process and the preservation of personal identity (and particularly of homosexual identity). In *The Magician*, these themes find expression in the struggles Thomas Mann experienced with each. It's a poignant portrayal and a pleasure to read.

Reviewed by Rod McLary. This review was originally published in *The BookBrowse Review* in October 2021, and has been updated for the October 2022 edition.

LIGHTNING STRIKE

by William Kent Krueger

BookBrowse Rating: 5/5
Critics' Consensus: 4.5/5
Readers' Rating: 4/5

Published July 2022 in Paperback, 400 pages

> ## Summary
>
> The author of the instant *New York Times* bestseller *This Tender Land* returns with a powerful prequel to his acclaimed Cork O'Connor series - a book about fathers and sons, long-simmering conflicts in a small Minnesota town, and the events that echo through youth and shape our lives forever.

Aurora is a small town nestled in the ancient forest alongside the shores of Minnesota's Iron Lake. In the summer of 1963, it is the whole world to twelve-year-old Cork O'Connor, its rhythms as familiar as his own heartbeat. But when Cork stumbles upon the body of a man he revered hanging from a tree in an abandoned logging camp, it is the first in a series of events that will cause him to question everything he took for granted about his hometown, his family, and himself.

Cork's father, Liam O'Connor, is Aurora's sheriff and it is his job to confirm that the man's death was the result of suicide, as all the evidence suggests. In the shadow of his father's official investigation, Cork begins to look for answers on his own. Together, father and son face the ultimate test of choosing between what their heads tell them is true and what their hearts know is right.

In this masterful story of a young man and a town on the cusp of change, beloved novelist William Kent Krueger shows that some mysteries can be solved even as others surpass our understanding.

BookBrowse Review

The popular Cork O'Connor detective series takes readers back to the beginning in this introspective, coming-of-age prequel that explores not only a mysterious death but the mysteries of fathers and sons.

It is the summer of 1963 in Tamarack County, Minnesota. Just outside the small town of Aurora, nestled next to shimmering Iron Lake, 12-year-old Cork O'Connor makes a grisly discovery. Hiking into the infamous burned-out logging camp called Lightning Strike, Cork and his friend, Jorge, find the body of Big John Manydeeds hanging from a tree near the edge of the forest. Scattered beneath his lifeless, dangling feet, are empty bottles of the whiskey he swore off months ago. Sheriff Liam O'Connor, Cork's father, is called out to the scene to investigate, with all the evidence pointing toward suicide. But those who knew Big John in life don't believe it, including Cork, who plunges into a summer of sleuthing to find answers to the senseless death of his revered older friend.

Big John's death rocks the close-knit Ojibwe community on the Indian Lake Reservation and presents a powder keg puzzle for Liam O'Connor. Krueger deftly portrays the lingering and fiery resentment of the Native community to white authority. Even though Liam is married to Colleen, who is half Ojibwe, he feels the continuing sting of the community's rejection because of his whiteness. These longstanding tensions ratchet up exponentially as Big John's body is laid to rest and a local Ojibwe girl is found murdered, with local authorities eager to pin the crime on Big John. Tempers run high on all sides in the steamy summer of 1963 as Cork and his friends begin to "follow the crumbs," searching for fleeting scraps of evidence, information, and motive. It's a defining moment for Cork, who readers of Krueger's other novels in this series know will grow up to become a sheriff.

A fitting element to this creation story is Krueger's touching portrayal of a father and son seeing each other for the first time. Liam wants to protect his son, who is quarter Ojibwe, from the endemic racism in the white community, but also the disdain that "mixed bloods" receive from the Ojibwe people. On the cusp of becoming a teenager, Cork in turn wants to prove to his father that he can help in the investigation, no matter the slights he receives. As Cork talks to neighbors and collects money for his paper route among the locals — many endearing, others reprehensible — the crumbs he gathers start to suggest Big John was murdered. Sharing information and theories at the morning breakfast table, father and son unwittingly help each other in their separate quests for the truth.

Krueger delivers a masterful strike down the middle with the riddle of Big John's death; *Lightning Strike* will keep experienced mystery readers guessing until the very end about who was responsible and how it was engineered. Spooling out the mystery among the thick pines of the North Woods, the atmosphere is ripe for both exploration and danger, acting as a tantalizing proving ground for Cork and his friends. In these moments, Krueger summons a hazy nostalgia for long-ago summers of adventure, where boys could take canoe trips and camp overnight by themselves. But there will be a price to pay for their fearless inquisitiveness.

For those new to the series, *Lightning Strike* is a prequel that also works as a powerful standalone novel, richly told and sensitive to the issues of race and class between "The First People" and their white neighbors. It also reveals the epic events that shaped a young, malleable Cork O'Connor into the man he becomes. Longtime fans of the series will rejoice at the evocative backstory, while new readers (of which I am one) will finish this book and eagerly seek out the others.

Reviewed by Peggy Kurkowski. This review was originally published in *The BookBrowse Review* in October 2021, and has been updated for the August 2022 edition.

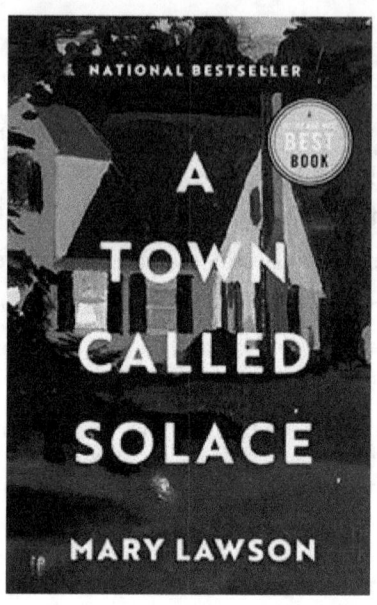

A TOWN CALLED SOLACE

by Mary Lawson

BookBrowse Rating: 5/5
Critics' Consensus: 5/5
Readers' Rating: 5/5

Published June 2022 in Paperback, 304 pages

Summary

Mary Lawson is back after almost a decade with a fresh and timely novel that is different in subject but just as emotional and atmospheric as her beloved earlier work.

A Town Called Solace, the brilliant and emotionally radiant new novel from Mary Lawson, her first in nearly a decade, opens on a family in crisis. Sixteen-year-old Rose is missing. Angry and rebellious, she had a row with her mother, stormed out of the house and simply disappeared. Left behind is seven-year-old Clara, Rose's adoring little sister. Isolated by her parents' efforts to protect her from the truth, Clara is bewildered and distraught. Her sole comfort is Moses, the cat next door, whom she is looking after for his elderly owner, Mrs. Orchard, who went into hospital weeks ago and has still not returned.

Enter Liam Kane, mid-thirties, newly divorced, newly unemployed, newly arrived in this small northern town, who moves into Mrs. Orchard's house—where, in Clara's view, he emphatically does not belong. Within a matter of hours he receives a visit from the police. It seems he is suspected of a crime.

At the end of her life, Elizabeth Orchard is also thinking about a crime, one committed thirty years previously that had tragic consequences for two families, and in particular for one small child. She desperately wants to make amends before she dies.

Told through three distinct, compelling points of view, the novel cuts back and forth among these unforgettable characters to uncover the layers of grief, remorse, and love that connect them. *A Town Called Solace* is a masterful, suspenseful, darkly funny and deeply humane novel by one of our great storytellers.

BookBrowse Review

A novel of love and loss set in Canada's far north.

Mary Lawson's novel, *A Town Called Solace*, is set in a small town several hours north of Ontario, Canada. The narrative unfolds from the perspectives of three individuals whose lives are in upheaval: Seven-year-old Clara, whose teenage sister Ruby has run away; Elizabeth, Clara's elderly neighbor, now hospitalized; and Liam, a 35-year-old man who leaves his home in Toronto for the refuge of

Elizabeth's house in Solace, thereby deferring decisions he must make about his failing marriage and the job he hates.

The book's plot was somewhat of a surprise to me because, well, there actually isn't much of one. Readers might expect, for example, that Ruby's disappearance and ultimate fate would be central to the story, but it receives only minimal attention. The author's considerable talent instead lies in creating unique and memorable characters, and she's at her best here. She brilliantly breathes life into Clara, Elizabeth and Liam as they experience losses, which they meet with resilience, making the most of their situations even as they struggle to understand how they've arrived at this point in their lives. The characters are unrelentingly realistic and sympathetic, and, while the concerns of each might seem mundane on the surface, their inner turmoil is completely relatable. Indeed, I'm hard-pressed to think of many other novels that reach the high character-development standard the author sets here.

In spite of a rather run-of-the-mill plot, the book is quite the page-turner. Lawson captures the reader's attention by raising questions that pull us into each character's story. It's soon apparent, for example, that Elizabeth has had a complex history with Liam (who she hasn't seen in 30 years), but that part of the plot unfolds slowly as she reminisces about her past and contemplates her impending death. By the time this and other tensions are resolved, readers are so heavily invested in the characters themselves that the original plot points seem inconsequential.

Lawson doesn't paint a comprehensive portrait of Solace itself, but she definitely nails its small-town feel. Minor details conjure up the atmosphere of the rural community, adding a sense of authenticity without explicitly describing the physical aspects of the environment. We learn, for instance, that there are only two restaurants in town, just one of which is open in the off-season when vacationers cease driving through, and which only serves two menu items. While Lawson's portrayal isn't groundbreaking in any way – readers encounter nothing unexpected – her sketches are perfect and avoid cliché.

One of my favorite parts of this novel, one of the aspects that make it a real stand-out, is its ending. As in real life, there are no hard and fast resolutions here. Lawson doesn't wrap up her tale in a neat little package, tying up each loose end, but leaves readers with the hope that the future holds good things for all concerned. She has created a feel-good novel without allowing it to devolve into a trite "happily ever after" conclusion, and it cements her reputation as a masterful storyteller.

My only complaint is that the timeline isn't clear, with large chunks occurring in the past without that being obvious at first. At the end of a chapter told from Clara's point of view, for example, she finally comes face to face with Liam. The following section is narrated by Elizabeth from her hospital bed, and then the next opens with Liam speaking to a contractor about repairs to the house. Only at the end of that lengthy chapter does Liam encounter Clara, at which point readers realize the chapters overlap, with the time frame backing up to show the day from his perspective. I found the technique confusing and largely unnecessary, something that could have easily been clarified in the chapter title if not within the narrative itself.

That said, *A Town Called Solace* is a quick, pleasant read, and I highly recommend it to those looking for a quiet, character-driven novel. Its subject matter makes it appropriate for all audiences, and it would make a great selection for book groups in particular.

Reviewed by Kim Kovacs. This review was originally published in *The BookBrowse Review* in December 2021, and has been updated for the July 2022 edition.

THE SECRET KEEPER OF JAIPUR

by Alka Joshi

BookBrowse Rating: 4/5
Critics' Consensus: 4.5/5
Readers' Rating: 5/5

Published June 2022 in Paperback, 384 pages

Summary

In *New York Times* bestselling author Alka Joshi's intriguing new novel, henna artist Lakshmi arranges for her protégé, Malik, to intern at the Jaipur Palace in this tale rich in character, atmosphere, and lavish storytelling.

It's the spring of 1969, and Lakshmi, now married to Dr. Jay Kumar, directs the Healing Garden in Shimla. Malik has finished his private school education. At twenty, he has just met a young woman named Nimmi when he leaves to apprentice at the Facilities Office of the Jaipur Royal Palace. Their latest project: a state-of-the-art cinema.

Malik soon finds that not much has changed as he navigates the Pink City of his childhood. Power and money still move seamlessly among the wealthy class, and favors flow from Jaipur's Royal Palace, but only if certain secrets remain buried. When the cinema's balcony tragically collapses on opening night, blame is placed where it is convenient. But Malik suspects something far darker and sets out to uncover the truth. As a former street child, he always knew to keep his own counsel; it's a lesson that will serve him as he untangles a web of lies.

BookBrowse Review

Alka Joshi's follow-up to *The Henna Artist* provides a dash of adventure and romance.

Alka Joshi's *The Secret Keeper of Jaipur* is the sequel to her 2020 bestseller *The Henna Artist* and the middle entry in the planned Jaipur Trilogy. The story opens in 1969, 12 years after the conclusion of the earlier work, and the three main characters (henna artist Lakshmi, her younger sister Radha and Lakshmi's ward Malik) have experienced great changes in their lives. Lakshmi is now married to Dr. Jay Kumar, a physician in remote Shimla (an Indian city in the foothills of the Himalayas). She works alongside him, balancing his formal medical skills with her knowledge of herbal remedies. Radha has become a perfumer living overseas with her French husband and their two daughters. And Malik has graduated from private school and returned to Jaipur (see Beyond the Book) at Lakshmi's insistence, apprenticing as an accountant at the Jaipur Royal Palace.

Most of the minor characters who played significant roles in *The Henna Artist* (the Singh family, Maharanis Indira and Latika, Manu and Kanta Agarwal) are represented in the sequel. While *The Henna Artist* is primarily relayed in the first person by Lakshmi, in this novel Joshi chooses to divide the narration between Lakshmi, Malik and a new character, Nimmi, a young widow from a Himalayan hill tribe whom Lakshmi invites to work at the Shimla clinic.

The bulk of the plot revolves around Malik and his new position in Jaipur. The Maharani Latika commissions the construction of a grand cinema, and he is present on opening night, granted the honor due to his apprenticeship with the palace architects. When the unthinkable happens and part of the structure collapses, blame lands where convenient, on those close to Malik. Sensing an injustice in progress, he seeks to uncover clues that point to those truly responsible. A secondary storyline concerns the relationships between the three main characters, as Malik and Nimmi fall in love and Lakshmi comes to realize that she must let the young man live his own life.

Joshi's writing shines as she describes the streets of Jaipur and the Himalayan countryside, as well as those who inhabit both environs. At one point Lakshmi thinks:

> I'm looking out the window, enjoying the choreographed chaos of the city: a lipsticked hijra on her way to market, slim hips swaying; a wagon drawn by a bony laborer carrying old tractor tires; children flicking marbles on a dusty street corner…

Indian terms often appear without much context for readers who are unfamiliar with them, but a dictionary is included at the end of the book. The author also comments on cultural social norms in a way that feels natural.

> Manu looked so lost; I wished that I had words to help him…He'd been raised to never question his superiors…For fifteen years, the royal family had employed him. He'd sooner cut his arm off than question their decisions or blame them for anything inappropriate.

Unfortunately, I didn't find Joshi's sophomore effort up to the standard set by the first book of the series. What made *The Henna Artist* so appealing was the strong, long-suffering Lakshmi, able to overcome all obstacles placed in her path with grace, fortitude and cleverness. That book was character-driven with very little action, yet its gossipy nature propelled the plot forward in a way that kept me rapt. I didn't like this version of Lakshmi as much — she's more reactionary and less self-reliant — and Nimmi often comes across as shrill and unnecessarily distrustful. Joshi has attempted to create a more plot-driven novel here, but there's no mystery, no tension; the outcome is a foregone conclusion that surprises no one. And finally, the sex scenes simply don't work; one in particular is completely gratuitous, being neither necessary nor a good fit for the rest of the story. The book is still certainly entertaining — it's just not at the level of *The Henna Artist*.

The author provides enough background information (including a helpful "who's who" at the front of the book) that for the most part the novel can be read as a stand-alone work. Indeed, there's some argument to be made that one might enjoy it more without the inevitable comparisons to the earlier book. Tackling the series in order, though, will allow readers to understand the characters and their motivations better, and for that reason I'd recommend the latter approach.

The Secret Keeper of Jaipur is a fast-moving, entertaining novel, and is recommended for most audiences looking for a light read. Readers who are interested in learning about Indian culture will find the author includes many interesting tidbits that will add to their knowledge. Those who enjoyed Joshi's earlier book will likely appreciate this new entry in the series.

Reviewed by Kim Kovacs. This review was originally published in *The BookBrowse Review* in September 2021, and has been updated for the July 2022 edition.

THREE GIRLS FROM BRONZEVILLE

by Dawn Turner

BookBrowse Rating: 5/5
Critics' Consensus: 5/5
Readers' Rating: 4/5

Published June 2022 in Paperback, 336 pages

> ## Summary
>
> A "beautiful, tragic, and inspiring" (*Publishers Weekly*, starred review) memoir about three Black girls from the storied Bronzeville section of Chicago that offers a penetrating exploration of race, opportunity, friendship, sisterhood, and the powerful forces at work that allow some to flourish…and others to falter.

They were three Black girls. Dawn, tall and studious; her sister, Kim, younger by three years and headstrong as they come; and her best friend, Debra, already prom-queen pretty by third grade. They bonded—fervently and intensely in that unique way of little girls—as they roamed the concrete landscape of Bronzeville, a historic neighborhood on Chicago's South Side, the destination of hundreds of thousands of Black folks who fled the ravages of the Jim Crow South.

These third-generation daughters of the Great Migration come of age in the 1970s, in the warm glow of the recent civil rights movement. It has offered them a promise, albeit nascent and fragile, that they will have more opportunities, rights, and freedoms than any generation of Black Americans in history. Their working-class, striving parents are eager for them to realize this hard-fought potential. But the girls have much more immediate concerns: hiding under the dining room table and eavesdropping on grown folks' business; collecting secret treasures; and daydreaming about their futures—Dawn and Debra, doctors, Kim a teacher. For a brief, wondrous moment the girls are all giggles and dreams and promises of "friends forever." And then fate intervenes, first slowly and then dramatically, sending them careening in wildly different directions. There's heartbreak, loss, displacement, and even murder. Dawn struggles to make sense of the shocking turns that consume her sister and her best friend, all the while asking herself a simple but profound question: Why?

In the vein of *The Other Wes Moore* and *The Short and Tragic Life of Robert Peace*, *Three Girls from Bronzeville* is a piercing memoir that chronicles Dawn's attempt to find answers. It's at once a celebration of sisterhood and friendship, a testimony to the unique struggles of Black women, and a tour-de-force about the complex interplay of race, class, and opportunity, and how those forces shape our lives and our capacity for resilience and redemption.

BookBrowse Review

Dawn Turner, Kim Turner and Debra Trice, adventurous black girls raised in the historical section of Chicago known as Bronzeville, are tested as their

difficult and turbulent environment demands strength, perseverance and toughness.

Friendship is an intimate experience. Dawn Turner and Debra Trice, two black girls living the same have-not ordeal, are guardians of each other. Dawn is an excellent writer and suffocatingly smart, while Debra is beautiful, spirited and impulsive. They are inseparable and live in the Lawless Gardens apartment complex in the Bronzeville section of Chicago, a historical black neighborhood once called the Black Belt, where Southern dreamers who migrated north plopped their tired bodies in the run-down part of town.

At the age of ten, Dawn and Debra spend a lot of time at their "love spot," a roof ledge where they read and dream. Dawn wants to be a doctor. Debra says that this is what she wants too. Baby sister Kim, stubborn and rebellious, wants to be a teacher. Three Girls From Bronzeville: A Uniquely American Memoir of Race, Fate, and Sisterhood is their heartbreaking story, richly written by older sister and best friend Dawn Turner. Dawn is the story's anchor. While her resilience is the stuff of legends — the poor girl who tramples class barriers to write for the Chicago Tribune — her success isn't contagious. Debra and Kim have a tumultuous and predictable struggle, beginning in adolescence.

Take ninth grade. Debra has a knack for falling in with the wrong crowd and her family, probably at their wits' end, abruptly moves to Indiana. In a way, this feels appropriate, but what the Trices don't consider is that removing Debra from such loyal attachments as those she has with Dawn and Kim can also have negative consequences. Fourteen is a difficult age. It's not easy to find devoted friends in a new place.

Social scientists have been studying working class communities for over a century, attempting to answer questions of prediction. Can we project who will thrive and achieve and who will be dragged down the poverty gutter? While Dawn gleefully embraces every educational opportunity put before her, her saucy-mouthed sister is a disinterested student and a party girl. The death of Kim's infant son kickstarts her depression and alcohol dependency. A few hundred miles away in Indiana, Debra's struggles are unseen but present. She waitresses, then strips while on coke. Then she kills a man.

Raymond Jones is a friend of Debra's and his shooting is accidental, one of those tragic stories where a loaded gun goes off seemingly on its own. But while the circumstances are chaotic, particularly for Debra, it feels predictable. She is a substance abuser and continually makes the wrong choices. She was pushing the envelope. It was inevitable something unforeseen was going to happen. And just like that, the romantic notion that all three girls will shake off oppression is gone. Debra is arrested and handed a harsh 50-year sentence.

Because I lived in Bronzeville for the first eight years of my life, I read Turner's memoir with wide eyes, and I questioned myself. What would have become of me had I stayed? Who would I have been in this story? Ambitious Dawn? Grieving Kim? Or incarcerated Debra? I alternated my affections between the three girls as if each was their own separate tree, each leaning into the wind a little differently. I found myself looking at the title again. Despite a certain resonance and romanticism, the word "fate" felt misleading. Confused, I messaged the author to ask what she meant.

"When I talk about fate in the book," Turner wrote in an email, "[I]t's less about where we land because we were pointed toward the sun. It's more about Debra and me becoming friends and our apartments being one atop the other. It's about the choices we made, and the ones made for us." A similar thought was expressed by Joyce Carol Oates, who said in an interview with Anita Sethi of the Guardian, "I believe in particular destinies - people who are 'made for each other' and only have to discover each other."

And yet Turner's memoir isn't just about destiny and friendship. Her ability to masterfully dissect racialized Chicago, her parents' marriage and her father's flaws give the story its strength. Those who appreciate language will enjoy her examples of often comical one-liners from adults to children: "Get out from under grown folks' business." "Low-income people don't have to be low-ceilinged people." "That girl is wearing a hole in my patience." "Kind takes to kind."

In our society, we are repeatedly told that children of the working class have damaged psyches. Turner wants us to know there is more to it than that. There are girls who are strivers and then things go wrong for them. Most readers will want to save Debra and Kim from themselves and from the structures that toss them aside. Most readers will have their hearts broken. The memoir is dramatic, and often sad. It's fast-paced storytelling for which Turner deserves a lot of credit. After all, this was her life. Entertaining, teary and very redemptive, it is an excellent read. It reminds me of the advice aunties like to give when sitting around the kitchen table. Be like me. Survive it all, baby, even when it hurts.

Reviewed by Valerie Morales. This review was originally published in *The BookBrowse Review* in November 2021, and has been updated for the July 2022 edition.

THE PERSONAL LIBRARIAN

by Marie Benedict, Victoria Christopher Murray

BookBrowse Rating: 5/5
Critics' Consensus: 4.5/5
Readers' Rating: 4.5/5

Published June 2022 in Paperback, 352 pages

Summary

The remarkable, little-known story of Belle da Costa Greene, J. P. Morgan's personal librarian--who became one of the most powerful women in New York despite the dangerous secret she kept in order to make her dreams come true, from *New York Times* bestselling author Marie Benedict and acclaimed author Victoria Christopher Murray.

In her twenties, Belle da Costa Greene is hired by J. P. Morgan to curate a collection of rare manuscripts, books, and artwork for his newly built Pierpont Morgan Library. Belle becomes a fixture on the New York society scene and one of the most powerful people in the art and book world, known for her impeccable taste and shrewd negotiating for critical works as she helps build a world-class collection.

But Belle has a secret, one she must protect at all costs. She was born not Belle da Costa Greene but Belle Marion Greener. She is the daughter of Richard Greener, the first Black graduate of Harvard and a well-known advocate for equality. Belle's complexion isn't dark because of her alleged Portuguese heritage that lets her pass as white--her complexion is dark because she is African American.

The Personal Librarian tells the story of an extraordinary woman, famous for her intellect, style, and wit, and shares the lengths to which she must go--for the protection of her family and her legacy--to preserve her carefully crafted white identity in the racist world in which she lives.

BookBrowse Review

A fictional glimpse into the life of Belle da Costa Greene, a Black woman passing as white who managed banker J.P. Morgan's private library.

The Personal Librarian drew a robust positive response from our First Impressions reviewers, receiving a rating of 4 or 5 stars from 70 out of 77 readers. The book is a collaboration between the novelists Marie Benedict and Victoria Murray.

What the book is about:

The fascinating story of Belle da Costa Greene begins for the reader in 1905. She went from working at the library at Princeton University to becoming the personal librarian to J.P. Morgan. Even though her father was the first African

American man to graduate from Harvard University, she lived her whole life as a white woman (Elizabeth K). The story provides a fascinating look at the process of building and collecting a library of rare books, manuscripts and art. But, it is also the story of a beautiful, intelligent and witty black woman, living as white (Sherilyn R).

Readers enjoyed peering into the world of art and antiquities in early-1900s New York high society.

The characters with whom Belle mingles have volumes written about them — Vanderbilt, Elsie de Wolfe, Lillian Russell, Oscar Wilde, Steichen, Stieglitz, Bernard Berenson and of course the collector himself, J.P. Morgan (Margaret S). I found the book to be particularly interesting in the descriptions of the sumptuousness of the library, the fashions of the time, the paintings and other artifacts owned by the Morgans and their friends, and the preciousness of the manuscripts and tomes sought for the collection (Dorinne D).

Many were pleased to discover a captivating protagonist based on a fascinating real-life figure.

I came to love the heroine's balance of professional chutzpah and vulnerable heart (Jessamyn R). Belle da Costa Greene was, historically, a very powerful woman and yet has never crossed my radar. The authors describe a woman of great intelligence, style and depth one can never know enough about (Carole A). This portrayal of the diminutive (in stature only) Greene and her ability to navigate a purely (white) man's world with her wit, tenacity and intelligence is unforgettable (Patricia L).

Some felt the book dragged at times despite its interesting characters and subject matter.

I felt that the characters were well-drawn, but thought that the book moved very slowly from major issue to major issue without sufficient build-up to propel the story forward (Erica M). The style of writing in this book reflects the restricted customs and repressed emotions... which makes it a slower and perhaps less exciting read (Karen W).

However, readers saw the novel's great potential for stimulating book club discussions, with some suggesting it would pair well with Brit Bennett's *The Vanishing Half*.

This book is an interesting counterpoint to *The Vanishing Half*, since the time and financial status are so different (Karen W). Coincidentally, both of my book groups had just finished reading and discussing *The Vanishing Half*. Hours could be spent discussing these two books together, even though they are different in many ways. This is a terrific book club book (Marianne D).

Ultimately, reviewers felt that *The Personal Librarian* **is an important work for its social and political context, with many layers that make it worth the read.**

Focusing on both racial and gender rights in the first half of the 20th century, the story line shows both the progress we've made and the work still ahead. I feel certain that both book clubs I'm involved in — one for women only and the other for both men and women — would be pleased with this selection (Patricia E). *The Personal Librarian* not only shows us how far we have come in our struggle against racial inequality and injustice, but also reminds us how much more is left to be done. ... It's a great story and the discussion possibilities are endless (Christine P).

Reviewed by First Impressions Reviewers. This review was originally published in *The BookBrowse Review* in July 2021, and has been updated for the June 2022 edition.

THE LOVE SONGS OF W.E.B. DU BOIS

by Honorée Fannone Jeffers

BookBrowse Rating: 5/5
Critics' Consensus: 5/5
Readers' Rating: 5/5

Published May 2022 in Paperback, 816 pages

Summary

The 2020 National Book Award–nominated poet makes her fiction debut with this magisterial epic - an intimate yet sweeping novel with all the luminescence and force of *Homegoing*; *Sing, Unburied, Sing*; and *The Water Dancer* - that chronicles the journey of one American family, from the centuries of the colonial slave trade through the Civil War to our own tumultuous era.

A New York Times Book Everyone Will Be Talking About • A People 5 Best Books of the Summer • A Ms. Most Anticipated Book of the Year • A Goodreads Most Anticipated Book of the Year • A Book Page Writer to Watch • An Essence Book of the Summer

The great scholar, W. E. B. Du Bois, once wrote about the Problem of race in America, and what he called "Double Consciousness," a sensitivity that every African American possesses in order to survive. Since childhood, Ailey Pearl Garfield has understood Du Bois's words all too well. Bearing the names of two formidable Black Americans—the revered choreographer Alvin Ailey and her great grandmother Pearl, the descendant of enslaved Georgians and tenant farmers—Ailey carries Du Bois's Problem on her shoulders.

Ailey is reared in the north in the City but spends summers in the small Georgia town of Chicasetta, where her mother's family has lived since their ancestors arrived from Africa in bondage. From an early age, Ailey fights a battle for belonging that's made all the more difficult by a hovering trauma, as well as the whispers of women—her mother, Belle, her sister, Lydia, and a maternal line reaching back two centuries—that urge Ailey to succeed in their stead.

To come to terms with her own identity, Ailey embarks on a journey through her family's past, uncovering the shocking tales of generations of ancestors—Indigenous, Black, and white—in the deep South. In doing so Ailey must learn to embrace her full heritage, a legacy of oppression and resistance, bondage and independence, cruelty and resilience that is the story—and the song—of America itself.

BookBrowse Review

A dazzling coming-of-age novel exploring the life of a young Black girl growing up in the Southern United States.

Honorée Fannone Jeffers' *The Love Songs of W.E.B. Du Bois* explores the Black experience in America through the lens of a middle-class girl and her family. Ailey is the youngest of three daughters born to Belle and Geoff Garfield, and we meet her when she is just three years old. Through her first-person account, we watch her mature from naïve child to confident and capable young woman, sharing her joys, sorrows, triumphs and failures along the way.

Although at its heart the novel is a coming-of-age story, that's not apparent until late in the book due to the various narrative techniques the author employs. A large and equally engaging portion of the story is historical fiction, following Ailey's ancestors from village life in Africa to their experiences being enslaved on a Georgia plantation and beyond. These sections have a mythic feel to them, their unnamed narrator weaving the early stories into the type of tale one might spin around a campfire. As the audience, we're aware that we're reading about Ailey's forebears, but their relevance isn't completely clear until the lineage catches up with what she knows of her family tree. Other chapters are relayed from the points of view of Belle and Lydia, Ailey's eldest sister. These third-person accounts fill in gaps in Ailey's knowledge while providing us with a comprehensive understanding of how she grows into the person we know at the book's conclusion. *Love Songs* contains an enormous cast, but all the characters' voices are unique and authentic — a truly remarkable feat.

Jeffers covers a wide range of topics throughout the novel, taking a finely nuanced approach to many of them. As one might expect, racism is a major theme: Some characters react to casual racism with anger or resentment, while others approach it as an annoyance — a day-to-day common occurrence to be expected and dealt with accordingly. The author also explores colorism within the Black community, where some seem to feel lighter-toned skin is more desirable. Another key theme centers on the sexual abuse of children and the ways such harm can manifest differently in individuals. The author additionally touches on subjects such as Black education, the importance of family (in particular, reverence for one's mother), marital fidelity, drug abuse, sexuality, interracial marriage and a host of other issues, some specific to the Black community, others universal.

I'd generally opine that when a work is this massive — over 800 pages — it perhaps would have been stronger had the author concentrated on fewer topics. But although *Love Songs* is big, sprawling and multi-faceted, there's not a sentence in it I'd have edited out. It's messy in the same way the experiences of most lives are messy — one goes through phases, finds romance, makes bad choices — but combine to form a whole. Jeffers brilliantly reflects these experiences throughout the novel, but her depiction of Ailey's growth in particular is perfect. That said, the book does require some patience and persistence, especially at first, when the reader has yet to become familiar with the characters (the family tree inserted at the front of the book is very helpful with keeping people straight).

I've found myself thinking about *The Love Songs of W.E.B. Du Bois* for many days after completing it, and consider it one of the most well-crafted, entertaining novels I've encountered in quite some time. I highly recommend it for readers who appreciate complex, adult themes and enjoy big, meaty generational stories. Book groups who are able to select a novel of its length will find it yields many great topics for discussion as well.

Reviewed by Kim Kovacs. This review was originally published in *The BookBrowse Review* in September 2021, and has been updated for the May 2022 edition.

THE FOREST OF VANISHING STARS

by Kristin Harmel

BookBrowse Rating: 5/5
Critics' Consensus: 5/5
Readers' Rating: 5/5

Published May 2022 in Paperback, 384 pages

Summary

The *New York Times* bestselling author of the "heart-stopping tale of survival and heroism" (People) *The Book of Lost Names* returns with an evocative coming-of-age World War II story about a young woman who uses her knowledge of the wilderness to help Jewish refugees escape the Nazis—until a secret from her past threatens everything.

After being stolen from her wealthy German parents and raised in the unforgiving wilderness of eastern Europe, a young woman finds herself alone in 1941 after her kidnapper dies. Her solitary existence is interrupted, however, when she happens upon a group of Jews fleeing the Nazi terror. Stunned to learn what's happening in the outside world, she vows to teach the group all she can about surviving in the forest—and in turn, they teach her some surprising lessons about opening her heart after years of isolation. But when she is betrayed and escapes into a German-occupied village, her past and present come together in a shocking collision that could change everything.

Inspired by incredible true stories of survival against staggering odds, and suffused with the journey-from-the-wilderness elements that made *Where the Crawdads Sing* a worldwide phenomenon, *The Forest of Vanishing Stars* is a heart-wrenching and suspenseful novel from the #1 internationally bestselling author whose writing has been hailed as "sweeping and magnificent" (Fiona Davis, *New York Times* bestselling author), "immersive and evocative" (*Publishers Weekly*), and "gripping" (*Tampa Bay Times*).

BookBrowse Review

A young woman raised by her kidnapper in an eastern European forest becomes a hero of the Resistance in this moving World War II novel.

Kristin Harmel's historical novel *The Forest of Vanishing Stars* was very well-received by our First Impressions readers, who gave it an average rating of 4.6 out of 5 stars.

What it's about:

The Forest of Vanishing Stars is a captivating read. The book is about a young girl, Yona, who was kidnapped when she was a baby and raised by her kidnapper in the forest. Yona is taught everything she needs to know to live there and stay hidden. These skills become immensely important to the Jews who hide in the forest from the Nazis during World War II (Colleen L).

First Impressions reviewers felt *The Book of Vanishing Stars* is a unique entry in the crowded field of historical fiction about the Holocaust:

The story is told in such an interesting and unique way. Avid readers should read it for that reason alone. Kristin Harmel has made my list of favorite authors. I'm looking forward to her next book! (Maureen M). Beautifully written, well researched and inspired by incredible true stories. A great addition to my Holocaust library and highly recommended (Esther L). Although this is just one of the multitude of books I've read about WWII over the years, it was one that will not soon be forgotten (Freya H). This book is based on true stories of survival in the forests of eastern Europe during WWII. I have read many books that take place during this era but I'd never heard about some of the Jews escaping the ghettos and fleeing into the surrounding wilderness. The setting was unique and I'm surprised that it never occurred to me that there would be thousands driven into the forests (Rosemary S).

Many appreciated Harmel's strong, well-crafted protagonist:

The survival experiment is led by Yona, an unusual adolescent woman, abducted and raised without family or social ties, who seeks to overcome her personal fears. Her resilience and leadership instincts lead to a storyline with engaging twists and turns (Mary F). I highly recommend this book for readers who enjoy historical fiction, who want to learn more about WWII from a new perspective, and those who enjoy strong female lead characters (Stephanie Z). Yona was extraordinary. I rooted for her survival, her success in saving others and her happiness. Readers will undoubtedly join Yona's cheering club (Maureen M).

The book was praised by Kristin Harmel fans and those new to her work who plan on reading more:

I had read and appreciated three earlier books by Kristin Harmel, so I was expecting to also enjoy this book. However, *The Forest of Vanishing Stars* is so, so much more than I was expecting (Stephanie Z). Harmel writes a well-researched book with amazing detail for her characters and the period. I have had many a sleepless night reading her other books, and this one was no different (Susan H). I LOVE Harmel's writing. It is beautiful, lush, eloquent and gripping. It is so engaging that you want to race along to see what happens (Colleen L).

The book is highly recommended, especially for book clubs:

This extraordinary novel draws you in from the very first page. I believe *The Forest of Vanishing Stars* will appeal to history fans, book clubs and anyone who likes suspense. I thoroughly enjoyed it and highly recommend it (Laurette A). Applause to Kristin Harmel, this is one book that is extremely difficult to put down. I loved how she brought the characters in the story together to fight for survival. I believe this would be a great selection for a book club, as it will generate so many thoughts and opinions (Cheryl P).

Reviewed by First Impressions Reviewers. This review was originally published in *The BookBrowse Review* in July 2021, and has been updated for the May 2022 edition.

THE CODE BREAKER

by Walter Isaacson

BookBrowse Rating: 5/5
Critics' Consensus: 5/5
Readers' Rating: 5/5

Published May 2022 in Paperback, 560 pages

Summary

Winner of the 2021 BookBrowse Nonfiction Award

The bestselling author of *Leonardo da Vinci* and *Steve Jobs* returns with a gripping account of how Nobel Prize winner Jennifer Doudna and her colleagues launched a revolution that will allow us to cure diseases, fend off viruses, and have healthier babies.

When Jennifer Doudna was in sixth grade, she came home one day to find that her dad had left a paperback titled *The Double Helix* on her bed. She put it aside, thinking it was one of those detective tales she loved. When she read it on a rainy Saturday, she discovered she was right, in a way. As she sped through the pages, she became enthralled by the intense drama behind the competition to discover the code of life. Even though her high school counselor told her girls didn't become scientists, she decided she would.

Driven by a passion to understand how nature works and to turn discoveries into inventions, she would help to make what the book's author, James Watson, told her was the most important biological advance since his co-discovery of the structure of DNA. She and her collaborators turned a curiosity of nature into an invention that will transform the human race: an easy-to-use tool that can edit DNA. Known as CRISPR, it opened a brave new world of medical miracles and moral questions.

The development of CRISPR and the race to create vaccines for coronavirus will hasten our transition to the next great innovation revolution. The past half-century has been a digital age, based on the microchip, computer, and internet. Now we are entering a life-science revolution. Children who study digital coding will be joined by those who study genetic code.

Should we use our new evolution-hacking powers to make us less susceptible to viruses? What a wonderful boon that would be! And what about preventing depression? Hmmm…Should we allow parents, if they can afford it, to enhance the height or muscles or IQ of their kids?

After helping to discover CRISPR, Doudna became a leader in wrestling with these moral issues and, with her collaborator Emmanuelle Charpentier, won the Nobel Prize in 2020. Her story is a thrilling detective tale that involves the most profound wonders of nature, from the origins of life to the future of our species.

BookBrowse Review

Walter Isaacson presents an illuminating biography of Nobel Prize winner Jennifer Doudna, whose work in gene editing has revolutionary implications for modern science.

Voted 2021 Best Nonfiction Award Winner by BookBrowse Subscribers

What makes humans human? It's a mystery that has inspired philosophers and driven scientific endeavor. The discovery of DNA in the 1950s provided a giant leap forward in answering that question, and today's genetic researchers continue to explore it. Concurrently, they are also learning how to potentially edit or improve a human's basic genetic makeup.

It is through gene editing and discovering the means of how humans could potentially alter themselves at the basic genetic level that *The Code Breaker* introduces the reader to some of the most updated advancements. Biographer Walter Isaacson describes the quest that begins with the discovery of DNA and ends with the winner of the 2020 Nobel Prize in Chemistry, Jennifer Doudna (who shared the prize with her French colleague, Emmanuelle Charpentier). In particular, the Nobel Committee recognized their work with a CRISPR associated enzyme (Cas9) that can change genetic information.

DNA contains the genetic instructions for living organisms. As its role became clearer, scientists speculated about the possibility of "editing" DNA to open up incredible opportunities — such as genetically modifying crops and animals to make them more productive and resistant to diseases and pests, and potentially to treat genetic conditions in humans, such as sickle-cell anemia and blindness. But how to achieve this? Several approaches were investigated, but the discovery of a naturally occurring gene editing system in bacteria led to the identification of the protein CRISPR-Cas9, which proved to be the key. Faster, cheaper, more accurate, and more efficient than other genome editing methods, CRISPR-Cas9 is revolutionizing — and turbocharging — research, giving scientists their first practical tool for gene editing.

Isaacson narrates Jennifer Doudna's life, beginning with her upbringing in Hawaii and the inspiration she found in Dr. James Watson's book *The Double Helix*, an autobiographical narrative of the author's discovery of the structure of DNA. Driven to succeed in science, Doudna rose in her field to eventually become a leader in genetic research. Isaacson covers in detail how she collaborated with other scientists to make the advances that led to the discovery of CaS9. However, this book is as much a history of genetic research as it is a biography of Doudna. Along with offering accessible explanations of what Doudna and her peers discovered and developed, this work also explores some of the less commonly discussed aspects of modern science: the struggle to get money for research, the friction between the objectives of academic research (advancements in science) and the objectives of the private sector (scientific discovery for profit), the arduous process to get discoveries published and patented, and the in-fighting between scientists.

These aspects can be the most engaging for the non-scientific reader. No sooner did Doudna and her team publish their results in 2012 when another scientist, Feng Zhang, made his claim to being the rightful discoverer of CRISPR (see Beyond the Book). The years-long battle between these two, along with various other stakeholders in genetic editing, takes the reader from learning about science to patent law and litigation.

The Code Breaker also considers the ethical angle of this discovery. While Issacson notes that the CRIPSR-inspired advancements can help those with sickle-cell anemia, he also describes how one Chinese scientist used this technology to conceive genetically modified babies. As humans learn what they can do with gene editing, there is the equally important challenge of learning what we must not do.

The last portion of the book examines how Doudna and her peers turned their research attention to COVID-19. The lessons learned from the discovery of CaS9 and gene editing played a major role in scientists' efforts to understand the new coronavirus and to develop the vaccines to suppress it. While this section can feel like an afterthought, its relevance given the significant impact COVID-19 has had on the world cannot be discounted.

Overall, this is an outstanding combination of biography, current events and science writing all in one volume. Being an Isaacson work, there is a lot of material to get through, but it is incredibly readable and engaging. The visual aids (including a graphic that describes exactly how CRISPR works) are especially insightful. While it is a substantial book, *The Code Breaker* is worth the time investment.

Reviewed by Scott C. Martin. This review was originally published in *The BookBrowse Review* in May 2021, and has been updated for the May 2022 edition.

THE SWEETNESS OF WATER

by Nathan Harris

BookBrowse Rating: 5/5
Critics' Consensus: 5/5
Readers' Rating: 5/5

Published May 2022 in Paperback, 368 pages

> ## Summary
>
> A profound debut about the unlikely bond between two freedmen who are brothers and the Georgia farmer whose alliance will alter their lives, and his, forever.

In the waning days of the Civil War, brothers Prentiss and Landry—freed by the Emancipation Proclamation—seek refuge on the homestead of George Walker and his wife, Isabelle. The Walkers, wracked by the loss of their only son to the war, hire the brothers to work their farm, hoping through an unexpected friendship to stanch their grief. Prentiss and Landry, meanwhile, plan to save money for the journey north and a chance to reunite with their mother, who was sold away when they were boys.

Parallel to their story runs a forbidden romance between two Confederate soldiers. The young men, recently returned from the war to the town of Old Ox, hold their trysts in the woods. But when their secret is discovered, the resulting chaos, including a murder, unleashes convulsive repercussions on the entire community. In the aftermath of so much turmoil, it is Isabelle who emerges as an unlikely leader, proffering a healing vision for the land and for the newly free citizens of Old Ox.

With candor and sympathy, debut novelist Nathan Harris creates an unforgettable cast of characters, depicting Georgia in the violent crucible of Reconstruction. Equal parts beauty and terror, as gripping as it is moving, *The Sweetness of Water* is an epic whose grandeur locates humanity and love amid the most harrowing circumstances.

BookBrowse Review

A moving debut set in Reconstruction-era Georgia.

Nathan Harris's dazzling first novel, *The Sweetness of Water*, is set in the American South just after the Civil War. As the story opens, the African American population has been freed from slavery, but no provisions have been made to accommodate the thousands of newly liberated men, women and children; young troops are returning from combat to find their society has changed; and those who have managed to retain their wealth and power are maneuvering to maintain their influence.

It's a time of reckoning, too, as some begin to realize just how much they've lost and how hard it will be to rebuild their lives. George Walker is one of these; a farmer who was too old and infirm to take part in the war himself, George is told that his only son was killed near the end of the conflict. In addition, his relationship with his wife Isabelle is complicated, so much so that whole days go by without them speaking, and he delays telling her of their son's demise. On a stroll around his property to contemplate what he'll say to her, he stumbles upon two recently liberated men, brothers Prentiss and Landry, who have set up a camp in his woods. The pair are cold and hungry, and George provides them with food and shelter, paying them to work his property. This doesn't sit well with residents of the nearby town, who resent the good wages given to these men, and conflict ensues.

This description may make it sound like the plot is relatively straightforward, but that's definitely not the case. Very little of the narrative unfolds as one might expect, and indeed, that's one of the many highlights of Harris's debut. Events and actions always make sense, but the author eschews the standard paths other storytellers have taken, creating a unique piece of literature that's utterly surprising, start to finish.

There are so many aspects of this novel I felt were sheer perfection. The plot is intricate and unpredictable, the characters have remarkable depth, and there's enough detail about the era for wonderful historical fiction. Harris's portrayal of the grieving process is dead-on, as is his perception of the complexities of human nature. Perhaps the biggest standout, though, is the writing style. The author captures the cadence of 19th-century prose, adding to the story's authentic feel while spinning lush descriptions of time and place. Harris writes of George's first encounter with the brothers:

> The log beneath him yawned and George's rear end sank into the waterlogged mess. Only as he moved to stand, to pat himself dry, did he see them sitting before him. Two Negroes, similar in dress: white cotton shirts unbuttoned, britches as ragged as if they'd fitted their legs into intertwined gunnysacks. They stood stock-still, and if the blanket before them

had not swayed in the wind like some flag to signal their presence, they might have disappeared in the foreground entirely.

The book's cover mentions a "forbidden romance between two Confederate soldiers" and a murder that occurs when the liaison is discovered. This relationship isn't a major thematic component, though the one scene regarding the young men's tryst is pivotal, as it connects to the main storyline and fuels the rest of the novel.

The Sweetness of Water isn't a fast read. This is partly due to the author's narrative technique, particularly at the start of the book as one adjusts to the rhythm of the text. But some readers may also find the novel's intensity necessitates slower reading; there were several times when I had to set it down for the day because an unexpected twist left me reeling. There were other times when I stepped away because I anticipated a tragic end to a storyline, only to find when I resumed reading that the author veers away from the assumed trajectory. Still, there were certainly scenes that were painful to read, and overall, it was an unforgettable, deeply emotional experience.

In short, *The Sweetness of Water* is one of the finest novels I've read this year, and certainly worthy of all the attention it's garnering. I highly recommend it to anyone with an interest in the time period and those looking for a truly memorable story.

Reviewed by Kim Kovacs. This review was originally published in *The BookBrowse Review* in December 2021, and has been updated for the June 2022 edition.

GREAT CIRCLE

by Maggie Shipstead

BookBrowse Rating: 5/5
Critics' Consensus: 5/5
Readers' Rating: 5/5

Published April 2022 in Paperback, 672 pages

Summary

An unforgettable story of a daredevil female aviator determined to chart her own course in life, at any cost - *Great Circle* spans Prohibition-era Montana, the Pacific Northwest, Alaska, New Zealand, wartime London, and modern-day Los Angeles.

After being rescued as infants from a sinking ocean liner in 1914, Marian and Jamie Graves are raised by their dissolute uncle in Missoula, Montana. Thereafter encountering a pair of barnstorming pilots passing through town in beat-up biplanes--Marian commences her lifelong love affair with flight. At fourteen she drops out of school and finds an unexpected and dangerous patron in a wealthy bootlegger who provides a plane and subsidizes her lessons, an arrangement that will haunt her for the rest of her life, even as it allows her to fulfill her destiny: circumnavigating the globe by flying over the North and South Poles.

A century later, Hadley Baxter is cast to play Marian in a film that centers on Marian's disappearance in Antarctica. Vibrant, canny, disgusted with the claustrophobia of Hollywood, Hadley is eager to redefine herself after a romantic film franchise has imprisoned her in the grip of cult celebrity. Her immersion into the character of Marian unfolds, thrillingly, alongside Marian's own story, as the two women's fates--and their hunger for self-determination in vastly different geographies and times--collide. Epic and emotional, meticulously researched and gloriously told, *Great Circle* is a monumental work of art, and a tremendous leap forward for the prodigiously gifted Maggie Shipstead.

BookBrowse Review

This stellar historical novel explores the lives of a groundbreaking aviatrix in the first half of the 20th century and the actress slated to play her a century later.

Maggie Shipstead's *Great Circle* follows the lives of two fictional women: Prohibition-era aviatrix Marian Graves and contemporary actress Hadley Baxter, who lands the role of Marian in an upcoming movie. When approached about the film, Hadley has just blown up her life by creating a scandal she knew would likely get her ousted from the franchise that made her career. Feeling a certain kinship with Marian (both were orphaned as infants and raised by dissolute uncles), she accepts the role, dreaming of Oscar glory for her participation in her first "serious" film. Alternating with Hadley's first-person account is the third-person narration of Marian's life, from the circumstances surrounding her birth to her fate decades later.

The bulk of the story is Marian's, and Shipstead fleshes out her life in such believable detail I found it hard to remember the character wasn't a real person. Although Marian's passion for flying underlies every part of her narrative, the book is less about her exploits as a pilot and the lengths she goes to achieve her aims and more about her journey of self-discovery. The author brilliantly illustrates the many factors in Marian's life that mold her into the person she becomes by her last flight. We develop an in-depth understanding of this remarkable character and are loath to let her go.

Hadley's chapters are briefer, and although they cover a shorter time period, her journey feels just as real as Marian's. She's pretty obnoxious at first, a stereotypical entitled Hollywood starlet, but as she becomes more involved with the film and the people behind its production, she develops a complexity that ultimately makes her more sympathetic. As with Marian, the author creates a multifaceted character in Hadley, one who feels real to the reader.

Shipstead's writing is gorgeous from start to finish, whether she's describing the countryside ("October leans into November. The trees are topped with gold, the cottonwoods bright as apricot flesh. The landscape flares and shimmers"); Marion's observations ("With the right instruments, you have a fighting chance of leveling out even if the cloud goes all the way down and brushes the earth like the marabou hem of a diaphanous white robe worn by God"); or Hadley's perceptions ("[S]he just sat there and stared like she was trying to turn me to stone with her mind. Or maybe she couldn't move her face. She's starting to have work done. In twenty years she'll be a skin balloon with eyeholes").

There's just enough of this lush writing to entertain, but not so much that it bogs down the narrative. Also interspersed are bits of aviation history as they occurred during Marion's timeline. For example, the author inserts a couple of paragraphs about Charles Lindbergh's historic transatlantic flight in 1927 that occurs just as

13-year-old Marion is becoming acquainted with a pair of barnstormers who take her on her first flights.

I occasionally find dual timelines confusing or annoying (sometimes the characters are too similar, sometimes the jump between them happens too frequently, sometimes I feel one or more storyline could have been jettisoned, etc.). Such was not the case with *Great Circle.* Switches between the two stories are so expertly crafted I'm hard-pressed to name a novel that accomplishes this feat more skillfully. At around 600 pages, the book is also quite long; however, I never felt like it was a slog. I'll sometimes come across a doorstopper and think about how it could have been edited into a more manageable length, but not this time; there's not a single sentence I'd have wanted left out. Although I wouldn't call it a page-turner, its pacing is excellent and it kept me engaged, start to finish.

Great Circle is one of my favorites of the year so far, and I'd unhesitatingly suggest it to anyone looking for an exquisite, character-driven work of literature.

Reviewed by Kim Kovacs. This review was originally published in *The BookBrowse Review* in July 2021, and has been updated for the May 2022 edition.

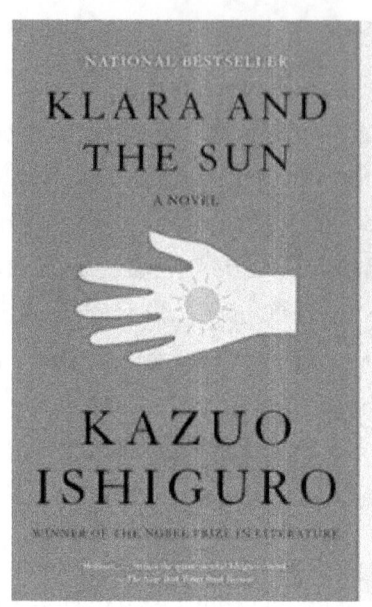

KLARA AND THE SUN

by Kazuo Ishiguro

BookBrowse Rating: 4/5
Critics' Consensus: 5/5
Readers' Rating: 4/5

Published March 2022 in Paperback, 320 pages

Summary

Klara and the Sun is a magnificent novel from the Nobel laureate Kazuo Ishiguro--author of *Never Let Me Go* and the Booker Prize-winning *The Remains of the Day*.

Klara and the Sun, the first novel by Kazuo Ishiguro since he was awarded the Nobel Prize in Literature, tells the story of Klara, an Artificial Friend with outstanding observational qualities, who, from her place in the store, watches carefully the behavior of those who come in to browse, and of those who pass on the street outside. She remains hopeful that a customer will soon choose her.

Klara and the Sun is a thrilling book that offers a look at our changing world through the eyes of an unforgettable narrator, and one that explores the fundamental question: what does it mean to love?

In its award citation in 2017, the Nobel committee described Ishiguro's books as "novels of great emotional force" and said he has "uncovered the abyss beneath our illusory sense of connection with the world."

BookBrowse Review

A bittersweet foray into questions of humanity and loyalty that follows the life of an artificially intelligent being and her relationship with her adolescent companion.

Klara and the Sun by Nobel Prize-winning author Kazuo Ishiguro drops the reader into a fictional universe that could be our own, save for scientific developments that have changed the course of events in drastic ways. For those familiar with Ishiguro's previous works, being placed in this type of altered and somewhat mysterious parallel reality will be familiar.

The story is told from the perspective of Klara, an Artificial Friend (AF). Klara is uncommonly bright for an AF, and catches the eye of her future companion, a girl named Josie, while displayed in a store window. Unlike many other AFs, Klara possesses an uncanny knack for observation and understanding. Though Josie immediately chooses Klara, her mother must be persuaded to take Klara home with them. The plot appears to take place in the not-so-distant future, and Josie's mother's reluctance mirrors a broader reticence toward AFs amongst older generations in society.

Some aspects of the novel's world are concealed; as in Ishiguro's *Never Let Me Go*, many facets of reality are merely hinted at, glossed over or elusive until later, if not for the entire story. For example, children and adolescents are educated virtually from their respective homes; and by way of some unclear alteration, some are "lifted" and receive special access to quality education, while others are not. However, unlike *Never Let Me Go*, *Klara and the Sun* focuses on the sacrifices and inner lives not of human beings, but of artificial intelligence (AI).

What is perhaps most disturbing about the story is its proximity to the current state of the world in the time of COVID-19. AFs accompany some adolescent children in order to assuage the loneliness they feel due to relative isolation from others their age, the reasons for which are not obvious. Children learn via "oblongs," which appear to be like smart tablets, and virtual tutors who instruct them from their homes. They must attend "socialization" events organized by their parents to develop social skills and interact with peers, but rarely see anyone other than their own parents and AFs in person. Indeed, it can feel like the story is a little *too* on the nose given our present circumstances.

While the uneasy mood of *Klara and the Sun* is partly due to these blatant parallels to today's world, it also results from the novel's somewhat traditional depiction of the relationship between humans and AI. On this front, Ishiguro's work does not break any new ground; the tensions present in many other stories are implicit here, too. Can AI feel? Can they love or have genuine experiences that we would recognize as human? Can they have faith or experience loyalty? These questions have formed the basis of countless works of science fiction. Even Klara's ostensibly uncommon curiosity is a well-worn trope present in many similar investigations into the nature of AI.

Yet despite drawing on previously explored themes, Ishiguro is generally able to avoid falling into cliché. This is partly because of the emphasis the author places on faith. AFs are solar powered, and exercise a sort of belief in the sun that resembles religious worship, largely stemming from it being their source of energy. Klara views the sun as an omnipotent force capable of healing humans and AFs alike. This allows for a degree of spirituality not often seen in stories about AI, and imbues Klara's experiences and outlook with a very human inclination.

One of the questions central to the story is whether human beings really do contain some ineffable quality that cannot be replicated artificially. The answer, perhaps reassuringly, is that yes, regardless of how advanced or studied AI becomes, there will always be a certain humanness that cannot be reproduced outside of a person. However, that difference is not in the capacity for love, faith, loyalty or empathy, as is demonstrated through Klara's experiences.

In *Klara and the Sun*, Ishiguro has designed neither a utopia nor a dystopia. Compellingly, it is a world much like our reality, one that augments and is augmented by technology in ways that are frightening and exhilarating. While the novel invokes recognizable philosophical queries, the author's characteristic melancholy and relatable use of memory and empathy reinvigorate otherwise tired concepts. It is unlikely that readers will tire of the seemingly endless nuances inherent to possible relationships between AI and humans anytime soon, but it is Ishiguro's inimitable storytelling that sets this story apart from its thematic predecessors.

Reviewed by Elspeth Drayton. This review was originally published in *The BookBrowse Review* in March 2021, and has been updated for the March 2022 edition.

STORIES FROM SUFFRAGETTE CITY

by M.J. Rose, Fiona Davis

BookBrowse Rating: 5/5
Critics' Consensus: 4.5/5
Readers' Rating: 5/5

Published March 2022 in Paperback, 272 pages

Summary

Stories from Suffragette City is a collection of short stories that all take place on a single day: October 23, 1915.

It's the day when tens of thousands of women marched up Fifth Avenue, demanding the right to vote in New York City. Thirteen of today's bestselling authors have taken this moment as inspiration to raise the voices of history and breathe fresh life into their struggles and triumphs.

The characters depicted here, some well-known, others unfamiliar, each inspire and reinvigorate the power of democracy. We follow a young woman who is swept up in the protests when all she expected was to come sell her apples in the city. We see Ava Vanderbilt as her white-gloved sensibility is transformed over the course of the single fateful day. Ida B. Wells battles for racial justice in the women's suffrage movement so that every woman's voice can be heard. Each story stands on its own, but together *Stories From Suffragette City* becomes a symphony, painting a portrait of a country looking for a fight and ever restless for progress and equality.

BookBrowse Review

In this anthology, short stories by authors including Paula McLain, Christina Baker Kline and Fiona Davis imagine the events of a 1915 march for women's suffrage through different perspectives.

Our First Impressions readers were fascinated by the historical fiction from a range of authors presented in *Stories from Suffragette City*, edited by M.J. Rose and Fiona Davis, collectively awarding the book 4.7 out of 5 stars.

What it's about:

Thirteen talented and well-known authors contribute to the anthology, and all of the stories have some connection to October 23, 1915, the day a large group of U.S. women marched together in New York City in an effort to earn the right to vote. The characters of these tales are varied, coming from all over the country and representing very different ages and economic groups. In some instances, real historical figures are incorporated into the fictional narratives (Patricia E). The stories are vignettes about women and girls participating in the parade, with a few of the stories having threads of connection. Authors include Chris

Bohjalian, Jamie Ford, Paula McLain and Christina Baler Kline. Highly recommended for book clubs and young adult readers (Judith C).

Many readers appreciated that the book offers a broad spectrum of experiences:

While I liked all the stories, I think my favorites were 'Apple Season' and 'The Last Mile.' The first features a main character who is impoverished; the last features characters who are privileged. I enjoyed seeing that the right to vote was important to all women, not just those of a certain social class (Gail K). I was particularly struck by the diverse reactions of the men in the lives of these women — from the husband whose zoo trip to see the Thylacine marsupial becomes a life-changing experience for him and an awakening for his wife, to Charles Tiffany of jewelry fame who is opened reluctantly to a new vision of the future for himself and his seven-year-old niece, Grace (Carol S).

Several mentioned feeling inspired by the suffrage activists and their commitment to change:

It was moving to read about the determination and courageous spirit of these women who planned to march in New York City in 1915. Some of the marchers were familiar to me — Ava Vanderbilt and Ida B. Wells, for example. The characters represent different ages, ethnicities and motivations for adding their voices to this important cause for the democracy we enjoy today (Carol S). In these stories, we see women with the courage to act and the faith to believe in a better future for all women. They are not perfect, as they do not include women of color as equals. We do well to remember these stories as we face the challenges of our own time. Highly recommended (Lynn D).

Even those who do not usually read this genre were won over:

I don't read short stories very often, but I really enjoyed this collection. There is a lot of variety in the people who included in them, but they are tied together very well by the focus of the suffragettes' parade (Christine D). Although I rarely choose to read short stories, I'm so glad I made an exception in requesting *Stories from Suffragette City* (Gail K). I loved this book! Although I am not a fan of short stories, I was drawn to this book because of the authors. I didn't know much about the 1915 Women's Suffragette March. As a side note, I also learned reading short stories can be as fulfilling as reading a whole novel (Martha S).

Overall, readers felt this anthology was a timely and well-crafted distillation of the movement for women's suffrage:

Because of the 100th anniversary of the 19th Amendment this year, I've been reading a great deal of both fiction and nonfiction based on the women and men who were part of the more than 80-year struggle. Of all the volumes I've read, this will take pride of place on my shelves. I highly recommend it (Patricia E). A historic and tumultuous election year and the global pandemic back-burnered many of the centennial commemorations of the passage of the 19th Amendment. But this book has a message that perhaps becomes even more meaningful as political winds blow from different directions. Your favorite writers personalize a social upheaval that has shaped all our lives, writing short vignettes that can easily be wedged into your day. What could be better? (Carol P).

Reviewed by First Impressions Reviewers. This review was originally published in *The BookBrowse Review* in January 2021, and has been updated for the March 2022 edition.

A MILLION THINGS

by Emily Spurr

BookBrowse Rating: 5/5
Critics' Consensus: 4.5/5
Readers' Rating: 5/5

Published August 2021 in Paperback, 304 pages

Summary

Winner of the 2021 BookBrowse Debut Award

A soaring, heartfelt debut following fifty-five days in the life of ten-year-old Rae, who must look after herself and her dog when her mother disappears.

For as long as Rae can remember, it's been her and Mum, and their dog, Splinter; a small, deliberately unremarkable, family. They have their walks, their cooking routines, their home. Sometimes Mum disappears for a while to clear her head but Rae is okay with this because Mum always comes back.

So, when Rae wakes to Splinter's nose in her face, the back door open, and no Mum, she does as she's always done and carries on. She tends to the house, goes to school, walks Splinter, and minds her own business—all the while pushing down the truth she isn't ready to face.

That is, until her grumpy, lonely neighbor Lettie—with her own secrets and sadness—falls one night and needs Rae's help. As the two begin to rely on each other, Rae's anxiety intensifies as she wonders what will happen to her when her mother's absence is finally noticed and her fragile world bursts open.

A Million Things transforms a gut-wrenching story of abandonment and what it's like to grow up in a house that doesn't feel safe into an astonishing portrait of resilience, mental health, and the families we make and how they make us in return.

BookBrowse Review

An intense, atmospheric work of fiction about love, grief and resilience.

Voted 2021 Best Debut Award Winner by BookBrowse Subscribers

Our First Impressions reviewers were intrigued and captivated by Emily Spurr's debut novel *A Million Things*, awarding it an average rating of 4.7 out of 5 stars.

What the book is about:

This is a delightfully sad story about a 10-year-old girl (Rae), a dog (Splinter) and a hoarding old lady (Lettie) who lives next door. The resiliency of all three of them is what keeps this book interesting and from turning maudlin. Rae's mother disappears but Rae is used to being on her own, and carries on, taking care of herself and Splinter. When Lettie falls and needs Rae's help the storyline takes its most interesting turn. Watching Rae, Lettie and Splinter form their own family is the crux of the book. And, as with all families, there are ups and downs, yet they keep going (Mary S).

Reviewers were drawn in by the characters' lovable and compelling qualities.

I fell hard for Rae, the protagonist in this novel. What a strong, smart, scrappy, vulnerable and resourceful little girl. The relationship that develops between Rae and Lettie, the neighbor with a hoarding tendency, added such depth. Every character in this book, from Rae's teacher, Mrs. Pham, to Oscar, the boy down the street, lends something important to move the story along (Jennie R). The character development of the quirky people who live in this neighborhood is great. They are all very believable; they are compelling (Susan W). I won't soon forget narrator Rae, her neighbor Lettie or her sweet beast of a dog Splinter. But the nameless mother is also an interesting character, more so because she develops in the literary equivalent of negative space (Ann B).

They also appreciated the book's sensitive exploration of mental health issues.

I appreciate the light the author shines on mental health without being preachy (Susan W). Lettie and Rae's relationship, based on their shared experiences, will be eye-opening to those who have been blessed not to have to deal with mental health issues (Jo S).

Some felt that the plot took a while to pick up, and warned that details are revealed slowly.

It got a little bogged down and wordy in the beginning but then was hard to put down until I learned the outcome (Mary Jane D). The pacing was a bit slow at first, but I was captivated once Lettie and Rae began communicating in earnest (Kathy).

However, others enjoyed the author's lingering focus on the world of the story.

This book demands at least two readings. First Reading: Enjoy the story of a resilient little girl, a scruffy dog, a cranky old woman and a remarkable friendship. Second Reading: Slow down, stroll leisurely through the sensuous soundscape, filled with vivid imagery (Kathryn S). I found the writing to be beautifully evocative, especially as Rae describes the sights, smells and feel of her everyday life (Nancy L).

Despite the book's sad premise, readers ultimately found *A Million Things* hopeful and inspiring.

Emily Spurr explores grief and loneliness without melodrama, leaving room for hope and happiness (Karen B). This book! It will break your heart and put it back together again. Rae is a character you won't soon forget and this story of loss and resilience is a triumph (Danielle M). Rae's story of grief, love and resilience is both heartbreaking and inspiring (Sylvia T).

Reviewed by First Impressions Reviewers. This review was originally published in *The BookBrowse Review* in September 2021, and has been updated for the December 2021 edition.

BEST BOOKS OF 2020

THE SPLENDID AND THE VILE

by Erik Larson

BookBrowse Rating: 5/5
Critics' Consensus: 4.5/5
Readers' Rating: 4.5/5

Published February 2022 in Paperback, 624 pages

Summary

Winner of the 2020 BookBrowse Nonfiction Award

The #1 *New York Times* bestselling author of *The Devil in the White City* and *Dead Wake* delivers a fresh and compelling portrait of Winston Churchill and London during the Blitz.

On Winston Churchill's first day as prime minister, Adolf Hitler invaded Holland and Belgium. Poland and Czechoslovakia had already fallen, and the Dunkirk evacuation was just two weeks away. For the next twelve months, Hitler would wage a relentless bombing campaign, killing 45,000 Britons. It was up to Churchill to hold his country together and persuade President Franklin Roosevelt that Britain was a worthy ally—and willing to fight to the end.

In *The Splendid and the Vile*, Erik Larson shows, in cinematic detail, how Churchill taught the British people "the art of being fearless." It is a story of political brinkmanship, but it's also an intimate domestic drama, set against the backdrop of Churchill's prime-ministerial country home, Chequers; his wartime retreat, Ditchley, where he and his entourage go when the moon is brightest and the bombing threat is highest; and of course 10 Downing Street in London. Drawing on diaries, original archival documents, and once-secret intelligence reports—some released only recently—Larson provides a new lens on London's darkest year through the day-to-day experience of Churchill and his family: his wife, Clementine; their youngest daughter, Mary, who chafes against her parents' wartime protectiveness; their son, Randolph, and his beautiful, unhappy wife, Pamela; Pamela's illicit lover, a dashing American emissary; and the advisers in Churchill's "Secret Circle," to whom he turns in the hardest moments.

The Splendid and the Vile takes readers out of today's political dysfunction and back to a time of true leadership, when, in the face of unrelenting horror, Churchill's eloquence, courage, and perseverance bound a country, and a family, together.

BookBrowse Review

A fascinating account of Winston Churchill and those close to him during a critical period of WWII, *The Splendid and the Vile* holds strong appeal for history buffs and casual readers alike.

Voted 2020 Best Nonfiction Award Winner by BookBrowse Subscribers

An impressive 23 out of 24 reviewers rated Erik Larson's *The Splendid and the Vile* 4 or 5 stars, giving it an overall average of 4.6.

What the book is about:

This well-documented non-fiction work by Erik Larson was fascinating to read. Larson focuses on Winston Churchill's first year as prime minister during which time the British people faced brutal bombing by the Germans in an effort to get them to give up (Lorraine R). Larson weaves a narrative using threads of the lives of various personalities: Churchill himself, Lady Clementine, daughter Mary, and various aides and governmental figures (Emily C).

Readers found *The Splendid and the Vile* to be a highly engaging work of non-fiction…

Far from being a ponderous tome of non-fiction, this book reads more like a thrilling novel. Larson zeroes in on a critical year in WWII history, breathing life and insight into Churchill, his family and close associates. Larson's research creates a very detailed picture of a blitz-besieged England and the impact on everyday life. Even his footnotes are interesting (Lois K). Simply put, *The Splendid and the Vile* brings Churchill to life in a way only those who surrounded him could have shown. I would love to see this made into a movie (Yolanda M).

…and loved the intimate, personal feel that Larson brings to the book.

As I read each page, I felt as if Larson was speaking directly to me while sitting in my living room with a cup of tea (Emily C). Larson takes a moment in history and brings it to life in a way that makes you feel like you are there. You get a sense of the true emotion of the people living through the events of the time. I think everyone knows a little (or a lot) about World War II, however, Larson takes this one year in the beginning of the British entry into the war and tells it through the eyes of some of the people closest to the decision making process (Vicki R).

Some point out that the level of detail may require patience and commitment...

I found the length and number of details to be challenging. If this had been an academic publication much of the information would probably have been footnoted. At 500 pages, this is not a quick read but the careful reader will be rewarded (Dona N). The book begins with some scene-setting, and would benefit from a reader's patience during the first 50 or so pages as the threat increases (Janet T).

...but most were thoroughly absorbed.

Erik Larson is not capable of writing anything less than a gripping account of historical events as he has already demonstrated in his past books. This one is no exception. I found myself emptying the dishwasher and thinking, I can't wait to get back to WW2! (Peggy A). Lots of World War II novels and histories have been published lately, but Larson's is a compulsive, stay-up-way-past-bedtime read. He makes Churchill's political brinkmanship so thrilling, it's easy to forget everything you learned about history and turn each page waiting to see how each maneuver will turn out (Sarah M).

Reviewers recommend the book for history buffs...

I found many facts I had not previously known about how Churchill rallied the British people amid horrific times, to carry on. I enjoyed how the author quoted first hand accounts about how Londoners survived. I think history buffs will enjoy this book (Lorraine R). I'd recommend it to readers of history who appreciate a detailed account of the Churchill family under the toughest of circumstances (Janet T).

...and for those less familiar with the time period.

Recommended for history buffs and biography fans in particular, but anyone who loves a good story will enjoy it (Deborah C). Larson's writing introduces Churchill to readers less familiar with him and his times. For the more knowledgeable reader, Larson's writing adds to the Churchill story (Jill M). If you are a history fan or even if you just want to learn more about Winston Churchill and his first year in office, this book is for you (Victoria B).

Reviewed by First Impressions Reviewers. This review was originally published in *The BookBrowse Review* in March 2020, and has been updated for the December 2020 edition.

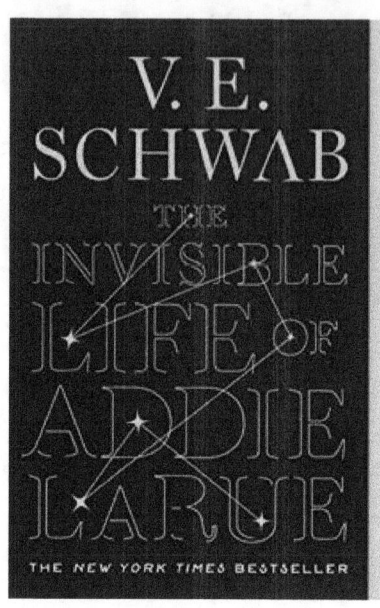

THE INVISIBLE LIFE OF ADDIE LARUE

by Victoria E. Schwab

BookBrowse Rating: 5/5
Critics' Consensus: 5/5
Readers' Rating: 5/5

Published April 2023 in Paperback, 464 pages

Summary

Winner of the 2020 BookBrowse Fiction Award

In the vein of *The Time Traveler's Wife* and *Life After Life*, *The Invisible Life of Addie LaRue* is *New York Times* bestselling author V. E. Schwab's genre-defying tour de force.

A Life No One Will Remember. A Story You Will Never Forget.

France, 1714: in a moment of desperation, a young woman makes a Faustian bargain to live forever—and is cursed to be forgotten by everyone she meets.

Thus begins the extraordinary life of Addie LaRue, and a dazzling adventure that will play out across centuries and continents, across history and art, as a young woman learns how far she will go to leave her mark on the world.

But everything changes when, after nearly 300 years, Addie stumbles across a young man in a hidden bookstore and he remembers her name.

BookBrowse Review

V.E. Schwab, author of children's books and the bestselling Shades of Magic series, returns with a magical realism novel geared toward adults.

Voted 2020 Best Fiction Award Winner by BookBrowse Subscribers

In *The Invisible Life of Addie LaRue*, readers follow the eponymous heroine through history, from rural 18th-century France to modern-day New York City. As a child, Addie is told by an older friend and mentor, "No matter how desperate or dire, never pray to the gods that answer after dark." When a crisis unfolds, though, she does the unthinkable and summons the type of being she was specifically told to avoid. She tells the creature (it's not clear if he's a demon, a god, or Satan himself), "I want a chance to live. I want to be free...I want more time," and with that, she sells her soul. Such Faustian bargains are never straightforward, and what Addie doesn't realize is that while the deal means she'll live precisely as long as she wants to, the flipside is that she will leave no mark of her passage, no proof she existed; she is cursed to be forgotten through all time. The story follows her escapades over the next 300 years until something remarkable happens in New York City in 2014: someone remembers her.

Addie's antagonist, whom she names Luc, always visits her on the anniversary of their agreement to ask if she's ready to give up her soul yet (at which point her body would die). Of course, the stubborn young woman refuses each time. The plot bounces back and forth between these visits and Addie's life in 2014. After the initial setup, the chapters occurring in the past illustrate how she learns to adapt to her curse while simultaneously exploiting its loopholes and actively seeking to thwart Luc's decree that she be completely forgotten. (She can't write a song, for example, but she can inspire others to do so, thereby leaving subtle traces of her presence throughout time.) Although she experiences history — she's in France for the Revolution and in Germany during World War II — the book contains surprisingly little historical background, with the focus of these chapters remaining solely on Addie, the curse and her love-hate relationship with Luc, the one "person" who knows her. As the plot progresses, the emphasis gradually shifts to the present and the mystery of why one person seems immune to the spell.

Everything about the novel is stellar, from the pacing to the characters to the exceptionally well-thought-out plot. Schwab's writing, too, is superb, convincingly reflecting the longing at her heroine's core while at the same time being beautifully descriptive:

> Addie misses stars. She met a boy, back in '65, and when she told him that, he drove her an hour outside of L.A., just to see them. The way his face glowed with pride when he pulled over in the dark and pointed up. Addie had craned her head and looked at the meager offering, the spare string of lights across the sky, and felt something in her sag. A heavy sadness, like loss. And for the first time in a century, she longed for Villon. For home. For a place where the stars were so bright they formed a river, a stream of silver and purple light against the dark.

Indeed, I'm hard-pressed to come up with any flaws in this novel at all. At times reading like a fairy tale, at others like a romance, I enjoyed every minute; I still smile when I think about it — truly the sign of a great read.

At the risk of pigeon-holing *The Invisible Life of Addie LaRue* as "chick lit" (a label that belies the book's depth), I imagine the plot, with its strong heroine and romantic leaning, will appeal most to female readers. I wholeheartedly recommend it for a broad audience, though, as a feel-good and overall charming read. The novel would also be an excellent choice for book groups, as it raises many wonderful topics for discussion, such as the lengths one might go to for love or what one might do with eternal life.

Reviewed by Kim Kovacs. This review was originally published in *The BookBrowse Review* in October 2020, and has been updated for the April 2023 edition.

THE MOUNTAINS SING

by Nguyen Phan Que Mai

BookBrowse Rating: 5/5
Critics' Consensus: 5/5
Readers' Rating: 5/5

Published March 2021 in Paperback, 368 pages

Summary

Winner of the 2020 BookBrowse Debut Award.

The Mountains Sing tells an enveloping, multi-generational tale of the Trần family, set against the backdrop of the Việt Nam War. "Both vast in scope and intimate in its telling ... Moving and riveting." - Viet Thanh Nguyen, author of *The Sympathizer*, winner of the Pulitzer Prize.

With the epic sweep of Min Jin Lee's *Pachinko* or Yaa Gyasi's *Homegoing* and the lyrical beauty of Vaddey Ratner's *In the Shadow of the Banyan*, *The Mountains Sing* tells an enveloping, multigenerational tale of the Trần family, set against the backdrop of the Việt Nam War. Trần Diệu Lan, who was born in 1920, was forced to flee her family farm with her six children during the Land Reform as the Communist government rose in the North. Years later in Hà Nội, her young granddaughter, Hương, comes of age as her parents and uncles head off down the Hồ Chí Minh Trail to fight in a conflict that tore not just her beloved country, but her family apart.

Vivid, gripping, and steeped in the language and traditions of Việt Nam, *The Mountains Sing* brings to life the human costs of this conflict from the point of view of the Vietnamese people themselves, while showing us the true power of kindness and hope.

The Mountains Sing is celebrated Vietnamese poet Nguyễn Phan Quế Mai's first novel in English.

BookBrowse Review

A vivid and poetic multi-generational saga, *The Mountains Sing* follows the experiences of a Vietnamese family through the 20th century.

Voted 2020 Best Debut Award Winner by BookBrowse Subscribers

All 23 of our First Impressions reviewers for *The Mountains Sing* by Nguyễn Phan Quế Mai rated the book 4 or 5 stars, with over half giving it 5 stars, resulting in an inspiring average rating of 4.6.

What the book is about:

This beautifully written historical novel tells the 20th-century Vietnamese history of conflict, famine and corruption through the lives of a resilient and loving grandmother, born in 1920, and her granddaughter, born in 1960, who long for a world without war. Their struggles to survive, and stay a family, portray the impact war can have for many generations (Lynn D).

Readers describe Nyugen's writing as beautiful and poetic...

This story is beautifully and compellingly told by Nguyễn Phan, whose family lived through Vietnam's 20th-century history, starting with the land reform, Communist rule and the Vietnam War (Margaret A). This is one of the best books I've read in a long time! The author Nguyễn Phan is a poet and it shows in her beautiful prose (Karen S). With power and poetry, Nguyễn Phan guided me onto lands and into cultures I had never before experienced. Her fresh imagery reflects a constant dependence on the earth for survival, passed down through generations of farmers (Ora J).

...and remark that the book is surprisingly engaging despite its painful subject matter.

It seems odd to note that a book about such painful events is "easy to read," but this poet, essayist and novelist tells her characters' story with clarity and beautiful language (Karen S). Nguyễn Phan gives us characters with depth and a storyline that is filled with action, insight and discovery (Molly K).

Some reviewers mention having gained a new perspective on the Vietnam War...

The story was an eye-opener for me, never having heard the Vietnam story from the point of view of the North Vietnamese. They struggled heroically to keep their way of life and their country whole in the face of incredibly bad odds forced on them by foreign powers (Liz D). As an American, I found this novel to be eye-opening about a country and people beyond just the "Vietnam War" I knew about. A full-bodied picture was presented, providing a depth of knowledge and emotion that was lacking in my previous thoughts of Vietnam (Kay D).

...as well as a sense of hope.

I was especially awed by the strength, courage and intelligence of Tran Dieu Lan, the matriarch of the Tran family. She shares her story with her young granddaughter, Huong, whose father has not returned from the war and whose mother is traumatized by her own war experiences. There is no one in the family not touched by the evils of war. But they have such strong love for each other. *The Mountains Sing* is truly inspiring (Gloria F). The examples of respect and honor for ancestors, devotion to family and persistence in the face of incredible odds are lessons for all. The hope and love shine through in this emotionally fulfilling novel. I look forward to hearing more from Nguyễn Phan either in new books or translations of some of her previous works (Mary G).

Reviewed by First Impressions Reviewers. This review was originally published in *The BookBrowse Review* in April 2020, and has been updated for the March 2021 edition.

WE ARE NOT FROM HERE

by Jenny Torres Sanchez

BookBrowse Rating: 5/5
Critics' Consensus: 5/5
Readers' Rating: 4.5/5

Published May 2021 in Paperback, 336 pages

Summary

Winner of the 2020 BookBrowse Award for Best Young Adult Novel

A poignant novel of desperation, escape, and survival across the U.S.-Mexico border, inspired by current events.

Pulga has his dreams.

Chico has his grief.

Pequeña has her pride.

And these three teens have one another. But none of them have illusions about the town they've grown up in and the dangers that surround them. Even with the love of family, threats lurk around every corner. And when those threats become all too real, the trio knows they have no choice but to run: from their country, from their families, from their beloved home.

Crossing from Guatemala through Mexico, they follow the route of La Bestia, the perilous train system that might deliver them to a better life--if they are lucky enough to survive the journey. With nothing but the bags on their backs and desperation drumming through their hearts, Pulga, Chico, and Pequeña know there is no turning back, despite the unknown that awaits them. And the darkness that seems to follow wherever they go.

In this striking portrait of lives torn apart, the plight of migrants at the U.S. southern border is brought to light through poignant, vivid storytelling. An epic journey of danger, resilience, heartache, and hope.

BookBrowse Review

Three teenagers escape Guatemala and attempt a perilous journey to the U.S. atop Mexico's infamous La Bestia train in this urgent and evocative YA novel.

Voted 2020 Best Young Adult Award Winner by BookBrowse Subscribers

Pulga and Chico are only dimly aware of the danger around them — the corruption, the drug dealing and the gang violence — as they grow up in a small town in Guatemala. But on the day their friend Pequeña has her baby, the three teenagers lose all semblance of innocence. The boys witness a murder, Pequeña wants nothing to do with the child of the man who holds her town hostage, and the friends realize that their lives depend on fleeing Puerto Barrios. Others from their village have made it to the United States on the back of the infamous train La Bestia; Pulga has been meticulously planning the trip north for as long as he can remember. And so, under cover of night, a teenage girl who gave birth days before, a gentle giant of a boy, and his best friend who feels the world too much, set off together on a journey many able-bodied men do not survive. Their story is told from two points of view — which is clear but heartbreaking foreshadowing.

The teens' harrowing trip north is full of chance encounters with the sorts of people who have made the plight of immigrants their business, some genuinely caring and helpful, others exploitative and opportunistic. Their ride through Mexico on La Bestia is depicted as a multisensory experience, sometimes nightmarish, sometimes triumphant. And the conclusion of that journey highlights the various ways a trip like this can end in these days of unaccompanied children waiting in cages on the border. The book avoids overtly politicizing the situation of these characters — an attorney volunteers to take their case, so they are safe from deportation, at least for a while — but it also makes clear that no sane person would repeatedly risk death in the desert or under the wheels of a train unless they had a desperate need to escape something terrible.

Pequeña, who disguises herself as a boy for her own safety, has a touch of second sight. Magical realism is not uncommon in books with Latinx characters, but it runs the risk of turning into a trope in the hands of a clumsy writer. Sanchez's hands are not clumsy; Pequeña believes in and trusts her visions, and they are described as vividly and beautifully as the horrors of La Bestia.

The ending of the journey is a bit too convenient to be fully believable, but it still feels right. And it is not a comfortable ending, though the most life-threatening moments may be behind these young people. It is also fitting that two characters who have frequently been called by somewhat juvenile, condescending nicknames finally come into their own, as if their ordeal has been a baptism.

Refugees have been traveling to what they hope will be a better life in the United States for generations, and the stream of undocumented immigrants continues. *We Are Not from Here*, with its young, sympathetic, genuinely desperate characters, is a heart-wrenchingly real novel to hand to any teen or adult who wonders how and why that journey can be so urgent and imperative for some.

Reviewed by Catherine M Andronik. This review was originally published in *The BookBrowse Review* in July 2020, and has been updated for the June 2021 edition.

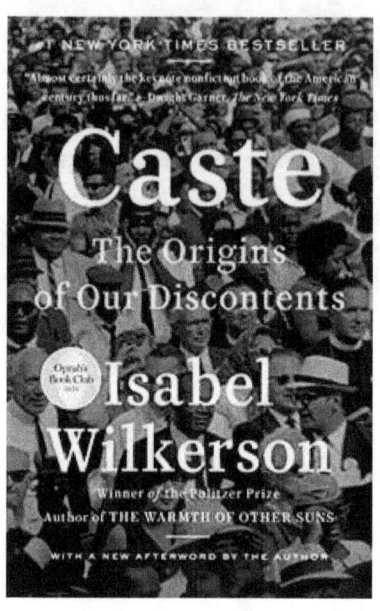

CASTE

by Isabel Wilkerson

BookBrowse Rating: 5/5
Critics' Consensus: 5/5
Readers' Rating: 4.5/5

Published February 2023 in Paperback, 512 pages

Summary

The Pulitzer Prize–winning, bestselling author of *The Warmth of Other Suns* examines the unspoken caste system that has shaped America and shows how our lives today are still defined by a hierarchy of human divisions.

"As we go about our daily lives, caste is the wordless usher in a darkened theater, flashlight cast down in the aisles, guiding us to our assigned seats for a performance. The hierarchy of caste is not about feelings or morality. It is about power—which groups have it and which do not."

In this brilliant book, Isabel Wilkerson gives us a masterful portrait of an unseen phenomenon in America as she explores, through an immersive, deeply researched narrative and stories about real people, how America today and throughout its history has been shaped by a hidden caste system, a rigid hierarchy of human rankings.

Beyond race, class, or other factors, there is a powerful caste system that influences people's lives and behavior and the nation's fate. Linking the caste systems of America, India, and Nazi Germany, Wilkerson explores eight pillars that underlie caste systems across civilizations, including divine will, bloodlines, stigma, and more. Using riveting stories about people—including Martin Luther King, Jr., baseball's Satchel Paige, a single father and his toddler son, Wilkerson herself, and many others—she shows the ways that the insidious undertow of caste is experienced every day. She documents how the Nazis studied the racial systems in America to plan their out-cast of the Jews; she discusses why the cruel logic of caste requires that there be a bottom rung for those in the middle to measure themselves against; she writes about the surprising health costs of caste, in depression and life expectancy, and the effects of this hierarchy on our culture and politics. Finally, she points forward to ways America can move beyond the artificial and destructive separations of human divisions, toward hope in our common humanity.

Beautifully written, original, and revealing, *Caste: The Origins of Our Discontents* is an eye-opening story of people and history, and a reexamination of what lies under the surface of ordinary lives and of American life today.

BookBrowse Review

Isabel Wilkerson provides a new language with which to talk about racial inequality, and offers a pathway towards deconstructing the hidden hierarchies that bind us.

In 2020, the word "racist" remains taboo. Conceptually, racism is so culturally unacceptable, so ugly and indefensible, that even the alt-right take pains to acquit themselves of accusations of it. However, despite the fact that almost nobody will admit to being racist nowadays, inequality and racial prejudice continue to exist. Resistance to the word does not address the problems it is meant to describe; it merely makes them more difficult to articulate.

In *Caste: The Origins of Our Discontents*, Pulitzer Prize-winning journalist Isabel Wilkerson offers an alternative language for these problems — that of caste. Through this conceptual shift, she is able to advance the conversation about the structural power imbalances that permeate American society and reveal the deeper machinations of racial hierarchy. "The modern-day version of easily deniable racism may be able to cloak the invisible structure that created and maintains...inequality," she writes. "But caste does not allow us to ignore structure. Caste *is* structure." According to Wilkerson, caste predates the notion of race. It is "insidious and therefore powerful because it is not hatred, it is not necessarily personal. It is the worn grooves of comforting routines and unthinking expectations, patterns of a social order that have been in place for so long that it looks like the natural order of things." Caste is, she claims, "the basis of every other ism."

A caste system, as defined in Wilkerson's remarkably in-depth and powerful study, is "an artificial construction, a fixed and embedded ranking of human value that sets the presumed supremacy of one group against the presumed inferiority of other groups." Wilkerson identifies eight "pillars" by which these systems are kept intact, a rigid set of beliefs designed to justify the natural superiority of the dominant caste as well as to distance and dehumanize the subjugated caste. These include divine law, notions of purity, endogamy and occupational hierarchy. She compares the race-based American caste system to two other prominent caste societies: those of India and Nazi Germany. This serves to show that while caste systems may come in different forms, using different arbitrary features to designate power, their structures are much the same. "Each version," she writes, "relied on stigmatizing those deemed inferior to justify the dehumanization necessary to keep the lowest-ranked people at the bottom and to rationalize the protocols of enforcement."

Wilkerson writes clearly and with a gravity that matches her subject matter. Her masterful and at times poetic use of allegory adds color and emotional resonance to her academic analysis, such as when she relates the story of a strange sickness that swept through Siberia in 2016, which eventually was discovered to have been caused by anthrax buried under permafrost. It had been there since World War II, but now, because a radical heatwave had hit the area, it had been released from the snow. The anthrax, she says, is "like the reactivation of the human pathogens of hatred and tribalism in this evolving century...It lay in wait, sleeping, until extreme circumstances brought it to the surface and back to life."

The book is painstakingly researched, with thousands of testimonials and case studies, both historical and contemporary. Each anecdote conveys an element of the barbarity and perversity of the caste system. Wilkerson relays these incidents with calm authority, equal parts blunt and tender, laying bare the exceptional cruelty that the delusion of caste can engender. The horror of descriptions of the Jim Crow South, in which the bodies of African Americans were dismembered after lynchings and distributed as souvenirs, is juxtaposed with more banal forms of subjugation in Wilkerson's own experience, such as the subtle prejudices she encounters while flying first class. Using the caste model, she is able to show the pervasive and harmful impact of this structure on how we all live, dominant and subdominant castes alike. The caste system rumbles beneath the surface, erupting occasionally when pressure is applied.

Although Wilkerson's book is steeped in suffering, her concluding message is one of hope. In the last chapters, she offers a glimmer of light, a future that could be brighter than the historical cruelties she portrays. To get there would require a kind of "radical empathy," the kind that is able to recognize "the pain of another as they perceive it." By educating ourselves and committing to a vigilant awareness of history, we can, she suggests, begin to deconstruct hierarchies. This remedial work, of which her book is a part, will lead us to a place of harmony. "In a world without caste," she writes, "instead of a false swagger over our own tribe or family or ascribed community, we would look upon all of humanity with wonderment."

Reviewed by Grace Graham-Taylor. This review was originally published in *The BookBrowse Review* in October 2020, and has been updated for the March 2023 edition.

HAMNET

by Maggie O'Farrell

BookBrowse Rating: 5/5
Critics' Consensus: 5/5
Readers' Rating: 5/5

Published May 2021 in Paperback, 320 pages

Summary

"Of all the stories that argue and speculate about Shakespeare's life ... here is a novel ... so gorgeously written that it transports you." —*The Boston Globe*

England, 1580: The Black Death creeps across the land, an ever-present threat, infecting the healthy, the sick, the old and the young, alike. The end of days is near, but life always goes on.

A young Latin tutor—penniless and bullied by a violent father—falls in love with an extraordinary, eccentric young woman. Agnes is a wild creature who walks her family's land with a falcon on her glove and is known throughout the countryside for her unusual gifts as a healer, understanding plants and potions better than she does people. Once she settles with her husband on Henley Street in Stratford-upon-Avon she becomes a fiercely protective mother and a steadfast, centrifugal force in the life of her young husband, whose career on the London stage is taking off when his beloved young son succumbs to sudden fever.

BookBrowse Review

Set in Stratford-upon-Avon in the 1590s, *Hamnet* imagines the impact of the death of their child on William and Agnes Shakespeare.

William Shakespeare's name is never used in *Hamnet* — a conspicuous absence around which Maggie O'Farrell forms her richly imaginative narrative. Instead, the novel tells the story of those closest to Shakespeare: his parents, John and Mary; his wife Agnes; his daughter Susanna; and his twin children Hamnet and Judith. Shakespeare himself features in the narrative, though he is only ever described in relation to those around him, referred to as the Latin tutor, the husband, the father, the son. The result of this narrative decision is twofold: it pushes Shakespeare's family to the foreground, but it also humanizes Shakespeare himself by reminding the reader that none of his works were created in a vacuum. This is the central conceit around which the novel's climax is formed, as O'Farrell imagines the potential influence of Hamnet's death in 1596 on *Hamlet*, written between 1599 and 1601.

Despite the novel's title, Agnes is its protagonist. O'Farrell draws on the limited historical detail that we have about the real Agnes as her backdrop, and then fleshes her out into a compelling character. Portrayed as a village outcast, there are whispers and rumors throughout the book that she's a witch; this is heightened by a hint of magical realism in which Agnes is able to divine certain details about the future. She knows, for example, that she will have two children standing at her bedside when she dies; she is shocked then when she gives birth to twins, already having one older child (the reader, of course, understands that her vision is accurate, knowing that Hamnet will die young).

The first two-thirds of the novel are split into a dual timeline, bouncing back and forth between the week of Hamnet's death (the present), and the blossoming romance between William and Agnes (the past). It's a tender yet fraught courtship, and the pacing here is slow and deliberate. The final third speeds up and takes place after the death of their son. Both parts are equally as successful — the languid pace is sustained by O'Farrell's lyrical prose, and the more frantic pace is made tense and urgent by it.

> Every life has its kernel, its hub, its epicenter, from which everything flows out, to which everything returns. This moment is the absent mother's: the boy, the empty house, the deserted yard, the unheard cry. Him standing here, at the back of the house, calling for the people who had fed him, swaddled him, rocked him to sleep, held his hand as he took his first steps, taught him to use a spoon, to blow on broth before he ate it, to take care crossing the street, to let sleeping dogs lie, to swill out a cup before drinking, to stay away from deep water. It will lie at her very core, for the rest of her life.

This novel is gentle and domestic and, in many ways, speaks to grief as a commonality of the human experience. But despite O'Farrell's light touch with historical detail, it's a novel that cannot be removed from its Shakespearean context. The allusions to Shakespeare's works are more hints and whispers than overt references, but any eagle-eyed Shakespeare fan will enjoy the way O'Farrell plays with expectations, ducking around moments that could be turned into fan service by an author with a heavier hand. *And what if I fail?* Shakespeare asks Agnes at one point, echoing Macbeth's line *If we should fail?* Agnes's response is not, however, Lady Macbeth's famous retort (*We fail!*) — instead she says *You won't fail. I know it.*

The point is clear — Shakespeare's plays were all works of fiction; Agnes likely never said the words *We fail!/ But screw your courage to the sticking-place, and we'll not fail* to her husband, thus inspiring Lady Macbeth's famous line. But as reality and fiction often exist in a symbiotic relationship, O'Farrell imagines the subtler influences of Agnes and Hamnet on Shakespeare in a novel that's as intimate and human as it is grandiose.

Reviewed by Rachel Hullett. This review was originally published in *The BookBrowse Review* in August 2020, and has been updated for the June 2021 edition.

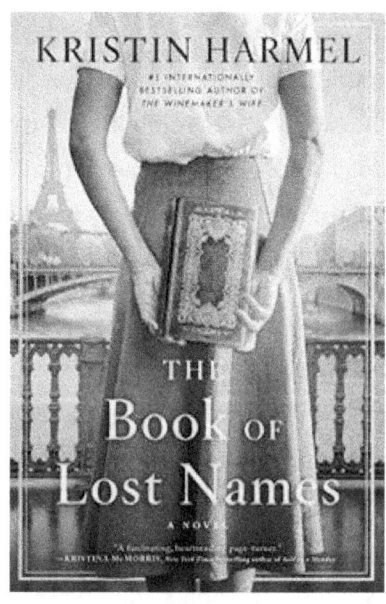

THE BOOK OF LOST NAMES

by Kristin Harmel

BookBrowse Rating: 4/5
Critics' Consensus: 4.5/5
Readers' Rating: 4.5/5

Published May 2021 in Paperback, 400 pages

Summary

Inspired by an astonishing true story from World War II, a young woman with a talent for forgery helps hundreds of Jewish children flee the Nazis in this unforgettable historical novel from the New York Times bestselling author of the "epic and heart-wrenching World War II tale" (Alyson Noel, #1 New York Times bestselling author) *The Winemaker's Wife.*

Eva Traube Abrams, a semi-retired librarian in Florida, is shelving books one morning when her eyes lock on a photograph in a magazine lying open nearby. She freezes; it's an image of a book she hasn't seen in sixty-five years—a book she recognizes as *The Book of Lost Names.*

The accompanying article discusses the looting of libraries by the Nazis across Europe during World War II—an experience Eva remembers well—and the search to reunite people with the texts taken from them so long ago. The book in the photograph, an eighteenth-century religious text thought to have been taken from France in the waning days of the war, is one of the most fascinating cases. Now housed in Berlin's Zentral- und Landesbibliothek library, it appears to contain some sort of code, but researchers don't know where it came from—or what the code means. Only Eva holds the answer—but will she have the strength to revisit old memories and help reunite those lost during the war?

As a graduate student in 1942, Eva was forced to flee Paris after the arrest of her father, a Polish Jew. Finding refuge in a small mountain town in the Free Zone, she begins forging identity documents for Jewish children fleeing to neutral Switzerland. But erasing people comes with a price, and along with a mysterious, handsome forger named Rémy, Eva decides she must find a way to preserve the real names of the children who are too young to remember who they really are. The records they keep in *The Book of Lost Names* will become even more vital when the resistance cell they work for is betrayed and Rémy disappears.

An engaging and evocative novel reminiscent of *The Lost Girls of Paris* and *The Alice Network*, *The Book of Lost Names* is a testament to the resilience of the human spirit and the power of bravery and love in the face of evil.

BookBrowse Review

In this moving work of historical fiction based on real events, a young Polish-French Jewish woman forges identification papers to aid Jews fleeing the Nazis during World War II.

There is certainly no shortage of books set in World War II Europe — from thrillers to family dramas — but even within this crowded setting, *The Book of Lost Names* stands out thanks to a strong sense of character and a compelling tale of love and survival.

While it doesn't carry the emotional or political weight of Hans Fallada's *Alone in Berlin* or Anthony Doerr's *All the Light We Cannot See*, Kristin Harmel's novel is tightly written and impressively affecting. *The Book of Lost Names* tells the story of Eva, a young Jewish Parisian and daughter of Polish migrants, that begins in 1942 and ends in 2005.

The novel flits back and forth between World War II Paris and 2005 Florida, with Eva now well into her eighties. When the titular Book of Lost Names — a book which Eva herself created during the war — turns up in Berlin, the events of this time in her life come rushing back to her.

In 1942, Eva is 23, living with her parents, and studying for her Ph.D. One night, she and her mother are babysitting the neighbor's children when Eva's father is pulled out of their apartment and stolen away by the Nazis. Eva and her mother escape to a quiet French town where Eva works to forge personal papers for those looking to flee into neutral Switzerland. It's here that Eva meets Remy, a fellow member of the resistance.

While *The Book of Lost Names* is set against the war-torn landscape of Nazi-occupied France and Eva is working as part of the resistance, this is, at its core, a love story — a book about how love can thrive even in the direst of circumstances.

It's also a book about identity. Eva creates new identities for those looking to escape and keeps their old ones safe, encoded within the Book of Lost Names.

Her mother no longer knows who she is without her husband, and Eva herself is, in her mother's eyes, is betraying the Jewish faith by falling in with a Catholic boy.

These themes hold together expertly, and the love story that unfolds is a true tearjerker. Every character in the novel is well-rounded and clearly defined, if a little one-dimensional. The plot is a bit reminiscent of a Disney movie, however; the main characters are good people with small interpersonal dramas and there is a looming villainous presence. Nothing here is narratively complicated or heavy, even given the wartime setting and high political stakes.

There are also a frustrating number of contrivances, with things falling into place a little too effortlessly. More than once, a challenge will rise up, only for a character to suddenly appear, equipped with the exact skillset to meet and defeat it. One other small bugbear is the fact that the present-day chapters are written in the first person while the flashbacks are in the third person. Narratively, I felt it would have made more sense for it to be reversed, with present-day Eva telling her own story of the past in the first person, thus creating a greater sense of intimacy with both the present and past versions of her character.

Despite these gripes, *The Book of Lost Names* is a pure kind of novel. It works spectacularly as a love story; its characters are lovable and easy to bond with. The highs and lows all hit hard because of the tight pacing. It flows well from chapter to chapter and from act to act, with every emotional punch landing perfectly. It's not the most thematically or politically deep story — every motif has a spotlight on it and every character is written to be wholly transparent — but everything works in service of an emotionally satisfying story of familial and romantic love in a time of war.

Reviewed by Will Heath. This review was originally published in *The BookBrowse Review* in December 2020, and has been updated for the June 2021 edition.

THE VANISHING HALF

by Brit Bennett

BookBrowse Rating: 5/5
Critics' Consensus: 5/5
Readers' Rating: 4.5/5

Published February 2022 in Paperback, 400 pages

Summary

From the *New York Times*-bestselling author of *The Mothers*, a stunning new novel about twin sisters, inseparable as children, who ultimately choose to live in two very different worlds, one black and one white.

The Vignes twin sisters will always be identical. But after growing up together in a small, southern black community and running away at age sixteen, it's not just the shape of their daily lives that is different as adults, it's everything: their families, their communities, their racial identities. Many years later, one sister lives with her black daughter in the same southern town she once tried to escape. The other secretly passes for white, and her white husband knows nothing of her past. Still, even separated by so many miles and just as many lies, the fates of the twins remain intertwined. What will happen to the next generation, when their own daughters' storylines intersect?

Weaving together multiple strands and generations of this family, from the Deep South to California, from the 1950s to the 1990s, Brit Bennett produces a story that is at once a riveting, emotional family story and a brilliant exploration of the American history of passing. Looking well beyond issues of race, *The Vanishing Half* considers the lasting influence of the past as it shapes a person's decisions, desires, and expectations, and explores some of the multiple reasons and realms in which people sometimes feel pulled to live as something other than their origins.

BookBrowse Review

Brit Bennett's *The Vanishing Half* explores issues of racism and identity in 20th-century America.

Brit Bennett's second novel, *The Vanishing Half* (after [The Mothers](), her 2016 bestselling debut), follows Desiree and Stella Vignes, identical twins born in 1938 in Mallard, Louisiana, a town so small it can't even be found on a map. Settled by the girls' ancestors, the town prides itself on its residents being primarily African Americans with very light skin tones (the lighter, the more prized). The girls run away to New Orleans when they turn 16. Desiree returns home 14 years later with her eight-year-old daughter, Jude, whose skin is so dark it's blue-black, touching off a firestorm of gossip and invective that impacts both mother and child. Stella, on the other hand, disappears without a trace, reinventing herself as a white woman with no family and no past. Marrying outside her race she gives birth to Kennedy, a blond, blue-eyed daughter. As Jude and Kennedy reach adulthood, each seeks to establish her place in the world and to uncover the secrets of her mother's past.

The narrative explores many important topics through the lives of these four women. Covering the time period from the World War II era through 1986, the author portrays the changing face of racism in the United States as exhibited not only by whites, but within Black communities as well, with light-skinned Blacks discriminating against those who are darker. Bennett also addresses the themes of family, identity and privilege, and illustrates the evolution of women's rights during this time period. That seems like a lot to tackle within one short novel, and in less-skilled hands the story might have become a slow plod, weighed down by its heavy themes. The author interweaves these subjects and others so skillfully, though, that the narrative soars, and it's only on reflection that one realizes its remarkable depth.

The Vanishing Half is captivating in large part because of the fully-realized characters Bennett has created. The women grow and change over the course of the story as they deal with loves and losses, joys and disappointments; they feel like real-life people we've met, and we grow to care deeply about them. Not only are the four central characters drawn with a fine pen, even minor characters are imbued with complexity, adding to the novel's richness.

The other highlight is the author's vivid writing style. While seldom using colloquialism in her text, she nevertheless captures the lyricism of Southern dialog throughout her prose:

> [The residents of Mallard] weren't used to having a dark child amongst them and were surprised by how much it upset them. Each time that girl passed by, no hat or nothing, they were as galled as when Thomas Richard returned from the war, half a leg lighter, and walked around the town with one pant leg pinned back so that everyone could see his loss. If nothing could be done about ugliness, you ought to at least look like you were trying to hide it.

Truisms abound, adding further flavor to the narration; for example, Desiree despises the local boys because "nothing made a boy less exciting than the fact that you were supposed to like him," and "the Mallard boys seemed as familiar and safe as cousins." Later, she doesn't tell her mother about her marriage because, she thinks, "What was the point of sharing good news with someone who couldn't be happy for you?"

My only complaint is that I found the plot overly dependent on coincidence. One accidental meeting over the course of a novel, OK, perhaps; maybe even two such encounters would be acceptable. But there were at least four major turning points that relied on unlikely circumstances, which seemed a bit much. I did enjoy the direction the author took her story, but the repeated reliance on this plot device cast a shadow on an otherwise exceptional work.

Regardless, *The Vanishing Half* is one of my favorite novels of the year; it's entertaining, fast-moving, has great characters, and Bennett's writing style is absolutely stellar from start to finish. Fans of novels such as Alice Walker's *The Color Purple*, Kathryn Stockett's *The Help*, or *The Secret Life of Bees* by Sue Monk Kidd will almost certainly enjoy this one as well, as will those interested in reading about mother-daughter relationships. The book would also be an ideal choice for book groups.

Reviewed by Kim Kovacs. This review was originally published in *The BookBrowse Review* in June 2020, and has been updated for the February 2022 edition.

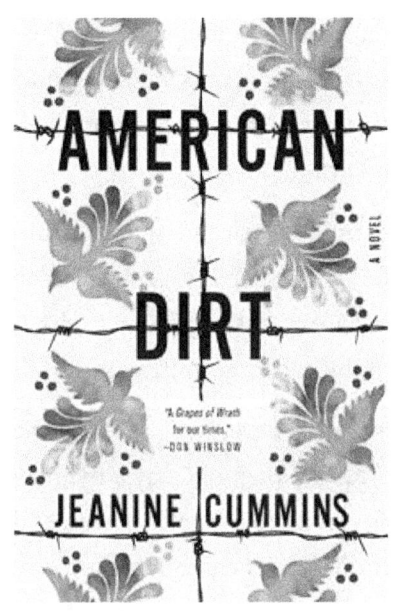

AMERICAN DIRT

by Jeanine Cummins

BookBrowse Rating: 5/5
Critics' Consensus: 3.5/5
Readers' Rating: 5/5

Published February 2022 in Paperback, 416 pages

Summary

Hailed as "a *Grapes of Wrath* for our times" and "a new American classic", *American Dirt* is a rare exploration into the inner hearts of people willing to sacrifice everything for a glimmer of hope.

También de este lado hay sueños.

On this side too, there are dreams.

If it's only a better life you seek, seek it elsewhere...This path is only for people who have no choice, no other option, only violence and misery behind you. And your journey will grow even more treacherous from here. Everything is working against you. —American Dirt

Lydia Quixano Perez lives in the Mexican city of Acapulco. She runs a bookstore. She has a son, Luca, the love of her life, and a wonderful husband who is a journalist. And while there are cracks beginning to show in Acapulco because of the drug cartels, her life is, by and large, fairly comfortable.

Even though she knows they'll never sell, Lydia stocks some of her all-time favorite books in her store. And then one day a man enters the shop to browse and comes up to the register with four books he would like to buy—two of them her favorites. Javier is erudite. He is charming. And, unbeknownst to Lydia, he is the jefe of the newest drug cartel that has gruesomely taken over the city. When Lydia's husband's tell-all profile of Javier is published, none of their lives will ever be the same.

Forced to flee, Lydia and eight-year-old Luca soon find themselves miles and worlds away from their comfortable middle-class existence. Instantly transformed into migrants, Lydia and Luca ride la bestia—trains that make their way north toward the United States, which is the only place Javier's reach doesn't extend. As they join the countless people trying to reach el norte, Lydia soon sees that everyone is running from something. But what exactly are they running to?

American Dirt will leave readers utterly changed. It is a literary achievement filled with poignancy, drama, and humanity on every page. It is one of the most important books for our times.

BookBrowse Review

The tense and engrossing story of a mother-and-son migrant journey, *American Dirt* is a truly groundbreaking work of fiction.

Jeanine Cummins' *American Dirt* hasn't just been positively reviewed by BookBrowse First Impressions readers—it's become our highest-rated book of all time! 33 out of 33 reviewers rated it five out of five stars, scoring it a perfect 5.0 average—the first book out of more than 600 titles to achieve this.

What *American Dirt* is about:

It tells the story of a mother and son as they flee drug cartel violence in their hometown of Acapulco. They head north, facing many dangers, and have to draw upon reserves of inner strength they did not know they had (Randi H). Imagine yourself at a family party in Acapulco. The festivities are underway, and everyone is having a wonderful time. In a split second, gunfire breaks out, leaving 16 members of your family dead. You and your son are alive only because he had gone inside and you went in to check on him. You hear the gunmen—cartel members you assume—looking around for survivors. By pure luck and instinct, the two of you survive. But this is only the beginning of the story (Nanette C).

Reviewers were immediately drawn in by Cummins' lifelike characters and captivating plot.

From the very first page to the last, I was hooked. The story of Lydia and Luca is so beautifully written. I felt I was actually with them on every step of their journey (Amber H). *American Dirt* captivated me from the moment I read the first page. There were so many twists and turns that were totally unpredictable (Antoinette B). This book has the key elements of what makes a great book—a plot-driven story with characters you care about (Michele H). *American Dirt* grabbed me from the very first sentence. I couldn't decide whether I wanted to rush through the book or savor every word (Marianne D).

While the book recounts traumatic events, readers found joy and beauty in it.

There are moments of abject terror, but there are also moments of joy. The way Lydia holds it together for her son reminded me a bit of the father in the movie *Life Is Beautiful*. *American Dirt* is a novel you will never forget (Nanette C). This book is compelling, frightening, heartwarming and unforgettable. The migrants can trust no one and yet they find hope, and the courage to keep living, and to love. Lydia and Luca are beautiful characters (Lynn D).

Some praise its potential for education and discussion...

This is that book. The one you will read and instantly want to share. The one that will spark the discussions we so need to have. I would so love to see this read in high schools across the country. This IS that book (Deborah H). If anything could have the power to change the debate about immigration in this country, it would be this book. It should be required reading for every U.S. citizen (Susan S). There will be some who will say it's too political but how can it not be? The migrant tragedy is real, political and complex and needs to be evaluated with compassion and realism (Margot P).

Many readers take pains to express just how highly they think of *American Dirt* and how deeply it has affected them.

There are a few times in your life when you read a book that transforms you. For me, this is one of those books. I found this book riveting from the very first sentence. I might add that I am a very critical reader but there is nothing I can say except to praise *American Dirt* (Dorothy L). This book actually gave me a book hangover that is making it difficult for me to move on to another story. I can't recommend it enough (Ilyse B). Blurbs have covered the stratosphere heralding the publication of this novel. I am here to tell you that these comments are not hyperbole; all of them are well deserved (Lani S). This will be without a doubt the best book I've read all year, and it has been a year of excellent novels for me. I could not stop reading, I felt so emotionally involved with the characters. My heart ached for them, I felt their terror and unbearable grief. I urge everyone to read this stunning and realistic book (Cheryl S).

Reviewed by First Impressions Reviewers. This review was originally published in *The BookBrowse Review* in January 2020, and has been updated for the February 2022 edition.

THE EXILES

by Christina Baker Kline

BookBrowse Rating: 5/5
Critics' Consensus: 5/5
Readers' Rating: 4.5/5

Published July 2021 in Paperback, 400 pages

Summary

The author of the #1 New York Times bestseller *Orphan Train* returns with an ambitious, emotionally resonant historical novel that captures the hardship, oppression, opportunity and hope of a trio of women's lives - two English convicts and an orphaned Aboriginal girl - in nineteenth-century Australia.

Seduced by her employer's son, Evangeline, a naïve young governess in early nineteenth-century London, is discharged when her pregnancy is discovered and sent to the notorious Newgate Prison. After months in the fetid, overcrowded jail, she learns she is sentenced to "the land beyond the seas," Van Diemen's Land, a penal colony in Australia. Though uncertain of what awaits, Evangeline knows one thing: the child she carries will be born on the months-long voyage to this distant land.

During the journey on a repurposed slave ship, the *Medea*, Evangeline strikes up a friendship with Hazel, a girl little older than her former pupils who was sentenced to seven years transport for stealing a silver spoon. Canny where Evangeline is guileless, Hazel—a skilled midwife and herbalist—is soon offering home remedies to both prisoners and sailors in return for a variety of favors.

Though Australia has been home to Aboriginal people for more than 50,000 years, the British government in the 1840s considers its fledgling colony uninhabited and unsettled, and views the natives as an unpleasant nuisance. By the time the *Medea* arrives, many of them have been forcibly relocated, their land seized by white colonists. One of these relocated people is Mathinna, the orphaned daughter of the Chief of the Lowreenne tribe, who has been adopted by the new governor of Van Diemen's Land.

In this gorgeous novel, Christina Baker Kline brilliantly recreates the beginnings of a new society in a beautiful and challenging land, telling the story of Australia from a fresh perspective, through the experiences of Evangeline, Hazel, and Mathinna. While life in Australia is punishing and often brutally unfair, it is also, for some, an opportunity: for redemption, for a new way of life, for unimagined freedom. Told in exquisite detail and incisive prose, *The Exiles* is a story of grace born from hardship, the unbreakable bonds of female friendships, and the unfettering of legacy.

BookBrowse Review

The Exiles is a story of oppression, endurance and hope featuring three women struggling to find the inner strength needed to survive their new lives in 19th-century Australia.

A young governess finds herself pregnant and in prison for theft and attempted murder. An Irish thief and herbalist finds her medical skills in high demand on a convict ship bound for Australia. A young Aboriginal girl is placed in the home of a British family where she is meant to become "civilized." *The Exiles* brings these three women together under bleak circumstances, and each must discover what she's willing to do to survive in Christina Baker Kline's novel of adversity and resilience.

The narrative is shared between Evangeline, Hazel and Mathinna, with each telling a different part of a larger story in a linear fashion — each character picks up where the last left off. When the narratives do overlap, it's only briefly and not until much later in the book. The characters' circumstances naturally lend themselves to this sort of narration; while Evangeline and Hazel are together on the convict ship, Mathinna is far away in Australia with her own story to tell.

Kline uses the three points of view to highlight the drastically different treatment of the three women at the hands of the British government. Evangeline, despite being a convict and an unwed soon-to-be mother, is educated and formerly of the middle class, so while she is still treated as a prisoner, she is often given special attention and preferential treatment by those in charge. Hazel, a thief of no social standing, is seen as a true criminal and is often treated cruelly or abusively by others. But once she proves her knowledge and skills as a midwife, she begins to earn respect and trust. Mathinna, despite being the daughter of a former chieftain, is seen as a savage by the British settlers. She is intelligent and curious, but considered uncivilized because she is Aboriginal. The implied importance of education is indicative of the classist and racist beliefs of British imperialist culture. Anyone who is not educated in their narrow sense of the word is deemed inferior.

The treatment of Evangeline, Hazel and Mathinna demonstrate that Britain's power in the 19th century was sustained by the colonization and destruction of other peoples and cultures. Kline shares a little-known piece of history through Mathinna's story, as she is based on a real person (see Beyond the Book), but she is also a representative of all the children lost to their families and their tribes at the hands of the British.

Although many are familiar with the British establishing a penal colony in Australia, few are likely as familiar with the stories of women sent there to serve out their prison sentences. The descriptions of Newgate Prison, the convict ship and the convict stations in Van Diemen's Land — now known as Tasmania — bring the harsh realities of these women's lives to light. The atmosphere of oppression, selfishness and sadness makes the narrative more realistic, and also more tragic. Kline isn't afraid to write unhappy endings for her characters, which adds an additional layer of authenticity, as many of the women convicts ended up leading sad lives even if they managed to survive.

Because the overall nature of the story is bleak, the small moments of hope and joy shine all the brighter. Despite their stories only just overlapping, the three women each learn about the importance of inner strength and carrying on, whatever the circumstances: the past is always carried within you like the rings of a tree, and both the good and the bad make you stronger. It's a surprisingly positive outlook, one with which the main characters find varying degrees of success. However, perhaps it's reflective of the attitude of many of the real-life women convicts upon their release as they learned to make the best out of any situation and move on. In fact, reality shares a similar outlook: many modern-day Australians take pride in their ancestors. No matter what these individuals may have done to become convicts, they also helped found and develop a prosperous country. As the story follows Hazel into her life of freedom, her inner strength comes to serve her time and again as, like the women convicts after whom she's modeled, she helps make her new home a better place.

The Exiles can't be described as a happy story, but it is inspiring and thought-provoking. Exploring historical events that may be unknown to some readers, Kline offers a unique look at the treatment of those outside of the strict rules and regulations of 19th-century British society. Furthermore, the three points of view tell three distinct stories that intertwine to create a larger picture of friendship, survival and hope. It's a fascinating tale that will appeal to readers with a taste for well-researched historical fiction and female friendships that can't be broken.

Reviewed by Jordan Lynch. This review was originally published in *The BookBrowse Review* in October 2020, and has been updated for the June 2021 edition.

HOW TO BE AN ANTIRACIST

by Ibram X. Kendi

BookBrowse Rating: 5/5
Critics' Consensus: 5/5

Published January 2023 in Paperback, 336 pages

> **Summary**
>
> From the National Book Award–winning author of *Stamped from the Beginning* comes a bracingly original approach to understanding and uprooting racism and inequality in our society - and in ourselves.
>
> "The only way to undo racism is to consistently identify and describe it—and then dismantle it."

Ibram X. Kendi's concept of antiracism reenergizes and reshapes the conversation about racial justice in America—but even more fundamentally, points us toward liberating new ways of thinking about ourselves and each other. In *How to Be an Antiracist,* Kendi asks us to think about what an antiracist society might look like, and how we can play an active role in building it.

In this book, Kendi weaves an electrifying combination of ethics, history, law, and science, bringing it all together with an engaging personal narrative of his own awakening to antiracism. *How to Be an Antiracist* is an essential work for anyone who wants to go beyond an awareness of racism to the next step: contributing to the formation of a truly just and equitable society.

BookBrowse Review

Part memoir, part electrifying treatise, *How to Be an Antiracist* challenges readers to recognize and resist racial inequity and injustice.

Ibram X. Kendi opens *How to Be an Antiracist* with a personal story he finds shameful in retrospect, recalling his participation in a high school oratorical contest named for Dr. Martin Luther King Jr. In his speech, Kendi excoriated Black youth for a higher rate of teen pregnancy and for valuing sports and music over schoolwork. "Who on earth did I think I was?" he wonders. The point he's making is that to argue that Black people should pull themselves up by the boot straps and improve their lives is to ignore the centuries of oppression and systemic racism that established a white supremacist society where Black people are not afforded anywhere close to the same opportunities as their white peers. Of course their lives and values will be different.

It's an effective hook on more than one level. First, the story is reassuring to the reader because Kendi is demonstrating that everyone can be racist, including the author of a book called *How to Be an Antiracist*. Second, it segues seamlessly into an explanation of the title:

> The opposite of 'racist' isn't 'not-racist.' It is 'anti-racist.' What's the difference? One endorses either the idea of a racial hierarchy as a racist, or racial equality as an antiracist. One either believes problems are rooted in groups of people, as a racist, or locates the roots of problems in power and politics, as an antiracist. One either allows racial inequities to persevere, as a racist, or confronts racial inequities, as an antiracist.

Kendi continues interspersing the personal with the political throughout the text. He recounts the early stages of his parents' relationship and incidents from his own life, and in doing so, he charts the history of racism and Black activism from the 1970s to the present. (He does reference events from earlier centuries, but readers interested in the history of racism would be better off seeking out his previous book, _Stamped from the Beginning_, for which he won the National Book Award.) He recalls growing up in the New York City borough of Queens and later moving to Manassas, Virginia as a teenager, where he attended a school called Stonewall Jackson High School. In both places, his education was often impeded by white teachers who rarely called on him or the few other Black students in class. This took place in the 1990s and Kendi remembers feeling an intense struggle while vacillating between the dueling cultural messages he absorbed about Black people — "we were either King's disciples or thugs killing King's dreams" — which would later inform his oratorical contest speech.

One of the most significant themes in the book, skillfully considered from multiple angles, is assimilation and respectability politics. In this context, respectability politics refers to the argument by Black leaders, thinkers and others with influence that engaging in irreproachable moral conduct will earn Black people respect and success. Likewise, white assimilationists believe (overtly or subconsciously) that Black people should make every effort to conform to the behavioral standards of white society. Again, neither of these attitudes takes into account the history of racism and how it is woven into the very fabric of American culture and institutions. These are precepts that blame the victim, conveniently ignore centuries of racist crimes and establish impossible expectations — no matter how "respectably" Black people may conduct themselves, they will still never be white and will therefore never be fully accepted into a white supremacist society.

Kendi also refutes some powerful myths, providing data, for instance, demonstrating that unemployment level is a much more likely predictor of a neighborhood's violent crime rate than the skin color of the residents living there. He explains that the achievement gap between majority-white and majority-black schools is the result of the underfunding of the latter, rather than some inherent difference in intelligence or ambition between white and Black students. This and many other discussions in the book explore the intersection between race and class and how, because of the policies of inequity built into the system from slavery to racial income disparities, "To love capitalism is to end up loving racism." An antiracist must be anti-capitalist as well, because both were "birthed together from the same unnatural causes."

In the book's final pages, Kendi recalls his recent battle with Stage 4 metastatic colon cancer, which has an 88 percent fatality rate over a five-year period after diagnosis. After six months of chemotherapy, he underwent surgery to have his tumors removed. An evaluation of his cells indicated he was cancer-free. This serves as an apt metaphor for the urgent need to excise racism from American society. Having essentially experienced a miracle, he expresses an inspiring message of hope: "Racism is not even six hundred years old. It's a cancer that we've caught early."

The author's contextualizing of the impact of systemic racism within his own life story is compelling and persuasive; his personal examples serve as proof of his claims regarding how racism affects Black people, and also invite the reader to conduct self-examination. Kendi demonstrates how antiracism is a lifelong commitment one must actively choose on a daily basis, and also how that choice is not only necessary but richly rewarding.

Reviewed by Lisa Butts. This review was originally published in *The BookBrowse Review* in June 2020, and has been updated for the February 2023 edition.

MIGRATIONS

by Charlotte McConaghy

BookBrowse Rating: 5/5
Critics' Consensus: 5/5
Readers' Rating: 5/5

Published July 2021 in Paperback, 288 pages

Summary

For readers of *Flight Behavior* and *Station Eleven*, a novel set on the brink of catastrophe, as a young woman chases the world's last birds—and her own final chance for redemption.

A MOST ANTICIPATED BOOK (*Entertainment Weekly, Vogue, Time, Vulture, Elle, Harper's Bazaar, Newsweek,* The Millions, *Library Journal, Maclean's,* and more)

Franny Stone has always been a wanderer. By following the ocean's tides and the birds that soar above, she can forget the losses that have haunted her life. But when the wild she loves begins to disappear, Franny can no longer wander without a destination. She arrives in remote Greenland with one purpose: to find the world's last flock of Arctic terns and follow them on their final migration. She convinces Ennis Malone, captain of the Saghani, to take her onboard, winning over his eccentric crew with promises that the birds she is tracking will lead them to fish.

As the Saghani fights its way south, Franny's new shipmates begin to realize that she is full of dark secrets: night terrors, an unsent pile of letters, and an obsession with pursuing the terns at any cost. When the story of her past begins to unspool, Ennis and his crew must ask themselves what Franny is really running toward—and running from.

Propelled by a narrator as fierce and fragile as the terns she is following, *Migrations* is both an ode to our threatened world and a breathtaking page-turner about the lengths we will go for the people we love.

BookBrowse Review

A complex, ambitious and captivating novel that considers troubling environmental destruction alongside poignant self-reckoning.

Migrations, Australian author Charlotte McConaghy's literary fiction debut, earned a notably high average rating of 4.8 out of 5 stars from our 41 First Impressions reviewers.

What the book is about:

Written with profound insight, *Migrations* tells the story of Franny Stone's quest to follow the endangered Arctic tern migration from Greenland to the Weddell

Sea near the Antarctic Peninsula (Marilyn G). *Migrations* is a compelling story of the possible future of wildlife extinction. As Franny follows the last of the Arctic terns during their migration we are drawn into her past story and yet apprehensive of her current journey (Carol F).

Readers found McConaghy's novel impressively ambitious in its variety of themes and subjects,

The author describes a future we do not want. But her bleak vision is only one element of this engrossing story. The novel is also a warm combination of a love story, a perilous journey, a dark back story that is only gradually revealed, echoes of classics (*Moby Dick*, Jules Verne and Hans Christian Andersen immediately come to mind, along with tales of orphans) and mesmerizing nature writing... Just as *Flight Behavior* changes the way its readers look at and think about butterflies, and *The Overstory* does that for trees, so does *Migrations* for birds (Deborah W). This book was a delicious "trail" of imagery, feelings, times and locations. It was like unwrapping a present (Linda V).

...and it helped some out of a reading slump.

In this time of coronavirus isolation, reading would seem the perfect antidote to our boredom and worries. And yet I've found myself lacking the concentration required as I tried various books on my "to read" pile. Until, that is, I came to *Migrations* by Charlotte McConaghy (Nanette C). This book captured me! So refreshing in a time of fear and uncertainty (Mary O). It has been awhile since I read a book that thoroughly captured me, but with *Migrations* I found that delight in reading again (Viqui G). What a good read. At first I thought it would be a little bit depressing for these days: Mass extinction, climate disruption, the end of the wild. But no, not at all! The story of Franny and her search for the last of the Arctic terns was engrossing (Gary R).

A few reviewers had difficulty connecting with the character of Franny,

I did not connect with Franny, the narrator, and thought she was unreliable (Jane C). Even though McConaghy's novel is a page turner that kept me reading too late many nights, I found myself not liking Franny at all. I feel she is supposed to be the sympathetic victim we are to root for and fall in love with, but I'm not sold (Melissa S).

...but many declared a special fondness for the book,

This novel is one of the better books that I've read in a long time; it even may be a look into our environmental future. I'm hoping *Migrations* will receive many honors. It is a special book (Suzanne G). I will carry this book with me a long time. I will reread it more slowly and deliberately (Carole R). I imagine in years to come I will remember *Migrations* as one of my most favorite books (Betty B).

...and felt it touched on important topics for discussion in current times.

I read this while "sheltering in place" during the coronavirus outbreak. It's too late to stop the global spread of the virus; but hopefully it's not too late to have a brighter future for our planet than the one *Migrations* paints. I have lots of time now, so I'll be thinking about what I can do about global warming, and I'll be thinking about Franny — what she was passionate about, where she ended up and how her tale can empower us. Book groups will find much to discuss here (Deborah W).

Reviewed by First Impressions Reviewers. This review was originally published in *The BookBrowse Review* in September 2020, and has been updated for the July 2021 edition.

THE BODY

by Bill Bryson

BookBrowse Rating: 5/5
Critics' Consensus: 4.5/5
Readers' Rating: 5/5

Published January 2021 in Paperback, 464 pages

Summary

Bill Bryson, bestselling author of *A Short History of Nearly Everything*, takes us on a head-to-toe tour of the marvel that is the human body. As addictive as it is comprehensive, this is Bryson at his very best, a must-read owner's manual for everybody.

Bill Bryson once again proves himself to be an incomparable companion as he guides us through the human body--how it functions, its remarkable ability to heal itself, and (unfortunately) the ways it can fail. Full of extraordinary facts (your body made a million red blood cells since you started reading this) and irresistible Bryson-esque anecdotes, *The Body* will lead you to a deeper understanding of the miracle that is life in general and you in particular. As Bill Bryson writes, "We pass our existence within this wobble of flesh and yet take it almost entirely for granted." *The Body* will cure that indifference with generous doses of wondrous, compulsively readable facts and information.

BookBrowse Review

In his latest work, bestselling author Bill Bryson guides readers through the wonders of the human body.

Many of Bill Bryson's fans first became familiar with his work through his autobiographical travel books, such as *Notes from a Small Island* or *A Walk in the Woods: Rediscovering America on the Appalachian Trail*. Bryson also famously delved into the world of science in *A Short History of Nearly Everything*, which breaks down scientific fields such as chemistry and biology so that the lay person finds them fascinating and entertaining. *The Body: A Guide for Occupants* marks the author's reentry into popular science. With his characteristic wit, he takes his readers on a survey of anatomy that successfully outlines what makes us human.

Bryson begins with a brief examination of what chemically makes up a person, and then he drills down to the workings of specific body parts and systems, such as the head or the digestive system. He later touches on the less physical aspects of being human, from sleep to sexuality, and he ends by considering how our bodies ultimately break down. While there is some order to the book's structure, with overarching chapters like "The Head," "The Guts" and "Nerves and Pain," each of these is wide ranging and encompasses an amazing range of subjects tangentially related to the main focus.

Bryson is a master at making arcane information accessible to a broad audience and keeping that audience engrossed from start to finish. Every page is jam-packed with interesting trivia that is fun to share with others. I constantly found myself turning to my husband and saying, "Huh—here's something cool—let me read you this paragraph!" The material Bryson presents ranges from obscure facts about the body (we blink about 14,000 times a day, so much that a person's eyes are closed for 23 minutes of every waking day) to things that make sense that most people just haven't thought about (unlike other organs of the body, the skin never fails) to intriguing bits of history that are not well known (the modern species of penicillin is descended from <u>a single moldy cantaloupe</u>).

What keeps the book from being a dry recitation of anatomy trivia is Bryson's light touch with the subject matter; he injects the text with wit at every turn:

> "Many authorities (for which possibly read 'science majors who don't have a date on a Friday') have tried at various times, mostly for the purposes of amusement, to compute how much it would cost in materials to build a human."

> "It's a little ironic that two of the lightest things in nature, oxygen and hydrogen, when combined form one of the heaviest [water], but that's nature for you."

> "Incidentally, the idea that we use only 10 percent of our brains is a myth...You may not use it all terribly sensibly, but you employ all your brain in one way or another."

> "You are 70% more likely to die from heart disease today than you were in 1900. That's partly because other things used to kill people first, and partly because a hundred years ago people didn't spend five or six hours an evening in front of a television with a big spoon and a tub of ice cream."

For more trivia about the body see Beyond the Book.

The downside to *The Body* is that there's no overarching narrative that ties all the fascinating parts together. There's consequently nothing to keep one reading "just one more chapter" late into the night, and there's simply too much information to absorb to move quickly through the book. This is a slow read, and one designed for sharing but not necessarily discussing or debating; it likely would not make a good selection for a book group.

Regardless, Bryson very likely has another hit on his hands. I've read everything he has written and believe it to be far and away his best work to date. It will certainly appeal to his ever-growing fan base and delight anyone who enjoys acquiring new information about a topic they think they know well; it would also make an ideal gift book for the trivia lover.

Reviewed by Kim Kovacs. This review was originally published in *The BookBrowse Review* in November 2019, and has been updated for the February 2021 edition.

HIDDEN VALLEY ROAD

by Robert Kolker

BookBrowse Rating: 5/5
Critics' Consensus: 5/5
Readers' Rating: 5/5

Published March 2021 in Paperback, 400 pages

Summary

The heartrending story of a midcentury American family with twelve children, six of them diagnosed with schizophrenia, that became science's great hope in the quest to understand the disease.

Don and Mimi Galvin seemed to be living the American dream. After World War II, Don's work with the Air Force brought them to Colorado, where their twelve children perfectly spanned the baby boom: the oldest born in 1945, the youngest in 1965. In those years, there was an established script for a family like the Galvins--aspiration, hard work, upward mobility, domestic harmony--and they worked hard to play their parts. But behind the scenes was a different story: psychological breakdown, sudden shocking violence, hidden abuse. By the mid-1970s, six of the ten Galvin boys, one after another, were diagnosed as schizophrenic. How could all this happen to one family?

What took place inside the house on Hidden Valley Road was so extraordinary that the Galvins became one of the first families to be studied by the National Institute of Mental Health. Their story offers a shadow history of the science of schizophrenia, from the era of institutionalization, lobotomy, and the schizophrenogenic mother to the search for genetic markers for the disease, always amid profound disagreements about the nature of the illness itself. And unbeknownst to the Galvins, samples of their DNA informed decades of genetic research that continues today, offering paths to treatment, prediction, and even eradication of the disease for future generations.

With clarity and compassion, bestselling and award-winning author Robert Kolker uncovers one family's unforgettable legacy of suffering, love, and hope.

BookBrowse Review

Hidden Valley Road **chronicles a family's struggle to cope with the effects of schizophrenia and how they, in turn, helped others understand the disorder.**

Don and Mimi Galvin thought they'd realized the American Dream when they purchased a newly-built home on Hidden Valley Road, just north of Colorado Springs, in 1963. The suburban development had enough room for their 11 rambunctious children (Mary, the 12th and youngest child, was born soon after their move) and was rural enough for them to pursue their hobby of training falcons. Their life seemed idyllic, but storm clouds lurked on the horizon. Their eldest son Donald began exhibiting troubling, sometimes violent behavior and was eventually diagnosed with schizophrenia, a serious neurological disorder that may result in hallucinations, delusions and an altered sense of reality. Over the next few years, five more of their children began displaying symptoms of the disorder as they hit their late teens or early 20s. Robert Kolker's *Hidden Valley Road* tells the Galvin family's story and explores how their experiences — as well as their genes — contributed to the ongoing effort to understand schizophrenia.

The book follows the Galvin children as they age, with half of them going on to live relatively normal lives while the others cycle in and out of various mental health institutions. The author points out that the well children also suffered, developing their own insecurities and fears. Each endured physical abuse at the hands of their ill brothers — unacknowledged by their parents — and as adults they were constantly concerned that any anxiety or depression they felt was a precursor to developing the disorder. As they had children of their own, they watched and worried about whether they'd passed a predisposition for the condition to their offspring (so much so that at least one child underwent a psychological evaluation that determined his acting out was only due to his parents constantly believing he was developing schizophrenia).

The author interweaves the history of the diagnosis and treatment of schizophrenia with the Galvins' story. The disorder affects some more than others, and, as illustrated by the six ill Galvin boys, manifests differently in each patient. In trying to determine if the disease could be genetic, beginning in the 1960s researchers started studying families where it was diagnosed in more than one sibling. The Galvin clan became a part of several of these studies, and their blood samples are still being used by scientists investigating the illness.

Kolker's writing is clear and concise throughout the narrative, with prose that keeps the nonfiction account moving at a good clip. He vividly describes the chaos of the Galvin homestead and the trauma of growing up in such an environment. The sections of the book that delve into the relevant medical research are equally fascinating and written in such a way that the science can be easily grasped by readers with no prior knowledge of the subject.

My biggest complaint about the narrative is that it seems clear that not all the surviving Galvin children cooperated equally with Kolker, so the account feels a bit slanted. Much of it, in fact, seems to be viewed through the lens of the youngest child, Mary (who changed her name to Lindsay as an adult). Because of that, the family matriarch, Mimi, garners a lot of the blame for the household turmoil. She's painted as being more concerned about producing babies than caring for them, being gone often, and ignoring the danger the older boys posed to her younger children. This comes across a bit one-sided, as presumably the children's father, Don, contributed equally to the problems, and certainly any parent would struggle with a household of 12 children, not to mention a family where half of them exhibit psychosis.

Although *Hidden Valley Road* is a page-turner, it's not an easy read emotionally. Nevertheless, it's highly recommended for those who enjoy science books that overlap with real-life family tragedy (it compares well to *The Immortal Life of Henrietta Lacks*).

Reviewed by Kim Kovacs. This review was originally published in *The BookBrowse Review* in December 2020, and has been updated for the March 2021 edition.

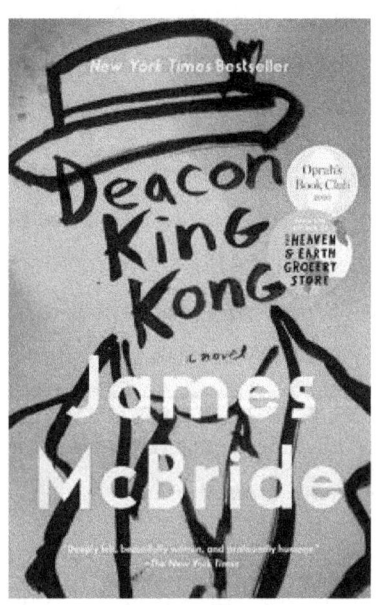

DEACON KING KONG

by James McBride

BookBrowse Rating: 5/5
Critics' Consensus: 5/5
Readers' Rating: 5/5

Published February 2021 in Paperback, 400 pages

Summary

From James McBride, author of the National Book Award-winning *The Good Lord Bird*, comes a wise and witty novel about what happens to the witnesses of a shooting.

In September 1969, a fumbling, cranky old church deacon known as Sportcoat shuffles into the courtyard of the Cause Houses housing project in south Brooklyn, pulls a .38 from his pocket, and in front of everybody shoots the project's drug dealer at point-blank range.

The reasons for this desperate burst of violence and the consequences that spring from it lie at the heart of *Deacon King Kong*, James McBride's funny, moving novel and his first since his National Book Award-winning *The Good Lord Bird*. In *Deacon King Kong*, McBride brings to vivid life the people affected by the shooting: the victim, the African-American and Latinx residents who witnessed it, the white neighbors, the local cops assigned to investigate, the members of the Five Ends Baptist Church where Sportcoat was deacon, the neighborhood's Italian mobsters, and Sportcoat himself.

As the story deepens, it becomes clear that the lives of the characters--caught in the tumultuous swirl of 1960s New York--overlap in unexpected ways. When the truth does emerge, McBride shows us that not all secrets are meant to be hidden, that the best way to grow is to face change without fear, and that the seeds of love lie in hope and compassion.

Bringing to these pages both his masterly storytelling skills and his abiding faith in humanity, James McBride has written a novel every bit as involving as *The Good Lord Bird* and as emotionally honest as *The Color of Water*. Told with insight and wit, *Deacon King Kong* demonstrates that love and faith live in all of us.

BookBrowse Review

James McBride's *Deacon King Kong* is a humorous take on Black life in "the Projects."

Cuffy Jasper Lambkin, better known as Sportcoat to his fellow members of the Five Ends Baptist Church and residents of the Causeway Housing Projects in South Brooklyn, is at the heart of James McBride's novel *Deacon King Kong*. The

71-year-old widower meanders through "The Cause," performing odd jobs when he's not too intoxicated by the local moonshine (which is rarely). He's the person everyone knows, trusts and calls on when they need help, the person who sets all to rights. "There is no job too small, no miracle too wondrous, no smell too noxious," McBride writes.

> [I]f your visiting preacher had diabetes and weighed 450 pounds and gorged himself with too much fatback and chicken thighs at the church repast and your congregation needed a man strong enough to help that tractor-trailer-sized wide-body off the toilet seat and out onto the bus back to the Bronx so somebody could lock up the dang church and go home – why, Sportcoat was your man.

Which makes it all the more surprising when this peaceful man beloved by all, out of the blue and without warning, shoots a 19-year-old drug dealer one afternoon at the flagpole where the old church women of the neighborhood congregate to exchange the daily gossip.

The book is to an extent about unraveling the mystery of what led Sportcoat to do such a thing, as well as detailing the consequences the attack sets in motion. Really, though, the plot is at times almost irrelevant, and in fact barely pokes its head up during the first half of the novel, only showing itself briefly now and then to remind readers that there truly is a unifying story here somewhere. The author embeds deeper topics into the overall narrative, taking on issues like the importance of friendship and trust, the need to be loved, the sense of caring that comes from being part of a community, the effect of racial disparities on communities of color and dealing with change.

Primarily, though, McBride seems intent on establishing an atmosphere, conveying the feel of the neighborhood and its residents. Page after page is devoted to character sketches and descriptions of the many tiny facets of life in the Projects. One chapter, for example, is about an annual invasion of ants. This laugh-out-loud account is completely peripheral to the book's storyline, but there's so much color in it, so much vivid detail, that one's mental image of the neighborhood is heightened considerably. Although the novel often feels a bit like a collection of short stories, all the little vignettes add up to an enormously effective portrait of the community as a whole as well as the people that comprise it. When the plot does kick in (somewhere around pages 200 to 250) it's engaging and moves along rapidly, if somewhat improbably.

Although the narrative is set in 1969, the issues it raises haven't changed much in the ensuing decades and seem particularly relevant in light of the current Black Lives Matter movement. Black vs. white racial conflict isn't a major theme — or, rather, it's so all-encompassing that it's more a state of being, an undercurrent humming along just below the surface of the entire story. There's a lot of justifiable anger evident under McBride's humor; as a white reader, there were times when I simultaneously found myself laughing and feeling ashamed of the racial disparities that exist and the privileges I have simply because of my skin color. It says a lot about the author's skill, though, that while the novel deepened my understanding of some of the issues Black communities face and left me thoughtful, it still ended up being a feel-good read that had me smiling at the end.

Comedy can be tricky to pin down; something one person finds amusing might leave another completely unaffected. Personally, I found *Deacon King Kong* to be one of the funniest books I've read (and typically I don't "get" a lot of what's billed as humor). I did think that at times the comic passages went on too long, and around the middle of the novel I found myself wishing the author would just get on with the story. Although these passages are quite entertaining, for the most part they do little to further the plot and I became a bit bored with the style. However, the narrative soon kicked into high gear and I was completely engaged from that point until the book's end.

Deacon King Kong has appeared on numerous "best of" lists (including BookBrowse's), and it's definitely a worthy entry; it has my vote for one of the best books of the year, at any rate. I highly recommend it to those looking for an exceptionally well-written, light-hearted take on serious subjects. Book groups will likely find many great topics of discussion here.

Reviewed by Kim Kovacs. This review was originally published in *The BookBrowse Review* in December 2020, and has been updated for the April 2021 edition.

MEMORIAL DRIVE

by Natasha Trethewey

BookBrowse Rating: 5/5
Critics' Consensus: 4.5/5
Readers' Rating: 4/5

Published June 2021 in Paperback, 320 pages

> **Summary**
>
> A chillingly personal and exquisitely wrought memoir of a daughter reckoning with the brutal murder of her mother at the hands of her former stepfather, and the moving, intimate story of a poet coming into her own in the wake of a tragedy.

At age nineteen, Natasha Trethewey had her world turned upside down when her former stepfather shot and killed her mother. Grieving and still new to adulthood, she confronted the twin pulls of life and death in the aftermath of unimaginable trauma and now explores the way this experience lastingly shaped the artist she became.

With penetrating insight and a searing voice that moves from the wrenching to the elegiac, Pulitzer Prize-winning poet Natasha Trethewey explores this profound experience of pain, loss, and grief as an entry point into understanding the tragic course of her mother's life and the way her own life has been shaped by a legacy of fierce love and resilience. Moving through her mother's history in the deeply segregated South and through her own girlhood as a "child of miscegenation" in Mississippi, Trethewey plumbs her sense of dislocation and displacement in the lead-up to the harrowing crime that took place on Memorial Drive in Atlanta in 1985.

Memorial Drive is a compelling and searching look at a shared human experience of sudden loss and absence but also a piercing glimpse at the enduring ripple effects of white racism and domestic abuse. Animated by unforgettable prose and inflected by a poet's attention to language, this is a luminous, urgent, and visceral memoir from one of our most important contemporary writers and thinkers.

BookBrowse Review

Pulitzer Prize-winner and former U.S. Poet Laureate Natasha Trethewey navigates grief and residual trauma 30 years after her mother's murder in this devastating and lyrical memoir.

On June 5, 1985, Natasha Trethewey's mother, Gwendolyn Turnbough, was murdered by her ex-husband, Joel Grimmette. It took Trethewey 30 years to feel ready to truly reckon with the trauma of this event and the years of abuse that preceded it. In a piercing, extraordinary memoir, she excavates the chasm of the loss and holds its terrible artifacts up to the light of day.

Memorial Drive begins with the author's childhood in Mississippi in the late 1960s and early '70s, where she grew up surrounded by doting family who could not entirely shield her from the racism of the time and place. Trethewey is the biracial child of a Black mother and a white father, and the family was often subjected to threats and intimidation. (She notes that her mother gave birth to her in a hospital that was still segregated on April 26, 1966, the 100-year anniversary of Mississippi's celebration of Confederate Memorial Day.) Her parents divorced when she was six years old and Trethewey and her mother moved to Atlanta; Gwendolyn met Joel soon after and the two got married. Joel was often left to babysit Trethewey while Gwendolyn was at work. When she upset him, he forced her to pack a bag and get in the car, then drove her in a loop around the city, claiming he was going to leave her somewhere alone. She was in the fifth grade the first time she heard Joel hitting her mother in the next room.

Amid the horrors recounted in the memoir is Trethewey's coming-of-age story, as the person she is today — the writer she is today — was forged in the fire of this trauma. She recalls receiving a diary from her mother at age 12, only to discover a short time later that Joel had picked the lock and read her private thoughts. Her response was to turn her diary entries into a virulent direct address to her abuser, telling him exactly what she thought of him. "In my first act of resistance," she writes, "I had inadvertently made him my first audience...I had begun to compose myself."

In 1983, when Trethewey was a senior in high school, Gwendolyn left Joel, taking the author and her little brother Joey with her. Shortly thereafter, Joel showed up at a high school football game looking for Trethewey. Uncertain how to react, she greeted him as she always did, "Hey, Big Joe." She later learned that Joel told a psychologist while he was hospitalized that he'd brought a gun and planned to shoot her but couldn't go through with it after she said hello to him. On the one hand, this was certainly a blessing. On the other, she notes that had he killed her that night, he would have been arrested and almost definitely imprisoned, perhaps never finding the opportunity to murder her mother. It is a chilling realization and the author's struggle with survivor's guilt is rendered with forthright clarity.

In the two years that followed, Joel tried to kill Gwendolyn, served a year in prison, and then immediately began threatening her life again when he got out. Trethewey includes evidence from her mother's case, such as police reports and transcripts of phone conversations between Joel and Gwendolyn in the days leading up to the murder that are hard to read but essential to understanding how difficult it is for a victim of abuse to get help. Even in this case, when the police took the situation seriously (it is not at all uncommon for victims to be ignored or disbelieved by the authorities), they did not adequately protect Gwendolyn.

The memoir is bookended by the author's recounting of a recurring dream. She and Gwendolyn walk around a circular path. Joel steps out of the shadows, Trethewey greets him as she always did, "Hey, Big Joe," and they continue walking. Shortly thereafter, he appears again, this time holding a gun. She shouts "No!" and tries to shield her mother, waking herself up in the process. It is a representation of her guilt, and one repeated symbol among many in the memoir. Of this dream and a particularly vivid and traumatic memory from childhood, she writes, "What matters is the transformative power of metaphor and the stories we tell ourselves about the arc and meaning of our lives." For a writer especially, metaphor is a powerful tool. But *Memorial Drive* offers insight and instruction for anyone who has experienced trauma. The memories, dreams and other ephemera that haunt us may ultimately prove key to finding meaning and hope (or perhaps just the ability to put one foot in front of the other) in our darkest hours. It's a powerful record of grief, abuse and the cleaving of the self that often occurs in conjunction with a life-altering tragedy, an acute and far-reaching manual for making sense of the senseless.

Reviewed by Lisa Butts. This review was originally published in *The BookBrowse Review* in September 2020, and has been updated for the June 2021 edition.

TRANSCENDENT KINGDOM

by Yaa Gyasi

BookBrowse Rating: 5/5
Critics' Consensus: 5/5
Readers' Rating: 5/5

Published July 2021 in Paperback, 304 pages

Summary

Yaa Gyasi's stunning follow-up to her acclaimed national bestseller *Homegoing* is a powerful, raw, intimate, deeply layered novel about a Ghanaian family in Alabama.

Gifty is a sixth-year PhD candidate in neuroscience at the Stanford University School of Medicine studying reward-seeking behavior in mice and the neural circuits of depression and addiction. Her brother, Nana, was a gifted high school athlete who died of a heroin overdose after an ankle injury left him hooked on OxyContin. Her suicidal mother is living in her bed. Gifty is determined to discover the scientific basis for the suffering she sees all around her. But even as she turns to the hard sciences to unlock the mystery of her family's loss, she finds herself hungering for her childhood faith and grappling with the evangelical church in which she was raised, whose promise of salvation remains as tantalizing as it is elusive.

Transcendent Kingdom is a deeply moving portrait of a family of Ghanaian immigrants ravaged by depression and addiction and grief--a novel about faith, science, religion, love. Exquisitely written, emotionally searing, this is an exceptionally powerful follow-up to Gyasi's phenomenal debut.

BookBrowse Review

In this tenderly wrought exploration of the workings of grief, addiction and spirituality, Yaa Gyasi creates human subjects worthy of wonder.

Yaa Gyasi's (pronounced "yah jessie") *Transcendent Kingdom* is, among other things, a meditation on science and religion. However, this cursory description doesn't do justice to the full contents of the novel any more than the scientific method encompasses the human quest for knowledge, or than the practice of prayer explains the human impulse to seek guidance from a higher power.

Gyasi's book follows a woman named Gifty as she cares for her depressed, bedridden mother and attempts to reconcile her present existence as a graduate student studying neuroscience with her past existence as a fervently religious child. A series of flashbacks swirl around the present timeline, covering key events that have produced profound effects on Gifty: her father's decision to return to his home country of Ghana, leaving his family behind in Alabama; her brother Nana's opioid addiction and death; and the subsequent breakdown of her mother's mental health, which now seems to be recurring.

As first-person narrator, Gifty takes the methodical approach one might expect of a scientist to understanding the raw material of her life. The author takes a similar approach to dissecting and arranging events in a logical (if not always chronological) order. A tendency towards systematic, evidence-based thinking is also visible in younger Gifty, whose journal entries, in which she writes to God, read as experiments in defining and communicating with the unknown. That the result of all of this is an emotionally evocative text may appear paradoxical, but this seems to be the point; the main character's strong spiritual experiences and her scientific outlook on life are not in conflict but firmly intertwined.

Gifty is both a fascinating observer and a strangely likable person — strangely because her likability is at odds with the way she treats others. She struggles with expressing herself romantically and sexually, has a habit of ghosting friends and lovers, and keeps details of her brother's death and life from those who seek to be close to her. She has a tendency towards self-deprivation, developed in response to Nana's addiction as well as the rigidity instilled by her evangelical past, which lives on in the beliefs of her still-evangelical mother, who is now barely speaking to her. But from the inside perspective the reader is given, Gifty isn't only sympathetic and comprehensible, she is a warm and funny character with touching quirks and vulnerabilities, one who explains her job on first dates by saying she gets mice hooked on cocaine (when in fact she has switched to feeding them Ensure because it is more easily accessible and the mice find it just as addictive) and avoids a certain Safeway because she is afraid the intimidatingly beautiful cashier who works there will judge her shopping choices.

The work that Gifty is struggling to complete in grad school, which she hopes will lead to better methods of treatment for addiction, is — like her forays into faith — an attempt to understand and gain mastery over the mechanisms of desire and restraint. But it is also an outlet for her genuine curiosity, as well as a way of feeling close to her brother, of whom she eventually reaches an understanding that stretches far beyond the question of his lack of self-control:

> Forget for a moment what he looked like on paper, and instead see him as he was in all of his glory, in all of his beauty. It's true that for years before he died, I would look at his face and think, *What a pity, what a waste.* But the waste was my own, the waste was what I missed out on whenever I looked at him and saw just his addiction.

The flipside of Gifty's wish for control, and her most sympathetic trait, is her willingness to remain open to reevaluation. This is what ultimately allows her to come to terms with her brother's death, her father's estrangement, her mother's state of mind and the loss of her own younger self.

The expected route for the novel to take would be to reveal Gifty's work as a futile attempt to "fix" her world. But Gyasi lets her protagonist's science remain as multitudinous as her self, lets the reader experience the same quiet struggles and occasional sense of wonder that Gifty does. Similarly, her childhood belief in God does not exist for the sake of mere character definition; religion acts with agency upon her life, an entity in itself. This generous approach to concepts that are often reduced to stereotypes or mere facets of identity is striking, and it forms the core of a novel that is humbling in its uncompromising wholeness.

Reviewed by Elisabeth Cook. This review was originally published in *The BookBrowse Review* in September 2020, and has been updated for the August 2021 edition.

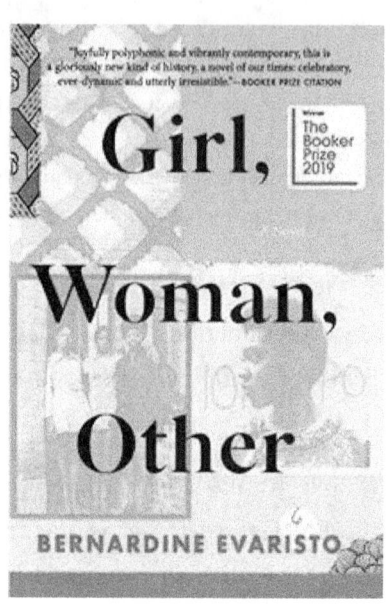

GIRL, WOMAN, OTHER

by Bernardine Evaristo

BookBrowse Rating: 5/5
Critics' Consensus: 5/5
Readers' Rating: 4/5

Published November 2019 in Paperback, 464 pages

> **Summary**

"Joyfully polyphonic and vibrantly contemporary, this is a gloriously new kind of history, a novel of our times: celebratory, ever-dynamic and utterly irresistible." —Booker Prize citation

From one of Britain's most celebrated writers of color, *Girl, Woman, Other* is a magnificent portrayal of the intersections of identity and a moving and hopeful story of an interconnected group of Black British women. Shortlisted for the 2019 Booker Prize and the Gordon Burn Prize, *Girl, Woman, Other* paints a vivid portrait of the state of post-Brexit Britain, as well as looking back to the legacy of Britain's colonial history in Africa and the Caribbean.

The twelve central characters of this multi-voiced novel lead vastly different lives: Amma is a newly acclaimed playwright whose work often explores her Black lesbian identity; her old friend Shirley is a teacher, jaded after decades of work in London's funding-deprived schools; Carole, one of Shirley's former students, is a successful investment banker; Carole's mother Bummi works as a cleaner and worries about her daughter's lack of rootedness despite her obvious achievements. From a nonbinary social media influencer to a 93-year-old woman living on a farm in Northern England, these unforgettable characters also intersect in shared aspects of their identities, from age to race to sexuality to class.

Sparklingly witty and filled with emotion, centering voices we often see othered, and written in an innovative fast-moving form that borrows technique from poetry, *Girl, Woman, Other* is a polyphonic and richly textured social novel that shows a side of Britain we rarely see, one that reminds us of all that connects us to our neighbors, even in times when we are encouraged to be split apart.

BookBrowse Review

A sprawling patchwork of stories from a varied ensemble of characters, *Girl, Woman, Other* explores marginalized identities and the intricate and often uncomfortable ways people navigate them.

As we meet Amma, a 50-something playwright finally experiencing mainstream success in Bernardine Evaristo's Booker Prize-winning novel *Girl, Woman, Other*, her thoughts flow over the page in a poetic form littered with frequent line breaks and lacking standard punctuation. At first glance, this might seem like a challenge posed to the reader, a work that might be labeled as "modern" or "experimental."

If Evaristo's novel is experimental, though, it's been rigorously tested and is well out of the trial phase. This book is genuinely readable in the purest sense. Characters' speech, ruminations and backstories blend together naturally, proceeding in a version of the off-the-cuff style many of us write in daily as we text or tweet messages that roll out by their own logic, making complete sense to us even if they don't follow traditional formatting. The author has harnessed the easy expressiveness of this style and applied it to a polished and complex narrative.

Within the novel's digestible casing are the stories of 12 distinct characters, most of whom are Black British women. In addition to Amma, who takes us through her early days of feminist politics and promiscuity, we meet her 19-year-old daughter Yazz, socially progressive in her own way but eager to develop language and beliefs distinct from her mother's. We also encounter Amma's erstwhile business partner Dominique, and learn of a difficult past relationship she had with an African American woman from which it took her years to recover. Amma's childhood friend Shirley recalls her own long struggle as a teacher for underprivileged children, while a prize student of Shirley's, Carole, shares the traumatic adolescence she suffered and how this led to her determination to pursue a successful career at all costs.

Some of the characters are bound to one another in ways that aren't always made clear to us—or them—upfront. In fact, discerning who's related to whom makes up what loose semblance of a plot exists in *Girl, Woman, Other*. For a book that glides with such majesty on its characters' individual stories, any intentional attempt to tie them together might seem heavy-handed. But along with Amma's play, *The Last Amazon of Dahomey*, which draws many of the characters together for its opening night, the mystery surrounding certain familial relationships exists naturally inside of the novel's broad focus on community of all kinds. Within this focus, we see the power that both reunification and forming new connections can have, even when these processes initially feel awkward and jarring.

Evaristo's novel contains plenty of uneasy moments. Some of these have to do with trauma sustained from assault and abuse, but the author also has a knack for portraying a specific type of discomfort that occurs in political discussions. Morgan, a non-binary character seeking a broader understanding of their gender with the help of strangers on the internet, tries to hold a dialogue with a trans woman who they simultaneously clash with and are drawn to. Yazz, at university, tries on a variety of views surrounding topics of racial and class privilege, feminism and identity. In one instance, a white girl named Courtney shuts down Yazz's assertion that, as a Black person, she's "more oppressed than anyone who isn't" by citing Roxane Gay, resulting in an interaction that makes both girls seem naive:

> ...Yazz, I mean, where does it all end? is Obama less privileged than a white hillbilly growing up in a trailer park with a junkie single mother and a jailbird father? is a severely disabled person more privileged than a Syrian asylum-seeker who's been tortured? Roxane argues that we have to find a new discourse for discussing inequality
>
> Yazz doesn't know what to say, when did Court read Roxane Gay - who's amaaaazing?
>
> was this a student outwitting the master moment?
>
> #whitegirltrumpsblackgirl

I was initially uncomfortable with how relatively unchecked this moment goes, even with the very youthful vibe between the characters, wondering if some people might read it as Courtney really having schooled Yazz. It seems fine for Courtney to challenge Yazz's comment, but she does this by cherry-picking language from Gay's actually much more complex ideas about race and privilege to move the spotlight off herself. Evaristo doesn't exactly go out of her way to show this, but it's also hard not to read the above passage as intentionally ridiculous. Also, in the next section, Courtney adds that she "only fancies black men" and will lose at least 50% of her white privilege by having mixed-race children. At this point, it's obvious that the author is making fun of Courtney just as much as, if not more than Yazz, while also allowing readers to consider whether there may still be some legitimacy to the relatively unformed opinions of both. This sense of humor that's more expansive than reductive continues to accompany awkward moments throughout *Girl, Woman, Other*.

I also came to feel that discomfort (the characters' and my own) was part of the point of this reading experience and that, to borrow a phrase from a social media platform the novel both references and stylistically resembles, retweets don't equal endorsements. Thoughts and opinions are produced with such spontaneity and plurality, and over such a wide span of time and experiences, that it's impossible not to encounter some that are cringe-worthy. Again, though, this is just part of the nature of Evaristo's book. It's about the actuality of getting from Point A to Point B without always having all of the necessary tools and language, whether from a loveless marriage to a fulfilling relationship, or from internalized misogyny to self-acceptance.

Even in its title, *Girl, Woman, Other* makes it clear that the author's intention is to address specific experiences of marginalization. It's refreshing to read a book that encompasses such a variety of human perspectives and flaws but that still unequivocally centers Blackness, non-male genders and queer sexualities, as well as non-traditional relationships and family arrangements. While Evaristo's novel entertains many points of view, it doesn't stumble into moral vagueness or the idea that all opinions and experiences are the same. Instead, it chooses motion over stagnation, self-awareness over denial. It insists on pushing through discomfort and moving forward.

Reviewed by Elisabeth Cook. This review was originally published in *The BookBrowse Review* in January 2020, and has been updated for the December 2020 edition.

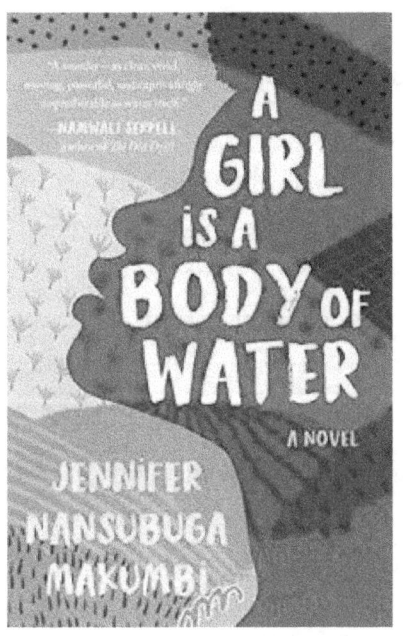

A GIRL IS A BODY OF WATER

by Jennifer Nansubuga Makumbi

BookBrowse Rating: 5/5
Critics' Consensus: 4.5/5
Readers' Rating: 4.5/5

Published June 2021 in Paperback, 450 pages

Summary

International-award-winning author Jennifer Nansubuga Makumbi's novel is a sweeping and powerful portrait of a young girl and her family: who they are, what history has taken from them, and--most importantly--how they find their way back to each other.

Published as *The First Woman* in the UK.

In her twelfth year, Kirabo, a young Ugandan girl, confronts a piercing question that has haunted her childhood: who is my mother? Kirabo has been raised by women in the small village of Nattetta—her grandmother, her best friend, and her many aunts, but the absence of her mother follows her like a shadow. Complicating these feelings of abandonment, as Kirabo comes of age she feels the emergence of a mysterious second self, a headstrong and confusing force inside her at odds with her sweet and obedient nature.

Seeking answers, Kirabo begins spending afternoons with Nsuuta, a local witch, trading stories and learning not only about this force inside her, but about the woman who birthed her, who she learns is alive but not ready to meet. Nsuuta also explains that Kirabo has a streak of the "first woman"—an independent, original state that has been all but lost to women.

Kirabo's journey to reconcile her rebellious origins, alongside her desire to reconnect with her mother and to honor her family's expectations, is rich in the folklore of Uganda and an arresting exploration of what it means to be a modern girl in a world that seems determined to silence women. Makumbi's unforgettable novel is a sweeping testament to the true and lasting connections between history, tradition, family, friends, and the promise of a different future.

BookBrowse Review

In Jennifer Nansubuga Makumbi's luminous second novel, a young woman comes of age in Uganda in the 1970s while searching for her missing mother.

First Impressions readers were fascinated by *A Girl Is a Body of Water*, a riveting and nuanced novel set in Uganda, awarding it an average score of 4.5 out of 5 stars.

What it's about:

Kirabo is a 'special child.' She was born with 'the original state' inside her, a consciousness going back to Ugandan origin myths. It allows her to leave her body and fly, swinging from the church steeple until, 'like a canon, she launched into the sky.' Kirabo is conflicted because her Christian upbringing tells her these powers are evil. In secret, she consults Nsuuta, the village witch. She has two requests: to lose her original state and to find her birth mother, who deserted her when she was a newborn. These conflicts propel Kirabo forward as she leaves the village for boarding school in Kampala, falls in love, and survives Idi Amin's reign of terror (Naomi B).

Readers appreciated the opportunity to learn about Ugandan culture and language...

A fascinating journey into Ugandan culture. The author uses her gifts for crafting narrative and language to examine the particulars of a patriarchal and storytelling culture and how Christianity impacts and challenges families and social structures (Claire M). It was quite an experience traveling to Uganda through this book, learning about this rich culture: family, village life, beliefs and the unrest and civil war in the 1980s. I loved the storytelling within the storytelling. It was like sitting around a fire and listening to your grandmother tell tales of long ago about why life is the way it is now. A very captivating story of a young girl coming of age: falling in love, attending school, experiencing pain. But through it all, she endures (Sonia F).

...particularly the author's approach to the experiences of women in Uganda:

There's such a contradiction between the expectations and demands and treatment of Ugandan women (by the men of course) vs. the raw internal strength and impenetrable will of these women when the men aren't around. But even though the men and the culture take what appears to be everything from the women (including losing both their first and last names upon marriage) the women always persevere, and beautifully. It's ultimately an incredibly informative, educational and uplifting story that feels so very real (Shaun D).

Some found the novel a little difficult or felt it took some time to get invested...

Maybe it's my choice of books lately but I haven't been anywhere near this challenged by a book, start to finish, in a very long time. My advice is to stick with it because it's hands-down one of the best books I have ever read. It challenged me in myriad ways, from the language (which is so beautifully lyrical) to the cultural references to the geography and history of Uganda, all of which forced me to read at a much slower and more careful rate than usual, pausing frequently to do research. This frustrated me at first but ultimately benefited my understanding and appreciation of the book as a whole (Shaun D). It took about 75 pages for the story to hook me and then I couldn't stop reading. I cared about each character (Sandy F). I found the first part (200 pages) to be very slow. I actually put the book down for a few weeks. I picked it up again about a week ago and flew through the last part. It was beautifully written and took me away to Uganda in the 1970s and '80s. That is no mean feat during these trying times so I applaud the author. I look forward to her next book (Susan C).

...but most found the challenge more than worthwhile and recommend *A Girl Is a Body of Water*, especially for book clubs:

Makumbi weaves a thoughtful tale with the threads of clan relationships and rivalries, with strong elements of expanding feminism, with the values of schooling all set against a political background of government vs. rebellion. Book clubs should find rich material for discussion. In my view this is an excellent novel and a good read, albeit at times the path is strewn with unfamiliar language. Readers should feel rewarded for traveling on these Ugandan roads in Kirabo's shoes (Darrell W). Young women especially may identify with the theme of coming of age, regardless of culture. The main family characters are strong and thoughtful. The novel shifts between past and present to support a tender story highly recommended for book club discussion (Margaret F). I cared about each character — and there are many. I enjoyed this book and highly recommend it. This is not an easy read but it is worth it. A rich and compelling story (Sandy F).

Reviewed by First Impressions Reviewers. This review was originally published in *The BookBrowse Review* in September 2020, and has been updated for the July 2021 edition.

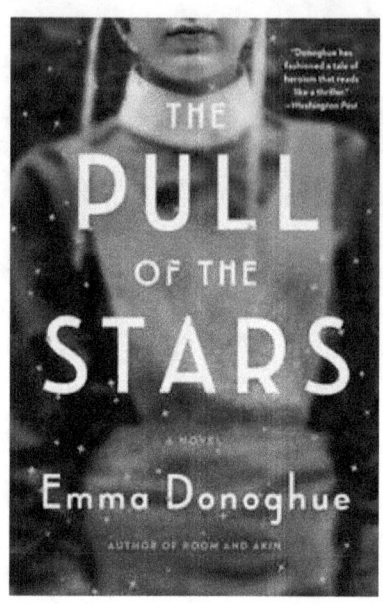

THE PULL OF THE STARS

by Emma Donoghue

BookBrowse Rating: 5/5
Critics' Consensus: 4.5/5
Readers' Rating: 5/5

Published July 2021 in Paperback, 320 pages

Summary

In Dublin, 1918, a maternity ward at the height of the Great Flu is a small world of work, risk, death, and unlooked-for love, in "Donoghue's best novel since *Room*" (*Kirkus Reviews*).

In an Ireland doubly ravaged by war and disease, Nurse Julia Power works at an understaffed hospital in the city center, where expectant mothers who have come down with the terrible new Flu are quarantined together. Into Julia's regimented world step two outsiders -- Doctor Kathleen Lynn, a rumoured Rebel on the run from the police, and a young volunteer helper, Bridie Sweeney.

In the darkness and intensity of this tiny ward, over three days, these women change each other's lives in unexpected ways. They lose patients to this baffling pandemic, but they also shepherd new life into a fearful world. With tireless tenderness and humanity, carers and mothers alike somehow do their impossible work.

In *The Pull of the Stars*, Emma Donoghue once again finds the light in the darkness in this new classic of hope and survival against all odds.

BookBrowse Review

Set during the final months of World War I just as the so-called Spanish Flu was hitting its peak, *The Pull of the Stars* chronicles three harrowing days in a makeshift maternity ward in Dublin.

Julia Power is a skilled nurse working in a dangerously understaffed hospital in Ireland's capital. With the population already decimated by war, the arrival of a deadly flu pandemic is the last thing the hospital is equipped to deal with, but on a tiny improvised ward for heavily pregnant women who have contracted the virus, Julia continues to serve with compassion. Throughout the three intense days depicted in the novel, she is aided by Kathleen Lynn, a political radical and pioneering female doctor, and Bridie Sweeney, a novice volunteer with a tragic past and a big heart. The contrasting trauma and beauty of what they experience together will teach them as much about themselves as each other; their unwavering dedication a testament to the endurance of hope even in the darkest of times.

Donoghue succeeds in capturing the abject horror of a city blighted by the cumulative effects of war and disease. Though she never shies away from detailing the utter devastation racking people's bodies (indeed, there are several deeply upsetting and visceral sequences), there's a tenderness to Julia's perspective that grounds the narrative and stops it from tipping into gratuitous suffering. As well as being set against the backdrop of actual historic events, the inclusion of real-life doctor and rebel Kathleen Lynn further emphasizes the story's factual basis. Couple this with the author's sensitive handling of difficult subject matter and every instance of heartbreak feels earned.

The decision to focus on a restricted timeframe of just three days allows Donoghue to show how relentless a nurse's work really was during this time. Distressing scenes are presented in excruciating detail, drawn out to an almost painful extent, but this makes the vital tension-breaking moments of friendship, love and light all the more poignant and impactful.

Due to the intensity with which it attacked the immune system, the strain of flu spreading in 1918 was known to hit pregnant women particularly hard — their bodies already operating in overdrive. This often led to deadly complications for both mother and child. As such, parallels are drawn throughout the novel between the experiences playing out on Julia's ward and the brutality of the battles unfolding on mainland Europe. If men were suffering on the frontline in the name of freedom, women in maternity wards were paying an equal debt in blood, pain and misery to keep the spark of human hope alive.

Aside from the historical significance of being set at the crossroads between the war and the flu pandemic, the novel captures Ireland during a period of great transition socially. Women have just won the right to vote in elections for the first time and hospitals are finally employing female doctors. And yet, tensions remain: nurses are still denied decision-making power, their medical expertise underestimated; Catholics and Protestants are still at loggerheads; controversial mother-and-baby homes continue to exploit society's most vulnerable by separating unmarried women from their children; soldiers are returning from the trenches with PTSD; and the fight for political independence from the UK leads to violent protests and bitter division. All of these notions are woven into the narrative in a seamless way that grants them equal room to breathe. The novel serves as a fascinating window into Irish society at the time and reflects the idea that life endures in all its nuance and complexity no matter the obstacles faced by the wider world.

The Pull of the Stars takes us from despair right through to euphoria and back again, but the presiding tone throughout is always fiercely feminine. Beyond the gripping narrative and its endearing characters, the book serves as a love letter to all the women who sacrifice themselves mind, body and soul in the name of caring for others — a theme that resonates as powerfully today as it ever did.

Reviewed by Callum McLaughlin. This review was originally published in *The BookBrowse Review* in August 2020, and has been updated for the October 2021 edition.

BEST BOOKS OF 2019

WITH THE FIRE ON HIGH

by Elizabeth Acevedo

BookBrowse Rating: 5/5
Critics' Consensus: 5/5
Readers' Rating: 5/5

Published March 2021 in Paperback, 416 pages

Summary

From the New York Times bestselling author of the National Book Award title The Poet X comes a dazzling novel in prose about a girl with talent, pride, and a drive to feed the soul that keeps her fire burning bright.

Ever since she got pregnant freshman year, Emoni Santiago's life has been about making the tough decisions—doing what has to be done for her daughter and her abuela. The one place she can let all that go is in the kitchen, where she adds a little something magical to everything she cooks, turning her food into straight-up goodness.

Even though she dreams of working as a chef after she graduates, Emoni knows that it's not worth her time to pursue the impossible. Yet despite the rules she thinks she has to play by, once Emoni starts cooking, her only choice is to let her talent break free.

BookBrowse Review

A teenage mother finds new horizons opening up before her when she signs up for a cooking class at school.

From *Like Water for Chocolate* to *Ratatouille*, writers have recognized the power of food to evoke strong feelings and nostalgic memories. Elizabeth Acevedo explores this theme in *With the Fire on High*, her second young adult novel after the multi-award winning *The Poet X*.

Emoni is a senior in a Philadelphia high school, and she has more on her plate than many of her classmates. She had a baby at the end of her freshman year, and has been raising little Emma (a.k.a. "Babygirl") with the help of her grandmother. Emma's father is present in their lives—but maybe a little too forcefully present, especially when a new boy enters the picture. Emoni's mother died when she was very young, after which her father, more interested in social causes than his own family, returned to Puerto Rico. Bringing all these issues to a head is a new culinary elective, perfect for Emoni's natural talents in the kitchen, which opens up unexpected educational and professional horizons.

Teen parenthood is not a new subject in YA novels, but *With the Fire on High* offers a refreshing perspective. Raising a baby has certainly changed Emoni's life, and Babygirl is the center of her world, but at heart she is an ordinary high school senior who opted out of a "special" teen parent track in favor of a regular school day and curriculum. She has an amazing support system to help her with Emma, from her beloved, young-at-heart grandmother; to her lesbian best friend Angelica; and even her ex Tyrone and his overbearing mother, who have partial custody of Emma. Emoni is building a life for herself that is self-affirming as well as loving and positive for her baby. Her growing relationship with patient, gentle Malachi, her new beau, inspires hope that Emoni will eventually open herself up to love as well, despite her less-than-stellar experience with selfish Tyrone.

Food is at the center of the novel. Emoni has a natural gift for pairing flavors—especially Caribbean flavors—that do not ordinarily go together, tweaking classic recipes and making them her own. And her creative recipes act on the diner's brain and heart as well as the tongue, evoking long-forgotten memories and feelings. Her teacher, Chef Ayden, guides her to a respect for the essential basics of food preparation and cooking, while recognizing his pupil's extraordinary gift. Each of the book's three sections include one of Emoni's simpler recipes, all of which figure into the story itself.

Elizabeth Acevedo's previous novel, *The Poet X*, was written in verse; *With the Fire on High* is prose, but the writing is still very lyrical—sometimes as lush as a warm and sunny Caribbean afternoon in the midst of a Philadelphia winter. The author is as much a master of language as Emoni is a master of food. Even the cover art, with its blood oranges, vanilla flowers and fresh herbs, is evocatively mouth-watering.

In Emoni, Acevedo has created a strong, creative, resourceful urban Latina whose story will resonate with both teen readers and adults.

Reviewed by Catherine M Andronik. This review was originally published in *The BookBrowse Review* in July 2019, and has been updated for the April 2021 edition.

BECOMING

by Michelle Obama

BookBrowse Rating: 5/5
Critics' Consensus: 5/5
Readers' Rating: 5/5

Published March 2021 in Paperback, 464 pages

Summary

Winner of the 2019 BookBrowse Nonfiction Award

An intimate, powerful, and inspiring memoir by the former First Lady of the United States.

In a life filled with meaning and accomplishment, Michelle Obama has emerged as one of the most iconic and compelling women of our era. As First Lady of the United States of America - the first African-American to serve in that role - she helped create the most welcoming and inclusive White House in history, while also establishing herself as a powerful advocate for women and girls in the U.S. and around the world, dramatically changing the ways that families pursue healthier and more active lives, and standing with her husband as he led America through some of its most harrowing moments. Along the way, she showed us a few dance moves, crushed Carpool Karaoke, and raised two down-to-earth daughters under an unforgiving media glare.

In her memoir, a work of deep reflection and mesmerizing storytelling, Michelle Obama invites readers into her world, chronicling the experiences that have shaped her - from her childhood on the South Side of Chicago to her years as an executive balancing the demands of motherhood and work, to her time spent at the world's most famous address. With unerring honesty and lively wit, she describes her triumphs and her disappointments, both public and private, telling her full story as she has lived it - in her own words and on her own terms. Warm, wise, and revelatory, *Becoming* is the deeply personal reckoning of a woman of soul and substance who has steadily defied expectations - and whose story inspires us to do the same.

BookBrowse Review

Former First Lady Michelle Obama offers insight into her life and mind, discussing her education and career, motherhood, and maintaining decorum during politically divisive times.

Voted 2019 Best Nonfiction Award Winner by BookBrowse Subscribers

BookBrowse hosted a Book Club discussion early in 2019 about Michelle Obama's memoir *Becoming*, and participants overwhelmingly expressed their appreciation for the book. Here are some highlights from that discussion.

What it's about:

In *Becoming*, former First Lady Michelle Obama narrates her life story, from her upbringing in South Side Chicago, to her education at Princeton and Harvard, to meeting and marrying President Barack Obama. She further narrates the Obamas' eight years in the White House, explaining how she managed to juggle raising children with affairs of state, while also keeping her trademark composure and positive attitude in the face of criticism.

Many Book Club participants admired Mrs. Obama's honesty and candor:

Her decision to take a different path was inspiring, and she made some difficult choices. It's not easy to walk away from expectations that others have for you. Her honesty throughout the book was very refreshing (Auntie Mame). I was surprised when I got insight into their personal life issues and problems, such as marital difficulties. I feel many normal couples go through these things and they are very relatable (theavidbookerfly). It surprised me when she admitted she disliked being a lawyer, and I admired her courage to switch her "horizons" to working with the people. Her involvement with Public Allies impressed me. She utilized her inherent talents and expanded those assets with future projects, always with the idea of 'uplifting' people to believe in themselves (kathrynb). I found her memoir astounding. She writes with such honesty, passion and love. She recalls her feelings about her miscarriage, the deaths of her father and her friend Suzanne, and the difficulties in her marriage. She is also very funny and clear-eyed about trying to find a balance between career and motherhood (barbarae).

Readers also thought the former First Lady was a remarkably good writer:

I guess it's no surprise that someone who excelled in academics and in life is so skilled with the written word. *Becoming* was informative without being stuffy, casual without being chatty and so well-crafted overall (paulak). Michelle has always been one of my favorite First Ladies and now I feel I know her even better. The book is very well written and I felt like I was right in the moment with her and her girls (RuthEh).

Many commenters felt like *Becoming* helped them get to know Mrs. Obama on a personal level:

By the time I finished the book I felt as if I had just had a wonderful conversation with a friend (PTK). I really enjoyed it. She writes very well. She is very honest about her life and her family. It was like having a chat with a friend (karenrn). I felt I really got to know what kind of person Michelle was/is beyond her public life and image, and I found a woman who, like all of us, has had her share of ups and downs in life. She has shown us that "becoming" is always a work in progress (pate). I thoroughly enjoyed her story and the way she expressed it. I feel like I have gotten a wonderful glimpse into her life and it left me wanting to know what she is planning to do next. After reading *Becoming*, there's one thing I do know—she is definitely someone I would love to hang out and share ideas with (jamiek).

Overall, readers were very enthusiastic:

I could not have loved this book more than I did. It was presented in such a way that when I was finished, I felt I had full knowledge of what made Michelle tick (Carol R). It was like meeting a new friend and over time getting to know her through revelations of the stages of her life. It was easy and still thought-provoking (katherinep). I love Michelle Obama and I loved her book. She is a class act and it came through in her writing (djn). I found her memoir astounding. She writes with such honesty, passion, and love (barbarae). This is a fabulous, informative and uplifting book. I always had a good impression of Michelle Obama and this book enhanced it. I felt that Michelle really shared herself with her readers and offered an intimate look at her life (Lois I).

Reviewed by First Impressions Reviewers. This review first ran in the December 4, 2019 issue of BookBrowse Recommends.

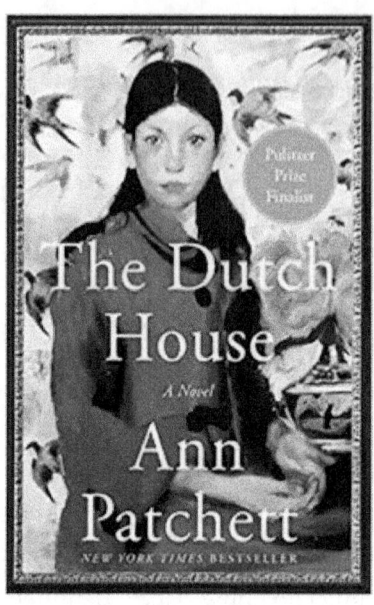

THE DUTCH HOUSE

by Ann Patchett

BookBrowse Rating: 5/5
Critics' Consensus: 4.5/5
Readers' Rating: 5/5

Published January 2021 in Paperback, 352 pages

Summary

Ann Patchett, the *New York Times* bestselling author of *Commonwealth* and *State of Wonder*, returns with her most powerful novel to date: a richly moving story that explores the indelible bond between two siblings, the house of their childhood, and a past that will not let them go.

"'Do you think it's possible to ever see the past as it actually was?' I asked my sister. We were sitting in her car, parked in front of the Dutch House in the broad daylight of early summer."

At the end of the Second World War, Cyril Conroy combines luck and a single canny investment to begin an enormous real estate empire, propelling his family from poverty to enormous wealth. His first order of business is to buy the Dutch House, a lavish estate in the suburbs outside of Philadelphia. Meant as a surprise for his wife, the house sets in motion the undoing of everyone he loves.

The story is told by Cyril's son Danny, as he and his older sister, the brilliantly acerbic and self-assured Maeve, are exiled from the house where they grew up by their stepmother. The two wealthy siblings are thrown back into the poverty their parents had escaped from and find that all they have to count on is one another. It is this unshakeable bond between them that both saves their lives and thwarts their futures.

Set over the course of five decades, *The Dutch House* is a dark fairy tale about two smart people who cannot overcome their past. Despite every outward sign of success, Danny and Maeve are only truly comfortable when they're together. Throughout their lives they return to the well-worn story of what they've lost with humor and rage. But when at last they're forced to confront the people who left them behind, the relationship between an indulged brother and his ever-protective sister is finally tested.

The Dutch House is the story of a paradise lost, a tour de force that digs deeply into questions of inheritance, love and forgiveness, of how we want to see ourselves and of who we really are. Filled with suspense, you may read it quickly to find out what happens, but what happens to Danny and Maeve will stay with you for a very long time.

BookBrowse Review

A pair of siblings with a close bond lean on each other throughout a lifetime of bitterness over the stepmother that wronged them, returning again and again to their childhood home.

The Dutch House is my introduction to Ann Patchett, which, after reading it, surprises me. I had only heard of her in passing, while always on the way to another author, another novel, never really turning her way. Why did it take me so long to discover her? As I see it now, Patchett is one of those novelists, like John Irving or Anne Tyler, who come to you at just the right time, when you didn't even know you needed them. During that initial encounter with the author, you realize that they're crucial to you in that time, a gentle guide through whatever problems you've been facing. They give you characters going through similar situations, not for comparison, as if to say, "Oh, I'm so glad that's not me," but to give hope. These characters have endured and have come through, and so will you.

> There are a few times in life when you leap up and the past that you'd been standing on falls away behind you, and the future you mean to land on is not yet in place, and for a moment you're suspended, knowing nothing and no one, not even yourself." - Danny Conry, *The Dutch House*

The main feature of the novel is the titular historical home, perched just outside Philadelphia, around which the lives of close siblings Danny and Maeve Conroy, seven years apart, revolve in a 50-year span. The house is so named because of the Dutch husband-and-wife VanHoebeeks who built and owned it from the end of World War I to the end of World War II. The siblings' father, Cyril, a burgeoning building magnate, bought it for their mother Elna, believing she would love it, but he was dead wrong. She hated every moment she was there and eventually left the family. Since their emotionally-unavailable father was not up to the task, Maeve was then forced to raise Danny largely on her own.

Their lives become even more complicated when Cyril marries Andrea. She brings her daughters, Norma and Bright, in tow, and it becomes clear early on she only married Cyril to have the house. When Cyril suddenly dies, Andrea feels no further obligation toward his children. She sends Danny away to stay with Maeve, who is already living on her own. The siblings soon realize Andrea now owns the house and their father's building business, and what follows is a delicate ballet of the two trying to forge ahead. Life goes on, because it has to. Danny endures medical school in New York City, simply because Maeve wants to drain the educational trust their father set up for all the children so there's nothing left for Norma and Bright. And time and time again, the siblings find themselves sitting together in cars of various makes over the years, looking at the Dutch House from the street. The varying descriptions of the house, inside and outside, before and after the siblings' exile, are atmospheric. It looms over everything that goes on, and it's easy to see why Danny and Maeve have remained so deeply affected by it (though the trauma of their mother leaving likely contributed to this as well).

Patchett has considerable talent for unobtrusive writing; she doesn't call attention to what the reader should know, trusting that we'll pick up on certain cues. The years in the novel intertwine in such a way that the present often darts right back into the past and vice versa, and in less capable hands, it would be confusing. The story is so deeply absorbing, it hardly feels like years and years of the protagonists' lives are passing before your eyes. This is also the kind of novel you might put down many times after a certain line or two, thinking back to your own experiences and wondering how she could possibly know a piece of your life or your family so well.

A little over three months ago, my father died of colon cancer, leaving behind me, my mother and my sister, five years younger than me. While his chemotherapy sessions and many hospital stays felt like dress rehearsals for what we knew was coming, his death was still devastating, much like Patchett portrays it here. She illustrates how completely numbing it can be, too. In fact, through all the paperwork and legal clean-up duties I had to do after he died, reading *The Dutch House* was the first time I was able to sit down and think about what I had been through, what I felt, alongside Danny and Maeve dealing with the aftermath of their father's death. I'm grateful to Ann Patchett for the time and space to work out tangled tentacles of emotions that I might not have processed at length outside these 352 pages.

The Dutch House is an exceptional journey for those who might not have siblings, especially heartfelt for those who do, and gives me a little more courage to keep going. That's the greatest gift a book can give.

Reviewed by Rory L. Aronsky. This review was originally published in *The BookBrowse Review* in October 2019, and has been updated for the January 2021 edition.

THE WATER DANCER

by Ta-Nehisi Coates

BookBrowse Rating: 4/5
Critics' Consensus: 4.5/5

Published November 2020 in Paperback, 432 pages

Summary

In his boldly imagined first novel, Ta-Nehisi Coates, the National Book Award–winning author of *Between the World and Me,* brings home the most intimate evil of enslavement: the cleaving and separation of families.

Young Hiram Walker was born into bondage. When his mother was sold away, Hiram was robbed of all memory of her—but was gifted with a mysterious power. Years later, when Hiram almost drowns in a river, that same power saves his life. This brush with death births an urgency in Hiram and a daring scheme: to escape from the only home he's ever known.

So begins an unexpected journey that takes Hiram from the corrupt grandeur of Virginia's proud plantations to desperate guerrilla cells in the wilderness, from the coffin of the deep South to dangerously utopic movements in the North. Even as he's enlisted in the underground war between slavers and the enslaved, Hiram's resolve to rescue the family he left behind endures.

This is the dramatic story of an atrocity inflicted on generations of women, men, and children—the violent and capricious separation of families—and the war they waged to simply make lives with the people they loved. Written by one of today's most exciting thinkers and writers, *The Water Dancer* is a propulsive, transcendent work that restores the humanity of those from whom everything was stolen.

BookBrowse Review

National Book Award-winning author Ta-Nehisi Coates' much-anticipated first novel is a dynamic slave narrative with a tinge of the supernatural.

For close to two decades, Ta-Nehisi Coates has been two writers. There's the celebrated essayist and author of influential nonfiction works, including the National Book Award-winning *Between the World and Me*, written as a heart-wrenching letter to his son about the realities of being Black in America. Then there's Coates the successful comic book writer, who in 2016 reinvigorated Marvel's floundering Black Panther series a couple of years before the character clawed his way to pop culture phenomenon status in a $1 billion grossing blockbuster. (The author has since taken on Marvel's goody two-shoes poster boy Captain America.)

Now, with the launch of *The Water Dancer*, we have the long-awaited third string to Coates' writer-bow – the novelist. If you were a betting person, you might have put money on Coates' major fiction debut to arrive weighted with the gravitas of his nonfiction best. Surprisingly, the novel attempts to merge both the author's political and comic book worlds, but ends up skewing towards the caped crusader camp, albeit without the genre's penchant for crotch-tight spandex.

What begins as an antebellum South slave narrative that's all wispy Toni Morrison-esque flourishes, drifts into a tale of espionage and rescue, before suddenly, in the blink of an eye, revealing itself to have been a version of a superhero origin story all along. There's even a sprinkling of meta-human powers thrown in for good measure. The about-turns are clunky, but it somehow pulls together in the end.

Hiram Walker is born a biracial slave on the tobacco plantation of Lockless, Virginia. After his mother is sold off, his plantation owner father takes pity on young Hiram and invites him to live in the big house as the servant to his airheaded half-brother Maynard. Years later, the two brothers almost drown and, through the accident, Hiram discovers strange gifts within him connected to the water, his highly-developed photographic memory and a mysterious blue mist. On recovering, he resolves to escape Lockless and his enslavement.

Hiram's grueling search for freedom leads him to the Underground, a secret society whose mission is to smuggle slaves from the deep South to the safety of the North. As an Underground agent, Hiram works tirelessly to rescue the loved ones he has left behind in Virginia, while striving to master the primitive power he possesses known as Conduction, which could facilitate the emancipation of thousands of slaves.

For all its supernatural dealings, *The Water Dancer* is, oddly, quite a formally voiced book. Told in the first person from Hiram's point of view, the writing is taut and precise, almost Victorian in tone. Perhaps this is meant to echo the style of two of Hiram's favorite books - indeed the only two explicitly named - Sir Walter Scott's historical romance novels *Ivanhoe* and *Rob Roy*. It certainly has an adventurous and exciting rhythm. But what's gained in pace is lost somewhat in emotion.

Hiram is noble, patient, stoic. Too stoic to be moved at times. This is a man who is beaten and broken, who suffers and is witness to immense atrocities. Yet, as readers, we're kept at bay from his anguish. The formality of the writing doesn't help here. You wish Coates would have allowed Hiram to unbridle his frustrations more, to unleash a fire-and-brimstone fury upon his subjugators. Instead, there are too many instances where feelings are bottled up and hurts are needlessly left unsaid.

Coates skillfully explores the many horrors of slavery. Through his journeys, Hiram comes in contact with countless former slaves who share their heartbreaking stories in great detail. These voices widen the scope, and it's in these testimonials where this novel truly comes alive.

The sensitive representation of female characters and their gender specific persecutions during the 1800s is also to be commended. When Hiram discloses his love for Sophia, a black slave mistress owned by a neighboring plantation owner, she lets her feelings on marriage be known: "Ain't no freedom for a woman in trading a white man for a colored." Later in the North, Hiram observes two shaven-headed proto-suffragettes who "essayed on the rights of women to appear with all the freedoms of men, in all the same spheres." Then there's Moses, a sort of Conduction sorceress supreme who befriends Hiram: "Knives melt upon the garments of Moses. Bullwhips turn to ash in the slave-master's hand." She may be a contrivance, but it is joyous to read a powerful female character loom large in a world dominated by male slavers.

Those waiting for Coates' great state-of-the-nation novel will have to wait a while longer it seems. For now they'll have to settle on this fantasy-tinged neo-slave narrative that is quietly touching in its strange ways.

Reviewed by Dean Muscat. This review was originally published in *The BookBrowse Review* in October 2019, and has been updated for the December 2019 edition.

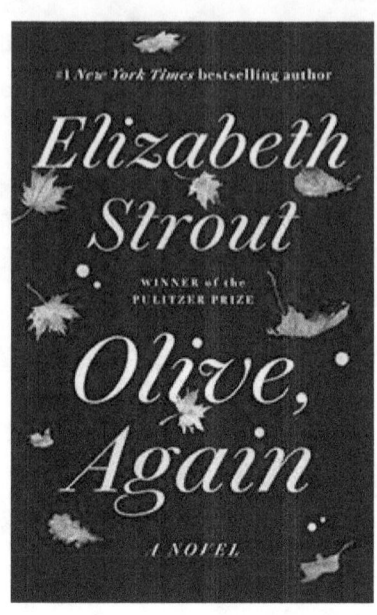

OLIVE, AGAIN

by Elizabeth Strout

BookBrowse Rating: 5/5
Critics' Consensus: 5/5
Readers' Rating: 5/5

Published November 2020 in Paperback, 320 pages

Summary

Winner of the 2019 BookBrowse Fiction Award

Prickly, wry, resistant to change yet ruthlessly honest and deeply empathetic, Olive Kitteridge is "a compelling life force" (*San Francisco Chronicle*).

The *New Yorker* has said that Elizabeth Strout "animates the ordinary with an astonishing force," and she has never done so more clearly than in these pages, where the iconic Olive struggles to understand not only herself and her own life but the lives of those around her in the town of Crosby, Maine. Whether with a teenager coming to terms with the loss of her father, a young woman about to give birth during a hilariously inopportune moment, a nurse who confesses a secret high school crush, or a lawyer who struggles with an inheritance she does not want to accept, the unforgettable Olive will continue to startle us, to move us, and to inspire moments of transcendent grace.

BookBrowse Review

In a long-awaited sequel to the Pulitzer Prize-winning *Olive Kitteridge*, Elizabeth Strout revisits the curmudgeonly Olive as she remarries and approaches very old age.

Voted 2019 Best Fiction Award Winner by BookBrowse Subscribers

2019 was a big year for literary sequels, with the publications of *Find Me* by André Aciman, *The Testaments* by Margaret Atwood and *Olive, Again* by Elizabeth Strout. In all three cases, readers have had to wait more than a decade to return to a familiar setting and set of characters—but in the meantime there has been a film or television adaptation to tide them over. It was 11 years ago that we first met Olive Kitteridge, a grumpy retired math teacher in the fictional town of Crosby, Maine, through the Pulitzer Prize-winning *Olive Kitteridge* (2008).

Like several of Strout's novels, this sequel is a collection of linked short stories. The stories are connected by the Maine setting and by references to Olive, who is often the main character but sometimes only mentioned in passing, such as through a piece of advice she gave her math students several decades ago, or a brief encounter with a local acquaintance. All is not cozy in this small town; Crosby's residents are struggling with illness, addiction, dementia, domestic violence, poverty and ailing marriages. Yet Strout balances out tragedy with humor, as in "The End of the Civil War Days," a story about a husband and wife who have barely spoken in 35 years—they even divided their house down the middle with yellow duct tape—but are reunited by their mutual dismay about their daughter's unconventional career choice.

If it's been years since you've read *Olive Kitteridge*, you may want to reread its final story, "River," as the sequel picks up immediately where this one left off. (That said, Strout provides enough background information that familiarity with the first book is not an absolute requirement.) After her pharmacist husband Henry dies in a nursing home following a stroke, Olive entertains the prospect of a romance with widower Jack Kennison. The challenge of adjusting to a second marriage with someone who exasperates you is a major theme of *Olive, Again*. For starters, Jack is a Republican, while Olive is an outspoken Democrat. "God, Olive, you're a *difficult* woman," Jack exclaims just before he proposes. Although he wishes she "could be a little less Olive," he is sure they should get married—"Because I love you," he says, "and we don't have much time."

As Olive drifts from her 70s into her 80s, the ravages of old age become inescapable. She faces the return of widowhood—along with infirmity and the specter of death—with her usual mixture of stoicism and bad temper. You may hear more about her bowels than you'd like, but Strout, it seems, is determined to be realistic about the indignities of aging. Crucially, Olive has started, very late in life, to have compassion for others, including her daughter-in-law and the caregivers she meets after her heart attack. "Tell me what it's like to be you," she requests of her Somali nurse; "You're having a hell of a time," she says to a former student with cancer. Comparing other people's lives with her own, she realizes how lucky she's been. Yet somehow that doesn't make preparing for death any easier.

Besides Olive Kitteridge, there are references to a couple of other Strout novels. In the story "Exiles," Bob and Jim Burgess of *The Burgess Boys* (2013) are reunited in Maine, while in the final piece, "Friend," Olive befriends a new fellow nursing home resident, who turns out to be Isabelle Daignault of *Amy and Isabelle* (1998). The connections, not just between the Olive stories, but also across Strout's various novels, are satisfying; readers who are reasonably new to Strout will undoubtedly be compelled to seek out her other work.

Older characters are still fairly rare in literature (see Beyond the Book), so it's refreshing to encounter a protagonist in her 80s. Crosby feels like a microcosm of modern society, with Olive as our Everywoman guide. She hasn't lost her faculties or her spirit, but the approach of death lends added poignancy to her story. "I am scared to death to die, is the truth," she tells a former student. Nor has she figured it all out by the end of the book: "*I do not have a clue who I have been. Truthfully, I do not understand a thing,*" she thinks. Haven't we all felt the same at some point? Strout is a master of psychological acuity and mixing hope with the darkness. Those who are wary of sequels need not fear: *Olive, Again* is even better than *Olive Kitteridge*, and one of the most profound and worthwhile books of the year.

Reviewed by Rebecca Foster. This review was originally published in *The BookBrowse Review* in December 2019, and has been updated for the November 2020 edition.

BUTTERFLY YELLOW

by Thanhha Lai

BookBrowse Rating: 5/5
Critics' Consensus: 5/5

Published October 2020 in Paperback, 320 pages

Summary

Winner of the 2019 BookBrowse Award for Best Young Adult Novel

Perfect for fans of Elizabeth Acevedo, Ibi Zoboi, and Erika L. Sanchez, this gorgeously written and deeply moving own voices novel is the YA debut from the award-winning author of *Inside Out & Back Again*.

In the final days of the Việt Nam War, Hằng takes her little brother, Linh, to the airport, determined to find a way to safety in America. In a split second, Linh is ripped from her arms—and Hằng is left behind in the war-torn country.

Six years later, Hằng has made the brutal journey from Việt Nam and is now in Texas as a refugee. She doesn't know how she will find the little brother who was taken from her until she meets LeeRoy, a city boy with big rodeo dreams, who decides to help her.

Hằng is overjoyed when she reunites with Linh. But when she realizes he doesn't remember her, their family, or Việt Nam, her heart is crushed. Though the distance between them feels greater than ever, Hằng has come so far that she will do anything to bridge the gap.

BookBrowse Review

Set in 1981, a Vietnamese refugee seeks her little brother in Texas with the help of a wannabe rodeo star in this radiant YA debut.

Voted 2019 Best Young Adult Award Winner by BookBrowse Subscribers

As readers, many of us hope for lasting images from books, for thoughts expressed by authors that might match what we've believed in our souls, but couldn't articulate ourselves. Encounters with books like these become deeply imprinted.

Butterfly Yellow, the young adult debut of Thanhhà Lại, author of two highly-acclaimed books for middle grade readers, offers all of that and more. Born from the ashes of the Vietnam War, it gently, poetically reminds us that the current national clamor and debate over immigrants and refugees arriving in the United States is nothing new. The book is not overtly political, though; Lai is more interested in exhibiting human kindness and understanding.

This poignant, heartfelt novel begins in the summer of 1981 from the perspective of 18-year-old LeeRoy (whose given name is Leslie Dwight

Cooper), a longtime Texas resident with University of Texas professor parents. He started going by "Lee" in junior high after being teased on the playground, and added Roy, after his grandfather, on the very day the story begins. After graduating high school, LeeRoy sets out to follow and emulate his hero, rodeo bareback rider Bruce Ford. Nothing is going to stop him, not even his lack of experience with animals, which he tries to gloss over with a brand-new outfit and Ford F-350 truck.

Real life interferes in a convenience store parking lot when a Good Samaritan couple suddenly thrusts upon him the responsibility of driving a stranded Vietnamese refugee to Amarillo. Hằng was separated from her brother a little over six years earlier, and believes he ended up in Amarillo after being swept up in Operation Babylift (see Beyond the Book), a government program that sought to bring Vietnamese orphans to the United States (though these particular siblings were not actually orphans). Hằng's younger brother was taken, but at 12, she was rejected for being too old. After that came an escape from Vietnam on a small, overcrowded fishing boat, and a horrific experience on an island. Hằng made it to a refugee processing camp in the Philippines, and was eventually sent to the U.S. under Extreme Trauma status to stay with family who had gotten out of Vietnam long before; she was with them for only a day before going in search of her brother. This backstory is gracefully interwoven throughout the book.

Wisely, Lại divides *Butterfly Yellow* between LeeRoy and Hằng's perspectives in order to capture her reactions to the new, strange country and vast Texas land she encounters, and his gradual acclimation to the unorthodox situation he's found himself in. Soon enough, LeeRoy forgets his Bruce Ford dreams as he gets more deeply involved in Hằng's quest to find her brother.

Besides the languid stretch of summer that Lại portrays so well — even as family drama mounts — her fascination with the English language gives *Butterfly Yellow* its lasting power. Ordinary moments provide touching beauty, such as Hằng speaking English phonetically in Vietnamese as she learns it, and lingering over the Vietnamese words she teaches LeeRoy. Lại bottles these moments in such a way that we also linger over them, not moving on to the next paragraph or the next chapter until we note how interesting it is that the word "trái," for example, is "fruit," and that a word placed after it characterizes the type, i.e. "trái mít" means "jackfruit." There's also a wondrous section in a chapter midway through about Hằng trying to understand more English by using word trees to break up each sentence, and the process involved.

Above all, *Butterfly Yellow* seeks to remind us that a genuine and profound human connection can happen anywhere, at any time, with anyone. It doesn't matter who we are or where we've come from; we are all human and therefore we already know something of each other.

Reviewed by Rory L. Aronsky. This review was originally published in *The BookBrowse Review* in October 2019, and has been updated for the November 2020 edition.

THE SEINE

by Elaine Sciolino

BookBrowse Rating: 5/5
Critics' Consensus: 5/5
Readers' Rating: 5/5

Published October 2020 in Paperback, 304 pages

Summary

A vibrant, enchanting tour of the Seine from longtime *New York Times* foreign correspondent and best-selling author Elaine Sciolino.

Elaine Sciolino came to Paris as a young foreign correspondent and was seduced by a river. In *The Seine*, she tells the story of that river from its source on a remote plateau of Burgundy to the wide estuary where its waters meet the sea, and the cities, tributaries, islands, ports, and bridges in between.

Sciolino explores the Seine through its rich history and lively characters: a bargewoman, a riverbank bookseller, a houseboat dweller, a famous cinematographer known for capturing the river's light. She discovers the story of Sequana—the Gallo-Roman healing goddess who gave the Seine its name—and follows the river through Paris, where it determined the city's destiny and now snakes through all aspects of daily life. She patrols with river police, rows with a restorer of antique boats, sips champagne at a vineyard along the river, and even dares to go for a swim. She finds the Seine in art, literature, music, and movies from Renoir and *Les Misérables* to Puccini and *La La Land*. Along the way, she reveals how the river that created Paris has touched her own life. A powerful afterword tells the dramatic story of how water from the depths of the Seine saved Notre-Dame from destruction during the devastating fire in April 2019.

A "storyteller at heart" (June Sawyers, *Chicago Tribune*) with a "sumptuous eye for detail" (Sinclair McKay, *Daily Telegraph*), Sciolino braids memoir, travelogue, and history through the Seine's winding route. *The Seine* offers a love letter to Paris and the most romantic river in the world, and invites readers to explore its magic for themselves.

BookBrowse Review

A vibrant tour of the Seine from a bestselling *New York Times* foreign correspondent based in France.

Of the 24 members who reviewed Elaine Sciolino's *The Seine: The River that Made Paris* for BookBrowse's First Impressions Program, 23 gave it a 4+ rating, for an overall average of 4.6 out of 5.

What it's about:

From the source of the Seine in Burgundy to its ultimate destination in the English Channel, Elaine Sciolino takes us on a glorious journey. We visit barge operators and people living on house boats, as well as vineyards, chateaus, and fascinating spots along the river in Paris (Joy E). The book covers topics such as the river's source, history, geographic features, influence on the arts, and iconic status as a symbol of Paris (Mary Jane D). There are stories of wineries, fishing, barge life, songs, and movies (Colleen T); readers will discover lots of well-researched facts and interesting historical anecdotes about what has drawn so many people to Paris and made the River Seine world renowned (Barbara O).

Many praised the book as detailed and well researched:

Sciolino has written an exhaustive volume, viewing the Seine from virtually every angle (Mary A). This history is rich and bound to entice anyone to at least imagine seeing this river in their lifetime, if only in the many films in which the Seine plays a part (M K). The book is filled with fascinating facts related to the River Seine (Sandra L). It is so thorough that it is most rewarding to take it in by small mouthfuls, so as to prolong the enjoyment and also to fully digest the information (Katherine P). Sciolono has stitched the past and present together into an easy-to-read story; the delights keep coming as she digs deeper, and it's a useful journey to take (Rory A). This is a marvelous history of a river and the people it has touched throughout the centuries (Christine B).

Readers enjoyed the stimulating style of writing:

Sciolino writes in a breezy and very engaging style, and she includes loads of interesting and little known details about the river (Barbara E). The beautiful way the book is written makes you feel that you are following the river (Veronica E). The writing style is easy to read and makes all the facts flow like a comprehensive story (Mary Jane D); the book has a journalistic style, but some portions actually read more like a novel than a travelogue (Susan N). Sciolino's love of every inch of the Seine, 777 kilometers (483 miles), shows in her lovely descriptions of the river (Lee M).

Overall, our readers loved *The Seine*:

As a Francophile, I enjoyed this book very much. It is very well written and filled with interesting facts and stories about the Seine (John A). It was a real treat to read this book! The author's passion for France and the Seine is very much apparent (Karen S). There are so many interesting things about the Seine that one would never think of. Even if one has never seen the river, the author brings it to life (Carolyn S). A good book prompts questions and explorations, and I can easily imagine a book group discussion on the many topics presented here (Mary G). I loved this fascinating exploration of the Seine (Carol C).

The book comes highly recommended, especially for travelers to France:

This wonderful book provides a rich history of the extraordinary places along this river (Deanna W). Every serious traveler to France should read this book before leaving home (Mary A); those traveling to France would find much to enhance their travels here (Chris W). I recommend this to romantics, travelers, history buffs and anyone else looking for a good book (Portia A).

Reviewed by First Impressions Reviewers. This review was originally published in *The BookBrowse Review* in October 2019, and has been updated for the November 2020 edition.

THE WORLD THAT WE KNEW

by Alice Hoffman

BookBrowse Rating: 5/5
Critics' Consensus: 5/5
Readers' Rating: 4/5

Published September 2020 in Paperback, 400 pages

Summary

In 1941, during humanity's darkest hour, three unforgettable young women must act with courage and love to survive, from the *New York Times* bestselling author of *The Dovekeepers* and *The Marriage of Opposites* Alice Hoffman.

In Berlin, at the time when the world changed, Hanni Kohn knows she must send her twelve-year-old daughter away to save her from the Nazi regime. She finds her way to a renowned rabbi, but it's his daughter, Ettie, who offers hope of salvation when she creates a mystical Jewish creature, a rare and unusual golem, who is sworn to protect Lea. Once Ava is brought to life, she and Lea and Ettie become eternally entwined, their paths fated to cross, their fortunes linked.

Lea and Ava travel from Paris, where Lea meets her soulmate, to a convent in western France known for its silver roses; from a school in a mountaintop village where three thousand Jews were saved. Meanwhile, Ettie is in hiding, waiting to become the fighter she's destined to be.

What does it mean to lose your mother? How much can one person sacrifice for love? In a world where evil can be found at every turn, we meet remarkable characters that take us on a stunning journey of loss and resistance, the fantastical and the mortal, in a place where all roads lead past the Angel of Death and love is never ending.

BookBrowse Review

This moving magical realist novel follows a group of teens as they resist Nazi forces and aid Jewish refugees in Europe at the height of WWII.

Alice Hoffman's sparkling prose and immersive descriptions of place summon readers into World War II. Chapters are place- and time-marked from 1941-1944, to guide readers through a suspenseful journey. Told by an omniscient narrator, the novel begins in Berlin, 1941, and swiftly moves to France, where Nazis control most of the territory including Paris. Typical of stories set during wartime, there is much death. Yet, the novel also flows with lyrical imagery, and flashes of magical realism are common. A few supporting characters—the Angel of Death, a heron, and a golem—reveal explicit magical powers, while the leads all have what I call "ordinary-super powers," exhibiting traits such as bravery under trying circumstances. As the plot unfolds, Hoffman chronicles many forms of resistance and develops a vivid cast of characters, most of them teens; they are often separated, but reconnect in unexpected, memorable ways.

Ettie, 17, German-born daughter of a rabbi, has one of the strongest arcs. Near the story's start she embraces prayer and sacred ritual to create a magical being from clay, a golem named Ava. She casts the golem spell in order to show off her intellect, and also to protect a neighbor's child, Lea, from Nazi forces. The pragmatic teen also bargains for jewels and two train tickets to Paris, intending to run away from Berlin with her little sister, Marta. Neither sister arrives to Paris. Marta is killed, and Ettie decides to seek revenge. She dedicates herself to the Resistance, and remains empowered by her faith.

Brothers Victor, 17, and Julien, 14, Lévi develop distinctly different qualities. Victor, physically strong and daring, runs away from his wealthy Parisian family to join friends in the Jewish Resistance. They use lessons from science class to build explosives and set traps for Nazis and the Milice (French militia collaborating with Nazis). Julien is the quieter brother, training to be a mathematician. His analytical skills prove useful in imagining strategies for escape and survival. When Julien finds temporary refuge in a boarding school for children whose parents were deported to Nazi camps, he tutors kids in math; he also turns to the arts for comfort and develops his own talents as an artist and writer.

Berlin-born Lea, by contrast, embodies heroic powers of endurance. From age 12, she faces trauma after her father is killed and a soldier assaults her. Lea's mother sends her away, to stay with relatives who might protect her in Paris. In order to survive, Lea invokes deep memories and the fables her mother, Hanni, and grandmother, Bobeshi, have often told her:

> She understood her grandmother's stories. Demons were on the streets. They wore brown uniforms, they took whatever they wanted, they were cold-blooded, even though they looked like young men. This is why Lea must learn how to survive.

In Paris, Lea befriends Julien, who happens to be her distant cousin. Their friendship grows to love, and the power of love fortifies them, even as the plot thickens with danger.

Lea's plot involves many magical realist elements. Whenever she and Julien are separated, a magical heron carries messages and sketches between them, carrier-pigeon style. The heron is also devoted to Ava, the super-human golem created by Ettie's magical ritual to be Lea's guardian. Ava appears to be an ordinary woman; yet she can talk with birds and defeat enemies with a glance—or if that fails, with her physical strength. She is also a healer. Her entire destiny is to be a surrogate mother, protecting Lea and her allies. The relationship between Ava and Lea becomes especially complex and nuanced as the novel advances.

Marianne, a maid at the Lévi home in Paris, shares the other protagonists' fortitude. Early in the novel, she returns to her home in rural Haute-Loire to help her ailing father manage. Marianne's an expert in rural, earthy skills, able to make do with scarcity, to see in the dark, to navigate difficult terrain, to endure extreme weather. She's devoted to her father, and equally dedicated to the Allies when she joins the Resistance. Marianne's unique skillset allows her to help guide refugee children to safety in Switzerland. Marianne also embraces the power of love; she and Victor become lovers despite barriers of class and religion that might impede their affair if not for wartime.

Ordinary heroes are omnipresent in the novel, including priests, nuns, teachers, and farmers who shelter children and families on the run. Dr. Girard secretly passes messages between members of the Resistance, while also healing the sick and wounded. He mentors Ettie in both callings. I bonded with every character; of course, many don't survive.

Despite the painful wartime setting, full of sorrow and family separations, the beauty of Hoffman's prose and themes delivers a sense of hope. Even if humanity continues to engage in war and atrocity, the novel suggests, perhaps art, stories, and love can endure. There are parallels between the protagonists' bravery and today's wave of teen activism, for example, those committed to #UnitedWeDream or #MarchForOurLives and other global movements. Juxtaposing historical fact with a well-crafted story, *The World That We Knew* is sure to appeal to readers new to Alice Hoffman's work as well as her longtime fans.

Reviewed by Karen Lewis. This review was originally published in *The BookBrowse Review* in October 2019, and has been updated for the October 2020 edition.

THE TESTAMENTS

by Margaret Atwood

BookBrowse Rating: 5/5
Critics' Consensus: 4.5/5
Readers' Rating: 5/5

Published September 2020 in Paperback, 448 pages

Summary

In this brilliant sequel to *The Handmaid's Tale,* acclaimed author Margaret Atwood answers the questions that have tantalized readers for decades.

When the van door slammed on Offred's future at the end of *The Handmaid's Tale*, readers had no way of telling what lay ahead for her—freedom, prison or death.

With *The Testaments*, the wait is over.

Margaret Atwood's sequel picks up the story fifteen years after Offred stepped into the unknown, with the explosive testaments of three female narrators from Gilead.

"Dear Readers: Everything you've ever asked me about Gilead and its inner workings is the inspiration for this book. Well, almost everything! The other inspiration is the world we've been living in." —Margaret Atwood

BookBrowse Review

Margaret Atwood's *The Testaments* returns to the Republic of Gilead first envisioned in *The Handmaid's Tale*. Whereas her 1985 work examined how totalitarian regimes gain control; here, she explores how they fail.

The Handmaid's Tale is narrated by Offred (known by no other name throughout the book, although the popular Hulu series gives her the moniker "June") and ends with the heroine getting into a black van, fate unknown. Although many readers had hoped for a continuation of this compelling woman's story, in *The Testaments* the author (probably wisely) chooses to continue Gilead's story 15 years after the events in the earlier book, employing three different female narrators. Two of these are teenagers, one raised within the male-dominated Gilead to be an obedient Wife, the other raised in Toronto, Canada, learning to hate the system created by her neighbors to the south. The third woman will be familiar to Atwood's readers and fans of the TV series: the formidable Aunt Lydia, who runs the Red Center, where she indoctrinates young women into becoming submissive Handmaids, enslaved fertile women who are to be impregnated by high-ranking Commanders whose Wives are infertile. It's this third voice that fills in the gaps in Atwood's earlier work, exploring how an intelligent, educated woman could be coerced into supporting a repressive regime.

Atwood brilliantly captures the two teenagers' voices, describing with complete authenticity that age when people often feel like they know everything but at the same time are vulnerable and insecure. The highlight, though is her portrayal of Aunt Lydia – older, wiser, more manipulative, and able to control her higher-ups and influence her place within the system. Although responsible for enforcing the policies penned by the powers-that-be, she doesn't embrace them. She has, however, learned how to survive within the toxic political regime, avoiding the purges that periodically thin the ranks of her male cohorts. She thrives on information and knows how to use it to better her position. I found her to be one of Atwood's most complex and compelling creations to-date.

The Testaments is without a doubt a five-star book; it's well-written, it's entertaining, and it moves extremely well. It's inevitable, though, that it will be compared to *The Handmaid's Tale*, and frankly it falls short of the bar. Atwood's earlier work is a more challenging book to read; it was frightening when it first came out, and in rereading it some 30-plus years later, it seems eerily prescient, far too accurate, and way too possible. It has depth, and I believe it ranks right up there with classic dystopian novels such as George Orwell's *1984*.

The Testaments may prove prophetic as well, but right now it feels too juvenile, too directed at a younger audience, and too positive and hopeful at the end.

For those curious, Atwood did work with the producers of the award-winning TV series, which moves well beyond events in *The Handmaid's Tale*, to make sure her current book dovetailed with where they were headed with their scripts (for example, they weren't allowed to kill off Aunt Lydia, since she's the star of the current novel). I can't help but feel this influenced Atwood's ultimate product, resulting in a book that feels somewhat predictable and, ultimately, less impactful; novels with a happy ending are entertaining and popular, but seldom are they the ones that provoke societal awareness and change.

Atwood, the author of over 40 books in various genres, is a master of the speculative fiction format (defined as a future that could happen with our existing technology, in contrast to science fiction, which relies on technology that hasn't been invented yet, such as speed-of-light space travel). *The Testaments* will surely please readers who appreciate this genre, particularly those who enjoy female-empowering stories such as *The Hunger Games* or *Divergent*. It's entertaining, and while not up to the standard of her earlier novel, still very much worth a read.

Reviewed by Kim Kovacs. This review was originally published in *The BookBrowse Review* in October 2019, and has been updated for the September 2020 edition.

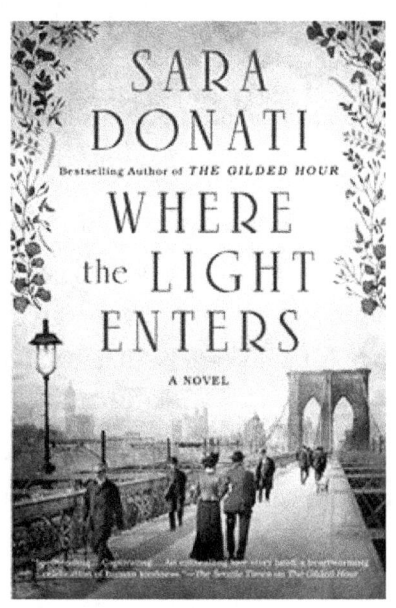

WHERE THE LIGHT ENTERS

by Sara Donati

BookBrowse Rating: 5/5
Critics' Consensus: 4.5/5
Readers' Rating: 5/5

Published August 2020 in Paperback, 672 pages

Summary

From the international bestselling author of *The Gilded Hour* comes Sara Donati's enthralling epic about two trailblazing female doctors in nineteenth-century New York.

Obstetrician Dr. Sophie Savard returns home to the achingly familiar rhythms of Manhattan in the early spring of 1884 to rebuild her life after the death of her husband. With the help of Dr. Anna Savard, her dearest friend, cousin, and fellow physician she plans to continue her work aiding the disadvantaged women society would rather forget.

As Sophie sets out to construct a new life for herself, Anna's husband, Detective-Sergeant Jack Mezzanotte calls on them both to consult on two new cases: the wife of a prominent banker has disappeared into thin air, and the corpse of a young woman is found with baffling wounds that suggest a killer is on the loose. In New York it seems that the advancement of women has brought out the worst in some men. Unable to ignore the plight of New York's less fortunate, these intrepid cousins draw on all resources to protect their patients.

BookBrowse Review

Having returned to New York, Dr. Sophie Savard and her cousin, fellow physician Anna, advise police on a murder case in this gripping historical drama.

In this thrilling follow-up to *The Gilded Hour*, doctors Sophie and Anna Savard take on a baffling murder case that leads them into the seedy underworld of 19th century New York. Dr. Sophie Savard has just returned from Europe after the death of her husband and is eager to continue her practice as an obstetrician in Manhattan. The year is 1884, and although great strides have been made in science and industry, the women's rights movement has yet to gain momentum. Basic health care needs unique to women, such as birth control (condoms and diaphragms were in use by this time, as well as an early version of the IUD) and gynecological exams, are not widely available, which is why both Sophie and her cousin Anna dedicate themselves to helping society's forgotten citizens. So when the mysterious murder of a young woman is brought to their attention, they can't refuse the chance to be consultants on the case. It soon becomes clear, however, that there's more to this crime than meets the eye; a string of other victims seem to be connected, and all of them were women seeking an abortion. As the two doctors begin to close in on the killer, they make a startling discovery that forces them to question their own ideas of right and wrong.

It's refreshing to read a novel with such resilient female characters who not only know their worth, they have no qualms about reminding the men in their lives of it as well. In one memorable scene, a gentleman expresses his surprise at Sophie's outspoken manner. After a laugh, she simply replies; "You might find this odd, but I'm not offended to be thought of as blunt. I like it." It's this spirit of boldness and self-assurance that make Sophie and Anna so fascinating in a profession filled to the brim with stuffy old men. On top of this, Sophie is African American, making her even more of an anomaly. There is a strong feminist undercurrent throughout the novel, also evident in the complex women's issues at the core of the plot regarding pregnancy and abortion at a time when little help was available to women in need. The natural desire many women feel to be a mother, and what happens when women are denied that impulse, are also explored in haunting detail.

The history of medicine in the 19th century is vividly brought to life. It's obvious that Donati did her research when it comes to medical terms and practices from the era, because the many instances of examination and diagnosis read like authoritative case histories. Descriptions of house-calls are stark and gritty in their portrayal of inner-city life: "The candlelight played over a litter of hypodermic needles on the floor, cast aside carelessly, along with gauze stained with dried blood." An interesting side-drama unfolds around Sophie's endeavor to teach medicine. The reader is given access to every triumph and struggle in her mission to train the next generation of female physicians. And because Donati keeps building new developments on previous chapters, the jumps between the women's personal lives and their professional pursuits feel relevant, while also adding more complexity to the narrative.

With its focus on smart, courageous women physicians, who were a rarity but certainly not unheard of in the late 19th century (see Beyond the Book), *Where the Light Enters* easily sets itself apart in the genre of historical fiction. It is an excellent followup to *The Gilded Hour*, but also can be read as a standalone novel. The controversial themes, headstrong heroines and gripping accounts of high-stakes medical trials all come together to create a winning combination.

Reviewed by Tara Mcnabb. This review was originally published in *The BookBrowse Review* in October 2019, and has been updated for the August 2020 edition.

DRIVE YOUR PLOW OVER THE BONES OF THE DEAD

by Olga Tokarczuk

BookBrowse Rating: 5/5
Critics' Consensus: 5/5
Readers' Rating: 4/5

Published August 2020 in Paperback, 288 pages

Summary

In a remote Polish village, Janina devotes the dark winter days to studying astrology, translating the poetry of William Blake, and taking care of the summer homes of wealthy Warsaw residents. Her reputation as a crank and a recluse is amplified by her not-so-secret preference for the company of animals over humans.

Then a neighbor, Big Foot, turns up dead. Soon other bodies are discovered, in increasingly strange circumstances. As suspicions mount, Janina inserts herself into the investigation, certain that she knows whodunit. If only anyone would pay her mind...

A deeply satisfying thriller cum fairy tale from the winner of the 2018 Nobel Prize for Literature, *Drive Your Plow over the Bones of the Dead* is a provocative exploration of the murky borderland between sanity and madness, justice and tradition, autonomy and fate. Whom do we deem sane? it asks. Who is worthy of a voice?

BookBrowse Review

Man Booker Prize winner Tokarczuk's latest is an unconventional murder mystery set in a remote village in southwest Poland that raises questions about justice and sanity.

A subversive feminist noir mystery set in a remote Polish village, *Drive Your Plow Over the Bones of the Dead* both dazzles and defies categorization. Olga Tokarczuk's seventh novel (her fourth to be translated into English) follows Janina Duszejko, an elderly woman living as a recluse on the outskirts of a Polish town close to the Czech border, who spends her days reading horoscopes and translating the poetry of William Blake. But it's a far cry from an idyllic life for Janina, whose beloved dogs have gone missing and whose neighbors keep mysteriously turning up dead.

The intelligent and eccentric Janina immediately recalls Agatha Christie's Miss Marple, but to call this one a mystery novel would be reductive. Janina is an unlikely heroine not only for her age, but because of the sundry ways in which she refuses to submit to societal standards; she's a vegetarian within a hunting community, she's outspoken about animal rights, she's a firm and unironic believer in astrology. As the murders begin to escalate, Janina becomes adamant that she knows who the culprit is, but she succeeds only in isolating herself further from those in her town who already doubt her sanity. The commentary on how the elderly – women in particular – are viewed with disdain and ridicule is the novel's focus, rather than the whodunit.

However, Tokarczuk's advocacy for the elderly isn't the only thematic thread that leaves a strong impression. Against the stark, dreary and frigid backdrop, an atmosphere rendered to perfection, the novel's driving conflict isn't so much with the climate and landscape, as one might expect, but with society at large. Tokarczuk deftly weaves together commentary on the limitations of the body, animal welfare, justice and the nature of violence – which all condense into a fundamental question about fate vs. free will, echoing back to Janina's obsession with the stars.

> "I think we all feel great ambivalence at the sight of our own Horoscope. On the one hand we're proud to see that the sky is imprinted on our individual life, like a postmark with a date stamped on a letter – this makes it distinct, one of a kind. But at the same time it's a form of imprisonment in space, like a tattooed prison number. There's no escaping it. I cannot be someone other than I am. How awful. We'd prefer to think we're free, able to reinvent ourselves whenever we choose. This connection with something as great and monumental as the sky makes us feel uncomfortable. We'd rather be small, and then our petty little sins would be forgivable."

Translated from the Polish by Antonia Lloyd-Jones, *Drive Your Plow Over the Bones of the Dead* is stylistically striking. With a pseudo-biblical flair, improper nouns are capitalized seemingly at random (a quirk that isn't consistent with Polish orthography, indicating this was an intentional choice made by Tokarczuk in the original language). Early in the novel Janina meditates on the nature of names: she often finds them ill-fitting and chooses to refer to people by a prominent characteristic instead. Her neighbors therefore have names like Oddball and Big Foot, but she also talks of Horoscopes and her Ailments, imbuing these words with an almost equal weight as that with which she considers her fellow men. What makes human life so special? This is the question that propels the novel forward, one that will continue to haunt its readers long after they finish.

Reviewed by Rachel Hullett. This review was originally published in *The BookBrowse Review* in August 2019, and has been updated for the November 2020 edition.

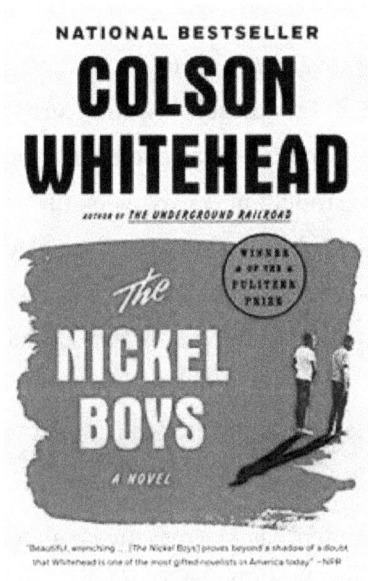

THE NICKEL BOYS

by Colson Whitehead

BookBrowse Rating: 4/5
Critics' Consensus: 5/5
Readers' Rating: 4.5/5

Published June 2020 in Paperback, 224 pages

Summary

In this bravura follow-up to the Pulitzer Prize, and National Book Award-winning #1 *New York Times* bestseller *The Underground Railroad*, Colson Whitehead brilliantly dramatizes another strand of American history through the story of two boys sentenced to a hellish reform school in Jim Crow-era Florida.

As the Civil Rights movement begins to reach the black enclave of Frenchtown in segregated Tallahassee, Elwood Curtis takes the words of Dr. Martin Luther King to heart: He is "as good as anyone." Abandoned by his parents, but kept on the straight and narrow by his grandmother, Elwood is about to enroll in the local black college. But for a black boy in the Jim Crow South of the early 1960s, one innocent mistake is enough to destroy the future. Elwood is sentenced to a juvenile reformatory called the Nickel Academy, whose mission statement says it provides "physical, intellectual and moral training" so the delinquent boys in their charge can become "honorable and honest men."

In reality, the Nickel Academy is a grotesque chamber of horrors where the sadistic staff beats and sexually abuses the students, corrupt officials and locals steal food and supplies, and any boy who resists is likely to disappear "out back." Stunned to find himself in such a vicious environment, Elwood tries to hold onto Dr. King's ringing assertion "Throw us in jail and we will still love you." His friend Turner thinks Elwood is worse than naive, that the world is crooked, and that the only way to survive is to scheme and avoid trouble.

The tension between Elwood's ideals and Turner's skepticism leads to a decision whose repercussions will echo down the decades. Formed in the crucible of the evils Jim Crow wrought, the boys' fates will be determined by what they endured at the Nickel Academy.

Based on the real story of a reform school in Florida that operated for one hundred and eleven years and warped the lives of thousands of children, *The Nickel Boys* is a devastating, driven narrative that showcases a great American novelist writing at the height of his powers.

BookBrowse Review

From Pulitzer Prize winning-author Colson Whitehead comes a compelling coming-of-age tale of an African-American boy unjustly sentenced to reform school.

In his last novel, The Underground Railroad, Colson Whitehead sketched an alternate version of the Civil War, in which the titular network of safe houses and escape routes transporting runaway slaves to Canada was an actual subterranean railroad system. Through the lens of the fantastical, the work examines the horrors of slavery, and offers a fresh perspective on American history.

Jumping a century forward, the author's follow-up, The Nickel Boys, takes place at the height of the Civil Rights Movement in the 1960s, depicting an entrenched system of institutionalized racism that's nearly as brutal and dehumanizing as slavery itself. The story follows Elwood, an idealistic young man preparing to attend college when a tragic misunderstanding lands him in an inhumane reformatory school, the Nickel Academy. Bringing to life the horrors of Jim Crow, the novel considers the possibility of maintaining hope in the face of racist terror and violence.

The plot opens by sketching a vivid portrait of Elwood's life in Tallahassee, Florida, circa 1963. The teenager devotes all his energy to working at a convenience store, studying for his exams and preparing to be the first in his family to attend college. Raised in a home without a television and forbidden from listening to Motown, Elwood's favorite pastime is playing his album of Martin Luther King at Zion Hill, a collection of the activist's speeches and a Christmas gift from his grandmother Harriet. Strict but loving, Harriet has raised Elwood since his parents abandoned him at an early age, heading west to live unencumbered by childcare.

Comprising the first part of three, these chapters abound with references to the life-affirming activism of the Civil Rights Movement. Elwood loves reading Life photo essays about anti-racist protests, seeks out Black-owned newspapers like The Chicago Defender, and finds inspiration to better himself and fight for a just future in the bravery of the Freedom Riders. Extremely idealistic, he prides himself on being thought of as having an "industrious nature and steady character."

In neat, understated prose, Whitehead sensitively renders an era of political optimism. At the time the story starts, the Civil Rights Act of 1960 had recently established much-needed federal oversight of local voter registration polls, and more legislative victories seemed likely; the movement hadn't yet become disillusioned with white liberal politicians like JFK and LBJ. Elwood's community brims with hope, and the teen's faith in patience, industry and nonviolence reflect the time's dominant ethos.

Then, in the span of a few pages, everything falls apart. Caught in the wrong place at the wrong time, Elwood is accused of being an accomplice to theft by racist police officers. Whitehead smartly elides the protagonist's trial, leaving the details of his sentencing to the imagination, and the second and longest part of the novel begins with Elwood entering the Nickel Academy, a horrendous segregated reformatory school based on an infamous real-life institution (See Beyond the Book).

"I am stuck here, but I'll make the best of it," Elwood tells himself, "and I'll make it brief." The teen's faith that, if he follows the rules of the system, he'll be recognized as virtuous and released is soon challenged, though, both by the cynicism of his closest confidante at the academy, Turner, as well as the unrestrained violence and surveillance of Nickel's guards, teachers and administrators.

The crux of the plot hinges on whether or not Elwood can survive the academy with his idealism intact. In this, he acts as a symbol for the entirety of the Civil Rights Movement, which faced intensifying state repression during the mid-60s. Is nonviolence an effective response, Whitehead wonders, to a government that beats and bloodies unarmed protesters? Should Black people play by the rules of a racist system in their fight for better lives, or aim to topple it?

The debate about the merits of respectability politics and integrating into white society versus an ideology of Black liberation is as timely as ever, in an era when unabashed white supremacy is on the rise across the globe, and Whitehead's critique of assimilationist politics is sharp. Part of what makes the novel so memorable is the way the ending explicitly ties past injustice to the present, refusing to quarantine racism to the realm of history. So, too, does the author's quiet style refuse to sensationalize anti-Black violence, in contrast to other historical works of this kind.

Thoughtful and engaging, The Nickel Boys offers astute observations about the history of race relations in America: it's sure to appeal to the author's devoted readers as well as those new to his work.

Reviewed by Michael Kaler. This review was originally published in *The BookBrowse Review* in July 2019, and has been updated for the July 2020 edition.

THE LAST YEAR OF THE WAR

by Susan Meissner

BookBrowse Rating: 5/5
Critics' Consensus: 4.5/5
Readers' Rating: 5/5

Published April 2020 in Paperback, 416 pages

Summary

From the acclaimed author of *Secrets of a Charmed Life* and *As Bright as Heaven* comes a novel about a German American teenager whose life changes forever when her immigrant family is sent to an internment camp during World War II.

Elise Sontag is a typical Iowa fourteen-year-old in 1943--aware of the war but distanced from its reach. Then her father, a legal U.S. resident for nearly two decades, is suddenly arrested on suspicion of being a Nazi sympathizer. The family is sent to an internment camp in Texas, where, behind the armed guards and barbed wire, Elise feels stripped of everything beloved and familiar, including her own identity.

The only thing that makes the camp bearable is meeting fellow internee Mariko Inoue, a Japanese-American teen from Los Angeles, whose friendship empowers Elise to believe the life she knew before the war will again be hers. Together in the desert wilderness, Elise and Mariko hold tight the dream of being young American women with a future beyond the fences.

But when the Sontag family is exchanged for American prisoners behind enemy lines in Germany, Elise will face head-on the person the war desires to make of her. In that devastating crucible she must discover if she has the will to rise above prejudice and hatred and re-claim her own destiny, or disappear into the image others have cast upon her.

The Last Year of the War tells a little-known story of World War II with great resonance for our own times and challenges the very notion of who we are when who we've always been is called into question.

BookBrowse Review

A touching work of historical fiction exploring the relationship between two teenagers confined to an American internment camp during World War II.

36 out of 37 First Impressions reviewers gave Susan Meissner's *The Last Year of the War* four or five stars, for an overall rating of 4.6.

What it's about:

The Last Year of the War follows the life of Elise Sontag and her family. When Elise's father is arrested by the FBI as an enemy alien during World War II, their peaceful life in Davenport, Iowa is disrupted. Poverty and uncertainty follow the family as they are separated from each other, reunited in an internment camp in Texas, and finally repatriated to Germany, where Allied pilots were still dropping bombs. The story is also about the friendship that arises between Elise and Mariko, a Japanese internee at the same camp in Texas. Sixty years later, at the age of 77, Elise has been diagnosed with Alzheimer's. She becomes determined to reconnect with Mariko, who she has not seen or heard from since the camp (Jean L). This moving narrative tells of Elise's search for home, happiness and a sense of identity that keeps her true to herself. This is the story of a woman who stayed the course throughout countless obstacles (Marcia C).

Most thought the book was superb historical fiction:

This was a truly outstanding book about a little-known series of events during WWII. I had no idea that American citizens of German heritage were interned at the same time as those of Japanese heritage. Nor did I know that some of these American citizens were "traded" for American citizens caught behind enemy lines. This excellent historical fiction explains how and why that came to pass, and what happened to two families who were repatriated to their parents' country of origin (Janet H). Meissner has brilliantly taken this dark period in America's history and made it accessible to the mainstream reader (Judi R).

The book touches on many important subjects:

The author explores issues of injustice, the hardships of war and feelings about "place" with an engaging story and well-developed characters (Rosemary C). There are broad themes of friendship, love, identity, family loyalty and the damages of war played out against an important historical backdrop (DeAnn A).

Many readers also compared Elise's situation to that of today's immigrants:

The parallels to present day immigration issues are unmistakable, and caused me to reflect upon the current plight of the DREAMers (Maribeth R). This book sheds light on a part of the immigration debate that most Americans never consider – what happens to ordinary people caught in untenable situations (Becky H).

First Impressions reviewers were also impressed with the author's characters:

Meissner's characters embody a sincerity and clarity that makes them come alive to the reader and remain memorable long after the book is read (Marianne L). They seemed so real! I really cared about both young girls, one from a German family and one from a Japanese family, and the friendship they forged in the internment camp (Jean N). Perhaps they should be re-named CAREacters because when you encounter them, you take them into your heart (Maribeth R).

Some felt the last third of the book was a let-down:

The story is a compelling and interesting piece of historical fiction, with a believable account of how an American-born teenager might have reacted. The book is less successful when it verges on soap opera after the war with the drama of Elise's marriages and interactions with her in-laws. The picture of Elise in old age feels contrived and does not add to an otherwise good book (Joy E). For the last 100 pages or so I felt too many serendipitous events took place for it to be a satisfying read (Henry W).

The general consensus, however, was that it was a wonderful, well-paced novel:

Warning: when you begin this volume, ensure your next day or two are unencumbered. It is guaranteed you will not want to stop reading once you begin Meissner's tale of tragedy, hope and reconciliation (Maribeth R). I was completely absorbed by this historically accurate novel about a young German American girl's experience during World War II and after (Rosemary C). Well-written and well-researched, this book is one that should not be missed (Becky H). It was very easy to read, very engaging and definitely hard to put down (Mary D).

Recommended for:

Fans of historical fiction are sure to love this exceptional novel and will add it to their favorites of the year (Judi R). There is much food for discussion here. It would be a great book club pick, especially in light of the internment camps once again being set up in Texas (Marcia C).

Reviewed by First Impressions Reviewers. This review was originally published in *The BookBrowse Review* in March 2019, and has been updated for the April 2020 edition.

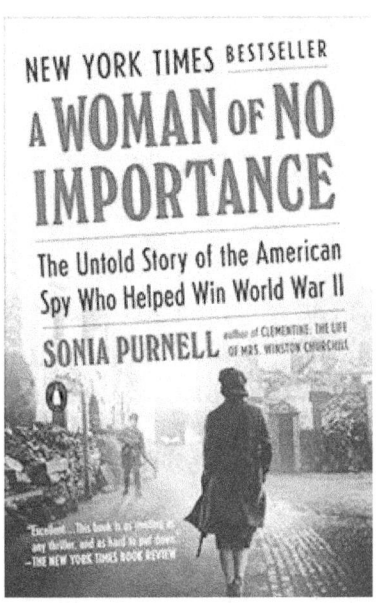

A WOMAN OF NO IMPORTANCE

by Sonia Purnell

BookBrowse Rating: 5/5
Critics' Consensus: 5/5
Readers' Rating: 5/5

Published March 2020 in Paperback, 368 pages

Summary

The never-before-told story of Virginia Hall, the American spy who changed the course of World War II, from the author of Clementine in 1942, the Gestapo sent out an urgent transmission: "She is the most dangerous of all Allied spies. We must find and destroy her." The target in their sights was

Virginia Hall, a Baltimore socialite who talked her way into Special Operations Executive, the spy organization dubbed Winston Churchill's "Ministry of Ungentlemanly Warfare." She became the first Allied woman deployed behind enemy lines and--despite her prosthetic leg--helped to light the flame of the French Resistance, revolutionizing secret warfare as we know it.

Virginia established vast spy networks throughout France, called weapons and explosives down from the skies, and became a linchpin for the Resistance. Even as her face covered wanted posters and a bounty was placed on her head, Virginia refused order after order to evacuate. She finally escaped through a death-defying hike over the Pyrenees into Spain, her cover blown. But she plunged back in, adamant that she had more lives to save, and led a victorious guerilla campaign, liberating swathes of France from the Nazis after D-Day.

Based on new and extensive research, Sonia Purnell has for the first time uncovered the full secret life of Virginia Hall--an astounding and inspiring story of heroism, spycraft, resistance, and personal triumph over shocking adversity. A Woman of No Importance is the breathtaking story of how one woman's fierce persistence helped win the war.

BookBrowse Review

This compelling biography paints a vivid portrait of a fearless American spy who helped sabotage Nazi forces, train Resistance fighters, and protect democracy.

Virginia Hall is largely unknown in the annals of history, but her World War II accomplishments were magnificent. *A Woman of No Importance: The Untold Story of How an American Spy Won World War II* lovingly bestows upon Virginia Hall the notoriety and acclaim she rightly deserves.

As a young woman, Hall studied at the École Libre des Sciences Politiques in Paris and was obsessed with the city and its stars. She found herself enchanted with the black entertainer Josephine Baker, writers Ernest Hemingway and F. Scott Fitzgerald, and feminist Gertrude Stein. What was not in Paris were rules, limitations, segregation. She felt free and wanted an adventurous life.

After school, Hall moved to Turkey, where she would suffer her greatest tragedy. During a hunting party, her gun accidentally discharged and put a hole in her foot. An infection spiraled upwards, and in the aftermath of hospitalizations and surgeries, her leg had to be amputated. When she returned to the United States for further care, Hall was somber and in misery. How was she to have adventures on one leg?

By making the best out of her circumstances: she quickly taught herself to walk on the wooden leg, which she named Cuthbert.

After Germany attacked Poland, Hall had her chance to pursue heroism: she went to work in London for the Special Operations Executive (SOE). SOE was created in June 1940 when newly appointed Prime Minister Winston Churchill ordered three existing organizations to be merged into one unit. It was to be a brutal group of undercover agents who bombed, stole secrets and caused Nazi havoc. In reality, SOE had trouble finding agents. They weren't in the position to reject a one-legged adrenaline junkie. So in 1941, Hall became SOE's first female agent in France. She was sent to France as Marie Monin, a *New York Post* reporter.

The spy's information smuggling, her secret communications and rescue missions—she coordinated a bold escape for 12 imprisoned men—made Marie Monin a legendary figure in France. The more successful she was at thwarting the Nazis, the more she was hunted.

If Hall had ever been caught there is little doubt she would have been tortured. French authorities under German occupation could be worse than the Germans, as they were trying to impress the Nazis to save their own necks.

Eventually, her cover was blown and she had to get out of France. Fast. A large reward was offered for her arrest. "I'd give anything to get my hands on that limping Canadian bitch" one of her enemies, Klaus Barber, known as The Butcher of Lyon, reportedly said. Thousands of wanted posters were taped to poles with her picture on it and the caption: 'The Enemy's Most Dangerous Spy. We must find and destroy her.'

Back in London, SOE forbade Hall from returning to France; but 16 months later she was back there, working for the Office of Strategic Services (OSS), the precursor to the CIA. She dyed her hair and filed down her teeth to disguise herself as a peasant woman. Her job was to coordinate sabotage operations and hit and run attacks on behalf of the Americans.

Hall began training men in four groups of twenty-five. Diane was her new code name and her trainees were called the Diane Irregulars. Their motto was: shoot, burn, destroy, leave. They paralyzed communications, packed explosives on roadways, removed road signs and replaced them with fake ones to confuse the Germans.

OSS's sabotage efforts were incredibly successful. Over the course of WWII, the organization recruited fearless saboteurs such as Hall, and it forced German prisoners-of-war to act as spies on counterintelligence missions. At its height, it employed close to 24,000 workers. Referring to partisan operations in general, President Eisenhower remarked that the ambush, harassment, and ruining of the Nazi morale shortened the war by eight months.

Page after page, Sonia Purnell delivers a breathless and breathtaking thriller. But as powerful as Hall's story is, and as much as it is a testament to fearless women, it doesn't answer a singular question about the spy. Why does a woman who summered on a Maryland farm leave her homeland to water down the evil of the Third Reich? She could have lived a life of comfort and safety. But she put everything on the line as she redirected the arc of evil and saved the lives of strangers. Hall was the only civilian woman honored with the Distinguished Service Cross, an award for heroism.

Virginia Hall the fighter is part of our rich story of dynamic women. She was a leader of men. A spy. A legend. We often hear the cliché of being the good we want to see in the world. 75 years ago that was the soul of a woman, a striking and attractive American, a woman with one leg and a purpose to free humankind.

Reviewed by Valerie Morales. This review was originally published in *The BookBrowse Review* in July 2019, and has been updated for the April 2020 edition.

A WOMAN IS NO MAN

by Etaf Rum

BookBrowse Rating: 4/5
Critics' Consensus: 5/5
Readers' Rating: 5/5

Published February 2020 in Paperback, 368 pages

Summary

"Garnering justified comparisons to Khaled Hosseini's *A Thousand Splendid Suns*... Etaf Rum's debut novel is a must-read about women mustering up the bravery to follow their inner voice." —*Refinery 29*

A *New York Times Book Review* Editors' Choice
A *Washington Post* 10 Books to Read in March
A *Marie Claire* Best Women's Fiction of 2019
A *Newsweek* Best Book of the Summer
A *USA Today* Best Book of the Week
A *Washington Book Review* Difficult-To-Put-Down Novel
A *Refinery 29* Best Books of the Month
A *Buzzfeed News* 4 Books We Couldn't Put Down Last Month
An *Electric Lit* 20 Best Debuts of the First Half of 2019
A *The Millions* Most Anticipated Books of 2019

In her debut novel Etaf Rum tells the story of three generations of Palestinian-American women struggling to express their individual desires within the confines of their Arab culture in the wake of shocking intimate violence in their community—a story of culture and honor, secrets and betrayals, love and violence. Set in an America at once foreign to many and staggeringly close at hand, *A Woman Is No Man* is an intimate glimpse into a controlling and closed cultural world, and a universal tale about family and the ways silence and shame can destroy those we have sworn to protect.

"Where I come from, we've learned to silence ourselves. We've been taught that silence will save us. Where I come from, we keep these stories to ourselves. To tell them to the outside world is unheard of—dangerous, the ultimate shame."

Palestine, 1990. Seventeen-year-old Isra prefers reading books to entertaining the suitors her father has chosen for her. Over the course of a week, the naïve and dreamy girl finds herself quickly betrothed and married, and is soon living in Brooklyn. There Isra struggles to adapt to the expectations of her oppressive mother-in-law Fareeda and strange new husband Adam, a pressure that intensifies as she begins to have children—four daughters instead of the sons Fareeda tells Isra she must bear.

Brooklyn, 2008. Eighteen-year-old Deya, Isra's oldest daughter, must meet with potential husbands at her grandmother Fareeda's insistence, though her only desire is to go to college. Deya can't help but wonder if her options would have been different had her parents survived the car crash that killed them when Deya was only eight. But her grandmother is firm on the matter: the only way to secure a worthy future for Deya is through marriage to the right man.

But fate has a will of its own, and soon Deya will find herself on an unexpected path that leads her to shocking truths about her family—knowledge that will force her to question everything she thought she knew about her parents, the past, and her own future.

BookBrowse Review

Etaf Rum's debut novel, *A Woman Is No Man*, explores the lives of three generations of Palestinian-American women as they struggle with questions of love and family in their Bay Ridge, Brooklyn home.

The chapters of *A Woman Is No Man* alternate between two time periods and the narrative viewpoints of three women. We are first introduced to 17-year-old Isra as she meets her soon-to-be husband, Adam, in Palestine in 1990. She was chosen by Adam's mother Fareeda to marry her son because she is quiet and obedient. Adam and his family live in America, and Isra returns there with them immediately after the wedding ceremony, hoping to be granted greater freedom than she experienced under her own mother's roof. She soon finds, however, that her role in the household is that of a servant, her husband is an abusive alcoholic, and her position becomes increasingly unbearable with each of the four girls she gives birth to, since she has not produced the all-important male heir.

The next voice we hear is that of Isra's eldest daughter, Deya, who in 2008 is only slightly older than her mother was when she married Adam. She lives with her grandparents and her sisters, and has grown up believing that her parents died when she was young. Fareeda is consumed with seeing Deya married and is constantly having her meet suitors, but Deya is disinterested, wanting to go to college and have a career.

Finally, readers experience Fareeda's perspective during both time periods as she ruminates on her life as a refugee, her culture and her changing family.

Rum adeptly explores many complicated and important themes throughout the novel, but primarily she focuses on the roles culture and family play throughout the lives of these individuals and, by extension, many others of Arab descent. Fareeda, representative of the older generation, reinforces the importance of tradition with those in her orbit, even when others view her espoused practices as unacceptable in modern society. She illustrates how harmful cultural traditions are repeated even by their victims. The other two women show how difficult it is to break free from this damaging cycle.

Although Rum's writing style is somewhat simplistic, her characters are extremely well-drawn and sympathetic across the board. The predicaments the women find themselves in could have been challenging for a Western audience to relate to, but the author skillfully guides her readers into understanding why they feel so boxed in and helpless. Also, although she clearly concentrates on the roles and experiences of women, one nice surprise is that she also touches on the challenges her male characters endure as they try to live up to cultural norms - something I'm not sure I've read often in books dealing with this sort of subject matter. Although Adam, for example, takes his rage out on his wife, one actually feels sorry for him, as he does everything in his power to live up to his family's expectations, in spite of their complete lack of gratitude for his sacrifices.

There were several aspects of the book that I feel could have been better. I did enjoy the storyline, but I found it utterly predictable. I also found the very short chapters somewhat annoying, frequently wishing the author had stuck with one woman's story longer before switching to another. And finally, the author formulated some interesting observations but overall labored the points she was trying to make, causing the plot to drag halfway through.

Readers should also keep in mind that, while *A Woman Is No Man* ends on a hopeful note, overall it's a pretty sad tale; Isra obviously suffers from worsening and untreated depression, and she is treated brutally by those around her. Still, it offers a nuanced picture of a woman's life within a traditional Arab-American family, and as such it's definitely worth a read. The book is highly recommended for those interested in learning more about the culture, and book groups in particular will find much fodder for discussion.

Reviewed by Kim Kovacs. This review was originally published in *The BookBrowse Review* in December 2019, and has been updated for the February 2020 edition.

INHERITANCE

by Dani Shapiro

BookBrowse Rating: 4/5
Critics' Consensus: 4.5/5
Readers' Rating: 5/5

Published January 2020 in Paperback, 272 pages

| Summary

A new memoir about identity, paternity, and family secrets--a real-time exploration of the staggering discovery Shapiro recently made about her father, and her struggle to piece together the hidden story of her own life.

What makes us who we are? What combination of memory, history, biology, experience, and that ineffable thing called the soul defines us?

In the spring of 2016, through a genealogy website to which she had whimsically submitted her DNA for analysis, Dani Shapiro received the stunning news that her father was not her biological father. She woke up one morning and her entire history--the life she had lived--crumbled beneath her.

Inheritance is a book about secrets--secrets within families, kept out of shame or self-protectiveness; secrets we keep from one another in the name of love. It is the story of a woman's urgent quest to unlock the story of her own identity, a story that has been scrupulously hidden from her for more than fifty years, years she had spent writing brilliantly, and compulsively, on themes of identity and family history. It is a book about the extraordinary moment we live in--a moment in which science and technology have outpaced not only medical ethics but also the capacities of the human heart to contend with the consequences of what we discover.

Timely and unforgettable, Dani Shapiro's memoir is a gripping, gut-wrenching exploration of genealogy, paternity, and love.

BookBrowse Review

A compelling exploration of paternity, identity and belonging from the best-selling author of *Devotion* and *Hourglass*.

Dani Shapiro's *Inheritance* begins with a shocking discovery. In the opening chapters Shapiro recounts how in early 2016, after submitting her DNA for analysis through Ancestry.com on a whim (See Beyond the Book), she found out that she is not in fact biologically-related to her deceased father, an Ashkenazi Jew. The test results understandably unsettled the acclaimed memoirist, who has spent her career writing about family history and Jewish culture. Shapiro cogently conveys the turmoil she felt upon learning that she is only 52% Jewish and unrelated to her dad, and then the main storyline of

Inheritance begins in earnest as she attempts to track down her biological father and reckon with what her finding means for her sense of herself as a proud Jewish woman.

Over the course of the memoir's first half, Shapiro details the steps she took to unravel her genealogical mystery in clear-cut, precise prose. Remarkably, her journey to find her biological father is not marked by frustration and pain as it is for many, but rather a surreal, almost unbelievable ease. The memory of a single conversation she had years ago with her deceased mother led Shapiro down a rabbit hole: her conception, her mother once told her, involved "a doctor—an institute—in Philadelphia." Shapiro describes how in mere months, using only those cryptic clues, she managed to find out that her parents used a sperm donor for her conception at a cutting-edge institute in Philadelphia back in the 1960s, making them one of the first infertile couples to risk the then-experimental procedure. More spectacularly, she even managed to learn the donor's name and contact information, an achievement that usually takes years.

The first half of the book, while interesting, is a bit repetitive. Shapiro alternates between painting vivid portraits of her parents, recollecting the history of artificial insemination in America, and, most often, considering what her discovery means for her sense of self. Despite speaking flawless Hebrew and being raised as Orthodox, the blonde-haired and blue-eyed Shapiro has never "looked the part" of a Jewish woman, "to such a degree that it became a defining aspect of [her] identity" and a point of insecurity early in her life. She spends most of the first two sections of her four-part memoir questioning whether or not her newly discovered ancestry makes her less Jewish. The author's anxiety is understandable, but her excessive worrying becomes monotonous. Thankfully, these chapters, like the rest, move at a fast pace, and the memoir's second half is more consistently engaging.

In the third and fourth parts, Shapiro shifts to narrating the thrilling tale of her attempt to contact and establish a relationship with her biological father, a renowned doctor living in Portland with his family. Here, Shapiro reflects on the visceral feeling of connection she experienced after studying videos of the man online and combing through his website, noting the similarities in their physical appearance, traits and mannerisms. An expert at storytelling, the author keeps readers in suspense as she reveals her story piecemeal, all the while asking, "What did I owe him? What did he owe me? Who were we to each other?"

Shapiro explores the ethical and existential questions at the heart of her journey with sensitivity and nuance. She occasionally belabors her points, but rarely do her musings about identity and ancestry read as simplistic or shallow. A complex and multifaceted memoir, interwoven with history and full of feeling, *Inheritance* is sure to appeal to loyal fans of the author as well as readers new to her thoughtful work.

Reviewed by Michael Kaler. This review was originally published in *The BookBrowse Review* in January 2019, and has been updated for the February 2020 edition.

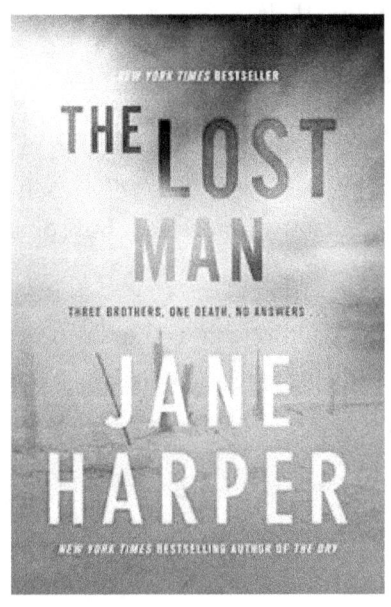

THE LOST MAN

by Jane Harper

BookBrowse Rating: 5/5
Critics' Consensus: 4.5/5
Readers' Rating: 5/5

Published December 2019 in Paperback, 368 pages

Summary

Two brothers meet in the remote Australian outback when the third brother is found dead, in this stunning new standalone novel from *New York Times* bestseller Jane Harper.

Brothers Nathan and Bub Bright meet for the first time in months at the remote fence line separating their cattle ranches in the lonely outback.

Their third brother, Cameron, lies dead at their feet.

In an isolated belt of Australia, their homes a three-hour drive apart, the brothers were one another's nearest neighbors. Cameron was the middle child, the one who ran the family homestead. But something made him head out alone under the unrelenting sun.

Nathan, Bub and Nathan's son return to Cameron's ranch and to those left behind by his passing: his wife, his daughters, and his mother, as well as their long-time employee and two recently hired seasonal workers.

While they grieve Cameron's loss, suspicion starts to take hold, and Nathan is forced to examine secrets the family would rather leave in the past. Because if someone forced Cameron to his death, the isolation of the outback leaves few suspects.

A powerful and brutal story of suspense set against a formidable landscape, *The Lost Man* confirms Jane Harper, author of *The Dry* and *Force of Nature*, is one of the best new voices in writing today.

BookBrowse Review

Two estranged brothers come together to investigate the death of a third brother on an Australian cattle ranch in this slow burn thriller from Jane Harper.

36 out of 37 First Impression reviewers gave Jane Harper's third novel, *The Last Man*, either four or five stars, for an overall rating of 4.7.

What it's about:

Jane Harper's latest book, *The Lost Man*, is a fantastic family drama/mystery that explores the consequences of both taking action and failing to do so. In the aftermath of the seeming suicide of Cameron Bright in a desolate part of the Australian Outback, his family must come to terms with his death and with what may have prompted it. Told from the point of view of Nathan, Cameron's older brother, the story slowly unfolds as Harper interweaves past and present and reveals dark family secrets (Terri O). Nathan and Cameron trade places as protagonist and antagonist throughout the book, posing the question: Which of the brothers was really lost? (Joan B).

At the core of the novel is the question of how a person's family history may affect their actions later in life:

The plot delves into how our childhoods define our family situations in the present (Mary O). The generational effects of living in a dysfunctional family and other events of the past influence how each character reacts to Cameron's death (Shirley T). I was reminded that we all carry our pasts with us, and that some are more successful in moving forward than others (Gina T).

Many reviewers mentioned Harper's writing skill:

The author has a talent for describing people and locations in such a way that one gets inside the heads of her flawed, and so very human characters (Sue P). They're very well developed, as is the plot. The sense of place is palpable, and the resolution, when it finally comes, is satisfying and believable (Terri O). Harper really deserves credit for building suspense. Atmospheric, anxious, ghostly, foreboding and fulfilling…this story checks a lot of boxes (Linda H).

***The Lost Man* compared favorably to Harper's previous books:**

I thought *The Lost Man* was a wonderful book and enjoyed it even more than Jane Harper's previous novels featuring Aaron Falk (Randi H). Although I was not a big fan of *The Dry*, I chose this based on the fact that it was a standalone and had some great advance buzz. To my mind, this book is MUCH better than her debut novel, with a greater emphasis on the characters, and less on the detective work (Jill S). Harper is a great storyteller, and I enjoyed her other two books, but somehow this one resonated more with me (Linda S). This was very different from Harper's first book, which I realized received rave reviews despite my less than enthusiastic opinion of it. This book on the other hand was terrific (Barry E).

As with Harper's previous works, the action is set in the Australian Outback:

Harper's images of the dry, vast Outback will leave you thirsty! (Diane D). She does an amazing job of describing the rugged—almost alien—terrain, as well as its impact on the people who live there (Deborah C). The lonely, desolate landscape mirrors the characters' lives and actions perfectly (Nikki M). The Australian Outback becomes a character itself; the descriptions of the environment bring an extra layer of bleakness and urgency to the story that keeps the pages turning faster and faster (Betsy H).

A few of our readers found the pacing problematic:

I thought this was a rather slow-moving mystery. I got impatient with trying to figure out what the crime was really about (Sara P). I felt like I was slogging through the mud for the first 50 pages (Richard N).

Most, however, thought it was a fast read:

Like Harper's first two books, *The Lost Man* seizes the reader's interest and doesn't let up until the final page (Sheryl M). I read this in one sitting, forgoing dinner and sleep to find out what secrets were hidden in this family (Elizabeth S). A page-turner that I did not want to put down! (Mary O). I think this book will end up being one of my year's favorites (Frances N).

***The Lost Man* is recommended by our First Impressions Reviewers to a wide audience:**

Strong characters, riveting plot and an honest look at life in the Australian Outback make it easy to give this book a 5-star endorsement (Norman G). I would highly recommend it to anyone who enjoys a suspenseful tale, well-told (Linda S). I thoroughly enjoyed it and would suggest it to anyone who enjoys layered family dramas and slow-burning mysteries (Terri O). It would be a great basis for a stimulating book club discussion (Joan B). I thoroughly enjoyed it and cannot wait to see what she does next! (Meara C).

Reviewed by First Impressions Reviewers. This review was originally published in *The BookBrowse Review* in February 2019, and has been updated for the January 2020 edition.

SOLITARY

by Albert Woodfox

BookBrowse Rating: 5/5
Critics' Consensus: 5/5
Readers' Rating: 5/5

Published December 2019 in Paperback, 448 pages

Summary

Winner of the 2019 BookBrowse Debut Author Award

A chronicle of rare power and humanity that proves the better spirits of our nature can thrive against any odds.

Solitary is the unforgettable life story of a man who served more than four decades in solitary confinement - in a 6-foot by 9-foot cell, 23 hours a day, in notorious Angola prison in Louisiana - all for a crime he did not commit. That Albert Woodfox survived was, in itself, a feat of extraordinary endurance against the violence and deprivation he faced daily. That he was able to emerge whole from his odyssey within America's prison and judicial systems is a triumph of the human spirit, and makes his book a clarion call to reform the inhumanity of solitary confinement in the U.S. and around the world.

Arrested often as a teenager in New Orleans, inspired behind bars in his early twenties to join the Black Panther Party because of its social commitment and code of living, Albert was serving a 50-year sentence in Angola for armed robbery when on April 17, 1972, a white guard was killed. Albert and another member of the Panthers were accused of the crime and immediately put in solitary confinement by the warden. Without a shred of actual evidence against them, their trial was a sham of justice that gave them life sentences in solitary. Decades passed before Albert gained a lawyer of consequence; even so, sixteen more years and multiple appeals were needed before he was finally released in February 2016.

Remarkably self-aware that anger or bitterness would have destroyed him in solitary confinement, sustained by the shared solidarity of two fellow Panthers, Albert turned his anger into activism and resistance. The Angola 3, as they became known, resolved never to be broken by the grinding inhumanity and corruption that effectively held them for decades as political prisoners.

BookBrowse Review

Albert Woodfox spent 43 years in solitary confinement for a murder he did not commit; in this memoir he shares his story of perseverance, growth and hope.

Voted 2019 Best Debut Author Award Winner by BookBrowse Subscribers

According to statistics from the United States Bureau of Labor, between 80,000 and 100,000 people are held in solitary confinement per year, a condition critics claim is specifically designed to break the human spirit through extreme isolation and restriction. Albert Woodfox spent 43 years in solitary, but he endured, and now shares his powerful story in this insightful memoir.

Born in 1947, Woodfox grew up in a time of openly state-sanctioned segregation and discrimination. When his family moved to a poor and working-class black ward in New Orleans, Woodfox began to see and feel these realities for the first time. He witnessed black men and boys harassed, assaulted and charged by police without cause (see "Black Incarceration and Sentencing" for more on this topic). Yet he would not learn the depth of these social issues for years. As an adolescent and young adult, he shoplifted food as a means of survival, but he quickly degenerated to more serious crimes, causing harm to a community already contending with poverty and police scrutiny/violence.

In and out of juvenile centers and prisons, Woodfox developed a criminal reputation, eventually entering Angola—the Louisiana State Penitentiary—in 1965, and returning in 1969. Angola was once a slave plantation. In 1869, a slave trader's widow leased the land to a former confederate major, who worked leased inmates under slave conditions to farm the land (see "The Legacy of Slavery and Prison Labor" for more on this topic). Hundreds died each year. In 1901, the state of Louisiana bought the land and turned it into a penitentiary, retaining the name "Angola," the country where the plantation's original slaves were born. When Woodfox arrived in the mid-60s, the prison was run by the "freemen"— white security guards who descended from generations of Angola workers. Inmates were regularly subjected to violence and brutality, gassed, beaten, harassed and raped.

After years of breaking laws, serving sentences and enduring police abuse, Woodfox fled to Harlem to escape another bid at Angola for armed robbery.

It was here that he was introduced to the Black Panther Party. They unified the city by engaging in community work, from free school breakfast programs to literacy, education and outreach efforts. He marveled at their confidence and lack of fear. Woodfox soon found himself back in prison in New York when the authorities caught up with him, and there he met more Black Panthers, many of whom would later be released, proven innocent of charges against them. Instead of engaging in the often violent, inhumane inmate culture, the imprisoned Black Panthers acted with respect and kindness. To Woodfox, "they acted like they weren't even in prison." The Black Panthers asked fellow inmates what they needed, sharing food and clothes; they asked who could not read and began educating and sharing books with those around them, including Woodfox. This was his turning point. He read, related, analyzed and debated the words of Mao Zedung, Ho Chi Minh, Chou En-lai, Fidel Castro, Che Guevara, George Jackson, Frantz Fanon and Kwame Nkrumah. In connecting to their words and learning from their teachings, Woodfox transformed: "We knew from experience that by changing, we gained more than we lost. We got more awareness. We got more compassion. We talked about how the entire human race needed to raise its consciousness, not as individual races or groups, but as humans, as a species."

Woodfox was transferred back to Angola for his third bid there, but this time he was armed with new morals, values and principles. He was radically different. Upon arrival, he connected with imprisoned Black Panthers and officially joined the Party. Together, they worked within the prison—through hunger strikes, protests, litigation, defiance and media outreach—to bring humanity back to Angola.

The unrest and solidarity of inmates was viewed as a threat to the prison system. When corrections sergeant Brent Miller was murdered in 1972, officials seized the opportunity to pin the crime on the Black Panthers. Woodfox was sent to solitary confinement, alongside two other Panthers, Herman Wallace and Robert King. These political prisoners became known as the Angola 3. One of the wardens would later describe Woodfox as a "hardcore Black Panther racist" in court.

Woodfox was convicted, despite there being no physical evidence and no reliable eyewitness testimony connecting him to Brent Miller's murder. In fact, the primary testimony used against him was given by a serial rapist who was proven to have been paid off and released by Angola officials. *Solitary* describes how this injustice happened: delays in gaining a lawyer of consequence; lack of random, unbiased jury selection; misconduct and false accusations from prison officials; failure to properly document, record and store evidence; negligence of proper conduct in the attempt to gain statements; and general prosecutorial misconduct. By the 2000s, countless human rights activists and organizations stood behind the Angola 3, including Critical Resistance, Amnesty International, the Malcolm X Grassroots Movement, Solitary Watch, and the National Association for the Advancement of Colored People.

In 2016, Woodfox was finally released, the result of decades of appeals to the courts. He plead no contest to reduced charges, meaning he did not admit guilt, but accepted he could not prove innocence, due largely to a number of people involved in the original trials being deceased and unavailable for questioning. This was Woodfox's final round of appeals, and he chose freedom over justice. Today, he is still adjusting to life outside of solitary confinement. Despite the decades spent in Angola, he maintains hope.

Relatively few people will ever experience the horrors of solitary confinement, but in this narrative reflection, readers will see themselves. This is what makes *Solitary* such a weighty and worthwhile read. Running parallel to Woodfox's experience with the judicial system is his trek into social activism. This subplot creates something of a redemption story, a moving testament to our potential for growth, regardless of circumstances and past decisions. It is proof that a strong belief system paired with a like-minded community can catalyze change. Woodfox's unwillingness to break—his strength and determination—is a lesson bestowed to those who are just entering the world of social struggle, as well as a reminder to those who have been fighting these battles for decades. Whether it's prison reform, racism, classism, or other ideologies and causes, the message is the same: Do what can be done, wherever it can be done, to better the world.

Readers curious to learn more about Albert Woodfox may wish to listen to his 2005 interview about activism with Prison Radio or read his recent interview about *Solitary* with NPR.

Reviewed by Jamie Chornoby. This review was originally published in *The BookBrowse Review* in March 2019, and has been updated for the January 2020 edition.

THE FAR FIELD

by Madhuri Vijay

BookBrowse Rating: 5/5
Critics' Consensus: 5/5
Readers' Rating: 4/5

Published October 2019 in Paperback, 448 pages

Summary

Gorgeously tactile and sweeping in historical and socio-political scope, Pushcart Prize-winner Madhuri Vijay's *The Far Field* follows a complicated flaneuse across the Indian subcontinent as she reckons with her past, her desires, and the tumultuous present.

In the wake of her mother's death, Shalini, a privileged and restless young woman from Bangalore, sets out for a remote Himalayan village in the troubled northern region of Kashmir. Certain that the loss of her mother is somehow connected to the decade-old disappearance of Bashir Ahmed, a charming Kashmiri salesman who frequented her childhood home, she is determined to confront him. But upon her arrival, Shalini is brought face to face with Kashmir's politics, as well as the tangled history of the local family that takes her in. And when life in the village turns volatile and old hatreds threaten to erupt into violence, Shalini finds herself forced to make a series of choices that could hold dangerous repercussions for the very people she has come to love.

With rare acumen and evocative prose, in *The Far Field* Madhuri Vijay masterfully examines Indian politics, class prejudice, and sexuality through the lens of an outsider, offering a profound meditation on grief, guilt, and the limits of compassion.

BookBrowse Review

In her highly-anticipated debut novel, Pushcart Prize-winning author Madhuri Vijay presents a meditation on grief and shifting identity set in Kashmir.

This substantial, character-driven debut novel invites readers to travel to places beyond roads. Its adventurous coming-of-age story follows first-person narrator Shalini on a quest to escape grief and to excavate family secrets, navigating between privilege and poverty, knowledge and self-doubt. Madhuri Vijay's prose is lyrical, descriptive and seasoned with terms from the Indian subcontinent, a region alive with diverse religious, cultural and linguistic currents.

> "The shops were open now, some owned by Muslims, others by Hindus who had lit sticks of incense in front of tinseled portraits of Lakshmi. The ground was littered with fruit rinds, plastic cups, pellets of goat shit, and runnels of brown water."

At age 8, Shalini witnessed something spark between her mother and a visiting Kashmiri sari salesman, Bashir Ahmed. Bashir was more than a salesman, he was a gifted storyteller, and entertained mother and daughter with dazzling tales, personal style, and flashing green eyes. Curious from the beginning, Shalini later noticed that her mother relied on Bashir in ways beyond a simple housewife listening to a visiting salesman. We meet Shalini in 2010 when she is 30, and reflecting back on her journey to Kashmir four years earlier. In the aftermath of her mother's death, on the run from grief, post-college job responsibilities, and a wealthy slacker boyfriend, Shalini is determined to find Bashir in Kashmir to let him know that her mother is dead. Traveling by taxi, train and on foot, the journey from Bangalore spans nearly 1900 miles, from urban affluence to subsistence village life in the Himalayan foothills.

> "I stopped and raised my face to the mountains. They were pink, shadows running like deep cracks down their slopes. I lifted my hand and traced their wavering peaks with a forefinger. Somewhere in those mountains, I sternly reminded myself, was Bashir Ahmed. That was why I had come. To find him."

There are many flashbacks, woven seamlessly and cinematically through the main narrative. The twists of past and present enhance tension and deepen all characters. Shalini recalls a complex and unstable childhood relationship with her mother, Amma. Shalini's parents were in many ways mismatched, yet joined by a traditional, arranged marriage. Amma, an alluring beauty, was a rural village girl with limited formal education. Shalini's father, Appa, attended university in the U.S. and owns a multinational business headquartered in affluent Bangalore. Shalini embodies elements of both parents, but during her trip to Kashmir, she begins to notice more similarities between herself and her volatile, unpredictable mother. In her earlier years, Shalini enjoyed a stronger bond with her father. Appa is a nurturing presence, a financial provider and an intellectually challenging friend. It's clear that Shalini is not expected to accept an arranged marriage, she is of a new generation, where previous rules no longer apply.

Upon first arriving in Kashmir, Shalini learns that Bashir has disappeared - one of many political dissidents who have been imprisoned, killed, or otherwise detained without recourse by the occupying Indian military forces. The Indian state of Jammu and Kashmir is claimed by both Pakistan and India, with many Kashmiri separatists wanting a sovereign state. (Political crosscurrents are carefully explored throughout the novel.) Shalini is eventually sheltered by Bashir's son, Riyaz Ahmed, and his effervescent wife Amina, who teaches her to milk cows and other survival skills, and nicknames her "Murgi" which means "chicken," as in "always running away."

Life in a rural Kashmiri village seems idyllic to Shalini at first, as she's befriending lovely people and admiring majestic natural scenery, especially in contrast to the cacophony of urban Bangalore. Soon, however, she notices that lack of access to basic medical care or education, and ever-present political disruptions mean that life in Kashmir is far from a Shangri-La utopia. People here are one injury away from starvation, one misspoken word away from detainment or death. She tutors the head of the village council's daughter, who aspires to learn enough English to enroll in a university. She's offered a position to teach at the local school, and considers staying, but the destabilization of both the region and her own life complicate this prospect.

Shalini steps into many frightening situations, which she navigates with unpredictable levels of confidence. She is often naive, making impulsive, dangerous choices, including instigating imprudent romantic encounters. Her actions (or failure to take action) cause hardship and danger for others. This is a reckoning that, as Shalini matures, haunts her. *The Far Field* exemplifies the power of story on many levels - to hold information, history and deep currents of emotion. Yet life is not like one of Bashir's fairy tales. Easy answers and absolute redemption remain elusive.

The novel offers elements of travelogue with the tone of a personal journal, where the narrator's emotions and ideas reveal insecurities and the intricacies of her consciousness without self-censorship. Intimate sensory details and emotional resonance flow on almost every page.

> "There had been no mirror in the house in the village, and this was the first time in weeks that I had looked at myself. I felt a brief shock of recognition, followed by an obscure disappointment. I was thinner, yes, my hair a bit longer, but other than that, I had not changed at all. But, then, what had I expected? A manic, holy gleam in my eye, as in the eyes of those ragged, hippie Westerners I sometimes saw around Bangalore...consecrated by their first exposure to yoga and the poor?"

On an important level, this book bears witness to complicated political injustices and territorial disputes in contemporary Jammu and Kashmir. It also portrays the heroic quest of a flawed and enduring heroine seeking her purpose in a difficult world. Raw edges of personal and cultural loss reverberate long after the last page is turned.

Reviewed by Karen Lewis. This review was originally published in *The BookBrowse Review* in January 2019, and has been updated for the December 2019 edition.

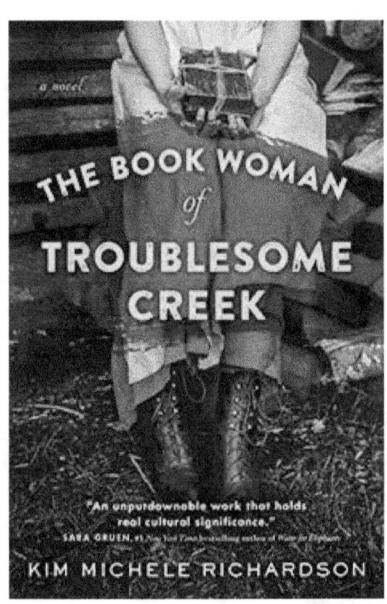

THE BOOK WOMAN OF TROUBLESOME CREEK

by Kim Michele Richardson

BookBrowse Rating: 4/5
Critics' Consensus: 5/5
Readers' Rating: 5/5

Published May 2019 in Paperback, 320 pages

Summary

Inspired by the true blue-skinned people of Kentucky and the brave and dedicated Kentucky Pack Horse library service of the 1930s, *The Book Woman* of *Troublesome Creek* is a story of raw courage, fierce strength, and one woman's belief that books can carry us anywhere—even back home.

The hardscrabble folks of Troublesome Creek have to scrap for everything -- everything except books, that is. Thanks to Roosevelt's Kentucky Pack Horse Library Project, Troublesome's got its very own traveling librarian, Cussy Mary Carter.

Cussy's not only a book woman, however, she's also the last of her kind, her skin a shade of blue unlike most anyone else. Not everyone is keen on Cussy's family or the Library Project, and a Blue is often blamed for any whiff of trouble. If Cussy wants to bring the joy of books to the hill folks, she's going to have to confront prejudice as old as the Appalachias and suspicion as deep as the holler.

BookBrowse Review

A heartfelt salute to the Pack Horse librarians of Depression-era Kentucky and to the act of reading itself, this eclectic novel is about and for book lovers.

A loyal animal companion, treks through gorgeous but forbidding wilderness, glimpses of larger historical events through personal and regional experiences: These components appear in many works of fiction intended to entertain and educate young people. They also emerge in Kim Michele Richardson's *The Book Woman of Troublesome Creek*, a novel set in the 1930s that is perfect for adults who grew up with the adventure and whimsy of books by Lucy Maud Montgomery and Laura Ingalls Wilder.

Cussy Mary Carter, known alternately as Bluet and Book Woman, is a blue-skinned Kentuckian of French descent—based on the Blue Fugates of Kentucky, a genetic ancestral line of people suffering from a rare blood disorder called methemoglobinemia that caused their skin to appear bluish-purple. She spends her days working as a Pack Horse librarian, toting books to the rural people of Troublesome Creek and surrounding areas amidst extreme poverty. Her job and way of life are threatened when her father, a struggling coal miner, marries her off to an abusive older man. However, a stroke of poetic justice soon enables Cussy to return to work with her newly adopted mule Junia, a fierce beast who will protect her mistress at all costs.

Despite the harsh and dangerous nature of Cussy's life and work, Richardson manages to infuse *The Book Woman of Troublesome Creek* with a sense of wonder. The characters along Cussy's route, each with their distinct dispositions and back stories, add to the novel's playful, picaresque feel. We journey with the protagonist as she visits children in a schoolhouse, an old woman with poor eyesight who depends on the Pack Horse librarian for regular Bible-reading sessions, a man sick from a gunshot wound and eligible bachelor Jackson Lovett—who we can guess from his first encounter with Cussy (or from his name alone) may be destined for a romantic future with our Book Woman.

As a Blue, Cussy experiences discrimination, which is informed by the anti-black racism of the time. The white townspeople and sheriff expect her to abide by the same segregation regulations as Black people in Troublesome, and many are afraid to touch her, fearing a contagion or some unknown consequence. She finds herself in a personal and moral dilemma when the local doctor assures her that he can "cure" her blueness.

Cussy's struggle with her appearance is believable, but the book never fully acknowledges the complexity of her relationship with historical racism. As a person of European ancestry rejected by a white community, she shares experiences with people of other races, but in a complicated and incomplete way. She privately sees herself as objectively worse off than her friend Queenie, a Black woman and fellow Pack Horse librarian, despite there being no evidence that the two have ever compared thoughts on the matter. It makes sense that Cussy would feel this way, having grown up as the only one of her kind in an isolated location and therefore having a limited perspective on race relations. It also seems possible that Queenie, who appears to keep a polite distance from Cussy while also showing genuine affection for her, might view Cussy as a fellow oppressed minority and yet, simultaneously, as a white woman. It would be interesting to explore this angle—however, Cussy's (understandably) simplistic thinking is never upset by a moment of conflict with Queenie or any other character. Even one short, strained exchange might have made for a less reductive presentation of systemic racism, and a more nuanced take on Cussy's feelings about her own identity.

At times, Richardson's novel also feels a bit shallow in the romance department, but this isn't necessarily a problem. Cussy isn't a particularly romantic individual after all, and frankly, she doesn't have time to undergo a fancy, languorous courtship. It's actually amusing to see her lingering interest in Jackson relegated to the background for much of the book as she crashes through the woods with bigger concerns on her mind, bringing deliveries to her patrons; spontaneously tending to the sick and hungry; and negotiating encounters with dangerous men, death-defying mountain paths and, at one point, a rattlesnake.

The Book Woman of Troublesome Creek puts its own offbeat spin not just on classic romance but also crime, action and adventure, suspense and, of course, historical fiction—all with a flawed but sympathetic lead at its center. In addition to spotlighting a fascinating phenomenon in book history, it is itself a book lover's book, a celebration of stories and genres, an exercise in reading nostalgia. It may just take you back to hushed afternoons in the school library, nights hiding with a flashlight and paperback under the covers, those magical days of discovering reading for pleasure.

Reviewed by Elisabeth Cook. This review was originally published in *The BookBrowse Review* in October 2019, and has been updated for the December 2019 edition.

BEST BOOKS OF 2018

EDUCATED

by Tara Westover

BookBrowse Rating: 5/5
Critics' Consensus: 4.5/5
Readers' Rating: 5/5

Published February 2022 in Paperback, 368 pages

Summary

Winner of the 2018 BookBrowse Nonfiction Award

An unforgettable memoir about a young girl who, kept out of school, leaves her survivalist family and goes on to earn a PhD from Cambridge University.

Tara Westover was seventeen the first time she set foot in a classroom. Born to survivalists in the mountains of Idaho, she prepared for the end of the world by stockpiling home-canned peaches and sleeping with her "head-for-the-hills" bag. In the summer she stewed herbs for her mother, a midwife and healer, and in the winter she salvaged metal in her father's junkyard.

Her father distrusted the medical establishment, so Tara never saw a doctor or nurse. Gashes and concussions, even burns from explosions, were all treated at home with herbalism. The family was so isolated from mainstream society that there was no one to ensure the children received an education, and no one to intervene when an older brother became violent.

When another brother got himself into college and came back with news of the world beyond the mountain, Tara decided to try a new kind of life. She taught herself enough mathematics, grammar, and science to take the ACT and was admitted to Brigham Young University. There, she studied psychology, politics, philosophy, and history, learning for the first time about pivotal world events like the Holocaust and the Civil Rights Movement. Her quest for knowledge transformed her, taking her over oceans and across continents, to Harvard and to Cambridge University. Only then would she wonder if she'd traveled too far, if there was still a way home.

Educated is an account of the struggle for self-invention. It is a tale of fierce family loyalty, and of the grief that comes from severing ties with those closest to you. With the acute insight that distinguishes all great writers, Westover has crafted a universal coming-of-age story that gets to the heart of what an education is and what it offers: the perspective to see one's life through new eyes, and the will to change it.

BookBrowse Review

This unforgettable memoir tells of a young woman's off-grid upbringing in Idaho and the hard work that took her from almost complete ignorance to a Cambridge PhD.

Voted 2018 Best Nonfiction Award Winner by BookBrowse Subscribers

Tara Westover had the kind of upbringing most of us can only imagine. She was the youngest of seven children raised in Buck Peak, Idaho by Mormon parents who distrusted the federal government and anticipated the end of days. Her father refused to register his children's births, so Westover had no birth certificate or knowledge of her exact birthday. Westover's dad also rejected formal education, so none of his children attended school. They could study at home from a meager selection of textbooks if they chose, but their father valued practical skills more. He put Westover to work in his junkyard, sorting scrap metal when she was merely 10. She also babysat, packed nuts, and worked in a grocery store. But she never went to school.

Few of the simple pleasures of childhood were available. Musical theater provided rare moments of joy in a life of hard labor that included assisting her mother, who was an unofficial midwife and herbalist (see 'Beyond the Book'). The family went through two serious car accidents and her brother Shawn suffered multiple head injuries at his father's construction site. Shawn's behavior grew cruel, especially after his brain damage. He would put Westover's head down the toilet, bend her wrist back until it nearly snapped, and call her a "whore" for wearing lip gloss. This sadistic pattern was repeated with another sister and later, with his wife, yet Westover struggled to convince her parents to believe her and do something, *anything*, about Shawn's manipulative violence.

Education was Westover's means of escape. Like her brother Tyler before her, she studied independently until she passed the ACT and earned acceptance to Brigham Young University. Here she was forced to wake up to her extreme ignorance. She raised a hand in history class to ask what "the Holocaust" meant, and learned who Martin Luther King, Jr. was. A study abroad year at King's College, Cambridge, opened her mind even more and paved the way for her return to England for Master's and PhD degrees in history. One professor told her she'd written one of the best essays he'd read in 30 years, and referred to her as his "Pygmalion" – a fresh mind that he could mold for success.

From an Idaho junkyard to the venerable halls of Cambridge—it was disorienting for Westover to think of how far she had come and truly believe she deserved to be there. Trips home plunged her back into family turmoil. Her parents disapproved of her pursuing education instead of marriage and motherhood, and her father was severely burned in a fuel tank explosion. He didn't believe in modern medicine, so never went to a hospital; his wife treated him at home with her herbal salves, a booming business that made them wealthy.

Westover's incredible story is about testing the limits of perseverance and sanity. Her father may have been a survivalist, but her psychic survival is the most impressive outcome here. Although this memoir represents Westover's own perspective, she strives to be rational and charitable by questioning her own memory and interpretation of events, often looking for outside confirmation from other family members who witnessed the same events. And though the temptation must have been strong, she doesn't portray her father as a villain; he's more like an Old Testament patriarch, fierce and unmovable. She is careful not to make hers a simple narrative about rejecting Mormonism – in fact, she opens with a disclaimer to that effect – because her parents' extremism was far beyond what is the norm for Mormons.

The writing takes this astonishing life story to the next level, making it a classic to sit alongside memoirs by Alexandra Fuller, Mary Karr and Jeannette Walls. Westover narrates with calm authority, channeling the style of the scriptures and history books that were formative in her upbringing and education. One of my favorite passages reflects on the fundamental differences between her father's viewpoint and her own: "My father and I looked at the temple. He saw God; I saw granite. We looked at each other. He saw a woman damned; I saw an unhinged old man, literally disfigured by his beliefs."

This is one of the most powerful and well-written memoirs I've ever read. In its first half a young girl spends lonely years in the wide-open sanctuary of the American West: "Her classroom was a heap of junk. Her textbooks, slates of scrap," Westover writes. In the second half the whole world and its history open up to her, but at a high price: "having sacrificed my family to my education." The author remains estranged from her parents, and the siblings have formed two factions: four work for her parents' herbal empire in Idaho; three left to pursue education, all obtaining doctoral degrees. Which route would you choose?

Reviewed by Rebecca Foster. This review was originally published in *The BookBrowse Review* in March 2018, and has been updated for the December 2018 edition.

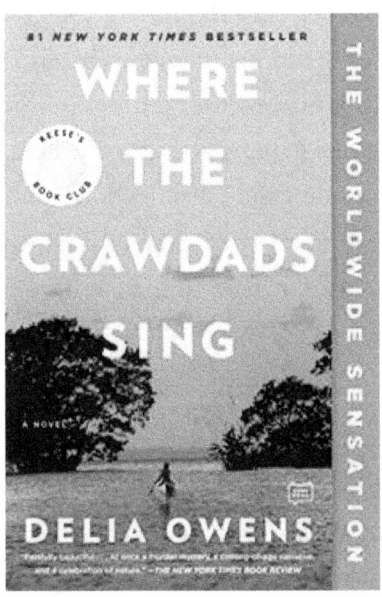

WHERE THE CRAWDADS SING

by Delia Owens

BookBrowse Rating: 4/5
Critics' Consensus: 5/5
Readers' Rating: 4.5/5

Published March 2021 in Paperback, 400 pages

Summary

Winner of the 2018 BookBrowse Debut Author Award

How long can you protect your heart?

For years, rumors of the "Marsh Girl" have haunted Barkley Cove, a quiet town on the North Carolina coast. So in late 1969, when handsome Chase Andrews is found dead, the locals immediately suspect Kya Clark, the so-called Marsh Girl. But Kya is not what they say. Sensitive and intelligent, she has survived for years alone in the marsh that she calls home, finding friends in the gulls and lessons in the sand. Then the time comes when she yearns to be touched and loved. When two young men from town become intrigued by her wild beauty, Kya opens herself to a new life - until the unthinkable happens.

Perfect for fans of Barbara Kingsolver and Karen Russell, *Where the Crawdads Sing* is at once an exquisite ode to the natural world, a heartbreaking coming-of-age story, and a surprising tale of possible murder. Owens reminds us that we are forever shaped by the children we once were, and that we are all subject to the beautiful and violent secrets that nature keeps.

BookBrowse Review

In Delia Owens's debut novel, a young woman who's survived a solitary childhood in a shack in North Carolina's marsh country looks for love and builds a career in science.

Voted 2018 Best Debut Award Winner by BookBrowse Subscribers

Where the Crawdads Sing was a hit even before being chosen for Reese Witherspoon's Hello Sunshine Book Club – and it's easy to see why so many have taken this debut novel into their hearts. It's a gripping mystery but also a tender coming-of-age story about one woman's desperately lonely upbringing and her rocky route to finding love and a vocation. Not only that, but its North Carolina marsh setting is described in lyrical language that evinces Delia Owens's background in nature writing (see Beyond the Book).

We first meet Kya Clark in 1952. The marshland surrounding the Clarks' shack has been a haven for fugitives and runaway slaves; though it's not far from Barkley Cove, it seems to have its own rules based on instinct and survival. Six-year-old Kya watches Ma leave with a blue suitcase in hand, and before long Pa's drunken violence has also driven off the last of her four older siblings, her brother Jodie.

Pa disappears for weeks at a time, leaving Kya to subsist on grits and soda crackers. The thought of a hot lunch lures her into attending second grade for a day, but after the kids call her "swamp trash" and make fun of her for not knowing how to spell, she vows to never set foot in school again. For years she survives by picking mussels and trading them for dry goods and kerosene at the general store run by Jumpin' and Mabel. As African Americans in the South, they know what it's like to be ostracized, and become like family to white Kya.

Kya's other source of support is Jodie's friend Tate, who shares her love of nature and teaches her to read when she's 14. Tate brings her rare feathers, science books and paint for her sketches. Their budding romance is cut short when Tate leaves for college. Although he promises to come back for Kya, the years pass and she's still alone, writing and illustrating field guides to the region's shells and birds. When she's 19, star quarterback Chase Andrews catches her eye and starts wooing her over picnics. Soon he's talking marriage, though he still hasn't introduced Kya to his parents or friends. Does he really love her, or is he just making a trophy out of "the Marsh Girl"?

Early on in the novel we learn that Chase Andrews will be found dead in 1969, having fallen from the fire tower into the swamp. No fingerprints or footprints are found; it doesn't seem like suicide or an accident. Soon rumor points to "the crazy lady on the marsh" because of her clandestine relationship with Chase. In between sections about Kya's childhood and adolescence, there are short updates on the 1969 investigation. As the two story lines converge, the chapters become more rapid-fire. Owens ramps up the tension, culminating in top-notch courtroom scenes as Kya stands trial for murder. The novel's third-person narration is coy, omitting certain scenes to allow readers to speculate right along with the prosecution.

Although the novel focuses on the years between 1965 and 1970, it encompasses the whole span of Kya's life. At times I found it hard to believe that the plucky urchin living off of grits and evading truant officers is the same character as the willowy nature writer wondering who will love her and never leave. Also, the chronology becomes slightly difficult to follow as it approaches 1969, and there are perhaps a few too many Amanda Hamilton poems. (You'll have to read the novel to find out more about who this fictional poet is!)

The use of animal behavior metaphors works very well, though. Kya understands her fellow humans by analogy, asking why a mother animal might leave her cubs or why males compete for female attention. The title refers to places where wild creatures do what comes naturally, and throughout the book we are invited to ponder how instinct and altruism interact and what impact human actions can have in the grand scheme of things, as in this passage about the marsh swallowing Chase's body: "the swamp is quiet because decomposition is cellular work. Life decays and reeks and returns to the rotted duff. ... A swamp knows all about death, and doesn't necessarily define it as tragedy, certainly not a sin."

In Kya, Owens has created a truly outstanding character. The extremity of her loneliness makes her a sympathetic figure in spite of her oddities. If you like the idea of a literary novel flavored with elements of mystery and romance, and of a poetic writing style tempered with folksy Southern dialect, *Crawdads* is a real treat.

Reviewed by Rebecca Foster. This review was originally published in *The BookBrowse Review* in December 2018, and has been updated for the April 2021 edition.

CIRCE

by Madeline Miller

BookBrowse Rating: 5/5
Critics' Consensus: 5/5
Readers' Rating: 5/5

Published April 2020 in Paperback, 400 pages

Summary

Winner of the 2018 BookBrowse Fiction Award

The daring, dazzling and highly anticipated follow-up to the New York Times bestseller *The Song of Achilles*.

In the house of Helios, god of the sun and mightiest of the Titans, a daughter is born. But Circe is a strange child - not powerful, like her father, nor viciously alluring like her mother. Turning to the world of mortals for companionship, she discovers that she does possess power - the power of witchcraft, which can transform rivals into monsters and menace the gods themselves.

Threatened, Zeus banishes her to a deserted island, where she hones her occult craft, tames wild beasts and crosses paths with many of the most famous figures in all of mythology, including the Minotaur, Daedalus and his doomed son Icarus, the murderous Medea, and, of course, wily Odysseus.

But there is danger, too, for a woman who stands alone, and Circe unwittingly draws the wrath of both men and gods, ultimately finding herself pitted against one of the most terrifying and vengeful of the Olympians. To protect what she loves most, Circe must summon all her strength and choose, once and for all, whether she belongs with the gods she is born from, or the mortals she has come to love.

With unforgettably vivid characters, mesmerizing language and page-turning suspense, *Circe* is a triumph of storytelling, an intoxicating epic of family rivalry, palace intrigue, love and loss, as well as a celebration of indomitable female strength in a man's world.

NPR's Weekend Edition "Books To Look Forward To In 2018"
Esquire's "The 27 Most Anticipated Books of 2018"
Boston Globe's "25 books we can't wait to read in 2018"
The Millions "The Most Anticipated: The Great 2018 Book Preview"
Cosmopolitan's "33 Books to Get Excited About in 2018"

BookBrowse Review

Madeline Miller follows up her prize-winning debut, *Song of Achilles*, with another dazzling Greek myth retelling that explores femininity and self-determinism through the lesser known figure of Circe the nymph.

Voted 2018 Best Fiction Award Winner by BookBrowse Subscribers

Towards the end of Madeline Miller's novel *Circe*, the titular nymph is questioned by her son about her life that has already spanned some thousand years. The teenaged Telegonus can hardly hide his astonishment upon discovering that his seemingly low-key mother, whom he has lived alone with for sixteen uneventful years on the secluded island of Aeaea, is related to illustrious gods and mighty Titans, and has been acquainted with already legendary figures in Greece's nascent history. "'Mother! You must tell me everything,'" he pleads.

Yet far from being flattered by this newfound interest in her marginal existence, Circe is almost resentful and retreats from this rare opportunity to shine: "My past was not some game, some adventure tale. It was the ugly wrack that storms left rotten on the shore."

It is a curious, somewhat unfair admission that exposes the mindset of this female divinity. Despite the mythic moments she was witness to and participated in, including being present for the punishment of Prometheus and daring to be the only one of all the gods to secretly offer the wounded Titan a merciful drink to ease his pain, Circe feels she administers no particular control over her destiny, she has no pride in her story. But make no mistake. Her tales are of similar stock to those other gods would eagerly rhapsodize over.

Circe's self-deprecation stems from a lifetime of being used, abused and belittled by gods and mortals alike. From birth, she is quick to realize that regardless of her divine heritage, she is little more than an inconsequence. Her mother, the nymph Perse, wrinkles her nose at her newly born daughter's sex.

Pasiphaë, her glory-seeking sister, treats her as a constant object of derision to taunt and mock. And in her adolescence, her sun god father Helios declares his daughter to be "the worst of my children, faded and broken, whom I cannot pay a husband to take."

Rejected, Circe finds solace in sorcery. She learns the power of herbs and potions and begins to surreptitiously use her newfangled witchcraft to self-serving advantage. She gifts her first love, the fisherman Glaucus, with divinity and turns a rival to her beau's affections into a grotesque six-headed sea monster. But even these impressive magical feats are not enough to garner Circe any particular prestige. Her own father dismisses these transformations as instances of fate that Circe was coincidentally spectator to and had no active hand in invoking. Circe soon begins to understand that her marginality is less to do with the fact that she is a nymph, "least of the lesser goddesses," than that she is a woman. This becomes especially apparent when, exiled on Aeaea, Circe offers drowning wayward sailors refuge in her home. Time and time again the sailors turn on their solitary hostess. Even displaying her divinity makes no difference: "I was alone and a woman, that was all that mattered." Her solution is to turn these lustful debauched men into swine.

Much of *Circe* is an exploration into what it means to be female in a world of men and monsters. While it is usually tenuous to compare an author's latest novel to previous work, it does feel as if Miller wrote *Circe* as a conscious inversion of her prize-winning debut *The Song of Achilles* in nearly every aspect. The pool of inspiration may be the same – primarily Homer's epics – but whereas *Achilles* was very much a book about mortal men coming to grips with their own version of masculinity, *Circe* is about a divine woman trying to consolidate her myriad feminine identities as daughter, sister, lover, mother, witch, and goddess.

Even the narrative frames in each of Miller's binary novels take on quasi-gendered forms. In *Achilles* the story arc is as steady and as unwavering as the trajectory of the sun. From the start the reader knows more or less where the tale will set. In *Circe* there's a fluidity to plot and narrative that is similar to the tides that surround the nymph's adopted home island. Characters come and go. Those well-versed in Greek myth will particularly delight in cameos from Jason of Argonauts fame, Minos and his namesake Minotaur, and Daedalus, father of that cautionary figure Icarus. That said, Miller provides plenty background for even those unfamiliar with Greek mythology to enjoy her adaptations of these classic myths.

By the end of her transformative tale, Circe comes to realize that she has far more control and power over her destiny than she was initially led to believe. Graceful and majestic in equal measures, *Circe* is sure to leave an indelible impression on readers both new and returning to Miller's singular reworkings of Greek myths.

Reviewed by Dean Muscat. This review was originally published in *The BookBrowse Review* in April 2018, and has been updated for the May 2020 edition.

BURIED BENEATH THE BAOBAB TREE

by Adaobi Tricia Nwaubani

BookBrowse Rating: 5/5
Critics' Consensus: 5/5

Published March 2020 in Paperback, 336 pages

Summary

Based on interviews with young women who were kidnapped by Boko Haram, a Muslim terrorist group, this poignant novel by Adaobi Tricia Nwaubani tells the timely story of one girl who was taken from her home in Nigeria and her harrowing fight for survival.

A new pair of shoes, a university degree, a husband - these are the things that a girl dreams of in a Nigerian village. And with a government scholarship right around the corner, everyone can see that these dreams aren't too far out of reach.

But the girl's dreams turn to nightmares when her village is attacked by Boko Haram in the middle of the night. Kidnapped, she is taken with other girls and women into the forest where she is forced to follow her captors' radical beliefs and watch as her best friend slowly accepts everything she's been told.

Still, the girl defends her existence. As impossible as escape may seem, her life - her future - is hers to fight for.

BookBrowse Review

Based on interviews with young women who were kidnapped by Boko Haram, this novel tells the timely story of one girl who was taken from her home in Nigeria and her harrowing fight for survival.

Ya Ta, the main character in Adaobi Tricia Nwaubani's novel, *Buried Beneath the Baobab Tree*, lives in rural northeastern Nigeria and is the first student from her village to gain a scholarship to boarding school. In this extremely rural region of the country, many children, both boys and girls, do not complete primary school. Some, like Ya Ta's brothers, stay home to help work the fields, while others are married young and quit school. Here, Christian and Muslim families have long coexisted in harmony, embracing traditional tribal rites while also attending church or mosque. The novel opens with Ya Ta's future plans being interrupted by Boko Haram, a violent militia, raiding her village.

Boko Haram is an armed insurgency that espouses a corrupted vision of Islam. Its name means "western school is forbidden" in the northern Nigerian language of Hausa. Over the past decade, it has gained traction in parts of Nigeria, Niger, Chad, and Cameroon in its attempt to impose Islamic law as the sole law by inflicting violent assaults, threats, and abduction to terrorize civilians and evade the rule of law. The group came to international media attention in 2014 after kidnapping 276 young girls from a school in Chibok, a town in northern Nigeria. As of September 2018, more than 100 Chibok girls remain missing. Thousands of other youth have been taken and more than two million people have been displaced by the Boko Haram terror. Characters in *Buried Beneath the Baobab Tree* are based on real people interviewed by the author. Historical background is detailed in the afterword, titled "The Chosen Generation," written by Italian journalist Viviana Mazza, who is one of Nwaubani's journalism colleagues.

The novel is set within this current political and cultural context. Ya Ta and her best friends, Sarah and Aisha, are abducted with dozens of other youth including Ya Ta's youngest brother, Jacob, and are held captive at Boko Haram camps hidden in Sambisa Forest. Narrated in first-person by Ya Ta, the story moves quickly through hundreds of very short chapters. Chapter titles such as "Tree of Life", "Once a Month," "The Voice on Papa's Radio," "Gossip," "The Pink Van," "This is Not Islam," "New Clothes," "Showing Off," and "Watching Men" carry readers deep inside this real-world test of survival.

Language is clear, and action is fast-paced. The girls become indoctrinated by their captors and eke out a bare-bones existence hidden away from the world: "'We do not intend to harm you,' the Leader says. 'We only want to make you good Muslim women.' Gripping each other's fingers tight, Sarah and I shift to his left-hand side with the other Christian women and girls, while Aisha stands on the right with the Muslims." Aisha, 14, is already married to a beloved husband arranged by her parents; she is determined to protect her own life and the life of her unborn child. The Christian girls are given new names. Ya Ta becomes Salamatu. Sarah is called Zainab. Captivity tests friendships. Zainab embraces most aspects of life with her new "husband" and camp rules, while Salamatu continues to resist in subtle ways. She seeks comfort in her memories of family, school, faith, and the way life used to be.

She imagines a future at university and dreams up ways to escape her "husband," one of the fighters who, for some mysterious reason, always wears a mask. "In any case, whether he chooses to bury his face in a mask because it looks like a hippopotamus bottom or whether he is wary of dazzling damsels with his divine beauty, I do not want to marry him," she says.

Occasionally the captive girls hear rumors that government forces are near and will save them. But rescue is elusive, food is scarce, and loyalties are constantly tested. One day, hunger prompts Salamatu and Zainab to gather edibles from the forest and they delight in discovering a baobab tree (see Beyond the Book). So many of their previous childhood pastimes involved the baobab, they plan to stand on each other's shoulders to harvest fruit. But the truth is soon revealed: their captors have turned the shady area beneath the sacred tree into a mass grave.

Even if liberated, most former captives find return to "normal" life extremely difficult, for a variety of reasons. In the chapter "Better Life" Salamatu wonders: "How will the mother of a child with bad blood lift her head high among normal human beings? Life in the forest might have been better for me."

References to traditional West African images and customs will appeal to readers who want to learn about life in this part of the world. *Buried Beneath the Baobab Tree* is an ideal choice for book clubs and classroom discussion, and because of its short chapters and clear writing it will engage reluctant readers. Themes in the novel are relevant to contemporary teens everywhere: violence (including school violence), religious freedom, rule of law, gangs, sexual violence, peer pressure, family duty, missing parents, family separation, and teen empowerment. Nwaubani's previous novel *I Do Not Come to You by Chance* won the 2010 Commonwealth Writers Prize (Africa) for best first book and was a finalist for the Wole Soyinka Prize in Africa - a pan-African writing prize awarded biennially to the best literary work produced by an African. Her journalism appears in many media outlets including *The New Yorker, Reuters,* and *BBC,* where she has reported on the Chibok kidnappings and Boko Haram among many other topics.

Ultimately, Nwaubani has created a novel that is a hopeful call out to the resilient human spirit, showcasing young people and their communities who struggle to create a path forward from a place of violence and despair.

Reviewed by Karen Lewis. This review was originally published in *The BookBrowse Review* in October 2018, and has been updated for the March 2020 edition.

BAD BLOOD

by John Carreyrou

BookBrowse Rating: 5/5
Critics' Consensus: 5/5
Readers' Rating: 5/5

Published January 2020 in Paperback, 368 pages

Summary

The full inside story of the breathtaking rise and shocking collapse of Theranos, the multibillion-dollar biotech startup, by the prize-winning journalist who first broke the story and pursued it to the end, despite pressure from its charismatic CEO and threats by her lawyers.

In 2014, Theranos founder and CEO Elizabeth Holmes was widely seen as the female Steve Jobs: a brilliant Stanford dropout whose startup "unicorn" promised to revolutionize the medical industry with a machine that would make blood testing significantly faster and easier. Backed by investors such as Larry Ellison and Tim Draper, Theranos sold shares in a fundraising round that valued the company at more than $9 billion, putting Holmes's worth at an estimated $4.7 billion. There was just one problem: The technology didn't work.

A riveting story of the biggest corporate fraud since Enron, a tale of ambition and hubris set amid the bold promises of Silicon Valley.

BookBrowse Review

The full story of the rise and then collapse of a multibillion-dollar biotech startup. Voted a BookBrowse 2018 Top 20 Book.

In February 2015, a blogger for a pathology website contacted John Carreyrou, a Pulitzer Prize-winning investigative journalist for the *Wall Street Journal*. He claimed that his recent post expressing skepticism about a company named Theranos had led to a group of people contacting him with information about the organization. They thought Carreyrou might be interested in following up. He did, and after months of careful research, countless interviews, and threats from Theranos lawyers, he published a series of damning articles about the company and its board. *Bad Blood: Secrets and Lies in a Silicon Valley Startup* is a book-length treatment of Carreyrou's *Wall Street Journal* exposé as well as further investigations sparked by his work.

Theranos was the brain-child of Elizabeth Holmes who at the age of 19 dropped out of Stanford University to pursue an idea of making blood tests easier and less expensive for consumers. An incredibly charismatic and driven woman, Holmes quickly raised $700 million to develop the technology. Eventually she asserted that the equipment she designed could run over 800 tests on a single drop of blood, that its technology was more accurate than traditional lab testing, and that results were ready in less than 30 minutes. The problem was that not one of those claims was true. Nevertheless, by the time Carreyrou exposed the company as a fraud its equipment was being widely relied on, such as by drug manufacturers to test blood during clinical trials.

Immunoassays are performed over 100 million times a year worldwide, and they're big business – companies that provide immunoassay services (for example, for physicians and pharmaceutical companies) earned an estimated $17 trillion in 2012. Theranos, of course, tried to get a slice of this very lucrative pie. At a very basic level, Theranos's technology failed because in order to run numerous tests simultaneously on a very small amount of blood (Holmes at one point claimed up to 800 tests from a simple finger-stick) the material had to be diluted extensively. With such a tiny sample to run against, the distribution of the specific analyte being measured became skewed, producing wildly varying and frequently inaccurate results.

The first part of Carreyrou's account outlines everything he was able to learn about Theranos, Holmes, and other principals responsible for the company's success, such as Ramesh "Sunny" Balwani, its president and COO at the time (and also Holmes' lover.) It's pretty much a non-stop, stomach-turning litany of deception and intimidation (one employee was driven to suicide by the strong-arm tactics employed against anyone who made waves.) By the point in the book where Carreyrou is tipped off, I found myself rooting for someone - anyone - to take these really repulsive people down; I almost cheered out loud at his involvement. The remainder of the book illustrates how he was able to glean enough information about the company to make his case, and the lengths to which Theranos went to keep from being outed.

This highly readable book may be about big business, but it reads like a true crime thriller. The pages flew by as I held my breath, waiting to see what unbelievable act Balwani would perpetrate next, or what incredible claim Holmes would make to secure funding. If the author wasn't such a well-regarded journalist this story would be hard to believe; some of the principals' acts are truly jaw-dropping. A film version of the story starring Jennifer Lawrence is in the works – a testament to the fact that this is truly a riveting tale.

Two areas in *Bad Blood* left me unsatisfied, however, neither of which can be blamed on the author. First, although Theranos was clearly on the verge of collapse when the book was published in May 2018, the story wasn't over; the company didn't shut its doors until August 2018 and legal action was still pending at of the end of 2018. I wanted the rest of the story and some sense of justice, but certainly that final chapter is years off. Secondly, I badly wanted to know if Holmes was a greedy sociopath or just a narcissist, either deliberately ignoring the potential harm she was causing others or simply living in her own reality. She wouldn't grant interviews, so we only get an outsider's sketch of her character, and good journalists don't speculate where no evidence exists – but I still wanted some clue as to why she felt her actions were reasonable.

Carreyrou's work has won many accolades; his *Wall Street Journal* articles on Theranos won the George Polk Award for Financial Reporting, and *Bad Blood* was awarded the *Financial Times* and *McKinsey Business* Book of the Year Award. It also appeared on many "best of" lists for 2018 - including BookBrowse's. My vote can be added; I certainly found it to be one of the finest non-fiction accounts I've read, and I highly recommend it to those interested in cautionary tales about the business world, or great non-fiction reads in general.

Reviewed by Kim Kovacs. This review was originally published in *The BookBrowse Review* in December 2018, and has been updated for the February 2020 edition.

UNSHELTERED

by Barbara Kingsolver

BookBrowse Rating: 4/5
Critics' Consensus: 5/5
Readers' Rating: 4/5

Published October 2019 in Paperback, 480 pages

Summary

A timely novel that interweaves past and present to explore the human capacity for resiliency and compassion in times of great upheaval.

Willa Knox has always prided herself on being the embodiment of responsibility for her family. Which is why it's so unnerving that she's arrived at middle age with nothing to show for her hard work and dedication but a stack of unpaid bills and an inherited brick home in Vineland, New Jersey, that is literally falling apart. The magazine where she worked has folded, and the college where her husband had tenure has closed. The dilapidated house is also home to her ailing and cantankerous Greek father-in-law and her two grown children: her stubborn, free-spirited daughter, Tig, and her dutiful debt-ridden, ivy educated son, Zeke, who has arrived with his unplanned baby in the wake of a life-shattering development.

In an act of desperation, Willa begins to investigate the history of her home, hoping that the local historical preservation society might take an interest and provide funding for its direly needed repairs. Through her research into Vineland's past and its creation as a Utopian community, she discovers a kindred spirit from the 1880s, Thatcher Greenwood.

A science teacher with a lifelong passion for honest investigation, Thatcher finds himself under siege in his community for telling the truth: his employer forbids him to speak of the exciting new theory recently published by Charles Darwin. Thatcher's friendships with a brilliant woman scientist and a renegade newspaper editor draw him into a vendetta with the town's most powerful men. At home, his new wife and status-conscious mother-in-law bristle at the risk of scandal, and dismiss his financial worries and the news that their elegant house is structurally unsound.

Brilliantly executed and compulsively readable, *Unsheltered* is the story of two families, in two centuries, who live at the corner of Sixth and Plum, as they navigate the challenges of surviving a world in the throes of major cultural shifts. In this mesmerizing story told in alternating chapters, Willa and Thatcher come to realize that though the future is uncertain, even unnerving, shelter can be found in the bonds of kindred—whether family or friends—and in the strength of the human spirit.

BookBrowse Review

Kingsolver's bold eighth novel has a dual timeline that compares the America of the 1870s and the recent past, revealing that they are linked by distrust and displacement.

Willa Knox's house is falling down. She recently inherited a Victorian residence in Vineland, New Jersey, and moved there with her husband Iano, a Greek-American political science professor. With them are their 26-year-old daughter, Antigone ("Tig"), who is a restaurant worker recently returned from Cuba, and Iano's ill father, Nick. A contractor tells Willa the house is beyond saving even if they did have money for repairs, and as the year progresses ceilings start caving in. But her family is also falling apart in metaphorical ways. Willa, in her mid-50s, is a veteran journalist, but after the magazine she edited folds she fears her career may be over. Early on she gets a call from her son Zeke, whose partner has just committed suicide, leaving him the single father of a several-week-old son. As Zeke tries to rebuild his life, baby Dusty joins Willa's ragtag household.

Nearly 150 years before, in the early 1870s, a house on this very plot is also falling down. It is the home of Thatcher Greenwood, who moves in with his bride Rose and her mother and sister. The structure that Rose's father built is crumbling already, and there is no money to shore it up. Thatcher's career as the new science teacher founders almost before it starts, too, with Principal Cutler undermining him at every turn and trying to force him to publicly deny Charles Darwin's principles. The only relief Thatcher can find from his troubled family and work life is at his neighbor Mary Treat's house. Mary (one of the book's handful of historical figures – see Beyond the Book) writes up her experiments on spiders and Venus flytraps for scientific journals and is in correspondence with Darwin himself.

The stories collide when Willa starts investigating her neighborhood's past at the Historical Society. The book's structure also emphasizes similarities between two time periods that might initially appear very different. Chapters alternate between the story lines, and the last words of one chapter form the title of the next. Kingsolver carries this all the way through the book: take a peek at the last page and you'll see that the final words are the title of Chapter 1. It's a clever and elegant connecting strategy, as is the habit of using variations on the title word as frequently as possible – something Jonathan Franzen also does in his novels. (I counted 22 instances of "shelter" and its variants in the text; how many can you spot?)

There are also strong thematic links between the eras. In the wake of the Civil War, America remained divided: "One in five of our young men died ... and we are still riven, north against south, countryman against immigrant, laborer against lord," as Cutler puts it. In the novel's recreation of 2016, immigration and economic inequality are still huge concerns. Willa's racist father-in-law, Nick, blames illegal immigrants for all of the country's problems. Meanwhile, the family is barely getting by on Iano's nontenured academic salary and Willa's freelancing. They have to enroll in Medicare to get Nick's health problems treated. Through Tig's descriptions, Kingsolver presents Cuba as a utopian alternative to how things work in the USA: access to free health care and higher education are a given, carpooling is mandatory, and, thanks to the deprivation of the embargo years, people don't treat everything as disposable.

Kingsolver is nothing if not heavy-handed with her messages: Thatcher and Mary Treat are enlightened scientists who value all of life, as opposed to the selfish, superstitious masses; the American health insurance system is byzantine and socialism would solve it; owning your own home and looking after your own family are not the be-all and end-all. Although Donald Trump is never named, he's clearly the outrageous "Bullhorn" figure, likened to real-life Captain Landis, the tyrannical creator/leader of Vineland in the 1870s. The danger is that readers who are ideologically opposed to Kingsolver may be annoyed by her overt taking of sides, while those who already agree with her could be impatient with what seem like statements of the obvious. I felt

Willa's conversations with Tig, a model of the future-minded human, were particularly unrealistic idea dumps.

All the same, *Unsheltered* is a rich, rewarding novel with so much going on that it feels like it encompasses all of human life: Willa's grief for her dead mother; the shifts in her marriage over time; the unexpected joy of her grandson becoming part of their everyday life; facing an uncertain future in which cooperation and creative cutting of consumption may be the only means of survival. In both time periods we see how suspicion and fear divide people and incite authoritarian leadership. We feel how precarious life can be without a safety net. It's not a subtle book, but it's an important one for our time, with many issues worth pondering and discussing.

Reviewed by Rebecca Foster. This review was originally published in *The BookBrowse Review* in October 2018, and has been updated for the October 2019 edition.

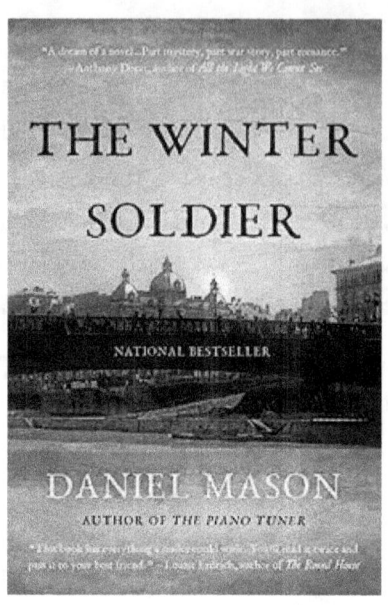

THE WINTER SOLDIER

by Daniel Mason

BookBrowse Rating: 5/5
Critics' Consensus: 4.5/5
Readers' Rating: 4.5/5

Published September 2019 in Paperback, 336 pages

Summary

By the international bestselling author of *The Piano Tuner*, a sweeping and unforgettable love story of a young doctor and nurse at a remote field hospital in the First World War.

Vienna, 1914. Lucius is a twenty-two-year-old medical student when World War I explodes across Europe. Enraptured by romantic tales of battlefield surgery, he enlists, expecting a position at a well-organized field hospital. But when he arrives, at a commandeered church tucked away high in a remote valley of the Carpathian Mountains, he finds a freezing outpost ravaged by typhus. The other doctors have fled, and only a single, mysterious nurse named Sister Margarete remains.

But Lucius has never lifted a surgeon's scalpel. And as the war rages across the winter landscape, he finds himself falling in love with the woman from whom he must learn a brutal, makeshift medicine. Then one day, an unconscious soldier is brought in from the snow, his uniform stuffed with strange drawings. He seems beyond rescue, until Lucius makes a fateful decision that will change the lives of doctor, patient, and nurse forever.

From the gilded ballrooms of Imperial Vienna to the frozen forests of the Eastern Front; from hardscrabble operating rooms to battlefields thundering with Cossack cavalry, *The Winter Soldier* is the story of war and medicine, of family, of finding love in the sweeping tides of history, and finally, of the mistakes we make, and the precious opportunities to atone.

BookBrowse Review

***The Winter Soldier* is a story of love, courage, and the fragile human psyche set in a small Eastern European hospital during World War I.**

Imagine the thousands of confounding cases doctors face routinely for which diagnoses are hard to come by. Now imagine an additional point of pressure on those decisions that must be made in a matter of seconds: the urgency of war. One wonders what mistakes are made and lived with under such harrowing circumstances, a question eloquently pondered by Daniel Mason in *The Winter Soldier*. It is a breathtaking and evocative novel on multiple fronts, but above all, it is the story of human frailty among those who have sworn to "first, do no harm."

The 22-year-old Lucius Krzelewski is born into a wealthy Polish family who have sunk roots in Vienna. Lucius finds medicine to be his way of giving back to society, but three years into his studies, World War I breaks out and he is caught in the whirlpool of history. Restless and in the prime of youth, he receives an additional boost when fellow Pole Madam Curie tells him at a professional dinner: "Save yourself. Genius favors the young. You are running out of time." These words inspire Lucius to join the war effort, where medical cases abound. After all, what better immersive experience for a young medical student like him than the battlefield trenches.

Lucius expects a fully staffed hospital, but he is instead posted to a small village in the Carpathian Mountains of Galicia (a former Eastern European country that straddled parts of modern day Ukraine and Poland). On the map it sat in a narrow valley on the northern slope of the mountains, "a finger's-breadth from Uzhok Pass on the Hungarian border." Here he must take charge of a makeshift hospital set up in a church where all the doctors have left and the only person in charge of operations is a mysterious nun, Sister Margarete. Under her brusque, take-no-prisoners tutelage, Lucius, who has never before handled a scalpel, quickly learns the tools of the trade.

The hospital squeaks along in "patch and send" mode on limited medical supplies (the only thing that flows in abundance is horilka, the local liquor, which Sister Margarete uses liberally as disinfectant and to buoy her own spirits). The somewhat predictable rhythm is upended when the titular "Winter Soldier" arrives, a Hungarian from Budapest, Sergeant Jozsef Horvath. The serviceman doesn't present with any immediate symptoms but it is very clear he is deeply damaged. The term PTSD was not a part of the medical lingo then, but Lucius classifies it as "nerve shock." The case intrigues him endlessly, and also tests him severely: ultimately he will make a decision that will compromise his oath and haunt him till the end. A slow-brewing romance between Lucius and Sister Margarete is also complicated by the chaos of war, as their simmering, half-baked intentions are dashed by the swallowing up of this small Galician town by Russian forces.

Author Daniel Mason is a Clinical Assistant Professor in the Stanford University Department of Psychiatry, and brings his own research interests to bear here. These include the subjective experience of mental illness and the influence of literature, history, and culture on the practice of medicine. *The Winter Soldier* weaves a spellbinding story, which draws you into another world from the very first page. At times the romance, also sensitively handled, overwhelms the central focus of the novel, which is trained on a doctor's remorse over a poorly handled decision. But the descriptions of wartime eastern Europe and the nuances of youth and inexperience and human error, are all hauntingly drawn to spectacular effect.

There is so much grandeur and sweep in these pages that you might be forgiven for not wanting to turn the last page. Few stories handle the human cost of war as delicately and perceptively as *The Winter Soldier* does. Read it. It's a bravura performance.

Reviewed by Poornima Apte. This review was originally published in *The BookBrowse Review* in September 2018, and has been updated for the October 2019 edition.

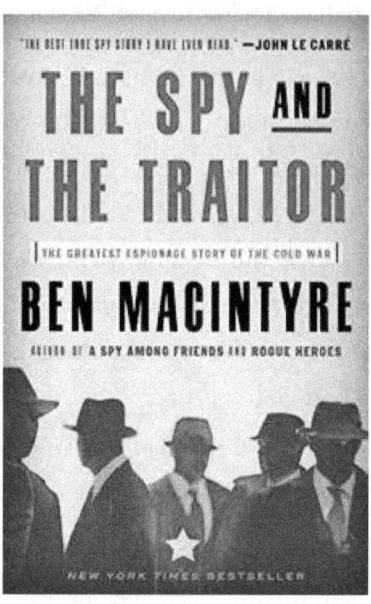

THE SPY AND THE TRAITOR

by Ben Macintyre

BookBrowse Rating: 5/5

Critics' Consensus: 5/5

Published August 2019 in Paperback, 384 pages

Summary

The celebrated author of *Double Cross* and *Rogue Heroes* returns with his greatest spy story yet, a thrilling *Americans*-era tale of Oleg Gordievsky, the Russian whose secret work helped hasten the end of the Cold War.

If anyone could be considered a Russian counterpart to the infamous British double-agent Kim Philby, it was Oleg Gordievsky. The son of two KGB agents and the product of the best Soviet institutions, the savvy, sophisticated Gordievsky grew to see his nation's communism as both criminal and philistine. He took his first posting for Russian intelligence in 1968 and eventually became the Soviet Union's top man in London, but from 1973 on he was secretly working for MI6. For nearly a decade, as the Cold War reached its twilight, Gordievsky helped the West turn the tables on the KGB, exposing Russian spies and helping to foil countless intelligence plots, as the Soviet leadership grew increasingly paranoid at the United States's nuclear first-strike capabilities and brought the world closer to the brink of war. Desperate to keep the circle of trust close, MI6 never revealed Gordievsky's name to its counterparts in the CIA, which in turn grew obsessed with figuring out the identity of Britain's obviously top-level source. Their obsession ultimately doomed Gordievsky: the CIA officer assigned to identify him was none other than Aldrich Ames, the man who would become infamous for secretly spying for the Soviets.

Unfolding the three-way gamesmanship between America, Britain, and the Soviet Union, and culminating in the gripping cinematic beat-by-beat of Gordievsky's nail-biting escape from Moscow in 1985, Ben Macintyre's latest may be his best yet. Like the greatest novels of John le Carré, it brings readers deep into a world of treachery and betrayal, where the lines bleed between the personal and the professional, and one man's hatred of communism had the power to change the future of nations.

BookBrowse Review

In this nonfiction Cold War espionage thriller, Ben Macintyre examines double-agent Oleg Gordievsky's monumental betrayal of Soviet and KGB intelligence by passing information to Western powers.

For over a decade, Oleg Gordievsky of the Soviet Union was a double-agent for the British, climbing the rungs of the Soviet KGB's political ladder while supplying the British MI6 with increasingly valuable information. Because of his impeccable language skills and his status as the son of a loyal KGB member, Gordievsky rose through the ranks of the organization with hardly a mark on his record, and seemed an unlikely candidate for treason. However, after witnessing the murder of innocent people trying to escape East Germany during the construction of the Berlin Wall in 1961 and uncovering the violence of the Soviet invasion of Czechoslovakia in 1968, Gordievsky sought new alliances in the West.

With his training in spycraft and a prodigious ability to retain, repeat and analyze dense intelligence information, Gordievsky is considered to be one of the most impressive and valuable double agents of the Cold War. He transferred thousands of documents to the British and provided hours upon hours of insight into the inner-workings of the KGB and Soviet Union. Gordievsky's contributions shaped history, aiding in the ejection of KGB spies who had infiltrated nations around the world. Of equal importance, Gordievsky's intimate understanding of the Soviet perspective fostered close relationships between himself and Western powers, wherein he advised top government officials on how to engage with the Soviet government during the Cold War. Both Ronald Reagan and Margaret Thatcher met with Gordievsky to discuss issues like the space race and the escalation of nuclear armament after he fled the USSR.

In 1985, after an information leak, Gordievsky was threatened with execution by the KGB. Facilitating an unlikely, miraculous escape plan called PIMLICO, the MI6 helped evacuate Gordievsky—and eventually his wife and two daughters—out of the Soviet Union and into British care. No one had ever been smuggled out of the Soviet Union before, and project PIMLICO hinged on a number of "what-ifs" that could easily have collapsed, costing Gordievsky his life. The suspense builds as Macintyre describes the intricate plan, down to the brand of chocolate bar that would signal a message received (Kit Kat or Mars) to the type of bag Gordievsky would use to initiate contact (Safeway) before traveling from the Soviet Union to Finland, passing five layers of border control while locked in a trunk. As Macintyre writes, "Outside fiction, spying rarely goes according to plan," a testament to the tension in these moments scattered throughout the book.

Contemporary spy stories are seldom conveyed with such accuracy and depth, since the documents pertinent to these cases are confidential, stored in intelligence agency archives around the world. However, in interviewing all of the officers involved in the case, including Gordievsky, Macintyre brings new information to the public about this concealed moment in international history. Herein lies the greatest strengths and weaknesses of the book: Although it is loaded with original, gripping information, the level of detail can be tedious to work through, particularly during lulls in Gordievsky's career. Governments and intelligence agencies are riddled with bureaucratic layers, the nuances of which are detailed in this book, weighing down the prose. Ultimately, this journalistic-historic approach pays off when Macintyre notes which Western political figures were entangled with the KGB and how contemporary leaders like Vladimir Putin fit into the tales of decades past.

Unlike many cut-and-dry renditions of history, *The Spy and the Traitor* approaches fact with style. By using Oleg Gordievsky's frame of reference as a funnel through which to explore espionage, international politics and the Cold War, Macintyre incorporates elements of literary finesse. Gordievsky's favorite censored writers and composers become allusions in the text, as the author references William Shakespeare's *Hamlet* and Somerset Maugham's short story "Mr. Harrington's Washing." Extended metaphors about long distance running and romance permeate the chapters, too. It is clear that Gordievsky's rebellion against the Soviet Union was as much an act of defiance against Russian culture as it was against Russian politics. Highly critical of the state-sanctioned censorship in Russia that limited his access to books, music, consumer goods and ideas, Gordievsky grew to resent the constant surveillance and control embedded in Russian society. This is an observation Macintyre explores in depth, noting the evolution of Gordievsky's character development in relation to his cultural and political awakening.

The Spy and the Traitor will appeal to readers with an interest in nonfiction books about politics and international affairs, as well as those who enjoy thrillers and crime fiction. Macintyre's prose reads somewhat like a novel, conjuring images with historical detail and weaving in illuminating symbols and allusions.

Reviewed by Jamie Chornoby. This review was originally published in *The BookBrowse Review* in October 2018, and has been updated for the December 2018 edition.

DOPESICK

by Beth Macy

BookBrowse Rating: 5/5
Critics' Consensus: 5/5
Readers' Rating: 4.5/5

Published August 2019 in Paperback, 400 pages

Summary

The only book to fully chart the devastating opioid crisis in America: An unforgettable portrait of the families and first responders on the front lines, from a *New York Times* bestselling author and journalist who has lived through it.

In this masterful work, Beth Macy takes us into the epicenter of America's twenty-plus year struggle with opioid addiction. From distressed small communities in Central Appalachia to wealthy suburbs; from disparate cities to once-idyllic farm towns; it's a heartbreaking trajectory that illustrates how this national crisis has persisted for so long and become so firmly entrenched.

Beginning with a single dealer who lands in a small Virginia town and sets about turning high school football stars into heroin overdose statistics, Macy endeavors to answer a grieving mother's question - why her only son died - and comes away with a harrowing story of greed and need. From the introduction of OxyContin in 1996, Macy parses how America embraced a medical culture where overtreatment with painkillers became the norm. In some of the same distressed communities featured in her bestselling book *Factory Man*, the unemployed use painkillers both to numb the pain of joblessness and pay their bills, while privileged teens trade pills in cul-de-sacs, and even high school standouts fall prey to prostitution, jail, and death.

Through unsparing, yet deeply human portraits of the families and first responders struggling to ameliorate this epidemic, each facet of the crisis comes into focus. In these politically fragmented times, Beth Macy shows, astonishingly, that the only thing that unites Americans across geographic and class lines is opioid drug abuse. But in a country unable to provide basic healthcare for all, Macy still finds reason to hope - and signs of the spirit and tenacity necessary in those facing addiction to build a better future for themselves and their families.

BookBrowse Review

Through unsparing, yet deeply human portraits of the families and first responders struggling to ameliorate this epidemic, *Dopesick* brings each facet of the crisis into focus.

Before Tess Henry was a heroin addict, she was a teenage girl who wrote poetry and loved the author David Sedaris. She played basketball and ran track. The daughter of a surgeon and a nurse, Tess studied French at Virginia Tech. She was one of the advantaged. Tess started with the narcotic Lortab, then graduated to Dilaudid, Roxicodone, and Opana. But it was her heroin descent that introduced her to the corrupt dealers, the predatory practices, the cruel punishment and the violent outcomes for addicts – the opioid culture.

When opioid abuse was a rural problem in forgettable places, Beth Macy began writing about it for the *Roanoke Times*. Six years later, opioid abuse is a national epidemic of 2.6 million addicts. Fluent in the crisis, Macy tells a layered tale of the history of morphine, children and their grieving families, and heroin highways. Absent ethnocentric and class judgements, *Dopesick* delivers a tragic story.

If nothing else, the numbers humanize the collapse. A stunning 300,000 have died in the past 15 years because of opioid abuse and 300,000 are projected to die in the next 5 years, more than gunshot wound deaths and even more than AIDS deaths in its most epic years. Opioid addiction is erasing those younger than 40. To put the devastation into context, Macy quotes a dealer who tells her that after an overdose, he has more customers, not less; a terrifying reality of opioids' appeal. It's not the drug that is erotic, but it is the high – and the high is what is drowning more than two million in a lethal culture.

There is no greater example of gods and monsters than opioids. Opioids, which act on receptors mainly in the nervous system to produce morphine-like effects, have been a great source of comfort for cancer patients, injured soldiers and everyone in between but simultaneously – and this is the devastation – opioids have destroyed the addicted like Tess Henry. Thousands have died because legal opioids have made heroin and fentanyl the pretty girl at the prom, a must have. "No one saw the train wreck coming – not the epidemiologists, not the criminologists, not even the scholars," Macy writes, as she explains the beginning of the crisis.

When it was launched in the mid-1990s, the legal opioid OxyContin was a time release drug that had a 12-hour potency and, according to the literature, was addictive less than 1% of the time. Unlike previous opioid pain relievers, Oxy wasn't just marketed for extreme pain but for moderate relief as well. Toothache, arthritis, muscle soreness, back pain--oftentimes doctors left it up to patients to decide how much they needed to take.

It didn't take long for addiction to surface. If you sucked the transparent coating off, what was left was a substance that could be crushed and snorted, or injected with a needle -80 milligrams of Oxy directly into the blood system. The high is glorious until it ends. Then the hunt for a repeat high begins. The fear of dopesickness begins too: hot and cold flashes, vomiting blood, spasms, dry mouth, migraines, not being able sleep or eat, sweating, agitation, paranoia and depression. There are no compromises, just horrors. To prevent dopesickness the drug has to never run out, even if that means selling your grandmother's wedding ring to pay for it or, as Macy describes, crawling through a ceiling vent to break into a pharmacy.

The mothers of the opioid dead are not hesitant to voice their outrage. They are sad, angry, resolute and filled with questions. Kristi Fernandez wants to know why her son Jesse died; she already knows the how, a narcotics overdose in the bathroom. She would later discover Jesse participated in pharm parties where opioids were traded. "I hurt as much today as the day my son died", she says. After Randy Nuss died, his grieving mother Lee placed a large magnet on her car, on the advice of her grief counselor, meant to serve as a warning to anyone who saw her car. Randy's photo accompanies the words: In love and memory of Randall Nuss and Others. Scott Roth, who loved to cook and rap, is dead because he bought heroin from a former classmate. His mother Robin says, "I wish I would have built him a stronger support system. I thought I could do it all as a single mom."

There are so many others.

Macy is able to paint a full picture here. She reveals how there are saints and villains in this venomous opiate war, people who inspire and people who are dangerous facilitators, but mostly she shines a spotlight on the fact that this is a policy and rehab failure. On average, it takes eight years and four or five attempts for an addict to become fully clean - if they become clean at all.

So how to cure addicts?

Macy argues on behalf of Medically Assisted Treatment (MAT). "If my own child were turning tricks on the streets, enslaved not only by the drug but also criminal dealers and pimps, I would want her to have the benefit of maintenance drugs, even if she sometimes misused them." She is dismissive of President Trump's non-policy policy that creates collateral damage for the chronically ill who are not given enough opioids to treat pain because addicts have hijacked opioids for themselves. Patients who truly need opioids to manage their disease have their treatment plans restricted because everyone is suspicious of everyone. Politicians who are dug in against the Affordable Care Act make the crisis even worse.

After reading Macy's chilling account, you can't help but wonder if we have reached the point of ordinary: the addicted dying before they reach the age of 40 while people run away – or look away or pretend they don't see. You can't help but wonder if they is actually we. It's not our fault a drug hit the market and was overprescribed, and the Center for Disease Control was apathetic. But it is our fault when we neglect the addicted.

Reviewed by Valerie Morales. This review was originally published in *The BookBrowse Review* in August 2018, and has been updated for the September 2019 edition.

MEET ME AT THE MUSEUM

by Anne Youngson

BookBrowse Rating: 4/5
Critics' Consensus: 4.5/5
Readers' Rating: 4.5/5

Published August 2019 in Paperback, 288 pages

> ## Summary
>
> Anne Youngson's *Meet Me at the Museum* is a celebration of long letters, kindred spirits, and the possibility of writing a new story for yourself, at any stage of life.

Tina and Kristian thought their love stories were over. Each on the other side of 60, they have lost a best friend and a wife, the ambitions of their youth, their hopes for a fresh start. Yearning for connection, they strike up a yearlong correspondence, brought together by a shared fascination with the Tollund Man, subject of Seamus Heaney's famous poem. As they open up to one another about their lives - daily routines, travel, nature, beauty, work, family - these two strangers become friends and then, perhaps, something more.

Full of insight, humor, and candor, Tina and Kristian's letters are a testament to the joy that can come from the meeting of two intensely curious minds.

BookBrowse Review

Anne Youngson's debut novel *Meet Me at the Museum* explores life and loss through the letters of two lonely and disparate individuals.

Of our 33 First Impression reviewers, 29 rated *Meet Me at the Museum* as four- or five-star, for an impressive average overall score of 4.4 out of 5 stars.

What it's about:

Meet Me at the Museum by Anne Youngson is a gentle story about second chances (Rebecca H). In this epistolary novel, letters are exchanged between two strangers who gradually develop a deep friendship through their correspondence (Melinda H). A chance inquiry from a woman in England reaches a Danish museum curator, and his reply launches a casual conversation that grows into the fulfillment of deep and previously unrecognized needs of both participants (Sheryl M).

Many reviewers found the author's observations astute:

Youngson's insights into human nature, love, what makes life meaningful, and the importance of family are remarkable. I turned down more than one page so that I could go back and reread something wise one character had written to another (Eileen C). Though this is the story of two people who are past middle age, most readers will realize that Tina's and Kristian's concerns, interests, opinions and ideas have parallels in all our lives. A careful reading will provide gems of wisdom, or at least stimulate thoughts and suggest new options or renewals in your life (Sheryl M). It reminded me to take time to step out of my daily routine, look around, listen, and reflect upon the world around me. (Wilhelmina H). It's a book that makes you think about your own relationships with family, music, poetry and other parts of your life (Joan V).

Several readers remarked on their appreciation of the older characters featured in the book:

I enjoyed the depiction of older middle-aged people coming to terms with their remaining time and being satisfied with what has occurred and what can occur. And yet something surprising (to them) can still happen (Elizabeth L). While love is not lost on the young, love between those with greater life experiences is delightfully multifaceted (Sheryl M). It is so nice to read a book about older people which does not ridicule them (Joan V).

Reviewers overwhelmingly considered it a quiet novel:

What a delightful book (Eileen C). It was gentle on my soul. It does not grab you and smack you, but leads you on a leisurely stroll into two people's lives and their growing friendship. It provided a welcome respite from some of the heavier genres that are popular right now, although it's certainly not fluff (Susan U). As I turned the last page, I found myself smiling gently, and I am still smiling (Gail K).

Most also mentioned that the novel is a leisurely read, and one that readers should take their time enjoying:

Meet Me at the Museum was a lovely, slower-paced read and a nice reminder that the paths we take through time have more "raspberries and ferns" to enjoy...no matter how old we become (Dorothy G). I liked the slower pace of this novel, which aligns with the slower pace of writing and posting handwritten letters instead of the more immediate forms of email or texting (Wilhelmina H). Go slowly with this book. Savor each page. Like a museum where each room and display holds a treasure, each page of this book inspires and links us to our humanity and oneness with time and place (Maureen R).

Some thought it started a bit too slowly but that it was worth the effort:

I have to say, if I hadn't agreed to review this book, I wouldn't have read beyond 20 pages. I felt the book got better as the letters became more personal and I began to see the characters more fully (Elyse G). When I first started reading it, I must admit I was a little bored. I didn't really understand where the writer was going with the story, but as I continued to read it I grew to love it (Colleen F).

Most enjoyed and would recommend it:

Meet Me at the Museum is one of my favorite books of all time (Maureen R). I liked it immensely (Marci G). I recommend it to those who are willing to read at a leisurely and thoughtful pace in order to appreciate each letter (Gail K). I think book clubs would really enjoy this book; it has much to offer and provides much to think about (Patricia W).

Reviewed by First Impressions Reviewers. This review was originally published in *The BookBrowse Review* in August 2018, and has been updated for the September 2019 edition.

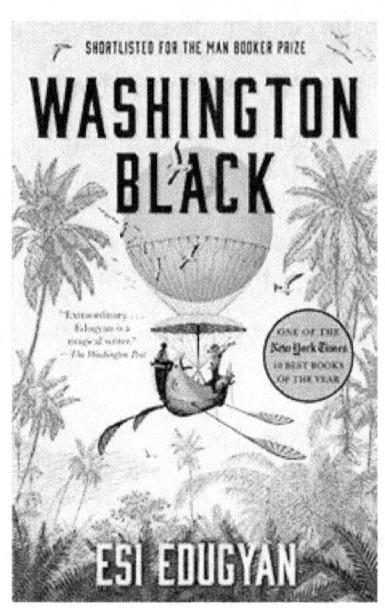

WASHINGTON BLACK

by Esi Edugyan

BookBrowse Rating: 5/5
Critics' Consensus: 5/5
Readers' Rating: 5/5

Published April 2019 in Paperback, 400 pages

Summary

A dazzling new novel about a boy who rises from the ashes of slavery to become a free man of the world.

George Washington Black, or "Wash," an eleven-year-old field slave on a Barbados sugar plantation, is terrified to be chosen by his master's brother as his manservant. To his surprise, the eccentric Christopher Wilde turns out to be a naturalist, explorer, inventor, and abolitionist. Soon Wash is initiated into a world where a flying machine can carry a man across the sky, where even a boy born in chains may embrace a life of dignity and meaning - and where two people, separated by an impossible divide, can begin to see each other as human. But when a man is killed and a bounty is placed on Wash's head, Christopher and Wash must abandon everything. What follows is their flight along the eastern coast of America, and, finally, to a remote outpost in the Arctic. What brings Christopher and Wash together will tear them apart, propelling Wash even further across the globe in search of his true self.

From the blistering cane fields of the Caribbean to the frozen Far North, from the earliest aquariums of London to the eerie deserts of Morocco, *Washington Black* tells a story of self-invention and betrayal, of love and redemption, of a world destroyed and made whole again, and asks the question, What is true freedom?

BookBrowse Review

Part adventure novel, part travelogue, part historical fiction, this is a story about a boy who rises from slavery to become a free man of the world.

Sometimes you just want a good adventure story. One that does not follow a predictable pattern and keeps the pages turning. There are many such stories, but few of them bring along the kind of depth and observation that Esi Edugyan brings to *Washington Black*.

Edugyan weaves a thrilling yarn that unfolds slowly, peeling back layers and revealing hidden depths. This is, at once, a coming of age tale, an exploration of slavery from inside and outside the plantation, and a skip-along through a variety of scientific discoveries. Washington Black, born a slave in Barbados in the 1830s, never expected much beyond a life of hard toil and pain. Yet he was rescued, suddenly, by the enigmatic brother of his master – a scientist in need of an assistant. Together they traverse the world, from the West Indies all the way to the Arctic Circle and beyond. Washington becomes a man of learning and an artist; he blazes a path that is unlike any he ever believed possible.

Washington is a compelling character because he not only escapes the bonds of slavery, he also participates in the latest scientific discoveries of his time. Given the tools to analyze and record, he feels both the thrill of his new life and its stark juxtaposition to what he's left behind. The resulting excitement and guilt are entirely believable and fully fleshed out throughout the course of the novel.

Beyond her strong characterization, Edugyan just plain writes well. Her story is bright and fresh, avoiding common clichés and building anticipation for the next bend in the story's road. Her descriptions of the Arctic cold and the dry heat of the desert are palpably real. What's more, she makes Washington's interests our own – many readers will likely spend some time exploring the marine life he studies or the aeronautic devices of the 19th century with which he comes into close contact. From the first page you are fully invested, ready and willing to follow the young protagonist wherever he may lead.

Washington Black is a study of a human life, with all its horrors, digressions and surprises. Read it for a good story, for a little bit of wonder or a good dose of thought-provoking narrative. Whatever your reason, read it.

Reviewed by Natalie Vaynberg. This review was originally published in *The BookBrowse Review* in October 2018, and has been updated for the June 2019 edition.

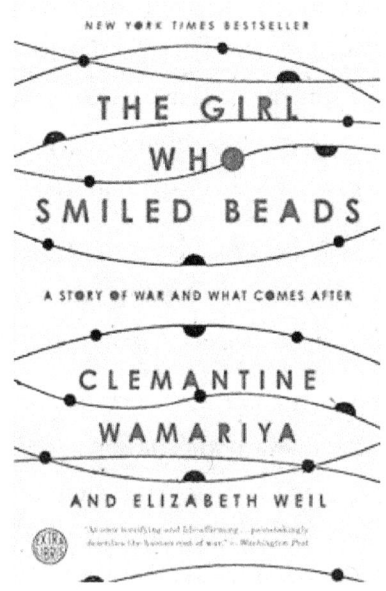

THE GIRL WHO SMILED BEADS

by Elizabeth Weil, Clemantine Wamariya

BookBrowse Rating: 5/5
Critics' Consensus: 5/5
Readers' Rating: 4.5/5

Published April 2019 in Paperback, 304 pages

Summary

A riveting story of dislocation, survival, and the power of stories to break or save us.

Clemantine Wamariya was six years old when her mother and father began to speak in whispers, when neighbors began to disappear, and when she heard the loud, ugly sounds her brother said were "thunder." In 1994, she and her fifteen-year-old sister, Claire, fled the Rwandan massacre and spent the next six years wandering through seven African countries, searching for safety—perpetually hungry, imprisoned and abused, enduring and escaping refugee camps, finding unexpected kindness, witnessing inhuman cruelty. They did not know whether their parents were dead or alive.

When Clemantine was twelve, she and her sister were granted asylum in the United States, where she embarked on another journey—to excavate her past and, after years of being made to feel less than human, claim her individuality.

Raw, urgent, and bracingly original, *The Girl Who Smiled Beads* captures the true costs and aftershocks of war: what is forever destroyed; what can be repaired; the fragility of memory; the disorientation that comes of other people seeing you only as broken—thinking you need, and want, to be saved. But it is about more than the brutality of war. It is about owning your experiences, about the life we create: intricately detailed, painful, beautiful, a work in progress.

BookBrowse Review

The Girl Who Smiled Beads **is an affecting memoir authored by a young survivor of the Rwandan genocide.**

Of the 26 First Impression readers who submitted reviews, 24 gave it four or five stars for an overall score of 4.4.

What it's about:

Clemantine Wamariya is an important writer who painfully, yet masterfully, exposes the atrocities of the Rwandan genocide and its effect on herself and her family (Rosemary C). This searing and personal account reveals much more than just a war-torn, conflicted country; it's the story of a girl who lost her family, her identity and her childhood. For six years Clemantine and her sister Claire moved from one refugee camp to another, seeking shelter but finding only hunger, disease and inhumane treatment. Throughout the book, told in alternating stories set in refugee camps in Africa, and in affluent American suburbs where the author lived as an immigrant and foster child, the reader comes to realize that even as a successful American citizen, Clemantine has yet to come to a place in her life where all the broken pieces fit together as a whole (Priscilla M). Despite the ugliness of genocide, this book describes human resilience and the strength of love and goodness and the determination to be counted (Barbara O).

Readers feel it is enlightening and timely:

The Girl Who Smiled Beads is beautifully written, disturbing and eye opening. We all need to know, on a personal level, what happens when human beings find themselves in the middle of conflict (Barbara O). Clemantine Wamariya writes about a life so foreign to me that I had to remind myself I wasn't reading fiction (Sandra H). She reminds us that millions of Africans have been affected by genocide, she is but one survivor and each survivor has had a different experience (Catherine O). Her memoir makes real what we only glimpse on nightly news. This story of child refugees tutors us in why we must save them, and in the strength they bring to our country (Paula B). It gives one hope that refugees can find a better life (Kate S).

Many found it a compelling read:

What a magnificently powerful and emotionally raw memoir. The book greatly impacted my entire being—down to the most basic fiber (Pattie P). It is a breathtaking and heartbreaking story (Peggy K). We feel the author's fear, insecurity and anger as she describes what she and her sister endured. It is heart-rending to learn that even today she struggles with her identity and her place in society; her anger is palpable on the pages (Diane H). Her story is one that is blisteringly ugly and yet at the same time triumphant and proud (Priscilla M). I found myself haunted by Claire's comment near the end of the book: "When I remember our experiences, I'm alone." Each family member has her own reality (Diane H).

The topic was challenging for some:

The descriptions of Claire and Clemantine's living conditions are beyond my ability to comprehend or even imagine. No human being should be subjected to the circumstances these two girls lived through (Laurie W). The subject matter was "hell on earth." The terrible things that people can inflict on one another for no reason strike me as insane and reading about the girls' experiences made this book difficult for me (Kate S).

Some felt the timeline unclear:

Wamariya's decision to alternate chapters between life as a refugee with life in the United States served to demonstrate her disorientation and confusion in her different worlds, but as a reader it made it hard to follow both tracks. I often had to refer back to previous chapters to remember her age, location and other important elements (Kathleen K).

Most reviewers highly recommended *The Girl Who Smiled Beads*:

This memoir is a must read, especially for those of us who live in the US. This is also a must read for all book groups and individuals who have the freedom to pick and choose what they read, but also, more importantly, have safe places to live and government intervention programs to help the less fortunate. I cannot recommend it strongly enough (Sandra H). I will be recommending this book to everyone I know who wishes to expand their view of the world. I know my book club will be reading it; it is exactly the type of thought provoking book we enjoy discussing (Catherine O).

Reviewed by First Impressions Reviewers. This review was originally published in *The BookBrowse Review* in May 2018, and has been updated for the June 2019 edition.

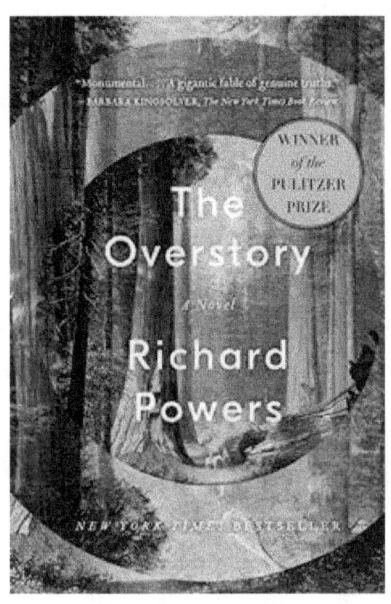

THE OVERSTORY

by Richard Powers

BookBrowse Rating: 5/5
Critics' Consensus: 5/5
Readers' Rating: 5/5

Published April 2019 in Paperback, 512 pages

Summary

"The best novel ever written about trees, and really just one of the best novels, period." —Ann Patchett

Winner of the Pulitzer Prize in Fiction

Shortlisted for the Man Booker Prize
New York Times Bestseller
A New York Times Notable Book and a Washington Post, Time, Oprah Magazine, Newsweek, Chicago Tribune, and Kirkus Reviews Best Book of 2018

The Overstory is a sweeping, impassioned work of activism and resistance that is also a stunning evocation of—and paean to—the natural world. From the roots to the crown and back to the seeds, Richard Powers's twelfth novel unfolds in concentric rings of interlocking fables that range from antebellum New York to the late twentieth-century Timber Wars of the Pacific Northwest and beyond. There is a world alongside ours—vast, slow, interconnected, resourceful, magnificently inventive, and almost invisible to us.

This is the story of a handful of people who learn how to see that world and who are drawn up into its unfolding catastrophe.

BookBrowse Review

In *Overstory*, a group of eco-activists plots to save the Pacific Northwest's precious forests from overzealous logging.

Many glowing adjectives can be used to describe a novel by Richard Powers: brilliant, moving, mesmerizing. But one word succinctly captures the feeling I come away with every time I put a novel of his down: awe. Of course, given that I look forward to a new Powers novel just as eagerly as my daughter waited for the next in the Harry Potters series, I will be the first one to admit I come to the table already biased. But Powers meets my ridiculously high expectations every single time. He does it again with *The Overstory*, a sprawling, messy, breathtaking and yes...awe-inspiring tome about trees.

If you're wondering how on earth an author can write a 500-page literary fiction volume about trees, consider this: Margaret Atwood is a huge fan. "It is not possible for Powers to write an uninteresting book," she once said. To its credit *Overstory* is more than merely *not* uninteresting: its very format – Roots, Trunk, Crown, Seeds – hints at the sprawling epic that is to come. Tucked in between the chapters Root and Trunk are the nine human branches: Nicholas Hoel, Mimi Ma, Adam Appich, Ray Brinkman and Dorothy Cazaly; Douglas Pavlicek, Neelay Mehta, Patricia Westford and Olivia Vandergriff, whose life histories intertwine to tell the story of how trees, in one way or another, profoundly root their everyday concerns. Nick Hoel, for example, is the scion of the Hoel family, generations of which have watched a single chestnut survive on their Iowa farm as the blight that scourged the rest of the country missed their precious tree. Mimi Ma is the daughter of a Chinese immigrant, an engineer who plants a mulberry in their Illinois backyard as a tenuous connection to her homeland.

If there is one flaw in this brilliant novel, it is that Powers throws in one or two characters too many. We could have easily done without Neelay Mehta or Ray and Dorothy, especially as it becomes clear that their stories are only tangential to the narrative that begins to take shape after we're a third of the way into the book.

As the story slowly gains momentum, five of the characters' paths intersect when they take a stand against indiscriminate logging in the Pacific Northwest. These sections are where the awe factor particularly kicks in. Powers is able to describe the breathtaking beauty that is being plundered and, equally important, he drives home the sobering scale of loss. As the five characters take on the Goliath, Powers zooms in and out to paint a picture of activism molded in the '90s that has urgent takeaway lessons for today.

Geeky details about trees – how sakaki tree is sacred in Shintoism, India's bejeweled wishing trees, Mayan kapoks – stud the narrative and never feel forced.

Readers will come away with a new respect for trees, and maybe even have some of the novel's activism brush off on them. Powers, a National Book Award winner for one of my all-time favorite novels, *The Echo Maker*, is to be commended for keeping the story front and center and not drowning it in his call to action. To apply a relevant metaphor, he does not lose the forest for the trees.

You don't have to be an environmentalist to love *The Overstory*. You will, however, come away with an overwhelming sense of awe. At one point, a character points out: "Humankind is deeply ill. The species won't last long. It was an aberrant experiment. Soon the world will be returned to the healthy intelligences, the collective ones. Colonies and hives." This will make you sit up and take notice. And surely that can only be a good thing?

Reviewed by Poornima Apte. This review was originally published in *The BookBrowse Review* in April 2018, and has been updated for the May 2019 edition.

A PLACE FOR US

by Fatima Farheen Mirza

BookBrowse Rating: 5/5
Critics' Consensus: 5/5
Readers' Rating: 5/5

Published March 2019 in Paperback, 400 pages

Summary

The first novel from Sarah Jessica Parker's new imprint, SJP for Hogarth, A Place for Us is a deeply moving and resonant story of love, identity and belonging.

A Place for Us unfolds the lives of an Indian-American Muslim family, gathered together in their Californian hometown to celebrate the eldest daughter, Hadia's, wedding – a match of love rather than tradition. It is here, on this momentous day, that Amar, the youngest of the siblings, reunites with his family for the first time in three years. Rafiq and Layla must now contend with the choices and betrayals that lead to their son's estrangement – the reckoning of parents who strove to pass on their cultures and traditions to their children; and of children who in turn struggle to balance authenticity in themselves with loyalty to the home they came from.

In a narrative that spans decades and sees family life through the eyes of each member, A Place For Us charts the crucial moments in the family's past, from the bonds that bring them together to the differences that pull them apart. And as siblings Hadia, Huda, and Amar attempt to carve out a life for themselves, they must reconcile their present culture with their parent's faith, to tread a path between the old world and the new, and learn how the smallest decisions can lead to the deepest of betrayals.

A deeply affecting and resonant story, A Place for Us is truly a book for our times: a moving portrait of what it means to be an American family today, a novel of love, identity and belonging that eloquently examines what it means to be both American and Muslim - and announces Fatima Farheen Mirza as a major new literary talent.

BookBrowse Review

A stunning debut novel in which an Indian Muslim family in the United States confronts cultural and generational issues.

A whopping 62 out of 66 of our First Impression reviewers gave *A Place for Us* by Fatima Farheen Mirza a four- or five-star rating – for an overall average of 4.7 stars.

What it's about

A Place for Us by Fatima Farheen Mirza is the story of one immigrant family trying to find a place in American society. Timely in its subject-matter and exquisitely written, the novel contains universal themes while highlighting the immigrant experience unique to Muslims (Sara L). The story opens with the wedding of the family's oldest daughter Hadia to Tariq, a modern marriage of love rather than the traditional arranged marriage. On her daughter's wedding day, mother Layla thinks back to the early days of her arranged marriage with husband Rafiq, an orphan who moved to America on his own, got a job, and established a good life for the two of them. Their three US-born children struggle with following their parents' religious and cultural practices, but the youngest, Amar, finds it especially challenging. He spends his entire life trying to find where he fits in and never truly feels that he belongs anywhere. Throughout the book Layla reflects back upon the lives of her children as they grew into adults and upon the stages of her own marriage (Betty T). This portrait of an Indian-American Muslim family, each struggling to reconcile personal choices with faith, clashing cultures, gender roles, family dynamics, and the world after 9/11, is at once engrossing, thought-provoking, heart-breaking and uplifting (Janice P).

Members remarked on the wide range of subjects explored by the author

The book encompasses such ancient themes as generational divides, father-son estrangement, patriarchal family culture and heartbreaking betrayals and misunderstandings (Ginny B). It also touches on sibling and parental relationships, gender, birth order, secrets revealed and withheld, guilt and adherence to religious restrictions (Beth B).

Readers felt the book was exceptional

A Place for Us is an amazing debut on many levels. It ticks off all the expected boxes for good fiction: it is well-written, plotted and paced and it's peopled with finely realized characters who speak with clarity and honesty. Perhaps most exciting of all is the discovery that an author so young could produce such a sure-handed, richly layered observation of the complex human condition in all its inherent beauty - and disappointments (Darra W). It is truly a beautifully written book that was a pleasure to read (Elizabeth V).

The character development was a highlight

This is a book where you really connect with and care about the characters (Beth M). They're so compelling and rich that they pull you along through a deep and complicated family history (Catherin O). I felt such empathy for them, they were fully realized and fleshed out (Cheryl S).

Many readers found it informative about Muslim culture

I was not very familiar with the culture and religion of the family portrayed in the book but I enjoyed learning more (Susan B). The parents' devout faith and their bonds within their religious community play a strong part in the story and may serve to educate some readers regarding Islam as a faith and the difficulties of raising children to be observant, particularly in this current age of intolerance and ignorance (Ginny B). I gained a tremendous amount of insight into Muslim customs and family life, but I also saw how divisive it can be trying to maintain a closed society in the midst of 21st century USA. According to your perspective the first generation born here becomes either a bridge to a different world or an ax dividing families and communities (Linda W).

The book's themes, however, are universal

The thing that impressed me most about the book is that it is the story about a family facing the problems that many of us have faced as our children form beliefs of their own which sometimes are at odds with the values and traditions that we, their parents, hold very close to our hearts. The author wrote this book about a Muslim family, but the book could have been about a Christian, Jewish, Buddhist or Mormon family (Virginia M). Many parts of the story resonated with me as a parent and sibling (DeAnn A). The more I read the more I was struck by how similar we all are (Barbara O).

A few complained about the narrative format and pacing

I was a little frustrated with the alternating flashback-present tense format. Sometimes the flashbacks went back to a younger age than the previous flashback, and I found myself underlining ages or grades in school to try and keep it straight (Rebecca R). The author's prose is littered with descriptive sentences that provide a vivid image but may or may not be germane to the action. Mirza also spends much time inside the head of her characters, switching people and time periods with little warning. These methods drag down an already slow-moving novel to a snail's pace (Patricia L).

***A Place for Us* is recommended to a wide audience**

I am so grateful this book came into my hands, it was a wonderful reading experience and I highly recommend it to all readers (Cheryl S). This is one of the best books that I have read in years. I'm pretty stingy with my stars but I would give this book six stars if I could (Joan P). It would be an excellent book club choice as it wrestles with cultural clashes, family dynamics and individual choices (Linda W).

Reviewed by First Impressions Reviewers. This review was originally published in *The BookBrowse Review* in June 2018, and has been updated for the March 2019 edition.

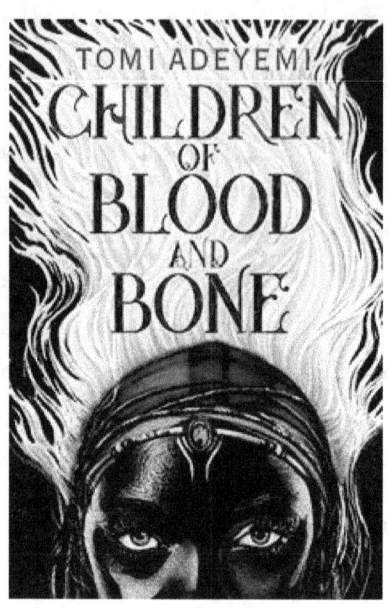

CHILDREN OF BLOOD AND BONE

by Tomi Adeyemi

BookBrowse Rating: 5/5
Critics' Consensus: 5/5
Readers' Rating: 5/5

Published March 2019 in Paperback, 560 pages

Summary

Winner of the 2018 BookBrowse Award for Best Young Adult Novel

Tomi Adeyemi conjures a stunning world of dark magic and danger in her West African-inspired fantasy debut, perfect for fans of Leigh Bardugo and Sabaa Tahir.

They killed my mother.
They took our magic.
They tried to bury us.
Now we rise.

Zélie Adebola remembers when the soil of Orïsha hummed with magic. Burners ignited flames, Tiders beckoned waves, and Zélie's Reaper mother summoned forth souls.

But everything changed the night magic disappeared. Under the orders of a ruthless king, maji were killed, leaving Zélie without a mother and her people without hope.

Now Zélie has one chance to bring back magic and strike against the monarchy. With the help of a rogue princess, Zélie must outwit and outrun the crown prince, who is hell-bent on eradicating magic for good.

Danger lurks in Orïsha, where snow leoponaires prowl and vengeful spirits wait in the waters. Yet the greatest danger may be Zélie herself as she struggles to control her powers - and her growing feelings for an enemy.

BookBrowse Review

A spellbinding debut fantasy that expands the boundaries of readers' imaginations while thrilling and delighting with captivating prose.

Voted 2018 Best Young Adult Award Winner by BookBrowse Subscribers

What would you do if, in a world filled with magic wielded by different clans, the magic disappeared over night? What would you do if it didn't just disappear, but a ruthless despot was trying to make sure that it died for good, and all who could practice died with it? And what would you do if you could stop it from disappearing? In her debut novel, *Children of Blood and Bone*, Tomi Adeyemi takes readers to Orïsha, a land ruled by a murderous king where those with the potential for magic, divîners, are ostracized and persecuted, and not allowed to pass on their traditions or their language, Yoruba.

Zélie is a divîner, and like all divîners, is easily distinguished from her countrymen by her dark skin and white hair. Before King Saran raided the lands killing all maji - active magic practitioners (including Zélie's mother) - Zélie would have one day grown into her powers. Since that raid, divîners' potential to wield magic can't come to fruition. But that changes with the appearance of a runaway princess, Amari, and a scroll that is part of the connection of the divîners and maji to Nana Baruku, the female deity from whom Zélie's people get their power. Zélie and Amari learn that there is a chance to restore the connection to Nana Baruku, and therefore the magic of Orïsha, before it is lost forever. As they set out on their journey, hunted by Amari's brother Inan, both are forced to take a hard look at the brutal realities of power when wielded with injustice, racism, and colorism, and the scars left by fear and genocide.

This work is timely – perhaps, overdue – not only because of the themes Adeyemi wields intellectually and accessibly, but because the young adult (YA) fantasy world has needed epic fantasies that root the concepts of magic, setting, and culture somewhere other than European, American, or generally "Western" locations. Rooted in West African and Yoruba religion, mythology, and magical traditions, Adeyemi gives readers a different way of experiencing wonder, a different way of sensing the world, which extends beyond representation and the presentation of diversity, though these are important. Adeyemi does not rely on the fantasy to give her prose strength; if the magic and the fantastic elements were stripped away, we would still be left with a story that touches upon the brutal elements of life that so many teenagers themselves face: inherited trauma, prejudice, isolation, facing down systems and institutions that are designed to keep them oppressed, and the fear and loneliness of families torn apart because of the inhumanity of others.

In *Children of Blood and Bone*, Adeyemi recognizes the maturity thrust upon contemporary youth and adolescents and has written them a book that doesn't offer false promise or hope of redemption through magic, but instead offers them a world that reflects, in many ways, the complexities of this one. And the idea that maybe, just maybe, injustices can be fought and triumphed over when we recognize the value of all to exist.

This is the first in a series that is going to challenge everything that readers know about what makes good YA fantasy. It's going to leave them demanding more, not only from the series, but from what the standard of "good enough" in publishing already is. Growth, confrontation, trauma, and the search for a better way by two strong women are all part of this epic fantasy. If I have any criticisms, it is that it ends on a cliff-hanger and 2019 is far too far away to wait for the next installment of what is sure to be the bestselling *Legacy of Orïsha* series.

Reviewed by Michelle Anya Anjirbag. This review was originally published in *The BookBrowse Review* in April 2018, and has been updated for the March 2019 edition.

AN AMERICAN MARRIAGE

by Tayari Jones

BookBrowse Rating: 5/5
Critics' Consensus: 5/5
Readers' Rating: 4.5/5

Published March 2019 in Paperback, 320 pages

Summary

An American Marriage is a masterpiece of storytelling, an intimate look deep into the souls of people who must reckon with the past while moving forward - with hope and pain - into the future.

A 2018 Oprah's Book Club Selection, and winner of the 2019 Women's Prize for Fiction

Newlyweds Celestial and Roy are the embodiment of both the American Dream and the New South. He is a young executive, and she is an artist on the brink of an exciting career. But as they settle into the routine of their life together, they are ripped apart by circumstances neither could have imagined. Roy is arrested and sentenced to twelve years for a crime Celestial knows he didn't commit. Though fiercely independent, Celestial finds herself bereft and unmoored, taking comfort in Andre, her childhood friend, and best man at their wedding. As Roy's time in prison passes, she is unable to hold on to the love that has been her center.

After five years, Roy's conviction is suddenly overturned, and he returns to Atlanta ready to resume their life together.

This stirring love story is a profoundly insightful look into the hearts and minds of three people who are at once bound and separated by forces beyond their control.

BookBrowse Review

This stirring love story is a profoundly insightful look into the hearts and minds of three people who are at once bound and separated by forces beyond their control.

Celestial Davenport and Roy Othaniel Hamilton were still navigating the contours of their new marriage one year in, and you could argue that the fault lines were already beginning to show. But Roy thought differently. "I believed that our marriage was a fine-spun tapestry, fragile but fixable. We tore it often and mended it again, always with a silken thread, lovely but sure to give way again." Celestial and Roy, graduates of historically black schools, are an upwardly mobile Atlanta couple, and at the novel's outset their lives lie ahead sparkling with promise. "We are not your garden-variety bush Atlanta

Negroes where the husband goes to bed with his laptop under his pillow and the wife dreams about her blue box jewelry," Roy reminds us. "I was young, hungry, and on the come-up. Celestial was an artist, intense and gorgeous."

It is against this landscape that life throws the couple a curveball. At a routine stay at a motel in Roy's native Louisiana, a white woman, mistaking one black face for another, accuses Roy of rape. And just like that, the marriage is put on hold. Roy gets twelve years in prison – "we would be forty-three when he is released", Celestial points out. The marriage is shattered.

As expected, from this point on Roy and Celestial's lives spool forward at different speeds. Roy is pretty much frozen in place, spending most of his time writing to a wife who is trying to come to terms with what she needs to do next. Many wives wait for their husbands, Roy has noticed, but then Celestial is not just another wife. Her earlier doubts about the marriage resurface, "Til death do us part" is unreasonable, a recipe for failure, she now believes.

Tayari Jones achingly explores what happens as our individual selves, slowly evolving over time, leave a marriage behind. A good marriage requires constant recalibration, embracing slowly changing personalities. But what if some of that change occurs at a remove? Neither Roy nor Celestial have any idea what the other is like now. All Roy has is hope, and in that hope he builds a glorified picture of his wife. Celestial, on the other hand, pieces together her artist career and finds support in an old friend, Dre.

In chapters alternately narrated by Roy, Celestial and Dre, *An American Marriage* challenges the reader to question what we buy into when we say "I do." Do we promise unending loyalty no matter what, even if that outcome is uncertain? As Celestial dithers, she also grapples with guilt over her changed self.

The title is particularly on point. Roy's only crime is to be a "a black man in the wrong place at the wrong time. This is basic," Jones writes. After all, in America, being a black man can mean that the chances you will be incarcerated is five times more than if you are a white man. Against this context, it is America to blame for the gradual fraying of Roy's and Celestial marriage. That result is the collateral damage from a society where systemic bias is ingrained. This, in other words, is the story of an American marriage.

Jones also teases apart the concept of class: "All my life I have been helped by programs like Head Start when I was 5 and Upward Bound all the way through," Roy explains, but Celestial grew up with more comforts. It's the slightest of disparities but one that gnaws at the marrow regardless.

At times the characters indulge in a little too much navel-gazing and seem to make the same points about marriage over and over again. These veer dangerously close to reading like platitudes: "Marriage is between two people. There is no studio audience." and "Human emotion is beyond comprehension and smooth and uninterrupted, like an orb made of blown glass." It is the novel's strength that you see the story from all three points of view, although I suspect readers will probably pick a favorite to root for.

All told, *An American Marriage* is a memorable dissection of one of society's most venerable institutions. Hard work or not, Jones brilliantly shows us just how easy it is for things to go awry in the blink of an eye, even in a happy marriage let alone in a less-than-perfect one.

Reviewed by Poornima Apte. This review was originally published in *The BookBrowse Review* in February 2018, and has been updated for the March 2019 edition.

ONLY CHILD

by Rhiannon Navin

BookBrowse Rating: 5/5
Critics' Consensus: 5/5
Readers' Rating: 5/5

Published February 2019 in Paperback, 304 pages

Summary

For fans of *Room* and the novels of Jodi Picoult, a dazzling, tenderhearted debut about healing, family, and the exquisite wisdom of children, narrated by a six-year-old boy who reminds us that sometimes the littlest bodies hold the biggest hearts, and the quietest voices speak the loudest.

Squeezed into a coat closet with his classmates and teacher, first grader Zach Taylor can hear gunshots ringing through the halls of his school. A gunman has entered the building, taking nineteen lives and irrevocably changing the very fabric of this close-knit community.

While Zach's mother pursues a quest for justice against the shooter's parents, holding them responsible for their son's actions, Zach retreats into his super-secret hideout and loses himself in a world of books and art. Armed with his newfound understanding, and with the optimism and stubbornness only a child could have, Zach sets out on a captivating journey towards healing and forgiveness, determined to help the adults in his life rediscover the universal truths of love and compassion needed to pull them through their darkest hours.

BookBrowse Review

A dazzling, tenderhearted debut about healing, family, and the wisdom of children.

Rhiannon Navin's debut novel, *Only Child* received an overall score of 4.8 out of 5 from BookBrowse members, one of the highest ever ratings for a First Impressions book.

What it's about:

The author takes us on a journey most are afraid to contemplate (Maureen R). *Only Child* is a powerful story of forgiveness and healing told through the dramatic experience of six-year old Zach Taylor. Set against the backdrop of a school shooting, the story reveals the tragedy of the loss of a child through inexplicable violence and the related impacts on marriage, family and community (Peggy C).

Most were impressed by how realistically the book's young narrator was voiced:

The concept of writing this book through the eyes of a 6 year old was brilliant. I felt the author truly captured a child's view of the events - his fears, guilt and loss. It was a good reminder to us that a child can see clearly right from wrong and the importance of love over hate; they don't get caught up in the outside opinions that can influence adults (Terrie J). Zach's innocent but wise perspective brought me to tears, to laughter and to a host of other emotions in between. I found myself pulling for him to show those much older and presumably wiser how to go on after such a loss (Carol S). His innocence proves to be both a safeguard and guiding light; and because he is able to find his way through the complexities of this tragedy, so are we. From first page to last, Zack is our champion, and we are his (Maureen R).

Reviewers commented on the challenging nature of the story:

It was sometimes hard to read because of the subject matter. Keep the tissue box handy (Doris K). While the topic of school shootings isn't a pleasant one, Rhiannon Navin does an amazing job with this difficult subject (DeAnn A).

Nevertheless, they found it to be a compelling story:

It is a sad but thought-provoking read that I found hard to put down (Peggy C). I read it in two afternoons (Anna R); it was riveting and enlightening. (Maureen R). I thought the story was well-executed and suspenseful but still "literary fiction" (Rebecca K). I will remember this story for a long time (Anna R).

A few reviewers voiced minor criticism of the characters:

I had a difficult time empathizing with Zach's mom Melissa, who is one of the main characters. I understand that every person deals with grief differently, but I could not agree with some of her decisions and even thought some of the choices she made were cruel to others (Rebecca K). I would have given it a 5 except that I found Zach painted a bit too mature for his age (Harriette K).

Highly recommended:

The fact that this is a debut novel blows me away! (Jill F). I have already recommended it to others (Terry J) Book clubs will have hours of discussion topics (Liz B).

Reviewed by First Impressions Reviewers. This review was originally published in *The BookBrowse Review* in February 2018, and has been updated for the February 2019 edition.

MOTHERS OF SPARTA

by Dawn Davies

BookBrowse Rating: 5/5
Critics' Consensus: 4.5/5
Readers' Rating: 4.5/5

Published January 2019 in Paperback, 272 pages

Summary

Some women are born mothers, some achieve motherhood, others have motherhood thrust upon them. Dawn Davies is in the third category. A six-foot-tall divorcee, she isn't chatty, couldn't care less about anyone's potty training progress, doesn't care to share her own children's milestones with people who don't love them. But even if she has never fit in with other moms, she has raised three children with her own particular brand of fierce, unflagging love.

In stories that cut to the quick, we see Davies grow from a young girl who moves to a new town every couple of years; to a misfit teenager who finds solace in a local music scene; to an adrift twenty-something who summons inner strength as she holds the hand of a dying stranger; to a woman dealing with difficult pregnancies and postpartum depression. And in her powerful titular story, we see Davies struggling with the weight of knowing that her son is deeply troubled.

Mothers of Sparta is not a blow-by-blow of Davies' life but rather an examination of the exquisite and often painful moments of a life, the moments we look back on and say, *That one, that one mattered*. Straddling the fence between humor and, well…not humor, Davies has written a book about what it's like to be a woman trying to carve a place for herself in the world, no matter how unyielding the rock can be.

BookBrowse Review

30 members reviewed Mothers of Sparta for First Impressions, rating it an impressive average of 4.5 out of 5

What it's about:

The tagline on the back cover of Mothers of Sparta says it all: "Some women are born mothers. Some achieve motherhood. Others have motherhood thrust upon them" (Linda J). Dawn Davies is a tough woman with a tender underside who paints a picture of her life through a series of autobiographical essays. The early chapters portray her great love and appreciation for the natural world around her juxtaposed with the heartbreak of frequent family uprooting. In later chapters she lays bare some of her most difficult times in beautifully written prose. She exposes small glimpses of her childhood, marriage, motherhood, divorce, and debilitating illness with honesty and quiet humor (Nancy L).

First Impression reviewers overwhelmingly approved of the book.

Memoirs are my preferred genre and this one is at the top of my list of favorites (Emily C). I cannot remember the last time I enjoyed a non-fiction book so much; I absolutely loved this book (Sally H). I couldn't put it down once I started (Kay D).

Reviewers applauded Davies' writing:

The author is a memoirist with a remarkable voice (Nancy L). Her writing style was captivating and drew me in to each chapter. I loved the way they held up as separate pieces, yet tied together to create an epic story; Davies has a gift for expressing herself (Kay D). She has such a sense of language that I was just left with my mouth open sometimes, wondering how she did it (Claire M).

The essays elicited wide range of emotions:

This is the first book I have read that both wrenches your gut with heartbreak and makes you laugh out loud at the humor at the same time (Lynne B). I laughed, I cried, and I was sympathetic to the pain and angst that Dawn Davies experienced throughout her life (Suzanne G). The range of emotions makes this book a worthwhile read for those of us who often think our joys, pains and victories are not shared by another (Liz D).

The author's candor was mentioned by nearly every reader:

Davies is irreverent, hilarious, unfailingly candid, and brutally honest in her descriptions of events in her life (Sally H). This memoir was not sugarcoated and it described life with honesty - the good, the bad, and the ugly (Miller W). The author makes herself totally vulnerable and opens up her life for all to see. It's deep, moving, brave stuff and I salute her for living her life with grace and courage (Monica P).

The book especially resonate with those who are mothers:

Mothers of Sparta appealed to me in particular due to my state in life--thirty something married mom. Any mom can relate and will appreciate this book (Miller W). Davies tells us we are not alone in our struggle to be great mothers (Liz D). I adore women who can look at their lives with clear eyes and a sense of humor even in the darkest moments and convey that sense of "me too, I get it, you're not alone" to their readers. Davies did that to perfection (Elizabeth F).

Some readers did not like the book's tone, primarily because of its shifting voice and its non-chronological chapters:

I understand the concept of the flawed mom but sometimes I felt little to no pity based on the author not taking responsibility for her decisions. I would have preferred the latter part of the book to be developed more than the first part which felt like a lot of complaining (Linda P). Some funny incidents are included, but overall the tone is of despair, anger, loneliness and frustration. Davies writes in both the first and second person, and for me this was a problem (Ruthie A). The book is not written in chronological order, and can be hard to follow at times (Linda J). Overall it felt chaotic (Alissa C).

However, most would recommend Mothers of Sparta to a broad audience:

I truly enjoyed reading this book and would certainly recommend it to anyone who enjoys memoirs of the not-rich and not-famous. It would be a great discussion selection for a reading group (Beth C). I believe it would raise some interesting points for conversation on motherhood, luck and the "payback fairy" (Carol F). Fans of Nora Ephron and Anne LaMott might recognize some of their traits in Davies' writing (Linda J). Definitely a book I will recommend to anyone (Diane T).

Reviewed by First Impressions Reviewers. This review was originally published in *The BookBrowse Review* in February 2018, and has been updated for the January 2019 edition.

FORCE OF NATURE

by Jane Harper

BookBrowse Rating: 5/5
Critics' Consensus: 4.5/5
Readers' Rating: 4.5/5

Published January 2019 in Paperback, 352 pages

Summary

From the *New York Times* bestselling author of *The Dry*, when a hiker goes missing, secrets and betrayal among friends are exposed, and Agent Aaron Falk will find out what happened.

Five women reluctantly pick up their backpacks and start walking along the muddy track. Only four come out the other side.

The hike through the rugged Giralang Ranges on the corporate retreat is meant to take the office workers out of their air-conditioned comfort zone and teach resilience and team building. But one of the women doesn't make it.

Federal Police Agent Aaron Falk has a particularly keen interest in the whereabouts of the missing hiker. Alice Russell is the whistleblower in his latest case - in just a matter of weeks she was due to help him bring down both the company she works for and the people she works with.

In an investigation that takes Falk from isolated bushland to city headquarters, he discovers secrets lurking in the mountains, and a tangled web of personal and professional friendship, suspicion, and betrayal among the hikers. But did that lead to murder? This is as atmospheric, tense, and explosive as the bestselling *The Dry*, and marks the continuation of a terrific new series.

BookBrowse Review

When a hiker goes missing in the Australian bush, secrets and betrayal among friends are exposed, and Agent Aaron Falk investigates.

Force of Nature, Jane Harper's sequel to *The Dry,* garnered 4+ stars from 33 out of 37 First Impression reviewers, for an impressive average score of 4.5.

What it's about:

Force of Nature centers around the disappearance of Alice Russell while she is on a team-building retreat in the Australian bush with four female colleagues. The women become lost in the wilderness and Alice goes missing. The others make it out of the forest but they all claim not to know what happened to Alice. Federal Agent Aaron Falk (first encountered in Harper's debut, *The Dry*) becomes involved because Alice is an informant in an ongoing case. The story switches between the current search for Alice and flashbacks to what happened to the five women in the bush. The flashbacks have a *Lord of the Flies quality* as the frightened women turn on each other as their situation becomes more desperate (Terri O). Falk, teamed with new partner Carmen Cooper, must solve a crime that originates as corporate misconduct and ends with possible murder (Maureen R).

Readers felt it compared favorably to the first entry in the series, while also working well as a stand-alone mystery:

Force of Nature is just as good, if not better, than her first novel, *The Dry* (Terri O). My test for a good read is that it must make me want to read the author's other work. I'll be reading Ms. Harper's first book, *The Dry*, soon (Lauren T).

Many found the mystery gripping:

It's a taut, suspenseful whodunit with lots of twists and turns—keeping me on the edge of my figurative seat until the end. The author keeps the intensity high and the story-line moving. I read the novel in one sitting. The unraveling of what happened with Alice and the other characters was a genuine surprise (Barbara F). This book was a compelling read; I could not guess what the ending was going to be (Constance C).

Harper's characters are a highlight, and Aaron Falk's return is welcome:

The characters are complex and multi-layered. Not one character in this novel is without purpose and as the layers are peeled back, secrets and truths and strengths and vulnerabilities are exposed (Lynda C). They are by far the strongest forces driving the mystery to its unsettling, yet satisfying end (Cheryl K). Harper's Detective Falk is intriguing (Barbara E). I hope the author continues this series with him, he's an excellent character (Constance C).

As with *The Dry*, Australia's landscape plays an important part in the story:

Harper's descriptions of the bush are vivid and downright terrifying, as the vegetation becomes more dense and the trees close in on the lost hikers (Terry O). The terrain and climate are described beautifully and I was left with a very clear vision of the land and the physical challenges her characters experienced (Laure R).

A few did not connect with the book:

The author spent a lot of time on the back stories of the women in the novel, and while this may have added to the mystery they seemed somewhat contrived and didn't hold my attention. I was much more interested in the parts of the novel about the detectives and I found myself skimming through the other parts (Julie G). The petty arguing and the dredging up of old grievances from years before became annoying. The women not only argued about grievances among them, but also their children. I felt relieved when the story turned from the lost women to Falk and Carmen solving the crime (MaryJane B).

But most recommend it highly:

For fans of well-written, plot and character-driven page-turners, this tense, atmospheric novel is an excellent choice (Barbara F). Harper has written an atmospheric novel that checks all the boxes of book worth reading. The locale, the characterizations, the interplay between the people, and the twist at the end all keep the story engaging up to the conclusion. A highly recommended book (Norman G). It was easy for me to give this one five stars, I struggled to find a flaw. Another marvelous book in the Aaron Falk series! (DeAnn A).

Book Reviewed by BookBrowse Review Team. This review was originally published in *The BookBrowse Review* in February 2018, and has been updated for the January 2019 edition.

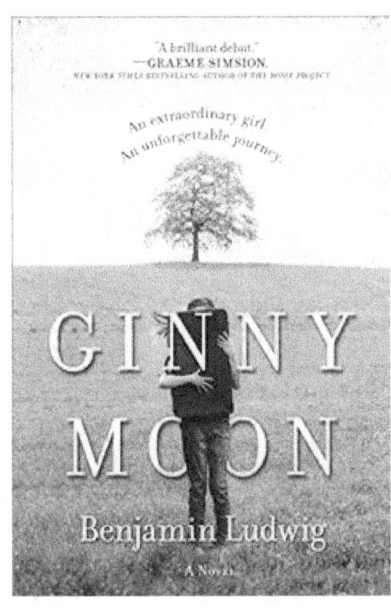

GINNY MOON

by Benjamin Ludwig

BookBrowse Rating: 5/5
Critics' Consensus: 5/5
Readers' Rating: 5/5

Published December 2017 in Paperback, 384 pages

Summary

Told in an extraordinary and wholly unique voice that will candidly take you into the mind of a curious and deeply human character.

Meet Ginny Moon. She's mostly your average teenager—she plays flute in the school band, has weekly basketball practice and reads Robert Frost poems for

English class. But Ginny is autistic. And so what's important to her might seem a bit…different: starting every day with exactly nine grapes for breakfast, singing along to Michael Jackson, taking care of her baby doll…and crafting a secret plan of escape.

Ginny has been in foster care for years and for the first time in her life she has found her "forever home." After being traumatically taken from her abusive birth mother and moved around to different homes, she is finally in a place where she'll be safe and protected, with a family who will love and nurture her. This is exactly the kind of home that all foster kids are hoping for. But Ginny has other plans. She'll steal and lie and reach across her past to exploit the good intentions of those who love her—anything it takes to get back what's missing in her life. She'll even try to get herself kidnapped.

Ginny Moon is at once quirky, charming, heartbreaking, suspenseful and poignant. It's a story of a journey, about being an outsider trying to find a place to belong and about making sense of a world that just doesn't seem to add up.

BookBrowse Review

The uniquely candid voice of Ginny Moon takes the reader into the mind of a curious and deeply human character.

In the tradition of Mark Haddon's *The Curious Incident of the Dog in the Night-Time,* Benjamin Ludwig's *Ginny Moon* gives us a novel written from the perspective of a child with autism.

Fourteen-year-old Ginny faces many challenges in life; not only is she autistic, but she was starved and beaten by her drug-abusing mother and subsequently removed from her home at the age of nine. She's been placed in at least three "forever homes," and has run away from each. Her current "forever parents" adopted her because they couldn't get pregnant at the time but eventually did conceive and now have an infant of their own. This places a new stress on their relationship with Ginny. Although her adopted parents attempt to help her have a normal life (e.g., helping her participate on a Special Olympics basketball team and taking her to flute lessons) she nevertheless does all she can to return to her birth mom, in spite of her love for her new sibling. The mystery of what exactly compels Ginny to return to her former home comprises much of the novel.

It's been a long time since I've read a first-person novel that made me care so much about the protagonist. Many books in recent years have featured young narrators in challenging circumstances, but *Ginny Moon* is absolutely one of the better written and most interesting of its type. Benjamin Ludwig has created a remarkable character in Ginny, making her realistic and completely bringing readers into her world. I experienced her frustration first-hand when she was unable to convey her inner fears to those who care about her. Her pain became my own and I wanted to hug her and explain her thoughts and feelings to those who just don't understand her.

One of the book's strongest features is how the author helps us view Ginny's parents, therapist, friends and teachers with a degree of clarity that eludes her because she is unable to pick up on the cues that most of us take into account during social interactions. Although Ginny doesn't understand how her actions impact those around her, readers readily grasp their exasperation through Ginny's own descriptions. I wanted to step into several scenes and play mediator between the parties involved, feeling like I was the only one perceiving each side's point-of-view. I think it's a rare novel that can elicit this kind of reaction from a reader, particularly when the story is narrated from a single point of view.

The plot, too, is intriguing and creative. On a few occasions, just when I felt that *Ginny Moon* was starting to lag or become predictable, the action took an unexpected but credible new direction, pulling me back into the narrative and keeping me hooked throughout. I was constantly on the edge of my seat as

Ginny made decisions that were completely logical to her but that would obviously have negative repercussions for her down the road.

Some readers may have concerns that, given Ginny's history, the book could be dark or disturbing; this is not the case by any means, and it is, in fact, quite uplifting overall. Although Ginny makes passing references to the abuse she suffered at the hands of her birth-mother, this is not dwelled on or described in-depth. One knows very bad things have happened to her but that's not the point of the book, other than to make it clear why she was removed from her home and, oddly, why she's so desperate to get back to it in spite of being in a safe and loving environment.

Benjamin Ludwig completely captures his young protagonist, and as a result *Ginny Moon* is without doubt one of the finest novels I've read all year. I whole-heartedly recommend it for a wide audience, including young adult readers; book groups in particular will find much material for discussion.

Reviewed by Kim Kovacs. This review was originally published in *The BookBrowse Review* in December 2017, and has been updated for the December 2018 edition.

BEST BOOKS OF 2017

LA BELLE SAUVAGE

by Philip Pullman

BookBrowse Rating: 5/5
Critics' Consensus: 5/5
Readers' Rating: 5/5

Published June 2019 in Paperback, 464 pages

Summary

Winner of the 2017 BookBrowse Award for Best Young Adult Novel

Philip Pullman returns to the parallel world of his groundbreaking novel *The Golden Compass* to expand on the story of Lyra

Malcolm Polstead is the kind of boy who notices everything but is not much noticed himself. And so perhaps it was inevitable that he would become a spy....

Malcolm's parents run an inn called The Trout, on the banks of the river Thames, and all of Oxford passes through its doors. Malcolm and his daemon, Asta, routinely overhear news and gossip, and the occasional scandal, but during a winter of unceasing rain, Malcolm catches wind of something new: intrigue.

He finds a secret message inquiring about a dangerous substance called Dust—and the spy it was intended for finds him.

When she asks Malcolm to keep his eyes open, he sees suspicious characters everywhere: the explorer Lord Asriel, clearly on the run; enforcement agents from the Magisterium; a gyptian named Coram with warnings just for Malcolm; and a beautiful woman with an evil monkey for a daemon. All are asking about the same thing: a girl—just a baby—named Lyra.

Lyra is the kind of person who draws people in like magnets. And Malcolm will brave any danger, and make shocking sacrifices, to bring her safely through the storm.

BookBrowse Review

Philip Pullman returns to the parallel world of his groundbreaking series *His Dark Materials* to expand on the story of Lyra, one of fantasy's best known and beloved characters.

Voted 2017 Best Young Adult Novel by BookBrowse's Subscribers

I wasn't quite sure what to expect when I heard that Philip Pullman would be revisiting the world he brought to life in the His Dark Materials series – not as a prequel or sequel series, but what he refers to as an "equel" – a series that is meant to stand on its own, yet as companion to the first. While I'm not sure if I agree that this is what he has achieved with the first installment of the new trilogy, I can say with certainty that *La Belle Sauvage* has left me excited for all that might come next in the series.

La Belle Sauvage is set in the same alternative universe as the earlier trilogy, and tells the story of how Lyra Belacqua - the protagonist in the first series - came to reside at Jordon College at Oxford University. While the beloved heroine is in the text, she is just a baby. It is the need to protect Lyra that drives the new young protagonists Malcolm Polstead and Alice Parslow on their epic journey from Godstow Priory to Oxford by canoe in a flood.

The book pulls from multiple literary styles: part spy novel, part bildungsroman, part adventure or quest tale, then, suddenly, glimpses of magical realism and embedded other-worlds. And while any one of these stylistic choices could have lent a very fascinating take on the narrative, there were places in which this mix of styles, combined with the detail paid to setting and sense of place, served to disrupt the pacing. As in the earlier series, the setting does help to draw the reader in, but here it is not seen through Lyra's eyes and is, instead, viewed from a wider, more distant lens, which made it distracting. So much detail is given that, at times, I felt my interest fading; it was less of a map leading me to the heart of the narrative and more like an inside conversation with those who know and love Oxford, leaving the rest of us who have never been there trying to keep apace with the conversation. The other drawback for me was that, at times, it felt like instead of letting the narrative lead him freely, Pullman was trying to tie up too many loose ends from the first series with regard to how Lyra, as a little girl, came to be living amongst the scholars.

That being said, this is a charming fantasy. Alice has quickly become one of my favorite characters ever written, and Pullman shows us again that he is a master of writing, not only for children, but for anyone. All readers who come to his books will find something for them. It is not a text that can be easily simplified to mean any one thing, and I am certain that those who come to this series first, and then look to read *His Dark Materials*, will have an utterly different experience. That is the mark of a good fantasy; it should be approachable for all, but not one-size-fits-all in what a reader might take from it. The narrative should provide us each with our own journey into our perceptions of the world. In a time of prescriptive fantasies, Pullman has once again given us an adventure that, for adults, appeals to the myriad complicated emotions we once had when we were young.

Reviewed by Michelle Anya Anjirbag. This review was originally published in *The BookBrowse Review* in December 2017, and has been updated for the July 2019 edition.

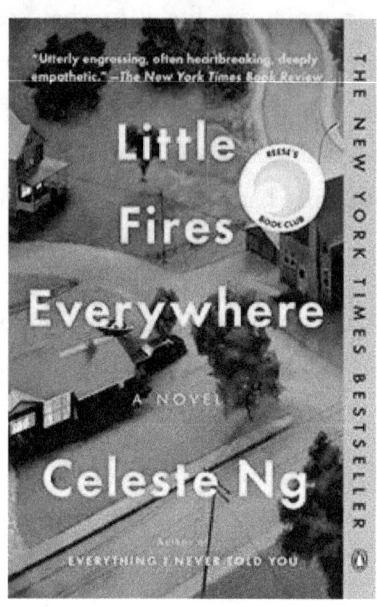

LITTLE FIRES EVERYWHERE

by Celeste Ng

BookBrowse Rating: 5/5
Critics' Consensus: 5/5
Readers' Rating: 3/5

Published May 2019 in Paperback, 368 pages

Summary

Winner of the 2017 BookBrowse Fiction Award

From the bestselling author of *Everything I Never Told You*, a riveting novel that traces the intertwined fates of the picture-perfect Richardson family and the enigmatic mother and daughter who upend their lives.

In Shaker Heights, a placid, progressive suburb of Cleveland, everything is planned – from the layout of the winding roads, to the colors of the houses, to the successful lives its residents will go on to lead. And no one embodies this spirit more than Elena Richardson, whose guiding principle is playing by the rules.

Enter Mia Warren – an enigmatic artist and single mother – who arrives in this idyllic bubble with her teenaged daughter Pearl, and rents a house from the Richardsons. Soon Mia and Pearl become more than tenants: all four Richardson children are drawn to the mother-daughter pair. But Mia carries with her a mysterious past and a disregard for the status quo that threatens to upend this carefully ordered community.

When old family friends of the Richardsons attempt to adopt a Chinese-American baby, a custody battle erupts that dramatically divides the town - and puts Mia and Elena on opposing sides. Suspicious of Mia and her motives, Elena is determined to uncover the secrets in Mia's past. But her obsession will come at unexpected and devastating costs.

Little Fires Everywhere explores the weight of secrets, the nature of art and identity, and the ferocious pull of motherhood – and the danger of believing that following the rules can avert disaster.

BookBrowse Review

In a vanilla Cleveland suburb, residents find that an obsession can have unexpected and devastating costs.

Voted 2017 Best Fiction by BookBrowse's Subscribers

Small towns, big drama. Acclaimed author Celeste Ng's *Little Fires Everywhere* occasionally reads like an upscale television show, with multiple plot lines interweaving to create a delicate dissection of suburban America.

The novel begins when artist Mia Warren, and her teenage daughter Pearl, rent Elena Richardson's second home. From there, it shifts into two divergent but interlocking story lines – the clashes between foils Elena and Mia, and Pearl's coming-of-age interactions with the Richardson children. The book gains a new sense of gravity when Mia's coworker, Bebe Chow, engages in a high-profile custody clash to regain the rights to her baby, May Ling. The infant had been adopted by Elena's closest friend, Linda McCullough, a woman unable to have her own children. And while Bebe had abandoned her baby during a time of crisis, she is now in a more stable position and desperate to get her daughter back.

The struggle divides the picture-perfect town of Shaker Heights, Ohio (a suburb of Cleveland), into two, and sparks resentment between Mia and Elena, leading to unforeseen consequences. While the entire novel is written extremely well, in the first half the tropes are somewhat tired—struggling artist protagonist, overbearing mom and her rebellious daughter—and the plot slow-moving. What sets *Little Fires Everywhere* apart is the custody battle. Bebe's desperation to regain her daughter adds a layer of emotional depth to the exploration of racial microaggressions. She fights for the rights to regain her Chinese daughter from a white family who thinks dining out at their favorite Chinese restaurant is enough to connect May Ling to her culture.

Bebe's struggles also push several moral questions to the forefront of both Shaker Heights and the reader's mind. The press points out that Bebe did abandon her baby, and the McCullough family would provide May Ling a privileged life. Then again, Bebe acted out of a larger concern about her child's future, and the McCulloughs, while affluent and loving, would deprive May Ling of experiencing her own culture. Who is "right?"

Emotionally, the reader – or, at least *this* reader – feels for Bebe. Mia sums up Bebe's loss beautifully: "To a parent, your child wasn't just a person: your child was a place, a kind of Narnia, a vast eternal place where the present you were living and the past you remembered and the future you longed for all existed at once." However, by making Linda McCullough desperate for children and extremely doting, Ng avoids spelling out how the reader should react, and instead paints a picture and leaves you to interpret the details.

This sense of delicacy and expert crafting is also on display with the cast of characters. With so many different viewpoints—from the four Richardson children, to Mia and Pearl, to Elena Richardson—it would be easy for the various characters to blur together, but Ng infuses each with their own personality, voice, and growth. I found myself perfectly okay with the multiplicity of voices. While it is the youngest Richardson child, Izzy, who is the most enchanting from the start—what with her black-sheep label, and her refusal to fit into the conventional Shaker Heights stereotypes – it is her older sister Lexie who surprised me the most. Arrogant and self-absorbed, Lexie also displays appealing hints of vulnerability. I wanted to know what other surprises she would serve up.

All the characters feel lifelike and balanced – everyone has their own strengths and flaws, and you sympathize even with the antagonists. Mia Warren and Elena Richardson are at opposite ends of the spectrum personality-wise – the former, artistic, eccentric, kind-hearted, spontaneous; the latter, grounded, ritualistic, scheming, determined—and their interactions form a subtle tension throughout the book, leaving the readers to wonder what cataclysmic event their polite animosity will lead up to.

Some of the story's plot does seem derivative. Even if this is not a novel for teens, the sections that feature Pearl and the Richardson children include many familiar tropes of young adult dramas – unrequited and requited love, teenage angst, the value and tensions of friendships, loners contrasted against the popular folk. Still, with its expertly done characterization, beautiful and often poignant writing, and subtle examination of suburban America, *Little Fires Everywhere* fills the reader with emotions and questions that linger long after the last page is finished.

Reviewed by Erin Szczechowski. This review was originally published in *The BookBrowse Review* in September 2017, and has been updated for the June 2019 edition.

HAPPINESS

by Heather Harpham

BookBrowse Rating: 5/5
Critics' Consensus: 4.5/5
Readers' Rating: 5/5

Published November 2018 in Paperback, 320 pages

Summary

A shirt-grabbing, page-turning love story that follows a one-of-a-kind family through twists of fate that require nearly unimaginable choices.

Happiness begins with a charming courtship between hopelessly attracted opposites: Heather, a world-roaming California girl, and Brian, an intellectual, homebody writer, kind and slyly funny, but loath to leave his Upper West Side studio. Their magical interlude ends, full stop, when Heather becomes pregnant - Brian is sure he loves her, only he doesn't want kids. Heather returns to California to deliver their daughter alone, buoyed by family and friends. Mere hours after Gracie's arrival, Heather's bliss is interrupted when a nurse wakes her, "Get dressed, your baby is in trouble."

This is not how Heather had imagined new motherhood – alone, heartsick, an unexpectedly solo caretaker of a baby who smelled "like sliced apples and salted pretzels" but might be perilously ill. Brian reappears as Gracie's condition grows dire; together Heather and Brian have to decide what they are willing to risk to ensure their girl sees adulthood.

The grace and humor that ripple through Harpham's writing transform the dross of heartbreak and parental fears into a clear-eyed, warm-hearted view of the world. Profoundly moving and subtly written, *Happiness* radiates in many directions - new, romantic love; gratitude for a beautiful, inscrutable world; deep, abiding friendship; the passion a parent has for a child; and the many unlikely ways to build a family. Ultimately it's a story about love and happiness, in their many crooked configurations.

BookBrowse Review

A compassionate, intelligent memoir of a family's attempt to parent a sick child. Highly recommended by First Impressions reviewers

Of the 53 reviews submitted for *Happiness*, 49 readers rated it a four- or five-star book for an average of 4.7, a score only achieved by one other non-fiction title in the 10 year history of First Impressions!

What it's about:

Heather Harpham's memoir, *Happiness: The Crooked Little Road to Semi Ever After*, is a compassionate, intelligent story of a family's attempt to parent a sick child. The non-fiction account begins with a delightful courtship between the author, a worldly California girl, and Brian, an intellectual homebody writer who doesn't want to change his New York lifestyle. Their magical interlude ends when she becomes pregnant and her newly acquired lover doesn't want children, even though he says he loves her. With the help of her family and friends, she returns to California to deliver their daughter alone. Within hours of her delivery she is told her baby Grace is perilously ill. As the child's condition becomes increasingly dismal, the father reappears and together they must decide what they will risk to ensure she will reach adulthood (Carol N).

The book covers many themes:

The author allows us to see her world from many different angles, all of them very personal (Dorothy G). She explores a multitude of subjects: romance, relationships, parental passion for one's children, and abiding friendships. It is ultimately a story about her family's search for love and happiness (Carol N).

Many found the book hit home:

Be prepared to be deeply moved (Monica P). I was absorbed by this heartwarming story and finished reading it with tears running down my face (Diane H). This book was absolutely incredible. Considering my 'season' in life--early 30s and having kids--I could easily put myself right in the author's shoes. She makes you want to enjoy each and every moment with your kids (Miller W). It truly speaks to the courage and strength we often don't believe we have, and the power of a child to evoke these qualities in the parents who love and vow to protect them, whatever it takes personally. I feel honored to have read their story (Diane W).

Harpham's writing was a highlight:

Although a difficult topic, Harpham portrays her deeply personal story with charm and grace. Her voice never loses its underlying positivity even in the face of traumatic medical decisions involving her children (Melinda H). She has a talent for great prose and description that made her memoir real

(Marion C). Her writing was full of pure and raw emotion which I found incredibly beautiful (Miller W). The highs and lows are presented as mini roller coasters which catapult the reader into what the family must be going through (Linda V).

First Impression reviewers also admired the author's candor:

I feel that it was brave and courageous for the author to share her emotional journey (Linda Z). The writer's honesty shone through (Gail H). Harpham's account felt authentic and real, and from the heart (Diane W).

Others found it enlightening and inspiring:

This book will enrich the lives of all readers (Myrna M). The story was an eye-opener as to what is involved in the care of desperately sick children (Arlene M). It made me think about the understanding and support parents, relatives, and friends need when facing a major medical crisis involving such a young child (Janice A). It left me with a desire to do my part and look into being a donor. The hard decisions made by Harpham and her partner were explained in such a way that I often had to stop reading and consider what I would do in such a situation (Dorothy G).

Overall our readers enjoyed *Happiness* and recommend it highly:

This is the best book I have read this year (Arlene M). I loved everything about it (Barbara O). I started it on a rainy night, thinking I would fall asleep quickly, and ended up reading the entire book (Diane W)! It's so good, you will want to read it twice (Sherri G). I highly recommend this memoir, it was a definite page-turner and tear jerker (Miller W). It's one I will never forget and without any reservation recommend to all my friends and family (Candace F). *Happiness* would make an excellent book club selection (Barbara O).

Reviewed by First Impressions Reviewers. This review was originally published in *The BookBrowse Review* in August 2017, and has been updated for the November 2018 edition.

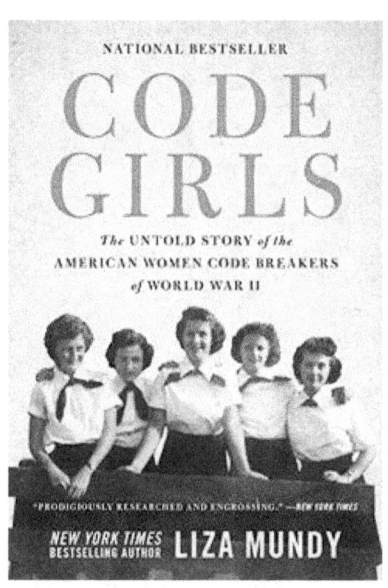

CODE GIRLS

by Liza Mundy

BookBrowse Rating: 5/5
Critics' Consensus: 5/5
Readers' Rating: 5/5

Published October 2018 in Paperback, 432 pages

Summary

"*Code Girls* reveals a hidden army of female cryptographers, whose work played a crucial role in ending World War II.... Mundy has rescued a piece of forgotten history, and given these American heroes the recognition they deserve." - Nathalia Holt, bestselling author of *Rise of the Rocket Girls*

Recruited by the U.S. Army and Navy from small towns and elite colleges, more than ten thousand women served as codebreakers during World War II. While their brothers and boyfriends took up arms, these women moved to Washington and learned the meticulous work of code-breaking. Their efforts shortened the war, saved countless lives, and gave them access to careers previously denied to them. A strict vow of secrecy nearly erased their efforts from history; now, through dazzling research and interviews with surviving code girls, bestselling author Liza Mundy brings to life this riveting and vital story of American courage, service, and scientific accomplishment.

BookBrowse Review

The little-known story of the young American women who cracked key Axis codes, helped secure Allied victory and revolutionized the field of cryptanalysis.

History books that focus on World War II are often peppered with accounts of military strategy and action, or reports of brave soldiers fighting and dying far from their homes to preserve freedom. Seldom featured are the everyday men and women who contributed to the war effort behind the scenes. Liza Mundy's latest work, *Code Girls*, takes advantage of recently declassified government documents to highlight the little-known work of the hundreds of women involved in cracking Japanese and German encryption to help bring WWII to a successful conclusion.

The code-breakers' stories are not only fascinating, they're enlightening; unbeknownst to most, their contributions had far-reaching effects long after the war and cannot be overstated. The author writes of these women: "They laid the groundwork for the now burgeoning field of cybersecurity, which entails protecting one's data, networks, and communications against enemy attack. They pioneered work that would lead to the modern computing industry...It was women who helped found the field of clandestine eavesdropping—much bigger and more controversial now than it was then—and it was women in many cases who shaped the early culture of the NSA."

Mundy highlights many individual women, and although a few "Eureka!" moments are illustrated (such as when Genevieve Grotjan, a 27-year-old-math teacher from Buffalo, found the key to a cypher used by Japanese diplomats), it's mostly a story of collective contribution. We learn that contrary to the popular myth of a lone genius who looks at a problem and figures it all out on his or her own, "codes are broken not by solitary individuals, but by groups of people trading pieces of things they have learned and noticed and collected."

Although readers will get to know some of them better than others, overall the author gives us a jigsaw puzzle-like picture of dozens of the young women – small tidbits that form an unexpected but captivating tableau. We learn about the many different types of people involved in the code-breaking effort – their backgrounds, their rationales for volunteering or enlisting, how they spent their limited free time, and how they contributed (even if it was just perusing endless streams of numbers, day after day, in search of a pattern). In spite of the vast cast of characters, the author really shines in her ability to bring each to life and give her a personality of her own.

Beyond a peek at the lives of the code-breakers themselves, readers get a real feel for America at war. She discusses the social changes that were taking place as a result of this all-encompassing event. "[N]ewfound freedoms were changing the women's lives," she writes. "Men, now, were the ones avid to get married. Men were the ones who wanted to have someone back home to write to; someone to produce an heir by; someone waiting when they came back from war, wounded or whole. Women—often—were the ones holding out for a bit more time to think."

There are several sections where Mundy goes into detail on how various cryptographic techniques were used to encrypt messages and how the codes were broken. I found these sections dragged somewhat, but I suspect many readers will appreciate the arcane information included on specific techniques, such as how versions of the Vigenère Square (a method of disguising letters using a tabular method dating back to the Renaissance, according to the author) were employed and ultimately cracked. Overall I found the book an absorbing portrait of not only these marvelous, brilliant, hard-working women, but of the era just before, during, and after WWII in the United States. It was intriguing to read an account of what it was like to live in the country during a time when every citizen contributed to the war effort in very tangible ways.

Code Girls will likely appeal to a wide audience; anyone with an interest in WWII history — both fiction and nonfiction readers alike — will find much to love here.

Reviewed by Kim Kovacs. This review was originally published in *The BookBrowse Review* in October 2017, and has been updated for the October 2018 edition.

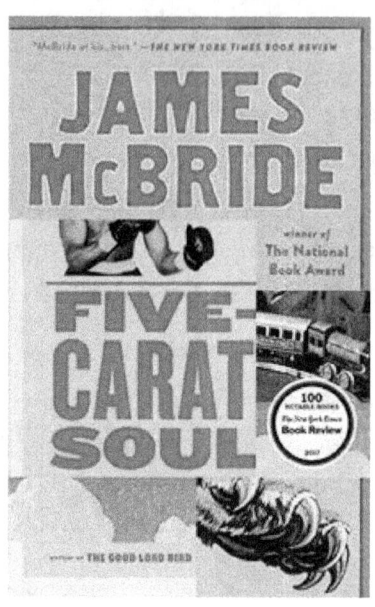

FIVE-CARAT SOUL

by James McBride

BookBrowse Rating: 5/5
Critics' Consensus: 5/5
Readers' Rating: 5/5

Published September 2018 in Paperback, 336 pages

Summary

Exciting new fiction from James McBride, the first since his National Book Award–winning novel *The Good Lord Bird*.

The stories in *Five-Carat Soul*—none of them ever published before—spring from the place where identity, humanity, and history converge. They're funny and poignant, insightful and unpredictable, imaginative and authentic—all told with McBride's unrivaled storytelling skill and meticulous eye for character and detail. McBride explores the ways we learn from the world and the people around us. An antiques dealer discovers that a legendary toy commissioned by Civil War General Robert E. Lee now sits in the home of a black minister in Queens. Five strangers find themselves thrown together and face unexpected judgment. An American president draws inspiration from a conversation he overhears in a stable. And members of The Five-Carat Soul Bottom Bone Band recount stories from their own messy and hilarious lives.

As McBride did in his National Book award-winning *The Good Lord Bird* and his bestselling *The Color of Water*, he writes with humor and insight about how we struggle to understand who we are in a world we don't fully comprehend. The result is a surprising, perceptive, and evocative collection of stories that is also a moving exploration of our human condition.

BookBrowse Review

James McBride, the National Book Award winner, explores the African American experience in this richly imagined collection of stories.

In the short story "Sonny's Blues," from the 1965 collection Going to Meet the Man, African-American author and social critic James Baldwin, known for his writing on race relations, explores the alienation between two brothers. The unnamed narrator is unable to understand his sibling Sonny, a musician and heroin addict, until he witnesses Sonny's remarkable performance at a jazz club. The resulting scene is one of the most memorable representations of music in literature. James McBride draws heavily from it in the opening story of Five-Carat Soul.

In McBride's version, a Jewish toy collector pursues the owner of a priceless model train all over New York City, finally catching up with him at a hip-hop club in Brooklyn. The owner turns out to be a rapping reverend, and the collector is shocked by the quality of his performance:

> ...a litany of nonstop cursing, roaring, funky, low-down, skuzzy, earth-scrapping, to-the-bone brilliant, rhyming lyrics that made the previous rappers before him seem like choirboys. His voice was unworldly. It sounded like sandpaper grinding on a gravelly road, yet smooth as a glass of water...

Next, in a series of linked stories, McBride takes readers to "The Bottom," an impoverished town on the outskirts of Uniontown, PA, where a twelve-year-old protagonist named Butter relates the chicanery of the town's children and adults alike with wry humor and precocious wisdom. Two other tales are set during the Civil War. In the first, an orphaned child seeks his father, whom he believes to be Abraham Lincoln. In the other, Lincoln himself finds inspiration in the words of a stable-hand while mourning the death of his son Willie. The collection tilts surreal with "The Moaning Bench," a story about a group of people appearing in purgatory before the gatekeeper of hell. Then there's "Mr. P & the Wind," a sharp satirical allegory about slavery and the dangers that befall captors and captives alike.

Where some authors excel at characterization, McBride's stories are often strongest because of their settings. "Ecosystems" is perhaps a more apt term. In the series of vignettes from which the collection takes its title, the protagonist's hometown "The Bottom," is an achingly real emblem of Rust Belt poverty. The kids hang out in the "Cool Out Spot," where rival groups get along, "so long as you brung soda or cakes or something to trade or share," while the adults struggle to pay the electricity bill and hope against all odds for a brighter future for the youth.

Five-Carat Soul is woven around themes of slavery and racial segregation — from the many references to Lincoln, to the story of an all African-American regiment that fought in World War II. These work in concert with the collection's religious overtones to assert the significance of the soul. In a world beset by differences (of skin color, of species), God is the great equalizer. McBride's superb wit and imagination ensure that this is accomplished without sermons or rhetoric. His glory is in the understated, showing the grandest creatures in their humblest moments, from Lincoln in the White House stable to the caged King of the Jungle in "Mr. P & the Wind." Several of the stories also serve as a celebration of African-Americans' contributions to history, which one character, a member of an all-black regiment of the Union army during the Civil War (see Beyond the Book), argues for passionately:

> The white folks'll know theirs, won't they? They'll write songs for 'em, and raise flags for 'em, and put 'em in books...ain't nobody but God gonna give more than a handful of feed to the ones of us who died out here fighting for our freedom.

McBride, much like James Baldwin, is a captivating storyteller using his imaginative talents to explore the African-American experience. It is a burdensome history, and its repercussions are very much alive today, but with his light touch and use of allegory, McBride brings enchantment to the onerous.

Reviewed by Lisa Butts. This review was originally published in *The BookBrowse Review* in October 2017, and has been updated for the October 2018 edition.

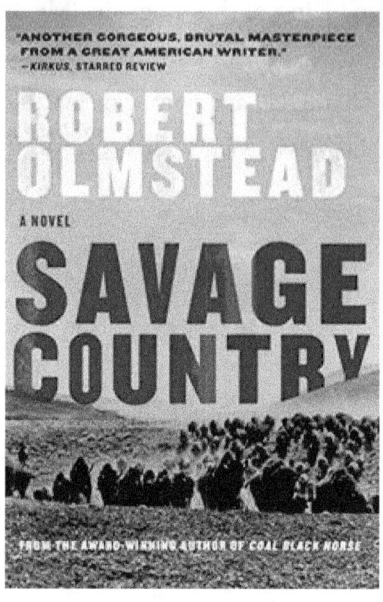

SAVAGE COUNTRY

by Robert Olmstead

BookBrowse Rating: 5/5
Critics' Consensus: 5/5

Published September 2018 in Paperback, 320 pages

Summary

A gripping narrative of the infamous hunt which drove the buffalo population to near extinction--the story of a moment in our history in which mass destruction of an animal population was seen as the only route to economic solvency. And the intimate story of how that hunt changed two people forever.

"For weeks countless swarms of locusts, brown-black and brick-yellow, darkened the air like ash from a great conflagration, their jaws biting all things for what could be eaten."

In September 1873, Elizabeth Coughlin, a widow bankrupted by her husband's folly and death, embarks on a buffalo hunt with her estranged and mysterious brother-in-law, Michael. With no money, no family, no job or security, she hopes to salvage something of her former life and the lives of the hired men and their families who depend on her. The buffalo hunt that her husband had planned, she now realizes, was his last hope for saving their land.

Elizabeth and Michael plunge south across the aptly named Deadline demarcating Indian Territory from their home state, Kansas. Nothing could have prepared them for the dangers: rattlesnakes, rabies, wildfire, lightning strikes, blue northers, flash floods, threats to life in so many ways. They're on borrowed time: the Comanche are in winter quarters, and the cruel work of slaughtering the buffalo is unraveling their souls. They must get back alive.

BookBrowse Review

This is a story about 19th century, Wild West America told through its land, its animals and its people.

In *Savage Country*, Robert Olmstead speaks to the American myths, legends, and ethos that originated with the Pilgrims and early settlers, was tested in the Civil War, and arrived at its last frontier with the expansion and settlements beyond the Mississippi River.

The plot of Olmstead's work is as simple as its theme is complex. In 1873, David Coughlin, a seemingly prosperous farmer-rancher on the Kansas prairie, has died after being kicked by "a big intractable stallion," one he was warned away from by his wife, Elizabeth. She's upset with her husband's carelessness, and then grows angry when she discovers that he was so deeply in debt to the local banker, Whitechurch, that she's now in danger of losing her land. Her worry is aggravated because so many people, mostly men who followed David into "the slaughterous American war," are dependent on the land's prosperity. David's brother, Michael, arrives, riding Khyber, a magnificent Arabian mare and accompanied by two loyal dogs. Michael has lived a life of adventure, traveling the world, of late mostly in Africa where "he thought to get rich in the ivory trade." Before even meeting Elizabeth, Michael pays off David's debts in gold, much to Whitechurch's chagrin. Later, not wanting to be obligated to Michael, Elizabeth decides to organize a buffalo hunt. There's a massive herd ranging south past the Deadline (demarcating Native American Territory from Kansas), into the Comanche country - that's north Texas and western Oklahoma, somewhere "between the north fork of the Canadian and Red Rivers, and from about the 100th meridian to the eastern border of New Mexico." Michael objects but Elizabeth is undeterred, so he decides to accompany her, fearing for her safety.

This simple plot frames an endurance story, an expedition lasting more than a year, with wild rivers to be crossed, prairie fires and blue northers (a sudden cold front) to be endured, bandits to be killed, and buffalo to be slaughtered by the hundreds on days when the big Sharps .50 caliber rifles grew so hot that hunters poured cooling canteen water down their barrels.

The big bull he shot, tormented and mystified, blew and pawed at the ground, throwing clumps of red earth high into the air ... Forming on the bulls lips and nostrils was a mass of bloody foam. This is a story of the snick-snick-snick of skinning knives being sharpened as blood-soaked men rip hides from magnificent beasts, careful to dig out the lead bullets to be melted and used to kill another animal. It is a tale of rag-clad freed slaves slipping from the lost woods where they've been hiding to ask to join the expedition.

Michael, silent, strong, tired of the killing yet obligated to Elizabeth, feeling "the passage of receding time," in spite of his moral qualms, is too real to be a John Wayne hero. Elizabeth, somewhat older than Michael, angry, growing into strength and independence as she endures privation, becomes heroic.

Others tag along, prosper, fail, die, or slink away like Reverend Doctor Purefoy, whose ambitions to marry Elizabeth began at the graveside; or a man with the singular name of Aubuchon, "educated for the priesthood, but had never taken holy orders," content now to serve as chef. There are misfits and men near feral. "The old man who wore blue jays in his hat was hired and with him came his woman without a nose" - they poison buffalo carcasses and then collect the pelts of the wolves and coyotes that come to eat their fill.

All together, they are the voice of a laconic, subtle poet, singing. There is a touch of Hemingway in the story's structure, more of Cormac McCarthy as it turns a cold eye toward the violence, all laced with spare stark sentences shaping images from our history too often obscured by myth. The book is an elegy for America, a continent subdued by hard men, Colt revolvers, and Sharps rifles.

Olmstead's *Savage Country* has a moral authenticity, but it's also a lament, an elegy for the beauty of what was and for what should have been.

Reviewed by Gary Presley. This review was originally published in *The BookBrowse Review* in September 2017, and has been updated for the September 2018 edition.

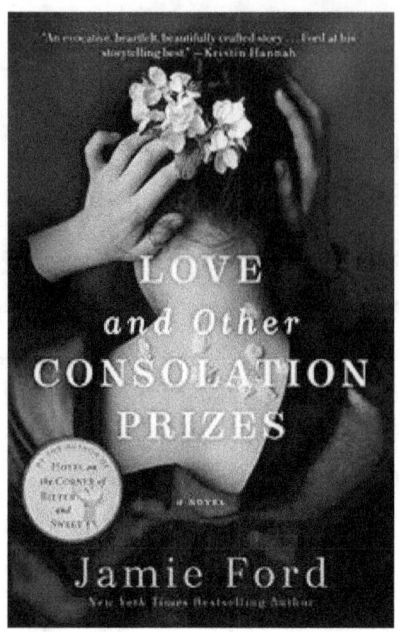

LOVE AND OTHER CONSOLATION PRIZES

by Jamie Ford

BookBrowse Rating: 5/5
Critics' Consensus: 4.5/5
Readers' Rating: 5/5

Published June 2018 in Paperback, 336 pages

Summary

From the bestselling author of *Hotel on the Corner of Bitter and Sweet* comes a powerful novel, inspired by a true story, about a boy whose life is transformed at Seattle's epic 1909 World's Fair.

For twelve-year-old Ernest Young, a charity student at a boarding school, the chance to go to the World's Fair feels like a gift. But only once he's there, amid the exotic exhibits, fireworks, and Ferris wheels, does he discover that *he* is the one who is actually the prize. The half-Chinese orphan is astounded to learn he will be raffled off—a healthy boy "to a good home."

The winning ticket belongs to the flamboyant madam of a high-class brothel, famous for educating her girls. There, Ernest becomes the new houseboy and befriends Maisie, the madam's precocious daughter, and a bold scullery maid named Fahn. Their friendship and affection form the first real family Ernest has ever known—and against all odds, this new sporting life gives him the sense of home he's always desired.

But as the grande dame succumbs to an occupational hazard and their world of finery begins to crumble, all three must grapple with hope, ambition, and first love.

Fifty years later, in the shadow of Seattle's second World's Fair, Ernest struggles to help his ailing wife reconcile who she once was with who she wanted to be, while trying to keep family secrets hidden from their grown-up daughters.

Against a rich backdrop of post-Victorian vice, suffrage, and celebration, *Love and Other Consolations* is an enchanting tale about innocence and devotion—in a world where everything, and everyone, is for sale.

BookBrowse Review

Jamie Ford, author of *Hotel on the Corner of Bitter and Sweet* returns with a Seattle-based epic inspired by a true story.

Love and Other Consolation Prizes was read and reviewed by 22 BookBrowse members for First Impressions, 21 of whom gave it four or five stars, resulting in an impressive overall rating of 4.7.

What it's about:

Jamie Ford's new novel, *Love and Other Consolation Prizes,* is a wonderful blend of historical fiction, coming of age and romance - with a smidgeon of mystery thrown in as well (Barbara Z). Based on real-life events, the plot centers on Ernest, the illegitimate son of a white missionary and a Chinese woman, as he tells his story to his adult daughter - a reporter who has uncovered that as a young boy her father was auctioned off at a raffle held at the 1909 World's Fair. Ernest's tale revolves around the madam who won him in the raffle and his life among the ladies of the night during a time when the women's suffrage movement was campaigning to shut down such houses of ill-repute (Arden A). The chapters alternate between the 1909 and 1962 World's Fairs, both of which were held in Seattle (Judi R). The author vividly describes the despair of a young orphan sold into slavery, the sights and sounds of the wondrous World's Fairs five decades apart, and the tender love that can exist between friends and family – as well as the fragile threads that connect them (Amy P).

The author's character development and writing is a highlight:

Ford provides deeply moving descriptions of each character, as well as their emotions and motives (Amy P). The cast of characters is actually very small, but we get to know them well (Sande O). I fell in love with the Young family and their search for true love both romantically and as part of a family (Lynn B). *Love and Other Consolation Prizes* is a well-written, moving book (Jean N). As always, Ford has crafted a heartfelt story (Carol S); this is a poignant and subtle novel (Deanna W).

Many also remark on how seamlessly the author incorporated the historical elements:

I really enjoyed the bits and pieces of historical events throughout the book; they grounded the story for me (Jean N). Ford takes stories he has read from old newspapers and documents and weaves a fantastically beautiful story with shreds of truth running throughout (Carm D). The book provides a colorful look at the "Old Seattle," and the two World's Fairs figure prominently throughout the novel (Susan R).

The book explores a great many themes:

The novel is a wonderful account of undying love and respect, heartbreak and unimaginable fear (Carm D). It deals with themes of family, prejudice, identity, and fitting in (Deanna W). Ford explores the racial and economic discrimination of the times as well (Lynne B). Additionally, it covers topics such as medical treatments, immigration and the Suffragette movement (Amy P).

A few feel it did not live up to the author's previous work:

The Hotel on the Corner of Bitter and Sweet was one of my favorite novels. Naturally I had high expectations for this novel. Unfortunately, *Love and other Consolation Prizes* did not move me in the same way (Vicki O). I hardly felt any connection. I couldn't feel empathy with some of the characters. I sometimes found myself very bored, skimming paragraphs, and would easily put the book down and not want to go back to it. I really craved more action (Lillian T). If I have a quibble with Ford it is with the pace of his narrative. A quickening might have enlivened several sections (Sande O).

Most, though, think *Love and Other Consolation Prizes* is sure to be a hit:

Jamie Ford has written another winner. I was a fan after *Hotel on the Corner of Bitter and Sweet*, and he does not disappoint with his latest (Roe P). There is nothing I didn't like about this book: the setting, the eras, the depth of the descriptions of both the times and the characters, the entertaining story, the history lesson... all meshed together to make an excellent read. I wish it had lasted another 100 pages (Arden A). This is a story not to be missed! (Lynne B). I found this engrossing book difficult to put down (Amber B). Readers are certainly going to be happy that Jamie Ford has given us another beautifully written novel (Judi R).

Recommended for a wide audience:

Everyone should do themselves a favor and read this book; it's also a great choice for book club discussions (Carm D). It will be a title that I will keep on my list to highly recommend to friends and family (Jean N). The book is appropriate for younger and older readers (Sande O). Historical fiction lovers will enjoy this novel (Shawna L).

Reviewed by First Impressions Reviewers. This review was originally published in *The BookBrowse Review* in October 2017, and has been updated for the July 2018 edition.

HUNGER

by Roxane Gay

BookBrowse Rating: 4/5
Critics' Consensus: 5/5
Readers' Rating: 5/5

Published June 2018 in Paperback, 320 pages

Summary

From the *New York Times* best-selling author of *Bad Feminist*, a searingly honest memoir of food, weight, self-image, and learning how to feed your hunger while taking care of yourself.

"I ate and ate and ate in the hopes that if I made myself big, my body would be safe. I buried the girl I was because she ran into all kinds of trouble. I tried to erase every memory of her, but she is still there, somewhere. ... I was trapped in my body, one that I barely recognized or understood, but at least I was safe."

New York Times bestselling author Roxane Gay has written with intimacy and sensitivity about food and bodies, using her own emotional and psychological struggles as a means of exploring our shared anxieties over pleasure, consumption, appearance, and health. As a woman who describes her own body as "wildly undisciplined," Roxane understands the tension between desire and denial, between self-comfort and self-care. In *Hunger*, she casts an insightful and critical eye on her childhood, teens, and twenties—including the devastating act of violence that acted as a turning point in her young life—and brings readers into the present and the realities, pains, and joys of her daily life.

With the bracing candor, vulnerability, and authority that have made her one of the most admired voices of her generation, Roxane explores what it means to be overweight in a time when the bigger you are, the less you are seen. *Hunger* is a deeply personal memoir from one of our finest writers, and tells a story that hasn't yet been told but needs to be.

BookBrowse Review

This honest memoir discusses the complex issues relating to weight and body image and shows how past trauma can color the present.

In this penetrating and fearless memoir, author Roxane Gay discusses her battle with body acceptance and PTSD stemming from her rape at age twelve by a group of boys. After using food and weight gain as a defense mechanism, she describes her journey of learning how to trust others, while recounting the myriad physical and psychological obstacles faced by obese individuals.

The first half of the memoir traces Gay's trajectory from being a happy, well-adjusted child to a very troubled young adult, as she was hesitant to seek help or tell friends or family about her rape. Left to her own devices at boarding school and then at college, Gay ate as a form of comfort, and used her weight gain as a way of becoming invisible to men, whom she found frightening after her attack. After quitting Yale and briefly spinning out of control in Arizona, Gay returned to school to get her undergraduate, and then graduate degrees elsewhere. She has since established herself as a talented and successful writer, but continues to be marked by the past. She describes, for example, Googling one of her attackers and imagining confronting him at his place of business on a near daily basis. However, she has learned to loosen her boundaries, to love and accept love in return, has opened up about her trauma, and is finding ways toward better health and happiness – the things she hungers for most of all.

Gay explores aspects of life as an overweight person that are rarely discussed, and these will hopefully spark conversation and greater sensitivity toward some important issues. For example, she speaks lovingly of her family, while wishing they would cease trying to intervene in issues surrounding her weight. She longs to wear bright colors, but sticks with a drab wardrobe so as not to draw attention to herself. Eating in a restaurant can be unbearable if the chairs have arms, and air travel is fraught with anxiety. Overall, she notes astutely, "The bigger you are, the smaller your world becomes."

Gay also discusses the unique difficulties in being a feminist and an obese woman. She recognizes that despite Western cultures' unreasonable beauty and size standards, all women deserve to feel comfortable and confident in their bodies. Yet she does not feel that way herself. "My body is a cage of my own making," she writes, "I am still trying to figure my way out of it." She sardonically ribs advertising aimed at women regarding weight loss and diet food, "Every time I watch a yogurt commercial I think, 'My god, I want to be that happy. I really do.'"

The titular hunger is metaphorical and stands in for many things, a hunger to be free from the trauma's long-lasting effects, the hunger to make better choices, to be normal (whatever that entails), to be happy, to be accepted. "My father believes hunger is in the mind," she explains, "I know that hunger is in the mind and the body and the heart and the soul."

Gay begins *Hunger* by insisting that hers is not a "success story," and she consistently refuses to acknowledge any part of her experience as profound or transformative. Even if Gay says that her narrative is not one of triumph, and that she is not a role model, she doesn't give herself enough credit. This lowers the stakes for the reader and makes the experience not quite as fulfilling as it could be. Nevertheless her candor is refreshing and commendable and other survivors of assault will certainly relate to, and perhaps find comfort in her struggle. She writes of it affectingly, particularly the difficulty in speaking up about the trauma, "We swallow it, and more often than not, that truth turns rancid. It spreads through the body like an infection." Those who struggle with their weight will also likely relate to Gay's story. But truly, everyone with a body and a history may easily relate. *Hunger* is an ardent expression of pain and longing, and a journey toward transcendence.

Reviewed by Lisa Butts. This review was originally published in *The BookBrowse Review* in August 2017, and has been updated for the July 2018 edition.

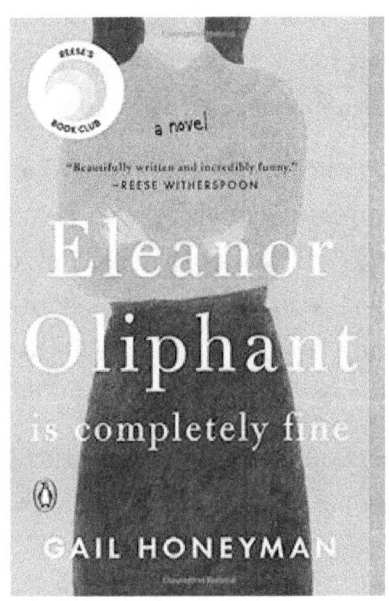

ELEANOR OLIPHANT IS COMPLETELY FINE

by Gail Honeyman

BookBrowse Rating: 4/5
Critics' Consensus: 4.5/5
Readers' Rating: 5/5

Published June 2018 in Paperback, 352 pages

Summary

Smart, warm, uplifting, *Eleanor Oliphant is Completely Fine* is the story of an out-of-the-ordinary heroine whose deadpan weirdness and unconscious wit make for an irresistible journey.

No one's ever told Eleanor that life should be better than fine.

Meet Eleanor Oliphant: She struggles with appropriate social skills and tends to say exactly what she's thinking. Nothing is missing in her carefully timetabled life of avoiding social interactions, where weekends are punctuated by frozen pizza, vodka, and phone chats with Mummy.

But everything changes when Eleanor meets Raymond, the bumbling and deeply unhygienic IT guy from her office. When she and Raymond together save Sammy, an elderly gentleman who has fallen on the sidewalk, the three become the kinds of friends who rescue one another from the lives of isolation they have each been living. And it is Raymond's big heart that will ultimately help Eleanor find the way to repair her own profoundly damaged one.

Smart, warm, uplifting, *Eleanor Oliphant is Completely Fine* is the story of an out-of-the-ordinary heroine whose deadpan weirdness and unconscious wit make for an irresistible journey as she realizes...

The only way to survive is to open your heart.

BookBrowse Review

Smart, warm, uplifting, this novel is about an out-of-the-ordinary heroine whose deadpan weirdness and unconscious wit make for an irresistible journey.

Eleanor Oliphant is, of course, completely fine. Because what else is she allowed to be? What other answer do you give to the question: "How are you?" Certainly not the real one. Certainly not when you have lived a life as damaging and fractious as that of Eleanor, and had to find your own way through it.

"The scalp massage at the hairdresser, the flu jab I had last winter – the only time I experience touch is from people whom I am paying, and they are almost always wearing disposable gloves at the time. I'm merely stating the facts. People don't like these facts, but I can't help that. If someone asks you how you are, you are meant to say FINE. You are not meant to say that you cried yourself to sleep last night because you hadn't spoken to another person for two consecutive days. FINE, is what you say."

Because she often doesn't recognize social norms, Eleanor Oliphant is told that she is a flawed misfit by the very people who were meant to look after her – her mother, social services, and foster families. She leads a controlled and isolated existence numbed by pizza, vodka, and a plant named Polly. Weekends are just empty spaces that break up the weekdays spent at a job surrounded by colleagues who mostly avoid her. These little routines keep her existing and muddling along.

Even if she is used to being alone, Eleanor recognizes that she's missing something. "There are days when I feel so lightly connected to the earth that the threads that tether me to the planet are gossamer thin, spun sugar. A strong gust of wind could dislodge me completely, and I'd lift off and blow away, like one of those seeds in a dandelion clock."

With no filters or ideas of social norms, Eleanor struggles to engage with other people. Excluded from water cooler conversations at work and communal gatherings, she has been so used to a solitary existence that she is baffled by the support from her colleague, Raymond. From how to order a drink to what family life can be like, from what to do when invited to a party to the etiquette of funerals, Eleanor learns a lot from Raymond. He brings Eleanor into a web of connections and she starts to slowly, accidentally, build relationships.

It's easy to laugh at Eleanor and how baffling she finds many things, but we might agree with the absurdities of the unspoken protocols of life she indirectly challenges. Through Eleanor's wry observations and uncensored honesty, Honeyman is able to question society. Take her assessment of the wedding gift list, for example. "Of all the compulsory financial contributions, this is the one that irks me most. Two people wander around John Lewis picking out lovely items for themselves, and then they make other people pay for them. It's bare-faced effrontery." The reader is also forced to ponder the dangers of loneliness and our attitudes toward those who seem to be outsiders.

Although she sometimes takes pride in describing herself as a "sole survivor...a self-contained entity," isolation hurts, and Eleanor knows this.

Odd Eleanor slowly enters a life that she never thought was for her. She remains quirky and unique, and the reader loves her for it, but her life becomes a little more expansive and contains a bit more opportunity. Gail Honeyman published this novel as she entered her forties, after a lot of rejection. Just like her protagonist, Honeyman's life changed after many trying years. Eleanor may be a social misfit, but she is an incredibly astute one. *Eleanor Oliphant is Completely Fine* is perceptive, wise, funny and utterly readable.

SING, UNBURIED, SING

by Jesmyn Ward

BookBrowse Rating: 5/5
Critics' Consensus: 5/5
Readers' Rating: 5/5

Published May 2018 in Paperback, 288 pages

Summary

A searing and profound Southern odyssey by National Book Award winner Jesmyn Ward.

In Jesmyn Ward's first novel since her National Book Award–winning *Salvage the Bones*, this singular American writer brings the archetypal road novel into rural twenty-first-century America. Drawing on Morrison and Faulkner, *The Odyssey* and the Old Testament, Ward gives us an epochal story, a journey through Mississippi's past and present that is both an intimate portrait of a family and an epic tale of hope and struggle. Ward is a major American writer, multiply awarded and universally lauded, and in *Sing, Unburied, Sing* she is at the height of her powers.

Jojo and his toddler sister, Kayla, live with their grandparents, Mam and Pop, and the occasional presence of their drug-addicted mother, Leonie, on a farm on the Gulf Coast of Mississippi. Leonie is simultaneously tormented and comforted by visions of her dead brother, which only come to her when she's high; Mam is dying of cancer; and quiet, steady Pop tries to run the household and teach Jojo how to be a man. When the white father of Leonie's children is released from prison, she packs her kids and a friend into her car and sets out across the state for Parchman farm, the Mississippi State Penitentiary, on a journey rife with danger and promise.

Sing, Unburied, Sing grapples with the ugly truths at the heart of the American story and the power, and limitations, of the bonds of family. Rich with Ward's distinctive, musical language, *Sing, Unburied, Sing* is a majestic new work and an essential contribution to American literature.

BookBrowse Review

A journey through Mississippi's past and present, examining the ugly truths at the heart of the American story, and the power - and limitations - of family bonds.

"I like to think I know what death is. I like to think that it's something I could look at straight." These haunting lines come from the mouth of 13-year-old Jojo. With an absent father and a drug-addicted mother, the mixed-race boy is forced to grow up in a hurry as he is often the sole caretaker of his toddler sister, Kayla. His black grandmother Mam is wasting away from cancer, and grandfather Pop is struggling with his own demons even as he tries to provide a measure of moral guidance to his grandson.

Jojo and his mother, Leonie, narrate most of *Sing, Unburied, Sing* in alternating chapters as the story travels back and forth in time, the past forever casting a shadow over the present. Like Jesmyn Ward's National Book award-winning <u>Salvage the Bones</u>, this novel, too, is set in the fictional town of Bois Sauvage, Mississippi, a place ravaged by poverty and subject to nature's cruel whims. The only escape from this harsh world seems to be meth, a release valve that Leonie grasps at readily. Racism is the other scourge that gnaws at the community's marrow, casting its grim shadow over every single person. It is the evil that irrevocably shapes Pop. His daughter, Leonie, has chosen a white man, Michael, as her husband and the father of her children, a relationship that destroys the family in more ways than one.

Sing, Unburied, Sing galvanizes into action when Leonie gets word that Michael is going to be released from jail after serving time for drug offenses. Her white friend Misty in tow, she brings both Jojo and Kayla along for the ride to pick up their father, a journey where misfortune and misery doggedly pursue them.

Ghosts of both the metaphorical and literal kind haunt these pages. Some of the most compelling chapters are narrated by Richie, the ghost of a boy who spent time at the notorious Parchman prison along with Pop, and whose spirit is linked to the family in many ways. Leonie also sees a ghost – that of her brother Given, who, like Richie, met an unnecessary and tragic end way too soon. He is her source of strength, a crutch she leans on to get through her muddled daily life. These elements of magical realism meld in seamlessly with the narrative - when real life becomes too difficult to bear, leaning on ghosts is a salve of its own.

Jojo and Pop are the most memorable characters of the story as they each struggle with their daily burdens of responsibility, guilt and wrenching family ties. Pop's story is richly layered, and one of the novel's many delights lies in getting to know this enigmatic man more closely and to lay bare the secrets that he holds dear, the same ones that have nearly done him in. Also brilliantly rendered is the Mississippi bayou — you practically suffocate under the weight of that stifling humidity and lush vegetation.

"Watching the family grabs me inside, twists, and pulls tight. It hurts. It hurts so much I can't look at it," Richie once says. The same could be said of the reader as misery after misfortune seems to pile on thick for Jojo and his loved ones. Yet despite their trying circumstances, the novel is nowhere near bleak. In fact, just as the title promises, it sings — the ghosts and the cast of characters together create a beautiful and haunting melody, one that resonates long after the last page is turned.

Will the secrets from the past that have forever been haunting this family finally be buried and put to rest? *Sing, Unburied Sing* is a moving and stark ode to the new South, a place where the present and past intertwine closely — so closely that it has become increasingly difficult to shake history's ugly stain and nature's brutal force to forge a new path. The residents, like Jojo and his family, just do what it takes to see the light of another day. That, in its own way, is its own kind of salvation.

Reviewed by Poornima Apte. This review was originally published in *The BookBrowse Review* in October 2017, and has been updated for the May 2018 edition.

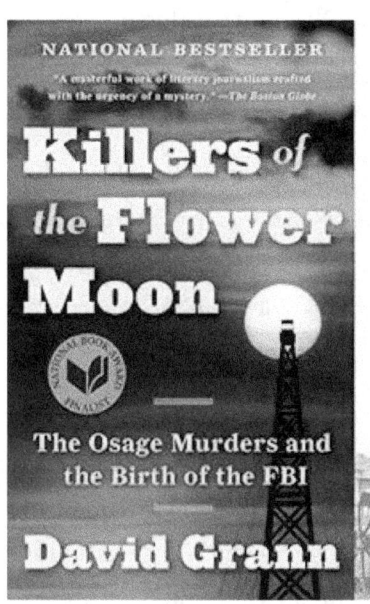

KILLERS OF THE FLOWER MOON

by David Grann

BookBrowse Rating: 5/5
Critics' Consensus: 5/5
Readers' Rating: 4/5

Published April 2018 in Paperback, 352 pages

Summary

Winner of the 2017 BookBrowse Nonfiction Award

A twisting, haunting true-life murder mystery about one of the most monstrous crimes in American history.

In the 1920s, the richest people per capita in the world were members of the Osage Indian nation in Oklahoma. After oil was discovered beneath their land, they rode in chauffeured automobiles, built mansions, and sent their children to study in Europe.

Then, one by one, the Osage began to be killed off. The family of an Osage woman, Mollie Burkhart, became a prime target. Her relatives were shot and poisoned. And it was just the beginning, as more and more members of the tribe began to die under mysterious circumstances.

In this last remnant of the Wild West - where oilmen like J. P. Getty made their fortunes and where desperadoes like Al Spencer, the "Phantom Terror," roamed - many of those who dared to investigate the killings were themselves murdered. As the death toll climbed to more than twenty-four, the FBI took up the case. It was one of the organization's first major homicide investigations and the bureau badly bungled the case. In desperation, the young director, J. Edgar Hoover, turned to a former Texas Ranger named Tom White to unravel the mystery. White put together an undercover team, including one of the only American Indian agents in the bureau. The agents infiltrated the region, struggling to adopt the latest techniques of detection. Together with the Osage they began to expose one of the most chilling conspiracies in American history.

In *Killers of the Flower Moon,* David Grann revisits a shocking series of crimes in which dozens of people were murdered in cold blood. Based on years of research and startling new evidence, the book is a masterpiece of narrative nonfiction, as each step in the investigation reveals a series of sinister secrets and reversals. But more than that, it is a searing indictment of the callousness and prejudice toward American Indians that allowed the murderers to operate with impunity for so long. *Killers of the Flower Moon* is utterly compelling, but also emotionally devastating.

BookBrowse Review

A twisting, haunting true-life murder mystery about one of the most monstrous crimes in American history, which birthed the FBI.

Voted 2017 Best Nonfiction by BookBrowse's Subscribers

The long, sorrowful list of injustices done to Native Americans by the U.S. Federal Government is well known by now. The wholesale relocation of tribes from their ancestral lands – and the subsequent violence and bloodshed that marked these tribes' trail of tears – is almost too large to get one's mind around. Maybe that's why smaller, localized campaigns of terror and intimidation against various Indian tribes are not so well known.

Most Americans have trouble processing the comprehensive horror of the centuries-long subjugation of the American Indian, a legacy of genocidal policies and human rights curtailment that still stains the psychic landscape today (and makes possible, for example, the thoughtless and offensive use of "Redskin" in the name of sports teams, an unequivocal legacy of disrespect and disdain for Native Americans, no matter how it is spun). Compared to the near-annihilation of many of the Plains Indian tribes, what's a few suspicious deaths anyway? In Oklahoma in the 1920s, the answer was a dismissive shrug: "White people in Oklahoma thought no more of killing an Indian than they did in 1724," said one hired gunman quoted by David Grann in his chilling and well-researched *Killers of the Flower Moon: The Osage Murders and the Birth of the FBI.*

Grann's book-length investigation of a series of suspicious murders among the Osage Indian Nation in Oklahoma in the 1920s tells a story that is so enraging and consequential that many readers will feel ashamed and alarmed that they've never known anything about this dark chapter of American history. The story Grann reports isn't new, exactly – his book recounts the investigations, trials, and legacy of these Osage murders, and the nationwide publicity they generated briefly in the 1920s. Grann not only provides a comprehensive overview of the crimes but also seeks to answer the question:

In the almost one hundred years since the suspicious shootings, poisonings, bombings, and disappearance of dozens of Osage tribe members, have we learned anything new about who might be responsible beyond those few who were tried and convicted?

The early chapters of the book constitute a primer on the history and culture of the Osage nation. In one of the most ironic twists in the history of Native Americans, when the Osage Indians were corralled after the U.S. Civil War from their native settlements across the Ohio and Missouri river valleys and forced into "Indian Territory" in northern Oklahoma, they were relocated on "rocky, presumably worthless" land that, in a few years, would prove to be some of the richest oil land in North America. Once oil was discovered there, the Osage flourished, owning the mineral rights of the property as part of the relocation treaty they were forced to sign.

How much wealth did these oil lands generate for the Osage? "After oil was discovered beneath their land, the Osage rode in chauffeured automobiles, built mansions, and sent their children to study in Europe." They enjoyed a lifestyle that, per capita, exceeded in terms of personal wealth any other similarly sized region in the United States. But the consequences of such affluence led to untold attempts to swindle or steal the land rights from the Osage, who often spoke little or no English and further, were frequently placed under the "guardianship" of white men appointed by the local government to ensure "proper" oversight of their wealth (the theory being that simple-minded Osages were incapable of discharging their own financial affairs). In other words, they were being robbed blind. Sometimes the thefts were given moral cover by local governments, corrupt judges, sheriffs, and barristers. Sometimes it was just outright theft:

> The passage of Prohibition had only compounded the territory's feeling of lawlessness by encouraging organized crime and creating, in the words of one historian, "the greatest criminal bonanza in American history." And few places in the country were as chaotic as Osage County, where the unwritten codes of the West, the traditions that bound communities, had unraveled.

Those Osage rights holders who refused to be tricked or intimidated into signing over their mineral rights were sometimes simply murdered, their rights reverting to a "guardian" (who, in most instances, had paid off the local authorities to be appointed to that role). Sometimes those murders were blatant: a shot between the eyes, or a house being blown to bits by dynamite. Sometimes, they were subtle: poisoned whisky, or injections from a "doctor" who was in the pay of a criminal syndicate. And sometimes, the Osage just disappeared. Dozens of Osage Indians were dispatched in this manner, their property rights by-passing their heirs and instead going directly to their "guardians." Grann suggests the actual number of Osage Indians who might have been killed for their land rights could number in the hundreds.

The murder of that many native Americans – even in Oklahoma at the time – could not be ignored, and after years of unsuccessful local and state investigations (almost all of which were doomed to fail because they were beset by corruption and bribery, and because "most officials seemed to have little concern for what they deemed a 'dead Injun'"), the federal government finally stepped in. The agency that would soon be known as the Federal Bureau of Investigation launched its first, widespread homicide investigation in Osage territory under the supervision of a young, ambitious federal investigator named J. Edgar Hoover.

Grann's recreation of the investigation is gripping. He recounts the details of the trial from published accounts at the time, and his years of archival research and interviews and the declassification of various documents once off limits allow him to provide a kind of annotation of the trial that lends both real-time excitement and the perspective of hindsight. Grann's shock at discovering that the murder plots against the Osage might have gone far beyond those outlined in the trial – and his zeal for discovering the parties responsible for the dozens of unprosecuted murders–makes *Killers of the Flower Moon* more entertaining than a book about such a dire subject should be. He seems driven to amend the historical record, to prosecute, even from the distance of several generations of history, those responsible for the deaths of these now-forgotten victims. Grann's powerful narrative resurrects a bitterly important chapter in American history, suggesting that the trail of tears doesn't have to lead to a dead end. It can circle back through justice, arriving, if not at reconciliation, then at least perhaps some closure.

Reviewed by James Broderick. This review was originally published in *The BookBrowse Review* in April 2017, and has been updated for the April 2018 edition.

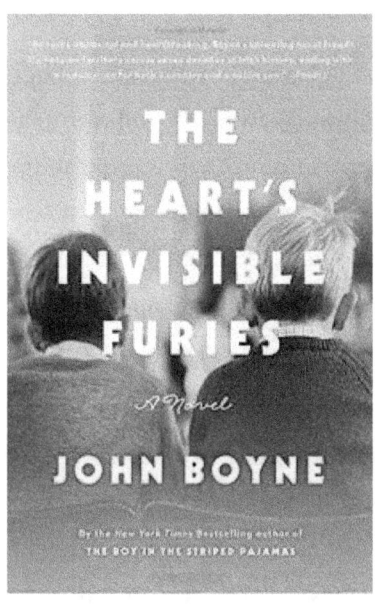

THE HEART'S INVISIBLE FURIES

by John Boyne

BookBrowse Rating: 5/5
Critics' Consensus: 5/5
Readers' Rating: 5/5

Published March 2018 in Paperback, 592 pages

Summary

From the beloved *New York Times* bestselling author of *The Boy In the Striped Pajamas*, a sweeping, heartfelt saga about the course of one man's life, beginning and ending in post-war Ireland

Cyril Avery is not a *real* Avery -- or at least, that's what his adoptive parents tell him. And he never will be. But if he isn't a real Avery, then who is he?

Born out of wedlock to a teenage girl cast out from her rural Irish community and adopted by a well-to-do if eccentric Dublin couple via the intervention of a hunchbacked Redemptorist nun, Cyril is adrift in the world, anchored only tenuously by his heartfelt friendship with the infinitely more glamourous and dangerous Julian Woodbead. At the mercy of fortune and coincidence, he will spend a lifetime coming to know himself and where he came from - and over his many years, will struggle to discover an identity, a home, a country, and much more.

In this, Boyne's most transcendent work to date, we are shown the story of Ireland from the 1940s to today through the eyes of one ordinary man. *The Heart's Invisible Furies* is a novel to make you laugh and cry while reminding us all of the redemptive power of the human spirit.

BookBrowse Review

A sweeping saga of one gay man's life over 70 years of Irish history, by the author of *The Boy In the Striped Pajamas*

Of the 20 First Impression reviewers of *The Heart's Invisible Furies* by John Boyne, 16 gave it four or five stars, netting an overall rating of 4.6 out of 5.

What it's about:

The Heart's Invisible Furies by John Boyne is a tragic, funny look into being gay in an evolving Ireland (Jill S). The story follows the life of Cyril Avery from 1945 to the present day, from his birth out of wedlock to his upbringing as an adopted, mostly neglected, closeted gay man in Dublin, and later, as life choices propel him far beyond Ireland itself. Cyril is an astute observer of the people he meets, the places he lives, and of history; through him we meet a wonderful cast of characters and observe sweeping social changes, even as Cyril matures, finds himself, and forges bonds he never expected (Janice P).

The author touches on a variety of subjects:

There are numerous themes at play here: obsession vs. love; bigotry vs. openness; and cultural influences vs individual integrity. Instead of being heavy-handed in dealing with such lofty topics, John Boyne employs a steady undercurrent of humor that is disarming in its subtlety but often laugh aloud funny. The thread of the mother/son connection knits together the story as it weaves in and out of the narrative (Peggy A).

Boyne dedicates his novel to John Irving, and there do seem to be similarities in writing style:

Irving's works are characterized by two key themes: the absent parent who looms large in his/her offspring's life, and the role of predetermination merged with coincidence. Both these themes are in ample display here (Jill S).

Readers felt enriched by the story:

Along the way, through Cyril's voice the author awakened me, more than any other writer has done, to what it is like, out of necessity or fear, to live every hour of every day in a lie. He takes the issue of homophobia out of the public arena and brings it into the human soul, making us feel the damage, the pain, and the ripple effect upon others. (Janice P).

Most felt the author excelled at character development, particularly concerning the main character:

The character development is superb (Carolyn S); they are interwoven in ways that delight and keep you reading (Nicole S). Each individual we are introduced to is struggling with some facet of acceptance of themselves because of societal pressures to conform (Susan P). Cyril is achingly human on his life's journey: he struggles; he loves imperfectly; he makes mistakes; he loves again and finds happiness only to have it snatched away (Lorri S). He is often lonely and isolated, but he is always likable to the reader, even when he makes poor decisions (Viqui G).

A few found the novel lacking:

Boyne is attempting something rather epic here, letting one man's story stand in for the history of homosexuality over the last five decades and in several locations. Sometimes it works, sometimes it doesn't. He also strives to bring the characters full circle; Cyril unknowingly keeps running across his birth mother, and the figure of Julian, his first crush, makes several reappearances. An interesting effort, if not always successful (Deborah M). Although I enjoyed the read, many themes were repetitive and too long. I think the novel would have been improved with tighter editing (Viqui G).

The majority, however, truly enjoyed *The Heart's Invisible Furies*:

This book grabs you from the first page and keeps your attention until the last. I enjoyed every minute of the rather complex story (Susan P). Boyne has written a remarkable novel that moved me to tears and made me laugh out loud (Barbara C). I was totally engrossed (Jill S); it's my vote for best book of 2017 (John W).

Recommended to a wide audience:

With big themes wrapped in a very human story, this would be a solid pick for readers and book groups who like family sagas with an edge (Lorri S). I would recommend this one to anyone (Susan P).

Reviewed by First Impressions Reviewers. This review was originally published in *The BookBrowse Review* in August 2017, and has been updated for the March 2018 edition.

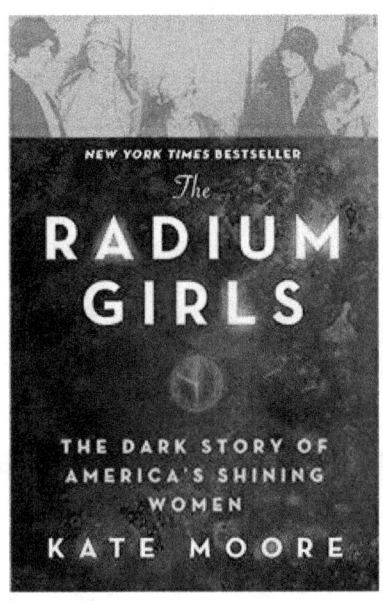

THE RADIUM GIRLS

by Kate Moore

BookBrowse Rating: 5/5
Critics' Consensus: 4.5/5
Readers' Rating: 5/5

Published March 2018 in Paperback, 480 pages

Summary

The incredible true story of the women who fought America's Undark danger.

The Curies' newly discovered element of radium makes gleaming headlines across the nation as the fresh face of beauty, and wonder drug of the medical community. From body lotion to tonic water, the popular new element shines bright in the otherwise dark years of the First World War.

Meanwhile, hundreds of girls toil amidst the glowing dust of the radium-dial factories. The glittering chemical covers their bodies from head to toe; they light up the night like industrious fireflies. With such a coveted job, these "shining girls" are the luckiest alive - until they begin to fall mysteriously ill.

But the factories that once offered golden opportunities are now ignoring all claims of the gruesome side effects, and the women's cries of corruption. And as the fatal poison of the radium takes hold, the brave shining girls find themselves embroiled in one of the biggest scandals of America's early 20th century, and in a groundbreaking battle for workers' rights that will echo for centuries to come.

Written with a sparkling voice and breakneck pace, *The Radium Girls* fully illuminates the inspiring young women exposed to the "wonder" substance of radium, and their awe-inspiring strength in the face of almost impossible circumstances. Their courage and tenacity led to life-changing regulations, research into nuclear bombing, and ultimately saved hundreds of thousands of lives...

BookBrowse Review

Part medical mystery, part courtroom drama, *The Radium Girls* by Kate Moore chronicles a tragic true story.

In 1915, Austrian-born Sabin von Sochocky developed a luminescent paint that used radium to create a glow-in-the-dark effect. Realizing the material could be used for many purposes, he opened the U.S. Radium Corporation in Orange, New Jersey, to produce the substance, and as a side business, contracted with manufacturers to create watch faces that could be read in the dark.

He hired girls – some as young as 14 – to work in the shop as dial painters. Using fine brushes, the girls delicately traced the timepiece's hands and numerals with the glowing substance. The instruments weren't quite sharp enough to achieve the precision required, so they employed a technique called "lip pointing," whereby the brush was put in the mouth before being dipped in the radium: "lip-dip-paint"...and repeat. Over time, ingesting the radioactive substance caused radium poisoning, and many of the girls in Orange — as well as those at a competing business, the Radium Dial Company in Ottawa, Illinois — died horrible deaths. The companies involved knew about the dangers of radium, but denied culpability, in some cases outright lying about the harm they caused.

While the lawsuits brought against these two corporations have been widely documented, the stories of the individual women have never been central to the narrative. "I was struck," Moore writes, "by the fact that the books focused on the legal and scientific aspects of the women's story, and not on the compelling lives of the girls themselves." In collectively becoming known as "the Radium Girls," their individual struggles and experiences were lost. The primary goal here is to give them names, faces, personalities – in other words, to humanize the "radium girls" and give them back the voices they lost nearly a century ago. In this aim, Moore succeeds admirably; although the lives of perhaps thirty women are highlighted, each comes across with her own particular strengths, weaknesses, concerns and family life. I came to know them so well that I was truly saddened by their physical declines and deaths, even though I knew the outcome in each case was inevitable.

Beyond the focus on the individuals impacted by blatant corporate negligence, the author creates tension as the girls become ill. No one in Orange or in Ottawa had seen radium poisoning before, and doctors and dentists were puzzled by what could cause teeth to fall out with the sockets failing to heal, jaws to disintegrate, and joints to freeze in place. Indeed, as the girls died, their death certificates inaccurately listed causes such as syphilis and diphtheria. Although readers know that radium was the culprit, Moore still keeps the suspense high; I felt like I was reading a "whodunnit" in which I knew who the murderer was but had to wait for the lead detective to figure it out.

An enthralling drama unfolds as the incredibly ill women testify in court and impassioned lawyers battle it out before judges and the press, who often came to the aid of plaintiffs who were literally disintegrating over the weeks needed to try their cases. The bad guys abound in this horrific tale, from the scientist who knew the lip-pointing practice was dangerous, to the "doctor" who told radioactive women they were "completely healthy," to the corporate vice president who deliberately suppressed medical reports, to the men who fired women as soon as they became obviously ill – as well as many others who put profits above lives.

The Radium Girls will likely be an emotional experience for many; the agony the women endured as their bones deteriorated as well as their courage in continuing to fight even while on death's doorstep make for heartbreaking reading. As Moore's heroines seek justice in the face of overwhelming odds, readers come to know them and root for their triumphs and grieve their losses. This exceptionally compelling book should appeal to a wide audience, including those who typically don't read non-fiction. I can't recommend *The Radium Girls* highly enough.

Reviewed by Kim Kovacs. This review was originally published in *The BookBrowse Review* in June 2017, and has been updated for the March 2018 edition.

BEARTOWN

by Fredrik Backman

BookBrowse Rating: 5/5
Critics' Consensus: 4.5/5
Readers' Rating: 5/5

Published February 2018 in Paperback, 432 pages

Summary

The #1 New York Times bestselling author of *A Man Called Ove* returns with a dazzling, profound novel about a small town with a big dream - and the price required to make it come true.

People say Beartown is finished. A tiny community nestled deep in the forest, it is slowly losing ground to the ever encroaching trees. But down by the lake stands an old ice rink, built generations ago by the working men who founded this town. And in that ice rink is the reason people in Beartown believe tomorrow will be better than today. Their junior ice hockey team is about to compete in the national semi-finals, and they actually have a shot at winning. All the hopes and dreams of this place now rest on the shoulders of a handful of teenage boys.

Being responsible for the hopes of an entire town is a heavy burden, and the semi-final match is the catalyst for a violent act that will leave a young girl traumatized and a town in turmoil. Accusations are made and, like ripples on a pond, they travel through all of Beartown, leaving no resident unaffected.

Beartown explores the hopes that bring a small community together, the secrets that tear it apart, and the courage it takes for an individual to go against the grain. In this story of a small forest town, Fredrik Backman has found the entire world.

BookBrowse Review

***Beartown* explores the hopes that bring a small community together, the secrets that tear it apart, and the courage it takes for an individual to go against the grain.**

Beartown has almost nothing left except for hockey – but that could change. Because this year, they have a junior team that is good enough to go all the way. And if they do, this almost dead town could be saved. However, after they win the national semi-finals, something happens that changes everything. The question is, did that incident change Beartown for better or for worse?

I have read all of Fredrick Backman's books (see <u>Beyond the Book</u>), and with each and every one I am pleasingly surprised at just how consistently wonderful a writer he is. He takes a subject I have no interest in, and turns it into a story that grips me from the first page. This time, his story centers on the game of hockey, a sport that I not only don't care for, but also sometimes find appalling. Yet when Backman starts describing how his characters play the game, including the violence that comes with it, we understand that this novel isn't just about a sport. Rather, hockey is simply the metaphor used to explore the human condition.

One of the already oft quoted sentences from *Beartown* is "Never trust people who don't have something in their lives that they love beyond reason." This could very well be its theme, although it occurred to me that Backman doesn't seem to believe that loving something beyond reason is always a good thing. He gives us examples of the enormous love than can make some people capable of acting unreasonably, which can cause a whole lot of damage. On the other hand, he also seems to say that this same unconditional love can be a source of strength that helps us survive the damage caused by someone acting in that unreasonable way.

It is hard to explain why I'm certain readers will fall in love with this book, maybe because there are so many reasons. It could be because of the vivid portrayal of this unusually large cast of characters with all their flaws. Often when there are many characters in a book I get confused, but not so with *Beartown*. Backman has a deep, intimate understanding of each one of his characters, which comes through in how he gives their voices distinctive cadences and tenors. Some people will be brought to tears because they care so much about these characters – Backman certainly knows how to evoke that, along with some smiles.

Others will love *Beartown* because of the story's deceptively simple language, enhanced by hints of poetry, flashes of wisdom and even some sparkles of humor.

Another reason to love *Beartown* is because of the pace of the story. Listen to the opening lines:

"Late one evening towards the end of March, a teenager picked up a double-barreled shotgun, walked into the forest, put the gun to someone else's forehead and pulled the trigger. This is the story of how we got there."

With that incredible opening, Backman glides up to the climax on a very smooth, clear path; but once we get to that climax and through to the conclusion, the writing becomes vaguer, disjointed, and almost impersonal, and the whole atmosphere of the book changes. It's as if he's trying to show how this event shattered not only the individual lives of those involved, but also the town as a whole. Furthermore, after this event, Backman gives us shards of action where he exchanges the names of the characters with "a boy" or "a girl" or "a man" or "a woman." Since, until this point, the characters have been infused so perfectly with their distinctive personalities, we instinctively know which of them is being described. I found this to be pure genius.

Some people might feel that all of the descriptions of playing hockey in the beginning of the novel are a bit too much and slow the story down. Hang in there, though, because once that climax comes, as well as its dire consequences, they'll realize just how important each piece is to the overall story. In short, Backman has proven, once again, that he is a master storyteller.

Reviewed by Davida Chazan. This review was originally published in *The BookBrowse Review* in June 2017, and has been updated for the February 2018 edition.

THIS IS HOW IT ALWAYS IS

by Laurie Frankel

BookBrowse Rating: 5/5
Critics' Consensus: 5/5
Readers' Rating: 5/5

Published January 2018 in Paperback, 352 pages

Summary

This is how a family keeps a secret...and how that secret ends up keeping them. *This is how* a family lives happily ever after...until happily ever after becomes complicated. *This is how* children change...and then change the world.

When Rosie and Penn and their four boys welcome the newest member of their family, no one is surprised it's another baby boy. At least their large, loving, chaotic family knows what to expect.

But Claude is not like his brothers. One day he puts on a dress and refuses to take it off. He wants to bring a purse to kindergarten. He wants hair long enough to sit on. When he grows up, Claude says, he wants to be a girl.

Rosie and Penn aren't panicked at first. Kids go through phases, after all, and make-believe is fun. But soon the entire family is keeping Claude's secret. Until one day it explodes.

Laurie Frankel's *This Is How It Always Is* is a novel about revelations, transformations, fairy tales, and family. And it's about the ways this is how it always is: Change is always hard and miraculous and hard again; parenting is always a leap into the unknown with crossed fingers and full hearts; children grow but not always according to plan. And families with secrets don't get to keep them forever.

BookBrowse Review

This novel insightfully explores the effects of a child's changing identity on the members of a large family.

This is How it Always Is tells the story of the family of Rosie Walsh and Penn Adams, a doctor and a writer respectively, who fall in love, marry, and have five children. The novel opens with Rosie hoping that her fifth pregnancy will bring her a girl—a girl she might name Poppy, after her younger sister who died of cancer when Rosie was just twelve. But the baby is a boy, Claude. Claude is quick to walk and talk and by the age of three he is thinking about what he would like to be when he grows up—a cat, or a vet, a dinosaur, a scientist, or...a girl. So begins the transition of the youngest of the Walsh-Adams children to become a girl called Poppy.

The story that unfolds of Poppy's childhood is fascinating in many ways. First it's a window into the life of a transgender child. Although Poppy's early years are told from the point of view of her parents and their concerns, as she grows Poppy's perspective develops. Issues of schools, bathrooms, (see '<u>Beyond the Book</u>') and sleepovers inevitably arise. She is also part of a large family and the implications of having a transgender sibling affects everyone. Part of trying to create a safe and happy childhood for her involves uprooting the family and moving from Wisconsin to Seattle. And then there is the constant question of what to reveal—or not—about Poppy's past as a boy. It's a secret the whole family will struggle to keep.

The novel is also an insightful study of the more commonplace joys and perils of parenthood. Rosie and Penn have a family set-up that works for them. Rosie, as a doctor, works long hours so it makes sense that Penn, an aspiring writer, takes on the lion's share of laundry, cooking and homework. Their relationship is good-humored and tender but at times the responsibilities of parenting—particularly a child like Poppy—and the choices in terms of hormones and surgery, threaten to overwhelm them.

Over the years, Penn narrates a long-running fairy-tale to his wife and children that both entertains and informs their lives. His fictional characters, Grumwald and Princess Stephanie, face challenges that often parallel their own. Penn's stories help the family understand their lives in a world that makes innumerable judgments about people based on their gender and where change is always around the corner.

Certainly this is an issue-driven novel. The author, Laurie Frankel, is the parent of a transgender child. As her fictional creation Rosie makes clear, "this is a medical issue, but mostly it's a cultural issue. It's a social issue and an emotional issue and a family dynamic issue and a community issue." For all the sensitive and difficult nature of the subject, Frankel has written a novel that is above all endearing and at times witty. When, for example, Poppy is about to dance with a boy at a fifth-grade Valentine Party and she silently urges the school principal not to play a slow dance, we read that she is in luck, not because the principal would not want to, but because the music is on a playlist created by someone else on his phone. All the principal knows to do is make calls.

Frankel has brought a believable, lovable transgender child to life in a believable, lovable American family. This is thoughtful, insightful and pleasurable read. I highly recommend it for both adults and a YA audience.

Reviewed by Kate Braithwaite. This review was originally published in *The BookBrowse Review* in February 2017, and has been updated for the January 2018 edition.

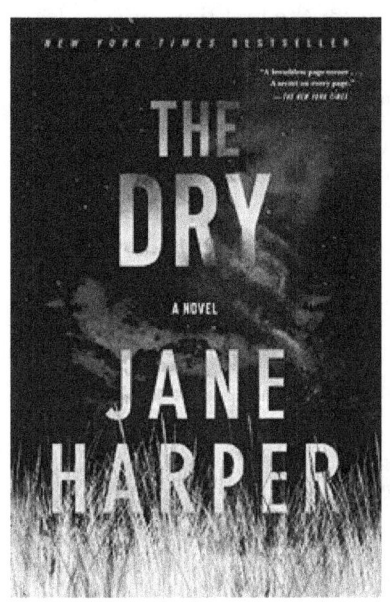

THE DRY

by Jane Harper

BookBrowse Rating: 5/5
Critics' Consensus: 5/5
Readers' Rating: 4.5/5

Published January 2018 in Paperback, 336 pages

Summary

Winner of the 2017 BookBrowse Debut Author Award

A small town hides big secrets in *The Dry*, an atmospheric, page-turning debut mystery by award-winning author Jane Harper.

After getting a note demanding his presence, Federal Agent Aaron Falk arrives in his hometown for the first time in decades to attend the funeral of his best friend, Luke. Twenty years ago when Falk was accused of murder, Luke was his alibi. Falk and his father fled under a cloud of suspicion, saved from prosecution only because of Luke's steadfast claim that the boys had been together at the time of the crime. But now more than one person knows they didn't tell the truth back then, and Luke is dead.

Amid the worst drought in a century, Falk and the local detective question what really happened to Luke. As Falk reluctantly investigates to see if there's more to Luke's death than there seems to be, long-buried mysteries resurface, as do the lies that have haunted them. And Falk will find that small towns have *always* hidden big secrets.

BookBrowse Review

A small town hides big secrets in this atmospheric, page-turning debut mystery by award-winning author Jane Harper.

Voted 2017 Best Debut Author by BookBrowse's Subscribers

After receiving a letter from his childhood friend's father, Aaron Falk, a Melbourne police officer specializing in financial fraud, drives five hours north to the drought-stricken town of Kiewarra for the funeral of that friend – Luke – who has allegedly murdered his wife and son and then killed himself.

The unraveling of this murder/suicide mystery, after Luke's father asks Falk to stay and investigate his concerns, takes place over the ensuing days as Falk and Raco, the new local police officer, unofficially investigate the crime. It is clear Falk feels very uncomfortable being back in his home town and is reluctant to stay any length of time.

Falk is an interesting choice of protagonist because his past, which he'd thought was well behind him, flashes back when he comes across various local characters and places that remind him of another tragedy – his and Luke's mutual friend Ellie Deacon, a teenager who died mysteriously, shortly before Falk and his father were run out of town. And now, while mourning Luke's death, it is coming back to haunt him:

> The funeral was starting. Gerry inclined his head in a tiny nod, and Falk unconsciously put his hand in his pocket. He felt the letter that had landed on his desk two days ago. From Gerry Hadler, eight words written with a heavy hand:
> *Luke lied. You lied. Be at the funeral.*
> He thought about the dark-eyed girl, and a lie forged and agreed on twenty years ago as fear and hormones pounded through his veins.
> *Luke lied. You lied.*

The Dry is a well-crafted debut and Jane Harper, while delivering the necessary twists and turns that make a good crime novel, also captures the tension created by the climatic and economic conditions of the area. Set in southeastern Australia, Harper paints a region in the grip of The Big Dry (See Beyond the Book), the most severe drought in living memory, which not only places a financial strain on farmers and local people's livelihoods, it's making people turn their guns on themselves.

The flashback scenes are displayed in italics, making an easy transition and distinction between the thoughts and events of the present and those of the past; between the mysterious deaths that have recently happened, and that remembered dreadful tragedy of the past. Harper explores, not only the economic effect of a community wedded to the land and dependent on water, but the social dysfunctions that endure and transmute when people stay in one place for too long; when a childhood bully turns into a gun-toting, grumpy old man and continues to menace those he hates; how people who might otherwise shine learn to dim their light; how witnesses know for their own good to keep their eyes down and their mouths shut.

The fictional town of Kiewarra contains a mix of traits plucked from the imagination and from rural communities Harper visited while working as a journalist. Its idiosyncrasies are exaggerated perhaps, though understandable in constructing the range of possible suspects, as nearly everyone has their secrets to bear, and any potential second-guessing by the reader is made all the more challenging knowing Falk has pre-conceived perceptions and an unclear past history with many of them. It highlights the often unbridgeable differences between locals and outsiders and why people might choose to come and live in such places, even if only temporarily.

With more than one mystery being unraveled simultaneously, *The Dry* keeps up a brisk pace, is full of surprises, and has the right balance of tension without overindulging in the brutal, tense-suspense formula of many potboilers today.

The Dry is a story that carries the reader to the arid, drought suffering region of Australia in a way that reminded me of Douglas Kennedy's thrilling debut novel set in the lesser known, slightly terrifying, remote and usually uninhabited Australian Outback, *The Dead Heart*. Jane Harper is already at work on her next crime and mystery novel which will also feature Aaron Falk. We are told it takes place in a different setting and can be read as a stand-alone rather than a direct sequel.

Reviewed by Claire McAlpine. This review was originally published in *The BookBrowse Review* in February 2017, and has been updated for the January 2018 edition.

GINNY MOON

by Benjamin Ludwig

BookBrowse Rating: 5/5
Critics' Consensus: 5/5
Readers' Rating: 5/5

Published December 2017 in Paperback, 384 pages

Summary

Told in an extraordinary and wholly unique voice that will candidly take you into the mind of a curious and deeply human character.

Meet Ginny Moon. She's mostly your average teenager—she plays flute in the school band, has weekly basketball practice and reads Robert Frost poems for

English class. But Ginny is autistic. And so what's important to her might seem a bit…different: starting every day with exactly nine grapes for breakfast, singing along to Michael Jackson, taking care of her baby doll…and crafting a secret plan of escape.

Ginny has been in foster care for years and for the first time in her life she has found her "forever home." After being traumatically taken from her abusive birth mother and moved around to different homes, she is finally in a place where she'll be safe and protected, with a family who will love and nurture her. This is exactly the kind of home that all foster kids are hoping for. But Ginny has other plans. She'll steal and lie and reach across her past to exploit the good intentions of those who love her—anything it takes to get back what's missing in her life. She'll even try to get herself kidnapped.

Ginny Moon is at once quirky, charming, heartbreaking, suspenseful and poignant. It's a story of a journey, about being an outsider trying to find a place to belong and about making sense of a world that just doesn't seem to add up.

BookBrowse Review

The uniquely candid voice of Ginny Moon takes the reader into the mind of a curious and deeply human character.

In the tradition of Mark Haddon's *The Curious Incident of the Dog in the Night-Time*, Benjamin Ludwig's *Ginny Moon* gives us a novel written from the perspective of a child with autism.

Fourteen-year-old Ginny faces many challenges in life; not only is she autistic, but she was starved and beaten by her drug-abusing mother and subsequently removed from her home at the age of nine. She's been placed in at least three "forever homes," and has run away from each. Her current "forever parents" adopted her because they couldn't get pregnant at the time but eventually did conceive and now have an infant of their own. This places a new stress on their relationship with Ginny. Although her adopted parents attempt to help her have a normal life (e.g., helping her participate on a Special Olympics basketball team and taking her to flute lessons) she nevertheless does all she can to return to her birth mom, in spite of her love for her new sibling. The mystery of what exactly compels Ginny to return to her former home comprises much of the novel.

It's been a long time since I've read a first-person novel that made me care so much about the protagonist. Many books in recent years have featured young narrators in challenging circumstances, but *Ginny Moon* is absolutely one of the better written and most interesting of its type. Benjamin Ludwig has created a remarkable character in Ginny, making her realistic and completely bringing readers into her world. I experienced her frustration first-hand when she was unable to convey her inner fears to those who care about her. Her pain became my own and I wanted to hug her and explain her thoughts and feelings to those who just don't understand her.

One of the book's strongest features is how the author helps us view Ginny's parents, therapist, friends and teachers with a degree of clarity that eludes her because she is unable to pick up on the cues that most of us take into account during social interactions. Although Ginny doesn't understand how her actions impact those around her, readers readily grasp their exasperation through Ginny's own descriptions. I wanted to step into several scenes and play mediator between the parties involved, feeling like I was the only one perceiving each side's point-of-view. I think it's a rare novel that can elicit this kind of reaction from a reader, particularly when the story is narrated from a single point of view.

The plot, too, is intriguing and creative. On a few occasions, just when I felt that *Ginny Moon* was starting to lag or become predictable, the action took an unexpected but credible new direction, pulling me back into the narrative and keeping me hooked throughout. I was constantly on the edge of my seat as

Ginny made decisions that were completely logical to her but that would obviously have negative repercussions for her down the road.

Some readers may have concerns that, given Ginny's history, the book could be dark or disturbing; this is not the case by any means, and it is, in fact, quite uplifting overall. Although Ginny makes passing references to the abuse she suffered at the hands of her birth-mother, this is not dwelled on or described in-depth. One knows very bad things have happened to her but that's not the point of the book, other than to make it clear why she was removed from her home and, oddly, why she's so desperate to get back to it in spite of being in a safe and loving environment.

Benjamin Ludwig completely captures his young protagonist, and as a result *Ginny Moon* is without doubt one of the finest novels I've read all year. I whole-heartedly recommend it for a wide audience, including young adult readers; book groups in particular will find much material for discussion.

Reviewed by Kim Kovacs. This review was originally published in *The BookBrowse Review* in December 2017, and has been updated for the December 2018 edition.

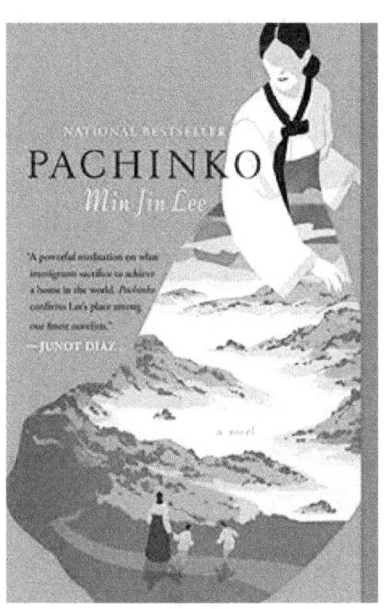

PACHINKO

by Min Jin Lee

BookBrowse Rating: 4/5
Critics' Consensus: 4.5/5
Readers' Rating: 5/5

Published November 2017 in Paperback, 512 pages

| Summary

A new tour de force from the bestselling author of *Free Food for Millionaires*, for readers of *The Kite Runner* and *Cutting for Stone*.

Pachinko follows one Korean family through the generations, beginning in early 1900s Korea with Sunja, the prized daughter of a poor yet proud family, whose unplanned pregnancy threatens to shame them all. Deserted by her lover, Sunja is saved when a young tubercular minister offers to marry and bring her to Japan.

So begins a sweeping saga of an exceptional family in exile from its homeland and caught in the indifferent arc of history. Through desperate struggles and hard-won triumphs, its members are bound together by deep roots as they face enduring questions of faith, family, and identity.

BookBrowse Review

Pachinko is a lush, expansive historical saga that explores the effects of world events and personal decisions on multiple generations of one Korean family.

Pachinko has one of the best opening lines I've encountered in some time: "History has failed us, but no matter." It's an unexpectedly cynical start to a historical novel, suggesting that every generation has to recreate itself after the letdown of the last one. For this fictional family, the pessimism is partially justified: although the specific challenges vary from one generation to another, being Korean in a foreign country is an ongoing struggle.

The novel opens in 1910, the year Japan annexed Korea, with an almost folktale-like scenario: in Yeongdo district, in the South Korean city of Busan, a fisherman and his wife have four sons, but only Hoonie, who has a cleft palate and clubfoot, survives. Hoonie marries and dies shortly thereafter leaving his 13-year-old daughter Sunja, and her mother, to run the family boardinghouse. During the hard winter of 1932, the sixteen-year-old Sunja becomes pregnant, but refuses to reveal the identity of the father - Koh Hansu. Hansu, a rich Korean businessman who meets Sunja while working in Busan, has a wife and children back in Japan, his adopted country, and so cannot marry Sunja. Instead, one of the boarding house guests, Presbyterian minister Baek Isak, comes to the rescue— he sympathizes with Sunja's predicament and offers to take her to Osaka as his wife.

Japan will be the family base for the next half-century or more, even though Koreans are treated as second-class citizens there. Isak and Sunja move in with his brother and sister-in-law in a squalid ghetto in Osaka. Soon Noa is born and, six years later, Mozasu. Sunja and her sister-in-law start selling homemade kimchi and black sugar candy for extra money. The family's prospects are a mixture of good and horrible: a restaurateur hires Sunja and her sister-in-law and gives them a generous salary, but Isak and his fellow churchmen are arrested for insufficient devotion to the Emperor, who, at that time, was considered divine.

As World War II closes in, the family escapes the coming bombardment of Japan's cities by sheltering on a sweet potato farm out in the countryside. Afterwards, they consider returning to famine-ridden Korea, but a fellow native warns them: "For people like us, home doesn't exist." Mozasu quits school and becomes a foreman at a pachinko parlor (see 'Beyond the Book'), while Noa goes to university in Tokyo.

Although some of the central events of the novel, like World War II and the atomic bomb drop at Nagasaki, are familiar territory for fiction, Lee prioritizes out-of-the-ordinary perspectives: her Korean characters are first the colonized, and then the outsiders trying to thrive in a foreign country despite segregation and persecution. Those who can pass for Japanese have the best chance for success, so Koreans like Noa pretend to be Japanese. Food, language, names, dress, and manners all take on extra significance in this context: you can tell whether the characters are proud or ashamed of their Korean origins by what they let others see. Will they take on new names and try to get rid of their accent? Or will they proudly eat kimchi and talk about their former life in Korea?

In the acknowledgments, Lee writes that the idea for this novel came in 1989, when she heard the story of a middle-schooler in Japan who committed suicide after being bullied for his Korean background. Lee herself was born in South Korea and moved to the United States with her family when she was seven. I wondered to what extent two of the young people in the novel's 1980s storyline shared her experience. The novel is an intriguing glimpse at how stories that start in the same place can diverge wildly.

Much as I enjoyed this generational saga, it went downhill in Part III. Here the novel speeds up, jumping ahead several years with every chapter and lurching from one melodramatic occurrence to another. Overall, I felt less of an emotional connection to this youngest generation. Sunja's early relationship with Hansu and the time on the sweet potato farm were my favorite parts, and nothing that followed felt *quite* as interesting. Still, I was eager to find out what would happen to all of the members of this clan. I recommend *Pachinko* to readers of family sagas and anyone who wants to learn more about the Korean experience.

Reviewed by Rebecca Foster. This review was originally published in *The BookBrowse Review* in February 2017, and has been updated for the January 2018 edition.

IF THE CREEK DON'T RISE

by Leah Weiss

BookBrowse Rating: 4/5
Critics' Consensus: 4.5/5
Readers' Rating: 5/5

Published August 2017 in Paperback, 320 pages

Summary

With a colorful cast of characters that each contribute a new perspective, *If The Creek Don't Rise* is a debut novel bursting with heart, honesty, and homegrown grit.

He's gonna be sorry he ever messed with me and Loretta Lynn.

Sadie Blue has been a wife for fifteen days. That's long enough to know she should have never hitched herself to Roy Tupkin, even with the baby.

Sadie is desperate to make her own mark on the world, but in remote Appalachia, a ticket out of town is hard to come by, and hope often gets stomped out. When a stranger sweeps into Baines Creek and knocks things off kilter, Sadie finds herself with an unexpected lifeline...if she can just figure out how to use it.

This intimate insight into a fiercely proud, tenacious community unfolds through the voices of the forgotten folks of Baines Creek.

BookBrowse Review

If the Creek Don't Rise **is a bold debut about a dusty, desperate town finding the inner strength it needs to outrun its demons.**

A chorus of voices tells this contemporary story from the mountain town of Baines Creek, North Carolina. Sadie Blue, a young pregnant teen, opens the novel in the midst of a beating by her moonshiner husband, Roy Tupkin. From the opening lines, life looks grim for Sadie, and, as it turns out, for many of Baines Creek's inhabitants.

As we hear from various members of this rough and gritty town, we see Sadie's situation through different perspectives. Her grandmother, Gladys, is a hard and gruff woman, due to a rough marriage and life much like the one Sadie seems destined for. Sadie's aunt Marris has a brighter perspective, though she too has experienced losses of her own. The town preacher, Eli Perkins, has seen Sadie's predicament too many times to be shocked, but he has his hopes set on the new schoolteacher, Kate Shaw, making a difference. Facing a daunting challenge, Kate is surprised to discover she feels at home here, despite the uncertain reception she receives from a community not used to outsiders.

Kate serves as a catalyst in Sadie's life. First, she begins teaching her to read and then asks for Sadie's help in the humble classroom. In a later chapter, Kate is there to help the medicine woman Birdie Rocas care for the teen after a particularly injurious beating from Roy. That experience spurs Sadie into action. Bolstered by her dead father's spirit and the song lyrics of Loretta Lynn, she is determined to change her fate.

Sadie's troubled relationship with Roy serves as the plotline, but it's the varying characters, each with his or her own needs and desires, that bring this small town to life. Their care and concern for Sadie speaks to her appeal, and the warmth of this town despite the hardships faced on a daily basis. The youngest, and most charming narrator is Tattler Swan, the medicine woman's assistant and fellow ginseng hunter. In addition to Sadie's kind-hearted supporters, we also see the darker underbelly of this place when we hear from the preacher's bitter and small-minded sister, Prudence, as well as the evil Roy and his moonshiner partner, Billy.

For readers of Appalachian literature, the characters here will be familiar, perhaps even stereotypical. Although there is authenticity; in my mind, their representations are of limited scope. As someone who has lived in Appalachia, I would have liked to see some of these common stereotypes to surprise me in some small way instead of simply filling their expected roles in the community.

Although the message seems to be that the outsider, teacher Kate, incited change within this town, that idea was dropped toward the end, when the novel narrates Roy and Billy's story. They are not influenced by the new teacher—or even by the changes occurring within their community. In these chapters, even though Sadie is hinted at in the background, her story is not woven in as fully as I would have liked, which is surprising especially seeing as Sadie is the focal point at the novel's beginning.

Appalachian life is foreign even to most Americans. In many ways, it's easy to think the people of these mountains don't have much in common with the rest of the country. I worry that the novel's conclusion might leave readers' prejudices and stereotypes intact, rather than creating an appreciation and respect for a different pace of life while seeing commonalities in our humanity. That being said, the novel's clear and evocative prose ultimately creates a portrait of a town both beautiful and harsh. *If the Creek Don't Rise* transports readers to a specific time and place, where they can spend time with a variety of characters.

Reviewed by Sarah Tomp. This review was originally published in *The BookBrowse Review* in September 2017, and has been updated for the December 2017 edition.

CASTLE OF WATER

by Dane Huckelbridge

BookBrowse Rating: 5/5
Critics' Consensus: 5/5
Readers' Rating: 5/5

Published April 2017 in Hardcover, 288 pages

Summary

Two very different people, one very small island.

For Sophie Ducel, her honeymoon in French Polynesia was intended as a celebration of life. The proud owner of a thriving Parisian architecture firm, co-founded with her brilliant new husband, Sophie had much to look forward to--including a visit to the island home of her favorite singer, Jacques Brel.

For Barry Bleecker, the same trip was meant to mark a new beginning. Turning away from his dreary existence in Manhattan finance, Barry had set his sights on fine art, seeking creative inspiration on the other side of the world--just like his idol, Paul Gauguin.

But when their small plane is downed in the middle of the South Pacific, the sole survivors of the wreck are left with one common goal: to survive. Stranded hundreds of miles from civilization, on an island the size of a large city block, the two castaways must reconcile their differences and learn to draw on one another's strengths if they are to have any hope of making it home.

Told in mesmerizing prose, with charm and rhythm entirely its own, *Castle of Water* is more than just a reimagining of the classic castaway story. It is a stirring reflection on love's restorative potential, as well as a poignant reminder that home--be it a flat in Paris, a New York apartment, or a desolate atoll a world away--is where the heart is.

BookBrowse Review

***Castle of Water* is more than just a reimagining of the classic castaway story. It's a reminder that home is where the heart is.**

When a whopping 24 out of 27 readers give a book 4 or 5 stars, you know you have a winner on your hands. Here's why our First Impression book reviewers enjoyed *Castle of Water*.

Readers were delighted by the story of two castaways

Dane Huckelbridge has written a captivating book about two people stranded on a miniscule island after a plane crash, who slowly go from being antagonists whose sole thoughts are survival, to caring helpmates who establish a "home" under the most primitive conditions possible (Arlene M).

How [two unlikely castaways] manage to survive, physically, emotionally and mentally in total isolation on an island small enough to walk around on an evening stroll is an absorbing story. It is full of all the stages of a developing relationship—getting to know each other, disagreements, compromise, thoughtful gifts, humor, teasing, insults—culminating in a partnership with depth and caring. As the reader looking in, you are sensitive to their fears, frustrations, hopes and love and you root for their survival (Katherine P).

...and appreciated that the story went beyond familiar tropes

Castle of Water does the impossible: transcend its seemingly generic premise of two people stuck in an island. It's far deeper than that. The book deals with stereotypes that we all have of other cultures and countries and how we can break these notions and even learn to see our differences as positive attributes. There is also the theme of expectations, like that of employment, that one is expected to fulfill in society. It tackles the notion that in a society, the happiness of the individual comes second to duty and finding long-term stability (Christopher R).

More than just another castaway story, *Castle of Water* is the story of differences. Sophie and Barry are forced to overlook theirs and to work together in order to survive (Maureen S).

Many thought the writing was stellar

This is one of the most well written and engaging novels by a first-time novel writer I have read. It is not simply a usual castaway story with a predictable plot and ending. The characters are engaging, intelligent and have a depth of personality you can imagine very distinctly (Carolyn S). Although it is a novel, the book has many well researched areas that will keep the reader turning the pages and in the end wishing for more (Arlene M).

...but a few thought the story was watered down

Castle Of Water is a good beach read. There is nothing too deep about it. I know the author was writing a castaway story but in my opinion it was a little too unbelievable (Maggie S). *Castle of Water* is a pastiche with a tongue-in-cheek tone. It gives a nod and a wink to previous castaway stories but never delves deeply enough into the tradition to truly come into dialogue with them. This may have proved charming and fresh if Barry and Sophie were less self-absorbed and more likable characters (Sarah M).

The general consensus was that *Castle of Water* is a winner...

From the minute I read the first few pages I was in love with the writing style and luxuriated in reading each page. Yes, the storyline was good, but the writing...now that was to die for (Terri C).

Great for book clubs, romance novel lovers and anyone just wanting a wonderful and engaging story (Elizabeth P).

Reviewed by First Impressions Reviewers. This review was originally published in *The BookBrowse Review* in April 2017, and has been updated for the December 2017 edition.

BEST BOOKS OF 2016

A GENTLEMAN IN MOSCOW

by Amor Towles

BookBrowse Rating: 5/5
Critics' Consensus: 4.5/5
Readers' Rating: 4.5/5

Published March 2019 in Paperback, 496 pages

Summary

From the *New York Times* bestselling author of *Rules of Civility* - a transporting novel about a man who is ordered to spend the rest of his life inside a luxury hotel.

With his breakout debut novel, *Rules of Civility*, Amor Towles established himself as a master of absorbing, sophisticated fiction, bringing late 1930s Manhattan to life with splendid atmosphere and a flawless command of style. Readers and critics were enchanted; as NPR commented, "Towles writes with grace and verve about the mores and manners of a society on the cusp of radical change."

A Gentleman in Moscow immerses us in another elegantly drawn era with the story of Count Alexander Rostov. When, in 1922, he is deemed an unrepentant aristocrat by a Bolshevik tribunal, the count is sentenced to house arrest in the Metropol, a grand hotel across the street from the Kremlin. Rostov, an indomitable man of erudition and wit, has never worked a day in his life, and must now live in an attic room while some of the most tumultuous decades in Russian history are unfolding outside the hotel's doors. Unexpectedly, his reduced circumstances provide him a doorway into a much larger world of emotional discovery.

Brimming with humor, a glittering cast of characters, and one beautifully rendered scene after another, this singular novel casts a spell as it relates the count's endeavor to gain a deeper understanding of what it means to be a man of purpose.

BookBrowse Review

A *Gentleman in Moscow* features one of literature's more memorable characters and gives a peek into Stalinist Russia rarely seen before.

It is June 21, 1922, and 33-year-old Count Alexander Ilyich Rostov is convicted of being a class enemy of the Soviet Socialist Republic. Instead of being shot as would normally be the result, he is sentenced to live the rest of his life in his current residence: Moscow's Hotel Metropol (see 'Beyond the Book'). So begins Amor Towles' novel, *A Gentleman in Moscow*. What follows is an account of Rostov's life over the next thirty-plus years as he makes friendships, finds ways to occupy his days, and watches a slice of the history of Stalinist Russia unfold from the relative safety of the Metropol.

The Count is handsome, charming, wealthy, erudite and witty. He conquers every situation with aplomb, and following his adventures is a fun ride. The novel feels very innocent, harkening back to a time when books and movies contained good clean fun; totally absent are the cruder forms of comedy one often finds in today's entertainment media.

While *A Gentleman in Moscow* includes some account of changing conditions in the USSR (for example, a minor plotline concerns idealistic youths heading out to collectivize the farms, and another touches on the repression of artistic expression), history isn't the book's primary concern. The main focus is on the Count and those who move in and out of his orbit over the years, such as Andrey, the hotel restaurant's maître d'; and desk clerk Arkady, whose talent is to know where everyone in the hotel is at all times. Not only are these portraits brilliantly drawn, they're not static. Over the course of the novel the characters grow and mature, giving them a realistic touch.

The novel was a bit of a surprise as I was expecting something much darker and more reflective of the terror and paranoia rampant in Soviet Russia during the period. I have not read a book set in this era and locale that is lighthearted; *A Gentleman in Moscow* is likely the first. That's not to say that it doesn't have its tragic moments and poignant scenes, but overall it's pretty upbeat. Once I dropped my preconceived ideas of what the book should be about (i.e., horror stories about Stalin's regime) and simply let things unfold, I found myself enjoying it a lot more. *A Gentleman in Moscow* is fast-paced, aided by the fact that Towles keeps the use of patronymics and honorifics to a minimum, abandoning the use of four or five different names for each character as is so common in Russian literature.

There's not a lot of plot here, particularly as the narrative begins; in fact it's somewhat anecdotal until a little more than halfway through when an unexpected arrival at the hotel disrupts the Count's routine, at which point the action feels more focused. Around page 200, I found myself wondering whether or not the book was going anywhere, as frankly I was beginning to get a little bored. After the midpoint though, I found the novel increasingly hard to put down; the pages fly as the plot speeds to its conclusion.

Although getting to the meat of the book requires some patience, it's definitely worth it. The Count is one of literature's more memorable characters, and *A Gentleman in Moscow* is a well-written novel worthy of one's time. The book is sure to win Towles new fans as well as satisfy those already familiar with his writing.

Reviewed by Kim Kovacs. This review was originally published in *The BookBrowse Review* in September 2016, and has been updated for the December 2016 edition.

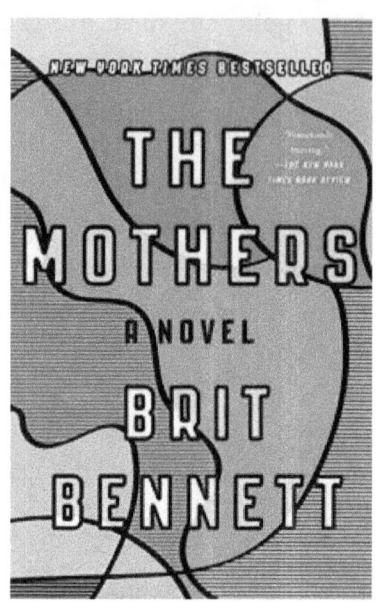

THE MOTHERS

by Brit Bennett

BookBrowse Rating: 5/5
Critics' Consensus: 5/5
Readers' Rating: 4/5

Published October 2017 in Paperback, 288 pages

Summary

A dazzling debut novel from an exciting new voice, *The Mothers* is a surprising story about young love, a big secret in a small community - and the things that ultimately haunt us most.

Set within a contemporary black community in Southern California, Brit Bennett's mesmerizing first novel is an emotionally perceptive story about community, love, and ambition. It begins with a secret.

"All good secrets have a taste before you tell them, and if we'd taken a moment to swish this one around our mouths, we might have noticed the sourness of an unripe secret, plucked too soon, stolen and passed around before its season."

It is the last season of high school life for Nadia Turner, a rebellious, grief-stricken, seventeen-year-old beauty. Mourning her own mother's recent suicide, she takes up with the local pastor's son. Luke Sheppard is twenty-one, a former football star whose injury has reduced him to waiting tables at a diner. They are young; it's not serious. But the pregnancy that results from this teen romance - and the subsequent cover-up - will have an impact that goes far beyond their youth. As Nadia hides her secret from everyone, including Aubrey, her God-fearing best friend, the years move quickly. Soon, Nadia, Luke, and Aubrey are full-fledged adults and still living in debt to the choices they made that one seaside summer, caught in a love triangle they must carefully maneuver, and dogged by the constant, nagging question: What if they had chosen differently? The possibilities of the road not taken are a relentless haunt.

In entrancing, lyrical prose, *The Mothers* asks whether a "what if" can be more powerful than an experience itself. If, as time passes, we must always live in servitude to the decisions of our younger selves, to the communities that have parented us, and to the decisions we make that shape our lives forever.

BookBrowse Review

A brilliant debut novel about motherhood, young love, community and ambition.

Every now and then the publishing industry gushes about a young author destined to become the next sensation in literary circles. Hardened cynics like yours truly invariably roll their eyes and try to take the adulation with a pinch of salt. I am embarrassed to admit that I had not read any of Brit Bennett's perceptive essays about race before I finished her incredibly brilliant, sage and moving debut novel, *The Mothers*. But now that I have read almost all her work, I am here to tell you: this phenom is the real thing.

The titular Mothers are a group of older African American women whose sole succor is Upper Room, a black church in Oceanside, a satellite of San Diego. Having being battered down by years of institutionalized racism, they have now retreated to the quiet refuge of Upper Room to live out their last days and to wring their collective hands or gossip over the young 'uns in the flock: "We tried to love the world. We cleaned after this world, scrubbed its hospital floors and ironed its shirts, sweated in its kitchens and spooned school lunches, cared for its sick and nursed its babies. But the world didn't want us, so we left and gave our love to Upper Room."

Prime among the Mothers' concerns is 17-year-old Nadia, a black high school senior with infinite promise caught in the throes of grief after her young mother commits suicide. Her supportive but reticent dad notwithstanding, Nadia can't find the ground beneath her feet, but she discovers a measure of escape in Luke Sheppard, Upper Room's pastor's son. Just a couple of years older than Nadia, Luke's promising career in football – and university scholarship – was cut short after a devastating leg injury. Nadia's classmate, and church faithful Aubrey Evans, nurses her own psychological injuries. The three young characters weave in and out of each other's lives in a complex and tangled web of friendship and secrets that Bennett teases apart with subtlety and a wisdom far beyond her 26 years.

Early on, Nadia's dalliances with Luke leads to pregnancy and then she becomes "unpregnant," undergoes an abortion. Having been granted a prestigious scholarship to attend college at the University of Michigan, Nadia is convinced about her decision: "She couldn't let this baby nail her life in place when she'd just been given a chance to escape."

This is not a plot spoiler. In fact, much of the story focuses on the effects from this singular, carefully deliberated decision that will reverberate over many years and wrap the characters in an unknowable and suffocating grip. Mothers and motherhood form the scaffolding of this emotionally pithy novel and Bennett's superlative gifts are visible in her nuanced handling of issues that are ripe for histrionics and melodrama. There's Nadia's motherhood cut short of course, but Bennett searingly places Nadia's story squarely in the womb of her mother's ultimate abandonment. Nadia is devastated by her mom's suicide and is convinced that she was the root cause of it: "Sometimes I wonder...If my mom had gotten rid of me, would she still be alive? Maybe she would've been happier. She could've had a life." It is difficult to overstate the depth of guilt burrowed deep in Nadia, it's a lurking monster that overshadows practically every major decision she makes. Then there are the collective Mothers who might care but also suffocate Nadia with their passive-aggressive manipulation and petty gossip.

Even in faraway Michigan, Nadia finds she can't escape family, community, Oceanside. "Grief was not a line, carrying you infinitely further from loss. You never knew when you would be sling-shot backward into its grip." When she eventually returns years later to tend to her ailing father, she is promptly sucked back into a complex whirlpool of emotions spiked with jealousy, rivalry, and tempered by nostalgia.

Bennett superbly dusts each character's life with the central motherhood theme, blended in so expertly that it is never jarring. Her decision to alternate the young characters' stories with a chorus of the elder mothers' voices in second person, allows the "kids" time to grow into their more mature skins against the larger canvas of the omnipresent mothers' concerns.

Bennett, who started work on *The Mothers* nine years ago when she was seventeen, walks a high-wire act: treading complicated story arcs, maturing characters and voice and tone with impressive panache. I can't wait to see this young author's career ripen and evolve and see what she comes up with next.

Believe the hype. Read this book. Be prepared to be floored.

Reviewed by Poornima Apte. This review was originally published in *The BookBrowse Review* in October 2016, and has been updated for the October 2017 edition.

ALL THE UGLY AND WONDERFUL THINGS

by Bryn Greenwood

BookBrowse Rating: 5/5
Critics' Consensus: 5/5
Readers' Rating: 4.5/5

Published October 2017 in Paperback, 432 pages

Summary

A beautiful and provocative love story between two unlikely people and the hard-won relationship that elevates them above the troubled Midwestern backdrop of their lives.

As the daughter of a drug dealer, Wavy knows not to trust people, not even her own parents. It's safer to keep her mouth shut and stay out of sight. Struggling to raise her little brother, Donal, eight-year-old Wavy is the only responsible adult around. Obsessed with the constellations, she finds peace in the starry night sky above the fields behind her house, until one night her star gazing causes an accident. After witnessing his motorcycle wreck, she forms an unusual friendship with one of her father's thugs, Kellen, a tattooed ex-con with a heart of gold.

By the time Wavy is a teenager, her relationship with Kellen is the only tender thing in a brutal world of addicts and debauchery. When tragedy rips Wavy's family apart, a well-meaning aunt steps in, and what is beautiful to Wavy looks ugly under the scrutiny of the outside world. A powerful novel you won't soon forget, Bryn Greenwood's *All the Ugly and Wonderful Things* challenges all we know and believe about love.

31 Books Bringing the Heat this Summer —Bustle
Top Ten Hottest Reads of 2016 —New York Daily News
Best Books of 2016 —St. Louis Post Dispatch

BookBrowse Review

A provocative look at the love between two people in extremely tough situations.

Bryn Greenwood's debut, All the Ugly and Wonderful Things, is a harsh, raw, and ultimately, truthful exploration of an unlikely pair as they find and desperately hold onto love. Our member-reviewers were challenged by this complicated, beautiful novel: 23 out of 28 gave it a 4 or 5 star rating.

The Ugly – Strung out, abusive, uncaring parents who also deal drugs and engage in "open" marriage among other things; relatives who are too eager to condemn and not eager to listen; law enforcement that wants to believe the worst; and more. The Wonderful – sincere friendship; true, faithful love;

caring teachers; and more. Beautifully written with well developed, complex characters and believable, if truly awful situations, Bryn Greenwood's debut book is mesmerizing (Becky H). Both Wavy and Kellan are living proof that if a person has one other person to love and care about her it can literally save a life no matter what else happens (Julie M). A love story, a drama, even a little mystery (Roe P). I couldn't put this one down. The characters are unusual, but they feel like real people, and the story is compelling (Elizabeth K). I found myself asking, am I rooting for the love story of a tattooed bruiser of a biker and the way underage child of a meth dealer? Yes. Yes, I am (Ann B). This is about what trust looks like. What love looks like. And it's about what family can mean and look like to those who live on the periphery of love. This is a brave story to tell. One that brushes up against what most would consider immoral and indecent behavior. It was hard to read emotionally, and I am glad I did (Jan B).

Some of our readers feel it is critical to mention that the novel deals explicitly with an underage sexual relationship:

At the beginning, you may not want to continue reading All the Ugly and Wonderful Things. Wavy is nearly mute, speaking monosyllabically, so traumatized by her bi-polar, self-centered and indifferent mother and her physically abusive meth-dealing father with his own harem. The only bright point in her life is Kellen, a giant, tattooed motorcycle mechanic twelve years her senior from his own alcoholic, abusive family. There are definite questions of whether their relationship is pedophilia, but the reader will have to decide what constitutes love after getting to know them and the situations in which they find themselves (Barbara G). What a difficult book to review. It began promising and was very well written but ultimately I could not get over the inappropriate and overly sexual relationship between a child and a very grown man. How can you root for a thirteen year old girl and a 25-year-old man to get together? (Sylvia G) At many times I was made uncomfortable by the burgeoning sexuality of Wavy, and the wildly inappropriate actions of Kellen and Wavy. Perhaps because their world was so devoid of a moral compass it was easier to deal with what in any other situation would be simply unacceptable. It was critical to have multiple voices narrating events to provide balance - sort of a "Greek Chorus" for the reader. I devoured this book - every ugly wonderful bit of it (Kenan R).

They all agree, though, that the writing is powerful:

Wow! Greenwood's style of writing allows you to feel as if you are inside of the skin of Wavy and Kellen and sharing their experiences. The book is raw, sensual and touching. I could not put it down (Diane H). Greenwood uniquely uses multiple narrators to tell her story, some in the first person, others in the third person. It is this writer's gift and allows the characters' stories to join and flow (Carol N). There is crude language and explicit sexual references, but if you can handle that you may find the story as gripping as I did (Carolyn L). Oh my, I thought I was going to dislike this book. I was very wrong, it is very well written, and the author knows her subject very well. The story line moved so fluidly, I found myself rooting for characters that I had no intention of liking. I couldn't put it down. The moral – don't rush to judge what you do not know or understand (Carm D).

Who do our readers believe would like novel?

This is an unusual book that will find its way to book groups eager to be challenged and willing to discuss drugs, law enforcement, child endangerment, felons, desperation, murder, family relationships, perseverance and hope (Becky H). Those who like stories of children surviving terrible childhoods in unthinkable conditions (think The Glass Castle by Jeannette Walls) will enjoy this story (Carole R). Definitely a book to read if you're looking for a happy ending (Jill F).

Reviewed by First Impressions Reviewers. This review was originally published in *The BookBrowse Review* in August 2016, and has been updated for the October 2017 edition.

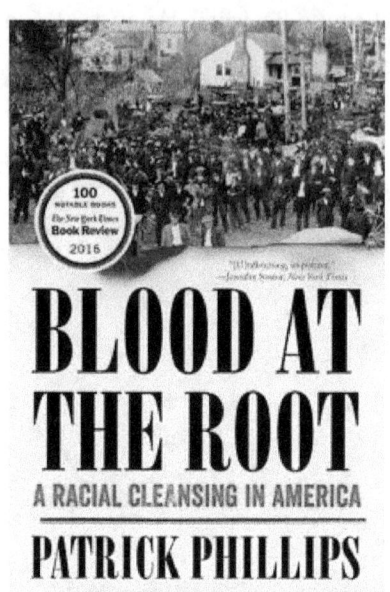

BLOOD AT THE ROOT

by Patrick Phillips

BookBrowse Rating: 5/5
Critics' Consensus: 5/5

Published September 2017 in Paperback, 320 pages

Summary

A gripping tale of racial cleansing in Forsyth County, Georgia, and a harrowing testament to the deep roots of racial violence in America.

Forsyth County, Georgia, at the turn of the twentieth century was home to a large African American community that included ministers and teachers, farmers and field hands, tradesmen, servants, and children. Many black residents were poor sharecroppers, but others owned their own farms and the land on which they'd founded the county's thriving black churches.

But then in September of 1912, three young black laborers were accused of raping and murdering a white girl. One man was dragged from a jail cell and lynched on the town square, two teenagers were hung after a one-day trial, and soon bands of white "night riders" launched a coordinated campaign of arson and terror, driving all 1,098 black citizens out of the county. In the wake of the expulsions, whites harvested the crops and took over the livestock of their former neighbors, and quietly laid claim to "abandoned" land. The charred ruins of homes and churches disappeared into the weeds, until the people and places of black Forsyth were forgotten.

National Book Award finalist Patrick Phillips tells Forsyth's tragic story in vivid detail and traces its long history of racial violence all the way back to antebellum Georgia. Recalling his own childhood in the 1970s and '80s, Phillips sheds light on the communal crimes of his hometown and the violent means by which locals kept Forsyth "all white" well into the 1990s.

Blood at the Root is a sweeping American tale that spans the Cherokee removals of the 1830s, the hope and promise of Reconstruction, and the crushing injustice of Forsyth's racial cleansing. With bold storytelling and lyrical prose, Phillips breaks a century-long silence and uncovers a history of racial terrorism that continues to shape America in the twenty-first century.

BookBrowse Review

A gripping tale of racial cleansing in Forsyth County, Georgia, and a harrowing testament to the deep roots of racial violence in America.

On September 8, 1912, in Forsyth County, Georgia, Mae Crow, a white teenaged girl, was beaten and raped. The next day her battered body was discovered, and for nearly two weeks Mae lingered between life and death, finally succumbing to her injuries on September 23. Her brutal attack was the catalyst for an already simmering pot of racial hatred in Forsyth County because it came only days after another attack on a white woman, Ellen Grice, in the same area. With emotions already running high, a scapegoat for Crow's rape and death was needed, and fast. Three black men were accused of the crime. Her death, as well as the events that followed – including the executions of her supposed attackers, as well as the expulsion of a staggering number of black people from the county – would become the stuff of legend. Patrick Phillips revisits this horrific crime and its aftermath in his non-fiction book *Blood at the Root: A Racial Cleansing in America.*

Three men ended up accused of Crow's rape and death: "Big" Rob Edwards, who would be lynched shortly after his arrest, Ernest Knox, and Oscar Daniel. Knox and Daniel, only in their teens, were convicted of the crime and publicly hanged on October 25, 1912, witnessed by an estimated 5,000 people.

The deaths of Edwards, Knox, and Daniel seemed to whet the appetite for more violence from the white citizens of Forsyth County. Night riders began to appear at the homes of black families living in the county, and their message was clear: "Get out!" They did; some 1,100 people left. Over the next seventy-five years, Forsyth County remained predominantly white and, in January 1987, history seemed on the verge of repeating itself when a protest march for equality almost met with disaster. Chuck Blackburn, a white resident of Cumming in Forsyth County, proposed a unity march both in memory of the 1912 events and in honor of Dr. Martin Luther King, Jr.'s birthday. Other white residents of Forsyth County got wind of the plan and promptly organized a counter-protest rally to intimidate them. On the day of the march, things quickly got out of hand, and the sheriff at the time, Wesley Walraven, warned the marchers he could not guarantee their safety. Dispersing, the marchers returned on January 24 with a larger group and the National Guard for protection. Unfortunately, race relations in the county were slow to improve in the years that followed.

Patrick Phillips chronicles the dark history of Forsyth County. The book is steeped in research and includes a lengthy footnotes section that details his sources. He recounts the 1912 story as it happened, but with clear judgment and condemnation of some of its central figures, who either turned a blind eye or encouraged additional violence. Forsyth County Sheriff William "Bill" Reid was one of these figures, whose mismanagement and pettiness were almost certainly responsible for Edwards' lynching. Although the men were convicted of committing the crime against Mae Crow, an attack on a wealthy white planter, Dabner Elliot, after the executions of Knox and Daniel, suggests they may have been wrongly accused. Phillips writes, "When doctors announced that Elliot had died from his wounds, few whites were willing to even consider the possibility that someone other than a vengeful black assailant had killed Dabner Elliot, presumably in retaliation for the deaths of Edwards, Knox, and Daniel. But privately, some people must have shaken their heads at the fact that Elliot had died in the exact same fashion as Mae Crow and in almost the exact same place…There was still a murderer lurking somewhere in the woods of Oscarville." (Oscarville is the small community in Forsyth County where Mae Crow lived and was attacked.)

Phillips' language is, at times, moving, and his understanding of the conditions of Jim Crow South (see Beyond the Book) feels complete. For example, he writes: "In a Jim Crow South where African Americans were disenfranchised at the polls and powerless in the courts, landowners could hire and rent to poor blacks, secure in the knowledge that if there was ever a dispute over rent payments, crop shares, or wages, the white man's word was sure to prevail."

While the bulk of Phillips' book is spent on the 1912 events, the final sections are devoted to what happened next. Over the years that followed, Forsyth County remained almost one hundred percent white. When minority groups did attempt to move in, they met with harassment and violence. Phillips helps readers to understand how much racial intolerance continued to exist in the county, and the author encourages readers to realize how the past shapes the future.

An engaging portrait of the South's haunting legacy, the lessons of *Blood at the Root: A Racial Cleansing in America* will stick with readers long after they have completed the book. Regrettably, they are lessons Americans still need to learn, for many black Americans today continue to experience racial injustice. Incidents like Trayvon Martin's murder and the unrest in Ferguson, Missouri are modern reminders of how much work Americans need to do to eradicate racial intolerance. The plight for equality in the United States continues.

Reviewed by Mollie Smith Waters. This review was originally published in *The BookBrowse Review* in September 2016, and has been updated for the December 2016 edition.

THE INVISIBLE LIFE OF IVAN ISAENKO

by Scott Stambach

BookBrowse Rating: 5/5
Critics' Consensus: 5/5
Readers' Rating: 4.5/5

Published September 2017 in Paperback, 336 pages

Summary

The Invisible Life of Ivan Isaenko is comic and staggeringly tragic, often both in a single sentence… A grittier, Eastern European, more grown-up *The Fault in Our Stars*." – Eowyn Ivey, author of *The Snow Child*

Seventeen-year-old Ivan Isaenko is a life-long resident of the Mazyr Hospital for Gravely Ill Children in Belarus. Born deformed, yet mentally keen with a frighteningly sharp wit, strong intellect, and a voracious appetite for books, Ivan is forced to interact with the world through the vivid prism of his mind. For the most part, every day is exactly the same for Ivan, which is why he turns everything into a game, manipulating people and events around him for his own amusement. That is until a new resident named Polina arrives at the hospital. At first, Ivan resents Polina. She steals his books. She challenges his routine. The nurses like her. She is exquisite. But soon, he cannot help being drawn to her and the two forge a romance that is tenuous and beautiful and everything they never dared dream of. Before, he survived by being utterly detached from things and people. Now, Ivan wants something more: Ivan wants Polina to live.

BookBrowse Review

The story of one brave teenager's fight to live with daunting challenges demonstrates the sheer strength of the human spirit.

BookBrowse First Impression reviewers were uniformly impressed by this difficult yet heartwarming story, with 21 out of 23 rating it four stars and higher.

Readers love Ivan — and his friend's — indomitable spirit

Ivan has been living in a children's hospital in Belarus all of his life because he was born with only nubs for feet, one arm with three fingers; he has no recollection of a mother or father; he survives in a wheelchair; and he is very smart. He is a Class A snoop. And then Polina arrives. She has cancer, but they form an unstoppable duo (Judy B).

They appreciated the memorable characters and vivid writing

I felt this book reads like a memoir rather than fiction. I will never forget Ivan for being determined, adventurous, intelligent, witty and loving. Both the characters and the setting were very real to me (Jean N). The author conveys the raw realities with dignity and the disobedient vitality of those often invisible to us. While there are teary episodes, it is the heartwarming moments and the "normalcy" of Ivan and Polina that shows the strength of humanity to make lemonade when given lemons. Kudos to the author for such an impressively rich and rewarding read (Beverly J).

It was inspiring to follow Ivan's story. He is the voice of this book. Highly intelligent, he strives to make more of his life beyond the limitations of the hospital and his own body. This is a story of survival, but also of compassion, cruelty and finally, love. The entire book is breathtaking for its story, characters and writing. The writing is amazing (Carole P).

Sensitive readers, take note...

I would like to warn readers of the foul language and sex that are included in this book. To some, this may be offensive (Patricia W). I recommend the book with the disclaimer that there are a few graphic sex scenes that might be offensive (Jean N).

A few readers found the novel to be difficult but rewarding

I found *The Invisible Life of Ivan Isaenko* a hard book to read. It has the social outrage of Dickens and the brooding introspection of Dostoevsky. But the characters are unforgettable, and the book is a reminder that humans are the most adaptable of animals (Mark O). If you can get past the underlying tragic lives, you will find humor, love, and humanity. Due to the underlying darkness, there is no way I can call this an enjoyable book, but the writing and insights into human behavior are exceptional (Valerie C).

Many reviewers found *The Invisible Life of Ivan Isaenko* to be exceptional

Stambach brings the grace of human nature to such a level that I found myself engrossed from page one. There are so many good novels just waiting to be read, that I rarely read one twice. I will make an exception with this novel. Stambach is that rare author that can capture the beauty of the human spirit in the most ugly of places and people. True genius! (Melissa S). How to describe this book? Amazing! Breathtaking! Inspiring! Heartbreaking! (Carole P).

Reviewed by First Impressions Reviewers. This review was originally published in *The BookBrowse Review* in August 2016, and has been updated for the December 2016 edition.

ALL WE HAVE LEFT

by Wendy Mills

BookBrowse Rating: 5/5
Critics' Consensus: 5/5

Published August 2017 in Paperback, 368 pages

Summary

Winner of the 2016 BookBrowse Award for Best Young Adult Novel

Interweaving stories from past and present, *All We Have Left* brings one of the most important days in our recent history to life, showing that love and hope will always triumph.

Now:

Sixteen-year-old Jesse is used to living with the echoes of the past. Her older brother died in the September 11th attacks, and her dad since has filled their home with anger and grief. When Jesse gets caught up with the wrong crowd, one momentary hate-fueled decision turns her life upside down. The only way to make amends is to face the past, starting Jesse on a journey that will reveal the truth about how her brother died.

Then:

In 2001, sixteen-year-old Alia is proud to be Muslim ... it's being a teenager that she finds difficult. After being grounded for a stupid mistake, Alia decides to confront her father at his Manhattan office, putting her in danger she never could have imagined. When the planes collide into the Twin Towers, Alia is trapped inside one of the buildings. In the final hours, she meets a boy who will change everything for her as the flames rage around them ...

BookBrowse Review

Winner of the 2016 BookBrowse Award for Best Young Adult Novel

September 11, 2001 is a date that few Americans will ever forget. It was on this day that our country experienced its single greatest terrorist attack on home soil. It was a tragedy that rocked us to our very core, but – somehow, some way – the country felt united in those following days and weeks after the attack. Wendy Mills, in her excellent New York City-set YA novel, *All We Have Left*, explores this idea, showing how tragedy can aid in restoring the broken past.

Mills, in alternating chapters, tells her story using the voices of Alia and Jesse, two sixteen-year-old girls from different times and different backgrounds.

Alia's story begins in September 2001 just after the school year begins. She's a rebellious artist, with a desire to attend NYU and learn how to become a comic book illustrator. One day she gets caught smoking marijuana in the girls' bathroom, and the next day she decides to wear her hijab (head covering) in public, showing a declaration of her Islamic faith. It's strange timing, and her parents doubt her sincerity. Still, Alia bravely puts on the hijab and enters a world that's growing more weary of Muslims by the day.

She goes to visit her father at his office in one of the World Trade Center buildings to convince him that she's actually a responsible person who happened to have made a bad mistake. It's here that tragedy hits, and the following pages are where Mills does her best storytelling. Alia's sections manage the difficult task of being both heartwarming and heartbreaking.

Jesse's story is set in the present time. She's similar to Alia in that she's a good person who has a tendency to make bad choices. After befriending Nick Roberts, her school's bad boy, she goes on an anti-Muslim painting spree where she writes "Terrorists go home" on a wall. She gets caught by the police, and her punishment is to do community service hours at the Islam Peace Center. For Jesse, being around Muslims is a big deal: Her brother, Travis, was killed in the 9/11 attack when he was only nineteen, and her bigoted father blames all Muslims for his death. Jesse says, "Dad doesn't like anyone he considers a foreigner, but he carries a bottomless well of hate for Muslims, which he often vents in a rage-filled rant at the TV."

After spending time at the Islam Peace Center, Jesse's eyes open to a world far larger than the narrow view she held previously. The transformation in Jesse's outlook is so precise that the novel often feels like a work of narrative nonfiction.

As the story nears its ending, the two sections collide, and the impact is truly astonishing. There were moments where I felt breathless. *All We Have Left*, with its realism and genuine feelings, creates a rare kind of reading experience where you don't want to – no, I mean can't – put the novel down.

Mills eloquently captures the feelings of the early millennium. Culturally, she recreates the days of MTV's *Total Request Live* and of Blink-182's airwaves' hits. She writes with a heightened curiosity of religious otherness, and also brings back a sense of kindness that seems rare in our current society. For example, Alia, on multiple occasions, speaks about goodness being found in people who are inherently different than she is. She says, "Just because people do bad things in the name of religion doesn't make the religion bad. People do crappy things, people do awesome things. That's just people." She also states, "People do terrible things. People do beautiful things. It's against the black backdrop of evil that the shining light of good shows the brightest. We can't just focus on the darkness of the night, or we'll miss out on the stars." It's a striking reminder how a young teenager can be the wisest person around.

All We Have Left is about celebrating our differences and finding a way to connect. It's about love and life, and it's about uncovering new friends and possibilities. There can be hope; there can be a future. After all, all we have left is each other.

Reviewed by Bradley Sides. This review was originally published in *The BookBrowse Review* in September 2016, and has been updated for the August 2017 edition.

CRUEL BEAUTIFUL WORLD

by Caroline Leavitt

BookBrowse Rating: 5/5
Critics' Consensus: 4/5
Readers' Rating: 5/5

Published August 2017 in Paperback, 384 pages

Summary

Set in the early 1970s against the specter of the Manson girls, when the peace and love movement begins to turn ugly, this is the story of a runaway teenager's disappearance and her sister's quest to discover the truth.

Caroline Leavitt is at her mesmerizing best in this haunting, nuanced portrait of love, sisters, and the impossible legacy of family.

It's 1969, and sixteen-year-old Lucy is about to run away with a much older man to live off the grid in rural Pennsylvania, a rash act that will have vicious repercussions for both her and her older sister, Charlotte. As Lucy's default caretaker for most of their lives, Charlotte's youth has been marked by the burden of responsibility, but never more so than when Lucy's dream of a rural paradise turns into nightmare.

With gorgeous prose and indelible characters, *Cruel Beautiful World* examines the intricate, infinitesimal distance between seduction and love, loyalty and duty, and what happens when you're responsible for things you can't fix.

BookBrowse Review

This is a compelling tale of family cobbled together by circumstance and torn apart by the impetuous act of a teenager in love.

Caroline Leavitt's *Cruel Beautiful World*, which looks at the repercussions of the choices we make and the things we do in the name of love, is a runaway hit with many BookBrowse First Impression reviewers.

This is the story of a teenage girl who runs away with her high school teacher, and the book tracks the effect this act has on her, her teacher, their families and the people they meet along the way (Eve A). In *Cruel Beautiful World*, the reader is immediately absorbed by the main character, Lucy, and her life-altering decisions. However, somewhere along the way, the secondary characters and their struggles become just as absorbing (Melissa S).

Reviewers appreciated the novel's many layers...

Woven into this intricate web is the story of two sisters and the responsibilities of life and ultimately the decisions we make. The concept of family is redefined and the final pages are full of emotion and the realization that everything that makes us human also gives us purpose. (Dianna C). How many boys and girls have made a reckless decision at the age of sixteen and lived through the disastrous consequences? I think readers will relate to the consequences of Lucy's impulsive act on many different levels (Janis H). Layered and complicated, this novel draws readers in and keeps them there as characters' dreams die and secrets unfold (Madeline M).

Caroline Leavitt's ability to bring complex characters to life in a way that touches the reader to the core is amazing. I found myself completely immersed in each subplot as the novel progressed. This ability to engage the reader in such a complex way is the mark of a great novel. I will recommend Leavitt to all my fellow readers and can't wait to dive into her other books. I highly recommend this jolting and heartfelt novel. The unexpected twists and turns within the subplots make *Cruel Beautiful World* a complete success! (Melissa S).

A few readers wanted more…

Unless the author intends a sequel about Charlotte, the end left me wanting more (Cindy C). I would love to see another book with a continuation of the story (Eve A). This novel has great potential to be more of a psychological thriller but the storyline is kept too shallow for that to happen. The plot is interesting and keeps the reader turning pages. I would have liked more insight into what different characters were thinking throughout the story, and to know what happened to them after the novel ends (Liz B).

Most pronounced it a winner…

There is tragedy here, but also survival. I found it pretty impossible to put down. Leavitt is a very good writer and *Cruel Beautiful World* is a winner (Sylvia G). The author delights us page after page with tender insights into longing, love, and heartaches with the most endearing encounters occurring as the story closes (Terri C).

Reviewed by First Impressions Reviewers. This review was originally published in *The BookBrowse Review* in October 2016, and has been updated for the August 2017 edition.

MISS JANE

by Brad Watson

BookBrowse Rating: 5/5
Critics' Consensus: 4.5/5
Readers' Rating: 5/5

Published July 2017 in Paperback, 288 pages

Summary

Astonishing prose brings to life a forgotten woman and a lost world in a strange and bittersweet Southern pastoral.

Since his award-winning debut collection of stories, *Last Days of the Dog-Men*, Brad Watson has been expanding the literary traditions of the South, in work as melancholy, witty, strange, and lovely as any in America. Inspired by the true story of his own great-aunt, he explores the life of Miss Jane Chisolm, born in rural, early-twentieth-century Mississippi with a genital birth defect that would stand in the way of the central "uses" for a woman in that time and place - namely, sex and marriage.

From the country doctor who adopts Jane to the hard tactile labor of farm life, from the highly erotic world of nature around her to the boy who loved but was forced to leave her, the world of Miss Jane Chisolm is anything but barren. Free to satisfy only herself, she mesmerizes those around her, exerting an unearthly fascination that lives beyond her still.

BookBrowse Review

Jane's rich inner life overcomes the limits of her physical body.

National Book Award Finalist Brad Watson returns with an intimate novel about one woman's journey to live her life to its fullest. Hopeful, despite the challenges she carries, Miss Jane captured the hearts of our member-reviewers: 22 out of 24 gave it a 5-star rating.

Watson, inspired by his great-aunt, weaves a moving tale about Jane, who is born in rural Mississippi in 1915 with a genital birth defect (Sue J). A must-read! The writing in Miss Jane is beautiful and almost poetic – terse and imaginative. Born with a genital affliction that could have made her bitter, reclusive, and joyless, Jane showed extraordinary gumption. She was her own person and an inspiring one at that. In her quiet way she forged a full life for herself despite being "different." I loved the book and unequivocally recommend it (Florence K). The quiet flowing rhythm of Watson's words describing the landscape, the people in Jane's life, and the dignity she maintains throughout is remarkable (Laurie R). The book inspired and challenged me to reflect on how I've dealt with adversity in my life (John W). Reading this book is enveloping yourself in a cocoon of images and sensations (Linda P). It is not often that you happen upon a book so eloquently written, interesting in subject matter and overflowing with emotions. Simultaneously heartwarming and heartbreaking, this wonderful novel tapped every single feeling possible (Aleksandra E). It took me so long to write this review because I read Miss Jane as slowly as possible to savor it. It is a beautiful story with sadness, but tenderness and bravery as well (Barbara B). Never maudlin, Miss Jane is a memorable story of courage in the face of adversity (Anna S). This is historical fiction at its best (Lynne B).

Readers were especially taken by the rich language Watson uses to illuminate the equally rich landscape of the story:

I'd give this book six stars if I could. The language is sensual, and filled with beautiful descriptions of nature. The writer does a remarkable job presenting Jane Chisolm and her physical deformity with grace and dignity. The reader will appreciate the slow pace of this book with its beautiful language (Barbara O). I loved this book from the very beginning. The prose itself is astounding, especially with the descriptions of nature. I grew up in south Mississippi and it took me back to my youth (Carol N). Miss Jane is an exceptionally well-written book. The prose is beautiful and the novel has a gentleness about it. I especially enjoyed Jane's love of nature, inside of which she seemed to flourish (Meredith K). A portrait of the south that appealed to me through its gentle approach to the people and their land. Watson is a storyteller of great power and finesse (Claire M). A beautiful book. Calm as a deep river that flows on despite the occasional turbulence (Maggie R).

The characters in Miss Jane are exceptionally drawn:

This book is beautifully written with characters so real that I cared for each of them: Jane, the main character born with a birth defect that made her life different; her mother, who was beaten down by the hardness of farm life and her own personal loss; her hard working father, who was trying to do the right thing; and the caring gentle doctor who takes care of Jane (Donna W). The characters – from the loving, gentle doctor who delivered Jane and was a mainstay in her life, to her independent and brash sister Grace, to the solemn man of few words who was her father – were wonderful (Cam G). The author has created interesting and multi-dimensional characters in Jane's parents, sister and the doctor. Even the minor characters are interesting and add to the texture of the story (Susan R).

Our readers wholeheartedly recommend the novel:

I recommend this book to anyone who loves a good character study (Donna W). I can't wait to recommend this book to my book group. There is much to discuss and explore. Thank you Mr. Watson for a mesmerizing, thought-provoking book (Cheryl M). I loved this book for its simplicity and would highly recommend it to my book club and others who enjoy a good read (Meredith K). The story is one of a kind and I would definitely recommend this book to my book club, as I am sure the story would lead to discussion in many different directions. Well done, Brad Watson! (Laura E)

Reviewed by First Impressions Reviewers. This review was originally published in *The BookBrowse Review* in July 2016, and has been updated for the August 2017 edition.

BEHOLD THE DREAMERS

by Imbolo Mbue

BookBrowse Rating: 4/5
Critics' Consensus: 4.5/5
Readers' Rating: 4.5/5

Published June 2017 in Paperback, 416 pages

| Summary

Oprah Winfrey's Summer 2017 Book Club Pick

In the vein of Amy Tan and Khaled Hosseini comes a compulsively readable debut novel about marriage, immigration, class, race, and the trapdoors in the American Dream - the unforgettable story of a young Cameroonian couple making a new life in New York just as the Great Recession upends the economy.

Jende Jonga, a Cameroonian immigrant living in Harlem, has come to the United States to provide a better life for himself, his wife, Neni, and their six-year-old son. In the fall of 2007, Jende can hardly believe his luck when he lands a job as a chauffeur for Clark Edwards, a senior executive at Lehman Brothers. Clark demands punctuality, discretion, and loyalty - and Jende is eager to please. Clark's wife, Cindy, even offers Neni temporary work at the Edwardses' summer home in the Hamptons. With these opportunities, Jende and Neni can at last gain a foothold in America and imagine a brighter future.

However, the world of great power and privilege conceals troubling secrets, and soon Jende and Neni notice cracks in their employers' façades.

When the financial world is rocked by the collapse of Lehman Brothers, the Jongas are desperate to keep Jende's job - even as their marriage threatens to fall apart. As all four lives are dramatically upended, Jende and Neni are forced to make an impossible choice.

BookBrowse Review

Behold the Dreamers **shines light on an immigrant family's interactions with their wealthy American employers, even as they labor for a slice of the American dream.**

Behold the Dreamers, Cameroonian author Imbolo Mbue's debut novel, revolves around two very different families. Jende Jonga has emigrated from Cameroon to the United States, and as the story opens, has finally saved enough money working multiple low-income jobs to allow his wife and son to join him, and to rent a tiny apartment in Harlem.

He is in the process of navigating the complex legalities of staying in the country he loves when he lands his dream job: chauffeur to the wealthy Clark Edwards, a high-ranking member of the financial firm Lehman Brothers (see

'Beyond the Book'). Jonga initially believes the Edwards family is living the American Dream, but as the story unfolds, it becomes clear that it's on the verge of collapsing under its own very different series of stressors.

The narrative alternately relays the action from Jende's point of view and from that of his wife, Neni. Although told from the immigrants' perspectives, *Behold the Dreamers* is definitely not a one-sided story, instead it clearly reveals the similarities and contrasts between the Jonga and Edwards families as each attempts to achieve success – and to define what form that might take.

The plot follows the challenges they face, at first simply the day-to-day getting by, and later adapting to the scandal surrounding Lehman Brothers during the collapse of the U.S. housing market (2007-2009). The difficulties the Jongas face are what one might expect – long hours, low wages, dealing with immigration law – but certainly the Edwards family has its struggles as it deals with societal and domestic pressures. The plot isn't intricate, but it *is* engaging - particularly after the economic crisis, at which point the storyline veers dramatically from the expected narrative arc.

Mbue's main talent is her ability to bring her characters to life. I absolutely fell in love with Jende and his wife; the optimism with which the author infuses these characters is infectious. In spite of the challenges of making ends meet, the couple is excited about the benefits available to themselves and their children in the United States, opportunities they wouldn't have in their native country. At one point Jende tells Clark:

> "I thank God every day for this opportunity, sir," he said as he switched from the center to the left lane. "I thank God, and I believe I work hard, and one day I will have a good life here. My parents, they, too, will have a good life in Cameroon. And my son will grow up to be somebody, whatever he wants to be. I believe that anything is possible for anyone who is American. Truly do, sir. And in fact, sir, I hope that one day my son will grow up to be a great man like you."

Statements like these might come across as overly sentimental, but Mbue makes her readers feel like these characters truly mean it; they're not naïve, just very hopeful. They remind us how much many of us born in this country take for granted each day. Equally convincing are Clark and Cindy Edwards, whose failing marriage and inability to appreciate what they have are painted in stark contrast to the Jongas.

The book is not without its flaws. The characters' situations and attitudes during the first two-thirds of the book lack depth. The immigrants are happy and loving in spite of financial hardship, the stresses of dealing with the U.S. legal system, and working multiple jobs to make ends meet, while the Edwards family members are wealthy, unhappy and disconnected from each other. Although all the characters are well-drawn, they initially fit too neatly into their roles. It's only close to the end, as events start spiraling out of control, that the plot becomes more realistic, leading to a much stronger book.

Also, readers never really learn about realistic U.S. attitudes toward race or the immigrant community (improbably, practically everyone is extremely friendly to the Jongas). This is not to say I didn't enjoy the book. I did, and wouldn't hesitate to recommend it to those interested in reading about the immigrant experience. *Behold the Dreamers* is an especially good book group selection, as the choices made by each family would make great fodder for discussion.

Reviewed by Kim Kovacs. This review was originally published in *The BookBrowse Review* in August 2016, and has been updated for the July 2017 edition.

NEWS OF THE WORLD

by Paulette Jiles

BookBrowse Rating: 5/5
Critics' Consensus: 5/5
Readers' Rating: 5/5

Published June 2017 in Paperback, 224 pages

Summary

It is 1870 and Captain Jefferson Kyle Kidd travels through northern Texas, giving live readings to paying audiences hungry for news of the world. An elderly widower who has lived through three wars and fought in two of them, the captain enjoys his rootless, solitary existence.

In Wichita Falls, he is offered a $50 gold piece to deliver a young orphan to her relatives in San Antonio. Four years earlier, a band of Kiowa raiders killed Johanna's parents and sister; sparing the little girl, they raised her as one of their own. Recently rescued by the U.S. army, the ten-year-old has once again been torn away from the only home she knows.

Their 400-mile journey south through unsettled territory and unforgiving terrain proves difficult and at times dangerous. Johanna has forgotten the English language, tries to escape at every opportunity, throws away her shoes, and refuses to act "civilized." Yet as the miles pass, the two lonely survivors tentatively begin to trust each other, forging a bond that marks the difference between life and death in this treacherous land.

Arriving in San Antonio, the reunion is neither happy nor welcome. The captain must hand Johanna over to an aunt and uncle she does not remember - strangers who regard her as an unwanted burden. A respectable man, Captain Kidd is faced with a terrible choice: abandon the girl to her fate or become - in the eyes of the law - a kidnapper himself. Exquisitely rendered and morally complex, *News of the World* is a brilliant work of historical fiction that explores the boundaries of family, responsibility, honor, and trust.

BookBrowse Review

A brilliant work of historical fiction that explores the boundaries of family, responsibility, honor, and trust.

Paulette Jiles brings the landscape of late 19th century Texas to life in this novel long-listed for the National Book Award about an unlikely friendship that is formed between a former Civil War hero and a young abducted girl. 23 out of 25 gave it a 4 or 5 star rating.

Don't miss this rich historical fiction offering! (Bev C). *News of the World* centers around a 70-year-old man Captain Kidd, who carries news of the world to the people of Texas after the Civil War. Great premise in itself. He is a quiet hero, who is entrusted with returning a 10-year-old to her family. What ensues is an exploration of the history and cultures that made Texas (Pam L). Well-researched, filled with beautiful description and wry humor, the story is also highly suspenseful all the way to the Captain's terrible moral dilemma at the end (Dona H). I have found a new author to love! (Marcie M). This is a touching story filled with both humor and raw descriptions of Texas life. Every scene is described so clearly that the reader becomes part of the narrative (Marianne D). I remember enough of my Oklahoma and Plains Indians history courses to know the events ring true, related in such a way to have genuinely touched my heart (Pam M). Paulette Jiles has written a poignant story of learning to trust and, in the end, to love (Arlene M).

Our readers were captivated by the way Paulette Jiles crafted the rugged, raw landscape of Texas in the late 19th century:

This is a beautiful and spare novel. The landscape comes alive, as does the almost constant sense of desperation of being on the road during such dangerous times. The author has a true gift for description, we see, smell and feel the conditions the pair experience (Ruthie A). Top-notch author Paulette Giles…describes the beauty of the land with the eye of a true naturalist. Her prose is really lovely (Jeanne B). Jiles captures the feel of the Texas landscape, from the plains of north Texas to the Hill Country to the desert of San Antonio. Moreover, she writes a beautiful story of courage, acceptance, and love (Linda J). The beauty of unformed and wild Texas comes through in the author's stark descriptions of the landscape in every chapter, but as the leaves burst forth and the sun again warms the earth, the two travelers are also reborn and enter a new life phase. Highly recommended! (Sharon R).

Perhaps because of the strong visual components of *News of the World*, perhaps because the story is just action-packed with vivid writing, our readers are ready for this novel's movie version!

One of the most enjoyable facets of Jiles' writing is in its cinematic quality. This is a Western, albeit unconventional. What is it like to have to immerse yourself in a culture completely alien to what you are used to? A bond grows between two people who are unlikely to care for each other; how does that happen? I didn't want to see the novel end, the story of Judd and Johanna cries for more. I highly recommend this book, and will seek out other works by Paulette Jiles (Mary P-K). This book is a movie that should be made (Pamela F).

Finally, our readers recommend this novel to family – and everyone else!

Captain Kidd and Johanna will linger for some time in my recollections…I plan to pass this book along to my mother who currently lives in the Texas Hill Country which plays a prominent role in the story albeit quite unrecognizable but strangely familiar to today's Texas Hill Country (Kelli R). I would definitely recommend this to my sister to read. Thanks again for the opportunity to discover another author to love (Mary D). If you are interested in an unfamiliar view into history - this is a book for you. If you are interested in a familiar view into history - this is a book for you. If you are interested in unexpected moral complexities - this is a book for you. If you are looking for a book to suggest to your book club that offers a number of paths for discussion - read this book! (Carole A)

Reviewed by First Impressions Reviewers. This review was originally published in *The BookBrowse Review* in October 2016, and has been updated for the July 2017 edition.

THANKS FOR THE TROUBLE

by Tommy Wallach

BookBrowse Rating: 5/5
Critics' Consensus: 5/5

Published June 2017 in Paperback, 304 pages

Summary

Tommy Wallach, the *New York Times* bestselling author of the "stunning debut" (*Kirkus Reviews*, starred review) *We All Looked Up*, delivers a brilliant new novel about a young man who overcomes a crippling loss and finds the courage to live after meeting an enigmatic girl.

"Was this story written about me?"

I shrugged.

"Yes or no?"

I shrugged again, finally earning a little scowl, which somehow made the girl even more pretty.

"It's very rude not to answer simple questions," she said.

I gestured for my journal, but she still wouldn't give it to me. So I took out my pen and wrote on my palm.

I can't, I wrote. Then, in tiny letters below it: Now don't you feel like a jerk?

Parker Santé hasn't spoken a word in five years. While his classmates plan for bright futures, he skips school to hang out in hotels, killing time by watching the guests. But when he meets a silver-haired girl named Zelda Toth, a girl who claims to be quite a bit older than she looks, he'll discover there just might be a few things left worth living for.

From the celebrated author of We All Looked Up comes a unique story of first and last loves.

BookBrowse Review

From the celebrated author of *We All Looked Up* comes a unique story of first and last loves.

Tommy Wallach is a young writer who's not afraid to tackle big issues of life and death. His debut novel, We All Looked Up, focused on a group of teenagers doing normal teenage things while confronting their own mortality, in the form of an asteroid hurtling toward Earth. Now, in Thanks for the Trouble, Wallach offers another thoughtful novel that deals with issues of (im)mortality, loss, and change, all tinted with humor and a hint of magic.

Parker Santé is a senior in high school, but he would be the first to admit that he's not exactly Ivy League material. Ever since the death of his writer father several years earlier, Parker has lived on the fringes of his own life. He is physically unable to speak despite years of therapy, he feels detached from his grieving, alcoholic mother, and he's gotten into trouble more than once for fighting and stealing things.

It's while he's in the process of his next theft, however, that he encounters a girl who's about to change everything for him. Zelda is strikingly lovely, with unexpected silver hair and a way of talking that makes her seem older than she appears. Parker is intent on stealing the wad of cash she uses to pay for her coffee at the Palace Hotel – but before he can do so, she engages him in an intriguing conversation (Parker writes his contributions in the notebook he carries everywhere) during which she confesses that she's only biding time until she plans to kill herself by jumping off the Golden Gate Bridge. Before their coffee cups are emptied, the two make a deal – if Parker promises to change his mind and apply for college, Zelda won't kill herself... at least not yet.

Starting on Halloween and extending for about the next 48 hours, Thanks for the Trouble explores how Parker's unexpected encounter with Zelda, and her fearless willingness to tell the truth no matter how uncomfortable it is, allows him to open his eyes to a world he's been largely blind to since his father died. "Where have you been, Parker?" she asks him at one point. "How have you managed to hide out right in the middle of your own life?"

Structured as Parker's (60,209 words too long) college application essay, punctuated by Parker's clever and thematically rich fairy tales, the novel not only examines Parker's retreat from and rapid reentry into real life, it also continually questions who Zelda is, whether she's telling the truth about her past, and if it even really matters in the end. Readers, like Parker himself, will be second-guessing Zelda's stories and motivation right up until the last page, wondering if she's really magic... or if she's real at all. In the end, though, what matters is Parker's realization that "maybe the closest thing we mortals get to magic is just change." His whirlwind time with Zelda is full of changes and surprises – but perhaps what matters most of all is his willingness to embrace the kinds of changes, for better and for worse, that denote the passing of time and that make us fully human.

Reviewed by Norah Piehl. This review was originally published in *The BookBrowse Review* in March 2016, and has been updated for the June 2017 edition.

MISCHLING

by Affinity Konar

BookBrowse Rating: 5/5
Critics' Consensus: 5/5
Readers' Rating: 4.5/5

Published May 2017 in Paperback, 352 pages

Summary

"One of the most harrowing, powerful, and imaginative books of the year" (Anthony Doerr) about twin sisters fighting to survive the evils of World War II.

Pearl is in charge of: the sad, the good, the past.

Stasha must care for: the funny, the future, the bad.

It's 1944 when the twin sisters arrive at Auschwitz with their mother and grandfather. In their benighted new world, Pearl and Stasha Zagorski take refuge in their identical natures, comforting themselves with the private language and shared games of their childhood.

As part of the experimental population of twins known as Mengele's Zoo, the girls experience privileges and horrors unknown to others, and they find themselves changed, stripped of the personalities they once shared, their identities altered by the burdens of guilt and pain.

That winter, at a concert orchestrated by Mengele, Pearl disappears. Stasha grieves for her twin, but clings to the possibility that Pearl remains alive. When the camp is liberated by the Red Army, she and her companion Feliks--a boy bent on vengeance for his own lost twin--travel through Poland's devastation. Undeterred by injury, starvation, or the chaos around them, motivated by equal parts danger and hope, they encounter hostile villagers, Jewish resistance fighters, and fellow refugees, their quest enabled by the notion that Mengele may be captured and brought to justice within the ruins of the Warsaw Zoo. As the young survivors discover what has become of the world, they must try to imagine a future within it.

A superbly crafted story, told in a voice as exquisite as it is boundlessly original, *Mischling* defies every expectation, traversing one of the darkest moments in human history to show us the way toward ethereal beauty, moral reckoning, and soaring hope.

BookBrowse Review

Twin sisters become the object of horrific experiments at Auschwitz and yet succeed in crafting their own incredible survival stories.

Mischling begins when twelve-year-old twins Pearl and Stasha Zamborski arrive at Auschwitz in a cattle car with their mother and grandfather, where they are immediately separated from their family to become residents of a Human "Zoo" of sadistic experiments, run by Dr. Josef Mengele, who is commonly known as the "Angel of Death." However, the story really unfolds in the womb where, as Stasha tells us, the girls were "afloat in amniotic snowfall, two rosy mittens resting on the lining of our mother." This is a story where love and connection are so strong, they can — and must — withstand all manner of barbarity.

While in some ways the twins are protected as Mengele's prized "pets," they are subjected to horrifying physical and psychological experiments. One twin is locked in a cage and tormented, the other believes Mengele's claims that he has made her immortal. These are two distinct versions of hell, narrated in alternating chapters as the point of view shifts between Pearl and Sasha. Upon the liberation of Auschwitz, the girls are separated. One is on a mission to seek safety with a group of fellow survivors. The other, believing her sister to be dead, is on a mission to find Mengele and exact revenge. Their journeys intersect in literal and metaphorical ways as they try to reconstruct a life and identity amid the crumbling of Eastern Europe.

Full of rich historical detail, *Mischling* is a captivating story of survival in the worst circumstances imaginable. The author, Affinity Konar, makes these details visceral as we experience them through the sensibilities of the twin narrators, the scorched scent in the air from the crematoriums, a room with eyes pinned to the wall, and other unbelievable (but true) horrors taken from real accounts of survivors (see 'Beyond the Book').

Despite these atrocities, there is a mystical wonder present in the story — the world may be in flames, but the universe provides. When the travelers are most weary, a getaway horse appears. When Pearl desperately needs crutches, her prayers are answered. Jewish Resistance fighters emerge from the night like mythical heroes to slay an enemy. None of these instances feel silly or contrived. There are also compelling and well-developed supporting characters: a haunted Jewish doctor forced to work under Mengele's command, and other "Zoo" dwelling misfits, a grieving boy with a tail, and a tough-talking Russian albino with a loud mouth and secret gentle heart. There is even humor. Stasha in particular is funny, remarking that one of their large captors resembles "a wardrobe with a toupee." This is not to say that the book is not sad, just that it is not *only* sad.

The girls possess a startling and inspiring level of resolve. Stasha declares early on her determination to "be more than an experiment in this world." Both girls take solace in a game called "The Classification of Living Things," where people are judged by their animal characteristics, and the recitation of species, genus, family, order, and class is a calming mechanism. This family tradition, along with the twins' intuition links the two narratives in clever ways as they think similar thoughts and even feel each other's pain. The book's title comes from the German word for "mixed blood," which Stasha boldly reclaims to relate to herself as "of two parts," one of "loss and despair" and one of "wild hope."

This thread of "two parts" gets at the heart of the book. The horrors of the concentration camp are dwarfed by a greater conflict – the twins' separation: "I was a broken half afloat in a great nowhere," Stasha says. Everything inflicted on the girls by Mengele is survivable but to be apart from one another is not. As Pearl says: "this is not about that man, as much as he would have liked it to be." It is hard to describe the alchemy that Konar performs to make this story so uplifting. In a way, she has created a kinder, gentler twin experiment of her own: how will Sasha and Pearl, "two parts," so alike, but so different in disposition, face and overcome their traumas, with rage or with kindness, vengeance, or forgiveness. The results of this experiment, unlike those conducted at Auschwitz, actually has value for humanity.

Reviewed by Lisa Butts. This review was originally published in *The BookBrowse Review* in September 2016, and has been updated for the June 2017 edition.

THIS MUST BE THE PLACE

by Maggie O'Farrell

BookBrowse Rating: 5/5
Critics' Consensus: 5/5
Readers' Rating: 5/5

Published May 2017 in Paperback, 400 pages

Summary

A dazzling novel from bestselling writer Maggie O'Farrell, winner of the Costa Novel Award—an irresistible love story that crisscrosses continents and time zones as it captures an extraordinary marriage, and an unforgettable family, with wit, humor, and deep affection.

Meet Daniel Sullivan, a man with a complicated life. A New Yorker living in the wilds of Ireland, he has children he never sees in California, a father he loathes in Brooklyn, and a wife, Claudette, who is a reclusive ex-film star given to pulling a gun on anyone who ventures up their driveway. Claudette was once the most glamorous and infamous woman in cinema before she staged her own disappearance and retreated to blissful seclusion in an Irish farmhouse.

But the life Daniel and Claudette have so carefully constructed is about to be disrupted by an unexpected discovery about a woman Daniel lost touch with twenty years ago. This revelation will send him off-course, far away from wife, children and home. Will his love for Claudette be enough to bring him back?

This Must be the Place is a novel about family, identity, and true love: an intimately drawn portrait of a marriage, both the forces that hold it together and the pressures that drive it apart. O'Farrell writes with complexity, insight, and laugh-out-loud humor in a narrative that hurtles forward with powerful velocity and emotion. *This Must be the Place* is a sophisticated, spellbinding summer read from one of the UK's most highly acclaimed and best-loved novelists.

BookBrowse Review

This portrait of a marriage's ups and downs is tender-hearted and fleshed out with believable characters.

Maggie O'Farrell's latest novel may be a multi-perspective and time-shifting narrative, but above all, it is a moving love story about the lives of a married couple, Dan and Claudette. When *This Must Be The Place* opens, Dan, albeit fondly, is quick to point out that his wife — and the mother of two of his children — is crazy. True or not, Claudette, who was once a famous movie star, now shuns the spotlight (see 'Beyond the Book'), insisting on living in a remote farmhouse in Ireland.

As happy as they appear to be, problems soon arise. Dan hears a voice from his past on the radio: the voice of a woman he once loved and for whose death he may have been responsible. When he decides to find out what happened to her and also reconnect with the children from his first marriage, everything changes. As O'Farrell moves from past to present and into the future lives of Dan and Claudette, an absorbing portrait of a relationship in crisis develops.

Never trite, never predictable and never shying away from the difficulties of life, love and loss, O'Farrell creates characters who are believable and sympathetic. Both Dan and Claudette have flaws that have brought them together but may also keep them apart.

Although the novel opens with chapters from Dan and then Claudette's perspective, other family and friends take up the role of storyteller and subsequent chapters are told from many different perspectives and different time periods. There is Dan's teenage daughter Phoebe, in 2010, struggling with the pressures of teenage body changes and peer pressure. There is her clever older brother Niall, in 1999, suffering from extremely painful eczema. There is Claudette's sister-in-law, in 2003, going to China to adopt a baby. At times the narrative also switches out of the straightforward prose form. Claudette's previous life and first marriage, for example, are illuminated through a series of illustrated entries from an auction catalogue. Her first husband's perspective is relayed in the form of an interview recording. Changing time frames and perspectives can sometimes make for a disconnected reading experience but in this case O'Farrell's choices enrich her story, bringing greater understanding of the motivations and concerns of her characters and adding layers of tension as the past is explained and the future unfolds.

This Must Be the Place certainly confirms, if it were ever needed, that O'Farrell is a highly accomplished novelist. Her dialogue is crisp and witty and her ability to give individual voices to so many narrators is to be greatly admired. While this is clearly a very clever novel, it is never consciously literary or contrived. The tone is light and the story sparkles with moments of great comedy: for example Claudette meets Dan while he is traveling around Ireland looking for the lost ashes of his dead grandfather, only to leave the urn by the roadside after helping her with a flat tire.

Tenderhearted and character-driven, *This Must Be the Place* is entertaining, thoughtful and wise. Because the fictional portraits seem so real, it is impossible not to become caught up in Dan and Claudette's lives and read eagerly – and anxiously - to see how their story will be resolved.

Reviewed by Kate Braithwaite. This review was originally published in *The BookBrowse Review* in September 2016, and has been updated for the May 2017 edition.

THE MEMORY BOOK

by Lara Avery

BookBrowse Rating: 5/5
Critics' Consensus: 5/5

Published May 2017 in Paperback, 368 pages

Summary

They tell me that my memory will never be the same, that I'll start forgetting things. At first just a little, and then a lot. So I'm writing to remember.

Sammie McCoy is a girl with a plan: graduate at the top of her class and get out of her small town as soon as possible. Nothing will stand in her way - not even the rare genetic disorder the doctors say will slowly steal her memories and then her health.

So the memory book is born: a journal written to Sammie's future self, so she can remember everything from where she stashed her study guides to just how great it feels to have a best friend again. It's where she'll record every perfect detail of her first date with longtime-crush Stuart, a gifted young writer home for the summer. And where she'll admit how much she's missed her childhood friend Cooper, and the ridiculous lengths he will go to make her laugh. The memory book will ensure Sammie never forgets the most important parts of her life - the people who have broken her heart, those who have mended it - and most of all, that if she's going to die, she's going to die living.

This moving and remarkable novel introduces an inspiring character you're sure to remember, long after the last page.

BookBrowse Review

A journal written to teenager Sammie's future self, so she can die remembering her remarkable life.

Isn't hope the ultimate motivation? We challenge ourselves because we believe that the reward will be well worth the struggle. We fight because there's the possibility that we will win. This feeling of hope, and all of the dreams and promises that surround it, are at the center of Lara Avery's moving novel, *The Memory Book*.

Samantha "Sammie" McCoy is an overachieving senior at Hanover High in New Hampshire. She's the kind of young person who is a leader – a doer, and she's filled with hope for her future. When we meet her, she says, "I'm going to win the National Debate Tournament, get into NYU, and be a human rights lawyer." She stands apart from her other classmates because she is exceptional on every level. She is intelligent, kind, and fun. In all of her greatness, she's likeable and even relatable. Sammie shows her light side by admitting that she "laughs at SpongeBob and fart jokes even when stupid people make them." If a young person can have a perfect life, Sammie seems to have it – at least from the outside.

But there's something hiding beneath the surface. Sammie has trouble with her memory. She forgets. She stumbles. She can't always process like she should be able to. After undergoing medical tests, she is diagnosed with Niemann-Pick Type C (NPC), a rare genetic disorder that is "always fatal," and, suddenly her bright future appears much less certain.

Sammie, however, has a plan. She'll create a memory book to help her remember, and she'll do everything in her power to not forget.

Avery handles Sammie's inevitable downfall with grace, and she captures Sammie's worries beautifully. Sammie begins to panic when she notices the symptoms occurring more frequently: "If I don't get to finish out the school year, my grades go down. If my grades go down, Hanover will reconsider my valedictory status. If they take away my valedictory status, my parents will realize I'm losing control of things." It's such an emotional and heartbreaking experience to read, but it's one grounded in truth.

Sammie is among the very best (and most well-rendered) YA characters in recent memory. Her love of success is endearing, and her frequent citations of her "favorite feminist icons" list including Senator Elizabeth Warren, Beyonce, Malala Yousafzai, and Serena Williams only adds to her kind and well-meaning spirit. Avery has crafted an infectious young spirit, and readers will fall in love with her.

The supporting cast of characters is also quite remarkable. Stuart Shah and Cooper Lind serve as love interests that create a *Twilight*-esque Edward versus Jacob dynamic. Stuart is a talented writer and kind spirit who Sammie fantasizes about as having for a boyfriend. Cooper is a rougher, boy-next-door type who also vies for Sammie's attention. As Sammie begins her decline, the boys continue to support her. They will have readers swooning. Maddie,

Sammie's friend and debate partner, brings an added layer. She is a friend who isn't willing to let Sammie's illness serve as a crutch in their relationship. Sammie's imperfect parents and frustrated siblings also stand out as enjoyable characters.

The Memory Book has more than its share of pain, anger, and suffering, but it also has plenty of laughter, joy, and especially hope. It's a novel that touches on the full spectrum of adolescent (and adult) emotions. Sammie's story is special. It's the kind of book that readers will share among groups of friends during these last weeks of summer.

For readers looking for a contemporary, realistic novel with an abundance of heart to tide them over until John Green or Jandy Nelson can publish their next books, Lara Avery's *The Memory Book* is a more than a worthy title.

Reviewed by Bradley Sides. This review was originally published in *The BookBrowse Review* in August 2016, and has been updated for the May 2017 edition.

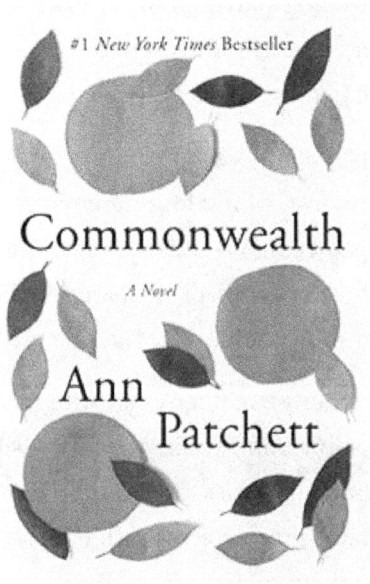

COMMONWEALTH

by Ann Patchett

BookBrowse Rating: 5/5
Critics' Consensus: 5/5
Readers' Rating: 5/5

Published May 2017 in Paperback, 336 pages

Summary

The acclaimed, bestselling author - winner of the PEN/Faulkner Award and the Orange Prize - tells the enthralling story of how an unexpected romantic encounter irrevocably changes two families' lives.

One Sunday afternoon in Southern California, Bert Cousins shows up at Franny Keating's christening party uninvited. Before evening falls, he has kissed Franny's mother, Beverly - thus setting in motion the dissolution of their marriages and the joining of two families.

Spanning five decades, *Commonwealth* explores how this chance encounter reverberates through the lives of the four parents and six children involved. Spending summers together in Virginia, the Keating and Cousins children forge a lasting bond that is based on a shared disillusionment with their parents and the strange and genuine affection that grows up between them.

When, in her twenties, Franny begins an affair with the legendary author Leon Posen and tells him about her family, the story of her siblings is no longer hers to control. Their childhood becomes the basis for his wildly successful book, ultimately forcing them to come to terms with their losses, their guilt, and the deeply loyal connection they feel for one another.

Told with equal measures of humor and heartbreak, *Commonwealth* is a meditation on inspiration, interpretation, and the ownership of stories. It is a brilliant and tender tale of the far-reaching ties of love and responsibility that bind us together.

BookBrowse Review

Spanning five decades, *Commonwealth* explores how a chance encounter reverberates through the lives of the four parents and six children involved.

Opening Ann Patchett's novel *Commonwealth* about two semi-functional mid-late 20th century families feels like sliding into a comfy chair in a quiet tearoom with an old friend. Not the kind of friend who finishes your sentences, but the kind who's got lots of stories to tell about her trips to Machu Picchu or sub-Saharan Africa. That is, if you've read one of Patchett's books before. If not, then you're in for a real treat as her intimate prose winds its way into your psyche and puts you at immediate ease. You can trust her. She knows her way around your feelings and treats them with tenderness and respect.

It's June in Los Angeles, on a Sunday afternoon in the early 1960s. There's a christening party going on at the home of one of LA's Irish cops. Fix and Beverly Keating are celebrating their youngest daughter Franny's big day with a houseful of friends and relatives. And one party crasher. The party is winding down; trays of food are running low, as is the liquor supply. Bert Cousins, the uninvited, shows up with the best and only christening gift he could lay his hands on as he hastily abandons his pregnant wife Teresa and the couple's three other children for the chaos of a party with a family he barely knows. Gin. He comes bearing a big bottle of gin.

I saw this as a Chekhov gun. There is no tonic to go along with the gin so Fix has to leave the party to go pick some up. While he's gone the inventive guests begin to harvest oranges from the burgeoning fruit trees in the Keatings' backyard. By the time Fix returns with the tonic, an assembly line has formed. There's Bert, a little too merrily slicing, squeezing, juicing and mixing gin-and-orange-juice cocktails alongside Fix's stunningly beautiful wife, Beverly. A woman he finds irresistible:

> He knew that making a move on a married woman was a bad idea, especially when you were in the woman's house and her husband was also in the house and the husband was a cop and the party was a celebration of the birth of the cop's second child. He knew all of this but as the drinks stacked up he told himself there were larger forces at work.

This day, Bert thought, was the beginning of his life. It was also the end of two marriages.

From here on the narrative voice switches between Fix at the end of his life, his and Beverly's youngest daughter Franny as an adult, and that of the blended children who spent summers together at Bert and Beverly's home in Virginia. "Here was the remarkable thing about the Keating children and the Cousins children: they did not hate one another, nor did they possess one shred of tribal loyalty...The six children had in common one overarching principle that cast their dislike for one another down to the bottom of the minor leagues: they disliked their parents. They hated them."

Though not told in chronological order, the story unfolds organically, each chapter building to the climax. And if it weren't for the fact that all of Patchett's books enjoy the same organic quality I might credit that to *Commonwealth*'s autobiographical inspiration. (See Beyond the Book.) But Patchett just seems to know all of her characters so intimately, and they move in a world we recognize and say things we might given similar circumstances. Even their bad decisions – and there are many here – make sense at the time. She is a master who can create passages that will be with you for the rest of your life.

Reviewed by Donna Chavez. This review was originally published in *The BookBrowse Review* in September 2016, and has been updated for the May 2017 edition.

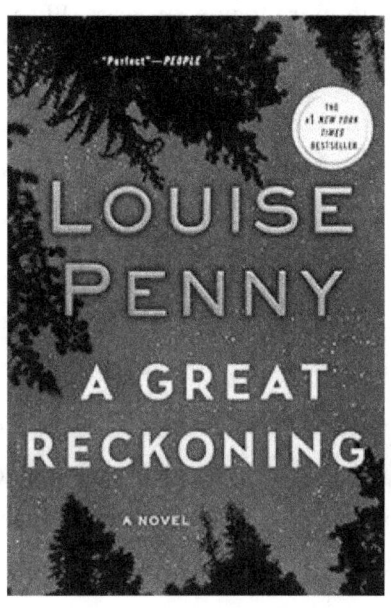

A GREAT RECKONING

by Louise Penny

BookBrowse Rating: 5/5
Critics' Consensus: 5/5

Published May 2017 in Paperback, 416 pages

Summary

Winner of the 2016 BookBrowse Fiction Award

Bestselling author Louise Penny pulls back the layers to reveal a brilliant and emotionally powerful truth in her latest spellbinding novel.

When an intricate old map is found stuffed into the walls of the bistro in Three Pines, it at first seems no more than a curiosity. But the closer the villagers look, the stranger it becomes.

Given to Armand Gamache as a gift the first day of his new job, the map eventually leads him to shattering secrets. To an old friend and older adversary. It leads the former Chief of Homicide for the Sûreté du Québec to places even he is afraid to go. But must.

And there he finds four young cadets in the Sûreté academy, and a dead professor. And, with the body, a copy of the old, odd map.

Everywhere Gamache turns, he sees Amelia Choquet, one of the cadets. Tattooed and pierced. Guarded and angry. Amelia is more likely to be found on the other side of a police line-up. And yet she is in the academy. A protégée of the murdered professor.

The focus of the investigation soon turns to Gamache himself and his mysterious relationship with Amelia, and his possible involvement in the crime. The frantic search for answers takes the investigators back to Three Pines and a stained glass window with its own horrific secrets.

For both Amelia Choquet and Armand Gamache, the time has come for a great reckoning.

BookBrowse Review

This novel in a beloved mystery series mixes old characters with new and is a satisfying addition from author Louise Penny.

Canadian author Louise Penny's twelfth entry in the Chief Inspector Armand Gamache series, A Great Reckoning, opens where her previous mystery, The Nature of the Beast, leaves off with Gamache retired from the homicide department of the Sûreté du Québec and living with his wife, Reine Marie, in the peaceful village of Three Pines. Readers soon find however that he has been convinced to return to the workforce, taking command of the Sûreté

Academy, the school that prepares new cadets to join the police force. Mysteries abound in this well-constructed complex novel, but at its core there are two: What is the origin and purpose of a WWI-era map found walled up in the Three Pines bistro, and who is responsible for the dead body discovered at the Academy?

As with Penny's previous books, A Great Reckoning is liberally sprinkled with red herrings, eccentric characters and the occasional dose of humor. Fans will be pleased that the residents of Three Pines whom they have come to know and love over the years are well-represented, playing a large role throughout. There are a lot of mystery series out there, but what has always made this one stand out are its recurring characters, utterly unique and yet familiar: bistro owners Olivier and Gabri; artist Clara Morrow; bookstore owner Myrna Landers; and of course the irascible poet Ruth Zardo and her duck Rosa. Long-time series readers encounter them as one might an old friend. In addition, setting the mystery in part at the Academy allows the introduction of several new equally intriguing players, which provides an opportunity to grow the series in future books.

The Great Reckoning is a perfect balance of old and new. This novel however, is not a good entry point to the series, which is worth getting into from the very first book, <u>Still Life</u>. Much of the plot here revolves around actions and events that occurred in earlier volumes, and without that background, most readers will likely feel they've missed something important. Gamache's decisions, too, only make sense in context, and those new to the series will lack that point of reference. I also think readers who haven't started from the first book might miss or misinterpret a lot of the subtle (and not-so-subtle) interactions between the characters. Their personalities are a large part of the author's success, and encountering them for the first time here may lead to misconceptions.

Readers who have kept up with the series, however, are in for a real treat. The novel is every bit as entertaining as Penny's previous works. The writing is lush and descriptive, creating beautiful scenes in exquisite detail.

The flurries had stopped in the night, leaving just a thin layer barely covering the dead autumn leaves. It seemed a netherworld. Neither fall nor winter. The hills that surrounded the village and seemed to guard it from an often hostile world themselves looked hostile. Or, if not actually hostile, at least inhospitable. It was a forest of skeletons. Their branches, gray and bare, were raised as though begging for a mercy they knew would not be granted.

The author's emphasis on quality writing and character development necessitates more setup on the front end of the narrative. The action doesn't get rolling until perhaps a third of the way in. These sections are so well written that the book never drags – I advise readers to set aside uninterrupted time to read the last 50 pages, as they likely wouldn't want to be disturbed as the book speeds to its conclusion.

Three Pines itself has always seemed somewhat of a throwback — a preternaturally quiet place isolated in time and space. In some respects the plot enforces this feeling; Three Pines doesn't have Internet access, it's a long, confusing drive to get there and it isn't registered on any map of Canada, making it appear almost mythical. Nevertheless, Penny goes out of her way to make the story relevant, addressing issues such as racism and gun control that strongly echo current social discussions. There are at least five different mysteries of varied seriousness embedded in the book (at the lowest tier: what is that little creature Reine Marie rescues and subsequently adopts?). While the major whodunit is exceptionally satisfying, I found one of the other plot lines less so.

Penny might just be my favorite mystery writer, and *A Great Reckoning* is certain to become a favorite entry in the series; it's highly recommended to those who've read the previous novels.

Reviewed by Kim Kovacs. This review was originally published in *The BookBrowse Review* in September 2016, and has been updated for the May 2017 edition.

HOMEGOING

by Yaa Gyasi

BookBrowse Rating: 5/5
Critics' Consensus: 4.5/5
Readers' Rating: 5/5

Published May 2017 in Paperback, 320 pages

Summary

Winner of the 2016 BookBrowse Debut Author Award

A novel of breathtaking sweep and emotional power that traces three hundred years in Ghana and along the way also becomes a truly great American novel. Extraordinary for its exquisite language, its implacable sorrow, its soaring beauty, and for its monumental portrait of the forces that shape families and nations, *Homegoing* heralds the arrival of a major new voice in contemporary fiction.

Two half-sisters, Effia and Esi, are born into different villages in eighteenth-century Ghana. Effia is married off to an Englishman and lives in comfort in the palatial rooms of Cape Coast Castle. Unbeknownst to Effia, her sister, Esi, is imprisoned beneath her in the castle's dungeons, sold with thousands of others into the Gold Coast's booming slave trade, and shipped off to America, where her children and grandchildren will be raised in slavery. One thread of *Homegoing* follows Effia's descendants through centuries of warfare in Ghana, as the Fante and Asante nations wrestle with the slave trade and British colonization. The other thread follows Esi and her children into America. From the plantations of the South to the Civil War and the Great Migration, from the coal mines of Pratt City, Alabama, to the jazz clubs and dope houses of twentieth-century Harlem, right up through the present day, *Homegoing* makes history visceral, and captures, with singular and stunning immediacy, how the memory of captivity came to be inscribed in the soul of a nation.

Generation after generation, Yaa Gyasi's magisterial first novel sets the fate of the individual against the obliterating movements of time, delivering unforgettable characters whose lives were shaped by historical forces beyond their control. *Homegoing* is a tremendous reading experience, not to be missed, by an astonishingly gifted young writer.

BookBrowse Review

A novel of breathtaking sweep and emotional power that traces three hundred years in Ghana.

It's all very well to challenge people to be the masters of their own destiny, but when you're a woman in 18th-century Ghana, your birth and beauty and tribe pretty much proscribe you from indulging in such flights of fantasy. So it is that just as the young and stunning Effia Otcher from the Fanteland region is promised in marriage to a white slave trader James Collins, a match that ensures the consolidation of her family's socioeconomic status, her half-sister Esi, belonging to another tribe, is swept up in the country's booming slave trade.

This roll of the dice, beyond either's control, will have the two siblings living their lives under entirely different circumstances and on two different continents. In a series of tightly knit chapters, *Homegoing* chronicles each sibling's descendants over seven generations as their paths diverge and interweave in surprising ways. Effia soaks in relative affluence and her immediate family members become key power brokers in the Gold Coast slave trade, even as later relatives want to have little to do with this stain of history. While bound in chains, Esi makes her way to the Deep South in America as a slave, a fate that will dog her family, shaping it with centuries of dark history.

Yaa Gyasi, herself a Ghanaian native brought up in Alabama, knows a thing or two about how the past casts a looming shadow over the present. "This is the problem of history," she writes. "We cannot know that which we were not there to see and hear and experience for ourselves. We must rely upon the words of others...whose story do we believe?" History, as *Homegoing* shows, is a living, breathing, fragile thing exerting its influence and marking its presence in small but readily recognizable ways. The Jim Crow South, the Great Migration, the civil rights movement of the '60s in America and the Ashanti nation's geopolitical machinations with the British (see [Beyond the Book](#)) all play out here, but the characters are always central to the narrative. It is this focus that makes for strikingly realistic fiction — the kind that works large scale events into the quotidian details of the everyday lives of people. When Kojo, a descendant of Esi, walks up to the seafront in Baltimore during the onset of the Great Migration, for example, he finds that what once used to be a sea of black faces had "turned into nothing" and knows that he too must travel North.

To capture two continents' history over three centuries is no easy feat, and Gyasi pulls it off by assigning each generation (and therefore, each character) the responsibilities of that time's corresponding historical arc and narrative. Every chapter is deliberately and carefully tailored to move the clock forward. There are times when this method — of creating panorama by cobbling together a whole series of short vignettes — feels much too tidy and convenient a ruse. Gyasi's crisp stories are sometimes wound a little *too* tight, one wishes for a little slack in the reel, to linger and learn more about the characters than what their carefully crafted roles allow them room for. The sheer number of players is also occasionally daunting; the family chart included at the beginning proves to be a necessary and handy guide.

Nevertheless this marvelous debut succeeds in creating an impressive sweep by the sheer dint of powerful writing and narrative scope. "In my village we have a saying about separated sisters," Esi's mom tells her. "They are like a woman and her reflection, doomed to stay on opposite sides of the pond." An ambitious saga that moves back and forth across these "opposite sides of the pond" and weaves a rich and colorful tapestry, *Homegoing* is an emotionally resonant debut that hints at great things yet to come from an immensely talented storyteller.

Reviewed by Poornima Apte. This review was originally published in *The BookBrowse Review* in June 2016, and has been updated for the May 2017 edition.

EVICTED

by Matthew Desmond

BookBrowse Rating: 5/5
Critics' Consensus: 5/5
Readers' Rating: 4/5

Published February 2017 in Paperback, 448 pages

Summary

From Harvard sociologist Matthew Desmond, a landmark work of scholarship and reportage that will forever change the way we look at poverty in America

In this brilliant, heartbreaking book, Matthew Desmond takes us into the poorest neighborhoods of Milwaukee to tell the story of eight families on the edge. Arleen is a single mother trying to raise her two sons on the $20 a month she has left after paying for their rundown apartment. Scott is a gentle nurse consumed by a heroin addiction. Lamar, a man with no legs and a neighborhood full of boys to look after, tries to work his way out of debt. Vanetta participates in a botched stickup after her hours are cut. All are spending almost everything they have on rent, and all have fallen behind.

The fates of these families are in the hands of two landlords: Sherrena Tarver, a former schoolteacher turned inner-city entrepreneur, and Tobin Charney, who runs one of the worst trailer parks in Milwaukee. They loathe some of their tenants and are fond of others, but as Sherrena puts it, "Love don't pay the bills." She moves to evict Arleen and her boys a few days before Christmas.

Even in the most desolate areas of American cities, evictions used to be rare. But today, most poor renting families are spending more than half of their income on housing, and eviction has become ordinary, especially for single mothers. In vivid, intimate prose, Desmond provides a ground-level view of one of the most urgent issues facing America today. As we see families forced into shelters, squalid apartments, or more dangerous neighborhoods, we bear witness to the human cost of America's vast inequality—and to people's determination and intelligence in the face of hardship.

Based on years of embedded fieldwork and painstakingly gathered data, this masterful book transforms our understanding of extreme poverty and economic exploitation while providing fresh ideas for solving a devastating, uniquely American problem. Its unforgettable scenes of hope and loss remind us of the centrality of home, without which nothing else is possible.

BookBrowse Review

A landmark work that will change the way we look at poverty.

We routinely hear talk about the one percent and the growing divide between the rich and the poor, yet it is difficult to fathom just exactly what extreme poverty looks like or how it can manifest itself. This is exactly what Matthew Desmond, a MacArthur genius who is recognized for his work on the impact of eviction on the urban poor, helps us with so well. Poverty, Desmond argues, is not just about poor people, but also about the relationship between the rich and poor. "To understand poverty, I needed to understand that relationship," he writes in his book *Evicted: Poverty and Profit In the American City*. "This sent me searching for a process that bound poor and rich people together in mutual dependence and struggle. Eviction was such a process."

Through years of intensive work on the ground, Desmond's essential book tells an American story focusing on two landlords in Milwaukee, the fourth poorest city in the United States: Sherrena Tarver, a black schoolteacher turned inner-city businesswoman who owns a number of properties in the city's ghettos, and Tobin Charney, a white man, who owns a rundown trailer park. Among their many tenants who are constantly evicted or in danger of being thrown out are Arleen, a young black woman with two boys; Lamar, a black disabled man with two sons struggling to find a place of his own; Larraine, a white woman struggling to make rent with no job prospects, and Scott, a white gay drug addict who loses his nursing license.

By focusing on these eight people's everyday lives, Desmond shows us the complexities of poverty and eviction, a problem that cuts across racial lines. Desmond, who moved into the Tobin trailer park in 2008 for his work, steers clear of sensational or exploitative writing. These are nuanced portraits of people, painted with all their frailties and strengths. Desmond's light touch weaves in social commentary without much grandstanding. When Larraine, for example, spends the last of her money and food stamps on a lobster and crab dinner, Desmond brilliantly explains why: "the distance between grinding poverty and even stable poverty could be so vast that those at the bottom had little hope of climbing out even if they pinched every penny. So they chose not to. Instead, they tried to survive in color, to season the suffering with pleasure. They would get a little high or have a drink or do a bit of gambling or acquire a television. They might buy lobster on food stamps. If Larraine spent her money unwisely, it was not because her benefits left her with so much but because they left her with so little."

In a book filled with deeply moving images, one of the most touching is of a school-aged child, Ruby Hinkston, visiting a local library in Milwaukee and checking in on her "house" which she builds through a free online game called Millsberry, a marketing tool created by General Mills. Ruby's make-believe house had "clean, light-reflecting floors, a bed with sheets and pillowcases, and a desk for doing schoolwork." The tragedy implicit in Ruby's seemingly routine pastime is that the real house that her family rents from Sherrena was stunningly deplorable: it had a non-functioning toilet, a kitchen sink brimming with gray water and lined with a rust-orange film. The house got so bad that everyone became withdrawn and lethargic. We might ask why the Hinkstons just couldn't ask their landlord to fix at least the toilet and the kitchen sink. The answer? Money. They were told they already owed $2,494.50 in back rent and other payments, so asking for repairs would only invite more scrutiny. They were, in fact, prime targets for eviction.

Evicted switches back and forth between different sets of people, which sometimes makes it difficult to keep everyone's story straight. But a positive outcome of this technique is that the accounts end up sharing many common threads: the same desperation, the same hand-to-mouth existence, the same bargains struck to stay on.

Evicted is an unforgettable portrait of class divides which also shines light on how race skews the equation to even worse outcomes. For example, some properties are designated "nuisance" when an excessive number of 911 calls issue from them – the onus falls on the landlord to clear things up. "In white neighborhoods, only 1 in 41 properties that could have received a nuisance citation did receive one," Desmond points out. In black neighborhoods, that number was 1 in 16. African American women, afraid of inviting landlords' wrath because of 911 calls they place, often suffered abuse silently as a result. *Evicted* is also impressive in its portrayal of the landlords as pragmatic people who are trying to make money while keeping a stable roster of tenants. Sherrena, for example, is not an evil person; she often makes concessions until events force her hand.

Desmond's important book might set out practical prescriptions for solutions such as improving the size of the housing voucher program (See Beyond the Book), but the deeply touching portraits are what really make *Evicted* the heavyweight that it is. It should be mandatory reading for everyone, especially politicians and others who walk the corridors of power. That such bruising poverty can exist in the world's richest country is a scathing indictment of our regulatory policies.

At one point in the narrative, a frustrated tenant, bemoaning her situation, breaks down and screams: "This is America! This is *America*!" Damn right. It is.

Reviewed by Poornima Apte. This review was originally published in *The BookBrowse Review* in March 2016, and has been updated for the March 2017 edition.

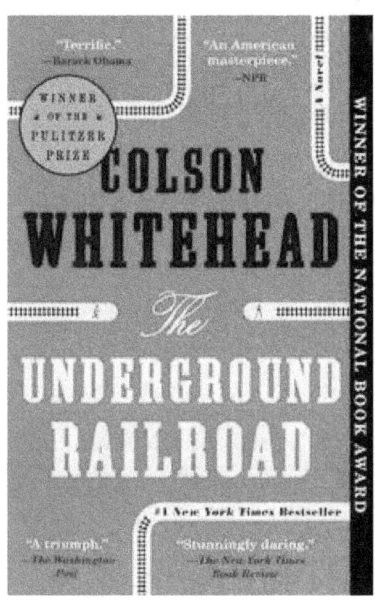

THE UNDERGROUND RAILROAD

by Colson Whitehead

BookBrowse Rating: 5/5
Critics' Consensus: 5/5
Readers' Rating: 4.5/5

Published January 2016 in Paperback, 336 pages

Summary

From prize-winning, bestselling author Colson Whitehead, a magnificent tour de force chronicling a young slave's adventures as she makes a desperate bid for freedom in the antebellum South

Cora is a slave on a cotton plantation in Georgia. Life is hell for all the slaves, but especially bad for Cora; an outcast even among her fellow Africans, she is coming into womanhood—where even greater pain awaits. When Caesar, a recent arrival from Virginia, tells her about the Underground Railroad, they decide to take a terrifying risk and escape. Matters do not go as planned—Cora kills a young white boy who tries to capture her. Though they manage to find a station and head north, they are being hunted.

In Whitehead's ingenious conception, the Underground Railroad is no mere metaphor—engineers and conductors operate a secret network of tracks and tunnels beneath the Southern soil. Cora and Caesar's first stop is South Carolina, in a city that initially seems like a haven. But the city's placid surface masks an insidious scheme designed for its black denizens. And even worse: Ridgeway, the relentless slave catcher, is close on their heels. Forced to flee again, Cora embarks on a harrowing flight, state by state, seeking true freedom.

Like the protagonist of *Gulliver's Travels,* Cora encounters different worlds at each stage of her journey—hers is an odyssey through time as well as space. As Whitehead brilliantly re-creates the unique terrors for black people in the pre–Civil War era, his narrative seamlessly weaves the saga of America from the brutal importation of Africans to the unfulfilled promises of the present day. *The Underground Railroad* is at once a kinetic adventure tale of one woman's ferocious will to escape the horrors of bondage and a shattering, powerful meditation on the history we all share.

BookBrowse Review

A young slave makes a desperate bid for freedom in the antebellum South.

Even when he's writing about zombies (like in Zone One) or poker (like in The Noble Hustle), Colson Whitehead demonstrates stunning intellectual and linguistic dexterity, often making unexpected connections and bridging gaps which cause readers to look, with fresh eyes, at things they might have thought they already knew everything about. The buzz for his new novel, The Underground Railroad, was already intense after fans learned that it would be a sort of alternative history of slavery in America; a return to the kind of social observation and rich historical reimagining that first gained him critical acclaim in books like John Henry Days and The Intuitionist. And then Oprah Winfrey chose The Underground Railroad to relaunch her book club – and it's no exaggeration to say that Colson Whitehead's novel has become one of the most talked about books of the year.

The Underground Railroad centers on Cora, a third-generation slave on a Georgia cotton plantation. Cora's only possession (in a manner of speaking), the one thing in the world she prizes above all else, is a small patch of land that her grandmother and then her mother Mabel also guarded and defended, carving out a small garden plot and nurturing what grew there. The yams from the plot, Cora believes, nourished Mabel during her successful escape from the Randall plantation when Cora was just a small child.

As the novel opens, Cora, who is still a very young woman, is offered the opportunity to escape. Another slave, Caesar, has learned that a new spur of the underground railroad - in Whitehead's world it is an actual railroad with tracks and trains - has been extended as far south as Georgia. A sympathetic white man has offered to help Caesar escape, and he wants to bring Cora – the legendary Mabel's daughter – along "for luck." At first, Cora declines, but after conditions on the plantation continue to deteriorate, she reluctantly agrees to accompany Caesar, filling her bag – as her mother did before her – with every last vegetable from her plot.

What follows is a journey both harrowing and exhilarating, as Cora travels through South and North Carolina, and as far away as Tennessee and Indiana. In nearly every place, she experiences both kindness and betrayal, fragile hope and staggering loss – and, of course, danger at every turn, right up to the final page.

Whitehead's novel is the best kind of historical fiction, one that prompts the reader to draw vital connections between past and present. It is suffused with real, true history, the history of slavery and its aftermath, whose painful and horrific stories are essential for modern-day readers to continue to confront. But it also is an alternative history, one in which an entire state bans black people on penalty of death while its neighboring state affords (on the surface anyway) more egalitarian options. And, of course, there's the physical underground railroad itself, which is, in Whitehead's telling, running on unpredictable schedules and routes through tunnels built by mysterious hands. "Look outside as you speed through," the conductor tells Cora before she embarks on her first voyage, "and you'll find the true face of America." Is that "face" the varied landscapes and social experiments she finds herself traveling through, Cora wonders much later, or is it the pure darkness of the tunnel walls? That question is left up to readers to interpret, as are the novel's numerous reflections on the ugly truths of slavery, racial tensions, and nation-building, many of which still resonate today.

Near the end of the novel, one character offers Cora perhaps the most hopeful statement in the book, adopting the outlook that whites and blacks hold the keys to create and define their own future in this young, newly forming nation: "We are Africans in America," he tells her. "Something new in the history of the world, without models for what we will become…All I truly know is that we rise and fall as one, one colored family living next door to one white family. We may not know the way through the forest, but we can pick each other up when we fall, and we will arrive together." This ultimately optimistic vision for what America could become is, of course, palpably bittersweet for modern-day Americans to read. Reading The Underground Railroad offers plenty of reminders of just how far our nation has come since these darkest years in our history, but also countless reminders of just how far we have yet to travel before we arrive at any destination resembling that hopeful vision.

Reviewed by Norah Piehl. This review was originally published in *The BookBrowse Review* in September 2016, and has been updated for the February 2018 edition.

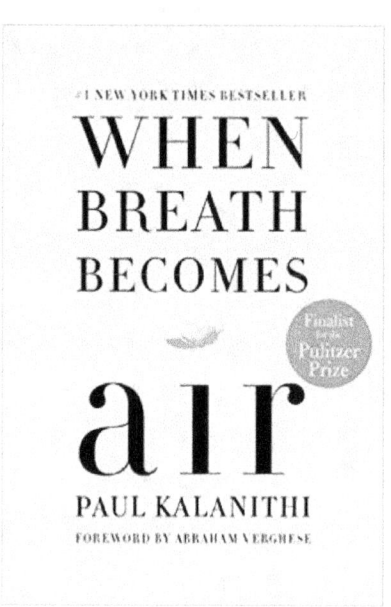

WHEN BREATH BECOMES AIR

by Paul Kalanithi

BookBrowse Rating: 5/5
Critics' Consensus: 5/5
Readers' Rating: 4.5/5

Published January 2016 in Hardcover, 256 pages

Summary

Winner of the 2016 BookBrowse Nonfiction Award

For readers of Atul Gawande, Andrew Solomon, and Anne Lamott, a profoundly moving, exquisitely observed memoir by a young neurosurgeon faced with a terminal cancer diagnosis who attempts to answer the question *What makes a life worth living?*

At the age of thirty-six, on the verge of completing a decade's worth of training as a neurosurgeon, Paul Kalanithi was diagnosed with stage IV lung cancer. One day he was a doctor treating the dying, and the next he was a patient struggling to live. And just like that, the future he and his wife had imagined evaporated. *When Breath Becomes Air* chronicles Kalanithi's transformation from a naïve medical student "possessed," as he wrote, "by the question of what, given that all organisms die, makes a virtuous and meaningful life" into a neurosurgeon at Stanford working in the brain, the most critical place for human identity, and finally into a patient and new father confronting his own mortality.

What makes life worth living in the face of death? What do you do when the future, no longer a ladder toward your goals in life, flattens out into a perpetual present? What does it mean to have a child, to nurture a new life as another fades away? These are some of the questions Kalanithi wrestles with in this profoundly moving, exquisitely observed memoir.

Paul Kalanithi died in March 2015, while working on this book, yet his words live on as a guide and a gift to us all. "I began to realize that coming face to face with my own mortality, in a sense, had changed nothing and everything," he wrote. "Seven words from Samuel Beckett began to repeat in my head: 'I can't go on. I'll go on.'" *When Breath Becomes Air* is an unforgettable, life-affirming reflection on the challenge of facing death and on the relationship between doctor and patient, from a brilliant writer who became both.

BookBrowse Review

Winner of the 2016 BookBrowse Nonfiction Award

When Breath Becomes Air is the autobiography of Paul Kalanithi, written in the time period between his being diagnosed with cancer and his death from the disease twenty-two months later at the age of 37.

Kalanithi's career was about to take off in 2013 as he was finishing his residency in neurological surgery and completing a postdoctoral fellowship in neuroscience at Stanford. His future seemed very bright, the possibilities endless. His resume was impressive: he had graduated from Stanford with degrees in English literature and human biology; earned a Master of Philosophy in history and philosophy of science and medicine from Cambridge, and graduated cum laude from the Yale School of Medicine. Tragically, Kalanathi's prospects were completely derailed when he began to have health issues, particularly excruciating back pain that was so bad he could barely stay upright for long periods of time. He began to suspect that he had cancer but delayed having his diagnosis confirmed until it could wait no longer. One look at his CT scan and he knew: he had metastatic lung cancer, for which there was no cure.

Kalanithi always loved the written word and hoped to write – later in his life, when his medical career was winding down. Realizing he was dying, he began penning his personal story in the hours after completing his surgeries. The book begins with his childhood in Arizona and progresses through his decision to switch from literature to science, eventually pursuing neurosurgery. Underlying the bare biographical narrative is the author's incredible curiosity about the meaning of life. "Where did biology, morality, literature, and philosophy intersect?" he ponders. As the book progresses, it becomes more philosophical, searching for what it takes for people to find significance in their existence as it becomes apparent their time is finite.

The writing can at times be a little clinical and abstruse as Kalanithi dips into metaphysical questions (e.g., if science provides no basis for God, does it logically follow that life has no meaning?). For the most part, the account is highly personal and moving, particularly as Kalanithi becomes increasingly ill:

> Time for me is now double-edged: every day brings me further from the low of my last relapse but closer to the next recurrence – and, eventually, death. Perhaps later than I think, but certainly sooner than I desire. There are, I imagine, two responses to that realization. The most obvious might be an impulse to frantic activity: to "live life to its fullest," to travel, to dine, to achieve a host of neglected ambitions. Part of the cruelty of cancer, though, is not only that it limits your time; it also limits your energy, vastly reducing the amount you can squeeze into a day. It is a tired hare who now races. And even if I had the energy, I prefer a more tortoise-like approach. I plod, I ponder. Some days, I simply persist.

In the book's afterword, Kalanithi's wife Lucy writes: "What happened to Paul was tragic, but he was not a tragedy" – and the narrative bears that out. The prose is contemplative but its tone isn't elegiac. At the conclusion I did feel a sense of sorrow at the loss of so talented a person, but more than that I found myself marveling at the author's courage and his willingness to share his experiences and thoughts. It also kept me thinking about my own transience. The book will certainly stay with readers for a long time, perhaps even change them permanently.

Lucy also explains why her husband chose to spend his last days writing *When Breath Becomes Air*:

> He wanted to help people understand death and face their mortality. Dying in one's fourth decade is unusual now, but dying is not. "The [thing about] lung cancer is that it's not exotic," Paul wrote in an email to his best friend, Robin. "It's just tragic enough and imaginable enough. [The reader] can get into these shoes, walk a bit, and say, 'So that's what it looks like from here… sooner or later I'll be back here in my own shoes.' That's what I'm aiming for, I think. Not the sensationalism of dying, and not the exhortations to gather rosebuds, but: Here's what lies up ahead on the road."

Mission accomplished.

Reviewed by Kim Kovacs. This review was originally published in *The BookBrowse Review* in February 2016, and has been updated for the December 2016 edition.

BEST BOOKS OF 2015

GOODBYE STRANGER

by Rebecca Stead

BookBrowse Rating: 5/5
Critics' Consensus: 5/5
Readers' Rating: 5/5

Published May 2017 in Paperback, 304 pages

Summary

Winner of the 2015 BookBrowse Award for Best Young Adult Novel

This brilliant novel by Newbery Medal winner Rebecca Stead explores multiple perspectives on the bonds and limits of friendship.

Bridge is an accident survivor who's wondering why she's still alive. Emily has new curves and an almost-boyfriend who wants a certain kind of picture. Tabitha sees through everybody's games - or so she tells the world. The three girls are best friends with one rule: No fighting. Can it get them through seventh grade?

This year everything is different for Sherm Russo as he gets to know Bridge Barsamian. What does it mean to fall for a girl—as a friend?

On Valentine's Day, an unnamed high school girl struggles with a betrayal. How long can she hide in plain sight?

Each memorable character navigates the challenges of love and change in this captivating novel.

BookBrowse Review

Multiple middle school perspectives on love, friendship and change all leading up to Valentine's day.

Winner of the 2015 BookBrowse Award for Best Young Adult Novel

Middle school is nothing if not a time of changes. Weirdly changing bodies, quickly changing interests, and, of course, friendships that can change – or disappear or self-destruct – at the drop of a hat. Rebecca Stead generously and thoughtfully addresses all these changes in *Goodbye Stranger*.

Most of the novel is told from the point of view of Bridge Barsamian, a seventh-grader who asks herself every day why she's alive. Not out of some abstract existentialist impulse, though, but because she is genuinely lucky to be alive after being hit by a car five years earlier. At times, a busy street, a honking horn, or even a tough decision can still paralyze Bridge with fear and flashbacks. What's saved her is the support and love of her best friends, Emily and Tabitha (Tab for short). Long ago they made a pact never to fight, and they've stuck to it.

But as their seventh grade year starts, all those changes start to creep up on them. Emily's newly developed body is attracting a lot of attention, from an eighth grade boy in particular, who wants Emily to text him some revealing photos. Tab is embracing feminism by way of a human rights club she's joined (and seems to have a little bit of a crush on her club's activist advisor). Sometimes Bridge feels like she's being left behind. But when she meets a boy, Sherman, who makes her laugh and think and talk about things she's never shared with anyone, she wonders: Is it ok to just want to be friends and not introduce one more scary change into her life?

Chapters told in the third person, primarily by Bridge and Sherm, alternate with chapters narrated in the second person by a slightly older girl who is unnamed for most of the novel. Her chapters take place on Valentine's Day, and the other narrative leads up to that day, too – but how are the two stories connected? Some savvy readers will figure out the identity of the unnamed narrator quite early, while others may be initially frustrated by the disorienting chapters, wondering what they're doing there. But readers who are familiar with Stead's approach to story writing from her previous novels such as the Newbery Medal–winning *When You Reach Me* will know enough to just sit back, relax, and let the story run its satisfying course, as the two narratives gradually merge and illustrate that even older kids don't always have all these questions figured out.

Goodbye Stranger, in its Manhattan setting, has a cast of characters whose diversity feels unforced and natural. As in her previous novels, Stead also depicts family relationships that, while realistically imperfect, serve as genuine sources of support and comfort for kids in the midst of their own questioning. She addresses issues such as sexting and cyberbullying in ways that are completely age-appropriate for her audience and that never threaten to eclipse storytelling with preaching. Stead also writes convincingly from the points of view of both male and female characters – Bridge and Sherm share a vulnerability, introspection, and kindness that will win over all kinds of readers. *Goodbye Stranger* is a winsome, at times outright funny book that also offers serious messages about loyalty, independence, and the preciousness of friendships new and old.

Reviewed by Norah Piehl. This review was originally published in *The BookBrowse Review* in September 2015, and has been updated for the May 2017 edition.

THE NIGHTINGALE

by Kristin Hannah

BookBrowse Rating: 5/5
Critics' Consensus: 4.5/5
Readers' Rating: 5/5

Published April 2017 in Paperback, 592 pages

Summary

Winner of the 2015 BookBrowse Fiction Award

Vivid and exquisite in its illumination of a time and place that was filled with great monstrosities, but also great humanity and strength, a novel that will have readers talking long after they turn the last page.

From the #1 New York Times bestselling author comes an epic novel of love and war, spanning from the 1940s to the present day, and the secret lives of those who live in a small French town.

Viann and Isabelle have always been close despite their differences. Younger, bolder sister Isabelle lives in Paris while Viann lives a quiet and content life in the French countryside with her husband Antoine and their daughter. When World War II strikes and Antoine is sent off to fight, Viann and Isabelle's father sends Isabelle to help her older sister cope. As the war progresses, it's not only the sisters' relationship that is tested, but also their strength and their individual senses of right and wrong. With life as they know it changing in unbelievably horrific ways, Viann and Isabelle will find themselves facing frightening situations and responding in ways they never thought possible as bravery and resistance take different forms in each of their actions.

Vivid and exquisite in its illumination of a time and place that was filled with great monstrosities, but also great humanity and strength, Kristin Hannah's novel will provoke thought and discussion that will have readers talking long after they turn the last page.

BookBrowse Review

The Nightingale **captures the epic panorama of WWII and illuminates an intimate part of history seldom seen: the women's war.**

Winner of the 2015 BookBrowse Fiction Award

BookBrowse readers were challenged and moved by Kristin Hannah's unique World War II novel, *The Nightingale*. Each and every one of our member reviewers rated it 4 or a 5 stars.

What makes the story of two sisters in Occupied France so different from other World War II novels? Why did our reviewers feel so connected to it?

Kristin Hannah has reached a new level with this strong and enduring cast of characters and themes. I would challenge anyone to read *The Nightingale* and not feel deeply moved by its message. I felt proud of these women, struggling to survive in times of war and wondered what I would do to save my family, my freedoms and all that I hold dear. Beyond that question looms another: "Do I have that deep core of bravery so desperately needed in the darkest of hours?" Relevant today and always, this story will stay with me a long time. It has my strongest recommendation (Virginia W). *The Nightingale* is easily the best book I have read in a very long time. I became a woman in occupied France and steeled myself as each new horrible circumstance confronted me (Nancy L). This is a story of love and sacrifice during the horror of the German occupation of France. It is a story of love - particular of family - and how sad and beautiful it can be (Marjorie W). This is a very special book! (Cam G)

Our readers felt that Kristin Hannah's focus on women during World War II was unique:

The Nightingale is about two sisters who lived in France during World War II, and weaves back and forth through time, with most of the emphasis in the '40s during the war. I have read many World War II books but few that place special emphasis on the heroism and courage of women fighting the war in their own ways (Colleen L). Kristin Hannah is known for her contemporary fiction so I was blown away by this meticulously researched work of historical fiction set in France during WWII. It speaks to the strengths of women who were willing to put their lives on the line because it was the right thing to do (Lisa G). Hold the phone, cancel appointments and have some tissues handy for a well-researched novel of the very disturbing years of Nazi occupied France. It is not only about the occupation, but about the brave women who risked their lives and lives of their families to save strangers (Kathy G).

And her take on the Holocaust novel genre is unique as well:

I was skeptical that *The Nightingale* was yet another novel about the Holocaust, but do yourself a favor and read this one. The characters are so richly developed that the reader can't help but keep turning the pages! (Diane

D) A wonderfully told story, totally engaging - and the saddest part is that even if it is fiction, we know too well the awful truth of what happened, and that the author has embedded that truth in this novel (Arden A). Hannah was particularly good at introducing lesser known historical events from World War II: the exodus from Paris, the Vichy collaboration with the Nazi's, the betrayal of the Parisians by the French Police, the events at the Velodrome d'Hiver (see "beyond the book"), retaliation against French resistance, and the dangers of the Pyrenees escape routes (Sherilyn R).

Our readers found the story to be relevant to today:

In these days of beheadings and innocents caught up in war zones, this is an essential book to read. Kristen Hannah's *The Nightingale* transcends the pages of historical fiction and poses the question, "When evil is everywhere around you, what would you do?" (Gwen C) A well-written book that helps us remember this period of history and all the extremes people went through. It is important to remember the contributions of the women of that time. Reflecting on my life makes me realize how much I have taken for granted (Sandra C). A thank you to Kristin Hannah for this awesome book written not a moment too soon - as so few people who will recognize the truth in it are left. May this story keep their experiences alive even longer. Memories matter. Love lasts. We remain. What a brilliant message (Lesley F).

And they wholeheartedly recommend *The Nightingale*:

I would heartily recommend this novel to anyone who loves historical fiction. It is well-researched and presents a solid look at the French Resistance (Colleen L). I recommend this book to lovers of historical fiction and to others who enjoy a book that promises to captivate! (Frances B) I have read many books about World War II - fiction and non-fiction - but never anything like this. The sense of place, the relationships between the women, their children and the German soldiers in the town make this a story you will remember for a long time. I recommend it for a different perspective on the toll of war (Eve A). I recommend *The Nightingale* if you like sister stories, France, romance and history (Barbara Z). Everyone – everyone – needs to read this book, to get into the parts of the characters, and try to feel just an iota of what they felt during this time in their lives (Annie P).

Reviewed by First Impressions Reviewers. This review was originally published in *The BookBrowse Review* in February 2015, and has been updated for the May 2017 edition.

THE TIGHTROPE WALKERS

by David Almond

BookBrowse Rating: 5/5
Critics' Consensus: 5/5

Published November 2016 in Paperback, 336 pages

Summary

In a raw and beautifully crafted bildungsroman, David Almond reveals the rich inner world of a boy teetering on the edge of manhood.

A gentle visionary coming of age in the shadow of the shipyards of northern England, Dominic Hall is torn between extremes. On the one hand, he craves the freedom he feels when he steals away with the eccentric girl artist next door, Holly Stroud - his first and abiding love - to balance above the earth on a makeshift tightrope. With Holly, Dom dreams of a life different in every way from his shipbuilder dad's, a life fashioned of words and images and story. On the other hand, he finds himself irresistibly drawn to the brutal charms of Vincent McAlinden, a complex bully who awakens something wild and reckless and killing in Dom.

In a raw and beautifully crafted bildungsroman, David Almond reveals the rich inner world of a boy teetering on the edge of manhood, a boy so curious and open to impulse that we fear for him and question his balance - and ultimately exult in his triumphs.

BookBrowse Review

A moving coming-of-age novel that draws on memories of David Almond's early years in Tyneside.

David Almond has crafted just about the finest young fictional character I have ever seen. From the moment Dominic (Dom) Hall introduces himself he is so likable and relatable that I immediately cared what happened to him. He's not perfect. He's often confused. Sometimes he is badly behaved, shockingly so. But he has heart. And as he narrates his story, his humanity is so winning that I couldn't help but want to know that he ends up okay.

Dom is the only child of a laborer who works in the shipyards on the River Tyne, northern England. Born just after World War II, he lives with his mam and dad in cheap, lower-class housing. It's the mid-20th century though and things are changing. Laborers and their children have a vastly improved opportunity to advance in life. So even though Dom's best friend Holly Stroud lives in an identical house across the narrow street, her father has a white-collar job as a ship draughtsman. Holly and Dom play together, attend the same Catholic school and share their dreams. They also share a nemesis, Vincent McAlinden, class bully.

Right from the get-go McAlinden is a stinker and troublemaker. He lobs a sharp rock at five-year-old Dom and cuts the boy's head. Dom calls it McAlinden's mark. There will be more as the kids grow and Vincent careens in and out of their lives. He's three years older and can't seem to keep from harassing them. While Dom's father doesn't necessarily approve of Vincent's bullying, he does wish his *bairn* was a tad tougher. "Seems to me there should be a bit more of that Vincent McAlinden in him, and a little bit less of that Holly bliddy Stroud."

See there? Almond has an awesome ear for the dialect of this northern England working class. But more on that later.

At the opening of *The Tightrope Walkers*, Dom is starting to struggle with his identity. He is not like Vincent, nor is he even remotely like his own father. You see, Dom loves to write. "I loved to copy the letters and make the shapes," he says, "to hear the sounds and the rhythms, to see the visions that my words made in my brain. The ship sails. The bird flies....to write, to be allowed to write words of my own, sentences of my own, tales of my own."

Holly is an artist; maybe more like her draughtsman father than Dom is like his. And so the two bond over their shared creative abilities - Dom spinning stories, Holly drawing pictures. And when the circus comes to town they are both awed and inspired by the tightrope walkers; *funambules*, Holly's father Bill uses the French word. They add this to their joint play, stretching a rope in Dom's backyard, enlisting their dads' help to put a sturdier rope – eventually a wire – in place. They practice; Holly getting more and more graceful, Dom with the Hall family body type not so graceful, but skilled nonetheless.

Then some subtle and not-so-subtle changes occur as the kids take on the heavy mantle of adolescence. Dom becomes confused, overwhelmed with ideas and wild notions he's never experienced, and he hangs out for a few dreadful months with Vincent. It's a period during which Vincent inflicts more marks on Dom – though this time not on his head but inside it. And

Holly fades into the background of Dom's life. There is heartbreak and there are hard times. It all unfolds so beautifully, punctuated by the rhythm and music of that dialect. Dom takes a temporary job at the shipyard and he writes about it:

> "I scribbled in my book. 'He's putting us in a b-book,' said Jakey." Norman, "leaned in close, shyly, afraid to be intrusive.... I touched his arm, pointed to his name, then showed him Jakey's and Silversleeve's. They shuffled closer, looked as well.
> "T-telt ye,' said Jakey.
> "ARE YEZ OOT?" [Shouted their boss]
> "'Bugger off,' I muttered.
> "I copied his words in capitals.... They watched....'AA SAID ARE YEZ OOT?' I wrote his words again. They watched."

As an American I am fascinated, and even a little mesmerized, by the beauty of this dialect. Between the *nowts* and the *owts* and the *oots* and the *bliddys*, there is such a lovely rhythm. Of course, while watching a BBC program I need captions because my ear can't keep up. But as Almond/Dom writes it, the dialect becomes almost its own character, or, most certainly, it gives great depth to the characters speaking it.

I truly loved this book, loved Dom and Holly and even Dom's dad who is so baffled that a son of his can write with such skill. But better than merely loving it, this is an especially good book; a well-written, great story, with fantastic characterization and important themes. I miss Dom already.

Reviewed by Donna Chavez. This review was originally published in *The BookBrowse Review* in April 2015, and has been updated for the November 2016 edition.

BULL MOUNTAIN

by Brian Panowich

BookBrowse Rating: 5/5
Critics' Consensus: 5/5
Readers' Rating: 5/5

Published June 2016 in Paperback, 320 pages

Summary

Winner of the 2015 BookBrowse Debut Author Award

From a remarkable new voice in Southern fiction, a multigenerational saga of crime, family, and vengeance.

Clayton Burroughs comes from a long line of outlaws. For generations, the Burroughs clan has made its home on Bull Mountain in North Georgia, running shine, pot, and meth over six state lines, virtually untouched by the rule of law. To distance himself from his family's criminal empire, Clayton took the job of sheriff in a neighboring community to keep what peace he can. But when a federal agent with the Bureau of Alcohol, Tobacco, and Firearms shows up at Clayton's office with a plan to shut down the mountain, his hidden agenda will pit brother against brother, test loyalties, and could lead Clayton down a path to self-destruction.

In a sweeping narrative spanning decades and told from alternating points of view, the novel brilliantly evokes the atmosphere of the mountain and its inhabitants: forbidding, loyal, gritty, and ruthless. A story of family - the lengths men will go to protect it, honor it, or in some cases destroy it - *Bull Mountain* is an incredibly assured debut that heralds a major new talent in fiction.

BookBrowse Review

This debut novel might be studded with plenty of gore but there's a strong story and evocative writing buried underneath it all.

Winner of the 2015 BookBrowse Debut Author Award

Brian Panowich's debut novel, *Bull Mountain*, follows three generations of small-time drug-runners as their enterprise begins to crumble around them.

Bull Mountain, an isolated peak in Georgia, is home to the Burroughs family — men who make their living selling illegal substances, first producing moonshine during the Prohibition, branching out to marijuana the following generation, and finally turning to meth production in the book's present. One scion of this clan, Clifford Burroughs, has turned his back on his criminal past and kin to become the county sheriff. Clifford is approached by ATF agent Simon Holly, who is aware of what the Burroughs family is up to and wants

Clifford to convince his lawless elder brother (the current head of the family) to help him go after a much larger operation. Clifford agrees, setting off a disastrous chain of violence that threatens to engulf the sheriff's family and friends as they're forced to take sides. As the plot follows his attempts to keep the situation contained, it also skips back in time to illustrate the characters of those involved and to help readers understand what brings each to their ultimate fate.

The story itself is utterly absorbing and enough of a reason to read the book, but as a bonus Panowich's writing is also exceptional, particularly for a genre in which action sequences typically take precedence over quality narrative. The author is equally adept at portraying scenes that can only be described as horrific as well as creating passages of great beauty:

> This early, the sky was a purple bruise. The churning chorus of frogs and crickets was beginning to transition into the scurry of vermin and birdsong – a woodland changing of the guard. On frigid mornings like this one, the fog banked low over the veins of kudzu like a cotton blanket, so thick you couldn't see your feet to walk through it. It always made [him] smile to know that the clouds everyone else looked up to see, he looked down on from the other side. He reckoned that must be how God felt.

In addition, Panowich is an expert at turning the perfect phrase — succinct but completely apt:

> Val was solid-muscled farm boy...He was also black as night, no stars. He looked like a mountain of Kentucky coal in a flannel shirt.
>
> Clayton's drinking wasn't a wildfire turning his life into a blazing inferno, it was a fine layer of rust slowly decaying and dissolving his marriage.
>
> The place used to be a symbol of her childhood, of summer, something dear. Now it was the burial ground of murderers and thieves. She was surprised that the lush grass and bright green moss around the pond wasn't rotting and brown, considering the amount of bad blood in the dirt.

The author strikingly conveys the simmering rage that resides just under the surface of most of his characters. It's ever-present, like a heartbeat or electrical current, bubbling away in the background and influencing every aspect of the plot, constantly threatening to erupt in violence with little or no warning. The tension is palpable and never lets up for a second, even during the relatively calm scenes.

The book won't appeal to everyone due to its exceptionally violent nature; it has a body count that rivals that of the best Shakespeare tragedies, and the deaths relayed are quite messy (think a Quentin Tarantino movie in novel form). Most of the women in the story are treated heinously, which many readers will find too upsetting to be able to enjoy the story.

The biggest challenge I had with *Bull Mountain* was that the time period changed from chapter to chapter, which made it difficult to follow at times. With most of the main characters having the last name "Burroughs," I had to make a conscious effort to remind myself which generation was the current focus. I'd normally consider this technique too confusing and consequently a weakness, but late in the book it became apparent that the story wouldn't have had the same impact if it had been laid out chronologically. It might have helped to have had more differentiation between the three generations of the Burroughs family patriarchs. I'm fairly sure the author wanted to demonstrate that each man was just like his father, but more variation in their characters might have gone a long way toward lessening the occasional confusion I felt as the book jumped around in time.

For me, *Bull Mountain* is an absolute winner; I haven't enjoyed a novel this much in years. Readers who can tolerate violent scenes will find a brilliant story and top-notch writing buried under the gore. Highly recommended.

Reviewed by Kim Kovacs. This review was originally published in *The BookBrowse Review* in September 2015, and has been updated for the July 2016 edition.

THE MARRIAGE OF OPPOSITES

by Alice Hoffman

BookBrowse Rating: 5/5
Critics' Consensus: 5/5
Readers' Rating: 5/5

Published June 2016 in Paperback, 384 pages

Summary

A forbidden love story set on the tropical island of St. Thomas, about the extraordinary woman who gave birth to painter Camille Pissarro - the Father of Impressionism.

From the *New York Times* bestselling author of *The Dovekeepers* and *The Museum of Extraordinary Things*: a forbidden love story set on the tropical island of St. Thomas about the extraordinary woman who gave birth to painter Camille Pissarro - the Father of Impressionism.

Growing up on idyllic St. Thomas in the early 1800s, Rachel dreams of life in faraway Paris. Rachel's mother, a pillar of their small refugee community of Jews who escaped the Inquisition, has never forgiven her daughter for being a difficult girl who refuses to live by the rules. Growing up, Rachel's salvation is their maid Adelle's belief in her strengths, and her deep, life-long friendship with Jestine, Adelle's daughter. But Rachel's life is not her own. She is married off to a widower with three children to save her father's business. When her husband dies suddenly and his handsome, much younger nephew, Frédérick, arrives from France to settle the estate, Rachel seizes her own life story, beginning a defiant, passionate love affair that sparks a scandal that affects all of her family, including her favorite son, who will become one of the greatest artists of France.

Building on the triumphs of *The Dovekeepers* and *The Museum of Extraordinary Things*, set in a world of almost unimaginable beauty, *The Marriage of Opposites* showcases the beloved, bestselling Alice Hoffman at the height of her considerable powers. Once forgotten to history, the marriage of Rachel and Frédérick is a story that is as unforgettable as it is remarkable.

BookBrowse Review

Veteran author Alice Hoffman's latest novel returns with some of her familiar themes — strong Jewish women, a touch of magical realism — applied to a tropical island setting.

Alice Hoffman's latest work, *The Marriage of Opposites*, is a historical fiction novel focusing on the life of Rachel Pomie Petit Pizzarro, the real-life mother of famed Impressionist painter Camille Pissaro. In a first-person account, Rachel relays her life on the small island of St. Thomas in the Virgin Islands during the 19th century. She talks about her hopes and desires, of her relationship with her family and with her best friend Jestine, and how she first obeys tradition – and later defies it. As the book progresses, the story transitions to that of her youngest son, Jacobo (who prefers his middle name, Camille) as he grows into an adult with many of the same yearnings his mother experienced in her youth - particularly the longing to break free from convention and expectation.

Hoffman builds the narrative around many of the elements readers have encountered in her previous works: a strong, independent female Jewish protagonist; the intersection and overlapping of the lives of the women in the community; secrets of paternity and love; and just a touch of magical realism. The novel has its basis in history — the bare-bones of Rachel's life were well documented through letters, particularly between her and Camille. The setting, however, differs radically from Hoffman's other novels; the author brings to life the beauty and color of the tropical world into which Rachel is born.

Without a lot of action, the novel is driven by complex and convincing relationships, and reading about the characters' cares and perceptions is quite involving. Much of the story is told in the first person, authentically relaying Rachel's interactions. The author's ability to convey Rachel's voice is a true highlight, particularly in the realistic way the character's tone ages. When we first meet her, Rachel is determined and willful and sees magic in the world around her, but by the novel's end she's become sadder, quieter, a bit more bitter toward life in general but considerably more appreciative of her family. Early on, she describes how she copes with her frustrations at being stuck on the small island:

> I spoke to the old ladies in the market and began to write down the small miracles common only in our country, For as long as I was trapped here, I would write down these stories, along with a list of the wondrous things I myself had seen...In our world there had been pirates with more than a dozen wives, parrots who could speak four languages, shells which opened to reveal pearls, birds as tall as men who danced for

each other in the marshes, turtles that came to lay their eggs on the beach in a single mysterious night. On these occasions I would wait in the twilight with Jestine, watching as the shoreline filled with these lumber creatures, all so intent on their mission on the worn path they always took that they didn't notice us among them. We were turtle-girls. If we had been inside of a story we would surely have grown shells and claws. In silence, we studied the beach through the falling dark.

Camille's narration, too, has a depth that draws readers completely into his world as he describes his youth and early adulthood. Although Camille relates how his interest in painting developed and the frustrations of convincing others that art is not only his passion but a valid career, the novel doesn't delve much into Pissarro's technique, influences or his ultimate role as an early and respected Impressionist. The story really is predominantly Rachel's and she takes over the narration later in the book.

The novel has long sections of text that shift to the third-person perspective. While this makes sense in some instances — for example the chapters in which the focus moves away from Rachel to record her future husband's arrival on St. Thomas — in others, the action remains primarily on one of the two main characters, so this narrative choice is puzzling. It placed more distance than was necessary from the characters and caused me to become less engaged; I'd gotten used to "hearing" their voices and actually missed them when reading the third-person parts of the book.

Nevertheless *The Marriage of Opposites* is another fine addition to Hoffman's oeuvre and will please fans and new readers alike. Historical fiction aficionados in particular will want to pick up a copy.

Reviewed by Kim Kovacs. This review was originally published in *The BookBrowse Review* in August 2015, and has been updated for the July 2016 edition.

CIRCLING THE SUN

by Paula McLain

BookBrowse Rating: 5/5
Critics' Consensus: 5/5
Readers' Rating: 5/5

Published May 2016 in Paperback, 400 pages

Summary

The extraordinary adventures of a woman before her time, the exhilaration of freedom and its cost, and the tenacity of the human spirit.

Paula McLain, author of the phenomenal bestseller *The Paris Wife*, now returns with her keenly anticipated new novel, transporting readers to colonial Kenya in the 1920s. *Circling the Sun* brings to life a fearless and captivating woman—Beryl Markham, a record-setting aviator caught up in a passionate love triangle with safari hunter Denys Finch Hatton and Karen Blixen, author of the classic memoir *Out of Africa*.

Brought to Kenya from England as a child and then abandoned by her mother, Beryl is raised by both her father and the native Kipsigis tribe who share his estate. Her unconventional upbringing transforms Beryl into a bold young woman with a fierce love of all things wild and an inherent understanding of nature's delicate balance. But even the wild child must grow up, and when everything Beryl knows and trusts dissolves, she is catapulted into a string of disastrous relationships.

Beryl forges her own path as a horse trainer, and her uncommon style attracts the eye of the Happy Valley set, a decadent, bohemian community of European expats who live and love by their own set of rules. But it's the ruggedly charismatic Denys Finch Hatton who ultimately helps Beryl navigate the uncharted territory of her own heart. The intensity of their love reveals Beryl's truest self and her fate: to fly.

Set against the majestic landscape of early-twentieth-century Africa, McLain's powerful tale reveals the extraordinary adventures of a woman before her time, the exhilaration of freedom and its cost, and the tenacity of the human spirit.

BookBrowse Review

Set against the majestic landscape of early-twentieth-century Africa, McLain's powerful tale brings Beryl Markham to life.

Paula McClain's *Circling the Sun* is a dynamic portrait of Beryl Markham (see Beyond the Book), a woman true to her nature and ahead of her time. Twenty-three of 24 reviewers gave this riveting historical fiction a 4 or 5.

What are our readers saying about this adventurous tale?

Having read and enjoyed *The Paris Wife*, I was anxious to read Paula McLain's book on Beryl Markham. It did not disappoint! McLain captured Beryl the woman who interacted with her peers, family and royalty in foreign lands as we can hardly imagine. The trip was exciting. We were there through all the record-setting exploits and achievements and day-to-day life of a remarkable woman (Alyce T). Paula McLain has done it again, crafting a dynamic fictional account of an historical woman. From the very beginning of Beryl Markham's story of her childhood years in Africa, I was hooked (Nancy L). I read it straight through (Lesley F). The writing is flawless – reading this literature is like holding a strand of pearls in your hand – silky smooth and warm (Hazel R). I fancied Beryl as "the sun." Her life evolved, and thus rotated around herself, her friends and her loves (D.J. K). Success and scandal – it's all here in this portrayal of a woman who "charged headlong into the world even – or especially – when it hurt to do so." (Sue Ellen S)

Readers felt like they got an excellent glimpse of early 20th century Kenya, especially the dynamics between Africans and Europeans:

In the novel we get to hear the voice of Markham, meet her friends, understand the African-English society of the time, learn the difficulties of sustaining a living in Africa, and see the beauty of the continent (Barbara H). I found the portrayal of life in 1920s Kenya to be fascinating, especially the vast divide between the European settlers and the indigenous people (Nancy L). I found many surprises in Paula McLain's newest book, *Circling the Sun*. Not only did I learn of an exceptional, pioneering, adventurous woman, but I was able to make many comparisons to the expat lifestyle occurring with Brits in Africa, to the Americans living in Paris during the 1920s (Barbara H).

They also felt like McClain brought the story to life with just-right sensory details:

McClain has done an outstanding job of describing in detail things like the tangible feel of the horses as they trotted and raced, the smells of the paddocks, the rain, and even the taste of the salt flats (Nancy L). The writing is excellent with especially vivid descriptions of the people and places (Sandra G). You can see and feel the whole area through the descriptions of the topography, weather, wildlife, and people and how all are shaped by the environment (Brenda D).

Beryl Markham was a strong woman in a time when women weren't supposed to be strong, and McClain brings her beautifully to life:

Beryl Markham was a remarkable woman, not afraid to make her own way in a man's world. Her story is compelling and is well told by Paula McClain. This book will give this brave and pioneering woman a great deal of well-deserved visibility (Patricia W). Markham was a trailblazer and, having read Markham's autobiography, I feel that McClain successfully captures her personality and spirit (Karen B). It would be impossible to exaggerate any aspect of Beryl's life; she was one of a kind, infamous rather than famous, a freeloader and a free spirit, a woman who completely ignored all the conventions to get where she wanted to go. Her life makes for a cracking good story (Patricia T). Beryl Markham was a remarkable woman. She had the courage and initiative to become a renowned horse trainer and pilot at a time when these aspirations were unheard of for a female, and one cannot help but admire such a self-sufficient, free-spirited, and determined individual (Sandra G).

Finally, our readers recommend *Circling the Sun* to many kinds of people:

I thoroughly enjoyed this book and it is a perfect read for fans of *Out of Africa* (Brenda D). I hope my book club will read it because there is a lot for book clubs to discuss here (Andrea S). If you enjoy fictional depictions of real people, this story will keep you engrossed to the end (Wendy W). I recommend *Circling the Sun* to any reader interested in strong female characters, sweeping descriptions of beautiful African vistas, horses, or anyone who has succeed and failed and still able to retain their dignity until the end of their life (Amy G).

Reviewed by First Impressions Reviewers. This review was originally published in *The BookBrowse Review* in July 2015, and has been updated for the July 2016 edition.

DID YOU EVER HAVE A FAMILY

by Bill Clegg

BookBrowse Rating: 3/5
Critics' Consensus: 5/5
Readers' Rating: 5/5

Published May 2016 in Paperback, 320 pages

Summary

The stunning debut novel from bestselling author Bill Clegg is a magnificently powerful story about a circle of people who find solace in the least likely of places as they cope with a horrific tragedy.

On the eve of her daughter's wedding, June Reid's life is completely devastated when a shocking disaster takes the lives of her daughter, her daughter's fiancé, her ex-husband, and her boyfriend, Luke - her entire family, all gone in a moment. And June is the only survivor.

Alone and directionless, June drives across the country, away from her small Connecticut town. In her wake, a community emerges, weaving a beautiful and surprising web of connections through shared heartbreak.

From the couple running a motel on the Pacific Ocean where June eventually settles into a quiet half-life, to the wedding's caterer whose bill has been forgotten, to Luke's mother, the shattered outcast of the town - everyone touched by the tragedy is changed as truths about their near and far histories finally come to light.

Elegant and heartrending, and one of the most accomplished fiction debuts of the year, *Did You Ever Have a Family* is an absorbing, unforgettable tale that reveals humanity at its best through forgiveness and hope. At its core is a celebration of family - the ones we are born with and the ones we create.

BookBrowse Review

A celebration of family - the ones we are born with and the ones we create.

Oh, families. They are the people who can sometimes hurt us the most, calling us out for our weaknesses and mistakes. However, when we are down, they are the ones who can help us heal the most too. For the most part, living without a family would be tough. Bill Clegg's *Did You Ever Have A Family* explores how losing one's family can tear a person apart.

Clegg's novel begins with the greatest of all family events: a wedding. June Reid, a rather dynamic, middle-aged woman, living in a small Connecticut town, is hosting a wedding for her daughter. The night before the wedding, after all of the rehearsal activities are over, the unthinkable happens. A fire consumes the Reid house, killing everyone except June. Broken, she flees across the country to the west coast.

Surprisingly – and, in my opinion, unfortunately – *Did You Ever Have A Family* doesn't solely focus on June's reaction to the loss of her family. Instead, Clegg delivers something unusual. He gives us a novel that doesn't really focus on June at all. Sure, her voice appears occasionally to narrate a chapter or two. We get glimpses that she's hurting and that she's lonely, but we never really get to know her. We never get to know anybody all that well – and that's the problem.

Did You Ever Have A Family's short chapters are told from the perspectives of many different characters. All of the individual voices connect with June (or her location) in some way. Some are family members whom she knows, but others are faces that she'll never meet. They seem interesting enough; for example, Dale, a father, is a character whom I'd very much like to know more about. He seems like a caring and intelligent man. Lydia is another interesting character. She's a mother who struggles with making good decisions. I want to know more about what made her the way she is. But the quick and episodic structure of Clegg's novel doesn't allow for enough development. That said, I don't think he intentionally neglects his characters. Rather, it seems like the emotional separation he gives us is intentional. It feels as if the overwhelming density of characters and circumstances is supposed to be a metaphor for the larger loss of life that pervades the novel, a sort of suffocation in grief.

However, there is still a lot to admire in *Did You Ever Have A Family*. Clegg's prose flows beautifully. The descriptions he paints are simultaneously lyrical and delicate. When describing June's act of leaving after the fire, Clegg writes, "That she has her cash card and car keys with her is luck – they had been in the jacket pockets – but she does not think of herself as lucky. No one does. Still, these stowaways from her old life allow her now to leave town, which is all she wants. It isn't restlessness, or a desire to be somewhere else, but a blunt recognition that her time in this place has expired." He goes deeper, creating vivid imagery to tell of her pain: "The house without sound is now loud with nothing, no one. A molten ache returns, turns in her chest, scrapes slowly. Outside, the daylilies flail in the morning wind." There is no doubt that Clegg is a brilliant wordsmith and one whom I'll read again.

The ending, like the prose itself, is also quite successful. All the many voices come together, and we get a closing that does create some semblance of a catharsis. We see happiness. We see life beyond the past. We see that families do matter and how important they are if we are to survive merrily in the often tedious world.

Reading *Did You Ever Have A Family* isn't the smoothest ride you'll ever take, but it's one that should prove worthy of your time.

Reviewed by Bradley Sides. This review was originally published in *The BookBrowse Review* in October 2015, and has been updated for the May 2016 edition.

GIRL WAITS WITH GUN

by Amy Stewart

BookBrowse Rating: 4/5
Critics' Consensus: 5/5
Readers' Rating: 4.5/5

Published May 2016 in Paperback, 448 pages

Summary

An enthralling novel based on the forgotten true adventures of one of the nation's first female deputy sheriffs.

Constance Kopp doesn't quite fit the mold. She towers over most men, has no interest in marriage or domestic affairs, and has been isolated from the world since a family secret sent her and her sisters into hiding fifteen years ago. One day a belligerent and powerful silk factory owner runs down their buggy, and a dispute over damages turns into a war of bricks, bullets, and threats as he unleashes his gang on their family farm. When the sheriff enlists her help in convicting the men, Constance is forced to confront her past and defend her family - and she does it in a way that few women of 1914 would have dared.

BookBrowse Review

At the beginning of the twentieth century, one strong-willed woman, with the backing of her sisters, proves she doesn't need a man to make her way in life.

Girl Waits With Gun, a historical fiction novel based on the first woman deputy sheriff in the United States (see 'Beyond the Book'), hit the target for many BookBrowse First Impression reviewers with 19 out of 22 of them giving the book 4 or 5 stars.

A story of sisters struck a chord

Sometimes you choose your profession, sometimes your profession chooses you. Such is the case in this entertaining and enjoyable read by Amy Stewart. The Kopp sisters, driving to town in their buggy in 1914 are hit by a motorcar driven by Henry Kaufman, a silk factory owner. He is a man of means used to getting his way. When Constance Kopp, the oldest sister, sends him an invoice for repairs, all hell breaks loose (Francine E).

I thoroughly immersed myself in this intriguing and delightful story of the Kopp sisters, each vulnerable yet strong in her own right. I particularly loved the oldest, Constance, who with true grit, courage, cleverness, resourcefulness and independence, meets the challenges that threaten her family (Linda N).

An intriguing slice of history whets appetite for more

Girl Waits with Gun is the fictionalized story of one of the first women deputies in the country. Constance is imposing, strong-willed, and ready to take on obstacles that lesser women or men would never tackle. She must defend her family and home from aggressive and brutal men, and she will not back down. Based on newspaper accounts and family interviews, Amy Stewart replays history and creates a gripping story along the way (Becky M).

I was very surprised when I read in the acknowledgements that the story was based on true events. I was thrilled when I read that it would be a series (Dianne S). The writing is bright, crisp, and conversational. I am looking for a sequel. A woman like Constance will surely have more adventures as a deputy sheriff (Mary P).

Readers appreciated the window into women's struggles...

Since it was a time in our country when a woman's place was in the home, the Kopp ladies are indeed an anomaly. Constance is strong-willed and imposing, ready to take on obstacles lesser ladies would not tackle (Carol N).

A well-researched work of historical fiction that also exposes the beginnings of the long road ahead for women who desired to be independent (Barbara Z). The early twentieth century was not a welcome place for women on their own. Not having a man meant no protection from the numerous dangers, either real or perceived, that could be encountered (Patricia L). Although a bit dragged out in places, worth reading for a view of what our women ancestors had to endure (Donna H).

...and the vibrant characters complemented by vivid writing

Stewart blends humor with the time period in a wonderful way. Ladies were ladies, but they could also be independent and feisty. Her characters are well drawn and she creates suspense since you don't know what is going to happen next (Joyce W). The writing was wonderful, the characters came alive and I could "see" the farm where the women lived (Anna R).

This was a refreshing, enjoyable peek into what a woman's world was like at the turn of the century. Stewart's descriptions brought to life the streets of chaos and turmoil from the new age of industry and all its consequences. One could almost taste the acrid air within the factories and the character development allowed the reader to feel them (Duane F).

Needs editing?

I could easily see 50-100 pages being edited out of this book and it being a much stronger work. It felt like the same thing kept happening over and over and it became tiresome (Wendy W).

Overall readers gave *Girl Waits With Gun* their stamp of approval...

This is a good choice for book clubs, lovers of historical fiction, and any reader who loves seeing difficult challenges met by strong female protagonists (Linda N). I would recommend this novel for historical fiction lovers, young adults and book clubs and people from New Jersey! (Beverly D).

Reviewed by First Impressions Reviewers. This review was originally published in *The BookBrowse Review* in September 2015, and has been updated for the May 2016 edition.

WHEN THE MOON IS LOW

by Nadia Hashimi

BookBrowse Rating: 4/5
Critics' Consensus: 4.5/5
Readers' Rating: 4.5/5

Published April 2016 in Paperback, 384 pages

Summary

Mahmoud's passion for his wife Fereiba, a schoolteacher, is greater than any love she's ever known. But their happy, middle-class world—a life of education, work, and comfort—implodes when their country is engulfed in war, and the Taliban rises to power.

In Kabul, we meet Fereiba, a schoolteacher who puts her troubled childhood behind her when she finds love in an arranged marriage. But Fereiba's comfortable life implodes when the Taliban rises to power and her family becomes a target of the new fundamentalist regime. Forced to flee with her three children, Fereiba has one hope for survival: to seek refuge with her sister's family in London.

Traveling with forged papers and depending on the kindness of strangers, Fereiba and the children make a dangerous crossing into Iran under cover of darkness, the start of a harrowing journey that reduces her from a respected wife and mother to a desperate refugee.

Eventually they fall into the shadowy underground network of the undocumented who haunt the streets of Europe's cities. And then, in a busy market square in Athens, their fate takes a frightening turn when Fereiba's teenage son, Saleem, becomes separated from the rest of the family. Without his mother, Saleem is forced, abruptly and unforgivingly, to come of age in a world of human trafficking and squalid refugee camps.

Heartbroken, Fereiba has no choice but to continue on with only her daughter and baby. Mother and son cross border after perilous border, risking their lives in the hope of finding a place where they can be reunited.

BookBrowse Review

The impact of the Afghanistan war and the rise of the Taliban is told through the lens of one middle-class family who decide to leave for the safety of a foreign land.

When the Moon is Low, a story about an Afghani family fleeing persecution after the Taliban takeover, resonated soundly with many First Impression reviewers with more than half giving it a full five stars. Love, death, birth, chaos in a rocket-ravaged Kabul, and the fortunes of a family emigrating from the turmoil of Afghanistan are the themes of this book. It is also a coming-of-age story as a young man separated from his family tries desperately to rejoin them, the obstacles he encounters are many (Florence K).

Readers were engrossed by one family's struggle for survival

When the Moon is Low is one of those books where you lose track of time and become totally engrossed in a family's journey from the terrors of the Taliban in Afghanistan to eventual reunion with family in England. But the journey is difficult as they are either cared for or persecuted by those they meet along the way. The read is a roller coaster of emotions as Nadia Hashimi teases us with their safety and then their near tragedies throughout the escape from their homeland (Laurie F). The story alternates between the viewpoints of Fereiba, a young Afghan widow, and her teenage son Saleem. Along with daughter Samira and baby Aziz, they make the perilous journey from Kabul into Iran, then to Turkey and on to Athens, where Saleem is arrested. The story then follows the separate journeys, perils, friendships and heartbreak of Fereiba and Saleem. Hashimi's writing is spare and poetic, and the story, moving and suspenseful (Rebecca H).

The story brought to life issues of refugees and immigration

This book also shows us a side of what the Afghan people have had to deal with that is not always portrayed. It certainly made me look at immigration in a different way (Laura E). With refugees and migrants struggling to escape misery and death, this book captures the reality of what that means in a way that gets under your skin and into your heart (Sandy F). With the world's eyes upon the situation of the refugees from many countries, this novel reveals the souls of our brothers and sisters searching for a life of hope free from oppression (Mary Anne R).

A few thought the story could have used more depth

While this story reveals some of the horrors refugees experience, I'm inclined to think it doesn't go nearly deep enough (Ginny B). My biggest criticism was the ending, which left me worrying about the fates of the family and some of those we met along the way (Beth W). I couldn't help feel that this lovely book was missing something. Something that took me deeper into the characters and their struggle (Sharon P). The story itself is compelling as well as timely, particularly as the world is in the midst of a crisis involving Syrian refugees. But the family's experiences were fairly tame compared to the horrors that real-life refugees live through every day (Sally H).

Yet most came away with new knowledge and hope

Depressing yet hopeful in the face of great odds is how I would describe this wonderful book (Loren B). [Afghan] women are allowed no freedom, yet Fereiba took it upon herself to make sure her family could enjoy a safe life in the future. A love story — and as the author wrote "love grows wildest in gardens of hardship." Everyone should be reading this book (Patricia S). The unbelievable love, courage and tenacity of being a refugee as well as the smell of fear is all in this book. Yet it is somehow hopeful. I learned a great deal about so much and enjoyed this book immensely. Somehow every nation must find a way to welcome and support refugees — they are leaving a hell we can't imagine (Sandy F).

Reviewed by First Impressions Reviewers. This review was originally published in *The BookBrowse Review* in October 2015, and has been updated for the May 2016 edition.

LUSITANIA

by Greg King, Penny Wilson

BookBrowse Rating: 5/5
Critics' Consensus: 4.5/5
Readers' Rating: 4.5/5

Published April 2016 in Paperback, 416 pages

Summary

On the 100th Anniversary of its sinking, King and Wilson tell the story of the Lusitania's glamorous passengers and the torpedo that ended an era and prompted the US entry into World War I.

Lusitania: She was a ship of dreams, carrying millionaires and aristocrats, actresses and impresarios, writers and suffragettes – a microcosm of the last years of the waning Edwardian Era and the coming influences of the Twentieth Century. When she left New York on her final voyage, she sailed from the New World to the Old; yet an encounter with the machinery of the New World, in the form of a primitive German U-Boat, sent her – and her gilded passengers – to their tragic deaths and opened up a new era of indiscriminate warfare.

A hundred years after her sinking, Lusitania remains an evocative ship of mystery. Was she carrying munitions that exploded? Did Winston Churchill engineer a conspiracy that doomed the liner? Lost amid these tangled skeins is the romantic, vibrant, and finally heartrending tale of the passengers who sailed aboard her. Lives, relationships, and marriages ended in the icy waters off the Irish Sea; those who survived were left haunted and plagued with guilt. Now, authors Greg King and Penny Wilson resurrect this lost, glittering world to show the golden age of travel and illuminate the most prominent of Lusitania's passengers. Rarely was an era so glamorous; rarely was a ship so magnificent; and rarely was the human element of tragedy so quickly lost to diplomatic maneuvers and militaristic threats.

BookBrowse Review

The story of the Lusitania's glamorous passengers and the torpedo that ended an era, prompting the U.S. entry into World War I.

Greg King and Penny Wilson's *Lusitania* placed our readers smack in the middle of history. They smelled the sea water, tasted the decadent food - and felt the horrific explosion as a torpedo hit and then sank the mighty boat. In fact, 18 out of 21 reviewers gave this historical non-fiction 4 or 5 stars.

What are our readers saying about this gripping, true tale?

Lusitania is amazing. I knew just a little about the sinking of the Lusitania and after reading this book I feel as if I were there on the ship. The rich details and tremendous research that obviously went into writing this book make for great reading…I have never read a book before where I felt that it was happening to me. This book really is remarkable (Anita S). The narrative is riveting and well paced throughout, and the analysis of the tragedy is thorough and thought-provoking. In short, I couldn't put it down until I had read it all (Jane A). The tragic story is told in suspenseful and riveting detail. The reader, as an unbooked passenger, observes from a safe distance as the disaster plays out day by day – while helpless to intervene! (Marie D) I do read some books twice…this will be one that I will read again (Dorothy C).

The sinking of the Lusitania is a lesser-known tragedy than the *Titanic*, and our readers feel as though this book could – and should – change that:

Lusitania, by Greg King and Penny Wilson, is one of the most enjoyable historical books I've read in a while. A lot has been written about the *Titanic*, but little about the luxury liner torpedoed as WWI was building up. This book is an education. Vividly written with beautiful descriptions of the opulence of the age, I enjoyed every page (Marjorie H). Almost everyone in the world knows the story of the tragic collision of the *Titanic* and an iceberg in the North Atlantic. This is the story of an equally elegant ship populated by equally affluent and influential people sailing in unbelievable opulence in the opposite direction during a period when most of the Western world was at war (Katherine P). History remembers the *Titanic* well but the Lusitania is another tragic sea disaster that is equally real and full of loss. This book is brilliantly laid out and full of mesmerizing historical detail (Melissa M).

Most of our readers felt like this book was a unique combination of great research that reads like a story:

I don't read much non-fiction, and I love getting lost in a story. Fortunately for me (and for any other readers) *Lusitania* tells a story – a riveting, transfixing story. Greg King and Penny Wilson did their homework. This book is so well researched, I can't imagine anything was overlooked. I felt like I was on the ship myself, and the story read like one of my beloved novels instead of a factual presentation of an historical event (Judy K). Were the Lusitania and her passengers exposed/sacrificed to danger in order to involve America in World War I? Did the Cunard Line, British Admiralty, and Captain William Turner deliberately place the Lusitania in danger? These questions and more are dealt with in King and Wilson's very informative book…their extensive research help readers arrive at their own conclusions (Annette S). I appreciate how much research these authors put into solving the mysteries surrounding the story and feel as though they gave me a front seat to people's lives as the story unfolded. The story is well written and companionable (Monica G).

Although some readers did feel differently about this fact-packed story:

The book was very interesting to read, however I think it would have worked better as historical fiction. It seemed like they felt they had to include every quote they found. As a result they couldn't weave in an extended story line, which would have made a good book a great book (Carolyn S). I recommend this book as a reference book, not a good story to read. It is full of facts, but there is not the flow of a good, readable story (Jan H). While clearly heavily researched and informational, I found it impossible to find a good reading flow to this book. Details taken in snapshots and corroborated with copious notes were great in small doses (Yolanda M).

But all in all, they recommend *Lusitania* to many kinds of readers:

Anyone who enjoys the stories of the Edwardian Age and all its apparent splendor, who is fascinated by the social and technological changes of the early 20th century and who is interested in great human tragedies will find this book extremely rewarding and a fast read (Katherine P). I've never been in a book club, but I think this book would spark a spirited discussion. Good read! (Judy K) I recommend this book to anyone interested in history or just wanting to read a great story (Darshell S). Anyone interested in World War I history will likely find this a good read (Rosanne J). Would recommend it for book clubs, history lovers and even to be used as reading for history classes (Kristen H).

H IS FOR HAWK

by Helen Macdonald

BookBrowse Rating: 5/5
Critics' Consensus: 5/5
Readers' Rating: 4/5

Published March 2016 in Paperback, 320 pages

Summary

Winner of the 2015 BookBrowse Nonfiction Award

Obsession, madness, memory, myth, and history combine to achieve a distinctive blend of nature writing and memoir from an outstanding literary innovator.

When Helen Macdonald's father died suddenly on a London street, she was devastated. An experienced falconer—Helen had been captivated by hawks since childhood—she'd never before been tempted to train one of the most vicious predators, the goshawk. But in her grief, she saw that the goshawk's fierce and feral temperament mirrored her own. Resolving to purchase and raise the deadly creature as a means to cope with her loss, she adopted Mabel, and turned to the guidance of *The Once and Future King* author T.H. White's chronicle *The Goshawk* to begin her challenging endeavor. Projecting herself "in the hawk's wild mind to tame her" tested the limits of Macdonald's humanity and changed her life.

Heart-wrenching and humorous, this book is an unflinching account of bereavement and a unique look at the magnetism of an extraordinary beast, with a parallel examination of a legendary writer's eccentric falconry. Obsession, madness, memory, myth, and history combine to achieve a distinctive blend of nature writing and memoir from an outstanding literary innovator.

BookBrowse Review

An improbable companion becomes a vehicle to process mind-numbing grief in this compelling memoir.

Winner of the 2015 BookBrowse Non-Fiction Award

It is difficult to categorize Helen Macdonald's debut, *H Is for Hawk*; it is simultaneously a natural history, a literary biography, a memoir, and a chronicle of bereavement. It's also a thoughtful inquiry into the — often imagined or imaginary — relationship between people and wild animals and an intriguing glimpse into a world many of us probably didn't even know existed.

If your knowledge of falconry is limited to images from medieval romances, you will no doubt be fascinated to discover that a subculture of falconry is alive and well all over the world. Most present-day falconers use their birds for hunting small game, but it seems that others use them as an unusual way to interact with the wild, or to keep the dying sport alive. When Helen Macdonald, an historian and academic lecturer at Cambridge University, learns of the sudden death of her father, a photojournalist, she is driven by her grief to immerse herself in the great pastime and passion of her youth. This time, however, Macdonald is not drawn to the smaller and more manageable hawks or falcons; instead, she is determined to train and hunt with a goshawk, birds she had previously thought of as "things of death and difficulty: spooky, pale-eyed psychopaths that lived and killed in woodland thickets."

But as she grows inexplicably intent on obtaining and training a goshawk, she turns again to one of the books that shaped her understanding of the responsibilities of the falconer: *The Goshawk* by T. H. White. White, most famous for writing the modern Arthurian adaptation *The Once and Future King*, memorably turned young Arthur into a hawk as part of his fictional education under the tutelage of the wizard Merlyn.

But White himself was also an amateur falconer (or, more properly, an austringer, a keeper of goshawks). His account of trying — and largely failing — to train a goshawk proves both instructive and maddening to Macdonald as she embarks on the process of training a young goshawk named Mabel. As she struggles to understand what motivated White — and where he fell short of his own ambitions — Macdonald also eventually strives to understand the complex blend of emotions that has caused her to throw herself headlong into this renewed passion, at times at the expense of her human relationships and, when she essentially abandons her career in favor of time with her hawk, even her livelihood.

Some readers may be perplexed by the technical jargon such as "bating," "mutes," and "jesses," detailed accounts of Mabel's training with which Macdonald peppers her memoir. Regardless, her story is worthwhile reading for anyone who harbors more than a passing fancy for nature or who longs to understand the often inexplicable journey of grief. Macdonald is, in her fearlessly honest portrayal of herself, not always likeable or admirable; nonetheless, she eventually comes to see her own motivations with (dare I say?) eagle-eyed clarity.

Macdonald's relationship with Mabel helps her grieve, initially allowing Macdonald to pretend she is not human and therefore not subject to human emotions. As she comes to spend more time with Mabel, though, she realizes that humans' experience of loss — and their ability to reflect on it — is far more complicated than that of the hawk, which is really a plain and simple instrument of death.

Macdonald shies away from easy metaphors — when she is tempted simply to equate herself and her desire for invisibility with the hawk, to anthropomorphize Mabel or to conflate their experiences as they grow into a unified hunting team. In the end, Macdonald — as she begins to emerge from the grief that has almost consumed her — is able to reflect on larger questions, such as how and why we imbue wild creatures with human qualities and whose version of "nature" is worth preserving. Most of all, she realizes that — her genuine and hard-won affection for Mabel notwithstanding — she needs more than a raptor counterpart to find herself truly human: "Hands are for other human hands to hold. They should not be reserved exclusively as perches for hawks. And the wild is not a panacea for the human soul; too much in the air can corrode it to nothing."

Reviewed by Norah Piehl. This review was originally published in *The BookBrowse Review* in March 2015, and has been updated for the March 2016 edition.

A LITTLE LIFE

by Hanya Yanagihara

BookBrowse Rating: 5/5
Critics' Consensus: 5/5
Readers' Rating: 5/5

Published January 2016 in Paperback, 736 pages

Summary

Brace yourself for the most astonishing, challenging, upsetting, and profoundly moving book in many a season. An epic about love and friendship in the twenty-first century that goes into some of the darkest places fiction has ever traveled and yet somehow improbably breaks through into the light. Truly an amazement - and a great gift for its publisher.

When four classmates from a small Massachusetts college move to New York to make their way, they're broke, adrift, and buoyed only by their friendship and ambition. There is kind, handsome Willem, an aspiring actor; JB, a quick-witted, sometimes cruel Brooklyn-born painter seeking entry to the art world; Malcolm, a frustrated architect at a prominent firm; and withdrawn, brilliant, enigmatic Jude, who serves as their center of gravity. Over the decades, their relationships deepen and darken, tinged by addiction, success, and pride. Yet their greatest challenge, each comes to realize, is Jude himself, by midlife a terrifyingly talented litigator yet an increasingly broken man, his mind and body scarred by an unspeakable childhood, and haunted by what he fears is a degree of trauma that he'll not only be unable to overcome - but that will define his life forever.

In rich and resplendent prose, Yanagihara has fashioned a tragic and transcendent hymn to brotherly love, a masterful depiction of heartbreak, and a dark examination of the tyranny of memory and the limits of human endurance.

BookBrowse Review

A tragic and transcendent hymn to brotherly love, and a dark examination of the tyranny of memory and the limits of human endurance.

"The past is a foreign country. They do things differently there." These memorable opening lines might belong to another brilliant novel (*The Go-Between*, by L. P. Hartley) but they could well form the essential scaffolding for *A Little Life*, a wrenching yet illuminating exploration of how child abuse can exert a suffocating grip on adulthood.

Jude St. Francis is at the center of *A Little Life's* vast 700+ page canvas, a brilliant mind and tortured soul who endured unimaginable horrors as a child: "...fifteen years whose half-life have been so long and so resonant, that have determined everything he has become and done." The novel opens with a group of newly minted college graduates trying to make their way in present-day New York City. In addition to Jude, who is armed with a degree from Harvard Law, there's his closest friend Willem, who has his sights set on an acting career, and JB and Malcolm, who dabble in other creative pursuits. These four continue to be close friends in the city post-college, making do while keeping their eyes on the prize. Yanagihara sets up this essential framework, and then brilliantly explores the dynamics of these four friends, their loves and petty rivalries over the course of three decades. The focus fades in and out from each, even as the group's friendship is kept alive "by dropping bundles of kindling onto a barely smoldering black smudge of fire."

Right from the outset, we know Jude has been marked by tragedy. Whatever happened was brutal enough to leave him dealing with chronic pain, and his halting gait, coupled with a stoic silence, is a visible reminder of a past he desperately wants to forget. Yanagihara keeps us hooked by hinting at the menace that will soon rear its ugly head and by painting such comprehensive character pictures that the reader gets invested in their eventual outcomes. *A Little Life* is also remarkable in its portrayal of male friendships, for the empathy writ large on every page and is studded with writing so pitch-perfect, it requires a great deal of restraint not to highlight practically every paragraph as a perfect specimen of evocative prose. Every descriptor is perfect: even a plate falling loudly on a kitchen floor makes a "timpanic" sound.

Given how measured and even-keeled the rest of the novel is, the story of Jude's physical abuse stands out in stark contrast. Readers be warned: the horrors are rendered in vivid detail (I'll admit I skipped a couple of pages) and they are relentless. At one point, a character quotes a line from The Odyssey: "We have still not reached the end of our trials. One more labor lies in store – boundless, laden with danger, great and long, and I must brave it out from start to finish." This pretty much sums up Jude's trials too. The adult Jude is understandably haunted by his childhood and cuts himself regularly, but he is also a brilliant and ruthless litigator. Still, it becomes hard to believe that anybody could suffer from *such* a miserable childhood. Perhaps Yanagihara could have edited some of Jude's horrors. A little restraint here could have added a touch of nuance to the sections of the story that deal with children's abuse. While it is clear that Jude is a tortured soul, his essential character outline occasionally borders on caricature.

This is the only drawback in what is otherwise a marvel of a novel. Yanagihara's picturesque writing paints Jude's nightmares in such dramatic fashion, you can see the metaphorical hyenas tearing away at his soul. Equally remarkable is the exploration of Jude's abuse on his close relationships. This is a novel not just about the effects of abuse on the victim, but on everyone else dear to him. Weighed down with baggage of their own, Jude's inner circle – his Harvard Law professor, Harold (who will later assume a bigger role in his life) and friend Willem – struggle to deal with Jude's pain, his routine self-inflicted abuse as an adult, and his deepest fears and anxieties. Even his status at his high-powered job as one of the city's most successful and revered litigators, cannot solve these problems. "We were so ill-equipped. Most people are easy: their unhappinesses, their sorrows are understandable, their bouts of self-loathing are fast-moving and negotiable. But his were not. We didn't know how to help him because we lacked the imagination we needed to diagnose the problems," Harold says.

In its lighter moments, *A Little Life* is also one of the most brilliant examinations of the New York zeitgeist, a city where ambition is the only religion. "These were days of self-fulfillment, where settling for something that was not quite your first choice of a life seemed weak-willed and ignoble. Somewhere, surrendering to what seemed to be your fate had changed from being dignified to being a sign of your own cowardice. There were times when the pressure to achieve happiness felt almost oppressive, as if happiness were something that everyone should and could attain, and that any sort of compromise in its pursuit was somehow your fault."

To compensate for the story's bleakness, there's sunshine in equal measure. Harold once says: "things get broken, and sometimes they get repaired, and in most cases, you realize that no matter what gets damaged, life rearranges itself to compensate for your loss, sometimes wonderfully." So it is, that *A Little Life* gives us hope — that generous doses of love and friendship might give us enough tenacity to make it through our darkest hours.

Reviewed by Poornima Apte. This review was originally published in *The BookBrowse Review* in April 2015, and has been updated for the February 2016 edition.

A GOD IN RUINS

by Kate Atkinson

BookBrowse Rating: 5/5
Critics' Consensus: 5/5
Readers' Rating: 5/5

Published January 2016 in Paperback, 480 pages

Summary

The stunning companion to Kate Atkinson's #1 bestseller *Life After Life*, "one of the best novels I've read this century" (Gillian Flynn).

"He had been reconciled to death during the war and then suddenly the war was over and there was a next day and a next day. Part of him never adjusted to having a future."

Kate Atkinson's dazzling *Life After Life* explored the possibility of infinite chances and the power of choices, following Ursula Todd as she lived through the turbulent events of the last century over and over again.

A God in Ruins tells the dramatic story of the 20th Century through Ursula's beloved younger brother Teddy - would-be poet, heroic pilot, husband, father, and grandfather - as he navigates the perils and progress of a rapidly changing world. After all that Teddy endures in battle, his greatest challenge is living in a future he never expected to have.

An ingenious and moving exploration of one ordinary man's path through extraordinary times, *A God in Ruins* proves once again that Kate Atkinson is one of the finest novelists of our age.

BookBrowse Review

A companion to Kate Atkinson's *Life After Life*, *A God in Ruins* is a moving exploration of one ordinary man's path through extraordinary times.

The title of Kate Atkinson's latest novel, a companion of sorts to her 2013 *Life After Life*, is taken from a quote by Ralph Waldo Emerson, which Atkinson includes as an epigraph: "A man is a god in ruins. When men are innocent, life shall be longer, and shall pass into the immortal, as gently as we awake from dreams." Right from the start, then, Atkinson uses her fiction to explore the idea of the imperfection of humankind. The Fall of Man if you want to get more traditional about it: the idea that humans have, since the very dawn of creation, fallen short of their own ideals.

In *A God in Ruins*, Atkinson explores this idea through the story of one man's life: Edward (Teddy) Todd, younger brother of Ursula Todd, the heroine of *Life After Life*. Teddy's life story, as told in this novel, extends from childhood through extreme old age, centering on what happened to Teddy as a bomber pilot in the Second World War. Throughout, Atkinson suffuses her narrative with images of primeval woods and rambling gardens, of humans' affinity with animals - in short, with glimpses of the world before that catastrophic Fall.

While Teddy's story does indeed begin with childhood and end with agedness, its chronology hardly plays out so neatly. In *Life After Life,* Teddy's sister Ursula lived her own life many times over, learning and imparting new lessons each time. The complexity and playfulness of that novel may give readers some clues that Teddy's story - under Atkinson's masterful pen - is hardly as straightforward as it seems. Sections of *A God in Ruins* are labeled with dates, but those are merely touchstones for what is, in actuality, a story that moves freely forward and backward in time, one that includes flash-forwards as well as flashbacks. The narrative is continually interrupted by glimpses of a future that hasn't even happened yet, treated as if it were a reminiscence, not a premonition: "But that was several weeks away yet, in the future," Atkinson writes after a long digression, for example, bringing us back to the present with a jolt. These kinds of narrative disruptions offer a new form of stream-of-consciousness, one that will keep readers alert and interested - and wondering just what it is the author is up to.

Atkinson introduces us to Teddy's idyllic childhood - the Eden of his imaginings - his young adulthood; his service in the military during World War II (described in excruciating and emotional detail); his seemingly inevitable but largely unexciting marriage to the girl next door; and his eventual struggles to do the right thing for his free-spirited and blithely irresponsible daughter and her two children, both young adults at the novel's close. Just as *Life after Life* encouraged readers to imagine countless possible paths for one individual's life, *A God in Ruins* encourages readers to consider how the vagaries of fate might affect what comes afterwards - a possible future time that, in the midst of the war, Teddy finds virtually impossible to imagine.

"He had made a vow, a private promise to the world in the long dark watches of the night, that if he did survive then in the great afterward, he would always try to be kind, to live a good quiet life. Like Candide, he would cultivate his garden. Quietly. And that would be his redemption."

On the surface of things, Teddy's life "in the great afterward" is nothing particularly remarkable or noteworthy, perhaps not even anything that merits its own novel. But on balance, perhaps Teddy's life, as mundane as it is, is nothing short of miraculous - and perhaps that is true of all humans, with all their inadequacies. Atkinson's *A God in Ruins* is simultaneously a story of one man's harrowing journey through war, a family's journey through the twentieth century, and every person's journey through mistakes and shortcomings toward something resembling redemption, no matter how imperfect.

Reviewed by Norah Piehl. This review was originally published in *The BookBrowse Review* in May 2015, and has been updated for the January 2016 edition.

A MAN OF GOOD HOPE

by Jonny Steinberg

BookBrowse Rating: 5/5
Critics' Consensus: 4.5/5

Published December 2015 in Paperback, 336 pages

Summary

In January 1991, when civil war came to Mogadishu, two-thirds of the city's population fled. Among them was eight-year-old Asad Abdullahi.

In January 1991, when civil war came to Mogadishu, the capital of Somalia, two-thirds of the city's population fled. Among them was eight-year-old Asad Abdullahi. His mother murdered by a militia, his father somewhere in hiding, he was swept alone into the great wartime migration that scattered the Somali people throughout sub-Saharan Africa and the world.

This extraordinary book tells Asad's story. Serially betrayed by the people who promised to care for him, Asad lived his childhood at a skeptical remove from the adult world, his relation to others wary and tactical. He lived in a bewildering number of places, from the cosmopolitan streets of inner-city Nairobi to the desert towns deep in the Ethiopian hinterland.

By the time he reached the cusp of adulthood, Asad had honed an array of wily talents. At the age of seventeen, in the Ethiopian capital, Addis Ababa, he made good as a street hustler, brokering relationships between hard-nosed businessmen and bewildered Somali refugees. He also courted the famously beautiful Foosiya, and, to the astonishment of his peers, seduced and married her.

Buoyed by success in work and in love, Asad put twelve hundred dollars in his pocket and made his way down the length of the African continent to Johannesburg, South Africa, whose streets he believed to be lined with gold. And so began a shocking adventure in a country richer and more violent than he could possibly have imagined.

A Man of Good Hope is the story of a person shorn of the things we have come to believe make us human - personal possessions, parents, siblings. And yet Asad's is an intensely human life, one suffused with dreams and desires and a need to leave something permanent on this earth.

BookBrowse Review

***A Man of Good Hope* is the story of one man's life - and his need to make it something of worth.**

Almost anybody with an ear to international events is aware of the humanitarian crisis in Somalia where civil war since the early '90s has lead to the displacement of upward of a million Somalis.

Asad Hirsi Abdullahi is one such refugee. By the time the author Jonny Steinberg is introduced to him in 2010, Asad is in Blikkiesdorp, the ghetto "described as Cape Town's asshole, the muscle through which the city shits out the parts it does not want." Recognizing that there might be more to this refugee's story, Steinberg gives Asad seven thousand rand (nearly $600), enough to start a small business, in exchange for his life story, which forms the crux of *A Man Of Good Hope*.

When Steinberg first meets Asad, it had been two years since xenophobia spread through Cape Town forcing many foreigners like Asad to flee. As violent as those incidents were, Asad is sadly no stranger to such misery. He was just eight when militia forces overran his Mogadishu home and shot his mother. The rest of the family was displaced as a result. This seminal event sparked a series of temporary arrangements for the young Asad, who was forced to make do with the barest minimum of food, shelter and clothing and to rely on an extended safety net of Somali clansmen that provided very little real help.

Asad travels from town to town, and from country to country (highlighted by maps in the book). He finds some amount of succor in Somali camps, whether it be Eastleigh in suburban Nairobi (a neighborhood Asad mistakenly pronounces as *Islii*) or Bole Mikhael (also spelled *Bole Michael*) in Addis Ababa, Ethiopia, but his heart-wrenching losses might jade even the hardiest souls. However, Steinberg's narration is a brilliant piece of sleuthing, one that doesn't stop merely at shining light on Asad's myriad problems, but further positions them in the right context, showcasing the man's incredible resilience and spirit. Case in point: Since Asad can only depend on his street smarts to survive, he develops a keen sense of business acumen — making do by delivering large barrels of water to cafes in Nairobi or ferrying passengers between Cape Town and Pretoria for a lower price than what the South Africans charge.

The real touching moments in *A Man of Good Hope* are not the readily obvious ones of large and spectacular losses. They come, instead, in the smaller personal memories that Asad holds dear. These observations underscore his refugee status better than any grander events can. For example, in South Africa, he gets to visit his uncle Abdicuur, whose house is in a suburb in the white town of Uitenhage. When asked what struck him most about that visit, Asad says he remembers that the house was full of things. *What things?* Steinberg asks. "Asad is at a loss when I ask him to recall precisely what, but they were the sort of things, he says, that gradually fill a house inhabited by people who have money," Steinberg writes. It's a point of view that speaks volumes, not just about Asad's lack of money, but also about the constant displacement that has prevented him from setting roots down in any one place for long enough to accumulate "things." There are many such moments of discovery for both Asad and the reader — the time when Asad learns he is classified as black ("I am not black, I have my own culture," he responds) or the many shades of belonging that define the class and color-based society in South Africa.

Since Steinberg doesn't gloss over Asad's failings (his stubbornness for example), the portrait that emerges is all the better for it. Throughout, true to the book's title, Asad maintains his indomitable spirit. "You are only on this earth for a few years, How long? Sixty years? Maybe eighty years? For many of those years you are an old person," Asad points out. "The years in between: it is a small time, really; it goes fast. If you do not make something then, you have lost your opportunity. You die without having lived." Asad's constant drive at self-improvement is truly inspirational. His story is a must-read; it's an incredibly moving ride — a look at Africa's many social issues laid bare through the eyes of one everyday global citizen.

Reviewed by Poornima Apte. This review was originally published in *The BookBrowse Review* in February 2015, and has been updated for the January 2016 edition.

DESCENT

by Tim Johnston

BookBrowse Rating: 5/5
Critics' Consensus: 4/5
Readers' Rating: 4.5/5

Published December 2015 in Paperback, 400 pages

Summary

The stunning vistas of the Rocky Mountains reveal a dark and deadly side in this brilliantly conceived thriller about family ties and the fight for survival.

Descent, the story of a family undone by the disappearance of a daughter who went out for a morning run and didn't come back, is stunning in its emotional impact - a compulsively readable page-turner with a strong literary sensibility.

The girl's vanishing - on a sunny, late-summer vacation morning- - all the more devastating for its mystery, is the beginning of the family's harrowing journey down increasingly divergent and solitary paths, until all that continues to bind them to each other are the questions they can never bring themselves to ask: *At what point does a family stop searching? At what point does a girl stop fighting for her life?*

Johnston captures every emotion, every terrifying thought, every moment of loneliness, from the perspectives of everyone in the family - as each in his or her own way assumes responsibility for their collective loss. And in the father we see the last flicker of hope as he pursues every angle and refuses to give up in his belief that his daughter is still alive. Ultimately he finds an answer, in a climax that is stunning in both its execution and its resolution.

This combination of a great story and beautiful writing brings to mind the works of Tim Gautreaux, Dennis Lehane, and Russell Banks.

BookBrowse Review

Descent **is a perfectly crafted literary thriller that races to its heart-pounding conclusion**

Part literary novel, part thriller, part psychological drama, *Descent* **is a novel in a unique category unto itself. Tim Johnston's storytelling captured the hearts of 22 out of 23 of BookBrowse's readers, who gave it 4 or 5-stars - and made their hearts pound fast too! Here is why:**

Descent is the story of the Courtland family and their daughter Caitlin's abduction and the efforts to track her down. But on a deeper level, it is about the physical and emotional toll the abduction and its aftermath take upon the whole family; it's that descent that brings the title of this book into focus

(Kathleen S.) Tim Johnston has written a suspenseful kidnapping story while depicting the main characters' sadness, guilt and helplessness in a way that makes them real and unforgettable. This book makes a powerful impression on the reader. Bravo! (Linda K) *Descent*'s descriptions of isolation, coldness and loss are paralyzing, and the dialogue is tight and reflects the conservation of energy needed to exist in this landscape (Tracy N.) Every once in a rare while a book is written that fulfills every requirement a reader is looking for. Tim Johnston has mastered that in *Descent* (Lydia M.)

Readers were especially impressed with Tim Johnston's use of language in the book:

This book drew me in like a magnet. The story is simple. A girl disappears and her family searches for her. But what Tim Johnston does with this story is amazing – it is a wonderful language experience. Don't miss this one! (Patricia D) The author uses stunning, poetic prose to tell this brutal and heartbreaking story from multiple perspectives (Phyllis R.) Normally, I have little patience for so much descriptive writing, but this was executed so well that I found myself drawn into the moods of the characters and their surroundings (I could even smell the mountain pines.)…This is a thrilling, well-written work, which will have your heart pounding as you tear through to the end. It is one of the best I have read, and I am pleased to have found a new author (Elinor M.)

This is not your usual thriller:

To employ the term "lyrical thriller" might seem an oxymoron, but not after you have begun reading this extraordinary novel. The lyricism comes from Johnston's poetic descriptions of the natural world. The standard materials for a thriller - young woman mysteriously disappears, the resultant family fears, the seeming insolubility of the case - may ring distantly familiar, but Johnston adds elements of love and concern not often found in popular thrillers. His careful descriptions of individuals and their reactions to events lift this novel out of the ordinary (William Y.) *Descent* is an intelligent and riveting story. The author's descriptions of the characters and surroundings gave me the sensation of being there. I could smell the fragrances, feel the snow on my face and could hear the wind and the sound of metal links (Mary A.) Johnston is a master of prose and is able to paint a picture and to make you feel that you are actually a part of the action (Steve B). This is not what you'd expect from a thriller, but so much more (Lauren T.)

Some readers felt the story had a slow and confusing start, but picked up speed and clarity as the pages turned:

Descent is a psychological family study for the first half then picks up speed to become a true movie thriller by the end. I found the beginning to be a bit slow and had to adjust to the chapters alternating between various characters (Liz B.) I usually enjoy reading stories told from the perspectives of different characters, but this book was a bit choppy (Gail L.) If only the beautifully written passages of the landscape, the crime, and the chase had not been preceded by the confusing style in the beginning of the book, I would have given it a 5 (Janis H.) The first part of the book is a little confusing since it is told by many characters at different times in their lives, but you will soon put it together and sit down for a long and enjoyable ride (Roe P.)

***More* was a common word heard from these readers – they wanted to see more from Tim Johnston:**

Descent is a page turner and it kept my interest. The only fault I'd assign is that I would have liked to have known what happened next...what's the next chapter? (Diana J) I read this book in one day because I just needed to know how it ended. And I believe there could be a sequel in there too (Cindy C.) On the one hand, this masterful novel grabbed me from the first chapter and I didn't want to put it down. On the other hand, I didn't want to read too fast or too far so that I could dole out the pages like bites of a splendid meal! I want to meet the author and tell him to begin writing his next book immediately so that I don't have to wait too long for another serving of his gifted prose (Linda

K.) This book held my attention from the first page, and I'm hoping it is made into a film. It would be great! (Linda J)

Reviewed by First Impressions Reviewers. This review was originally published in *The BookBrowse Review* in January 2015, and has been updated for the December 2015 edition.

THE LAST UNICORN

by William deBuys

BookBrowse Rating: 5/5
Critics' Consensus: 4.5/5

Published October 2015 in Paperback, 368 pages

| Summary

An award-winning author's stirring quest to find and understand an elusive and exceptionally rare species in the heart of Southeast Asia's jungles.

In 1992, in a remote mountain range, a team of scientists discovered the remains of an unusual animal with beautiful long horns. It turned out to be a living species new to western science - a saola, the first large land mammal discovered in 50 years.

Rare then and rarer now, no westerner had glimpsed a live saola before Pulitzer Prize finalist and nature writer William deBuys and conservation biologist William Robichaud set off to search for it in the wilds of central Laos. The team endured a punishing trek, up and down whitewater rivers and through mountainous terrain ribboned with the snare lines of armed poachers.

In the tradition of Bruce Chatwin, Colin Thubron, and Peter Matthiessen, *The Last Unicorn* is deBuys's look deep into one of the world's most remote places. As in the pursuit of the unicorn, the journey ultimately becomes a quest for the essence of wildness in nature, and an encounter with beauty.

BookBrowse Review

The search for an elusive creature deep in the jungles of southeast Asia raises larger questions about nature and environmentalism.

"A thing of beauty is a joy forever," the poet John Keats famously wrote. "It will never pass into nothingness." Behind that idea lies a real puzzle: much that is beautiful is also ephemeral, doomed to disappear. Many once-beloved "things of beauty" are now long gone, existing only in one's memory. Even amid the seeming permanence of nature, seasons change, the metamorphosis of landscapes proceeds. And of course the march of civilization often tramples nature in its advance. Can the litany of near-extinct species, for example – Bengal tigers, African elephants…each a thing of beauty surely – be a joy forever if the existence of these natural wonders should cease entirely? Wouldn't that joy turn to sorrow, a lament for the permanence of their loss rather than their beauty?

Such lofty questions acquire a pragmatic urgency in William deBuys' *The Last Unicorn*, a travelogue-in-diary-format about the quest to find a creature called a <u>saola</u> (pronounced: sow-la, and meaning "spindle horns" in Vietnamese), an antelope-like mammal recognized by two parallel horns with sharp ends, found on both males and females. First documented by scientists in 1992, evidence of its continued existence in the wild has been as wispy and uncertain as the landscape it is believed to inhabit (an isolated mountain range between Laos and Vietnam). Often called the Asian unicorn, the saola is more talked about by local hunters and farmers than actually seen.

The Last Unicorn tells the story of a 2011 expedition undertaken by deBuys and well-respected conservationist William Robichaud, aided by a team of local guides drawn from Laotian villages along the trail to Nakai—Nam Theun, the primeval forest that, in name only, is a protected wildlife refuge straddling the mountainous Laos-Vietnamese border. Less than a handful of saola have been documented living there in the past two decades, and deBuys and his fellow trekkers face the very real prospect that they might be chasing a creature that no longer exists. As the author of six previous books and a finalist for the Pulitzer Prize in general non-fiction, deBuys brings to his work a seasoned conservationist's grim realism while still retaining a boyish enthusiasm for his current adventure.

The Last Unicorn offers the vivid scene-setting one expects from an experienced travel writer, but deBuys sees more in the landscape than mere flora and fauna, finding the pathos, humor, and meaning in a journey that left him seriously physically depleted (he was far and away the oldest member of the expedition). The joys of *The Last Unicorn* – its thoroughness of detail, cleverness of metaphor, and abundant good humor – compensate for the heartbreaking tale of the landscape's rape at the sullied hands of a trading network that values tigers for the powder that can be ground from their genitals, or rare golden turtles for their blood, peddled as a miracle of medical quackery. But deBuys' self deprecation – from his awkward climbing skills engendering barely muffled laughter among his experienced guides to the anecdote of his public inebriation after sampling way too much of local spirits at the hut of a Laotian village elder – gives the narrative an unexpected buoyancy.

Despite the arduousness of the journey, which took place in February and March of 2011, deBuys kept a closely observed record of what transpired. His renderings of the natural landscape are as bracing as a mountain zephyr: We're in a landscape where "glorious yellow sunlight drizzles down," illuminating "a cohort of purplish butterflies carpeting the limestone." DeBuys struggles to cross algae-smeared boulders awash in rust-colored rivers, his aides far more nimble, by age and familiarity, leaving him feeling like "a cart horse among Lipizzaners."

And then there's the saola, whose ghostly presence hovers over the narrative like the canopy of the Nakai—Nam Theun. The connection to the mythical creature in the title seems increasingly well founded as we venture further into the forest — and into uncertainty. deBuys is hopeful but not naïve about his quarry, acknowledging it might no longer exist. But like Saint George, the legendary dragon slayer of medieval lore who was protected by his faith, deBuys rushes deeper into the mist, ever more persuaded of the spiritual value of his travels:

> We are entranced by beautiful creatures not just because they give pleasure and inspire awe but because they carry a charge like an ionized particle. Beauty excites and glows. Put a horse in an empty meadow, and the meadow becomes animate. Put a saola, even a saola you cannot see, in a forest, and the forest, as though it held a unicorn, acquires an energy that cannot be named. It becomes numinous; it gains the pull of gravity, the weight of water, the float of a feather.

The Last Unicorn is an enthralling and sobering account of a modern-day quest with a mythic underpinning, a tale filled with grace and eloquence and despair. Is there any hope for the gentle saola? DeBuys provides his own answer at the very end. As Keats said later in his poem about the permanence of beauty, "We have imagined for the mighty dead/all lovely tales that we have heard or read/an endless fountain of immortal drink/ pouring unto us from the heaven's brink." *The Last Unicorn* deals movingly with a brink that is much less celestial but more consequential – for the creatures of the world, and for ourselves.

Reviewed by James Broderick. This review was originally published in *The BookBrowse Review* in April 2015, and has been updated for the December 2015 edition.

THE GAME OF LOVE AND DEATH

by Martha Brockenbrough

BookBrowse Rating: 5/5
Critics' Consensus: 5/5
Readers' Rating: 5/5

Published April 2015 in Paperback, 352 pages

Summary

Not since *The Book Thief* has the character of Death played such an original and affecting part in a book for young people.

Flora and Henry were born a few blocks from each other, innocent of the forces that might keep a white boy and an African American girl apart; years later they meet again and their mutual love of music sparks an even more powerful connection. But what Flora and Henry don't know is that they are pawns in a game played by the eternal adversaries Love and Death, here brilliantly reimagined as two extremely sympathetic and fascinating characters. Can their hearts and their wills overcome not only their earthly circumstances, but forces that have battled throughout history? In the rainy Seattle of the 1920s, romance blooms among the jazz clubs, the mansions of the wealthy, and the shanty towns of the poor. But what is more powerful: love? Or death?

BookBrowse Review

What if who you love is preordained and you are merely a pawn in a game that is played beyond your control? This intriguing premise forms the backbone of Brockenbrough's imaginative novel.

The Game is pretty simple. Death picks her player at birth. Love picks his. They wait until a prescribed time when their players must choose to allow the love they feel for one another to be realized – or not. If they do choose love, well, then Love wins the game. But if they don't...then Death wins. And with her win comes the price of one player's life. This is the game that has been played by Love and Death through eternity.

Flora and Henry are the chosen players in Martha Brockenbough's incredibly inventive and vibrant young-adult novel, The Game of Love and Death. The time is 1937, the place is Seattle. Flora is an African-American orphan, who lives with her grandmother and co-owns a jazz club with her uncle. By night she is a singer in the club, but by day she works as an airplane mechanic. She is also an aviatrix, deeply passionate about flying, and has aspirations to own a plane. Henry is a white orphan, who lives with his friend Ethan's family. He goes to school, plays baseball and also plays the bass. He knows he needs to earn a scholarship for college and follow, gratefully, the path that his benefactor family has allowed for him and yet he feels compelled to play his bass day and night. Henry and Ethan are asked by Ethan's newspaper-publisher father to interview the pilot of the plane that Flora works on. Henry and Flora lay eyes on one another. It is love at first sight.

Simple, as I said.

But The Game of Love and Death is far from it. Brockenbough creates a realistically complicated relationship between Henry and Flora. First, and most obvious, they have racial barriers to overcome. It is 1937, after all, and black and white communities in Seattle are segregated. No one wants the two seventeen-year-olds to be together. Second, Flora is a pragmatic and, at times, pessimistic person. While both she and Henry have experienced plenty of death (both have lost their parents, and Henry has also lost his sister), it is Flora who has built a fence around her heart as a result. (The only person she lets inside is her grandmother.) And Flora has lived with inequalities all her life, struggling in a world prejudiced against non-whites. Finally, the immortal characters of Love and Death are constantly present, shape-shifting into people with whom Flora and Henry interact, manipulating events and emotions in their fervent desire to win the game.

Brockenbough's imagining of Love and Death as living, breathing characters is nuanced and thoughtful and endlessly fascinating. Death feeds on people, which is gruesome, but also intriguing – as she sucks the life out of whomever is her present victim, the person's life bursts into color like fireworks: "Death took her hand. [her] soft arm wrapped around her shoulder, and her forehead touched Death's as the two leaned into each other. At the moment of contact, there was an explosion of memories, ...cut apart and stitched together...and then Death's eyes turned white as [her] life flowed into [Death], feeding that endless hunger until she felt as though she might burst." Death is ruthless, this is true, but she is also consciously aware of the value of the lives she takes, and the responsibility and weight she bears. Love, on the other hand, nurtures the magic of inevitable connection. He is wise (but so is Death) and he is hopeful. His understanding of Henry and Flora: "On the surface, they were an impossible pair. From two separate worlds. But Love knew something Death did not, at least when it came to hearts. Theirs were twins. He sent her [Death] an image of what it would look like when they locked on to each other. The light within them would burst out and rise, two columns of flame winding like the strands of matter that are the stuff of life itself. The image echoed the creation of the universe in miniature and the elements of life on earth writ large. It was the source of everything, including Love and Death themselves." Brockenbough also effectively places the game of Henry and Flora's courtship against the backdrop of many historical events; of many loves and deaths throughout time.

The story builds with perfectly placed obstacles, and suspense hangs on every page. Will Henry and Flora accept the love they feel for one another? Will they ultimately choose it, even if it means their path together in the world will not be easy? Suffice it to say the answer is worth the wait, and the last six chapters of the book create one of the most satisfying endings I have ever read. I can't say much about it but I will say this: Love and Death, like Henry and Flora, are inextricably entwined; they are a tender couple that fill, for one another, what the other so desperately needs. The Game of Love and Death is suited for kids in Grade 6 and up, but it is equally compelling for anyone who has experienced love, at any age.

Reviewed by Tamara Ellis Smith. This review was originally published in *The BookBrowse Review* in April 2015, and has been updated for the December 2015 edition.

www.ingramcontent.com/pod-product-compliance
Lightning Source LLC
Chambersburg PA
CBHW070322010526
44107CB00004B/389